S0-AZL-913

Studies in Eighteenth-Century Culture

Volume 52

Studies in Eighteenth-Century Culture

Volume 52

Editor

David A. Brewer
The Ohio State University

Associate Editor

Crystal B. Lake
Wright State University

Advisory Board

Wendy Bellion
University of Delaware

Sarah Benharrech
University of Maryland

Benjamin Breen
University of California, Santa Cruz

Daniel O'Quinn
University of Guelph

Olivia Sabee
Swarthmore College

Chloe Wigston Smith
University of York

Published by Johns Hopkins University Press for the
American Society for Eighteenth-Century Studies

Johns Hopkins University Press
Baltimore and London
2023

© 2023 American Society for Eighteenth-Century Studies
All rights reserved.
Printed in the United States of America on acid-free paper.
9 8 7 6 5 4 3 2 1

Johns Hopkins University Press
2715 North Charles Street
Baltimore, Maryland 21218-4363
www.press.jhu.edu

ISBN 978-1-4214-4537-3
ISSN 0360-2370

Articles appearing in this annual series are abstracted and
indexed in *America: History and Life, Current Abstracts, Historical
Abstracts, MLA International Bibliography, Poetry and Short Story
Reference Center, and RILM Abstracts of Music Literature*

Contents

Indigenizing the Eighteenth-Century American South

The Female *Wunderkind* in the Eighteenth Century

ASECS *Affiliate and Regional Societies*

American Antiquarian Society
Aphra Behn Society
Bibliographical Society of America
British Society for Eighteenth-Century Studies
Burney Society of North America
Canadian Society for Eighteenth-Century Studies
Daniel Defoe Society
Early Caribbean Society
East-Central ASECS
Eighteenth-Century Scottish Studies Society
German Society for Eighteenth-Century Studies
Goethe Society of North America
Historians of Eighteenth-Century Art and Architecture
Ibero-American Society for Eighteenth-Century Studies
International Adam Smith Society
International Herder Society
Johnson Society of the Central Region
Lessing Society
Midwestern ASECS
Mozart Society of America
North American British Music Studies Association
Northeast ASECS
North American Kant Society
Rousseau Association
Samuel Johnson Society of the West
Samuel Richardson Society
Society of Early Americanists
Society for Eighteenth-Century French Studies
Society for Eighteenth-Century Music
Society for the History of Authorship, Reading and Publishing
South Central Society for Eighteenth-Century Studies
Southeast Asian Society for Eighteenth-Century Studies
Southeastern ASECS
Western Society for Eighteenth-Century Studies

A Note from the Editors

In the three years that we've been editing this journal, almost every day has been defined by crisis. A global pandemic, unprecedented heat as the result of climate change, a coup attempt in the U.S., a series of extraordinarily callous and cruel decisions by the U.S. Supreme Court that already have a body count, a devastating and wholly unnecessary Russian invasion of Ukraine, mass shootings, a brutal crackdown against women and girls in Iran, a resurgence of unabashed racism, antisemitism, and Christian nationalism …. The list goes on. In such "interesting times" (as the apocryphal Chinese curse would have it), it would be easy to presume that we have more than enough to focus on in the present—and so we don't have the time or bandwidth to think seriously about, much less research and study, the eighteenth century. Engaging in the latter would be, according to this line of thought, an antiquarian indulgence that we cannot currently afford for fear that it might distract from the desperate urgency of now and the foreseeable future. But as the contributions to this volume demonstrate, again and again in many different ways, understanding the eighteenth century is integral to understanding our current moment and how we might best respond to it: in our professional practices as scholars; in our sense of what possibilities are available in the midst of inequity and suffering; in our ability to find solace, pleasure, and instruction in art; perhaps even in our thinking about alternatives to the petroleum-based plastics that are so ubiquitous (and unsustainable) in our world. This is not to say, of course, that the only value to studying the eighteenth century is to extract lessons for the present; much of the work in this volume is devoted to exploring the profound difference of the period: how it is not merely an easy precursor to "us" (to which, perhaps, we can then feel Whiggishly superior), nor simply a version of the present playing dress-up with wigs and beauty patches. But it is to say that the eighteenth century is an extraordinary resource that we (and the "we" here is far more encompassing than just professional scholars of the period) neglect at our peril. Bridget Brophy once proclaimed that "the two most fascinating subjects in the universe are sex and the eighteenth century." The latter, at least, may well also be among the most urgent.

David A. Brewer
The Ohio State University

Crystal B. Lake
Wright State University

Congo Winckelmann: Exploring African Art History in the Age of White Marble

ANNE LAFONT [TRANSLATED BY OLGA GRLIC]

Did something like African Art History exist over the course of the long eighteenth century? What kind of epistemological torsions are needed to consider an African Art History of the Enlightenment? It might be difficult to answer these specific questions and opinions may diverge, given that the very existence of Art History as a discipline before the foundation of its key institutions—museums and universities—in the nineteenth century has still to be discussed. That said, there are definitely eighteenth-century discourses, texts, and beliefs concerning African art and culture, however preliminary. In a word, there is a consciousness and a knowledge of objects, festivals, and rituals from communities on the African continent and from the African diaspora, which emerge in the writings of many eighteenth-century authors and on many levels fit into European artistic categories, if often incorrectly or incompletely.

First of all, one has to realize that, during this period, notions of African art and its history were entangled with the idea of Blackness, as conceptualized by a diverse ensemble of European textual sources, most of them not explicitly concerned with art. Many of these early modern texts ought, nonetheless, to be understood as fragments of a historical discourse on art—whether they describe African geography, natural history, or commerce; narrate African history; or catalog its objects in *cabinets de curiosités*. Of course, these narratives, which concern themselves with African material culture and ritual performances, would eventually be articulated in art-theoretical publications properly speaking, as eighteenth-century authors such as the abbé Dubos or Johann Joachim Winckelmann began to include Africa in their ambition to write a comprehensive, comparative art history grounded on a climatic explanation of style. This approach to art history understood artistic style, form, and content as products of the natural climate and atmosphere (today one would say the environment) in which art was created. As the title of my essay implicitly acknowledges, recent scholarship has demonstrated the centrality of Whiteness to the emergence of archeology in the middle of the eighteenth century. This essay aims to show how, at the very same historical moment, Blackness was being constructed, not only as a counterpart to Whiteness, but also, more generally, as a means of inscribing African rites and objects into the field of European fine art.

With this purpose in mind, my argument will rely on case studies of four prominent figures of the Enlightenment's intellectual production regarding early forms of Black Art: M. L. E. Moreau de Saint-Méry, a French settler in Saint-Domingue who wrote about dance and cultural hybridity; Olfert Dapper, a Dutch polymath who published the first compendium on Africa as a whole; Winckelmann, a German antiquarian living in Rome who theorized the interdependence of Whiteness and Blackness; and Henri Grégoire, a revolutionary priest in Paris, who published the first history of Black culture in 1808.

Art in the Colonies

Moreau de Saint-Méry is a key figure for understanding the motivations of the colonial lobby, both in the Caribbean and in Paris, in all aspects of his work as a lawyer, scientist, and politician.[1] Nevertheless, of particular interest is his *Discours sur l'utilité du musée établi à Paris* [*A Speech on the Utility of the Museum*], which he delivered publicly on 1 December 1784. Moreau de Saint-Méry was also the author of a 1789 choreographic treatise: *De la danse* [*On Dance*]. Both texts were eventually published—in 1805 and 1801, respectively—in Parma, where Moreau de Saint-Méry had been posted as Administrator-General by the French Foreign Minister, Charles-Maurice de Talleyrand-Périgord. In his *Discours sur l'utilité du musée*, Moreau de Saint-Méry expressed his delight in presiding over the Cercle des Philadelphes, a new learned society in Saint-Domingue devoted to scientific and artistic instruction "for public use."[2] The Cercle was to be a place in which the work of scholars, both past and present, would provide a foundation for the emulation essential to the advancement of the different branches of knowledge that he enumerated: physics, natural history, mathematics, astronomy, anatomy, chemistry, linguistics, French literature, history, and geography, followed by the arts of drawing, music, and dance, which he placed on an equal footing with the sciences. He concluded by adding that this "museum"—by which he meant, a club of scholars gathered together for public discussion in a place filled with specific objects—would guarantee a new efficiency in the arts and sciences by ensuring "public exhibition" of their results and their productions, without the mediation of criticism, which he perceived as having only a "deprecating" purpose.[3] Moreau de Saint-Méry concluded his presentation on a progressive note, praising the contributions of women to this enterprise and arguing that they should no longer be the object of men's envious mistrust as they added charm to the Cercle's investigations. The proposed museum and academy (which clearly anticipated the Musée du Louvre and Institut de France) were thus to be both edifying and stimulating.

Some fifteen years later, during the last throes of the Revolution in Saint-Domingue, Moreau de Saint-Méry tackled a treatise on choreography based on a comparative study of colonial dances, which combined European and African practices, despite racial segregation. Without praising the forms of hybridization specific to life on a colonial plantation, Moreau de Saint-Méry described and analyzed these cultural practices with great acuity. The text was originally part of a dictionary of *notions coloniales* [colonial concepts] that he never completed, although its first entries have been preserved in the Archives nationales.[4] However, Moreau de Saint-Méry thought his article on choreography important enough to publish it separately in 1801 and then reissue it in 1803. In this text, which aims to be a climatic study of dance in the Americas, he demonstrates how choreographic art "depicts the soul of all peoples" and that as an index of civilization, it can be measured by observing its practice among Creoles (white settlers born in the colonies) compared to that of Europeans (non-native white people), Indigenous communities, and enslaved Africans.[5] The best way to gauge the impact of the climate, understood as *milieu*, was to consider the Creole versions of dances that he knew in their original European context. The differences between European dances and Euro-American dances, or more precisely between metropolitan dances and how they were adapted in the colonies by Creoles, became the window through which Moreau de Saint-Méry could observe the role of climate in the artistic—and therefore civilizational—evolution of the Creoles, whom he admired. He described the choreographic practices of different social groups (in his classification we find Europeans, Creoles, savages, freedmen, servants, and Negroes) based on his observations in Saint-Domingue and, in so doing, endeavored to measure the comparative degrees (or "nuances") of Europeanness, Americanness, and Africanness in each group. Among these dances, there is at least one that exemplifies the process of recategorizing art as work in European discourses on the Americas that is the subject of both this essay and my ongoing research:

> The Creoles have adopted another exotic production which, also coming from Africa, had an even greater influence than any of the negro dances of which I have spoken. This dance is known generally in the American colonies by the name of Chica, which name it has in the Windward Islands and Saint Dominique.
>
> When a Chica is to be danced several instruments will play a certain melody, which is devoted uniquely to this kind of dance, and in which the rhythm is strictly observed. For the danseuse, who holds the corners of a handkerchief or the two ends of her apron, the art of this dance consists mainly in moving the lower part of the torso, while keeping the rest of the body almost motionless. To speed up the movement of the Chica, a dancer will approach his danseuse, throwing himself forward, almost touching her, withdrawing, then advancing again, while seeming to implore her to yield to the desires which invade them.
>
> There is nothing lascivious or voluptuous which this tableau does not depict. It offers a kind of contest in which every trick of love and every means of triumph are displayed: fear, hope, disdain, tenderness, caprice, pleasure, denial, delirium, flight, intoxication, despair—and the followers of Aphrodite surely would have celebrated the divinity of its inventor.[6]

Moreau de Saint-Méry here describes a dance that is no longer the prerogative of a particular social group, but rather belonged to Creole society as a whole, since its lasciviousness, as we learn a little later, ultimately caused it to be banned at balls reserved for white women, even though they had adapted and practiced it exclusively as something done with other women. This testifies to how a Creole, slaveholding, colonial, and segregationist society was nonetheless multicultural and mixed, despite forceful prohibitions aimed at preventing just that. Of particular interest are its artistic practices, which indicate the progress of civilization within human groups: "Of course, there is an immense gulf between [an] expression of joy by primitive men and the voluptuous graces of civilized people; but one can easily see that, as in many other matters, all art is based on natural laws. ... The proof is found in the round dance, necessarily a primitive one since it is really a dance champêtre, which is shared by people possessing the highest degree of civilization—as one can observe among the modern Greeks."[7] Moreau de Saint-Méry also lists characteristics of the dances of free people of color, servants (or urban slaves), and Negroes, which in his nomenclature means plantation slaves. The latter can supposedly make only crude gestures when they imitate European dances, but he nonetheless credits them for having their own dances, which originated in Africa, such as the Bamboula and Kalenda, and which have been faithfully continued in the colonies, as is documented in two 1788 watercolors by the Swiss artist François-Aimé-Louis Dumoulin: *Calinda, danse des Nègres en Amérique* and *Combats et jeux des Nègres*.[8] Moreau de Saint-Méry's investigation is based upon some assumptions widely held in the eighteenth century: that universal history depends on climate, that art is a sign of civilization, and that racial genealogies can be discovered through the "objective" study of cultural practices. In this, Moreau de Saint-Méry's text on dance is representative of European forms of knowledge about the Americas and discourse on the progress of humanity.

However, what I am interested in examining here is an apparently trivial detail in *De la danse*. It appears in the list of dances imported from Europe by the white colonial elite under a name that, though eloquent, goes unremarked by Moreau de Saint-Méry (and all of the subsequent historiography, so far as I know): the *Congo Menuet* [Congo Minuet]. Here is the passage in its entirety: "When one observes that the dancers have lost all but their courage and the ladies speak of rest, this is a signal for Allemandes, Anglaises and the Congo Minuet, and they spend several additional hours which are no less gay, and which pass very rapidly."[9] This dance was performed mainly in the southwest of France, not far from the slave-trade center of Bordeaux. If we remember the fantastical geography of certain words prominent in the history of art, such as *arabesque* or *chinoiserie*, it becomes easy to see how the name of the *Congo Menuet* does not record the importation of an African dance to Europe or its American colonies, but rather the ways in which the lexical imagination generated by the aura (from slaving) of the African coast in a French region linked by trade with the other side of the Atlantic gave rise to an elliptical abbreviation. The *Congo Menuet* is, I propose, a linguistic trace of this aura, especially since Moreau de Saint-Méry, who is so precise in his genealogies of other American choreographic practices (including the different regional origins specific to Africa—he evokes the stylistic singularities of the Gold Coast, Senegal, the Congo, and Guinea) and so attentive to the linguistic resonance of the names of these dances (e.g., the *Bamboula* is related to a drum made of bamboo and sheep skin that accentuates the dancers' movements), did not raise these issues at all in the case of the *Congo Menuet*. Instead, it is unequivocally included in the list of white Creole practices of exclusively European inspiration. In Antoine de Rivarol's *Mémoires*, the carnivalesque and exotic context in which the *Congo Menuet* was danced in Paris is clearly evoked: "A pas de quatre was then performed by four free dancers. The one dressed as a royal tiger with a Parisian bohemian mask was recognized as Monsieur le Comte de Mirabeau, the other, dressed as the Wandering Jew was Monsieur Brissot de Warville. Madame de Gouges, disguised as a young Indian, and Madame de Condorcet, disguised as the infanta of Zamora, completed the quadrille which performed the Congo Menuet very well. Several groups, among whom we noticed l'Abbé Grégoire, the priest of Souppes, etc., costumed as marabouts, danced the caloula, the fandango, and the bamboula in the corners and we understood none of that."[10]

A Congo Winckelmann

In this expressionist pirouette, I also see signs of a correspondence with the continuous conquering movement that will lead to the major museum collections of African objects assembled at the end of the nineteenth century. To ground this argument more specifically in the field of material culture, I would like to transform the title of the dance slightly by choosing a more adequate ellipsis, namely *Congo Winckelmann*, which signals how this guiding trope of art history is, first, part of the invention and creation of European whiteness within which a powerful Blackness, still diffuse in the eighteenth century, effortfully resists and unfolds and second, on the margins and with reference to the foundational Winckelmannian oeuvre, a development *avant la lettre* of forms of discourse on the history of African art.

I propose to reread modern artistic literature in this context but also, and perhaps above all, in the period before the establishment of Art History as a normalized and institutionalized discipline—that is, before the second half of the nineteenth century and the first French collecting campaigns in Africa—in order to point out the places and the forms in which these discourses arose in texts as different as the geographical work on Africa by an Amsterdam bibliophile and polymath, the first modern art historical narrative by a German antiquarian, and a metropolitan anti-slavery treatise by a revolutionary abbot.

These writings comprise what I would like to call early modern Black aesthetics. I am using this deliberately broad phrase so as not to impose a more rigorous classification on this material than what they themselves propose and because it assumes continuity and kinship between continental and diasporic African art. This was the early era of the slave trade and the distance and difference between sub-Saharan Africa and the Antilles had not yet been established. Thus, what I call Black aesthetics is the modern narrative and imaginary fabric (woven over the course of the long eighteenth century) devoted to the artwork, material culture, and images of the Black Atlantic, which prepares and founds an art history, in the strict sense, of continental Africa and its Atlantic diaspora around 1900.[11] From an abundance of sources, I have chosen my three exemplary cases of Dapper, Winckelmann, and Grégoire.

Dapper and the Geography of Africa

Olfert Dapper (1636–89), who appears in an engraved portrait with a book open not to a page of text, but to an illustration (to which I will return), was a Dutch humanist and polymath who wrote about many geographic areas far away from Amsterdam, where he nevertheless spent all of his life. He is a good example of a cabinet scientist, whose primary sources were the books he consulted.[12] According to recent historiography, he supplemented that written information with the conversations he had with missionaries and merchants who returned to the Netherlands after undertaking expeditions for the Dutch East India Company.[13] Dapper wrote the first modern compendium on the African continent as a whole. His *Description of Africa*, a volume of more than six hundred pages, also includes more than fifty plates—the work of Reinier Nooms (c. 1623–67), nicknamed Zeeman, a little-known engraver who specialized in marine scenes, but was also familiar with contemporary academic visual techniques. The work was published in Dutch in 1661 and soon translated into English and German and eventually into French as well in 1686.

Overall, if we were to use our current disciplinary divisions, the *Description of Africa* offers an anthropology and sociology of different communities on the African continent, with particular attention to their religious rituals, whether Christian, Muslim, or animist. Dapper specifically describes different customs linked to major stages of life (birth, circumcision, initiation, marriage, death, etc.) and the trades most important to the region. He takes exceptional care in his descriptions, identifying the most minute spatial and social units within a dozen large territories that make up the African continent. I will take my examples from his account of lower Ethiopia, which corresponds more or less to the present-day Republic of Congo.

Dapper's book is encyclopedic in the sense that it aims to be a complete summary of the available knowledge on Africa, as of the late seventeenth century, organized into a structure of essentially geographical categories. The information it offers on Africa allows European readers to distinguish the many different communities that inhabit the continent and so provides an alternative to what we might call the Hegelian representation of a monolithic, indistinct, ahistorical—and thus caricatural—Africa.[14] Dapper's account aims for nuance and accuracy. It establishes, if not a history of art as such, then a discourse on different artifacts whose presentation, both textual and pictorial, participates in their progressive recategorization as works of art.

However, this is not really a work of history since Dapper does not seek to construct a genealogy for the present or narrate the sequence of events over time, but rather, as his title suggests, describes African societies with all their customary practices and in all their social complexities. His approach is, therefore, rather horizontal or synchronic, and it aims to preserve a continental scale without losing sight of local particularities. However, over the course of this in-depth investigation, particularly in the chapters on mores and natural resources, Dapper pays close attention to a number of social facts that can be compared to the world of European art and so, as such, are part of the *Ancien Régime*'s knowledge concerning African art. He writes, "Negroes are inventive, some of them know how to make powders [and] herbal preparations, [and] make figures and draw."[15] In other words, though Dapper never identifies artists or authors by their names (that is, he does not individualize creation in the way that European art history had done since Vasari in the mid-sixteenth century), he nevertheless recognizes African inventiveness and, even more, its tendency to manifest itself in the making of figures—i.e., sculpture—and in drawing (the highest form of art according to academic theory), both of which are somehow parallel to the preparation of pharmaceuticals. Dapper thus insists on an alchemy specific to the manual and plastic dimension of artistic creation and inscribes African art within familiar forms of craftsmanship without neglecting the question of drawing, the mastery of which, in modern aesthetic theory, guaranteed the liberality of other art forms, including painting, sculpture, and architecture.[16] Dapper also pays close attention to the habitat, furnishings, and urban qualities of large ports like the town of Loango, of which he provides a magnificent engraving that corresponds in every detail to his narrative. It was probably his text that served as reference for the draughtsman, not the town itself.

One wonders what reality was being offered to readers and viewers in this chapter, which is ostensibly devoted to African society, but which Dapper endowed with a particularly important relationship to art in a general sense. I would speculate that they were above all encountering what I would call a style of appropriation: the formal process for acclimatizing the strangeness of African artifacts. In other words, it was a way to give access to or to help readers understand a different, unfamiliar reality (Africa). One can also imagine that, perhaps even more than the author, the draughtsman was involved in mediating this African strangeness so that it could be received by European elites at the end of the seventeenth century. The stylistic canon was the preferred tool for this transfer (or mutation) of a foreign reality into an intelligible motif. It was this means of visual intelligibility, this way of contextualizing African objects within the visual framework of European fine arts, that was a necessary precondition for the consumption of African objects by early modern Europe in the eighteenth century.[17] This process of detaching and remediating African objects through descriptive interpretation, both textual and pictorial, helped transmit a portion of reality, however minute, that would have otherwise remained inaccessible to European readers and viewers of the period. To make an object contemporary by familiarizing it is to appropriate and reformulate it in known stylistic terms, thereby facilitating, however unnaturally, the absorption of foreign elements by the viewer. In Dapper's work, the images themselves participate in this process of familiarization and naturalization. In other words, access to a foreign object is made possible thanks to the use of an already known framework of visuality—i.e., familiarization—and through highlighting its status with an act of ratification (the equivalent of naturalization in the domain of fine arts).[18]

As for Dapper's text, if we isolate the discourse that we can relate to art history in its earliest forms, it focuses on the description of ornaments (the *loci* of graphic invention *par excellence*), rites (magnificent occasions for public symbolic display) and precious materials (which render objects valuable and give them a distinctive quality). This basic artistic trinity of ornament, rite, and preciousness—all qualities important to the European fine arts—is found primarily in his account of what relates to the African body and its ornamentation, in particular textiles and clothing, but also jewelry, headdresses, make-up, and scarification. The same range of ornaments is, by the way, recognizable on both skin and textiles (for example, the same patterns are used in the body art and the basketry of Kongo-Central's populations, especially the Mayombe).[19]

We thus witness with Dapper, in this first example of an illustrated book on African geography (in the ancient sense of maps + sociology + history), both the artification of ritual objects and the indexation of an ornamental grammar. We also observe the process of visualizing Africa and its symbolic objects by means of a canonical stylistic technique specific to academic drawing. This textual and visual material marks one of the earliest forms of discourse on what will become African Art. These strategies allow Dapper to mitigate African strangeness, to remove its alterity, so to speak, by importing it into European conceptual categories by means of image and text. Dapper thus brings us to the dawn of the possibility of a history of African art.

Winckelmann and White Greece

The second example in this investigation of the ways in which a history of African art emerged in the eighteenth century is based on the work of a very different author: Johann Joachim Winckelmann (1717–68), an archaeologist and historian of ancient art whose career flourished largely in Italy, although he was Prussian. He was the author of two books widely considered to be the origins of the discipline of Art History—they stand out by their break with the Vasarian way of writing about art, that was based on artists' biographies and regional schools. Winckelmann's works are also revolutionary in their author's ambition to offer a theoretical grounding founded on the biological cycle—the birth, life, and death or "origin," "progress," "decadence," and "end" of forms—as well as the use of climate to explain styles. The two fundamental works by Winckelmann are the 1755 *Gedanken über die Nachahmung der griechischen Werke in der Malerei und Bidhauerkunst* [*Reflections on the Imitation of Greek Works in Painting and Sculpture*] and the 1764 *Geschichte der Kunst des Aterthums* [*History of the Art of Antiquity*]. They were translated into French and Italian in the years following their initial publication.[20] The second title is of particular interest for the question of Blackness because of its status as the cornerstone of what Philippe Jockey identified as "the Myth of White Greece."[21] Jockey describes the history of this myth, defining it as a specifically Western dream whose efficacy rested on, among other things, the work of Winckelmann, whom he nicknamed "the Cantor of White Greece." Jockey convincingly demonstrates the extent to which the imaginary whiteness of ancient Greek sculpture imposed itself on eighteenth-century Europe, despite knowledge and evidence of a polychrome antiquity on the ornamental level and the archaeological discoveries in Herculaneum and Pompeii that brought to light colored fragments. This putative whiteness was reinforced by the success and multiplication of plaster copies as well as the invention of diaphanously white porcelain by Josiah Wedgwood. German Romantic literature, attached as it was to a narrative of Greece as the origin of Europe and the Republic of the Arts, consolidated this myth of a white Greece as the birthplace of Western civilization.

As I have tried to show elsewhere regarding painting and makeup, the escalation of whiteness intensified even as the slave trade and racial mixing grew considerably, especially in the American colonies.[22] The stakes for the colonists were to establish their identities and define themselves in terms of pigmentation, in other words, through their whiteness and the power and privilege attached to it in this new transatlantic space. In his intellectual construction of whiteness and ideal beauty, Winckelmann resorted to arguments based on a type of relativism that offered him the opportunity to affirm that certain peoples "praise the color of their mistresses by comparing it to the shiny blackness of ebony, as we compare the skin of ours to the polished whiteness of ivory."[23] This comparatist diversion allowed him to introduce an implicit equivalence between white and Black women, an equivalence that can only be envisaged as a comparison of precious materials anchored by a rhetorical figure: glistening black ebony on one hand and polished white ivory on the other. For Winckelmann, the preciousness of these materials creates a possible space for comparison, even equivalence. However, that space does not necessarily expand according to the same modalities in the context of human diversity.

Indeed, Winckelmann continues his demonstration of the universal aspects of beauty by relying on a geometric analysis of the face, which disqualifies the "horizontal eyes" of the Chinese and the Japanese, the squashed noses of the Kalmyks who represent "gaps" and "deformities against beauty," and "the customary shape of our species."[24] He continues his inventory of anatomical imperfections, which he links to the climatic conditions of the populations that are tainted by them, adding that the more one moves away from a temperate climate, such as that found in Greece, the more deformities are amplified. Thus he writes: "the mouth swollen and raised, such as the Negroes have in common with the monkeys of their country, is a superfluous excrescence, a swelling caused by the heat of the climate."[25]

At the same time, Winckelmann offers—from a set of considerations grounded in what seems to me to be a composite Black aesthetic—the possibility of Black beauty. Indeed, the existence of African civilizations akin to those of Europe and Asia serves as an implicit claim that beauty is common to all three continents (and so is therefore universal). Finally, he returns to the beauty of black materials (bronze and basalt), which he regards as in no way inferior, from an aesthetic point of view, to white materials, such as marble: "Besides, most civilized nations, in Europe as well as in Asia and Africa, are more or less of the same sentiment on what constitutes Beauty in general. Their ideas should not be considered as completely arbitrary, even if we could not give a reason for all of them. ... A Negro can be beautiful, if his facial features are regular. A traveler assures us that daily conversation removes what is repulsive about the color of the Negroes at first sight, and lets one see the features of beauty that are in them. The color of bronze & that of black or greenish basalt are not disadvantageous to the beauty of ancient heads either. The beautiful female head of the statue of black basalt at the Villa Albani, would not be more beautiful in white marble."[26] This recognition of African civilization and of the beauty of both Black people and black materials founds an aesthetic that is at the core of the

a single one has ever been found who has accomplished something greater in art or science or shown any other praiseworthy quality."[29] Grégoire chose to ignore the presumptions that the cranial shape specific to Blacks does not allow for the development of certain spheres of the brain and that the African climate limited the physical, moral, and intellectual capacities of Blacks. Instead, Grégoire tackled the elementary contradiction—both quantitative and qualitative—of the assertion that Blacks lacked intellectual and imaginative faculties by compiling an inventory of their known creations: "The preliminaries that we have just read, are not foreign to my work, they only represent a glut of evidence; for I could have abruptly approached the question, and by a multitude of facts claimed the aptitude of the Negroes for virtues and talents: the facts answer everything."[30]

Unlike Winckelmann, for whom Blackness was inherent in the construction of an ancient, European, and white aesthetic ideal, Grégoire, as a positivist and a historian, introduced the work of Blacks into the history of the arts and letters, in particular, the work of Westerners of African origin: former slaves, literate and educated in Britain or British North America, such as Ottobah Cugoano, who were able to talk about and reflect on their condition. Grégoire thus opened the way, not so much to knowledge of artists per se (visual artists are almost nonexistent in his catalog with the exception of Scipio Moorhead, the alleged portraitist of the African American poet, Phillis Wheatley Peters), but rather to the hypothesis of art imagined and created by Blacks, despite the impediments caused by slavery. In Grégoire's project, the art of Africans, both from the continent and in the colonies (and he assumes a continuity between the two), was to testify to and guarantee the humanity of its creators and therefore make emancipation indispensable. If his demonstration of African inventiveness was accepted, then justifications of slavery on the basis of a Black essence that destined those who had it for servile status became illegitimate and indefensible. For Grégoire, the relation between freedom and creativity is imagined differently than it is by Winckelmann, but it responds to Winckelman's thinking: the German author invented a Black aesthetic intertwined with a white one, but did not explicitly relate it to slavery. Moreover, he confined his exploration to his chapter on the negative idea of beauty. Grégoire took up the idea that art was a mark of civilization and undertook to collect and enumerate proofs of Black creativity, proofs that could then serve as the basis for emancipation and freedom. In Grégoire's argument, the freedom of spirit necessary for creativity demands the political freedom of the individuals who possess it. Only a free man can conceive of the liberal arts, or even that where there are liberal arts, there is humanity, and humanity does not tolerate slavery.

Notes

1. Médéric-Louis-Élie Moreau de Saint-Méry was born in Martinique in 1750 and died in Paris in 1819. He was a colonist from the French West Indies, who forcefully defended the cause of white Creoles, slavery, and racial hierarchy based on skin color (the aristocracy of the epidermis), particularly in *Loix et constitutions des colonies françaises de l'Amérique sous le Vent*, 6 vols. (Paris and Cap Français: Barrois et Baudry des Lozieres, 1784–90). Additionally, he wrote a history of Saint-Domingue, where he lived from 1776 to 1785 before returning to Paris. He then embarked more vigorously on a political career, which led him, as a member of the French Revolutionary Assembly, to promote the importance of slavery and racial segregation in the colonies.

2. Moreau de Saint-Méry, *Discours sur l'utilité du musée établi à Paris* (Parma, 1805), 9.

3. Moreau de Saint-Méry, *Discours sur l'utilité du musée*, 27–28, 28.

4. Archives nationales d'outre-mer, Aix-en-Provence, *Répertoire des notions coloniales*, col F3 Moreau de Saint-Méry, registre 73–77, 247 MIOM 56–57.

5. Moreau de Saint-Méry, *Dance: An Article Drawn From the Work by M. L. E. Moreau De St.-Méry, Entitled Repertory of Colonial Information, Compiled Alphabetically (1796)* (Brooklyn: Dance Horizons, 1975), 21.

6. Moreau de Saint-Méry, *Dance*, 60–62. N.B. this translation gives the phrase in the last sentence as "the followers of Pan," whereas the French text refers to "les habitants de Paphos" [the worshipers of Aphrodite].

7. Moreau de Saint-Méry, *Dance*, 2–4 and 7–8.

8. Claire Brizon, "François Aimé Louis Dumoulin, ou les images d'un Suisse aux Caraïbes," *Journal18* (2018), https://www.journal18.org/3305.

9. Moreau de Saint-Méry, *Dance*, 28, 39–40.

10. Rivarol, *Mémoires de Rivarol avec des notes et des éclaircissements historiques, précédés d'une notice par M. Berville* (Paris, 1824), 347.

11. The foundational work here is Paul Gilroy, *The Black Atlantic*: *Modernity and Double Consciousness* (Cambridge: Harvard University Press, 1993).

12. Some hundred works, according to Adam Jones, "Decompiling Dapper: A Preliminary Search for Evidence," *History in Africa* 17 (1990): 171–209.

13. Elizabeth A. Sutton, *Early Modern Dutch Prints of Africa* (Farnham: Ashgate, 2012), 1–21.

14. See G. W. F. Hegel, *La raison dans l'histoire. Introduction à la philosophie de l'Histoire (cours de 1822 à 1830)* (Paris: Pocket, 2012), 277–305.

15. Dapper, *Description d'Afrique* (Amsterdam, 1686), 260.

16. "Liberal," in the early modern sense, means the product of a free spirit, an independent individual thinking by him/herself and producing a work of art based on his/her spirit, rather than on a manual skill acquired by training.

17. This process is obvious in well-known examples such as Cornelis de Man's painting, *An Interior with a Seller of Curiosities* (formerly in the Dapper Museum in Paris; current location unknown), in which one can see an Asante ceremonial

saber (Ghana) and traditional Congolese basketry. Africa is thus seen through the lens of a cabinet of curiosities that standardizes the objects by having them hung (in a Western manner not specified in Dapper's text) on the wall along the traditional picture rail.

18. Nathalie Heinich and Roberta Shapiro, *De l'artification. Enquête sur le passage à l'art* (Paris: éditions de l'EHESS, 2012).

19. Margaret Trowel, *African Design* (New York: Praeger, 1960), xxxiii–xxxv.

20. The first French edition of *Histoire de l'art chez les Anciens* was published in 1766 and the first French edition of *Réflexions sur l'imitation des artistes grecs* came out in 1786. An Italian edition of *Storia delle arti del disegno presso gli antichi* appeared in 1779. On these translations, see Alex Potts, "Introduction," in Winckelmann, *History of the Art of Antiquity* (Los Angeles: Getty Research Institute, 2006), 37–38 n4 and Winckelmann, *Geschichte der Kunst des Alterthums: Text*, ed. Adolf H. Borbein, et al. (Mainz: Zabern, 2002), pp. xxiii–xxvii.

21. Jockey, *Le mythe de la Grèce blanche: Histoire d'un rêve occidental* (Paris: Belin, 2013).

22. See my *L'art et la race. L'Africain (tout) contre l'œil des Lumières* (Paris: Presses du réel, 2019), 45–84, which builds upon Angela Rosenthal, "Visceral Culture: Blushing and the Legibility of Whiteness in Eighteenth-Century British Portraiture," *Art History* 27, no. 4 (2004): 563–92, and Melissa Hyde, *Making up the Rococo: François Boucher and his Critics* (Los Angeles: Getty Publications, 2006), 83–105.

23. Winckelmann, *Histoire de l'art chez les Anciens*, 2 vols. (Paris: Saillant, 1766), 1:248. "Comme il y a des peuples qui font l'éloge de la couleur de leurs maîtresses en la comparant au noir luisant de l'ébene, comme nous comparons la peau des nôtres à la blancheur polie de l'ivoire."

24. Winckelmann, *Histoire de l'art chez les Anciens*, 1:249.

25. Winckelmann, *Histoire de l'art chez les Anciens*, 1:250.

26. Winckelmann, *Histoire de l'art chez les Anciens*, 1:251–52. "Du reste la plupart des nations civilisées, tant en Europe qu'en Asie & en Afrique, sont à peu de choses près du même sentiment sur ce qui constitue la Beauté en général & considérée ensemble. Leurs idées ne doivent donc pas être regardées comme tout-à-fait arbitraires, quand même sous ne pourrions pas rendre raison de toutes. … Un Nègre peut être beau, si sa physionomie est régulière. Un voyageur assure qu'une conversation journalière fait disparaître ce que la couleur des Nègres a de rebutant au premier abord, & laisse apercevoir les traits de beauté qui sont en eux. La couleur de bronze & celle du basalte noir ou verdâtre ne sont point non plus désavantageuses à la beauté des têtes antiques. La belle tête de femme de la statue de basalte noir de la Villa Albani, ne serait pas plus belle en marbre blanc."

27. Winckelmann, *Histoire de l'art chez les Anciens*, 1:i.

28. See Hume, "Des caractères nationaux," in *Essais moraux, politiques et littéraires et autres essais* (Paris: PUF, 2001), 406–25; and Kant, *Observations sur le sentiment du beau et du sublime* (Paris: Vrin, 2008), 75–78. For a general discussion from the perspective of intellectual history, see Silvia Sebastiani, "Race et Lumières: histoire d'une controverse," in Jean-Frédéric Schaub and Silvia Sebastiani, *Race et*

histoire dans les sociétés occidentales (XVe–XVIIIe siècles) (Paris: Albin Michel, 2021), 315–85.

29. Kant, *Observations sur le sentiment du beau et du sublime*, 75–78.

30. See Grégoire, *De la littérature des Nègres*, in *Écrits sur les Noirs*, ed. Rita Hermon-Bélot, 2 vols. (Paris: L'Harmattan, 2009), 1:121–42 and the summary that opens the next chapter on 1:143.

DECOLONIZATION AND EIGHTEENTH-CENTURY STUDIES

Edited by Emily C. Casey and Tita Chico

Introduction: Decolonization and Eighteenth-Century Studies

EMILY C. CASEY

"Decolonization and Eighteenth-Century Studies" originated as a roundtable on "Decolonizing ASECS," sponsored by the Women's Caucus of the American Society for Eighteenth-Century Studies (ASECS) during its 2021 Virtual Annual Meeting. In its conference form, "Decolonizing ASECS" was designed to speak directly to the conditions of eighteenth-century studies as a field of inquiry and specifically to one of its principal learned societies, founded fifty years ago and based in the United States. As such, it contributed to calls from a growing number of scholars of the eighteenth century to connect the field's temporal focus and major concerns—among them concepts of enlightenment and liberty; histories of colonialism, enslavement, and genocide; and cultural productions including literature, political and economic writing, works of visual art, and material culture—with the current conditions of academic scholarship.[1] By drawing on the language of decolonizing, the roundtable rooted itself in an ongoing theory and practice that challenges the political norms of institutions and recasts the dynamics of power that still structure the modern world. The resulting essays that grew from that roundtable—presented in this cluster—not only point the direction for future efforts in decolonizing eighteenth-century studies, but also challenge and expand the original panel's premise. Can eighteenth-century studies be decolonized, and what is at stake in such a call?

21

In recent decades, eighteenth-century studies broadly has "gone global," attending to places and histories beyond the traditional European canon, especially as they are shaped by colonialism and empire. However, despite a diversification of geographies and materials, the discipline's knowledge production continues to be founded on a colonialist paradigm. Similarly, the field's membership is still overwhelmingly white, reflecting broader disparities in higher education. To connect the practice of decolonization with eighteenth-century studies is to question the field's rootedness in the institution of the academy and its privileging of a Western European construction of the long eighteenth century.

Calls to decolonize intellectual disciplines and their attendant institutions are varied in their meaning and intent, encompassing a broad array of antiracist and anticolonial interventions that might take place at the level of pedagogy, scholarship, or institutional activism. While these efforts are urgent and necessary, too often the mobilizing of the language of decolonizing theory as part of the response takes attention away from the specific, material needs of decolonization. As a movement, the heart of decolonial practice is the imperative to restore Indigenous sovereignty and return stolen land to Indigenous communities.[2] In the academy, where institutions of higher learning have historically built (and continue to build) their wealth and reputations through land speculation and acquisition that displaces marginalized communities, the urgency of material restoration and return can be quickly overridden by a quest to find a universal language to oppose all racist and colonialist forms of injustice. What is more, the infrastructure of the academy—both physical and intellectual—raises the real possibility that it is an institution that cannot be decolonized.

However, dwelling amidst the tension of decolonization's limits within higher education and its communities does not preclude the necessity and responsibility for action. Together these essays treat the historic legacy of Western scholarship—an early modern structure for knowledge production, intellectual community, and pedagogy that was intertwined with capitalist and colonialist enterprises—as of a piece with its contemporary practitioners and output. Within the field, they make room for the kinds of experiences, knowledges, and practices that a decolonized understanding of the long eighteenth century enables. Reflecting the perspectives of their respective authors—who represent multiple disciplines, varying stages of academic careers, and diverse cultural backgrounds—they do not offer a singular formula for decolonization in eighteenth-century studies, or even an assurance that such a transformation is possible. Rather, they open up a conversation about what we mean and intend when we discuss decolonization and eighteenth-century studies together. They offer touchstones for enacting anticolonial and antiracist action within the work of eighteenth-century studies, while providing guideposts for considering the complex histories and commitments that are gathered together in the name of decolonization. Pondering these questions while developing this cluster of essays prompted the editors to change the title to better reflect the tension and irresolution inherent in conversations about decolonization within academic disciplines that are so embedded in colonialist history and ideology. While "Decolonizing ASECS" (the conference roundtable) was intended as a clarion call for change in the field, "Decolonization and Eighteenth-Century Studies" acknowledges not only the urgency of these efforts, but also their limits.

Like all events sponsored by the ASECS Women's Caucus, the conference roundtable that ultimately became "Decolonization and Eighteenth-Century Studies" was conceived during a lightning-round brainstorming session at the Caucus's luncheon during the Society's 2019 Annual Meeting. A group of scholars from multiple disciplines and all stages of their careers—from graduate students to tenured professors—randomly sat down together at that luncheon and began one of many discussions about what it would mean for ASECS, as an intellectual and professional community, to divest itself of the colonialist structures and practices that have long ordered both academia in general, and eighteenth-century studies in particular. The group included international graduate students whose cultural backgrounds and areas of research had provided them with first-hand perspectives on eighteenth-century studies' marginalization of non-European histories and ways of knowing. It also included contingent scholars whose precarious position within the employment structure of higher education meant that while they were charged with the responsibility of reproducing the field through instruction, their visibility and security within the field was limited by a lack of permanent affiliation, time, and financial support. In the end, while the crucial perspectives of everyone in that discussion shaped our vision of the panel, only the two participants who were in tenured or tenure-track positions had the time and stability to be able to co-chair it. Most of the other participants were not sure that they would be able to attend the next year's Annual Meeting, or even whether they would still be in the field at that time.

Of course, in the twelve months between the genesis of the roundtable and its slated presentation at the March 2020 Annual Meeting, many things changed. As organizers worked to assemble the roundtable for an in-person conference in St. Louis, Missouri, valued speakers were unable to commit because they lacked professional development funds to support conference travel or because they were already over-committed with teaching and service at their institutions. Failed efforts to secure financial underwriting for the non-academic presenters on another panel (one devoted to Indigeneity) only confirmed what Robbie Richardson notes in this cluster has been a long-standing lack of support for Native scholars and anticolonial criticism in eighteenth-century studies, even as interest in including Indigenous topics in the field is growing.[3] In Spring 2020, a global pandemic postponed the scheduled Annual Meeting, and pushed those in contingent or precarious positions within the field even closer to the brink. In her piece, Chi-ming Yang takes up Arundhati Roy's characterization of the pandemic as a portal to ask what practices of academia must be reassessed or jettisoned for the futurity of our communities and planet.

Yang's invocation of Roy should serve as a reminder that the questions at the heart of "Decolonization and Eighteenth-century Studies" were not posed in the abstract intellectual sphere of a "normal" year or conference, but rather were tested under the pressures of a period that laid bare the unstable and unjust foundations of academia. In higher education, the pandemic's portal opened onto a redoubled investment in capitalist practice and an even greater focus on the bottom line. The sudden, forced adaptations to teaching and scholarship made in the interests of income over learning strained the physical, mental, and emotional wellbeing of scholars and students alike. By the time the "Decolonizing ASECS" panel met online in the April 2021 Virtual Meeting, the tenure-track job of one of the co-chairs had been terminated and her college's Art History program eliminated. The collective frustration and exhaustion of scholars who had been on the front lines as graduate teaching assistants, community college professors, and social justice activists was palpable in the Zoom room. Chronicling the genesis of the conference roundtable and these resulting essays highlights the interrelatedness of intellectual labor, institutional power, and community wellbeing. The contributors to this cluster approach the question of decolonizing eighteenth-century studies as a collective praxis, rooted in the discipline's structural and material history and opening out onto its future relevancy and survival.

In challenging the systems of privilege and power that underlie eighteenth-century studies as a field and ASECS as a professional organization, these contributors jettison complacency and comfort, reminding us that these strategies have only ever served the most powerful and privileged in the field. Now, more than ever, the permeability between the scholarly work of the field and the material and institutional conditions of those who work in it is evident. As the humanities are under fire, stable employment becomes ever scarcer, and college and university administrators use the language of diversity and inclusion while promoting austerity measures that disproportionately affect the most vulnerable, the future of the field—who is able to contribute and how—will be shaped by the collective purpose of its members in relation to institutional power. In this environment, there is no question that the harms of higher education impact everyone involved in this work. As we have seen in recent years, from a global pandemic to the financial and moral crises in higher education, emergencies tend to inspire individualist responses that protect the already powerful and seek to stabilize and perpetuate regimes of control. The collective action that decolonization represents should be led by the vision of the historically marginalized and focused on the most vulnerable—particularly faculty and students of color and those working in conditions of precarity.

It is important to stress that the practice of decolonization goes beyond the conventional rhetoric of representation and inclusion to argue for disrupting and dismantling Western knowledge practices that were concretized in the eighteenth century and that perpetuate colonial forms of social and cultural control. In her contribution, Pichaya Damrongpiwat critiques the ways in which expanded curricula may add non-Western texts and objects to their syllabi, but teach them through a framework of colonialist knowledge that does not trouble the inherent power dynamics of the system. Patrícia Martins Marcos adds that if its practitioners take up the challenge, eighteenth-century studies is particularly well-situated to do this work, as the objects of our study were enmeshed in early modern systems of thought that themselves were in a state of flux and formation. Looking to the condition and futures of the field, the participants in this cluster articulate with uncompromising clarity what eighteenth-century studies must divest itself of—materially, politically, and intellectually—in order to make space for the perspectives and leadership that will keep it relevant, necessary, and thriving for the next generations of scholars. As Kathleen Alves asks in her contribution, "What kind of ancestors do we want to be?"

"Decolonization and Eighteenth-century Studies" expressly posits decolonizing and anticolonial action as a praxis for the future of eighteenth-century studies. This focus on futurity belies the ways that Native peoples have been erased from contemporary Western discourse that associates Indigenous culture with the past. As part of contesting the stereotype of the "dead Indian"—a trope that emerged in the early modern period as a tool of settler-colonial enterprise across the Americas—the collectives that form contemporary decolonization movements powerfully demonstrate that the future of the planet and its peoples lies in knowledge ways and community practices that have their roots in Indigenous cultures.[4] In these essays, our contributors contend that the relationship between intellectual labor and its social, political, and economic contexts make what is past, future. Academia is not neutral; its embeddedness within capitalist systems of land seizure and development, Christian missionizing, and white male supremacy mean that its intellectual productions are linked to the colonialist history from which it was born.[5] Discussions around decolonizing the field are and should be open-ended and without resolution. As Elizabeth Hutchinson reminds us, quoting Linda Tuhiwai Smith, unsettling the colonialist paradigms of eighteenth-century studies is a project that will be "often fraught, never complete, but worthwhile." These pieces are the fruits of many conversations about how the intellectual work of eighteenth-century studies is situated in relation to the moral work of scholarship and the structures that order scholarly labor. They are intended to be generative, rather than conclusive—offering not consensus, but rather many pathways forward to a more just future.

Notes

Tita Chico, the co-editor of this cluster, and I would like to acknowledge the support of the ASECS Women's Caucus, which sponsored the roundtable in which these essays originated. In particular, we would like to recognize the contributions of the Women's Caucus members who helped develop our initial ideas back in 2019.

1. Recent publications that consider the role of decolonizing thought in eighteenth-century studies include "The Indigenous Eighteenth Century," ed. Eugenia Zuroski, special issue, *Eighteenth-Century Fiction*, 33, no. 2 (2021); Eugenia Zuroski, "The Ship We're In," *The Rambling*, no. 9 (2020), https://the-rambling.com/2020/08/07/issue9-zuroski/; and "Scholarship in a Time of Crisis," ed. Emily Hodgson Anderson and Steven Aaron Minas, special issue, *The Eighteenth Century: Theory and Interpretation*, 62, no. 2 (2021).

2. In the United States, the conditions for decolonizing theory and practice are informed by the nation's history as a settler-colonial enterprise, in which people of European descent laid claim to, settled, and developed land that was taken from Indigenous communities. A key essay on decolonization's application in pedagogy and scholarship, Eve Tuck and K. Wayne Yang's "Decolonization is not a Metaphor," critiques the tendency for the language of decolonization to be co-opted and metaphorized for other ends. See Tuck and Yang, "Decolonization is not a Metaphor," *Decolonization: Indigeneity, Education & Society* 1, no. 1 (2012): 1–40.

3. Eugenia Zuroski writes about the development and aftermath of "The Indigenous Eighteenth Century" panel in her "Editor's Preface," *Eighteenth-Century Fiction* 33, no. 2 (2021): 177–80.

4. This is a narrative that abounds in U.S. cultural forms that support early national settler colonialism and westward expansion. Examples include James Fenimore Cooper's *The Last of the Mohicans: A Tale of 1757* (1826) and Thomas Crawford's "Progress of Civilization" multi-figure sculpture on the east pediment of the U.S. Capitol Building (1863). For more on how this trope became embedded in U.S. cultural discourse, see Vivien Green Fryd, *Art and Empire: The Politics of Ethnicity in the United States Capitol, 1815–1860* (Athens: Ohio University Press, 2001).

5. The claim that "academia is not neutral" draws on the "Museums are Not Neutral" advocacy initiative developed by La Tanya S. Autry and Mike Murawski. The movement explicitly critiques the ways in which museums characterize themselves as politically and socially neutral. Activism associated with "Museums are Not Neutral," like the work of other movements such as "Decolonize This Place," highlights the ways in which institutional histories, collecting practices, and labor policies have made museums bastions of inequity. These concepts are easily transferred to academia, given the historic interlinking of museums with universities and the contemporary claims for neutrality that explicitly and implicitly order administrative actions at colleges and universities. See La Tanya S. Autry and Mike Murawski, "Museums are Not Neutral: We are Stronger Together," *Panorama: Journal of the Association of Historians of American Art* 5, no. 2 (2019).

Rebuilding Eighteenth-Century Studies as a Relational Ecology

KATHLEEN TAMAYO ALVES

I acknowledge that as an Asian immigrant, I have been brought into this settler-colonial nation-state and have invested in the mythologies of whiteness, even in the impossibility of fully becoming a white settler. I come from the Philippines, a land that has endured colonial violence since the sixteenth century. My grandparents survived a war of empire, and my parents lived through a tyrannical dictatorship supported by the United States government in order to maintain its economic and military foothold in Asia. The stories of my ancestors under empire color my way of knowing and my way of being.

My contribution here does not engage with the process of decolonization in the sense of repatriating land, for which Eve Tuck and K. Wayne Yang have called.[1] Instead, I would like to discuss the "moves to innocence" made by the American Society for Eighteenth-Century Studies (ASECS). Tuck and Yang define these moves as "those strategies or positionings that attempt to relieve the settler of feelings of guilt or responsibility without giving up land or power or privilege, without having to change much at all. In fact, settler scholars may gain professional kudos or a boost in their reputations for being so sensitive or self-aware. Yet settler moves to innocence are hollow, they only serve the settler."[2] This cluster, which originated in the "Decolonizing

ASECS" roundtable at the 2021 Virtual Annual Meeting of ASECS, could be considered just such a "move to innocence," unless we deliberately discuss how our contributions do not serve settler interests and futurity.

As a U.S. organization, ASECS is informed and structured by whiteness. The by-products and tools of settler colonialism can be distinguished in the racist, sexist, heterosexist, ableist, and classist practices of its members and structure. The founding of the Race and Empire Caucus in 2013 by Ashley Cohen and Suvir Kaul confirmed the whiteness of what was already (and remains) in place in ASECS: the necessity for the caucus demonstrates that the historical violence of colonization that defines the eighteenth century has not been adequately addressed or included in how the field operates. Recently, especially in the wake of the revolutionary energies brought together by the Black Lives Matter movement, BIPOC scholars have been called upon to share our experience of our realities, to assemble and write special issues of journals on race, to present at diversity and inclusion panels and sit on diversity and inclusion committees, to show white people the antiracist way. This is in some ways genuine and in some ways a transparent attempt by institutions to "cover their asses." And it is another "move to innocence," another way in which settlers look to insulate themselves from their complicity in historical and continued colonization. This collection's inclusion in this journal could be construed as a "performative utterance," in which "the issuing of the utterance is the performing of an action."[3] Institutions can leave it up to BIPOC scholars and faculty to do the painful emotional labor of thinking through our expertise and then claim credit for that labor because of our affiliation with the organization. Our affiliation and our pain become the substitute for transformative action. The allyship of the organization is not only passive, but comes at the cost of squandering BIPOC scholars' time and energy. And all the while, deeply cynical about the intentions of such requests for our labor, we ask ourselves, "Why now? And to what purpose?"

We are quarried for the knowledge we have accumulated as subjects at the intersection of settler-colonist discourses, and we are told that we are "invaluable" to the institution, whether it be ASECS or the university. But how invaluable are we, how invaluable is our knowledge, when this economic exchange of expertise fails to result in the egalitarian utopia that we want? That we *both* purportedly want?

The exploitative culture of hierarchy—it's in the taxonomy of our institutions: assistant, associate, full, adjunct, student; people measured, valued as parts—is based on the premise of settler structures in which we are in competition with each other, fighting over scraps of food because "them's the rules." We "win" when we survive. We are conditioned to believe that we must run the gauntlet of academia; otherwise, everyone would be doing it. Exclusionary institutions are inherently prestigious ones. As an instructor in a community college, I have long experienced the condescension of others, as though teaching in a public, accessible, and low-cost institution is supposed to make me feel inferior (and I did, for a long time). Eugenia Zuroski writes, "We are by now used to thinking about the future of our field and our profession in terms of survival. But any world in which mere survival is the horizon of hope is not, in fact, worth saving."[4] Radical transformation requires the absolute repudiation of existing systems in which survival is the endgame.

So shouldn't we be thinking about ourselves as an *ecology*—a system in which the production of knowledge works in relation, rather than in isolation? A system built to dismantle all forms of gatekeeping and exclusionary practices in classrooms, in hiring, in publishing? A system built to replace indifference with compassion, especially with regards to the material precarities of graduate students and contingent faculty? The inability to imagine a system beyond the hoarding of resources shows the limits of settler imagination.

I would like to emphasize that the answers, or at least the beginning of answers, for how to achieve real equity have always been here. In "We Have Always Been Here," Megan Peiser describes her experience as a white-passing Indigenous academic and observes, rightly, "I am tired, as a lifetime member of ASECS, of seeing this matriarchical organization—for indeed the real leading here is done by scholars speaking from disability, from gendered and queer identities—filled with scholars in positions of power who hoard their fortunes. Why, in every panel about pedagogy, about changing our discipline, about women writers, about POC, about disability studies, is the room filled *only* with marginalized and early career scholars?"[5] Peiser's point rings true. I have been in those rooms. I call these DEI efforts the "lead a horse to water" phenomenon, as the individuals who really need to be here aren't here. Black feminist, disability, and queer communities that rely on an ecological ethics of care continue to be a marginal afterthought in scholarship and pedagogy. Their inclusion in systems of able-bodied cis hetero male whiteness, if we can even call it "inclusion," could easily be construed as a "move to innocence." It is especially galling when this inclusivity depends on how well these voices fit settler narratives. Sara Ahmed observes, "People of color are welcomed *on condition* they return that hospitality by integrating into a common organizational culture, or by "being" diverse, and allowing institutions to celebrate diversity."[6] We bend and twist ourselves to fit these spaces so that we don't break.

When we are told that these spaces have limitations, that is a fiction of settler hypocrisy. These borders are imaginary, but are determined to be fixed by whoever stands to gain by their fixedness. Empire has no limits when it serves them.

In a 1781 speech to the United States Treaty Commissioners, Cherokee warrior and diplomat Nanye'hi uses the rhetoric of motherhood to demonstrate that kinship binds all, regardless of difference: "Women are always looked upon as nothing; but we are your Mothers; you are our sons. Our cry [is] all for Peace; let it continue because we are Your Mothers. This peace must last forever. Let your Womens sons be Ours, and let our sons be yours. Let your women hear our Words."[7] Speaking from matrilineal Cherokee sensibility, Nanye'hi asserts women's authority in political participation and underscores the common stakes of peace and reconciliation. Nanye'hi's proposal to change the way we think about our relationship with each other, the human ties that bind us, is one way in which we can reanimate the past to begin to solve the systemic problems of the present.

"Let your women hear our Words." The verb "let" can mean "to allow" but can also mean to express defiance. We can defy tradition to make space. While the problem of getting horses to drink may sound insurmountable, as it would require a radical dismantling of pervasive settler ways of thinking, ASECS can at least restructure itself to make the water more accessible. In 2021, there was some more deliberate, meaningful listening, which was long overdue. The Virtual Annual Meeting in April held two listening sessions and ASECS hosted a town hall in August. The town hall was organized by representatives from ASECS's various caucuses and included breakout rooms for attendees (it is worth noting that the attendees were the same people as Peiser identifies in her essay). ASECS hired Gladiator Consulting to conduct and analyze a membership survey to determine institutional demographics and to ask members how ASECS fails or serves their needs. Gladiator Consulting also conducted focus groups with ASECS leaders to help inform their findings and recommendations.[8] How the proposed actions will affect organizational structure and governance still remains unclear, but the organization's pivot to creating a space for listening should continue in future, post-pandemic years.

Unpaid or underpaid labor continues to be a common exploitative practice in academia. ASECS is no exception, although board members are compensated for travel to the Annual Meeting and for two nights' lodging at the conference hotel. There is an assumption that officers or committee members will receive some form of compensation from their home institutions. Most of the people I know who serve as leaders do so out of a genuine desire to facilitate positive change or to see justice and fairness served in the organization. But as the landscape of academia is changing, with more faculty in precarious career and financial positions than ever, a situation only exacerbated by the pandemic, is that enough of an incentive to do this difficult work? Perhaps it is time for ASECS to defy conventions and to consider compensating leaders in recognition of the time, labor, and, sometimes, risks that they take.

A recent essay by Suvir Kaul urges us to hold institutions accountable for progressive change: "Which eighteenth century do we inhabit in our scholarship and pedagogy?"[9] As scholars of the period in which colonialism and early capitalism planted the poisonous seeds of today's institutional racism and ecological devastation, what are our ethical responsibilities? And to think even more broadly, what kind of ancestors do we want to be?

Notes

1. Tuck and Yang, "Decolonization is not a Metaphor," *Decolonization: Indigeneity, Education & Society* 1, no. 1 (2012): 1–40.

2. Tuck and Yang, "Decolonization," 10.

3. J. L. Austin, *How to Do Things with Words* (Oxford: Oxford University Press, 1975), 6.

4. Zuroski, "This Ship We're In," *The Rambling*, no. 9 (2020). https://the-rambling.com/2020/08/07/issue9-zuroski/

5. Peiser, "We Have Always Been Here: Indigenous Scholars in/and Eighteenth-Century Studies," *Eighteenth-Century Fiction* 33, no. 2 (2021): 181–88.

6. Ahmed, *On Being Included: Racism and Diversity in Institutional Life* (Durham: Duke University Press, 2012), 43.

7. *Report of Proceedings of a Commission Appointed by General Nathanael Greene on 26 February 1781 to Conduct Talks with the Cherokees,* Nathanael Green Papers, 1775–85, folder 5, Library of Congress.

8. Rebecca Messbarger, "President's Introduction to ASECS Town Hall," https://www.asecs.org/single-post/president-s-introduction-to-asecs-town-hall

9. Kaul, "Reading at Odds," "Scholarship in a Time of Crisis," supplement issue, *Eighteenth Century: Theory and Interpretation*. https://ecti.english.illinois.edu/files/2020/09/CFP.9._Reading-at-Odds_.pdf

Decolonizing Eighteenth-Century Studies: An Indigenous Perspective

ROBBIE RICHARDSON

It's very clear from the high attendance numbers at the "Decolonizing ASECS" roundtable at the 2021 Virtual Annual Meeting of the American Society for Eighteenth-Century Studies and the continuing expansion of the number of panels with Indigenous, global, and transatlantic foci that decolonization is a topic of interest to many people in our field. Over the last few years, I have been often asked to speak on this subject, primarily because I am Mi'gmaq and a member of Pabineau First Nation (Oinpegitjoig L'Noeigati) and have been writing about Indigenous people in the eighteenth century for some time. Native people and issues around Indigeneity have not received very much attention in eighteenth-century studies until fairly recently; we are often considered a subject more suitable for so-called Early American Studies. Yet Indigenous people exist outside the paradigms and histories of settler nation-states and were active agents in the transatlantic world and beyond. To my mind, part of the process of decolonizing the field, whatever that ultimately means, is to recover this sense of agency, to discuss the historical and continuing impact of the colonization of the Americas on both Indigenous people and the cultural imaginary and wealth of Europeans, and to tell stories of Indigenous knowledge and survival. All of this should be in service of the sovereignty and decolonial goals of Indigenous nations today. But I am at the same time highly suspicious of this sudden attention to Native people in an environment in which words have replaced action and scholarship often serves as a stand-in for material political commitments and activism, and I wonder how this energy can serve the Native people and communities who need it most, rather than boost the careers of academics or the legitimacy of universities.

The pandemic has exposed and exasperated vast inequalities, both nationally and internationally. In the face of this economic gulf and the expanding precarity of so many people, I wonder what academics mean by "decolonization" and what are the limits of that understanding? Does it mean tweaking curricula to add more diverse authors, or does it mean material practices that can benefit people outside of our narrow institutional worlds? Academia has a long history of appropriating the language of liberation struggles, but too often this serves to defang such struggles. In our present moment, university administrators, politicians, even sports teams with racist logos, are using the vocabulary and symbols of decolonizing, but radical words or land acknowledgements underpinned by empire, neoliberal capitalism, and settler colonialism do not feel like Indigenous liberation to me.[1]

Eve Tuck and K. Wayne Yang's "Decolonization Is Not a Metaphor" was published in 2012 and is still heavily cited, but, if anything, the "easy adoption of decolonizing discourse" that they describe has vastly expanded in recent years.[2] I noticed many scholars at the 2021 Virtual Annual Meeting of ASECS giving land acknowledgements, a practice toward which Native people in Canada have grown deeply skeptical. We cannot help but feel such acknowledgments are often a textbook example of what Tuck and Yang describe as "settler moves to innocence."[3] I appreciate that the motives for such gestures are good, but I don't understand to whom they are addressed or the purpose they are meant to serve other than to absolve the speaker and their institution.

In 2015, the Truth and Reconciliation Commission of Canada (TRC) released its final report on the establishment and legacy of Canada's Indian residential schools, concluding that they were an act of "cultural genocide."[4] The recent and ongoing discoveries of mass unmarked graveyards of Indigenous children at the sites of these schools has revealed to non-Indigenous people around the world that what happened to us was a genocide that need not be qualified with an adjective.[5] Canada's failure to implement the TRC's 94 calls to action to help guide the future toward reconciliation, and its ongoing efforts at resource extraction on Native land, led Indigenous activists blockading an oil pipeline at Wet'suwet'en to declare in 2020 that "Reconciliation is dead."[6] The rhetoric of truth and reconciliation has been appropriated by individuals and institutions while Native people across North

America, particularly poor Native people, continue to be incarcerated and killed by police at high rates, have worse health outcomes, and lack access to clean drinking water on many reserves (as has been the case for nearly twenty years in my community), all the while resisting the incursions of the oil and gas, logging, and other extractive industries. It's frustrating to see the failed practices of liberal reconciliation being repurposed in academic circles that are only now turning to Indigenous peoples. If an academic is inclined to give a land acknowledgement, I propose that they additionally contribute materially to an Indigenous cause, or actively engage with Indigenous scholarship and thought.

Frantz Fanon notes, in *The Wretched of the Earth*, that intellectuals outside of actual liberation struggles or political activism represent the "narcissistic monologue [of] the colonialist bourgeoisie."[7] The stated social justice concerns of academics in the humanities frequently align with mainstream corporate and institutional priorities, or at least get easily repurposed into the discourse of diversity and inclusion. And within academia, as Fanon reminds us, even the colonized intellectual is forced to believe in "the notion of a society of individuals where each is locked in his subjectivity, where wealth lies in thought."[8] Academics often focus on individual, rather than systemic critique, and, instead of attempting to build or contribute to movements of solidarity, they can filter energy away from Indigenous and other radical struggles and take up valuable space and resources. This includes Indigenous academics, and we must work hard to decenter ourselves and amplify the voices of Indigenous elders, artists, activists, and movements if decolonization is to mean anything other than hearing the opinions of a select few privileged people and ignoring the needs of living communities.

While I am skeptical of the benefits that the performance of political action and decolonizing rhetoric in academia can have for Indigenous people and solidarity movements, I do not mean to diminish the work of scholars in the field who are looking to make our departmental and organizational structures more equitable. This is difficult and often unrewarding work, and I am thankful to those who undertake it. Most importantly, those people are holding institutions to account for their rhetoric of justice and equality and finding ways to better distribute those institutions' resources. On a more modest, pedagogical level, there are some changes that can be made in the classroom to expand the field and include Indigenous voices. I don't think that this is "decolonization" per se, but rather a commitment to expanding not only *what* we teach and learn, but also *how* we teach and learn. Eighteenth-centuryists should read scholars in both Indigenous and Early American studies in devising their curricula and also make transatlantic and other global connections in their teaching. We should include early Indigenous writers like

Samson Occom, Hendrick Aupaumut, and William Apess, but also treaties, museum collections, wampum, other forms of material culture, and so forth. How did people tell stories and make meaning in ways other than printed books, and how and why were these alternate systems so often willfully ignored or suppressed? What role did the collection of Indigenous objects as curiosities or ethnographic items play in obscuring their epistemological functions, and how can the latter be recovered? Perhaps most importantly, how might Indigenous notions of relationality embedded in our languages and cosmologies inform both our scholarship and our way of being in the world? The stakes for many Indigenous people pursuing scholarship and telling our stories are high since, as Māori educator Linda Tuhiwai Smith reminds us, we have "a very powerful need to bring back into existence a world fragmented and dying."⁹ Academics who are seriously interested in "decolonizing" their classrooms should connect with local Indigenous communities, learn their histories, invite them to speak to their classes, and read some scholarship from those nations. They need to challenge the structure of settler colonialism in more meaningful ways, in part by understanding its history, but also by studying and critiquing its current form, both in North America and around the world. To suggest that everybody can and should be doing Indigenous Studies is to diminish the many years of work by Native scholars. But I think that expanding the global eighteenth century to seriously engage with Indigenous thought and radical hope can help make the discipline more future-oriented in this troubling time.

Notes

1. The Chicago Blackhawks added a land acknowledgement before home games in 2020. See https://nativenewsonline.net/currents/chicago-blackhawks-land-acknowledgement-an-empty-gesture-for-local-native-people

2. See Tuck and Yang, "Decolonization is Not a Metaphor," *Decolonization: Indigeneity, Education & Society* 1, no. 1 (2012): 1–40. The quotation is from their abstract (1).

3. Tuck and Yang, "Decolonization is Not a Metaphor," 10. On land acknowledgments, see Joe Wark, "Land Acknowledgements in the Academy: Refusing the Settler Myth," *Curriculum Inquiry*, 51, no. 2 (2021), 191–209.

4. *Honouring the Truth, Reconciling for the Future: Summary of the Final*

Report of the Truth and Reconciliation Commission of Canada (July 2015), 1. https://ehprnh2mwo3.exactdn.com/wp-content/uploads/2021/01/Executive_Summary_English_Web.pdf

5. See Erica Violet Lee, "Native children didn't 'lose' their lives at residential schools. Their lives were stolen," *The Guardian*, 6 July 2021. https://www.theguardian.com/commentisfree/2021/jul/06/native-children-didnt-lose-their-lives-at-residential-schools-their-lives-were-stolen

6. "'Revolution is alive': Canada protests spawn climate and Indigenous rights movement," *The Guardian*, 28 February 2020. https://www.theguardian.com/world/2020/feb/28/canada-pipeline-protests-climate-indigenous-rights

7. Fanon, *The Wretched of the Earth* (New York: Grove Press, 2004), 11.

8. Fanon, *The Wretched of the Earth*, 11.

9. Smith, *Decolonizing Methodologies: Research and Indigenous Peoples* (New York: St. Martin's Press, 1999), 28.

Notes on Abolitionist Pedagogy from Philadelphia

CHI-MING YANG

"We're all systematically miseducated."

— Josh Glenn

"We have to redefine what work is, and what our education is teaching us."

— Ghani Songster

The 2021 Annual Meeting of the American Society for Eighteenth-Century Studies (ASECS) convened virtually amidst the COVID-19 pandemic and after nearly a year of widespread racial justice protests in response to the murder of George Floyd by police officers on 25 May 2020 and the fatal shootings of hundreds of other unarmed Black Americans before him. Like many, I had been in the streets by day and otherwise quarantining at home, attending expert grassroots webinars on defunding police violence, and rethinking the role of academia and academic research during a state of emergency. I kept returning to Arundhati Roy's inciting words, "the pandemic is a portal."[1] What might have opened up during this time of closures and social trauma? What practices had emerged that could help ensure we would not go back to doing business as usual? To a degree, the heightened awareness of systemic racism, failed capitalist infrastructure, and the legacies of slavery, combined with the availability of videoconferencing to bridge physical distances, were breaking down pedagogical boundaries between the university and various publics. It became possible, even *safe*, to invite more guest speakers than usual into the classroom's shared virtual space and to divert unspent academic budgets toward compensating public intellectuals for their labor.

In April 2021, organizers with Philadelphia's Youth Art & Self-Empowerment Project (YASP) shared with my undergraduate students their efforts to dismantle Pennsylvania's corrupt juvenile sentencing and detention system.[2] Their work illuminated a timeline of criminalizing Black children that stretched back to the runaway slave advertisements we had studied as documents of both slavery and resistance. With over 48,000 young people behind bars in the U.S., youth incarceration is a symptom of the racist police state in which we live, a state that disproportionately relies on law enforcement to deal with the social crises of housing insecurity, mental illness, sexual violence, and poverty more generally.[3] From the vantage point of an eighteenth-century studies scholar, our contemporary system, which continues to foreclose the futures of the most vulnerable, was developed in tandem with the vagrancy laws, enclosure acts, and plantation slave codes of the British and American Empires.[4] We know that the plantationocene was reshaped into the prison-industrial complex and criminal justice system that touch every workplace and walk of life.[5] We know these facts even as we conduct our research and teaching about the history of colonialism within corporatized universities that reproduce the lineages of racial, class, and sexual discrimination.

All too often, universities perpetuate inequality under the guises of progress, excellence, and efficiency—the logic of the market. The past years' pandemic austerity measures are only the most recent instance of universities punishing workers while making millionaires of administrators. Keeanga-Yamahtta Taylor puts this into stark focus when she writes, "There are 400 American billionaires *because* there are 45 million people living in poverty. Profit comes at the expense of the living wage. Corporate executives, university presidents, and capitalists in general are living the good life— *because* so many others are living a life of hardship."[6] In divorcing our historical studies from current social realities we perpetuate the "systemic miseducation" that plagues well-funded and underfunded schools alike, as one YASP organizer pointed out.

What does this mean for eighteenth-century studies, especially when it is reconceived as "the long abolitionist project," to borrow from Dylan Rodríguez?[7] As scholars, we can help correct mainstream denialism of the legacies of settler-colonialism and genocide, and further connect those histories to current institutional practices of labor and land management. Our knowledge work is situated within spaces that hide material inequities behind the corporate brandishing of Enlightenment principles of religious toleration, free markets, and possessive individualism. Some of us work at schools founded in the eighteenth century, whose ties to slavery and the dispossession of Indigenous people continue in the form of unethical practices in our museums and medical schools, as well as the exploitation of poor communities and Black and Brown residents displaced by university real estate ventures and terrorized by campus police patrolling far outside campus.[8] However, if we understand abolition to mean eliminating unjust structures of policing, we must not only grapple with the place of our schools in the material environment, but also ask how "we" construct the parameters of our discipline. This means leading difficult conversations about Indigenous landback campaigns and reparations for slavery, as Georgetown University, Princeton Theological Seminary, Virginia Theological Seminary, and others have begun.[9] It also means confronting the infrastructure of dispossession as it functions today.

In his piercing diagnosis of the university as a "mechanism of power," Davarian Baldwin underscores the interlocking operations of "land, labor, and commercial development" that locate the roots of miseducation far beyond matters of curricula, disciplinarity, or classroom pedagogy.[10] An institution like the University of Pennsylvania, one of the nation's richest universities in one of its poorest big cities, regularly exploits its non-profit status by refusing to make payments in lieu of taxes (PILOTs) to the city of Philadelphia in the way that other wealthy Ivy League institutions that are similarly exempt from paying property taxes have done.[11] Penn masks this predatory relationship by making philanthropic donations, establishing diversity task forces and community outreach centers, and touting its civic mindedness. In reality, the university profits from the grave underfunding of public schools, and thus participates in the school-to-prison pipeline that criminalizes children at alarming rates.

As universities gentrify working-class neighborhoods, they perpetuate the violence of segregation, surveillance, evictions, and homelessness.[12] Instead of investing in permanent, affordable housing for low-income families, urban universities direct money into their police budgets to fortify campuses against the communities they have impoverished, which only extends the cycles of crime and punishment. The University of Pennsylvania, for example, has long reneged on its commitment to stop the displacement of the residents of the Black Bottom neighborhood in its midst.[13] As I write, the University City Townhomes, one of the historic, remaining examples of federally subsidized, low-income housing in "University City," is about to be demolished, and seventy households will be forced out amidst a Philadelphia-wide housing crisis and pandemic.[14] University pledges of civic engagement bear strange fruit.

Activists and scholars of the history of racism and policing remind us that abolitionism is neither a thing of the eighteenth-century past nor limited to the elimination of prisons or police forces. Housing justice, for example, is central to the struggle for a safe and equitable world. The long, unfinished, abolitionist eighteenth century might best be characterized by M. Jacqui Alexander's concept of "palimpsestic time." The past becomes visible as a set of imperfect erasures from the perspective of a "rescrambling" of the ideas of "here and now" and "then and there," to "here and there" and "then and now."[15] Alexander's 2005 study of U.S. Empire spans colonial, neo-colonial, and neo-imperial histories; its critique of institutional and state power, heterosexism, and heteropatriarchy through a Black feminist frame feels newly urgent in 2022. A pedagogy of crossing, she argues, is premised upon the primordial crossings of Atlantic slavery, but encompasses a number of other key boundary crossings, including that of academic and community work. Alexander writes that "this moment not only challenges but also undermines epistemic frameworks that are simply inadequate to the task of delineating ... itineraries of violence that are given other names such as democracy and civilization; ... probing our function and location as radical intellectuals (and I intend the term intellectual in the broadest sense of a commitment to a life of the mind whether or not one is linked to the academy) ... that is, our ethical commitments, the contours and character of our class affiliations and loyalties, and the interpretive frameworks we bring to bear on the histories to which we choose to be aligned."[16]

How might we take up abolition, reparations, and palimpsestic time in our own institutional practices of studying and being? We could begin pragmatically by addressing the contours of eighteenth-century studies through the structure of ASECS gatherings. To break out of the Eurocentric mold, might we periodically hold joint meetings with an Area Studies association? Or host a two-speaker keynote that pairs an eighteenth-centuryist with a scholar or public intellectual from a different historical field? To attend to the material conditions of the gathering, we might invite as a keynote speaker a representative of a local Indigenous or labor organization from whichever city hosts the conference. What would it look like for ASECS to have a capacious and inclusive definition of academic labor at a moment when the majority of university employees live precariously and when our conferences often take place in hotels where the workers may not be unionized?

Following Alexander, one mode of decolonizing our field would be to refuse the "fictitious" boundary between community work and academic work.[17] By recognizing the commonality of laboring bodies and knowledge production across different spheres, we also engage in a rigorous form of historical inquiry, what Paulo Freire described as "History [as] time filled with possibility and not inexorably determined."[18] Whether at an academic conference, in the classroom, or in the streets, social justice and abolitionist perspectives make newly visible the connections between our capitalist present and the eighteenth-century past and the relations of mutualism, patronage, and predation that structure our university communities.

Notes

I would like to acknowledge the wonderful comradeship of my fellow abolitionists with Police Free Penn and the Cops off Campus Coalition.

1. Roy, "The Pandemic is a Portal," *Financial Times*, 3 April 2020. https://www.ft.com/content/10d8f5e8-74eb-11ea-95fe-fcd274e920ca.

2. For more on YASP, see http://www.yasproject.com. For the campaign to end youth incarceration, see Care, Not Control, https://carenotcontrol.com.

3. See Wendy Sawyer, "Youth Confinement: The Whole Pie 2019," *Prison Policy Initiative.* https://www.prisonpolicy.org/reports/youth2019.html.

4. See Peter Linebaugh, "Police and Plunder," *CounterPunch*, 13 February 2015. https://www.counterpunch.org/2015/02/13/police-and-plunder/.

5. See Donna Haraway and Anna Tsing, *Reflections on the Plantationocene: A Conversation with Donna Haraway and Anna Tsing* (https://edgeeffects.net/haraway-tsing-plantationocene/) and Katherine McKittrick, "Plantation Futures," *Small Axe* 17, no. 3 (2013): 1–15.

6. Taylor, *From #BlackLivesMatter to Black Liberation* (Chicago: Haymarket Books, 2016), 194.

7. Rodríguez, "Abolition as Praxis of Human Being: A Foreword," *Harvard Law Review* 132, no. 6 (2019), 1575. See also Charmaine Chua, "Abolition is a Constant Struggle: Five Lessons from Minneapolis," *Theory & Event*, 23, no. 4 supplement (2020): S127–S147.

8. See the recent ACLU report to the United Nations on human rights violations by University of Pennsylvania and Philadelphia police (https://www.aclupa.org/en/un-report). For reporting on university medical ethics violations and calls for reparations, see https://billypenn.com/2021/07/31/philadelphia-brains-medical-examiner-university-pennsylvania-lawsuit-move-remains/. See also https://www.thedp.com/article/2021/06/kligman-prison-experiments-petition-police-free-penn

and https://www.inquirer.com/news/mortion-collection-skulls-upenn-museum-repatriation-racial-justice-20210405.html.

9. See https://www.aaup.org/article/bringing-abolition-ivory-tower#. YQp70y1h2X0

10. Baldwin, *In the Shadow of the Ivory Tower: How Universities are Plundering our Cities* (New York: Bold Type Books, 2021), 38, 42.

11. See https://www.pennforpilots.org. Penn's retiring President, Amy Gutmann, nominated by President Joe Biden to be the next U.S. ambassador to Germany, paid Biden over $900,000 in 2018–19 to be a "Professor of Practice" who taught zero classes. Gutmann, the highest-paid Ivy president, has had an annual salary of $3.6 million dollars. Even as many university workers are undercompensated, in fiscal year 2021 the University's endowment grew 41.1% to over $20 billion. See https://www.inquirer.com/news/joe-biden-penn-salary-lectures-20190712.html and https://www.thedp.com/article/2021/09/penns-2021-endowment-fund-rises-41-1.

12. See Sophie House and Krystle Okafor, "Under One Roof: Building an Abolitionist Approach to Housing Justice," *N.Y.U. Journal of Legislation & Public Policy* (1 November 2020). https://nyujlpp.org/quorum/house-okafor-building-abolitionist-approach-housing/

13. Statement by the University of Pennsylvania Trustees from February 23, 1969. https://archives.upenn.edu/exhibits/penn-history/science-center/part-3. See also, https://theblackbottom.wordpress.com/communities/blackbottom/history/.

14. See https://www.thedp.com/article/2022/01/upenn-broken-promises-university-city.

15. Alexander, *Pedagogies of Crossing: Meditations on Feminism, Sexual Politics, Memory, and the Sacred* (Durham: Duke University Press, 2005), 190.

16. Alexander, *Pedagogies of Crossing*, 3.

17. Alexander, *Pedagogies of Crossing*, 112.

18. Freire, *Pedagogy of Freedom: Ethics, Democracy, and Civic Courage*, trans. Patrick Clarke (Lanham: Rowman & Littlefield, 1998), 26.

Two #BIPOC Objects: Cultivating Epistemic Disobedience in the Undergraduate Classroom

PICHAYA DAMRONGPIWAT

As the "Decolonizing ASECS" panel at the 2021 Virtual Annual Meeting of the American Society for Eighteenth-Century Studies (ASECS) demonstrates, decolonizing eighteenth-century studies entails decolonizing curricula and research methodologies at every level. As an individual scholar and teacher, my pedagogical practices took shape—and continue to transform—within a climate of racial reckoning and in witness of urgent calls for individual and organizational accountability. Though the call to "decolonize stories" has become incredibly fraught, in lieu of a theoretical intervention, this essay develops an accessible, pedagogically oriented framework for power analysis via the concept of the epistemically disobedient object, a concept that may be applied to a broad range of texts, genres, works of visual art, and historical artifacts. I will present two such objects as examples from my undergraduate classroom: a speech by the Cherokee matriarch Nanye'hi and the figure of Br'er Rabbit, the trickster.

In the context of eighteenth-century coloniality, non-Western objects and artifacts, because of the ways in which they do not conform to Western-based ways of knowing, inherently question the twin consequences of eighteenth-century epistemology: the ossification of Western knowledge-making practices and colonial logic into knowledge per se and the rhetoric of Enlightenment modernity that continues to shape our notions of sociality, political participation, moral reasoning, and scientific logic. While epistemically disobedient objects expose the triangulation and mutual reinforcement of white supremacy, capitalism, and patriarchy posed by the BIPOC framework, they also suggest that another triangulation exists between racial justice/solidarity, survival, and decolonial epistemologies. Indeed, political calls for "unity" often ring hollow alongside calls for a kind of color-blind epistemology, a search for universality, or an underlying equivalence between different, culturally inflected systems of knowledge. Rather, due to their embeddedness in the eighteenth century and its diverse socio-political and epistemological legacies, BIPOC texts and objects are well-poised to help us think through these issues in a decolonial way.

In 2017, the Department of Literatures in English at Cornell University (formerly the Department of English) consolidated its introductory survey course offerings. Prior to the change, there were two distinct surveys, one British and one American, each two semesters long. After the change, the two surveys were combined into one year-long sequence. While surveys in the past, at this institution and certainly many others, ordinarily omit the early American period in favor of Romanticism, the first half of the survey course was revised to include early American materials, including Indigenous texts, up through 1800.

In Fall 2018, the faculty who designed the new syllabus made conscious efforts to juxtapose Indigenous and colonial voices. One significant pairing was that of *The Autobiography of Benjamin Franklin* (1791) with the Seneca orator Sagoyewatha's speech, "Reply to Missionary Jacob Cram," in which Sagoyewatha responds to a Boston missionary's proselytizing among the Seneca. Apart from the insights it offers, this pairing is also an acknowledgment that the lands and waters on which Cornell is located were originally populated by the Haudenosaunee people. Also known as the Six Nations, the Haudenosaunee were comprised of six distinct nations in upstate New York, including the Seneca.

In this case, the juxtaposition of Franklin and Sagoyewatha is predicated upon the existence of Indigenous-white settler relations, and its study illuminates the dynamics that organized the increasingly complex socio-political, religious, and cultural effects of settler colonialism in this geographical area and period: a potent concoction of Christian religiosity and Native logical inquiry that confronts many of the received stereotypes of Native cultures as not fundamentally based on reason, stereotypes that then served as justification for eroding Indigenous claims to political and cultural sovereignty. Yet I wondered whether teaching non-Western texts produced under coloniality via the lens of their own non-Western epistemological framework would be sufficient to successfully disentangle non-Western art objects from coloniality.

Toward this end, I introduced students to the idea of "disobedient objects," which derives from the framework of decolonial thinking put forward by Walter Mignolo, specifically his concept of "epistemic disobedience," though I did so with the recognition that Mignolo himself belongs to a white settler community in South America. Yet while Mignolo's framework emerged during the collapse of First/Second/Third World distinctions, I apply the concept of epistemic disobedience to the eighteenth century precisely in order to center non-Western artifacts and the epistemologies from which they originate. Of course, this model does not apply to every teacher in every educational setting. Each teacher's positionality (especially in relation to settler colonialism) interacts differently with the diversity of students they serve—including my own. The dilemma that I confront as a non-Native teacher serving very few Native students is to find a sustainable balance between emphasizing inter- and multiracial entanglements, especially in lieu of "authentic" insights into Native cultures, and the epistemic disobedience that non-Western texts bring to the classroom, including the fact that, in many cases, these texts are more responsive to pedagogical approaches that center their non-Western properties—epistemological, political, cultural, and so forth.

With all of this in mind, I'd like to offer two case studies as models for pedagogical practice. The first is a speech given by Nanye'hi, a Cherokee matriarch and political representative, to Benjamin Franklin. The epistemic disobedience of Nanye'hi's speech lies in its resistance to Western patriarchal norms, which may be captured in brief via the distinction between *maternalizing* political relations (in the Cherokee case) and *politicizing* maternal relations, with the latter a very familiar—and familiarly dangerous—tendency in Western discourse. The second involves the cultural fluidity and vexing complexity of the Br'er Rabbit figure, whose full legacy spans Africa, Indigenous North America, and the African American imagination. In his journey—perhaps better described as his emergence, disappearance, and re-surfacing—across continents and historical periods, Br'er Rabbit becomes a crux for critically reexamining the longstanding desire for coherence and cogency in the originary narratives surrounding most cultural artifacts, not just Indigenous ones. These narratives are, in other words, the stories we tell about our most ubiquitous or beloved cultural touchstones that nonetheless reveal more about our own desires than about the history of the touchstones themselves. As a trickster figure,

Br'er Rabbit offers an alternate way of thinking about survival in Black and Native cultures, in a world of increasing white-settler cultural and socio-political dominance—with the latter best described by considering the figure's appropriation in Joel Chandler Harris's Uncle Remus stories.

On 8 September 1787, representatives of the Cherokee Women's Council delivered a plea for peace to Benjamin Franklin, who was then governor of Pennsylvania and a delegate to the Constitutional Convention. Chief among them was Nanye'hi, known in English as Nancy Ward, who held the title of *Ghighua*, or Beloved Woman, a high-level political office in the Cherokee Nation. Born in 1738 into a politically prominent family in the Cherokee city of Chota (aptly described as a "mother town" because it was a place of refuge), Nanye'hi's legacy includes both bravery in war and shrewd negotiations in peace. Among other accomplishments, she is remembered for her advocacy for protecting Cherokee lands from increasing encroachment by white settlers. Nanye'hi's address illustrates how the matriarchal Cherokee Nation conceived of political ties in terms of the physical and emotional bonds between mothers and children. The existence of the Women's Council itself attests to the major role that women played not only in their individual families, but also as political officers and ambassadors. The speech's key intervention in relation to Western epistemology is the way in which political relations are maternalized, in contrast to the Western, patriarchal tendency to politicize maternal relations. In other words, the claim to power lies not in the political *use* or *efficacy* of maternal relationships, but rather derives from the women's ability to (pro)create. Nanye'hi begins, "I am in hopes if you Rightly consider it that woman is the mother of All—and that woman Does not pull Children out of Trees or Stumps nor out of old Logs, but out of their Bodies, so that they ought to mind what a woman says, and look upon her as a mother."[1] With this premise of maternal authority in mind, Nanye'hi then extends these relations to Franklin and those that he represents, as part of the practice of creating and sustaining peace, now infused with familial advice on morality: "I have Taken the privelage to Speak to you as my own Children, & the same as if you had sucked my Breast—and I am in hopes you have a beloved woman amongst you who will help to put her Children Right if they do wrong, as I shall do the same."[2] In the context of decolonial thinking, the Beloved Woman's address illustrates how relations that Western thinking has taken for granted—in this case, the relationship between familial and political relations—can be reconfigured as part of the ongoing effort to decolonize epistemology. The address also urges us to consider the modes of relation-making that shore up our ethics, specifically those that govern the ways by which people may be related to one another, interrogating not only how these relations encode and sustain power, but also revealing the generosity and sincerity with which these relations are extended by Nanye'hi to others across difference.

Br'er Rabbit is best known as a character in Joel Chandler Harris's book series, published in the 1870s and subsequently incorporated into Disney's Uncle Remus stories, including that of the Tar-Baby. He survives to this day primarily as an example of Southern Americana. However, his complicated origins involve numerous African traditions from West, Central, and South Africa, as well as Native American parallels, including stories of rabbit tricksters from the Algonquin, Cherokee, and other nations in Eastern North America. Br'er Rabbit exudes epistemic disobedience because of his composite, multi-cultural origins as well as his history of being later co-opted and appropriated by white American culture. The crux of my reading—and the key to mobilizing this figure within the pedagogical framework of epistemic disobedience—is casting the Rabbit-as-Trickster as representing or modeling practices of survival. Numerous scholars have pointed out how the trickster serves as a point of contact with the sacred, facilitated via laughter and ideas of transformation, such as sudden upset or reversal.[3] The cultural affinity between African American and Native American legends of the trickster, then, indicate a shared, though differently inflected, impulse for survival and resilience. To survive, the trickster assumes many forms, continually shape-shifting, disguising, and outwitting.

Perhaps the most striking pairing in the Br'er Rabbit stories is not his rivalries with Br'er Wolf and Br'er Fox, or even his maneuvers with the enigmatic Tar Baby, but rather his conversations with Miss Meadows [see Figure 1]. Here, Br'er Rabbit is trying to woo Miss Meadows with his skillful talk—perhaps echoing the kind of story that Uncle Remus tells the Little Boy in order to introduce him to the "ways of the world." Br'er Rabbit, even after his appropriation in the Uncle Remus Stories, still has the power to introduce us to his world—and thereby to reorient and help decolonize our own.

Figure 1. Frontispiece from Joel Chandler Harris, *Nights with Uncle Remus: Myths and Legends of the Old Plantation* (1883). Courtesy of the William Charvat Collection of American Literature, in the Rare Books and Manuscripts Library, Thompson Library Special Collections, The Ohio State University.

Notes

I thank Rayna Kalas, for whom I was a Teaching Assistant in the newly revamped survey course, as well as numerous other colleagues in the Department of Literatures in English at Cornell University for their guidance and vision on curricular reform.
1. Nancy Ward/Nanye'hi, "Cherokee Women to Governor Benjamin Franklin," in *Transatlantic Feminisms in the Age of Revolutions*, ed. Lisa L. Moore, Joanna Brooks, and Caroline Wigginton (Oxford: Oxford University Press, 2012), 181.
2. Ward/Nanye'hi, "Cherokee Women," 181.
3. In some cases, the trickster figure is itself divine. For example, Eshu is a Yoruba "trickster god" who demands sacrificial offerings on par with those of other deities (Eugenio Matibag, "Ifá and Interpretation: An Afro-Caribbean Literary Practice," in *Sacred Possessions: Vodou, Santería, Obeah, and the Caribbean*, ed. Margarite Fernández Olmos and Lizabeth Paravisini-Gebert [New Brunswick: Rutgers University Press, 1997], 156–58). Nimachia Howe's *Retelling Trickster in Naapi's Language* (Louisville: University Press of Colorado, 2019) is a recent study of Indigenous linguistics and the philosophy of Naapi, the trickster figure who appears in Nitsitapiisinni (Blackfoot) origin stories. Howe's "re-telling" reveals how many narratives associated with Naapi depend on a series of fundamentally linguistic misunderstandings of the Blackfoot language, to which most non-Native scholars lack access. The sacrality of the trickster figure has also endured into modernity, albeit in increasingly diffuse and diverse formations. See, for example, David Afriyie Donkor's *Spiders of the Market: Ghanaian Trickster Performance in a Web of Neoliberalism* (Bloomington: Indiana University Press, 2016) and Babacar M'Baye's *The Trickster Comes West: Pan-African Influence in Early Black Diasporan Narratives* (Jackson: University Press of Mississippi, 2009). In the latter, the trickster creates a "third space" between white supremacy and Black radicalism that, at the very least, gestures toward the figure's extraordinary capabilities—and thereby harkens back to its original associations with the sacred.

Unsettling our Classrooms

ELIZABETH HUTCHINSON

I write as an art historian working at a white-majority private liberal arts college in the unceded territory of the Lenape people, in a city full of museums with encyclopedic collections that are the result of imperial and colonial violence. I teach courses centered on the art and visual culture of Indigenous and Black America as well as the visual archives of settler colonialism, slavery, and other forms of social violence from the eighteenth through the twentieth centuries. I have been active for years in initiatives to increase diversity, equity, and inclusion at my school and have served on several advisory boards dedicated to similar work at museums. But I have come to be ambivalent about the goal of "decolonizing" the institutions with which I work.

In "Refusing the University," Quechua critical theorist Sandy Grande has identified the university as "an arm of the settler state—a site where the logics of elimination, capital accumulation, and dispossession are reconstituted."[1] One can say the same thing about museums, as Amy Lonetree has demonstrated.[2] Grande's critique relates to, but is distinct from other critiques of the academy as "neoliberal, Eurocentric, and/or patriarchal" that seek remedies in changing personnel and curricula. Finding common ground with Black radicals promoting abolitionism, such as Robin D. G. Kelley, Grande questions how our institutions can resolve historical injustices through recognition-based reform projects.[3] By "recognition," Kelley refers to acts of acknowledging and respecting difference that are limited and often reinforce existing systems of domination.[4] In "Decolonization is not a Metaphor," Eve Tuck and K. Wayne Yang describe the "long and bumbled history of non-Indigenous peoples making moves to alleviate the impacts of colonization," including "the too-easy adoption of decolonizing discourse" in gestures that serve as settler "*moves to innocence ...*, which problematically attempt to reconcile settler guilt and complicity, and rescue settler futurity."[5] From this perspective, it is valuable to consider whether our institutions even can be decolonized or if, instead, we need to adopt different strategies. Grande proposes the "politics of refusal," a concept devised by Audra Simpson to describe diverse historic and ongoing Haudenosaunee ways of resisting Canadian and American colonial forces.[6] Similarly, Tuck and Yang propose the idea of "unsettling" our work, resisting the incorporation of Indigeneity within settler institutions and instead making room for cultural incommensurability.[7] Importantly, these theorists create room for us to serve as accomplices to parallel social justice movements that recognize the distinctiveness of diverse struggles, but are grounded in shared commitments to anti-capitalism, feminism, and anti-colonialism.

The goal of unsettling is not reforming institutions, but remaking the world. How can we support this work in our teaching and scholarship? Métis anthropologist Zoe Todd offers some strategies. The first is what she calls "citational rebellion." She underscores Sara Ahmed's insight that one way the university reproduces itself is through the practice of ensuring that all new scholars, including scholars of color, cite "white men generation after generation, reinforcing the white, patriarchal Eurocentrism of our disciplines."[8] As Todd notes, this practice serves to reinforce academia as a "white public space." It also fails to engage with, or even recognize, BIPOC concepts and theories. As Todd points out, regarding such urgent contemporary topics as climate change, Indigenous thinkers have decades of work as observers, analysts, and theorists that could enrich the discussion of how to conceive of the other-than-human world.[9] She encourages scholars to expand their reading and whom they affirm as authorities through citation. I would argue that this is a practice that goes beyond scholarship and reaches into our classrooms, compelling us to rethink our syllabi. For the past several years, I have worked to not only add more BIPOC subject matter to my courses, but also to assign more Indigenous and Black scholars' work as models for the interpretation of objects. For, as Todd points out, implementing Indigenous thought in colonial contexts often involves appropriation. Building on the work of Anishinaabe and Haudenosaunee scholar Vanessa Watts, she writes, "the appropriation of Indigenous thinking in European contexts *without Indigenous interlocutors present to hold the use of Indigenous stories and laws to account* flattens, distorts, and erases the embodied, legal-governance, and spiritual aspects of Indigenous thinking."[10] Increasing the presence of Indigenous interlocutors requires more than just expanding reading lists. Whenever possible (i.e., whenever I can secure compensation), I bring community leaders, scholars, and/or artists into the classroom or take students to meet them. When that's not an option, I look for videos and recordings that allow students to hear the languages and perspectives of the makers, users, and *relatives* of the work we are studying and to see the land on which it has been created.

Another vital strategy identified by Todd is unsettling colonial ideas about how knowledge is produced. She points to the work of Kwakwaka'wakw geographer Sarah Hunt on how Western academic treatments of Indigenous ontologies translate them into information to be analyzed in ways that reify and distort their value in the service of legitimizing academic study. Hunt turns to embodied practice, specifically dance, as a mode of Kwakwaka'wakw knowledge production that "negotiate[s] the demands of colonial academic institutions and praxis, for it is through dance that Indigenous ontologies are brought to life."[11] Storytelling might be understood as a similar practice. This perspective can help illuminate how creating classroom activities that defy Western academic norms can help students gain a richer understanding of knowledge production and embrace modalities that challenge the traditional emphasis on the research paper and the valuing of individually accumulated authority that goes with it. Multi-media projects, student involvement in creating programming, group projects, and the like can be more than just fashionable pedagogical trends; they can contribute to unsettling our classrooms. In my own experience, these strategies have served to improve the classroom experience for all students, including students of color and other minoritized students. For, as Megan Peiser has reminded us, BIPOC interlocutors "have always been here" in the academy, and it is our responsibility to make room for them to be heard and to find and listen to one another.[12] This works even better when I invite my students to use what they have learned from our reading, discussion, and visiting to help to develop the shape of our projects and the criteria we will use to assess them. In this process, they are called to consider our relationships with and our responsibilities to our objects of study and what kinds of work might help equip us to engage meaningfully in social change.

At the same time, it is vital to remember that the academy is inherently colonial and that our students need us to value knowledge production that takes place in other contexts. Here it is good to keep in mind Leanne Betasamosake Simpson's reminder that, if the goal is to restore Indigenous sovereignty, "Indigenizing the academy" will not get us there. What's needed is to legitimize education that takes place in communities and on the land, that is grounded in tribal values and modes of knowledge production.[13] This doesn't mean that we shouldn't try to unsettle our classrooms (and museums); it simply calls us to be clear-eyed about what we can and cannot accomplish by it. As Linda Tuhiwai Smith, whose *Decolonizing Methodologies* has been a watershed for this kind of discussion, has argued, "Research for social justice expands and improves the conditions for justice; it is an intellectual, cognitive and moral project, often fraught, never complete, but worthwhile."[14]

Notes

1. Grande, "Refusing the University," in *Toward What Justice? Describing Diverse Dreams of Justice in Education*, ed. Eve Tuck and K. Wayne Yang (New York: Routledge, 2018), 47.

2. Lonetree, *Decolonizing Museums: Representing Native America in National and Tribal Museums* (Chapel Hill: University of North Carolina Press, 2012).

3. See Kelley, "Black Study, Black Struggle," *The Boston Review* (2016). https://www.bostonreview.net/forum/robin-kelley-black-struggle-campus-protest/.

4. For more on this issue, see Glen Coulthard, *Red Skin, White Masks: Rejecting the Colonial Politics of Recognition* (Minneapolis: University of Minnesota Press, 2014).

5. Tuck and Yang, "Decolonization is not a metaphor," *Decolonization: Indigeneity, Education & Society* 1, no. 1 (2012), 3.

6. Grande, "Refusing the University," 50. Cf. Simpson, *Mohawk Interruptus: Political Life across the Borders of Settler States* (Durham: Duke University Press, 2014).

7. Tuck and Yang, "Decolonization is not a metaphor," 28.

8. Todd, "Indigenizing the Anthropocene," *Art in the Anthropocene: Encounters Among Aesthetics, Politics, Environments and Epistemologies,* ed. Heather Davis and Etienne Turpin (London: Open Humanities Press, 2015), 247. She is referencing Ahmed's blog post "White Men," Feminist Killjoys Blog, 4 November 2014. www.feministkilljoys.com/2014/11/04/white-men.

9. Todd, "An Indigenous Feminist's Take on the Ontological Turn: 'Ontology' is just another word for Colonialism," *Journal of Historical Sociology* 29, no. 1 (2016), 4–22. "Citational rebellion" is defined on 19.

10. Todd, "Ontological Turn," 9.

11. Todd, "Indigenizing," 245. She is referencing Sarah Hunt, "Ontologies of Indigeneity: The Politics of Embodying a Concept," *Cultural Geographies* 21, no. 1 (2014): 27–32.

12. Peiser, "We have always been here: Indigenous Scholars in/and Eighteenth-Century Studies," *Eighteenth-Century Fiction* 33, no. 2 (2020–21), 181–88.

13. Simpson, "Land as Pedagogy: Nishnaabeg Intelligence and Rebellious Transformation," *Decolonization: Indigeneity, Education & Society* 3, no. 3 (2014): 1–25.

14. Smith, *Decolonizing Methodologies: Research and Indigenous Peoples*, 2nd. ed. (New York: Zed Books, 2012), 341.

Praxis is no Metaphor: Diasporic Knowledges and Maroon Epistemes to Repair the World

PATRÍCIA MARTINS MARCOS

"I refuse the prison of 'I' and choose the open spaces of 'we.'"
— Toni Morrison, *The Source of Self-Regard*

"The West does not exist. I know. I've been there."
— Michel-Rolph Trouillot, *Silencing the Past*

Start with yourself. That must always be the first iteration—always. Collective change cannot happen without broad coalitions premised on the discomfort prompted by the willingness to listen, by the difficult decentering of oneself, and by the acknowledgement that power operates through us too, try as we may to resist it. Learn, unlearn, relearn. Be open to that difficult confrontation. Be prepared, also, to eschew familiar categories—they too reify power, silently, insidiously, and with the seeming innocence conferred only by the tacit conflation of the "normal" with the "natural." Accept this questioning—if not the outright abandonment—of inherited categorical certainties. Be prepared for radical change, for abolition, for the transformation of resistance into a realm of plural and protean reexistences. Recreate and reimagine the world, reconstitute and resignify a commons not structured by the scaffold of scarcity. Think with abundance. Economies of prestige confer legibility, but their attachment to rank and hierarchical clarity also hinder solidarity. They thwart our capacity to think from and with, instead teaching us to simply research about. Unborder the world and jettison strict dichotomies between subject and object, the West and the Global South, the "civilized" and the "savage." Accept and embrace these open-ended processes starting with and from you.

This preamble serves both as a ritual and a reminder. As a scholar of Portuguese colonialism, and as someone raised and educated in Portugal, colonialism and coloniality have come to represent far more than mere objects of disciplinary interest. In fact, the grip exercised by coloniality over the uninterrogated structures of my quotidian life forms the essence of my own project of unlearning imperialism—a project incorporated, both through praxis and hexis, into my intellectual and lived experience. Here, I echo Ariela Aïsha Azoulay's desire to repair the world by forging solutions devised outside of the existing terms—be they epistemic or political— afforded by imperialist structures.[1] That is the positioning I write from and with. Moreover, it is also the reason why I regard imperialism as a genre of storytelling that thrives on the promise of futurity and has no qualms about using all the violence it needs in order to will that "ideal" into being. Empire was a lie compelled onto me, too—a deceit of neat order, fixity, universal yearnings, clear-cut demarcations, and linear futurity. Until we are ready to face its silent workings within ourselves, decolonization will be nothing more than an empty gesture.

Both as individual scholars and members of the idiosyncratic field of eighteenth-century studies, we are often moored to the grandiose birthing myths of modernity. Here, the eighteenth century seemingly has it all: a spirit of secularism and equality, a *bonhomie* about progress, science, universal human rights, the ascendency of reason, and the collapse of the divine right of kings. Yet even as our field today confronts the many silences produced by these stories through its critiques of heteropatriarchy and imperial whiteness, it also tacitly reifies a canon whose core texts and working languages continue to largely overlap with the modern imaginary of the "developed" West. This privileging of the United Kingdom, France, and the United States—with perhaps a bit of Italy or Germany here and there—forces us to confront the weight of imperial hegemony within our own field. Or, to put matters somewhat differently, it may force us to consider what would an Afrocentric eighteenth century look like? Would the field be recognizable to its current active participants if we were to be asked to engage an eighteenth century shaped by Asian perspectives, Latin American experiences, and Indigenous worldviews? Speaking as a scholar of Portuguese eighteenth-century colonialism, I remain skeptical, but hopeful.

Both skepticism and hope serve as a reminder that we must start from our own positionality while aiming to privilege intentional praxis. As a junior scholar whose work weaves together a lesser-known part of Europe, West Africa, and the Americas, the *habitus* of asking if X place has any legitimate claim to an "Enlightenment"—or any other recognizable grand eighteenth-century narrative—still remains, in my experience, deeply ingrained. In this regard, there are small gestures scholars could adopt, if not to decolonize, then at least to open the field to new possibilities. For example, to abandon the habit of asking colleagues who study non-canonical sites, problems, or authors to justify why they belong—especially when "why" amounts to a demand for self-justification, rather than a proposition for mutual engagement. More than representing an unfair burden placed onto scholars already dedicated to the study of marginalized problems and communities, this question also expresses a hierarchy of scholarly priorities: who is seen as a "natural fit" versus who, conversely, will be asked to explain why their work matters or belongs. Gestures like this work in a way that is akin to the canon pushing back. In their most benign iteration, they may simply aim for commensurability: i.e., they're trying to make the unfamiliar legible in terms they already understand. But when borne out of a spirit of scarcity and moored to liberal fantasies of individual genius, they may serve to exclude by enforcing a narrow vision of the discipline.

This is where an intentionally decolonial scholarly praxis must intervene through the upending of perspectives, the dismantling of disciplinary hierarchies, the rejection of economies of prestige, and a refusal to engage in the extractivism of either knowledge or labor. Any effort to decolonize must commit to decentering whiteness as well as the structures through which it is reproduced as power, property, or epistemic force. Thus, decolonization does not—or cannot—be accomplished by the mere addition of marginalized identities to the eighteenth-century pot. For if those identities—Black, queer, Indigenous, among others—continue to figure as deviant epiphenomena set against the established norm, then the field will continue to manifest a fundamental commitment to its epistemic whiteness. To decolonize, therefore, requires not just seeing or imagining the world differently. In a more fundamental way, it demands the development of a new politics of collective life and mutual rapport—or what Kathleen Tamayo Alves calls, in her essay in this cluster, a move toward a "relational ecology."

Drawing on this invitation to think together rather than as discrete beings, I want to draw from the epigraph from Toni Morrison with which I began, her call to "refuse the prison of 'I' and choose the open spaces of 'we.'" The sentiment contained in this gesture reminds me of subjects who, although chronologically part of the eighteenth century, have not traditionally been made part of the field. I am thinking about the *quilombos*, Afrodiasporic maroon communities that have existed in Brazil since the colonial period. *Quilombos*, as the Brazilian Black feminist scholar Beatriz Nascimento recounts, were spaces of reconstitution for Black life and being.[2] They were not merely spaces of flight, although they were that as well. Rather, *quilombos* were spaces in which new potentialities were forged through the recreation of Black life as it existed both before and outside of colonial domination. Although, as Nascimento carefully notes, *quilombos* cannot be reduced to a single model or system, they nonetheless offer a heuristic for how sociality can interrupt colonial structures. Spatially instantiating sovereignty through both individual flight and the collective reconfiguration of relations outside of imperial structures and the ways of thinking that they impose, *quilombos* manifest the power of refusal. This is not to romanticize *quilombos*. African societies also know hierarchies and unfreedom. Yet, as Nascimento insists, the longevity and changes experienced by Afro-Brazilian maroon societies demonstrate how liberation comes to fruition when metaphor and matter meet. That is, when decolonization aims to repair, restitute, and reconfigure reality.

Any effort to decolonize and therefore liberate and abolish existing matrices of power must seek to rebuild the world from the perspectives of Indigenous peoples. Sometimes this exercise will entail reading documents against the grain. At other times, it will force one to accept that African or Amerindian intellectuals were, far before Western academics, committed to creating deeply incisive analyses of colonialism's intersecting oppressions. Adopting citation practices that decenter Western knowledges and recalibrate epistemes towards Indigenous thought, lifeworlds, and ways of living is therefore an imperative. This gesture demands the abolition of existing hierarchies of intellectual production. Withholding recognition from Indigenous thinkers/makers is paternalist and extractive and so would both reproduce a hierarchical mode of thought and reiterate a key method of dispossession.

Colonialism operates by transforming life—anthropocentric or not—into property. If eighteenth-century studies is to have a future, the colonial moorings of devices as central to Western epistemology and state formation as scientific reason, economic progress, state sovereignty, and natural law jurisprudence must continue to be excavated. Slavery and dispossession were not just routine in the eighteenth century, they were state sanctioned and, thus, part and parcel of a legal scaffold of legitimate subjugation. For this reason, a decolonial vision of knowledge production within Western academia must start by decentering itself. To abolish the taxonomical language of imposed normativities confining existence to the enclosure of biocentric fixity, biopolitical control, and classificatory certainty entails engaging with Indigenous pluriverses. If we are to unlearn imperialism and decenter epistemic whiteness, Indigenous, African, or "Ameroafrican" lifeways and intellectual production must become the kernel for our future growth.[3] This gesture is not simply one of negation; rather, it stems from an ethos of nurture and cultivation. Stewardship and caretaking must replace the claiming of ownership over fields of knowledge and the correct methods of delivering such knowledge. Gatekeeping, and the disciplining of approaches and topics into the performance of scholarly convention, must therefore be intentionally averted. Amid all this, we can never lose sight of the long history of colonial epistemicide, nor how Western "reason" and legal regimes were complicit in the legitimation of slavery, dispossession, racial capitalism, and heteropatriarchy.

The enduring coloniality of the available conceptual worlds forces a confrontation. It requires facing the epistemic attachment to methods whose idioms of rigor have upheld established hierarchies by recapitulating and reproducing power. It demands urgent and intentional action from us. We need to openly acknowledge who was centered by the canon and, conversely, who has historically been absented from the narrative—and why. The colonial matrix of power, to evoke Aníbal Quijano, organizes, disciplines, and endlessly replays a truncated vision of the human.[4] However, this "prototypical whiteness" also continues to endure through the tacit recapitulation of an uninterrogated universal template.[5] Katherine McKittrick terms this presumption of natural belonging and universal, unambiguous interpretation as "transparent space."[6] Inviting us to consider why some varieties of humankind—and their respective geographies of belonging and exclusion—seem to exist as something that "just is" and questioning the discipline's attraction to stasis as a necessary epistemic condition, McKittrick reveals the many hierarchies of being that sustain the Western knowledge-making matrix of power. McKittrick also cautions her readers that "description is not liberation."[7] Thus, she reminds readers to be on guard against the epistemic desire to incorporate identity into disciplines that seek to read people as enunciating observable truths. Rather than adding symbolic Blackness to frameworks that recapitulate—and therefore simply "describe" the world—liberation demands theoretical interventions that support material reconfigurations.

Tackling the ongoing grip of coloniality by abolishing its power to separate, commodify, and extract the resources of people and places, the problem of "reason"—so central to the eighteenth century—appears at the crux of our efforts to decolonize eighteenth-century studies. This challenge must be faced from new vantage points. Refiguring what "the" Enlightenment means for the field, what sort of labor that concept performs, from where it is imagined to who is included and excluded from its dominant field of vision—all these demand our immediate attention. This labor, which must start with ourselves, stems from our willingness to unlearn what we think we already know as certain. Yet, while starting with the "I," decolonization can only be practiced and imagined together. The work of the future is here—may we know to embrace it together.

Notes

1. See Azoulay, *Potential History: Unlearning Imperialism* (London: Verso, 2019).

2. See Nascimento, "O Conceito de Quilombo e a Resistência Cultural Negra," *Afrodiáspora* 3, no. 6–7 (1985): 41–49, and *Uma História Feita Por Mãos Negras* (Rio de Janeiro: Zahar, 2021).

3. See Lélia Gonzalez, *Por Um Feminismo Afro-Latino-Americano: Ensaios, Interenções e Diálogos* (Rio de Janeiro: Jorge Zahar, 2020); Keisha-Khan Y. Perry and Edilza Sotero, "Amefricanidade: The Black Diaspora Feminism of Lélia Gonzalez," *LASA Forum* 50, no. 3 (2019): 60–64.

4. See Quijano, *Ensayos En Torno a La Colonialidad Del Poder* (Buenos Aires: Ediciones del Signo, 2019).

5. See Simone Browne, *Dark Matters: On the Surveillance of Blackness* (Durham: Duke University Press, 2015).

6. Browne's "prototypical whiteness," Sylvia Wynter's "the dominant genre of being human," and McKittrick's references to "transparent space" all invite us to think about how modern scholarship tacitly centers whiteness as natural, while relegating forms of scholarship that intentionally refuse those parameters to the category of minor, parallel fields, rather than parts of a self-sustaining discipline. See Wynter, "Unsettling the Coloniality of Being/Power/Truth/Freedom: Towards the Human, After Man, Its Overrepresentation—An Argument," *CR: The New Centennial Review* 3, no. 3 (2003): 257–337; McKittrick, *Demonic Grounds: Black Women and the Cartographies of Struggle* (Minneapolis: University of Minnesota Press, 2006).

7. McKittrick, *Dear Science and Other Stories* (Durham: Duke University Press, 2021), 48.

Unclaimed Runways in Colonial Haiti: Law, Liberation, and Re-Enslavement in the Atlantic World

ERICA JOHNSON EDWARDS

In colonial Haiti, authorities attempted to regulate *marronage* [running away or self-liberation] by enforcing article 38 of Louis XIV's 1685 *Code Noir*, which defined it as a crime and outlined punishments for it.[1] For the first offense, authorities were supposed to cut off the enslaved person's ears and brand them on the shoulder with a *fleur-de-lys*. For a second transgression, the colonial administrators were expected to cut one of the enslaved person's hamstrings and brand them on the other shoulder with a *fleur-de-lys*. Upon running away a third time, officials were supposed to execute the fugitive.[2] Of course, practice differed from the law. Evolving over time from its establishment in the 1720s, the *maréchaussée* [the rural police force] was responsible for capturing fugitives from slavery—if they did not kill them in the process.[3] Although made up primarily of free men of color, enslaved men also enlisted, or more likely their enslavers enrolled them, in the *maréchaussée* to earn their freedom, because it made tax-free manumission possible.[4] Allowing enslaved men to serve in the *maréchaussée* provided enslaved people of African descent with an opportunity for manumission, which, in turn, helped ensure the loyalty of *some* people of African descent, all the while protecting the institution of slavery by policing *marronage*.

Reports from enslavers or *gérants* [plantation managers] were also important for policing *marronage*. The *Code Noir* required that an enslaved person be absent for a full month after their enslaver reported them gone before they would be considered a maroon; however, there were many possible reasons an enslaver would not have reported or reclaimed a runaway. The most common was sheer ignorance, given the fact that many enslavers in colonial Haiti were absentees residing or traveling outside the colony. In addition, merchant houses in France's port cities owned plantations and enslaved people of African descent in colonial Haiti. Both relied upon *gérants* to maintain their holdings, which were often mismanaged.[5] Whenever an enslaver had to travel suddenly due to an illness or passed away without having made the necessary arrangements, their estates were left in a precarious position. Further, some enslavers and managers did not regularly update their registries because of the high mortality rates in colonial Haiti and the continuous sale and purchase of enslaved people.[6] Without an accurate registry, enslavers had no proof of *marronage* and no way to reclaim a self-emancipated individual. However, even if a plantation maintained an up-to-date registry, enslaved people could undermine efforts to police their flight through the information they chose to provide to colonial authorities, information that could prevent their enslaver from reclaiming them.

The *Code Noir* defined *marronage* in France's Caribbean colonies, but its authors in France did not anticipate a scenario in which enslavers would be unable to reclaim captured runaways. In colonial Haiti, unclaimed runaways were known as *nègres épaves*. Various eighteenth-century regulations addressed the imprisonment of unclaimed runaways, how their capture should be reported, how their labor should be used, and how their sale should be advertised, all of which subjected the *nègres épaves* to yet another round of enslavement. Neil Roberts contends that "during marronage, agents struggle psychologically, socially, metaphysically, and politically to exit slavery, maintain freedom, and assert a lived social space while existing in a liminal position."[7] For unclaimed runaways, their flight did not end with recapture. Advertisements for unclaimed runaways in the *Affiches Américaines* reveal how the enslaved continued to resist. Colonial authorities relied upon runaways to provide all nonvisible identifying information. This meant they could provide a name, ethnicity, and age other than what would be listed on a plantation registry, as well as misleading details about their enslaver. In this way, the enslaved had the power to claim an identity that could reflect their true selves, prevent an enslaver from reclaiming them, delay their reenslavement, and possibly improve their circumstances.

Even as studies of the French Caribbean have grown, especially those focused on colonial and revolutionary Haiti, scholars have not extensively researched or written about *nègres épaves*. Studies that mention the *nègres épaves* in colonial and revolutionary Haiti do so within the context of larger discussions of *marronage*, only providing a sentence or paragraph about these unclaimed runaways.[8] Even when pieced together, the studies of colonial Haiti merely provide hints regarding why enslavers did not claim runaways, how jailed runaways were treated, and the various changes in the laws related to unclaimed runaways throughout the eighteenth century. Similar gaps may be found in studies of eighteenth-century Guadeloupe and nineteenth-century Martinique and in work on the non-French portions of the Caribbean, Brazil, and the United States.[9] This essay works toward filling these lacunae in Atlantic historiography, offering an examination of unclaimed runaways that expands our understanding of *marronage* by highlighting how self-liberated individuals continued their struggle even after recapture. I explore the ways in which critical readings of sources, especially the *Affiches Américaines*, can offer insights into the lives of marginalized runaways and how their actions drove colonial policy.

Although fugitives from slavery rarely left accounts of their experiences, their stories can be accessed by reading against the grain of the laws and the advertisements in the *Affiches Américaines*. Despite the silences in the archive, it is possible to recreate elements of the lives of self-liberated people and how they attempted to reclaim their true selves.[10] Reactionary laws shed light on the resistance of the *nègres épaves*. For instance, authorities in France included *marronage* in the *Code Noir* because there was already a history of self-emancipation in the French Caribbean, even before Haiti became a French colony in 1697. Fugitives from slavery forced enslavers to respond to their acts of resistance, their "total refusal of the enslaved condition."[11] Further, once we recognize how authorities depended upon runaways for all nonvisible information, the voices of the self-emancipated emerge in the newspaper advertisements.[12] Even the absence of details, such as a name, reflected an identity crafted by a runaway. Lastly, after fugitives from slavery were captured, authorities would imprison them together and rely upon them to translate for one another, giving them space to create a "hidden transcript" of continued resistance.[13] In these ways, runaways helped shape the very laws and newspaper advertisements that were intended to oppress them.

Even before the newspaper advertisements, enslaved people influenced colonial laws regarding *marronage*. Since the *Code Noir* did not specify what to do in the event of runaways going unclaimed, colonial authorities in Haiti issued additional regulations responding to their local circumstances. The oldest surviving decree regarding *nègres épaves* came from the colony's capital, Cap Français, in the northeast. In early 1707, Cap's notary Noël Camusat ruled that, because of the cost to the public of their continued detention, unclaimed runaways should be sold by the *receveur des amendes et confiscations* [the receiver of fines and confiscations]. Based on what had recently become customary in Cap, he proposed that, after captured runaways had been imprisoned for one month, the authorities should advertise in all the surrounding parishes that they would sell any unclaimed runaways one month later.[14] Presumably, a month was thought to provide ample time for an enslaver or manager within that area to come forward to claim any runaways. However, if the fugitive from slavery came from outside the Cap region, enslavers and managers in other parts of the colony would not necessarily be aware that a person they enslaved had been arrested, nor of the impending sale. Furthermore, if an enslaver were out of the colony at the time, one month would not be enough time for any notification to reach them or them to send word. The enslaved could use this knowledge strategically to plan their flight. More importantly, any nonvisible information included in the authorities' advertisements would have come from the enslaved, who could have manipulated the details to prevent an enslaver from claiming them, regardless of the duration of their detention. Camusat's decision also did not specify a procedure for what to do if an enslaver or manager came forward at any time after the sale; similarly, there was no provision for them to recoup any unclaimed runaways sold at auction. While this decision aimed to address a local need, it did not account for all possible scenarios.

Although it was the first, Cap was not the only city in the colony to address the issue of unclaimed runaways. Léogâne, a port town in the West Province, addressed the sale of *nègres épaves* in the summers of 1711 and 1712. The acting *intendant* [the highest ranking civilian official in the colony], Jean-Jacques Mithon, issued an ordinance in June 1711 pertaining to the capture, imprisonment, and auction of unclaimed runaways around Léogâne.[15] In it, he referenced the runaways in Petite Rivière who had been imprisoned for "a very long time" without his knowing to whom they belonged. He insisted that their sale needed to be advertised on the door of the administrative office of Léogâne and at the entrance to the parish church. Although he did not specify how long the unclaimed runaways needed to be imprisoned before they would be sold, he was precise about their price. In addition to covering the cost of their nourishment while imprisoned, purchasing each unclaimed runaway required buyers to pay 12 livres to the seneschal, 8 livres to the clerk, and 6 livres to the bailiff.[16] In July 1712, Mithon issued another ordinance specifying that *nègres épaves* could only be sold after one month of imprisonment and three public advertisements.[17] Those advertisements likely provided some information about the enslaved persons intended for auction, and the enslaved would have had the power to give any nonvisible details they chose to the authorities who published them. The regulations for *nègres épaves* in Léogâne evolved as necessary to accommodate local circumstances.

The issue of *nègres épaves* drove some colonists to call for a royal jurisdiction around Cap in the 1730s. The *receveur des amendes, épaves et confiscations* [receiver of fines, unclaimed property, and confiscations], Julien Bornat, explained to the Council of Cap the need for an additional jurisdiction around Fort-Dauphin, near the Spanish border. He claimed that the *nègres épaves* being detained until auction in jails in Cap for as long as three months were malnourished and that some escaped, while others died before being sold. The previous regulations only required authorities to advertise the future auctions of *nègres épaves*, but Bornat requested that a registry of all jailed maroons be made public as well.[18] His proposals suggested that enslavers and managers did not have enough information or time due to the size of the jurisdiction to claim runaways and perhaps even that some officials had been withholding information to prevent claims and ensure sales. Therefore, if the jurisdiction of Fort-Dauphin were separated from that of Cap, and authorities provided public access to registries, the likelihood that enslavers and managers would claim runaways would increase. However, the authorities, enslavers, and managers failed to recognize how the enslaved shaped the registries in ways that could have prevented them from being reclaimed. Even with public access to the registries, jailed runaways could have hidden in plain sight if they provided false details to authorities for those registries. Although a new jurisdiction did not come to fruition, Bornat's pleas reveal the colonists' frustrations with the local regulations regarding *nègres épaves* and how those frustrations drove them, in desperation, to threaten royal interference.

Royal administrators in colonial Haiti answered Bornat's appeal with a broader ordinance in 1733. The highest-ranking colonial military officer, Governor Pierre Marquis de Fayet and *ordonnateur* [finance officer] Jean-Baptiste Duclos responded to the claims and offered remedies to what they saw as abuses. They stated that they had received "frequent complaints" about the mistreatment of imprisoned runaways held in jails for long periods and the inflated prices charged at auction for *nègres épaves*. They demanded that the officers in their jurisdictions investigate the colonists' claims, and they insisted that *nègres épaves* must be sold after one month in jail for only the cost of imprisonment.[19] Just over a year later, they issued additional instructions. They ordered each jurisdiction to report to the *intendant* all *nègres épaves* sold each month. This suggests that all jurisdictions were already selling or were expected to begin selling unclaimed runaways, making it another form of slave trade within the colony—one administered by the legal system.[20]

Colonial authorities in eighteenth-century Haiti imprisoned free and enslaved peoples in the same facilities, but their detention was far from equal. In 1740 and 1741, the Council of Cap issued regulations for the proper administration of the jails. Article IX stated that white and Black individuals, as well as free and enslaved prisoners, should be separated, if possible. Further, although they were all fed cassava and meat, the cost of nourishing prisoners depended upon their status. For example, the price to feed a free person for one month was 45 livres, while the price to feed an enslaved person was only 22 livres and 10 sols. There were 20 sols per livre, so they spent only half as much to feed an enslaved person. This meant either that they fed enslaved people less or that they fed them lower-quality food. Overall, they were trying to replicate among the prisoners the social and racial stratification outside the jails. The regulations were also relevant to *nègres épaves*. Article XXXV required jailors to keep a registry of maroons, including the enslaved person's name, condition, and brands. Although authorities could see their physical condition and any brands, an enslaved person could provide any name they chose. Authorities used the listed costs when selling *nègres épaves*. In addition to the cost of nourishment, jailors charged 1 livre and 10 sols for entering a maroon into their registers and the same amount again to release them from jail.[21] While detained in jail, unclaimed runaways had opportunities to exchange information about colonists, colonial geography, and colonial administration. As runaways, they could tell one another about their experiences with self-liberation. After being sold at auction, the unclaimed runaways took this information with them to their new location, where they could use it strategically and share it with other enslaved people.

Authorities also attempted to use unclaimed runaways in service of the colony and king while they were jailed. Article XXVI of the 1743 regulations for the *maréchausée* stated that after one month of imprisonment, *nègres épaves* would be taken to a chain gang to labor on fortifications or "other works of his majesty."[22] However, two years later, colonial Haiti's governor, Charles Brunier, Marquis de Larnage, and *intendant*, Simon-Pierre Maillart, claimed that the colony's plantation owners opposed the use of unclaimed runaways to labor on public works. They further suggested that it was extremely difficult to get the unclaimed runaways to work because of their "taste for *marronage*" and that their work was "mediocre" when it happened. The governor and *intendant* failed to recognize that these were intentional acts of resistance, what James C. Scott calls "infrapolitics."[23] Nonetheless, they decided not to enforce the "unhelpful provision." However, the colonial leaders stated their intention to continue selling unclaimed runaways after one month of detention. They would allow proprietors to reclaim and pay for any *nègres épaves* within one year of sale or be reimbursed for the price of their sale within five years.[24] In October 1746, Louis XV issued an ordinance supporting the governor and *intendant*'s decision to stop using imprisoned runaways on public works.[25] Intriguingly, the crown abandoned the use of convict labor in the royal galleys in France's Mediterranean fleet soon thereafter; after that, convicts labored on chain gangs on France's Atlantic coast.[26] Despite the efforts of officials to profit from *nègres épaves* in the 1740s, the royal administrators compromised after plantation owners raised opposition.

Authorities in the metropole and colonial Haiti issued conflicting ordinances affecting *nègres épaves* following the Seven Years' War (1756–63). In 1760, Caribbean property owner Jean Etienne Bernard de Clugny de Nuits was appointed as colonial Haiti's *intendant*, the "first high officer not to come out of the military."[27] He issued a new ordinance specific to *nègres épaves* in 1764, sending any captured runaways to jail and allowing the use of their labor for public works on one of three chain gangs: Cap, Port-au-Prince, or Saint-Louis. If the unclaimed runaways were not claimed within a month of being jailed, authorities would sell them for the cost of capture and their care during imprisonment.[28] In 1768, Louis XV put forth a comprehensive ordinance regarding *nègres épaves,* with ten articles addressing elements in all the previous eighteenth-century regulations. In the introduction to the articles, Louis XV condemned Clugny de Nuits's 1764 ordinance, because the provisions for using unclaimed runaways as laborers on public works contradicted his own prior ordinance from October 1746 forbidding it. Louis XV's regulations required sale after three months, with sales taking place four times a year on the second of January, April, July, and October.[29] In this case, the king's authority was final, and his regulations struck a balance between royal and colonial interests.

The colonial press aided in the administration of Louis XV's regulations for *nègres épaves* by advertising their recorded names, descriptions provided by jailors, and dates of scheduled auctions. Governor from 1764–66, Charles d'Estaing established a printing press in colonial Haiti, which produced a newspaper, the *Affiches Américaines*. Printed in Cap and Port-au-Prince, the newspaper had 1,500 subscribers at one point.[30] Article III of the king's ordinance of November 1767 required publication of lists of the unclaimed runaways in the *Affiches Américaines* before the sale.[31] In July of 1768, Port-au-Prince's edition of the *Affiches Américaines* reprinted a story from Cap's edition explaining the new legislation and that Cap's Superior Council had registered the king's ordinance in June.[32] On 26 October, the *Affiches Américaines* published the first list of unclaimed runaways from Cap, but the advertisement did not include an auction date. Of the five unclaimed runaways, all in their thirties, the newspaper listed four by name. They had each spent four to five months in jail at the time of publication, even though the legislation stated that they only needed to be jailed for three months before being auctioned.[33]

Advertisements for unclaimed runaways in the *Affiches Américaines* reveal the confusion and inconsistencies in the application of the king's 1767 ordinance. For instance, only Fort-Dauphin and Port-de-Paix listed *nègres épaves* in the *Affiches Américaines* in 1770. They advertised auctions in July and October. While these months accord with the regulations, authorities scheduled the sales for days other than the second. The listings included who captured the runaways and where they were arrested.[34] Although later listings sometimes included where authorities captured each runaway, they do not note the person or persons involved in the arrest. The listings also reveal the ways in which self-liberated people could control and manipulate the information included in the advertisements, as well as the uncertainty authorities initially had about what information to provide about each unclaimed runaway. It is understandable to omit the age of a runaway, as it might not be known or able to be accurately estimated (because gray hairs could be shaved or plucked, etc.). However, most of the advertisements in the 1770s also did not indicate the height or any other distinguishing physical characteristics of the *nègres épaves*. Enslavers and managers may have seen this lack of information as a way for the authorities to make it difficult for them to claim runaways, so that the colony and king could then profit from their sale. Therefore, by the 1780s, the listings consistently provided age and height, if not always any other physical description. Despite the inconsistency of the information in the advertisements in the *Affiches Américaines*, it is possible to learn significant details about who the unclaimed runaways were or claimed to be for their own benefit.

Self-emancipated individuals could omit certain kinds of information or provide misleading details in the hope of preventing their enslaver from claiming them. With many of those enslaved being African-born, there likely was a language barrier for some. For instance, an ad from 1779 explicitly stated that a *nègre nouveau* [a newly enslaved person] (Quimba) could not speak French.[35] Therefore, a translator would probably have been necessary for some of the captives to communicate with their jailors, and it is likely that the translator would have also been an enslaved person. The enslaved people could have communicated with one another without the jailor understanding, giving them an opportunity to collaborate in their resistance. Many of the advertisements stated that the unclaimed runaways could not say the names of their enslavers. On the surface, this suggests that they did not know how to pronounce French names. Indeed, people newly enslaved from Africa may not have even learned the name of their enslaver before their flight. However, it is also possible that runaways pretended not to know their enslaver's name or how to pronounce it, so that the newspaper would leave it out of the advertisement and thereby prevent their enslaver from claiming them. For example, Latremblé (Congo) told jailors that his enslaver was Alexandre when he was first jailed, but later told authorities that his enslaver was Bourgeois des Sources.[36] Perhaps he had been confused at first. Or perhaps he wanted to create confusion through what his captors might assume was a language barrier.

From 1768 to 1791, advertisements in the *Affiches Américaines* reveal how runaways could make use of a real or perceived language barrier. For instance, authorities listed some unclaimed runaways as *nègres nouveaux* instead of giving their names. The advertisements stated that the unclaimed runaways could not say their own names. This might indicate that enslavers assigned the runaway with a name, but the runaways could not remember it, or that they could not pronounce it, or that they chose not to identify themselves by it. This also suggests that jailors would only accept names given by enslavers and would not record an enslaved person's birth name, especially if it were of African origin. This is evident in the listings, where fugitives from slavery had French-language names like Julien, Jean-Pierre, Marie, or Dorothée. If the enslaved captives knew this, they could provide any French name they knew, not necessarily the one assigned by their enslaver, to make it harder for an enslaver to identify and reclaim them. Having the power to create a new identity gave runways some authority over themselves in eighteenth-century colonial Haiti.

As these advertisements show, age and gender were not a factor in *marronage*. Men, women, and children all attempted to liberate themselves from the horrors of slavery. The *Affiches Américaines* advertised unclaimed runaways of ages between 3 months and 70 years old. While most of those with a listed age were in their 20s or 30s, authorities did not provide an age for at least half of the runaways listed in the *Affiches Américaines*. In Cap, the baby of an unnamed eighteen-year-old woman (Congo) died within 3 days of their imprisonment.[37] The authorities provided the information that she had been pregnant and recently gave birth either to alert an enslaver or manager who might claim her or to promote her fertility to potential buyers at an auction. Indeed, a woman with a child would be appealing to enslavers for her fertility, but there were no guarantees that the auctioneers would sell them together. For example, having captured Nannette with her 4-year-old child in Dondon in early August 1773, authorities advertised them both for sale in January 1774, with nothing to indicate that they could not be purchased separately.[38] These two cases are striking because women represented less than 15% of the runaways reported captured, most likely because of their parenting roles.[39] In fact, most runaways were male. The *Affiches Américaines* advertised twelve-year-old Daniel (Congo), thirteen-year-old Charles (Nago), fourteen-year-old Jean-Jacques (Thiamba), fifty-five-year-old Jacques (Timbou), fifty-five-year-old Hardi (Arada), and sixty-six-year-old Jean-Baptiste (Miserable) among the *nègres épaves* to be sold in colonial Haiti.[40] While Daniel, Charles, and Jean-Jacques were still teenage boys, the advertisement described how Jean-Baptiste's and Hardi's advanced age physically presented in the form of white hair and grey beards.

In the decades leading up to the Haitian Revolution, the *Affiches Américaines* advertised unclaimed runaways who were Indigenous, creole, and African-born. In early September 1771, the newspaper listed a Carib fugitive from slavery named François. Although he was listed as "claiming to be free," without proof of his freedom and having been imprisoned for over four months, he was set to be sold on the first of October.[41] Similarly, Jean-Nicolas, a creole *mulâtre* [the offspring of one white parent and one Black parent] from Curaçao (a Dutch colony), was listed among the unclaimed runaways from Cap as "claiming to be free" in the *Affiches Américaines* in February of 1772.[42] Since the 1767 ordinance did not explicitly address runaways who were "claiming to be free," members of the justice system relied upon a law from 1713. The earlier ordinance stated that Black people who claimed to be free, but could not prove their freedom, would be "declared *épaves,* acquired and confiscated for sale for the profit of the king."[43] Further, each list of *nègres épaves* included self-liberated people of various ethnicities of West Africa. For example, in mid-May 1773, the newspaper listed an unnamed Cotocoli (Bight of Benin) man, Pierre and Cupidon as Ibo (Bight of Biafra), and Polite, César, Gaspard, and la Fortune as Congo (West Central Africa).[44] The ethnicities listed for each runaway could be inaccurate, because the authorities recording the information could have "labeled Africans" in a way that was convenient for them, but that "misrepresent[ed] African cultural diversity and reinforce[d] stereotypes of African cultures as static."[45] This could have resulted in the advertisements listing a different ethnicity for an enslaved person than that given in a plantation registry.

Whether born in the Caribbean or Africa, the unclaimed runaways advertised in the *Affiches Américaines* bore marks of their origins and their enslavement. Descriptions of Jean (Canga) and an unnamed *nègre nouveau* (Congo) included marks from their African homes as well as brands burned onto their skin by their enslavers. While the advertisement does not elaborate on the African markings, it does provide their locations on the runaways' bodies and the identifiable letters of the brands.[46] These markings remained a part of an enslaved individual's identity, tying them to their home, despite efforts by enslavers to impose a new identity upon them. Enslavers in colonial Haiti typically only branded African-born enslaved peoples.[47] Accordingly, not all fugitives from slavery had brands; Jean-Nicolas, the *mulâtre* creole from Curaçao mentioned earlier, did not. Most often, the brands were burned onto the chests and shoulders of the enslaved. Based on the advertisements, it appears that branding was often poorly done, leaving the letters and symbols illegible. Further, enslaved peoples could distort the brands by cutting or burning the skin around them. In this way, they asserted control over their physical identities.

Numerous advertisements for unclaimed runaways indicated that they had ailments. For instance, Jean-Philippe (Congo) was suffering from smallpox while captive, and Pierre (Bambara) and François (Caramenty) had scars from smallpox.[48] The advertisements do not indicate how long the enslaved people had been on the run, so there is no way to know when they got sick. There were several smallpox outbreaks in eighteenth-century colonial Haiti, and there were efforts to inoculate the enslaved.[49] It is also possible that Europeans used the enslaved to experiment with the disease and potential treatments.[50] Further, advertisements listed Victoire (Canga) as experiencing dropsy, now known as edema, and an unnamed runaway (Mosonga) as having yaws, a tropical skin infection.[51] Any illness or disability could have been the reason why authorities were able to capture a self-liberated person, as well as an additional reason for a fugitive from slavery to want to avoid being claimed (since their condition might well stem from or have been exacerbated by their enslavement).

The advertisements in the *Affiches Américaines* also highlighted the physical consequences the enslaved faced for having fled. When authorities arrested François (Congo) in late March of 1770, he was wearing a *nabot au pied* [ball and chain on the foot].[52] This suggests that he had previously made an unsuccessful attempt at *marronage*. While there were surely others who tried to run away more than once, none of the advertisements described any *fleur-de-lys* brands, as stipulated by the *Code Noir*. Further, it is likely that some runaways suffered injuries when the militias or *maréchaussée* violently captured them. For instance, Louis (Congo) had lash marks on his left shoulder, and someone had knocked out some of his teeth.[53] The enslaved struggled physically against recapture and continued their fight psychologically and politically once jailed.

The *Code Noir* defined and codified the consequences for *marronage* in the French Caribbean, but colonial authorities had to create laws to accommodate local circumstances that metropolitan leaders did not anticipate. However, in both places the free failed to understand the role that the enslaved would play in shaping laws regarding their own flight and reenslavement. While authorities and colonists wrote laws and advertised unclaimed runaways for sale as chattel, reading against the grain of the sources allows scholars to be accountable to the enslaved by recounting their histories of continued resistance. Colonial authorities and colonists carried out the process of detaining, advertising, and selling self-emancipated people. However, advertisements, such as those in the *Affiches Américaines*, reveal how fugitives from slavery took an active part in crafting their own identities, making them effectively coauthors of the very documents intended to control them. Although the authorities did not recognize any value in enslaved people beyond the physical and routinely underestimated the intelligence of runaways, enslavers nonetheless relied upon self-liberated individuals to provide details about their own identities. This allowed unclaimed runaways to manipulate the information in the advertisements. They used self-identification as a form of resistance, providing information or misinformation in ways that they believed could change their circumstances. Even while imprisoned and awaiting reenslavement, they continued to fight.

Notes

I am thankful to the many people who helped me develop this article. Early on, I corresponded with numerous scholars, including David Stark, Fernanda Bretones Lanes, and David Geggus. I also benefited greatly from workshopping my project with the members of David Andress's virtual Atlantic World group in the summer of 2020. And lastly, I am always grateful for Bryan Banks's insights on my analyses and writing.

1. Following the lead of Rob Taber, I use colonial Haiti instead of Saint-Domingue. See Taber, "Family Formation, Race, and Honor in Colonial Haiti's Communities, 1670–1789," in *French Connections: Cultural Mobility in North America and the Atlantic World*, ed. Robert Englebert and Andrew Wegmann (Baton Rouge: Louisiana State University Press, 2020), 164 n1.

2. Louis XIV, Jean-Baptiste Colbert, and François-Michel Le Tellier, "Code Noir ou Edit servant de Règlement pour le Gouvernement et l'Administration de la Justice et de la Police des Isles Françoise de l'Amérique, et pour la Discipline et le Commerce des Negres et Esclaves dans ledit Pays," in *Loix et Constitutions des Colonies Françoises de l'Amérique sous le Vent*, ed. Louis-Elie Moreau de Saint-Méry, 6 vols. (Paris, 1784), 1:420. For discussions of the drafting of the *Code Noir*, see Malick W. Ghachem, *The Old Regime and the Haitian Revolution* (Cambridge: Cambridge University Press, 2012), 58–63, 71–73, 178; and Brett Rushforth, *Bonds of Alliance: Indigenous and Atlantic Slaveries in New France* (Chapel Hill: University of North Carolina Press, 2012), 122–32.

3. Marquis de Sorel and Jean-Baptiste Duclos, "Ordonnance des Administrateurs, pour l'établissement d'une Maréchaussée," 27 March 1721, in *Loix et Constitutions*, 2:726–33; Moreau de Saint-Méry, *Description topographique, physique, civile, politique et historique de la partie française de l'isle Saint Domingue* (Paris, 1797), 449.

4. Stewart R. King, *Blue Coat or Powdered Wig: Free People of Color in Pre-Revolutionary Saint Domingue* (Athens: University of Georgia Press, 2001), 56–58; Moreau de Saint-Méry, *Description*, 450.

5. Laurent Dubois, *Avengers of the New World: The Story of the Haitian Revolution* (Cambridge: Belknap Press of Harvard University Press, 2004), 20, 37; Trevor Burnard and John Garrigus, *The Plantation Machine: Atlantic Capitalism in French Saint-Domingue and British Jamaica* (Philadelphia: University of Pennsylvania Press, 2016), 253–55.

6. Dubois, *Avengers*, 39–40; and Paul Cheney, *Cul de Sac: Patrimony, Capitalism, and Slavery in French Saint-Domingue* (Chicago: University of Chicago Press, 2017), 33–34, 59–60, 83–84.

7. Roberts, *Freedom as Marronage* (Chicago: University of Chicago Press, 2015), 10.

8. See for example, Gabriel Debien, "Le Marronage aux Antilles Françaises au XVIIIe siècle," *Caribbean Studies* 6, no. 3 (1996), 12; Dénétem Touam Bona, "Les Métamorphoses du Marronnage," *Lignes* no. 16 (2005), 38–39; and Crystal Nicole Eddins, "African Diaspora Collective Action: Rituals, Runaways, and the Haitian Revolution" (Ph.D. dissertation, Michigan State University, 2017), 126, 214, 216.

9. Frédéric Régent, "Résistances serviles en Guadeloupe à la fin du XVIIIe siècle," *Bulletin de la Société d'Histoire de la Guadeloupe* no. 140 (2005): 38; and John Savage, "Unwanted Slaves: The Punishment of Transportation and the Making of Legal Subjects in Early Nineteenth-Century Martinique," *Citizenship Studies* 10, no. 1 (2006), 40. For Cuba, see Manuel Barcia, *Seeds of Insurrection: Domination and Resistance on Western Cuban Plantations, 1808–1848* (Baton Rouge: Louisiana State University Press, 2008), 52–53. For the British Caribbean, see Gad Heuman, "Runaway Slaves in Nineteenth-Century Barbados," *Slavery and Abolition* 6, no. 3 (1985): 95–111; Bob Rees and Marika Sherwood, *Black Peoples of the Americas* (Oxford: Heinemann, 1992), 26–27; and Jim Piecuch, *Three Peoples, One King: Loyalists, Indians, and Slaves in the American Revolutionary South, 1775–1782* (Columbia: University of South Carolina Press, 2013), 42. For Brazil, see Stuart B. Schwartz, *Slaves, Peasants, and Rebels: Reconsidering Brazilian Slavery* (Urbana: University of Illinois Press, 1996), 110. For the U.S., see William R. Leslie, "The Pennsylvania Fugitive Slave Act of 1826," *Journal of Southern History* 18, no. 4 (1952), 437; Sylvia R. Frey, "Between Slavery and Freedom: Virginia Blacks in the American Revolution," *Journal of Southern History* 49, no. 3 (1983), 385; William P. Quigley and Maha S. Zaki, "The Significance of Race: Legislative Racial Discrimination in Louisiana, 1803–1865," *Southern University Law Review*, 24, no. 2 (1997), 152; Marion B. Lucas, *A History of Blacks in Kentucky: From Slavery to Segregation, 1760–1891,* 2nd ed. (Frankfort: Kentucky Historical Society, 2003), 61; and Darla Jean Thompson, "Circuits of Containment: Iron Collars, Incarceration and the Infrastructure of Slavery" (Ph.D. dissertation, Cornell University, 2014), 19, 135, 177–79.

10. My methodology aligns with that of the many scholars who center the enslaved despite the evidentiary difficulties. See, for example, Michel-Rolph Trouillot, *Silencing the Past: Power and the Production of History* (Boston: Beacon Press, 1995); Saidiya Hartman, "The Dead Book Revisited," *History of the Present* 6, no. 2 (2016): 208–15; Stephanie E. Smallwood, "The Politics of the Archive and History's Accountability to the Enslaved," *History of the Present* 6, no. 2 (2016): 117–32; Marisa J. Fuentes, *Dispossessed Lives: Enslaved Women, Violence, and the Archive* (Philadelphia: University of Pennsylvania Press, 2016); and Vanessa M. Holden, *Surviving Southampton: African American Women and Resistance in Nat Turner's Community* (University of Illinois Press, 2021).

11. Roberts, *Freedom as Marronage*, 13.

12. Simon P. Newman similarly reads advertisements against the grain to recognize the personhood of the enslaved. See "Freedom-Seeking Slaves in England and Scotland, 1700–1780," *English Historical Review* no. 570 (2019): 1136–68.

13. James C. Scott, *Domination and the Arts of Resistance* (New Haven: Yale University Press, 1990).

14. Noel Camusat was a royal attorney in Cap in 1685 and became a notary in April 1706. He died in 1707, likely just after this ruling, and his replacement assumed his position in October 1707. See François Maurice Lafillard, "Etats de services dit 'Alphabet Lafillard,' de 1627 à 1780," 185, D2 C222, Archives nationales d'outre-mer. Subsequent citations will be made as ANOM. For the custom Camusat referenced, see M. de Charitte, "Ordre du Commandant du Cap, pour indiquer qu'il y a des Negres Epaves au Corps-de-garde de la même Ville," 6 April 1704, in *Loix et Constitutions*, 2:8. For Camusat's decision, see Council of Cap, "Arrête du Conseil du Cap, touchant les Negres Epaves," 9 February 1707, in *Loix et Constitutions*, 2:92.

15. The French metropole did not appoint an official *intendant* for Saint-Domingue until 1718, but Mithon acted in that capacity in the preceding years. For more on Mithon, see François Maurice Lafillard, "Etats de services dit 'Alphabet Lafillard,' de 1627 à 1780," 525, D2 C222, ANOM, and Kenneth J. Banks, *Chasing Empire across the Sea: Communications and the State in the French Atlantic, 1713–1763* (Montréal: McGill-Queen's Press, 2002), 225–26. For more on the role of the *intendant*, see William S. Cormack, *Patriots, Royalists, and Terrorists in the West Indies: The French Revolution in Martinique and Guadeloupe, 1789–1802* (Toronto: University of Toronto Press, 2019), 16.

16. For the ordinance, see Jean-Jacques Mithon, "Ordonnance de M. l'Intendant, sur la Vente des Negres Epaves," 17 June 1711, in *Loix et Constitutions*, 2:261-62.

17. Jean-Jacques Mithon, "Ordonnance de M. l'Intendant, touchant les Negres Epaves," 12 July 1712, in *Loix et Constitutions*, 2:324–25.

18. Bornat refers to the new jurisdiction as the Siége de Bayaha. Bayaha was a Taíno name given to the French colonial town of Fort-Dauphin. Today, it is called Fort-Liberté. For more on Bornat, see François Maurice Lafillard, "Etats de services dit 'Alphabet Lafillard,' de 1627 à 1780," 143, D2 C222, ANOM, and "Bornat, greffier de la juridiction du Fort-Dauphin, à Saint-Domingue, sa place demandée par Cazin," COL E 42, ANOM. For Bornat's opinion, see "Arrête du Conseil du

Cap, touchant la Vente des Négres, Epaves, dans la Juridiction du Fort-Dauphin," 7 January 1731, in *Loix et Constitutions*, 3:296–97.

19. Le Marquis de Fayet and Jean-Baptiste Duclos, "Ordonnance des Administrateurs, touchant la vente des Négres-Epaves," 6 April 1733, in *Loix et Constitutions,* 3:355–56.

20. "Lettre du Ministre aux Administrateurs, concernant les Amendes, Confiscations, Epaves et Aubaines," 13 June 1734, in *Loix et Constitutions*, 3:399–400.

21. "Arrêts e Règlement du Conseil du Cap, pour la Police et l'Administration des Prisons, avec Tarif des droits du Geôlier," 12 September 1740 and 6 May 1741, in *Loix et Constitutions*, 3:625–35.

22. Louis XV, "Règlement du Roi, concernant la Maréchaussée de Saint-Domingue," 31 July 1743, in *Loix et Constitutions*, 3:754–59.

23. Scott, *Domination and the Arts of Resistance*, 183–201.

24. Brunier and Maillart, "Ordonnance des Administrateurs, concernant les Négres-Epaves," 2 July 1745, in *Loix et Constitutions,* 4:834–35.

25. Louis XV, "Ordonnance du Roi, qui confirme purement et simplement celle rendue le 2 Juillet 1745, par les Administrateurs, portant que les Négres fugitifs arrêtés, seront, faute de réclamation dans un mois, vendus comme épaves," 26 October 1746, in *Loix et Constitutions*, 3:852.

26. Albert H. Hamscher, *The Royal Financial Administration and the Prosecution of Crime in France, 1670–1789* (Newark: University of Delaware Press, 2012), 203.

27. John D. Garrigus, *Before Haiti: Race and Citizenship in French Saint-Domingue* (New York: Palgrave Macmillan, 2006), 114.

28. Jean Etienne-Bernard de Clugny de Nuits, "Ordonnance de M. l'Intendant, concernant les Negres Marrons," 23 March 1764, in *Loix et Constitutions*, 4:717–18.

29. Louis XV, "Ordonnance du Roi concernant les Negres épaves," 18 November 1767, in *Loix et Constitutions,* 5:139–41.

30. Dubois, *Avengers*, 19–20; Garrigus, *Before Haiti*, 124.

31. Louis XV, "Ordonnance du Roi concernant les Negres épaves," 18 November 1767, in *Loix et Constitutions*, 5:139–41.

32. "Amérique du Cap, le 30 juin," *Affiches Américaines*, 6 July 1768, 222–23.

33. "Etat des Negres épaves qui, suivant l'Ordonnance du Roi du 18 novembre 1767, doivent être vendus à la diligence du Receveur de ce droit, extrait des Registres du Greffe des Prisons Royales du Cap," *Affiches Américaines*, 26 October 1768, 352.

34. See *Affiches Américaines,* 25 April 1770 (202–3), 16 May 1770 (235), 1 August 1770 (322–23), and 29 August 1770 (352).

35. "Etat des Negres Epaves qui, conformément à l'Ordonnance du Roi du 18 novembre 1767, doivent être vendus le 7 octobre 1779, à la Barre du Siége Royal du Port-au-Prince, suite & diligence du Receveur de ce droit audit, lieu," *Affiches Américaines*, 10 August 1779, 255.

36. "Etat des Negres Epaves qui, conformément à l'Ordonnance du Roi du 18 novembre 1767, doivent être vendus le 7 octobre 1779, à la Barre du Siége Royal du Port-au-Prince, suite & diligence du Receveur de ce droit audit lieu," *Affiches Américaines*, 10 August 1779, 255.

37. "Etat des Negres Epaves qui, conformément à l'Ordonnance du Roi du 18 Novembre 1767, doivent être vendus le 27 Juillet prochain, à la Barre du Siege Royal du Cap, à la diligence du Receveur de ce Droit," *Affiches Américaines*, 22 May 1771, 207.

38. "Liste des Negres Epaves qui doivent être vendus à la Barre du Siege Royal du Cap le 28 dudit mois de janvier," *Affiches Américaines*, 17 November 1773, 551.

39. Eddins, "African Diaspora Collective Action," 130.

40. "Liste des Negres Epaves qui doivent être vendus à la Barre du Siege Royal du Fort-Dauphin, le 1 avril prochain, à la requête du Receveur de ce Droit," *Affiches Américaines*, 27 February 1773, 94; "Le lundi 4 du mois de Janvier prochain, il sera vendu à la Barre du Siege Royal de Jacmel, à la requête du Receveur des Epaves audit lieu, conformément à l'Ordonnance du Roi du 18 Novembre 1767," *Affiches Américaines*, 11 November 1772, 548–49; "Etat des Negres Epaves qui, conformément à l'Ordonnance du Roi du 18 Novembre 1767, doivent être vendus le samedi 7 Juillet prochain, à la diligence du Receveur de ce Droit. Extrait des Registres des prisons Royales du Port-de-Paix," *Affiches Américaines*, 16 May 1770, 235; and "Liste des Negres Epaves qui doivent être vendus à la Barre du Siege Royal du Cap le 28 dudit mois de janvier," *Affiches Américaines*, 17 November 1773, 551–52.

41. "Etat des Negres Epaves qui, conformément à l'Ordonnance du Roi du 18 Novembre 1767, doivent être vendus le premier Octobre prochain, à la Barre du Siege Royal de Saint-Louis, à la Requête du Receveur de ce Droit audit lieu," *Affiches Américaines*, 4 September 1771, 383.

42. "Etat des Negres Epaves qui, conformément à l'Ordonnance du Roi du 18 Novembre 1767, doivent être vendus le 28 mars prochain 1772, à la Barre du Siege Royal du Cap, à la Requête du Receveur de ce Droit audit lieu," *Affiches Américaines*, 22 February 1772, 95.

43. "Ordonnance des Administrateurs, touchant des Negres Epaves; Arrêtés relatifs à son enregistrement au Conseil du Cap, et Arrêtés du Conseil d'Etat portant cassation desdits arrêtés," 18 February, 4 April, 21 July, and 18 November 1767; 10 February, 8 March, and 6 June 1768, in *Loix et Constitutions*, 5:94.

44. "Etat des Negres Epaves qui, conformément à l'Ordonnance du Roi du 18 Novembre 1767, doivent être vendus le 2 Juillet prochain, à la Barre du Siege Royal du Petit-Goave, à la Requête du Receveur de ce Droit audit lieu," *Affiches Américaines*, 19 May 1773, 233–34.

45. David Northrup, "Igbo and Myth Igbo: Culture and Ethnicity in the Atlantic World, 1600–1850," *Slavery and Abolition*, 21, no. 3 (2000), 18.

46. "Etat des Negres Epaves qui seront vendus le 5 octobre prochain, à la Barre du Siege Royal de Saint-Marc, à la Requête du Receveur des Epaves," *Affiches Américaines*, 26 August 1772, 415–16.

47. Moreau de Saint-Méry, *Description*, 67.

48. "Etat des Negres épaves qui, conformément à l'Ordonnance du Roi du 18 novembre 1767, doivent être vendus le 7 octobre 1779, à la Barre du Siege Royal du Port-au-Prince, suite & diligence du Receveur de ce droit audit lieu," *Affiches Américaines*, 10 August 1779, 255; "Etat des Negres Epaves qui seront vendus le 3 octobre prochain, à la Barre du Siege Royal du Port-de-Paix, à la Requête du

Receveur des Epaves," *Affiches Américaines*, 5 August 1772, 380; and "Etat des Negres Epaves qui, conformément à l'Ordonnance du Roi du 18 Novembre 1767, doivent être vendus le 7 Octobre prochain, à la Barre du Siege Royal du Port-au-Prince, à la Requête du Receveur de ce Droit," *Affiches Américaines*, 25 August 1773, 404.

49. James E. McClellan III, *Colonialism and Science: Saint Domingue in the Old Regime* (Chicago: University of Chicago Press, 2010), 144.

50. See Londa Schiebinger, *Secret Cures of Slaves: People, Plants, and Medicine in the Eighteenth-Century Atlantic World* (Stanford: Stanford University Press, 2017).

51. "Etat des Nègres épaves qui doivent être vendus à la Barre de la Sénéchaussée de Saint-Marc," *Affiches Américaines*, 9 January 1790, 19, 597.

52. "Liste des negres marons que le Receveur des Epaves du Fort-Dauphin se propose de vendre à la Barre du Siege Royal dudit lieu le 5 juillet prochain," *Affiches Américaines*, 25 April 1770, 203. Gabriel Debien has suggested that a *nabot de pied* could weigh around 25 pounds. See "Les esclaves des plantations Mauger à Saint-Domingue (1763–1802)," *Bulletin de la Société d'Histoire de la Guadeloupe* no. 43–44 (1980), 70.

53. "Etat des Negres Epaves qui, conformément à l'Ordonnance du Roi du 18 Novembre 1767, doivent être vendus le 13 janvier prochain, à la Barre du Siege Royal du Port-au-Prince, à la Requête du Receveur de ce Droit," *Affiches Américaines*, 1 December 1773, 571.

"Something Else Ought Yet to be Done": Ottobah Cugoano's Critical Abolitionism

ALLISON CARDON

In his 1787 treatise, *Thoughts and Sentiments on the Evil and Wicked Traffic of the Slavery and Commerce of the Human Species*, Ottobah Cugoano points directly to the limitations of tropes that would eventually form the bedrock of abolitionist literature: humanitarian narrative and legal argumentation. In a critique of these approaches, Cugoano constructs linked theories of slavery and abolition beginning from the premise that slavery is a *wrong*—that is, a juridical violation that requires justice. His is a distinct and underappreciated framework: because neither humanitarian sentiment nor European legal codes can account for this wrong, even at the level of the individual, much less at the massive scale he identifies, he argues that righting the wrong of slavery requires an alternative juridical and political order.

The preponderance of the language of wrong, injury, restitution, and revolt in Cugoano's treatise demands attention: he argues that the law of God forbids theft, hence "it would be requisite to make restitution to the injured, and to bring about a reformation for themselves"; he calls for "the wise and considerate ... [to] make restitution for the injuries that they have already done"; and men who "find any wronged and injured by others ...

should endeavor to deliver the ensnared whatever their grievances might be."[1] He is deeply concerned with the related questions of revolt, retaliation, and punishment. Moreover, he repeatedly describes slavery as theft of a peculiar nature: slavers "do not take away a man's property, like other robbers; but they take a man himself, and subject him to their service and bondage, which is a greater robbery, and a greater crime, than taking away any property from men whatsoever" (*TS* 287). This conception of slavery as a network of personal, social, and political violations signals that, for him, accounting for wrong must be at the center of a just abolition.

What's more, Cugoano suggests that this orientation is precluded in most abolitionist writing, perhaps because of its tendency to rely on humanitarian sentiment: "the kind exertions of many benevolent and humane gentlemen" (*TS* 227). This line of thinking begins from the simple observation that the writing against slavery that had proliferated in the decade preceding the publication of *Thoughts and Sentiments* was strikingly ineffective: "notwithstanding all that has been done and written against it, that brutish barbarity, and unparalleled injustice, is still carried on to a very great extent in the colonies, and with an avidity as insidious, cruel, and oppressive as ever" (*TS* 228). He is particularly interested in how this writing tends to make abolition a matter of personal morality, rather than global politics: "It is therefore manifest that something else ought yet to be done; and what is required, is evidently the incumbent duty of all men of enlightened understanding, and of every man that has any claim or affinity to the name of Christian, that the base treatment which the African Slaves undergo, ought to be abolished; and it is moreover evident, that the whole, or any part of that iniquitous traffic of slavery, can nowhere or in any degree, be admitted, but among those who must eventually resign their own claim to any degree of sensibility and humanity, for that of barbarians and ruffians" (*TS* 227). By opposing the "kind exertions of many benevolent and humane gentlemen" to "the duty of all men of enlightened understanding, and of every man that has any claim or affinity to the name of Christian," Cugoano imagines the abolition of slavery as the result of a massive social movement. At three centuries' remove, his call for "something else" is an invitation to reevaluate the political vision of eighteenth-century abolitionism.

Cugoano's Critique of Humanitarian Narrative

Cugoano signals his ambivalence about humanitarian narrative very early on in *Thoughts and Sentiments*, and his point is underscored by how little we know about him. Quobna Ottobah Cugoano was kidnapped from the Fante people of the Gold Coast at age 13, taken first to Grenada, and then to England in 1772, where he was emancipated. In the 1780s, he was employed as a servant and came into contact with Olaudah Equiano and Granville Sharp. With Equiano, he founded the Sons of Africa, an abolitionist organization. He published *Thoughts and Sentiments on the Evil and Wicked Traffic of the Slavery and Commerce of the Human Species* in 1787 and disappeared from the historical record after the second edition of his book was published in 1791. It is unlikely that he lived to see the legal abolition of the slave trade (1807) and he almost certainly died before the abolition of the institution itself in 1833. The near-absence of personal narrative in his book is especially noticeable, given the ways in which personal narrative was becoming a cornerstone of abolitionist literature, defining Olaudah Equiano's *Interesting Narrative* and other writing by formerly enslaved Africans like John Marrant, Ukawsaw Gronniosaw, Phillis Wheatley Peters, and Ignatius Sancho. Personal narrative crops up as well in the work of white abolitionists like Thomas Clarkson, James Ramsey, and Anthony Benezet. Compared with these accounts, Cugoano's references to his own life are remarkably brief; he reports a bit about his childhood before relaying the details of his kidnapping, enslavement, and emancipation in just a few paragraphs. He specifically avoids any disturbing details, offering this rationale for his elision: "But it would be needless to give a description of all the horrible scenes which we saw, and the base treatment which we met with in this dreadful captive situation, as the similar cases of thousands, which suffer by this infernal traffic, are well known. ... Brought from a state of innocence and freedom, and in a barbarous and cruel manner, conveyed to a state of horror and slavery: This abandoned situation may be easier conceived than described" (*TS* 233). Though this might at first come off as a simple statement regarding the unrepresentability of atrocity (a familiar idea to modern readers), on closer reading, Cugoano's point seems to be not so much about unrepresentability as it is an assertion that representation is no longer necessary—in fact, it is "needless," given all the information to which his readers presumably have access. As the facts of the atrocity are "well-known," describing the grim details of the trade and the institution yet again belies the fact that it might be easier for his readers to imagine what has happened to him than for him to actually put his experience into words.[2]

Why does Cugoano reject humanitarian personal narrative as an abolitionist strategy? Looking at its conventions should begin to provide an answer. Thomas Laqueur lays these out: first, humanitarian narrative is characterized by a reliance on detail as the sign of truth; second, a focus on the "personal body, not only as the locus of pain but also as the common bond between those who suffer and those who would help and as the object of scientific discourse through which the causal links between an evil, a victim, and a benefactor are forged."[3] Lastly, it is connected to a reformist political orientation: "humanitarian narrative exposes the lineaments of causality and of human agency: ameliorative action is represented as possible, effective, and therefore morally imperative."[4] Laqueur takes Granville Sharp's conversion to abolitionism as an example of humanitarian narrative in action: "Sharp reports that he became involved with the plight of slaves when he discovered a black man, Jonathan Strong, waiting at the door of his brother William Sharpe, to be treated for wounds inflicted on his back by his West Indian owner. The wounds of one man, not the abstract wrongs of slavery, cried out, pierced his heart, and propelled him into the abolitionist cause."[5] If we take Sharp's conversion story as paradigmatic of abolitionist humanitarian narrative, Cugoano's eschewal of detail and the personal body sets him apart—prompting us to ask how and why would he want to disaggregate the narrative tropes of humanitarianism from abolitionism? What could he have against humanitarianism and what alternative approach to abolition does he imagine?

According to Julie Stone Peters, the rise of humanitarian narrative in this period meant that, in the minds of readers, narrative closure could stand in for political justice and leave the actual injustice in question materially unaddressed.[6] Lynn Festa's study of abolition echoes this point, showing how the sympathetic identification meant to expand the sympathizer's emotional and political consciousness can actually enclose the distant and unfamiliar within its sympathetic, self-referential circuit: "the imaginative placement of one's self in the position of another allows one provisionally to grasp his or her experience. And yet these sympathetic exchanges cannot be perfectly symmetrical; if they were, one would cease to be oneself. … Absolute equivalence does not secure identity; it menaces with total substitution."[7] Humanitarian narrative thus also requires a constitutively asymmetrical sympathy: the reading procedure collapses the imaginary distance between the reader and victim, such that the reader's agency is limited by the narrative's inevitable consolidation of their own identity. For Cugoano, this centering of the individual—and the European individual at that—means that abolitionist humanitarianism is limited by European ideas about suffering and political relationships—that is, it requires a model of slavery as *suffering*, not as a *wrong*. Righting wrongs requires not sympathy, but justice.

Cugoano's point is closer to Saidiya Hartman's observation that scenes of subjection meant to elicit sympathy for enslaved people eject actual Africans out of the equation: "empathy in important respects confounds [one's] efforts to identify with the enslaved because in making the slave's suffering [one's] own, [one] begins to feel for [oneself] rather than for those whom this exercise in imagination presumably is designed to reach."[8] A comparison with one of Cugoano's abolitionist allies, Thomas Clarkson, is instructive on this point. In his *Essay on the Slavery and Commerce of the Human Species*, Clarkson self-consciously sets himself up as an imagined humanitarian in conversation with another imagined humanitarian operating at a closer remove:

> To place this in the clearest, and most conspicuous point of view, I shall throw some of my information on this head into the form of a narrative; I shall suppose myself on a particular part of the continent of Africa, and relate a scene, which, from its agreement with unquestionable facts, might not unreasonably be presumed to have been presented to my view, had I been actually there.
>
> And first, I will turn my eyes to the cloud of dust that is before me. It seems to advance rapidly, and, accompanied with dismal shrieks and yellings, to make the very air, that is above it, tremble as it rolls along. What can possibly be the cause? I will inquire of that melancholy African, who is walking dejected upon the shore; whose eyes are steadfastly fixed on the approaching object. ...
>
> "Alas!" says the unhappy African, "the cloud that you see approaching, rises from a train of wretched slaves. They are going to the ships behind you. They are destined for the English colonies. ...
>
> The person you see in the middle, is the father of the two young men, who walk on each side of him. His wife and two of his children were killed in the attack, and his father being wounded ... was left bleeding on the spot where this transaction happened."[9]

The fictional African goes on to describe the kidnapping and suffering of several other fictional individual Africans, including details about their families and journeys. Clarkson's strategy here is interesting, for the nested imaginary interlocuters seem designed to pull readers' sympathies through layers of identification in order to collapse the distance between his audience and the imagined Africans in question. Equally significant, however, is the way that Clarkson includes fictional details "in agreement with unquestionable facts," as though his fictional narrative was truthful. The latter is exactly the kind of move that Cugoano suggests is "needless."

Indeed, Clarkson's model relies not just on sympathetic identification, but also on the assumption that the suffering of any particular African is interchangeable with that of other Africans—what better indication that humanitarian narratives did more to feed consumer appetites than to right wrongs?[10] Moreover, its central question concerns whether or not slavery is, in fact, atrocious—hence the attention to injured bodies and the destruction of family units. This approach simultaneously prioritizes verifying the fact of atrocity and proving that the trade is morally wrong. In doing so, it takes the limits of European capacities for identification as abolition's condition of possibility. For Cugoano, this is too low a bar.

Cugoano's Critique of the Law

In Cugoano's hands, humanitarian abolitionism is emblematic of a political minimalism anchored to the European individual as the agent of abolition, a politics that relies on a narrative form that sets up such an individual's understanding and need for information as its horizon of abolition. This is politically minimal both in terms of its ends—if humanitarian narrative is centered around scenes of suffering, then abolition itself is conceived of as the removal of that suffering—and in terms of its means: it imagines that a mass of individuals will be moved to advocate for a change within a political system that leaves that system intact. Effectively, humanitarian narrative tries to assimilate the cause and experience of enslaved Africans to that of Europeans who have for centuries ignored or even justified slavery. Cugoano's critique of legalist abolitionism parallels this line of thought: attempting abolition through British and European legal systems means assimilating the questions of slavery, abolition, and the humanity of Africans to legal, moral, and political forms very much tied up with the justification and protection of transatlantic slavery. Cugoano's comments on the *Zong* trial are an important case in point:

> The vast carnage and murders committed by the British instigators of slavery, is attended with a very shocking, peculiar, and almost unheard of conception, according to the notion of the perpetrators of it; they either consider them as their own property, that they may do with as they please, in life or death; or that the taking away the life of a black man is of no more account than taking away the life of a beast. A very melancholy instance of this happened about the year 1780, as recorded in the courts of law; a master of a vessel bound to the Western Colonies, selected 132 of the most sickly of the black slaves, and ordered them to be thrown overboard into the sea, in order to recover their value from the insurers. ... On the trial, by the counsel for the owners of the vessel against the underwriters, their argument was, that the slaves were to be considered the same as horses; ... But our lives are accounted of no value, we are hunted after as the prey

> in the desert, and doomed to appeal to the inhabitants of Europe,
> would they dare to say that they have not wronged us, and that the
> blood of millions do not cry out against them? And if we appeal
> to the inhabitants of Great-Britain, can they justify the deeds of
> their conduct toward us? (*TS* 301)

Cugoano's analysis targets not just the miscarriage of justice exemplified by the case itself, but also the legal fictions that made the ruling possible: a "conception" that makes it impossible to treat the massacre as a massacre, the murder of slaves as murder. Such a fiction is animated by a history that it necessarily obscures: enslaved Africans can be treated as horses for legal purposes because they had already been bestialized, "hunted after as the prey in the desert." Why, he wonders, would people whom the law treats as horses appeal to that same law for remedy? British law represents an impasse, not an avenue, for justice. By assimilating the injustices of slavery to the available legal categories, this form of abolitionism cannot address the actual history and injustice of slavery.

Compare his approach with that of Granville Sharp, whose argument about the *Zong* trial was that the crew should be tried for murder, an extension of his overall position that enslaved Africans were entitled to the protection of English law. In an essay on the injustice of slavery, Sharp argues that it amounts to a violation of both natural and positive law:

> True justice makes no respect of persons, and can never deny to any one that blessing to which all mankind have an undoubted right, their *natural liberty*.
> Though the law makes no mention of Negro Slaves, yet this is no just argument for excluding them from the general protection of our happy constitution. ...
> Now if Slavery in this kingdom is really an innovation unknown in law ... how can the vulgar plea *of private property in a Slave, as in a house or a dog*, avail any thing either in equity or law? ...
> Nay, it is an innovation of such an unwarrantable and dangerous nature, that besides the gross infringement of the common and natural rights of mankind, it is plainly *coutrary* [*sic*] to the laws and constitution of this kingdom.[11]

Sharp's argument here echoes the judgment that Lord Mansfield had made only a few years earlier in the Somerset case, in which he ruled that a West Indian slave owner could not compel a man to leave England because there was no positive law supporting slavery in England. Widely interpreted to outlaw slavery itself in England despite Mansfield's efforts to rule as narrowly as possible, the ruling represents the last in a series of juridical decisions either for or against the legality of slavery.[12] The effect of the Somerset case was arguably monumental, terrifying slave owners throughout the British Atlantic with the prospect that their property was in jeopardy; however, Mansfield's subsequent decision in the *Zong* trial underscored the point that even if a slave owner could not find legal protection for his property rights in England itself, enslaved people could still be murdered with impunity within English jurisdictions. Sharp's insistence that this same legal code should grant Africans the protections that it affords to any other Englishman is not naïve, according to Cugoano's critique, but it is inadequate because it does not account for the ways in which the law has enabled, rather than prevented, this and other monumental injustices.

Cugoano's point remains significant, as he is highlighting how, under English law, slave status was a matter of economic interests: "West Indian slaves were seen both as relics of social hierarchy grounded in the inherited possession of land or real property, and as emblems of commercial property that threatened that very land-based order."[13] This point, in turn, allows us to connect his critique of humanitarian abolitionism to legal abolitionism: both recognize the humanity of enslaved persons only as an effect of violation, effectively linking their political subjectivity to their capacity to be violated. Proposing that the recognition of this minimal personhood should be the horizon of abolition is ultimately tautological, obviating any justice or remedy that would presuppose a more expansive or self-evident African political subjectivity. As Saidiya Hartman puts it, "emancipation appears less the grand event of liberation than a point of transition between modes of servitude and racial subjection. As well, it leads us to question whether the rights of man and citizen are realizable or whether the appellation 'human' can be borne equally by all."[14]

For Cugoano, in fact, emancipation is no answer for the wrongs of slavery because those wrongs began in Africa: "The emancipation of a few, while ever that evil and predominant business of slavery is continued, cannot make that horrible traffic one bit less criminal. For, according to the methods of procuring slaves in Africa, there must be great robberies and murders committed before any emancipation can take place, and before any lenitive favours can be shown to any of them, even by the generous and humane" (*TS* 291). Because conventional approaches to abolition can only conceive of Africans in ways that perpetuate the legal and political fictions that have been used to justify slavery, Cugoano imagines his alternative version of abolition in spite of English law, not through it. His larger vision of abolition requires attention to a political relationship that both the law and humanitarian narrative continue to obfuscate: the relationship between the enslaved, their captors, and the stockholders who profited from their investment in the trade, a relationship wherein one party has wronged the other and so might owe them restitution, remedy, or repair.

Natural Law, Natural Rights, Human Rights

Conventional wisdom has it that natural law helps jurists think through legal and political relationships, events, or problems for which positive law lacks adequate terms or courses of action.[15] In the seventeenth and eighteenth centuries, natural-rights theorists were especially keen to sort out the relationship between natural law and positive law. Political theorists had long argued that positive law was under no obligation to follow the principles of natural law, but in the eighteenth century they began to argue that it should, in part because positive law had to find a new source of legitimacy after the decline of absolute monarchy made divine right an inadequate source of authority.[16] Amid this juridical transition, Cugoano's account makes two striking arguments: first, whereas many abolitionists argued that slavery violated natural law and so should be outlawed by positive law, he contends that the violation is of such significance as to invalidate European legal codes as such. Second, whereas political theory and jurisprudence were trending away from treating divine law as a source of legal authority and toward legal naturalism and even legal positivism, Cugoano treats divine law as the best resource for providing the type of remedy that slavery requires. He initiates this proposition by considering where to turn, given that neither positive law nor natural law can provide the requisite remedy:

> and who dare suppose, or even presume to think, that the inhuman ruffians and ensnarers of men, the vile negotiators and merchandizers of the human species, and the offensive combinations of slave-holders in the West have done no evil? And should we be passive, as the suffering martyrs dying in the flames, whose blood crieth for vengeance on their persecutors and murderers; so the iniquity of our oppressors, enslavers, and murderers rise up against them. For we have been hunted after as the wild beasts of the earth, and sold to the enemies of mankind as their prey ... we have been pursued after, and, by haughty mandates and laws of iniquity, overtaken, and murdered and slain, and the blood of millions cries out against them. ... the great distress and wretchedness of human woe and misery, which we are yet lying under, is still rising up before that High and Sovereign Hand of Justice. ... And should any of the best of them plead, as they generally will do, and tell of their humanity and charity to those whom they have captured and enslaved, their

> tribute of thanks is but small. … For as we have been robbed of our natural right as men, and treated as beasts, those who have injured us, are like them who have robbed the widow, the orphans, the poor and the needy of their right, and whose children are rioting on the spoils of those who are begging at their doors for bread. (*TS* 305)

At first, Cugoano's statement that "we have been robbed of our natural right as men" sounds very much like Olaudah Equiano's claim that slavery "violates that first natural right of mankind, equality and independency," or Clarkson's characterization of slavery as an invasion of "the liberties of mankind."[17] This is a straightforward recapitulation of the common idea that "haughty mandates and laws of iniquity" are out of sync with the principle in natural law that guarantees all men liberty. But as we have already seen, Cugoano is interested in doing "something else," something other than demonstrating that slavery is wrong in principle; he wants to demonstrate that it is a *wrong*: a violation, injury, or injustice that requires more than just new laws against it. It is a *wrong* that requires some profound collective action toward redressing what he sees as an atrocity: "the blood of millions cries out against them. … the great distress and wretchedness of human woe and misery, which we are yet lying under, is still rising up before that High and Sovereign Hand of Justice" (*TS* 305). This passage demonstrates Cugoano's vested interest not only in relief, but in justice—a justice that, for him, must be divine because it possesses political resources beyond those of either natural or positive law.

In this light, it is clear Cugoano is doing more than just emphasizing the disparity between common claims about natural rights and positive law: he is leveraging a more general critique of the European use of law to justify and obfuscate the domination and violence of slavery in particular. While he observes that enslaved Africans have been "robbed of our natural right as men, and treated as beasts," he also questions how one might restore and remedy the loss that results from the violation he describes. He often takes his point even further by highlighting the European arrogance behind the assumption that their law of nations should be recognized as a set of universal principles toward which all nations might aspire, even as it had, for centuries, permitted and enabled the injustice at issue: "For by some way or other every criminal nation, and all their confederates, who sin and rebel against God, and against his laws of nature and nations, will each meet with some awful retribution at last … the greater advantages of light, learning, knowledge, and civilization that any people enjoy, if they do not maintain righteousness … will meet with the more severe rebuke" (*TS* 304–5). Equally significant in the passage above is the way in which he reframes the perceived passivity of Clarkson's humanitarian victims; rather than making passivity tantamount to helplessness, he transforms it into an indication of martyrdom and therefore a contribution to the eventual retribution guaranteed by his theory of divine law. This zoomed-out, theological frame makes slavery much more than a humanitarian crisis; it is an injustice, biblical in scope, for which European legal codes have proven unable to account. To right these wrongs, he looks not to European jurisprudence, but rather to the "High and Sovereign Hand of Justice" (*TS* 305). The conventional abolitionist formulation of slavery as a violation of natural law helps Cugoano identify the injustice as such, but his vision of justice goes far beyond pleading for the recognition of Africans' natural rights. Divine law becomes a resource for assessing the wrong of slavery and imagining how it could be adequately remedied.

Because of the prevalence of natural-rights discourse and humanitarian narrative in abolitionist literature, scholars are often quick to treat the movement as an early or proto-human rights movement.[18] Whether or not one agrees with this assessment, Cugoano's account of natural rights in his broader, justice-oriented political vision highlights the complicated context of rights discourse, particularly abolitionist rights discourse, at the end of the eighteenth century. The lack of consensus about whether natural rights should be understood as normative or neutral principles in relation to other bodies of law meant that proslavery activists had centuries of jurisprudence and philosophy on their side when they argued that there was no actionable legal contradiction in their insistence on slavery's lawfulness, because it was permitted by positive law, despite its prohibition in natural law. In fact, it was only late in the century that some philosophers would argue that slavery should be outlawed on the basis that it was against natural law.[19] When abolitionists contended that slavery should be outlawed because it violated natural rights, they were participating in a juridically innovative trend that advocated for bringing natural and positive law into alignment.

What this innovation could mean for subject peoples, including African slaves, was less clear than such arguments might suggest. Although triumphalist accounts of natural rights champion their emergence in this period as the herald of a truly universal political equality, these same principles were thoroughly imbricated with the juridically justified forms of domination and colonialism that took shape under the aegis of the law of nations, which was also derived from natural law principles. Antony Anghie argues that the British abolitionist movement should be recognized as the first international human rights campaign because England used international courts and enforcement mechanisms to promote international abolition.[20] Others have noted that this moment is also rightly understood as one of

Britain's most successful bids to use the law of nations to solidify its juridical hold on its colonial interests under the pretext of defending natural rights. More to the point, many abolitionists retained a vision of British empire that in no way precluded the domination of peoples around the globe. In other words, abolitionist demands for the recognition of Africans' natural rights did not necessarily amount to a liberatory vision of abolition as such.

Anthony Bogues has argued that Cugoano should be appreciated as a natural-rights theorist because his political theory links natural liberty and rights to civilization—a move that distinguishes him from other natural-rights theorists who tend to define them in terms of various relationships between citizens and their governments.[21] For Cugoano, natural rights and liberty are the product of civilization itself. By focusing on his framing of slavery as an injustice, it becomes clear that civilization and slavery are mutually exclusive and that European society has thus not fulfilled its own vision of universal humanity in its continuing reliance on and acceptance of slavery. Bogues finds a contradiction, however, in Cugoano's contention that, according to divine law and the laws of civilization, the unlawful might need to be "suppressed, deprived of their liberty, and perhaps their rights" (*TS* 267). Bogues accounts for this contradiction by suggesting that Cugoano either did not believe that his proslavery readers would take his biblical injunction seriously or that he simply could not resolve the contradictions in his attempt to think both secularly and religiously at the same time. By my reading, however, this is less a contradiction than an indication of Cugoano's reliance on divine law as a resource for litigating a wrong for which secular law had proven unable to remedy.

Divine Law and the Conceit of Civilization

Treating slavery as an injustice leads Cugoano to recognize the shortcomings of natural rights—their imbrication within European concepts of civilization, governance, and the individual—and compels him to turn to the Bible to think about how to right such catastrophic wrongs. While humanitarian narrative and legalism frame abolition as a moral endeavor, Cugoano uses the Bible and Christianity as self-consciously political resources. As Stefan Wheelock explains, "theology provides a grammar of civilization and freedom in the Anglo world ... the exegesis of Scripture could perform as a way of setting the terms of modern cultures and their historical aims."[22] This political-theological vision puts Cugoano on what Bogues refers to as "a different track" from other natural rights thinkers and from his abolitionist counterparts.[23] Cugoano proclaims that "what I intend to advance against that evil, criminal and wicked traffic of enslaving men, are only some Thoughts and Sentiments which occur to me, as being obvious from the Scriptures of Divine Truth, or such arguments as are deduced from thence, with other such observations as I have been able to collect ... the production of slavery, the evil effects produced by it, must show that its origin and source is of a wicked and criminal nature" (*TS* 228). Rather than follow the traditional abolitionist route by using natural rights as a device for creating sympathy for the suffering caused by slavery, and rather than using scripture to condemn slavery as sinful, he brings the two discourses together in order to issue a clear judgment of slavers: "But the robbers of men, the kidnappers, ensnarers and slave-holders, who take away the common rights and privileges of others to support and enrich themselves, are universally those pitiful and detestable wretches; for the ensnaring of others is the worst kind of robbery, as most opposite every precept and injunction of the Divine Law ... that they should do unto others, as they would that men should do to them. As to any other laws slaveholders may make among themselves, as respecting slaves, they can be of no better kinds ... than what is implied in the common report—that there may be some honesty among thieves" (*TS* 229). Natural rights—"common rights and privileges"—are for him a threshold that, when trespassed, signal that a crime has been committed, a wrong has occurred, but divine law provides the language for ascertaining the scope and significance of that crime and wrong: "the worst kind of robbery, as most opposite every precept and injunction of the Divine Law" (*TS* 229).

Such judgments begin to point to the broader ramifications of Cugoano's theory of slavery: divine law not only gives him the purview to condemn slavers as criminals, it also gives him a position from which to critique the putative principles underwriting the European political order. If slavery is not just a moral failure, but a wrong—whether a civil injustice or a crime, an interpersonal injustice or a tort, and arguably both—and if European juridical systems were unable to identify, prosecute, or right this wrong, then perhaps it is because the institutions themselves have not succeeded in fostering civilization through adherence to divine law: "All the criminal laws of civilization seem to be founded upon that law of God which was published to Noah and his sons; and, consequently, as it is again and again repeated, it becomes irreversible, and universal to all mankind. ... But it is an exceeding impious thing for men ever to presume, or think, as some will say, that they would make it death as a punishment for such a thing, and such a trespass; or that they can make any criminal laws of civilization as binding with a penalty of death for any thing just what they please" (*TS* 270–71). Like slavery, the persistence of the death penalty is not only a violation of divine law, but also a sign of Europe's lack of civilization. He underscores the influence of Christianity in the development of English law, making note of hypocritical religious justifications for slavery in the midst of convenient juridical departures from Christian principles: "If this law of God had not been given to men, murder itself would not have been a crime; and those who punished it with death would just have been as guilty as the other" (*TS* 272). He also insists on the continuing relevance of scripture to political legitimacy, finding "a David, a Solomon, a Cromwell … and a Charles the Second" guilty of murder underwritten by religious hypocrisy: "But among all pretences for taking away the lives of men by any form or law, that for religion is the most unwarrantable" (*TS* 272).

Throughout *Thoughts and Sentiments*, Cugoano uses divine law to assess European legal practices. While he might tackle some individual issues not totally entwined with slavery, taken together, these assessments speak to the ways in which he sees the political fictions that justify slavery ramifying throughout European legal systems, revealing their fundamental illegitimacy. It's important to note that he is not simply identifying contradictions—that is, formal elements that are necessarily in conflict in any political system, but rather the way that what is often taken for granted as a necessary contradiction actually obfuscates how law shores up certain forms of political power: "But the laws of civilization must jar greatly when the law of God is screwed up in the greatest severity to punish men for their crimes on the one hand, and on the other to be totally disregarded. When the Divine law points out a theft, where the thief should make retribution for his trespass, the laws of civilization say, in many cases, that it is no crime. In this the ways of men are not equal; but let the wise and just determine whether the laws of God or the laws of men are right" (*TS* 273). God is a not just a devotional figure here, but the very source of political authority. "Screwing up" the law of God strains the laws of civilization, undermining not only their coherence, but also their legitimacy. Taking aim at the principle of formal equality, Cugoano directs his vision to the zone in which it fails to apply: criminal law and punishment. The link to his critique of slavery is clear: if slavers are, for him, first and foremost thieves, then what does the acceptance of slavery say about criminal law in general? The laws of civilization do not account for crime equally across different populations, and Cugoano targets the pure formalism of the rule of law, here clearly a masquerade for the rule of men—and barbarous men at that.[24]

Critical Abolitionism as Political Theology

It is tempting to treat Cugoano's abolitionist vision as eschatological: divine judgment circulates throughout the text as a distant, but certain eventuality: "And it cannot be thought otherwise, but that the abandoned aggressors, among the learned nations will, in due time, as the just reward of their aggravated iniquity, be visited with some more dreadful and tremendous judgments of the righteous vengeance of God, than what even befell to the Canaanites of old" (*TS* 264). However, such a reading risks reducing his analysis to a form of quietism that his treatment of the connections between slavery and colonialism cannot quite accommodate. I would propose instead that this vision of apocalyptic judgment reflects his sense of the enormity of the injustice at issue, which is both deeply embedded within the institutions of British civil society and fans out across the globe over several generations.

Having established that Cugoano avoids conventional approaches to abolition—eschewing humanitarian narrative in favor of legal and political analysis; relying on the retributive and remedial aspects of divine law, rather than the formal principles of natural law—we can now consider how his theory of slavery as a wrong requires an extraordinary, indeed revolutionary remedy. As he puts it:

> What revolution the end of the predominant evil of slavery and oppression may produce, whether the wise and considerate will surrender and give it up, and make restitution for the injuries they have already done, as far as they can; or whether the force of their wickedness, and the iniquity of their power, will lead them on until some universal calamity burst forth against the abandoned carriers of it on, and against the criminal nations in confederacy with them, is not for me to determine? ... And nothing else can be expected for such violations of taking away the natural rights and liberties of men, but that those who are the doers of it will meet with some awful visitation of the righteous judgment of God, and in such a manner as it cannot be thought that his just vengeance for their iniquity will be the less tremendous because his judgements are long delayed. (*TS* 277)

Cugoano recognizes slavery as a transnational injustice that cannot rely on the exigencies of international jurisdictions to be righted. Indeed, one important feature of his theory is the fact that he links the slave trade to colonialism in a way that abolitionists as a rule were unwilling to broach. As Christopher Leslie Brown has demonstrated, most abolitionists remained ideologically committed to the British empire as such, and their emancipation schemes never conveyed any sense that the British, or any other slave trading nation, could *owe* something to the Africans and African nations they had wronged. Instead, they came up with programs for incorporating previously enslaved populations into the imperial project itself—especially through the recognition of property, new ideas about the productivity of free labor, and the interpellation of cultural norms. Granville Sharp, for example, espoused the "Spanish regulations" (laws permitting enslaved people to earn or purchase their freedom), while Edmund Burke's Black Code allowed slaves to bequeath their property to their descendants.[25] Though Cugoano does, at one point, call for the "universal emancipation of slaves, and the enfranchisement of all the Black People employed in the culture of the colonies," arguing that their free labor would be "as useful as any other class of men that could be found" (*TS* 307), his position needs to be contextualized within his critique of colonialism and his demand for restitution. For him, this would amount to a different political order entirely. While abolitionists and imperialists and abolitionist-imperialists worked to rethink empire in the wake of the American Revolution, Cugoano's analysis of empire takes aim at the heart of their imperial anxieties.

In Cugoano's thinking, slavery forced questions of jurisdiction that brought the limits of imperial sovereignty to the fore. The prospect of abolition underscored the relationships between the metropole and its colonies, Europe and the globe.[26] In this light, jurisdictions become a method for creating legal boundaries around harm—whether through the nation-state, imperial jurisdiction, or rules dictating actionable harms according to political status—and these institutional forms occluded the illegitimacy of imperial projects. By connecting the harm endured by enslaved Africans to the harm endured by Indigenous peoples in the New World, Cugoano rejects these boundaries, suggesting that they serve to insulate responsible parties from liability. Beginning with Christopher Columbus, he traces the spread of colonial atrocities, including the betrayal of Anacoana, a Taino queen; Hernán Cortés's betrayal of Montezuma; and Francisco Pizarro's betrayal of Atahualpa. These cruelties, along with slavery, are acts of the Antichrist: "But all the nations have drunk the wine of that iniquity, and become drunk with the wine of the wrath of her fornication, whose name, by every mark and feature, is the Antichrist; and every dealer in slaves, and those that hold them in slavery, whatever else they may call themselves, or whatever else they may profess. And likewise, those nations whose governments support that evil and wicked traffic of slavery, however remote the situation where it is carried on may be, are, in that respect, as much Antichristian as any thing in the world can be" (*TS* 283–84). Cugoano here avoids the trope of the Black Legend—the common defense of English colonial practices by insisting on their mildness and benevolence compared to Spanish cruelty. Instead, he denationalizes slavery and colonialism, assessing their injustice in transnational terms.

By identifying disjunctions between legal and juridical definitions of wrong and the undeniable violation, atrocity, and injustice of slavery, Cugoano's political theory emerges as a form of political theology—that is, an investigation of "the theological legitimation or religious dimension of political authority."[27] Political theology often comes to the fore when philosophers examine the principles that legitimate modern political organization, particularly the principle of sovereignty.[28] Whereas a work of political theology often shows how a seemingly secular political principle is actually justified by a degree of theological mysticism, Cugoano's political theology instead delegitimizes secular political authority.[29] His willingness to recognize and affirm the relationship between wrongs and slavery give him access to the very categories and principles that the European imperialists are working to obfuscate and naturalize.[30]

Cugoano takes direct, explicit issue with the institutions that underwrite slavery—and in his account of revolution, the political will of the people is also the divine judgment of God, who offers a remedy to the harm caused by "subjection and oppression ... slavery and bondage" in the form of a new political order. This move is certainly rhetorical, but it's important to recognize that his purpose in invoking divine judgment here is to underscore the scale and scope of the wrong. This feature of his analysis has often been misunderstood: Keith Sandiford argues that his theological perspective is geared toward sympathy and evangelical identity.[31]

Indeed, Sandiford, Brycchan Carey, and Vincent Carretta all treat *Thoughts and Sentiments* as a jeremiad, but I think that categorization ultimately misses the political implications of Cugoano's reliance on divine authority. I follow Stefan Wheelock's connection of theology to political legitimacy and sovereignty: "Cugoano was not simply involved in the exercise of political sermonizing. ... he also wanted to point out the extent to which the Atlantic plantation complex was perverting the historical evolution of politics and religion in what was ostensibly an 'advanced Christian era' in the Atlantic."[32] Cugoano's definitions of slavery and restitution are based on his understanding of the thorough imbrication of the slave trade with politics and religion, and characterizing his treatise as a jeremiad unnecessarily limits the scope of his critique by defining slavery as sinful, rather than harmful and a *wrong*.

To Cugoano, abolition is neither a matter of conversion nor repentance. Instead, divine authority challenges the presumptions of British empire and brings up the possibility of revolution. Comparing positive law to divine law, he takes aim at the nation as a political fiction that limits responsibility for a fundamentally transnational wrong: "But the several nations of Europe that have joined in that iniquitous traffic of buying, selling, and enslaving men, must in course have left their own laws of civilization to adopt those of barbarians and robbers, and that they must say to one another, *When thou sawest a thief, and then thou consentest with him, and hast been partaker with all the workers of iniquity*" (*TS* 303).[33] These nations undermine their own civil ambitions not only by relying on slavery economically, but also by adopting laws that shore it up. Effectively, legalizing slavery negates Europe's claims to civilization. What's more, he challenges the idea that any European nation might tolerate the slave trade or the institution of slavery in isolation from the others because both the trade and the institution require some degree of permission from the others, even if they do not directly participate: "but whereas every man, as a rational creature, is responsible for his actions, and he becomes not only guilty in doing evil himself, but in letting others rob and oppress their fellow-creatures with impunity, or in not delivering the oppressed when he has it in his power to help them" (*TS* 303). If individuals have a divine responsibility not to allow the robbery and oppression of their "fellow-creatures," the nation has a political obligation to prevent or at least remonstrate with slaving nations: "And likewise that nation which may be supposed to maintain a very considerable degree of civilization, justice, and equity within its own jurisdiction, is not in that case innocent, while it beholds another nation or people carrying on persecution, oppression, and slavery, unless it remonstrates against that wickedness of the other nation, and makes every effort in its power to help the oppressed, and to rescue the innocent" (*TS* 303). For Cugoano, the tolerance of slavery reveals that the nation-state, acting out of mere economic self-interest, shields responsible parties from proper legal scrutiny and political repercussions. He instead imagines a just state that guarantees rights not only by protecting the property of its citizens, but also by making restitution for wrongs.

Political theorists, jurists, and imperialists were all searching for workable concepts of sovereignty in this period, and Cugoano's treatise includes a novel contribution to this political debate.[34] Rather than understanding political authority as political power over a people or a territory that has been legitimated by a constitution, treaty, or statute, for Cugoano sovereign power is tied to and limited by any state's capacity to redress the harm it has caused:

> But when a nation or people do wickedly, and commit cruelties and devastations upon others, and enslave them, it cannot be expected that they should be attended with the blessings of God, neither to eschew evil ... from hence that motly system of government, which hath so sprung up and established itself, may be accounted for, as being an evident and universal depravity of one of the finest constitutions in the world; and it may be feared if these unconstitutional laws, reaching from Great-Britain to her colonies, be long continued in and supported, to the carrying on that horrible and wicked traffic of slavery, must at last mark out the whole of the British constitution with ruin and destruction; and that the most generous and tenacious people in the world for liberty, may also at last be reduced to slaves. (*TS* 286)

Cugoano effectively here resanctifies sovereignty, stripping the state of political authority because of its violation of divine law. What's more, he frames political legitimacy as conditional on a state's response to the interlocking histories of slavery and colonialism. This is not just a different definition of sovereignty, but a concept of a different order than those developed in European thought and put to use in various European political conflicts—not least because it centers what has in Europe always been treated as peripheral. By linking his version of sovereignty to this particular history, Cugoano rejects both the Eurocentrism and the idealism that made the concept both so central and so unwieldly for his imperialist counterparts.[35] By tying sovereign authority not to the rights of political subjects, but rather to the state's capacity to remedy the harm it has authorized, Cugoano envisions a global political order that begins from its own historical enmeshment.

Notes

This article has benefited tremendously from the insight and support of George Boulukos, Seth Cosimini, Ruth Mack, Aaron Jay Neber, Ryan Sheldon, Charlotte Sussman, and Nicole M. Wright. I would also like to thank the Race and Empire Caucus of the American Society for Eighteenth-Century Studies for their recognition of my work.

1. Cugoano, *Thoughts and Sentiments on the Evil and Wicked Traffic of the Slavery and Commerce of the Human Species*, in Thomas Clarkson and Ottobah Cugoano, *Essays on the Slavery and Commerce of the Human Species*, ed. Mary-Antoinette Smith (Peterborough: Broadview Press, 2010), 273, 277, 303. Subsequent citations of this edition will be made parenthetically as *TS*.

2. Cugoano makes a similar point later, when he writes, "To give any just conception of the barbarous traffic carried on at those factories, it would be out of my power to describe the miserable situation of the poor exiled Africans, which by the craft of wicked men have daily became their prey, though I have seen enough of their misery as well as read; no description can give an adequate idea of the horror of their feelings, and the dreadful calamities they undergo" (*TS* 289).

3. Laqueur, "Bodies, Details, and the Humanitarian Narrative," in *The New Cultural History*, ed. Lynn Hunt (Berkeley: University of California Press, 1989), 177–78, 177.

4. Laqueur, "Bodies," 178.

5. Laqueur, "Bodies," 178.

6. See Peters, "'Literature,' 'The Rights of Man,' and Narratives of Atrocity: Historical Backgrounds for the Culture of Testimony," *Yale Journal of Law and Humanities* 17, no. 2 (2005): 253–83.

7. Festa, *Sentimental Figures of Empire* (Baltimore: Johns Hopkins University Press, 2006), 186.

8. Hartman, *Scenes of Subjection: Terror, Slavery, and Self-Making in Nineteenth-Century America* (New York: Oxford University Press, 1997), 19.

9. Clarkson, "Essay on the Slavery and Commerce of the Human Species," in Clarkson and Cugoano, *Essays on the Slavery and Commerce of the Human Species*, 147.

10. Such appetites were brought to the fore in the abolitionist movement itself, both through the campaign to boycott West Indian sugar and in the production of all kinds of merchandise branded with abolitionist slogans. See Charlotte Sussman, *Consuming Anxieties: Consumer Protest, Gender, and British Slavery, 1713–1833* (Stanford: Stanford University Press, 2000), and Patricia Matthew, "Serving Tea for a Cause," *Lapham's Quarterly*, 28 February 2018. https://www.laphamsquarterly. org/roundtable/serving-tea-cause.

11. Sharp, *A Representation of the Injustice and Dangerous Tendency of Tolerating Slavery, or of Admitting the Least Claim of Private Property in the Persons of Men, in England* (London: Benjamin White and Robert Horsfield, 1769), 38–40.

12. As Teresa Michals observes, Mansfield's "inability to control the meaning of his ruling ... reflects some of the tensions implicit in England's transformation to a commercial society" ("'That Sole and Despotic Dominion': Slaves, Wives, and Game in Blackstone's *Commentaries*," *Eighteenth-Century Studies* 27, no. 2 [1993], 195).

13. Michals, "'That Sole and Despotic Dominion,'" 196.

14. Hartman, *Scenes of Subjection*, 6.

15. See Richard Tuck, *Natural Rights Theories: Their Origin and Development* (Cambridge: Cambridge University Press, 1979), and Brian Tierney, "Natural Law and Natural Rights: Old Problems and Recent Approaches," *Review of Politics* 64, no. 3 (2002): 389–406.

16. See Dan Edelstein, *On the Spirit of Rights* (Chicago: University of Chicago Press, 2019), 1–21, 127–38.

17. Equiano, *The Interesting Narrative of the Life of Olaudah Equiano, or Gustavus Vassa, The African. Written by Himself*, ed. Vincent Carretta (New York: Penguin, 2003), 111; Clarkson, *Essay on the Slavery and Commerce of the Human Species*, 79.

18. This is the claim articulated most prominently by Lynn Hunt in *Inventing Human Rights: A History* (New York: W. W. Norton, 2007). Hunt is specifically interested in abolitionism as an enactment of sympathetic identification and the movement toward ever-expanding legal enfranchisement. Her account has been disputed by a number of scholars, including Samuel Moyn, in *Human Rights and the Uses of History* (London: Verso, 2014); Dan Edelstein, in *On the Spirit of Rights*; and George Boulukos, in his forthcoming *A Vindication of the Rights of Monsters: Conceiving Rights in the Anglophone Eighteenth Century*.

19. See Edelstein's account in *On the Spirit of Rights*, 127–38.

20. Anghie, "Slavery and International Law: The Jurisprudence of Henry Richardson," *Temple International and Comparative Law Journal* 31, no.1 (2017) 11–24.

21. Bogues, *Black Heretics, Black Prophets: Radical Political Intellectuals* (New York: Routledge, 2003), 36–45. Edelstein usefully divides the relationships between citizens and their governments into different regimes characterized as preservationist (it is the job of states to preserve the natural rights of their citizens), abridgement (states abridge certain natural rights of their citizens), or transference (citizens transfer their natural rights to the state). See *On the Spirit of Rights*, 3.

22. Wheelock, *Barbaric Culture and Black Critique: Black Antislavery Writers, Religion, and the Slaveholding Atlantic* (Charlottesville: University of Virginia Press, 2015), 34.

23. Bogues, *Black Heretics, Black Prophets,* 33.

24. We can historicize what Bogues calls the "narrow liberal conception of democracy as political equality" that addresses racial violence through the binary of inclusion and exclusion (*Empire of Liberty: Power, Desire, and Freedom* [Hanover: Dartmouth College Press, 2010], 26–47). Cugoano's reading of common law points to the way in which common law can only incorporate persons into its procedural view and cannot redress the atrocities it has not labeled as crimes.

25. Christopher Leslie Brown, "Empire Without Slaves," *William and Mary Quarterly* 56, no. 2 (1999): 286–94.

26. Carrie Shanafelt has recently argued that Cugoano recognizes how the imagined separation between metropole and colonies fostered financial crises. See "'A World of Debt': Quobna Ottobah Cugoano, *The Wealth of Nations*, and the End of Finance," *Eighteenth–Century Studies* 55, no. 1 (2021): 21–43.

27. Victoria Kahn, *The Future of Illusion: Political Theology and Early Modern Texts* (Chicago: University of Chicago Press, 2014), 1.

28. Perhaps the most famous trajectory runs from Carl Schmitt to Giorgio Agamben, each of whom theorize sovereignty as a concept inherited from a theological explanation of power that had to be redeployed to fit a modern, rationalized understanding of political power. For Schmitt, sovereignty may or may not be vested in the institutionalized political authority—it is expressed through the act of decision because making a political decision requires the power to enforce it. Ultimately, political power is guaranteed through sovereign violence. Agamben refines Schmitt's theory, arguing that the sovereign decision is the decision of exception—the designation of particular locations or populations as falling outside the purview of the body politic, but which are still subject to sovereign violence. When I argue that Cugoano is using political theology in his critique of slavery and liberal political institutions, however, I mean to complicate these theories of sovereignty by suggesting that Cugoano theorizes sovereignty from the position of the exception—he and other Afro-Britons and colonial slaves are subject to sovereign violence without being recognized as members of the body politic.

29. See, for example, Jacques Derrida, "Declarations of Independence," *New Political Science* 7 (1986): 7–15.

30. As Jennifer Pitts puts it, "European metropoles and extra-European states and societies, whether formally colonized or not, developed interdependently through a profoundly asymmetrical process, with international law playing an important role in justifying and stabilizing inequalities of wealth and power" (*Boundaries of the International: Law and Empire* [Cambridge: Harvard University Press, 2018], 14).

31. Sandiford, *Measuring the Moment: Strategies of Protest in Eighteenth-Century Afro-English Writing* (Selinsgrove: Susquehanna University Press, 1988), 97.

32. Wheelock, *Barbaric Culture and Black Critique*, 27.

33. The italicized portion of the quotation echoes Psalms 50:18.

34. To be sure, the concept of sovereignty has always been, and remains, ill-defined and controversial. For an overview of some aspects of the controversy, see the introduction to *Sovereignty in Fragments: The Past, Present, and Future of a Contested Concept*, ed. Hent Kelmo and Quentin Skinner (Cambridge: Cambridge University Press, 2010).

35. In an effort to correct the standard narrative that the concept and institution of sovereignty was consolidated through the Treaty of Westphalia in 1648, scholars of imperialism and international law, including David Armitage and Anthony Pagden, and more recently Antony Anghie, Lauren Benton, Ranajit Guha, and Jennifer Pitts, contend that both the political concept and its legal significance were subject to the exigencies of imperialism, including competing imperial powers, treaties, and cultures, networks of jurisdictions and different forms of legal pluralism, geography, etc. The upshot of these arguments is that the common conception of sovereignty as legitimate political authority over a given territory is both theoretically and historically inadequate because imperialist projects actually required many different constellations of political power, visions of territory, and ideas about relationships between a sovereign power and its subjects or citizens. Accounting for these variations not only makes it difficult to think about sovereignty as a uniform political principle, but also requires that we scrutinize some of its most basic premises: uniformity, indivisibility, legal legitimacy, and so on.

INDIGENIZING THE EIGHTEENTH-CENTURY AMERICAN SOUTH

Introduction: Indigenizing the Eighteenth-Century American South

ALEJANDRA DUBCOVSKY AND BRYAN C. RINDFLEISCH

"The history of Native people, just like American history, is a story of survival, not disappearance," Malinda Maynor Lowery powerfully writes. "The integrity and coherence of Native communities, even in the face of intense destruction and ambivalence of colonialism, is a fundamental principle rather than something to be proven or justified."[1] The papers in this cluster wholeheartedly agree. They do not endeavor to prove that the Native peoples of the American South were important, had tremendous agency, or maintained coherent communities; like Lowery, they assume that as "a fundamental principle." These four essays each take seriously Indigenous epistemologies in their research and writing about the past, and, in so doing, (1) they showcase the deep history of the Native South—and the American South more generally; (2) they demonstrate the centrality of gender and particularly womanhood to these Indigenous peoples and worlds; and (3) they explore the thoroughly interconnected nature of Indigenous and Euro-American societies—politically, economically, culturally, and sexually—before, during, and beyond the eighteenth century.

Collectively, this cluster brings together four different, yet deeply interrelated essays that explore the dynamic history of the Native South, a field that continues to evolve and redefine the history of the American

South more generally. Relying on foundational scholarship by Charles Hudson, Theda Perdue, Gregory A. Waselkov, and John Worth, among others, the four essays also showcase the expansion and growth of the field, highlighting groundbreaking recent scholarship by Sarah Deer, Malinda Lowery, Michelene Pesantubbee, and Christina Snyder, just to name a few. By seamlessly drawing on both older and newer contributions to the expanding scholarship on the Native South, these essays draw attention to the increasing sophistication of the study of the American South in both the past and present.[2]

This cluster thus forms part of an ongoing and rich conversation that seeks not only to understand the history of Native peoples in the American South, but also to prioritize the realities, concerns, and experiences of Native peoples. In other words, these four essays are not histories of the American South that just happen to include Native peoples; they are stories and arguments that center Indigenous peoples and their ability to shape the world and events around them throughout the eighteenth century. This particular conversation began as a panel on "Indigenizing the American South" at the virtual Annual Meeting of the Southeastern American Society for Eighteenth-Century Studies in February 2021, and although each presenter focused on a specific story and set of sources, it quickly became clear that the papers—especially as revised into the contributions to this cluster—had several overlapping and reinforcing arguments.

The first is about the depth of this rich and extensive history of the American South. While all of the essays stress the *longue durée* of the region and its peoples, it is Robbie Ethridge's contribution that truly grapples with what it means to think of the eighteenth-century South as a space that evolved over centuries and was shaped over millennia. By working through historical and archeological findings, Ethridge does much more than simply narrate an Indigenous history of the American South that began long before 1492; she shows how the common division that historians use between the "Pre-Columbian" and "Colonial" worlds (or, more problematically, between the "Pre-Contact" and "Post-Contact" worlds) means little when we center Indigenous histories of the American South. Ethridge's account of a long and dynamic Native history involving the rise and coalescence of Native societies effectively decenters Euro-American incursions and pressures upon the region, focusing instead on the millennia-long history of the Indigenous South.

The second theme that emerges from the cluster concerns the nuances and deeply engrained aspects of gender and womanhood in the Native South. For example, the essays of Alejandra Dubcovsky and Bryan Rindfleisch pull back the layers of historical erasure and revisionism to explore the often-obscured Indigenous female world. Dubcovsky effectively grounds her study in the early history of a colonial town in Florida, showing how different ideas about gender shaped the negotiated development of the Native-Spanish world in the American South. Meanwhile, Rindfleisch takes up the threads of Dubcovsky's work and carries it through the mid- to late eighteenth century as he attempts to give voice to the marginalized and tell the history of Indigenous women in the South, particularly among the Muscogee (Creek) Indians, through the story of an Indigenous woman by the name of Metawney, from the Lower Muscogee town of Coweta. Rindfleisch then connects this historical erasure and silencing to the modern-day Missing and Murdered Indigenous Women and Girls movement, demonstrating how the deep history of the eighteenth-century American South continues to shape the present. These two contributions in turn set up Jennifer McCutchen's essay on the centrality and importance of gunpowder in the eighteenth-century South to explore the gendered meanings and uses of that commodity.

Finally, these four essays explore the deeply entangled and interconnected nature of Indigenous and Euro-American worlds in the South and the utility of Indigenous epistemologies for understanding the eighteenth-century past. In McCutchen's case, this involves emphasizing how Indigenous leaders used commodities like gunpowder both to broker power and influence within their own worlds and to establish and maintain economic and political relationships with Europeans. McCutchen then traces these messy, complicated, and constantly renegotiated economic arrangements in order to make a much broader argument about the ways in which Indigenous and European peoples understood and forged connections with one another. In so doing, McCutchen challenges us to think critically about the deeply enmeshed and intimate interactions that defined the American South and its peoples during the eighteenth century. Similarly, Ethridge's deep history of the American South effectively demonstrates how we need to think more carefully about the long chronological arc of the South, dismissing any notions that this region began with or was shaped solely by Europeans. Meanwhile, Dubcovsky and Rindfleisch push us to consider Native women and how their voices and absences shape the framing, chronology, and connections central to the development of the American South. Altogether, as Daniel Heath Justice reminds us, these many stories of deep history that take seriously Indigenous understandings of the eighteenth-century past, and the interconnections and intimacies within and across Indigenous and colonial worlds "are the stories that matter most." These stories are reminders that the Indigenous peoples of North America are central to any and all stories about not only the American past, but also its present and future. In Justice's words, these stories "remind us (Indigenous peoples) who we are today, where we came from, and who we'll be in the generations to come." And while, in the present, "we might not all look the same as we did or as we will, some of us might speak a bit differently, dress a bit differently," these stories are ultimately about visibility, historical rootedness, and endurance, how "today, as yesterday and tomorrow, our fire survives the storm."[3] The essays in this cluster can only hope to add further fuel to that already blazing fire.

Notes

1. Lowery, *The Lumbee Indians: An American Struggle* (Chapel Hill: University of North Carolina Press, 2018), xv.

2. For an overview of the changing historiography of the Native South, see Angela Pulley Hudson, "Unsettling Histories of the South," *Southern Cultures* 25, no. 3 (2019): 30–45.

3. Justice, *Our Fire Survives the Storm: A Cherokee Literary History* (Minneapolis: University of Minnesota Press, 2006), 220.

The Origins and Coalescence of the Creek (Muscogee) Confederacy: A New Synthesis

ROBBIE ETHRIDGE

A s is well known by now, between the sixteenth and eighteenth centuries, the Native South was transformed. The polities of the pre-colonial South, the so-called "chiefdoms" of what archaeologists call the Mississippi Period (900 CE to 1600 CE), went through a succession of failures throughout the late sixteenth and seventeenth centuries, and by 1730 none remained [see Figure 1]. However, Native peoples did not disappear. Instead, a region-wide restructuring occurred, out of which arose the large Indian nations of the eighteenth and nineteenth centuries—the Catawbas, Cherokees, Chickasaws, Choctaws, Creeks, and others. In 1998, Charles Hudson and I referred to these new kinds of Indian polities as "coalescent societies" because they were all, to varying degrees, coalescences of people from various fallen chiefdoms, of various languages and kin groups, from multiple regions, and so on.[1] Since then, the terms "coalescent societies" and "coalescence" have become part of our scholarly vocabulary for the early colonial era of the American South. Even so, we still have a poor understanding of exactly how coalescences took place, the pushes and pulls of the various migrations that were attendant to coalescence, the processes involved, the political, social, and ideological transformations that occurred, and the glue that held these new societies together.[2]

Coalescence, as one scholar notes, is "one of the more important linchpins" of studies in Southeastern ethnohistory and archaeology, but the process is not limited to the colonial era, nor to the American South.[3] Coalescence is a common process that occurred when people of a region found themselves under such extreme duress that massive migrations resulted or when polities incorporated (either voluntarily or involuntarily) large numbers of foreign peoples into their social systems.[4] The result was a new type of community and social system, and sometimes a wholly new social and political identity.

The disturbances in Native life in the sixteenth- and seventeenth-century South have not been difficult to identify. The archaeological and documentary evidence attests to the disappearance of Native polities, movements of people into tightly compacted and heavily fortified towns, a dramatic loss of life, multiple migrations and splintering of groups, the coalescence of some groups, and the disappearance of many others—creating what I have called a "shatter zone."[5] Some of the forces that caused these disruptions and subsequent transformations include military losses and cultural exchanges with early Spanish colonizers; the introduction of Old World diseases; and the consequences of political and economic incorporation into the modern world economy through a trade in Indian slaves, skins, and guns.[6] Despite such disruptions, Native people did not disappear. Across the Native South, people responded to the European invasions in myriad ways from violence and resistance to accommodation and negotiation. One response was coalescence, and many Native groups coalesced into large, formidable polities that dominated the geopolitics of the American South for the next two hundred years.

Examinations of a few of the Native South coalescences indicate that the internal ascribed hierarchical organization of the Mississippian chiefdoms and especially the variations in political and economic stability, leadership patterns, location, and geopolitics within and between chiefdoms were foundational to how and why these chiefdoms fell apart and how the subsequent coalescent and other societies were put together.[7] If the foundation of each coalescent society was unique, it follows that the coalescent societies of the seventeenth- and eighteenth-century Native South also would be quite variable. Indeed, that was the case: the Creeks were different from the Cherokees, who were different from the Chickasaws, who were different from the Choctaws, who were different from the Caddos, and so on.

To understand coalescence then, one must examine each case of coalescence independently and comparatively. I would like here to take a close look at the origins of the best documented case of coalescence in the Native South—that of the eighteenth- and nineteenth-century Creek (Muscogee) Confederacy, which was located in present-day central Alabama and western Georgia. In recent years, archaeologists and ethnohistorians have combined the rich archaeological record with the colonial documentary evidence to craft a better understanding of the origins of the Creek Indians. In this essay, I collate this evidence into a single, coherent account of the Creek coalescence. Let me be clear, I am not contributing new evidence of my own; rather, I am synthesizing a body of disparate, mostly archaeological scholarship that has been published across a wide array of anthologies and journals into a single essay. In so doing, I also seek to render the arcane and specialized language of archaeology into a form more accessible to non-specialists.

Evidence now suggests that not only did the Creek Confederacy begin to form soon after Hernando De Soto and his army of six hundred-plus soldiers marched through present-day central Alabama in the mid-sixteenth century, but also that its formation may have been a result of people applying an old response to political instability to a new situation. Archaeologists believe coalescence to have been an ancient process and posit that it was at play throughout the Mississippi Period and was perhaps foundational to the formation of chiefdoms.[8] This is not to say that Native southern peoples had not gone through transformations, historical changes, and large and small events before Europeans came on the scene. We can easily pinpoint some of these: the end of the Ice Age, the Archaic Period revolution behind the archaeological site known as Poverty Point, the beginnings of agriculture, the spread of the Hopewell ideologies of the Ohio River Valley in the Woodland Period, the invention of the bow and arrow, the religious revitalization of the Mississippi Period, the collapse of the first Mississippian grand polity known today as Cahokia, the rise of the complex Middle Mississippi Period chiefdoms such as that of Moundville, the fifteenth-century drought, the political diversity of the Late Mississippi Period, and so on. Certainly, the history of the Native South has always been marked by monumental, transformative, world-shaping events, and European contact was but one of many.

The Mississippi Period was a dynamic period that saw the rise and fall of multiple polities throughout its seven hundred years. When Spanish explorers arrived in the mid-sixteenth century, they encountered a variety of chiefdoms across the Southeast, from paramount chiefdoms, such as Coosa, to the small, simple chiefdoms of the southern Appalachians. When these Late Mississippian chiefdoms failed, as they all ultimately did, it did not result in the rise of new Mississippian-era-type chiefdoms. Rather, out of their failures arose the great Indian coalescent societies of the eighteenth and later centuries—the Catawbas, Cherokees, Chickasaws, Choctaws, Creeks, Yamasees, and others—that became powerful players in the colonial South and would structure much about life for Europeans, Indians, and Africans in the South and beyond for two hundred years.

The seventeenth-century Creek Confederacy was divided into two divisions and composed of four provinces—the provinces of Abihka, Alabama, and Tallapoosa comprised the Upper Creeks and the province of Apalachicola comprised the Lower Creeks [see the bottom of Figure 1]. We will examine each in turn. Archaeological evidence shows that Abihka formed out of the collapse of the pre-colonial polity known as Coosa. At the time of the De Soto *entrada* [expedition] in the mid-sixteenth century, Coosa was a large paramount chiefdom that spanned about three hundred miles, from present-day eastern Tennessee into central Alabama, and had formed sometime in the late fifteenth or early sixteenth century [see the top of Figure 1]. We also know that Coosa was a multi-lingual polity that encompassed the smaller chiefdom of Coosa, as well as those of Chiaha, Coste, Itaba, Napoochie, Talisi, Tasqui, and Ulibahali.[9]

The rise of Coosa awaits deep scholarly analysis; however, a brief overview of the archaeological findings to date implies coalescence was actively practiced in the pre-colonial Mississippi Period and so was not merely a product of the colonial era. The predominant ceramic complexes of Coosa are variants of the Lamar, Dallas, and Mouse Creek ceramic complexes. The Lamar ceramics date to 1350–1600 CE and are found throughout much of present-day central and northern Georgia, southern Tennessee, eastern South Carolina, northeastern Alabama, and northern Florida. The chiefdoms of Coosa that had variants of the Lamar ceramics were located in the part of the paramountcy that lay in present-day western Georgia and northeastern Alabama. Dallas ceramics date between 1300 and 1600 CE and are found throughout much of eastern and central Tennessee and in southern Virginia. The chiefdoms of Coosa with Dallas ceramics were those in northeastern Tennessee. The dates of the Mouse Creek Phase are 1400–1600 CE, and its ceramics are found in a confined area of southeastern Tennessee. The chiefdoms of Coosa with Mouse Creek ceramics are found in the small area of Coosa that spilled into present-day southeastern Tennessee.[10] The Lamar ceramics of Coosa have their roots in the Middle Mississippian (1300–1450 CE) paramount chiefdom known today as Etowah, while the Dallas ceramics have their roots in the small Middle Mississippian chiefdoms of the southern Appalachians. The Mouse Creek ceramics, which are still a subject for debate, may have their roots in the non-mound towns of southeastern Tennessee.[11]

In 1450 CE, the Mississippian world withstood a massive failure of multiple chiefdoms across the South when both small, simple chiefdoms and large, complex, paramount chiefdoms, such as Etowah in northwestern

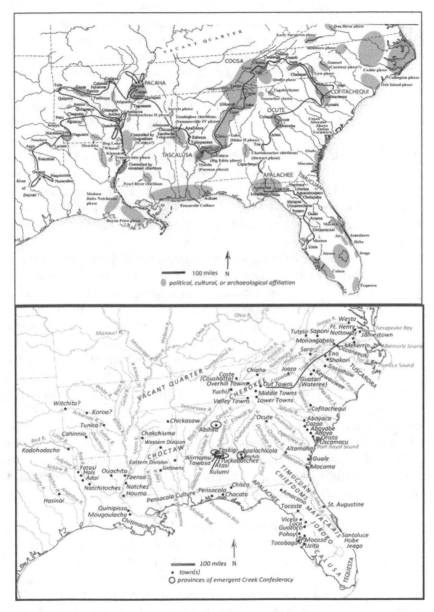

Figure 1. Transformation of the Native South, 1540–1650, showing (on the top) the 1540 route of Hernando de Soto and the pre-colonial Mississippian world, and (on the bottom) the provinces of the emergent Creek Confederacy, c. 1650. Maps by the author.

Georgia and Moundville in west-central Alabama, went into decline. Archaeologists attribute this massive disruption to a widespread climatic pulse that resulted in a prolonged drought across the American South.[12] Out of these failures, the paramount chiefdom of Coosa arose wherein several small chiefdoms from present-day eastern Tennessee to central Alabama (the Lamar, Dallas, and Mouse Creek peoples) banded together under a political pact that scholars still do not wholly understand. Although the Coosa paramount chiefdom was a single polity under a single leader, and although the whole of Coosa was alarmed, offended, and quickly militarized when de Soto kidnapped their chief, the paramountcy was apparently loosely organized. The chief Coosa may have been only the first among equals, rather than an autocrat.[13] Furthermore, recent studies indicate that, once under the umbrella of Coosa, the Dallas, Lamar, and Mouse Creek people had little close interactions with one other, with each maintaining distinctive cultural and ethnic identities.[14]

De Soto passed through the entire paramountcy of Coosa in 1540, and European eyewitnesses described it as an expansive, fertile province, with numerous large towns and abundant agricultural fields stretching from town to town.[15] Twenty years later, when a contingent from the Tristán de Luna y Arellano expedition surveyed Coosa, they were disappointed to find only small towns, many abandoned agricultural fields, and a much smaller population.[16] Additionally, archaeological evidence hints at the possibility that the leadership had passed from one chiefly lineage to another in those twenty years.[17] De Luna's contingent also aided the paramount-chief of Coosa in subjugating the rebellious Napochies, which further indicates political instability. Even so, when Juan Pardo's army encountered the northern edge of Coosa in present-day Tennessee in 1568, it was still a large, expansive polity, and the paramount chief at that time still commanded enough influence to organize a coalition of chiefs to threaten Pardo, so much so that he decided to return to Santa Elena, rather than risk a military altercation with the army of Coosa.[18]

As the accounts of the later de Luna expedition make evident, the encounter with de Soto destabilized Coosa. The paramountcy seems to have faltered for a few decades, recovered somewhat, and then, sometime after the Pardo expedition in 1568, Coosa went into steep decline. Archaeologists propose that Coosa's decline occurred because of the introduction of Old World diseases by the Spanish expeditions and a subsequent extreme loss of life.[19] I would argue, however, that Coosa, as a paramount chiefdom, would have been one of the most unstable political entities in the Mississippian world and could have fallen for any number of reasons, including the instability brought on by de Soto's march through and ransacking of the entire province.[20]

Archaeologist Marvin Smith pieced together a series of migrations for the people of Coosa, Itaba, and Ulibahali, three of the chiefdoms in the paramountcy. All of these polities were abandoned by the late sixteenth century, and the people began a hundred-year sojourn down the Coosa River valley. By around 1600, the survivors of these fallen chiefdoms had moved southwest about sixty miles and congregated together around present-day Weiss Reservoir on the Coosa River at the Georgia-Alabama border, where they amalgamated with local people known only by their archaeological name of the Kymulga-phase people. At the Weiss Reservoir, archaeologists have only found four or five town sites in total, indicating a serious contraction of the population. Then, around 1630, they moved downstream yet again, about thirty miles to Whorton's Bend, near present-day Gadsden, Alabama. Here they congregated into only three towns according to their old Coosa affiliations of Coosa, Itaba, and Ulibahali. The three towns would later be collectively known as the province of Abihka [see the bottom of Figure 1].[21]

Little else is known about the lives of these people over these sixty or so years except to say that they quit building mounds, moved into smaller towns, changed some of their pottery designs and the tempering agents for their ceramic paste, and began digging earthen pits, perhaps for storing (and hiding) foodstuffs. By the early seventeenth century, the people of these towns were placing prestigious European artifacts, obtained from Spanish Florida and the Atlantic trade, in a high percentage of their burials, suggesting that "virtually everyone had access to European goods." In other words, it appears as if the elite hierarchy was crumbling or had already crumbled when people from Coosa, Itaba, and Ulibahali moved to the Weiss Reservoir around 1600, less than sixty years after de Soto had passed through the paramount chiefdom of Coosa.[22]

The Alabama province formed on the upper Alabama River, just south of its confluence with the Coosa and Tallapoosa rivers [see the bottom of Figure 1]. At the time of de Soto, this region was home to the chiefdom of Tascalusa, ruled by a chief of the same name. By all contemporary accounts, Tascalusa was a powerful, authoritative chief.[23] Archaeologists now suggest that the chiefdom of Tascalusa was founded by people who left the grand chiefdom of Moundville after it collapsed around 1450 CE and merged with some local populations. The chiefdom location coincides with the archaeological ceramic complex known as the Big Eddy phase (1450–1575 CE).[24] In fact, Tascalusa may have been in the process of putting together his own paramountcy at the time of de Soto's visit by forging an alliance with the adjacent polity of Mabila to the west and by enticing the polity of Talisi, which lay on Tascalusa's eastern boundary, away from the paramount chiefdom of Coosa with whom it had been aligned [see the top of Figure 1].[25] Tascalusa also orchestrated a surprise attack against de Soto at a town in the chiefdom of Mabila.[26] The battle of Mabila was costly to the Indians of Tascalusa, but it did not spell immediate disaster, and afterwards people continued to put mantles on the mound at Atahachi, the principal town of Tuscalusa, at least until around 1560. We know this because some of the gifts brought by the later expedition of Tristán de Luna were buried in the mound. However, the de Luna reports on Tascalusa are curt; apparently it was not the noteworthy paramountcy that de Soto had encountered. The archaeology also suggests that the paramountcy, and perhaps the chiefdom of Tascalusa itself, disintegrated by 1575, if not earlier.[27]

This date marks the beginning of a new archaeological ceramic phase in the region, known as the Alabama River phase, which dates from 1575 to 1700. Unfortunately, the long span of time covered by this phase prevents us from getting a finely detailed view of an especially tumultuous time for Mississippian people. Suffice it to say that during these 125 years, the descendants of the former province of Tascalusa quit building capital towns with monumental earthworks and began living in smaller, compact towns with no mounds. They no longer practiced elaborate elite mortuary customs, and there is no evidence for social hierarchy among them. They stopped their extensive trade in exotic, prestige goods. They also went through a particularly bad period of poor health, probably resulting from a dramatic change in their diet from largely cultivated foods to mostly wild foods. And they began burying their children in urns. In time, they constricted their settlements to the northeast, at the confluence of the Coosa and Tallapoosa River.[28]

The chiefdom of Mabila, an ally of Tascalusa, had a similar history after the encounter with de Soto. Although the site of Mabila has yet to be found, archaeologists place it about twenty miles south of the Tascalusa chiefdom [see the top of Figure 1]. Mabila is most likely represented by the archaeological ceramic complex known as the Furman phase (1400–1575 CE).[29] The fate of Mabila after the battle with de Soto is unknown, except to say that the Furman-phase ceramics were replaced by a variation of the Alabama River-phase ceramics, suggesting that the fate of the Mabilans was somehow intertwined with and similar to the fate of the people of Tascalusa. In addition, around 1575 or a little later, the people of Apafalaya, a small chiefdom on the Black Warrior River, began to migrate out of the Black Warrior valley altogether.[30] Some were drawn east to the congregation of people at the confluence of the Coosa and Tallapoosa rivers. It is noteworthy that these three chiefdoms—Apafalaya, Mabila, and Tascalusa—all had roots in the fifteenth-century chiefdom known as Moundville and probably spoke variants of the same language, most likely the Alabama-Coushatta language.[31] When they coalesced on the upper Alabama River, they came to form the core of the Creek Confederacy's Alabama province.

The Tallapoosa province formed on the lower Tallapoosa River, where de Soto had encountered the Talisi chiefdom, which was a subject of the paramount chief of Coosa and yet was being courted by Tascalusa [see the top of Figure 1]. The Talisi chiefdom most likely corresponds to the archaeological ceramic complex known as the Shine II phase (1400–1575 CE) and extended from just east of the confluence of the Coosa and Tallapoosa rivers to the big bend in the Tallapoosa. The Talisi chiefdom, comprised of three towns, was a plural society formed around 1350 to 1400 CE, when one or more factions from the fallen fifteenth-century Etowah chiefdom of northwestern Georgia (Lamar phase-ceramics) migrated to central Alabama. There they incorporated a local simple chiefdom (Shine I-phase ceramics) and a local population (Autauga-phase ceramics) to become Talisi.[32] After de Soto departed central Alabama, the people of the Talisi province apparently stayed in place on the lower Tallapoosa, and they became an independent polity when both Coosa and Tascalusa fell. The archaeology also shows changes in the Talisi capital towns, suggesting shifts in hierarchical leadership. By 1575 or 1600, though, people began a new ceramic tradition by combining elements of Shine II ceramics with ones from the Big Eddy (Tascalusa) style. Archaeologists call this new ceramic type Atasi-phase ceramics. During this time, the people of Talisi also quit building mounds. In the early decades of the seventeenth century they began acquiring European trade goods from the Spanish in present-day Florida. The presence of Spanish items in many non-elite burials from Atasi-phase sites indicates a challenge to elite authority, a leveling of social status, and perhaps the beginnings of the end for the Mississippian political hierarchy in Talisi.[33] These three towns on the Tallapoosa were occupied until Removal; their historic names are Atasi, Kulumi, and the famous Tuckabatchee [see the bottom of Figure 1]. These and the other towns along the lower Tallapoosa comprised the province known as Tallapoosa, which would become one of the core nuclei of the eighteenth-century Creek Confederacy.[34]

The Apalachicola province was centered on the Chattahoochee River [see the bottom of Figure 1]. And although de Soto did not travel along the Chattahoochee, several chiefdoms existed there at the time, which are known by their archeological name of Stewart-phase sites (1475–1600 CE) [see the top of Figure 1]. Like the other chiefdoms we have discussed, the sixteenth-century Stewart-phase chiefdoms were also founded through an amalgam of local peoples and immigrants, including some with ancient connections to Moundville and Etowah. These Stewart-phase people were most likely the ancestors of the historic Hitchitis.[35]

Sometime between 1500 and 1585 CE, a group of people from Tascalusa established a town in the chiefdom of Talisi, and it looks as though some of this group, and perhaps others, moved east, eventually settling on the lower

Chattahoochee. We do not know whether the move to the Chattahoochee was before or after the battle at Mabila. Once on the Chattahoochee, these immigrants established a chiefdom with two town sites featuring mounds, one on either side of the river at present-day Columbus, Georgia. This immigration is marked by the archaeological ceramic complex known as the Abercrombie phase (1500–1600 CE). These two sites undoubtedly are the original sites of the towns known historically as Cusseta and Coweta, two major towns of the eighteenth-century Lower Creeks and the province known as Apalachicola.[36] When the immigrants moved to the Chattahoochee River, it profoundly affected the local Stewart-phase chiefdoms, and archaeologists report a dramatic reduction in the number of Stewart-phase sites. They interpret this to mean that either Stewart-phase people were incorporated into the new Abercrombie chiefdom or else they suffered some kind of population loss, most likely from disease or military confrontation. Even so, the two groups continued to live side-by-side. By 1630 or before, they would merge into a single multi-lingual polity, known as Apalachicola, and represented archaeologically by the Blackmon-phase ceramic complex (1600–1700 CE).[37] Apalachicola would later become the core nucleus for the Lower Creeks. Given the historical relatedness between the Chattahoochee people, the lower Tallapoosa people, and the upper Alabama people, it should not be too surprising that, by the eighteenth century, all of these groups would fuse into the Creek Confederacy.

By the early seventeenth century, these four provinces—Abihka, Alabama, Apalachicola, and Tallapoosa—began attracting immigrants and refugees from other collapsing polities. People were most likely attracted to this coalescence because of the plural roots of these polities, because of their relative distance from the colonial disruptions of disease and slaving that were erupting all along the Atlantic seaboard and in present-day Florida, and because these groups could offer some protection from the militarized Indian slaving societies, such as the Westos and Occaneechis, who were raiding far and wide for captives to sell to English slave traders.[38] Throughout the seventeenth century, a flood of migrants settled in central Alabama. Between the upper Alabama River and the big bend in the Tallapoosa River, these immigrants established a series of towns so archaeologically similar that it is difficult to discern one from the next. The towns in the Tallapoosa province grew in both size and number from the mid- to late seventeenth century. Tukabatchee, for instance, expanded from a small Shine II mound center in 1575 CE to a non-mound town four or five times its former size.[39] People fleeing the Piedmont also migrated down the Coosa River to join the groups coalescing with the Abihka province.[40]

In addition, during the mid-seventeenth century, we see a large migration of Coushatta-speaking people fleeing the lower Piedmont in the wake of Occaneechi, Westo, Iroquois, and perhaps Cherokee slave raiding.[41] When Marcos Delgado visited the Alabama province in 1686, he observed several towns of "Qusate," or Coushatta, speakers. These towns most likely represent Coushatta-speaking people from present-day eastern Tennessee who were once part of the Coosa paramount chiefdom.[42] The movement of the Coushatta-speaking people of present-day eastern Tennessee to the Alabama province has puzzled scholars for many years. Recent investigations, however, have shown the Coushatta and Alabama to have had mutual, albeit ancient, origins in the Middle Mississippian Shiloh mounds.[43] This ancient connection also helps explain the striking similarities between the Coushatta and Alabama languages.[44]

The number of towns in the Apalachicola province likewise expanded between 1630 and 1690, and a number of these new towns were settled by people moving out of the reach of Westo and Occaneechi slavers, such as the Yuchis and the Coushatta-speaking Chiahas who originated in present-day eastern Tennessee. People from the former Ocute paramount chiefdom on the Ocmulgee River in present-day central Georgia who, after the fall of Ocute, had consolidated with others into the Yamasee confederacy on the South Carolina coast now fled to Apalachicola in the 1680s. It may have been around this time that another province arose in northcentral Alabama, that of the Okfuskees. In the mid- to late eighteenth century, the Okfuskees lived in several towns on the upper Tallapoosa River where the Upper Trade Path crossed the river. Okfuskee was their largest town. Okfuskee origins, however, are murky since they have received little archaeological research. Whether they were the descendants of Mississippian polities on the upper Tallapoosa or later immigrated into the area from regions unknown has yet to be determined.[45]

We need to remember that most coalescent societies of the Native South formed in the seventeenth century and in the grip of a destructive commercial trade in Indian slaves and guns that swept across the American South at this time, causing the failure of multiple chiefdoms and the displacements and migrations that followed in their wake. Given this context, then, each coalescent society must have had certain mechanisms for admitting refugee groups under a political umbrella that, if nothing else, required mutual agreements that those in the alliance would not conduct slave raids against one another. In fact, the documentary record indicates that although each coalescent society eventually became a militarized slave trader, they did not raid groups within their own confederacies.[46] A need for mutual defense against Indian slave raiders, then, served as a centripetal force among the coalescent societies. In 1998, Charles Hudson and I suggested that the early iterations of coalescent societies may have resembled war leagues, or symmachys, in which disparate people were forced together against a common enemy—in this case, slave raiders from other Indian polities.[47]

This could also help explain the independence characteristic of some coalescent societies in the Native South. When the larger coalescent societies—such as the Creeks, Cherokees, and Choctaws—formed, people from a fallen chiefdom entered the union as an independent township. In the Creek Confederacy, for example, people retained a loyalty to and affiliation with their towns that superseded any loyalty to and affiliation with the confederacy as a whole. Until the nineteenth century, unless there was a crisis of international proportions, members of the Creek Confederacy rarely referred to themselves as Creeks or Muscogees, but rather as Alabamas, Coosas, Cowetas, Cussetahs, Yuchis, and so on. Throughout the eighteenth century, other groups sought admittance to the Abihka, Alabama, Apalachicola, Okfuskee, and Tallapoosa provinces. Such in-migrations would bolster their numbers and would eventually make the Creeks into one of the most formidable and populous Indian nations in the American South. We can now see that the coalescence of the Creeks was an imaginative and adaptive response to living in a shatter zone. The Creek coalescence also indicates that some coalescences were predicated on old Mississippian alliances and connections and, in fact, may have been an old solution to the new problems that came with colonialism.

Although we still have much to consider, this new synthesis of Creek origins makes clear that the Late Mississippian world, the consequences of early colonial encounters, and the subsequent restructuring of Native life are part of the same historical narrative. The conceptual divide between the pre-colonial and the colonial (or the prehistoric and the historic) needs to be abolished. We know that virtually every polity that existed during the Late Mississippi Period was transformed by the early eighteenth century and that the survivors found themselves on the edge of a powerful, global economic system and growing empires that could marshal far-flung resources. The survivors responded accordingly, building new kinds of societies both by appropriating useful remnants of the chiefly order and by fashioning altogether new ways of doing things. We can now recognize the absolute and inescapable connections between the pre-colonial Mississippian world and the colonial world. This realization, alone, is a major reckoning that lays a solid foundation for understanding and explaining coalescence in and the coalescent Native societies of the eighteenth-century colonial South.

Notes

This essay relies on the work of the many archaeologists who have spent decades pouring over and making sense of the myriad details of artifacts and complicated data from central Alabama and west-central Georgia. They are too numerous to name, but I thank each and every one of them for their commitments to the deep history of the Native South.

1. Hudson and Ethridge, "The Early Historic Transformation of the Southeastern Indians," in *Cultural Diversity in the U.S. South: Anthropological Contributions to a Region in Transition*, ed. Carol E. Hill and Patricia D. Beaver (Athens: University of Georgia Press, 1998), 4.

2. Charles R. Cobb, *The Archaeology of Southeastern Native American Landscapes of the Colonial Era* (Gainesville: University Press of Florida, 2019), 107–8.

3. Cobb, *Archaeology*, 104.

4. Robin Beck, *Chiefdoms, Collapse, and Coalescence in the Early American South* (Cambridge: Cambridge University Press, 2013), 7; Cobb, *Archaeology*, 105; Kathleen Duval, *The Native Ground: Indians and Colonists in the Heart of the Continent* (Philadelphia: University of Pennsylvania Press, 2006), 26; Stephen A. Kowalewski, "Coalescent Societies," in *Light on the Path: The Anthropology and History of the Southeastern Indians*, ed. Thomas J. Pluckhahn and Robbie Ethridge (Tuscaloosa: University of Alabama Press, 2006), 94–122.

5. Ethridge, "Introduction: Mapping the Mississippian Shatter Zone," in *Mapping the Mississippian Shatter Zone: The Colonial Indian Slave Trade and Regional Instability in the American South*, ed. Robbie Ethridge and Sheri M. Shuck-Hall (Lincoln: University of Nebraska Press, 2009), 1–62. See also my *From Chicaza to Chickasaw: The European Invasion and the Transformation of the Mississippian World, 1540–1715* (Chapel Hill: University of North Carolina Press, 2010).

6. Ethridge, "Introduction," 1.

7. Robin Beck, *Chiefdoms*; Denise I. Bossy, *The Yamasee Indians: From Florida to South Carolina* (Lincoln: University of Nebraska Press, 2018); Cobb, *Archaeology*; Ethridge, *From Chicaza to Chickasaw*; Martin D. Gallivan, *The Powhatan Landscape: An Archaeological History of the Algonquian Chesapeake* (Gainesville: University Press of Florida, 2016); Patricia Galloway, *Choctaw Genesis, 1500–1700* (Lincoln: University of Nebraska Press, 1995); Jon Bernard Marcoux, *Pox, Empire, Shackles, and Hides: The Townsend Site, 1670–1715* (Tuscaloosa: University of Alabama Press, 2010); Amanda L. Regnier, *Reconstructing Tascalusa's Chiefdom: Pottery Styles and the Social Composition of Late Mississippian Communities along the Alabama River* (Tuscaloosa: University of Alabama Press, 2014); Christopher B. Rodning, "Reconstructing the Coalescence of Cherokee Communities in Southern Appalachia," in *The Transformation of the Southeastern Indians, 1540–1760*, ed. Robbie Ethridge and Charles Hudson (Jackson: University Press of Mississippi, 2002), 307–46; John E. Worth, "Yamassee," in *Handbook of North American Indians*, vol. 14, *The Southeast*, ed. Raymond D. Fogelson (Washington: Smithsonian

Institution, 2004), 245–53. For a comparative study of coalescences from around the world, see Kowalewski, "Coalescent Societies."

8. Susan Alt, "The Power of Diversity: Settlement in the Cahokian Uplands, in *Leadership and Polity in Mississippian Society*, ed. Brian M. Butler and Paul D. Welch (Carbondale: Southern Illinois University, 2006), 289–308; Cobb, *Archaeology*, 104–7. For an examination of Mississippian chiefdom coalescences in central Alabama, see Ned J. Jenkins, "Tracing the Origins of the Early Creeks, 1050–1700 CE," in *Mapping the Mississippian Shatter Zone,* 188–249. It is worth noting that Mississippian polities showed so much variability through space and time that some think the term "chiefdom" an inadequate descriptor; see Charles R. Cobb, "History, Social Evolution, and the Culture Wars," *Native South* 2 (2009), 74–75; Timothy R. Pauketat, *Chiefdoms and Other Archaeological Delusions* (New York: Altamira Press 2007), 3, 81; and Lynne P. Sullivan, "Deposing the Chiefdom Model 'Monster-God,'" *Native South* 2 (2009): 88.

9. Marvin T. Smith, *Coosa: The Rise and Fall of a Mississippian Chiefdom* (Gainesville: University Press of Florida, 2000), 34–49, 85–87; Jenkins, "Tracing the Origins of the Early Creeks"; Chester B. DePratter, Charles M. Hudson, and Marvin T. Smith, "The De Soto Expedition: From Chiaha to Mabila," in *Alabama and the Borderlands: From Prehistory to Statehood*, ed. R. Reid Badger and Lawrence A. Clayton (Tuscaloosa: University of Alabama Press, 1985), 108–27. The Spaniards referred to the paramount chiefdom as "Coosa"; we do not know what the citizens of the polity called the alliance. There was a chiefdom within the paramountcy also called "Coosa," and the Spaniards, by convention, called the leader of both Coosas (who was the same person). See "Coosa"; Galloway, *Choctaw Genesis*, 111.

10. Charles Hudson, Marvin Smith, David Halley, Richard Polhemus, and Chester DePratter, "Coosa: A Chiefdom in the Sixteenth-Century Southeastern United States," *American Antiquity* 50, no. 4 (1985), 725, Figure 2.

11. For a succinct overview of these ceramic traditions, see Michaelyn S. Harle, "Biological Affinities and the Construction of Cultural Identity for the Proposed Coosa Chiefdom" (Ph.D. dissertation, University of Tennessee, 2010), 30–38.

12. Cobb, *Archaeology*, 146–51.

13. Charles Hudson, *Knights of Spain, Warriors of the Sun: Hernando de Soto and the South's Ancient Chiefdoms* (Athens: University of Georgia Press, 1997), 215–17.

14. Harle, "Biological Affinities," 149–52.

15. Luys Hernández de Biedma, "Relation of the Island of Florida," trans. John E. Worth, in *The De Soto Chronicles: The Expedition of Hernando de Soto to North America in 1539–1543*, ed. Lawrence A. Clayton, Vernon. J. Knight, Jr., and Edward C. Moore, 2 vols. (Tuscaloosa: University of Alabama Press, 1993), 1:232; Gentleman of Elvas, "The Account by a Gentleman from Elvas," trans. James Alexander Robertson, in *De Soto Chronicles*, 1:92–94; Rodrigo Rangel, "Account of the Northern Conquest and Discovery of Hernando de Soto," trans. John E. Worth, in *De Soto Chronicles*, 1:284–88.

16. *The Luna Papers: Documents Relating to the Expedition of Don Tritán de Luna y Arellano for the Conquest of La Florida in 1559–1561*, ed. and trans. Herbert I. Priestly, 2 vols. (Deland: Florida State Historical Society, 1928), 1:291–95.

17. Ned J. Jenkins and Craig T. Sheldon, "The Hernando de Soto and Tristán de Luna y Arellano Expeditions in Central Alabama, 1540–1560: Routes, Cultures, and Consequences," in *Modeling Entradas: Sixteenth-Century Assemblages in North America*, ed. Clay Mathers (Gainesville: University of Florida Press, 2020), 186–98, 200; Smith, *Coosa*, 32, 43–44.

18. Charles Hudson, *The Juan Pardo Expeditions: Exploration of the Carolinas and Tennessee, 1566–1568*, 2nd ed. (Tuscaloosa: University of Alabama Press, 2005), 39–46.

19. Smith, *Coosa*, 96–121.

20. Ethridge, *From Chicaza to Chickasaw*, 62–66. In this scenario, the paramountcy of Coosa fell, and it did so along the time line set by Smith in *Coosa*, 96–121. The difference is that I propose the reasons for the fall were not primarily episodes of disease and that Coosa's ruin should not be projected across the South as the total collapse of the Mississippian world. Jenkins and Sheldon share this interpretation in "The Hernando de Soto and Tristán de Luna y Arellano Expeditions," 195–98. These theories are in contrast with those of Paul Hoffman, who, after examining the documentary evidence, questioned whether or not Coosa actually fell in the first place. Hoffman, however, did not re-examine the archaeological evidence for the decline of Coosa that Smith used in his reconstruction. See Hoffman, "Did Coosa Decline Between 1541 and 1560?," *Florida Anthropologist* 50, no. 1 (1997): 25–29.

21. Jenkins, "Tracing the Origins of the Early Creeks," 218–19; Smith, *Coosa*, 103–4, 107–9; see also Ted Clay Nelson, "Material Evidence for Early Coalescence: The Hightower Village Site (1TA150) in the Coosa River Valley" (Ph.D. dissertation, University of Alabama, 2020).

22. Smith, *Coosa*, 105–7, 106, 110–11.

23. Biedma, "Relation," 1:232–33; Gentleman of Elvas, "Account," 1:95–99; Rangel, "Account," 1:290–94.

24. Jenkins, "Tracing the Origins of the Early Creeks," 214–16; Jenkins and Sheldon, "The Hernando de Soto and Tristán de Luna y Arellano Expeditions," 173–80. Amanda Regnier concludes that Tascalusa was a large, albeit loosely organized, plural society, made up of people from Moundville (Moundville III ceramics), northeastern Georgia (Lamar ceramics), and the coastal area (Pensacola ceramics) and that the connections between sites in this area extends geographically to the big bend of the Tallapoosa and further down the Alabama; see Regnier, "A Stylistic Analysis of Burial Urns from the Protohistoric Period in Central Alabama," *Southeastern Archaeology* 25, no. 1 (2006): 121–34; "What Indian Pottery of Sixteenth-Century Central Alabama Looks Like and Why It Matters," in *The Search for Mabila: The Decisive Battle between Hernando de Soto and Chief Tascalusa*, ed. Vernon James Knight, Jr. (Tuscaloosa: University of Alabama Press, 2009), 88–93; and *Reconstructing Tascalusa's Chiefdom*, 31–36, 132–135. Jenkins, in "Tracing the Origins of the Early Creeks," sees the same plurality in the region; however, he parses out the Shine II (derived from the Lamar Variant) and Furman (derived from the Pensacola Variant) phases as representing separate polities, Talisi and Mabila, respectively (207, 214–16). See also Craig T. Sheldon, "Introduction," in *The Southern and Central Alabama Expeditions of Clarence Bloomfield Moore*, ed. Craig T. Sheldon (Tuscaloosa: University of Alabama Press, 2001), 1–114.

25. Hudson, *Knights of Spain*, 231; Jenkins and Sheldon, "The Hernando de Soto and Tristán de Luna y Arellano Expeditions"; Regnier, *Reconstructing Tascalusa's Chiefdom*, 134–35; Ethridge, "When Giants Walked the Earth: Chief Tascalusa, Hernando de Soto, and the Precolonial Mississippian Borderlands of the Sixteenth-Century U.S. South," in *Indigenous Borderlands of the Americas*, ed. Joaquin Rivaya-Martinéz (Norman: University of Oklahoma Press, in press). See also the essays in Knight, *The Search for Mabila*.

26. Biedma, "Relation," 1:232–36; Gentleman of Elvas, "Account," 1:96–105; Rangel, "Account" 1:291–94.

27. Gentleman of Elvas, "Account," 1:104; Rangel, "Account," 1:294; Priestly, *The Luna Papers*, 1:291. Atahachi is most likely the Charlotte Thompson site; see Hudson, *Knights of Spain*, 230–31; Jenkins, "Tracing the Origins of the Early Creeks," 214–16, 221, 223; Regnier, *Reconstructing Tascalusa's Chiefdom*, 81; Sheldon, "The Present State," 120; and Gregory A. Waselkov, Linda Derry, and Ned J. Jenkins, "The Archaeology of Mabila's Cultural Landscape," in *The Search for Mabila*, 230–31. Regnier, in *Reconstructing Tascalusa's Chiefdom*, 44, suggests that the Big Eddy and Thirty Acre Field sites may also be contenders for the capital of Tascalusa.

28. On the disintegration of the Tascalusa chiefdom, see Jenkins, "Tracing the Origins of the Early Creeks," 223–27; Jenkins and Sheldon, "The Hernando de Soto and Tristán de Luna y Arellano Expeditions," 186–91; Regnier, "A Stylistic Analysis," 121, 127–32; and Regnier, "What Indian Pottery." The beginning date for the Alabama River phase is taken from Jenkins, "Tracing the Origins of the Early Creeks," 224; Regnier dates the beginning of the Alabama River phase at 1560 CE ("A Stylistic Analysis," 129). It should be noted that archaeologists have also found a few urn burials in which the disarticulated skeletons of adults have been placed. Typically, though, adults from the Alabama River phase were de-fleshed and then their bones were buried in an earthen grave; see Regnier, "A Stylistic Analysis."

29. In the last few years, archaeologists have found what they believe to be archaeological sites associated with the polity of Mabila and in the vicinity indicated by the archaeology of Jenkins and Regnier. They have named this archaeological complex and the associated ceramics the Marengo Archaeological Complex (MAC). How this relates to the Furman phase awaits further analysis; see Ashley V. Dumas and James Knight, Jr., "Ceramics and Chronology of the Marengo Archaeological Complex," and Charles Cobb, "Indigenous Settlements and Spanish *Entradas* in the Western Black Prairie" (both papers presented at the Southeastern Archaeological Conference, Durham, North Carolina, 24–27 October 2021).

30. Jenkins, "Tracing the Origins of the Early Creeks," 234. According to Regnier, "A Stylistic Analysis," 130–32, the Furman-phase people migrated out of Mabila, with some moving northeast to join citizens of the former Tascalusa chiefdom at the Coosa and Tallapoosa confluence and others returning south to the Gulf area. The middle Alabama River would not be re-occupied again until after the American Revolution.

31. Jenkins, "Tracing the Origins of the Early Creeks," 235.

32. DePratter, Hudson, and Smith, "The De Soto Expedition," 120, place Talisi on the Coosa River, near present-day Childersburg, Alabama, and argue that it probably corresponds to the Kymulga-phase people. However, a recent re-evaluation of central Alabama during the late sixteenth century, places Talisi on the lower Tallapoosa; see Jenkins, "Tracing the Origins of the Early Creeks," 205–8, 233–34; and Jenkins and Sheldon, "The Hernando de Soto and Tristán de Luna y Arellano Expeditions," 170–71. The Lamar culture encompassed several Mississippian polities over a large area covering parts of present-day eastern Alabama, northern Florida, North and South Carolina, Tennessee, and most of Georgia. See David J. Halley, "An Overview of Lamar Culture," in *Ocmulgee Archaeology, 1936–1986*, ed. David J. Halley (Athens: University of Georgia Press, 1994), 144–74.

33. Archaeologically, we see an *in situ* transition from the Shine II-phase complex to the Atasi phase (1575–1700 CE). Unfortunately, both the Shine II and the Atasi phases do not yet have exact chronologies, and so we cannot say with precision when certain transitions occurred. For instance, although we know that the largest Shine II mound center (the Jere Shine site) was abandoned sometime during Shine II, we do not yet know if people left before or after the de Soto *entrada*. After people abandoned the Jere Shine site, three smaller Shine II towns with mounds to the east continued to be occupied into the Atasi phase, perhaps indicating a shift in leadership either prior to or after de Soto's expedition; see Jenkins, "Tracing the Origins of the Early Creeks," 227–28; Gregory A. Waselkov and Marvin T. Smith, "Upper Creek Archaeology," in *Indians of the Greater Southeast: Historical Archaeology and Ethnohistory*, ed. Bonnie G. McEwan (Gainesville: University Press of Florida, 2000), 250–52; Vernon J. Knight, Jr., "The Formation of the Creeks," in *The Forgotten Centuries: Indians and Europeans in the American South, 1521–1704*, ed. Charles Hudson and Carmen Chaves Tesser (Athens: University of Georgia Press, 1994), 383; *Tukabatchee: Archaeological Investigations at an Historic Creek Town, Elmore County, Alabama, 1984* (Tuscaloosa: University of Alabama, Office of Archaeological Research, Report of Investigations, no. 45, 1985); and Cameron B. Wesson, "Prestige Goods, Symbolic Capital, and Social Power in the Protohistoric Southeast," in *Between Contacts and Colonies: Archaeological Perspectives on the Protohistoric Southeast*, ed. Cameron B. Wesson and Mark A. Rees (Tuscaloosa: University of Alabama Press, 2002), 118–20.

34. Jenkins, "Tracing the Origins of the Early Creeks," 228; Waselkov and Smith, "Upper Creek Archaeology," 250–52; Knight, "Formation of the Creeks," 383. Knight, in *Tukabatchee*, 9–12, gives slightly different dates for the phases; he dates the Shine II phase as 1400–1550 CE and the Atasi phase as 1600–1715 CE. Knight understands the fifty-year gap between the two to be due to a lack of data, rather than discontinuity. For a detailed listing of Creek ceramic phases, see Vernon J. Knight, Jr., "Ocmulgee Fields Culture and the Historical Development of Creek Ceramics," in *Ocmulgee Archaeology*, 186–89.

35. Knight, "Formation of the Creeks," 381.

36. The migration of people from Tascalusa (Big Eddy phase ceramics) comes from Jenkins, "Tracing the Origins of the Early Creeks," 214-15, 221. Others agree that the Abercrombie phase resulted from migrants joining extant populations on the

Chattahoochee, but submit that the migrants were not only from present-day central Alabama, but Tennessee as well (Alabama River-, Dallas-, and McKee Island-phase people); see John H. Blitz and Karl G. Lorenz, *The Chattahoochee Chiefdoms* (Tuscaloosa: University of Alabama Press, 2006), 70–72; Knight, "Formation of the Creeks," 383, 384; and John E. Worth, "The Lower Creeks: Origins and Early History," in *Indians of the Greater Southeast*, 268-69, 271–72, 274.

37. Blitz and Lorenz, *The Chattahoochee Chiefdoms*, 70–72; Jenkins, "Tracing the Origins of the Early Creeks," 228–29; Knight, "Formation of the Creeks," 383, 384; Worth, "The Lower Creeks," 269, 271–72, 274. There is some discrepancy in the dating of the Chattahoochee River phases. The dates here are from Jenkins, "Tracing the Origins of the Early Creeks," 228–29. In contrast, Worth, "Lower Creeks," repeats Knight's dates in "Formation of the Creeks." These are Stewart phase, 1475–1550 CE; Abercrombie phase, 1550–1650 CE; and Blackmon phase, 1650–1715 CE. Blitz and Lorenz date them as Stewart phase, 1550–1600 CE, and Abercrombie phase, 1600–1650 CE (*Chattahoochee Chiefdoms*, 71–72). Using these later dates, it is tempting to interpret the Big Eddy migration to the Chattahoochee as resulting from the fall of Tascalusa after the battle of Mabila. For the later archaeology of Apalachicola, see Thomas Foster, "The Identification and Significance of Apalachicola for the Origins of the Creek Indians in the Southeastern United States, *Southeastern Archaeology* 36, no. 1 (2017): 1–13.

38. Ethridge, *From Chicaza to Chickasaw*, 60–115.

39. Knight, "Formation of the Creeks," 384; Gregory Waselkov, "Seventeenth-Century Trade in the Colonial Southeast," *Southeastern Archaeology* 8, no. 2 (1989): 120–28; Waselkov, personal communication, 2008.

40. Sheri M. Shuck-Hall, "Alabama and Coushatta Diaspora and Coalescence in the Mississippian Shatter Zone," in *Mapping the Mississippian Shatter Zone*, 250–71. As we have seen, the northernmost edge of the paramount chiefdom of Coosa extended into present-day eastern Tennessee, where it encompassed the Coushatta-speaking chiefdoms of Coste and Chiaha. Coste and Chiaha, undoubtedly, felt the fall of Coosa, and after Coosa declined in the sixteenth century, the Coste and Chiaha chiefdoms also declined. Later documents reveal the Chiahas to have joined the Apalachicola. And seventeenth-century European eyewitnesses described pre-migration Coste as only a small town, which, given its proximity to both the Westo and the Occaneechi, left them extremely vulnerable to slave raiders; see Ethridge, *From Chicaza to Chickasaw*, 112–13.

41. Shuck-Hall, "Alabama and Coushatta Diaspora;" Hudson, *Knights of Spain*, 229; Worth, "Lower Creeks," 271–72. Worth includes Casiste as one of the Coushatta-speaking migrant towns, which he identifies as one of the towns in the province of Talisi at the time of de Soto. I agree that some people from the Talisi province migrated to Apalachicola; however, these people most likely did so soon after the de Soto *entrada* and, therefore, were not refugees from slaving.

42. Marcos Delgado, "The Expedition of Marcos Delgado From Apalachee to the Upper Creek Country in 1686," ed. and trans. Mark F. Boyd, *Florida Historical Quarterly* 16, no. 1 (1937), 14, 26; Patricia Galloway, *Choctaw Genesis,* 177–79; Smith, *Coosa*, 80. See especially Shuck-Hall, "Alabama-Coushatta Diaspora." The

main Coushatta town on the Alabama River was Coosada and likely was comprised of people from Coste. The smaller Coushatta towns of Tubani and Taskigi were nearby. De Soto and Pardo had found the towns of Tasqui and Tasquiqui on the Hiwassee River in present-day Tennessee and it is quite likely that some of the people from Tasqui and Tasquiqui had joined their former Coste neighbors on the Alabama.

43. Jenkins, "Tracing the Origins of the Early Creeks," 235–40; Shuck-Hall, "Alabama-Coushatta Diaspora," 252.

44. Shuck-Hall, "Alabama-Coushatta Diaspora."

45. Ethridge, *From Chicaza to Chickasaw*, 99–100, 112. Joshua Piker, in *Okfuskee: A Creek Indian Town in Colonial America* (Cambridge: Harvard University Press, 2004), 7, states that Okfuskee in the eighteenth century was a town in the Abihka ("Abeika") province; I understand Okfuskee to have been a separate province in the early nineteenth century (*Creek Country: The Creek Indians and Their World* [Chapel Hill: University of North Carolina Press, 2003], 90).

46. See my *From Chicaza to Chickasaw*.

47. Hudson and Ethridge, "The Early Historic Transformation," 42.

The Making and Unmaking of San Luis, an Apalachee-Spanish Town in Florida

ALEJANDRA DUBCOVSKY

Formal excavations of San Luis's Spanish structures, which date from what scholars call the San Luis Phase (1633–1704), began in the late 1940s, though the existence of Spanish structures and artifacts on this site near present-day Tallahassee, Florida, was well known before then.[1] In the 1950s, archaeologists excavated part of the Spanish fort: they located important architectural details, such as the moat around the blockhouse, and the remains of many artifacts associated with Spanish residency, including nails, bottles, and European weapons. The region saw new archeological exploration in the 1980s, especially after 1983, when the State of Florida purchased 50 acres and established a permanent and active archaeological site. Under the direction of Bonnie McEwan, C. Margaret Scarry, John Scarry, Gary Shapiro, and Richard Vernon, among others, the multi-faceted features of the city came to life.[2]

At the center of town there was a large, circular plaza bordered by an impressive Apalachee council house, a church, and various other structures, including a convent and a kitchen area. The excavations and findings at San Luis had many parallels to those spearheaded by Kathleen Deagan in

St. Augustine, the main hub of Spanish activities in colonial Florida.[3] The ongoing archaeological excavations in Mission San Luis have uncovered a wealth of artifacts, helping us reconstruct everyday life in this Apalachee-Spanish town. Although the European sites have been far more explored than the Apalachee ones, the archaeological findings regarding the latter both fill out and complicate a historical narrative focused on Spanish men.[4]

Combining both historical documents and archaeological findings not only offers a new understanding of San Luis, its structures, and its everyday operations, but also allows us to refocus the traditional narratives by highlighting the experiences and struggles of women. Women, and in particular Native women, were vital members of this town. They proved central both to the development of this contested Apalachee-Spanish space and to the abandonment of San Luis in 1704, after English-Native raids violently destroyed most of the surrounding towns.[5] Focusing on women shows how Spaniards and Apalachees interacted with one another, negotiated power, and made sense of their changing world.

In 1633, after over a century of intermittent contact and interaction, Apalachees welcomed the first Spanish Franciscans into their towns.[6] One of the earliest missions established was called San Luis de Anahica/Jinayca /Xinayaca. The location and name of this mission likely referenced Anhayca (also called Iniahico), a city visited by both Cabeza de Vaca, during the disastrous Pánfilo de Narváez expedition in 1528, and over a decade later by Hernando de Soto, who spent part of the winter of 1539–40 in the town. Both *conquistadores* met violent opposition in and near this prominent town. In the hundred years after the *entradas* [Spanish expeditions], Apalachee had undergone many important changes, not least of which were a sharp demographic decline and increased external, as well as internal, pressures on their power.[7] Yet it seems that this town remained a center for Apalachee politics. The archaeological work done on San Luis de Anahica/Jinayca/ Xinayaca not only affirms the endurance of Apalachee communities, but also highlights the long and layered process of early contact with Spanish colonialism.[8]

Apalachees decided when and where Spaniards entered their towns. This political maneuvering enabled Apalachees to use Spanish involvement to reclaim and retain their authority, but many of their actions and efforts were directed at Timucuas and other Indian groups, rather than exclusively at the Spaniards.[9] While Spanish efforts in San Luis are often framed in terms of Spanish-Apalachee relations, Apalachees participated in and were shaped by a larger Indigenous world that included Apalachicolas, Chacatos, Chines, Yamasees, and many other groups. More pressingly, Apalachee relations with Spaniards had a lot to do with their Timucua neighbors.[10] From Apalachees' first peaceful overture towards the Spaniards in 1612, which came during Friar Martín Prieto's peace accord between Timucua and Apalachee in Ivitachuco, to the relocation of San Luis from Anahica/Jinayca/Xinayaca to Talimali closer to the *camino real* [the Royal Road] during the so-called Timucua Rebellion in 1656, the relations between Apalachees, Timucuas, and Spaniards had been closely interconnected.[11] These multidirectional interactions add a level of complexity and messiness to an already complex and messy milieu, one that is evident in both the archival sources and the archaeological artifacts.[12]

From 1656 to 1704, San Luis de Talimali, never again referred to as San Luis de Jinayca, became the main hub of Spanish economic, military, and religious activity in the area.[13] Bishop Calderón surveyed the region in 1675, revealing that San Luis boasted a population of 1,400 people, by far the most populous town in Apalachee. Fourteen years later, a census of the region described 300 families and a total of 1,500 people living in the town. San Luis's seven-percent increase paled in comparison to the rise of Bacuqua, Cupaica, Oconi, and Ocuia, which all almost doubled in size, but was significant compared to the towns of Aspalaga or Tomole, which saw sharp population declines. Even with the variability of each individual town, the Native population of Apalachee remained around 10,000 in this period, with a growing number of non-Apalachee Indigenous populations living in the region.[14]

The Spanish and *criollo* [people of Spanish descent born in the Americas] population in the San Luis remained relatively small. Soldiers, government officials, and enterprising ranchers quickly followed the small Franciscan contingency into the region. In the 1670s, military activity increased, especially with the building of a small fort nearby at the confluences of the Wakulla and St. Marks Rivers. The garrison in San Luis also expanded to about forty-five soldiers; it then quickly contracted to a mere twelve in the late 1680s. During the 1702 English siege of St. Augustine, San Luis claimed to have sent a relief force of about ninety armed men, but in 1704, when the city was evacuated, the number of active Spanish officials listed was closer to forty.[15]

Although there are almost no descriptions of the town's physical space, the constant requests to reinforce its military buildings hint at their rudimentary nature.[16] In 1697, forty years after the founding of the city, a wooden blockhouse finally stood in San Luis, but this structure lacked proper roofing.[17] In 1702, after the English besieged St. Augustine, the Spaniards feared a similar attack in San Luis and erected a palisade around the 70- by 40-foot garrison, but as the excavations of the fort revealed, "the relationship of the military complex within the larger Spanish-Indian community was somewhat specialized. Because the town of San Luis had well-established religious, domestic, and public areas, the fort complex played a relatively limited role as a workplace for the garrison, a storehouse for supplies and munitions, and a safehouse in the event of a siege."[18] At the start of the eighteenth century, the defenses around the garrison grew, but it is unclear how much impact that palisade had on everyday life or even if neighboring Apalachees took the decision to strengthen the fort as an act of militarization.

The church was the other main Spanish structure in town. The San Luis church was comparable in size to the one erected in St. Augustine. Its large and easily recognizable footprint showed the importance of the Catholic enterprise and of religious life in San Luis. But its size and shape also made it an anomaly. The San Luis church was strikingly different from the other, smaller mission structures in Apalachee.[19] It was clear that San Luis was the hub for all missionary activities and festivities in the region: Franciscan friars had to report in and out of San Luis, and the church saw active Native and *criollo* participation in the town.[20] There are also hundreds of superimposed burial sites under the church; women, men, and children are all interred alongside each other. Many of the dead are buried in alignment with the long axis of the church (east to west) with their arms crossed to make the sign of the cross; archaeologists have used these graves to explore the influence of Christianity and religious conversion in San Luis.[21]

But most Apalachees did not encounter Catholicism, Franciscans, or the church in this large, rectangular setting. They likely went to the missions in their own towns. The churches in smaller Native towns had no Spanish or *criollo* participation, and the friar was likely the only European for tens of miles. Similar to other Native structures, these missions in Apalachee towns outside San Luis were differentiated only by a wooden cross and some ceremonial artifacts found inside.[22] Spanish missions in Apalachee towns thus looked little like a Spanish structure and instead resembled other Apalachee dwellings. Apalachee interaction with Catholic practices varied widely. San Luis offers a fascinating case study, but only one, and a very particular one, among many more that still need to be explored.[23]

The findings and ongoing work at Mission San Luis suggest that it seems to have been like the mission complexes found throughout Spanish Florida. In other words, San Luis resembled other places in La Florida: it had "a fort with a blockhouse, fortified country house, church, *convento* [convent], cemetery, central plaza, council house, public granary, and village."[24] But Bonnie McEwan, one of the principal archeologists for San Luis, argues that the archaeological focus on these particular structures has not only produced "knowledge [that] is heavily biased toward men and their activities," but also fostered very particular narratives about San Luis that insist on the presence of Native and Spanish women, while denying them their subjectivity.[25]

The standard narratives go something like this: women lived in San Luis, for, surely, they had to. In all likelihood, they made pottery and maintained their homes; they gathered water and cleaned; they cared for children and went to church; and in 1704 when San Luis was evacuated, they left as well. The inclusion of Apalachee and *criolla* women broadens and varies the experiences of this mission town without altering the entrenched military and religious narratives of San Luis. In other words, even when women are included, San Luis remains a town of men. Except it was not.

Doña Juana de Florencia offers a telling example. She lived most of her adult life in San Luis. The exact location of her residence is unknown, and none of the excavations in the town have been linked to a specific family.[26] Juana was probably the wealthiest and most recognizable Spanish-descended woman living in San Luis. Like most Spaniards and *criollos* in town, she lived close to the circular plaza. Her immediate neighbors were likely other Spaniards or *criollos*. A tiny segment of the population, they remained close to one another and attempted to create exclusive Spanish spaces within an imposing Native world. Though Juana likely employed Apalachee women within her home and used Native pottery to cook, she and her neighbors might have gone for an entire day hearing mostly Spanish being spoken.

In San Luis, unlike St. Augustine, there was a clear division between the Native and European sections of town. Doña Juana's neighborhood was not only apart from the main Apalachee residential areas in San Luis, but it also looked different. John Scarry and Bonnie McEwan argue that "shapes and spatial arrangement of native and European domestic structures changed very little as a result of contact [in San Luis]. This suggests that each group maintained a distinct identity in the realm of residential organization."[27] In other words, San Luis was a spatially segregated town.

San Luis was likely not built on a grid. The two main home structures excavated in town are of different sizes and have different orientations. McEwan contends that "if the residential area was gridded, it must have been flexible enough to allow for second generation buildings to be significantly modified from their earlier counterparts."[28] Spanish-style houses had rectangular structures made either of wood or of wattle-and-daub with palm-thatched roofs.[29] Juana's house, although made from these materials, was in all likelihood bigger than the average two-room *casita*; her family also owned several ranches beyond town.[30] The excavations of San Luis indicate that the residential areas were slightly larger than those in St. Augustine and had extensive outdoor areas.

Perhaps one of the biggest surprises from the excavations of the Spanish portion of San Luis was the high percentage of personal objects uncovered, especially compared to findings in St. Augustine. Many of these items, including rings, pendants, beads, and amulets, come from Feature 6 (a trash pit in the Spanish residential area). These uncovered artifacts hint at both the affluence of a certain portion of the population and at the gendered dimension of that wealth, since a large number of these items were likely worn by or intended for women. The implication of these artifacts is not necessarily that women controlled more wealth or owned more things than men in San Luis, but rather that the display of these items—especially on the hands, necks, and bodies of Spanish and *criolla* women— helped convey Spanish colonial power. The presence of women and families in San Luis signaled the expansion of Spanish influence over Apalachee, a region that had long resisted European incursions.

The archaeological findings have not only confirmed the presence of women and families in San Luis that are hardly mentioned in the documentary record, but have also helped recreate a sense of the wealth and status that the Spanish minority was able to mobilize. With over 25,000 artifacts categorized, and ongoing investigations of Feature 73 (a larger trash pit near Ocala Road), the material record has shown that San Luis was not an impoverished, disconnected mission town. Its Spanish residents ate better, adorned themselves more lavishly, and seemed to have had a better quality of life than in St. Augustine.[31]

Excavations have also uncovered a large number and variety of pottery in the Spanish sections of town. Ceramics account for roughly 90% of all artifacts recovered in San Luis, and 90% of those ceramics were Native-made. Colonoware ["pottery produced using traditional aboriginal techniques and exhibiting European form characteristics that differ from Native vessel form"] appears extensively and almost exclusively in San Luis's Spanish residences.[32] Apalachee sites, like the council house, contained very little colonoware and instead showcase Apalachee pottery unmodified, either in shape or decoration, by European influence. Richard Vernon and Ann Cordell, who have done extensive categorization of these artifacts, argue that "the mere fact that large quantities of colono-wares were found in contexts associated with the Spanish village at San Luis suggests that these wares were being used by Spaniards or their Apalachee wives and servants."[33]

Kathleen Deagan has made similar arguments for St. Augustine. She posited that the assorted pottery traditions found within Spanish households had everything to do with Native women. Native women married Spanish and *criollo* men and brought their own pottery traditions, techniques, and preferences into their new living arrangements. For Deagan, these Native-made artifacts found in Spanish homes help to counter a narrative of Spanish domination and control.[34] She contended that the prevalence of this archaeological style and these goods shows the powerful influence of Native women within Spanish homes. Deagan's arguments remain incredibly influential, and have only recently been challenged.

Barbara Voss has offered one of the most powerful reappraisals of Deagan's model to date. Voss's first critique focuses on place. Voss found that the St. Augustine model and its well-defined roles for Native women and Spanish men could not readily transfer to other places in Latin America.[35] But the crux of Voss's argument relied on labor. Voss argued that Native women entered Spanish households not as equal partners, but as concubines, slaves, and servants. They were likely not equal partners or wives—existing evidence shows that intermarriage accounted for only a small percentage of marriages in St. Augustine (and the numbers might be even smaller in San Luis).[36] In Deagan's story, Native-made goods for Spanish consumption revealed Native agency and influence; in Voss's story, those same artifacts show the unequal power dynamics and labor arrangements that Native women faced. This debate over material goods has forced scholars either into a story that privileges the agency of Native people, in particular women, but fails to properly account for the violence of colonialism, or into a history that demonstrates the abusive, asymmetrical power of Spanish colonialism, but struggles to account for the lives and experiences of Native people.[37] To tell the stories of women, Native as well as European, in La Florida, these seemingly conflicting narratives must find some balance.

The case of Marcos Delgado, a leading colonial official in Apalachee, provides some insight into the complex power structures that governed Spanish-Apalachee relations in San Luis. Apalachee leaders accused Delgado of enslaving Native women. They claimed that the Spanish officer had carried off "a family of three women," one elderly and another two much younger, and required them to work on his ranch.[38] Although it is unclear what labor Delgado planned for these women to perform, he intended to keep them for a long time. After all, he had kidnapped the entire family, even the woman who was too old to work. Perhaps Delgado had merely taken what he had found. But it's more likely that the capture of at least two generations of a single family had been a calculated act. Delgado had allowed them to stay together not simply out of convenience. The women all knew the area and the younger ones might have the opportunity to escape, but in so doing, they would likely have to leave behind their older relative. Delgado thus took advantage of these Native women, who had found themselves without protection since their male kin were serving the *repartimiento* [labor draft] mandated by the Spanish Crown. He also manipulated their efforts and desire to remain with their kin. The Native women thus continued living in his household despite the abuse because, by doing so, they could stay together and preserve their matrilineal connections.[39]

Diego Jiménez was another Spanish officer accused of enslaving Apalachee women. His illegal activities came to light during the official 1695 Visitation of Apalachee. The Spanish *visitador* [surveyor] traveled from town to town assessing the state of affairs. In the town of Candelaria, the principal cacique "beg[ged] that his Excellency deign to order that Spaniards who live in this province *not carry the women to serve them with the use of violence and against their will.*"[40] Jiménez was guilty on all counts. He had taken a Native woman and compelled her to work in conditions that were clearly abusive. Jiménez had not relied on the same level of inter-generational violence and intimidation employed by Delgado, but he had kept Chuguta Francisca in his household for a long time. She had been "assisting him in the preparing of his meals on his ranch," until "he dismissed her without paying anything." Chuguta Francisca had performed intensive work while living away from her kin and hometown, only to be "dismissed" suddenly and without pay. She thought Jiménez's actions punishable. She complained about her work conditions and lack of recompense to the chief of her town, who in turn presented her case to San Luis officials. The Spanish *visitador* listened to her accusations and reprimanded Jiménez, but little changed. The forced labor of Apalachee women kept Spaniards in San Luis comfortable, fed, and in control.[41]

Don Patricio, the leading Apalachee cacique of Ivitachuco, noted the growing violence against Native women. Though at first he claimed that all was well in his town, "nothing occurred to them to petition for relative to their government or their village," he went on to list the names and locations of nine married men who were compelled to find work away from the town. He explained how these men's wives "beg of his excellency that he, for his part, use his authority so that they may come back to resume the aforesaid marital life and to dwell in their village."[42] Don Patricio appealed to the patriarchal sensibility of the Spanish officials. The Native women of Ivitachuco were "in great need" without their husbands. Don Patricio downplayed the Spaniards' role in taking these men far from home, framing their actions instead as protective and caring. He used gendered and familial requests to subtly critique the Spanish disruption of Apalachee life.

Hinachuba Adrian, cacique of Santa Cruz de Capole, spoke far more candidly about the disappearing population of his town. He also asked for the return "of four married Indians. ... Who are Chuguta Marcelo, Chinocossa Jucepe, Abaiaga Axnd, and Vicente Abaiaga, who are married and who, in addition to being missed by their wives, *are missed also by the village* because it has no more than twenty men and of these some are elderly."[43] The leading men of San Martín de Tolomi took their complaints a step further. "There were four married men at the presidio, who are: Paslali Alonso, Pansaca Juan Mendosa, Pansacola Julian, and Ocolasli Baltassar ... and because of their absence a field is not planted ... and they and their children find themselves perishing."[44] Since women could not perform their labor in a safe manner, Apalachee communities were failing to meet their most basic needs. They did not have enough food, shelter, or protection. Spanish men recorded and listened to the Apalachee pleas without understanding the gravity of the situation. Apalachee leaders, on the other hand, had no doubt that their declining population numbers were a direct affront to their power and their ability to govern the region; they began to openly state that what hurt Apalachee women hurt all of Apalachee.

In 1704, Spanish officials decided to abandon San Luis. At the time, the town had over 1,400 inhabitants and was an important hub in a growing trade network that extended not only to the interior and the coast, but also to Spanish cities in the Caribbean. But the expansion of English-sponsored and supplied slaving raids into Spanish Florida had left San Luis increasingly exposed. In the summer of 1704, English forces led by Colonel James Moore, former governor of Carolina (which had not yet been divided into North and South), launched a violent campaign against Apalachee. The object of these raids was to capture and enslave as many people as possible. And though there is a growing scholarship on these successful and devastating slaving campaigns, far less attention has been paid to the gendered ways in which Apalachee communities experienced this mounting violence.[45]

Indian slavery deeply affected the everyday lives of Native women. Native women in the sixteenth and seventeenth century tended to enjoy far more mobility than their European counterparts. They were responsible for preparing and planting fields, gathering fruits and nuts, and bringing water to their communities; in other words, Native women were expected to labor and spend a large part of their days away from their homes. But at the close of the seventeenth century, as the Apalachee population declined rapidly, Native women found themselves increasingly vulnerable when doing the tasks they needed to perform. As they tended fields, traveled to waterways, collected nuts, and moved about the land without male protection, they could be captured by slave raiders. Women's lives and daily activities became increasingly dangerous in the context of Indian slavery.[46]

In the eighteenth century, Indian slavery led to the capture and enslavement of thousands of Apalachees, who were torn apart from their homelands and families. As slave raiders marched Apalachee men and women to Carolina, they left a wake of devastation. They burned towns, killed and tortured those who resisted, and created an outmigration of people desperately seeking safety elsewhere.[47] In other words, the violence of Indian slavery upended the lives of those enslaved, but also of those who had managed to avoid captivity. Native women could no longer plant fields or gather food, Apalachee children were kept close to town, and family life became an impossibility for most Apalachees.[48]

In 1704, as Spanish officials debated whether the situation was too volatile to remain in the area, they hardly mentioned Native women. They worried about English manpower and ammunition, eventually deciding that the poorly equipped Spanish fort in San Luis was no match for the coming attack. Ultimately, they decided it would be better for Spanish forces to destroy and leave San Luis than to have it fall into enemy hands. Apalachee leaders saw this threat differently.[49]

Don Patricio, cacique of Ivitachuco, vowed support for the Spanish Crown, but then requested to move his family and the women in his community to a safer location.[50] The Spanish could only imagine the end of Apalachee after the evacuation of San Luis in 1704; the chief of Ivitachuco still envisioned a place in which his people could live and work without the constant threat of violence. He asked Governor Zúñiga y Cerda "for permission so that his wife and children might travel to Pensacola for a short time until this province's condition changes in some way."[51] To protect Apalachee in general and his own town of Ivitachuco in particular, he needed to provide a safe haven for "his wife and children"—he needed to take care of Native women, for they sustained, in every possible meaning of that word, Apalachee communities.[52]

At first glance, women hardly appear in descriptions of San Luis. They were rarely mentioned in the *entradas* into Apalachee. They were not featured in Apalachee petitions for Spanish missions. And they have no place in the brief accounts of the San Luis blockhouse or mission. Their absence is owed in part to the lack of baptismal, marriage, and death records from the region. Since the documents in which women normally appear in the Spanish colonial archive are missing for Apalachee, women are also missing from San Luis's history. But their histories are neither gone, nor inaccessible. In the crevices of the documentary and material record, Native women, along with their stories, decisions, and actions can be found. And they offer much more than a unique voice and perspective on a poorly studied time and place. They make legible the relations, personal as well as communal, that structured both Apalachee life and Apalachee-Spanish interactions.

Notes

I would like to acknowledge Robin Beck as well as the participants and audience members of the *William and Mary Quarterly*-Early Modern Studies Institute 2019 Workshop: "Archaeology, History, and the Problem of 'Early America,'" who provided valuable feedback on an earlier version of this work.

1. Gordon Willey, *Archaeology of the Florida Gulf Coast* (Washington: Smithsonian Institution, 1949): 285–86; John W. Griffin, "Excavations at the Site of San Luis," in *Here They Once Stood*, ed. Mark F. Boyd, Hale G. Smith, and John W. Griffin (Gainesville: University of Florida Press, 1951): 139–60.

2. Gary Shapiro, *Archaeology at San Luis: Broad Scale Testing, 1984–85* (Tallahassee: Florida Bureau of Archaeological Research, 1987); Gary Shapiro and Bonnie McEwan, "Archaeology at San Luis: The Apalachee Council House," *Florida Archaeology* 6 (1991): 107–17.

3. See Deagan, *Spanish St. Augustine: The Archaeology of a Colonial Creole Community* (New York: Academic Press, 1983); and Deagan, *America's Ancient City: Spanish St. Augustine, 1565–1763* (New York: Garland, 1991). For an overview of the archaeological developments, see Rochelle A. Marrinan and Tanya Peres, "Unearthing the Missions of Spanish Florida," in *Unearthing the Missions of Spanish Florida,* ed. Rochelle A. Marrinan and Tanya Peres (Gainesville: University of Florida Press, 2021): 1–34.

4. Marrinan and Peres, "Unearthing the Missions of Spanish Florida"; Suzanne M. Spencer-Wood, "Feminist Theory and Gender Research in Historical Archaeology," in *Handbook of Gender in Archaeology*, ed. Sarah M. Nelson (Lanham: Alta Mira Press, 2006), 59–104.

5. Pamela L. Geller, "Identity and Difference: Complicating Gender in Archaeology," *Annual Review of Anthropology* 38 (2009): 65–81. For slaving raids that targeted the Apalachee, see Alan Gallay, *The Indian Slave Trade: The Rise of the English Empire in the American South, 1670–1717* (New Haven: Yale University Press, 2002): 127–54.

6. Charles R. Ewen, "The DeSoto-Apalachee Project: The Martin Site and Beyond," *Florida Anthropologist* 42, no. 4 (1989): 361–68; Governor Luis de Horruytiner, letter to the King, 15 November 1633, Archivo General de Indias (AGI) Santo Domingo (SD) 223.

7. John E. Worth, *The Timucuan Chiefdoms of Spanish Florida*, 2 vols. (Gainesville: University of Florida, 1998), 2:9–10, 2:35–65, 2:66–87.

8. John Hann, *Apalachee: The Land between the Rivers* (Gainesville: University Presses of Florida, 1988), 88.

9. Bonnie G. McEwan, "San Luis De Talimali: The Archaeology of Spanish-Indian Relations at a Florida Mission," *Historical Archaeology* 25, no. 3 (1991), 37; Hann, *Apalachee,* 13. For a general discussion, see Robin Beck, *Chiefdoms, Collapse, and Coalescence in the Early American South* (Cambridge: Cambridge University Press, 2013), 1–23.

10. For Timucua, see Jonathan DeCoster, "Entangled Borderlands: Europeans and Timucuans in Sixteenth-Century Florida," *Florida Historical Quarterly* 91, no. 3 (2013): 375–400; and Jerald T. Milanich, *The Timucua* (Cambridge: Blackwell Publishers, 1996), 187–88, 198–212. For Apalachee, see Joseph Hall, "Anxious Alliances: Apalachicola Efforts to Survive the Slave Trade, 1638–1705," in *Indian Slavery in Colonial America*, ed. Alan Gallay (Lincoln: University of Nebraska, 2009), 147–84; James W. Covington, "Apalachee Indians, 1704–1763," *Florida Historical Quarterly* 50, no. 4 (1972): 366–84; Hann, *Apalachee,* 106; and John

Hahn, *The Invention of the Creek Nation, 1670–1763* (Lincoln: University of Nebraska Press, 2004), 40–47.

11. Bonnie G. McEwan, "Colonialism on the Spanish Florida Frontier: Mission San Luis, 1656–1704," *Florida Historical Quarterly* 92, no. 3 (2014), 595.

12. Hann, *Apalachee*, 17; Amy Bushnell, "The Menéndez Marquéz Cattle Barony at La Chua and the Determinants of Economic Expansion in Seventeenth-Century Florida," *Florida Historical Quarterly* 56, no. 4 (1978): 407–31; John F. Scarry, "The Apalachee Chiefdom: A Mississippian Society on the Fringes of the Mississippian World," in *The Forgotten Centuries: Indians and Europeans in the American South, 1521–1704*, ed. Charles Hudson and Carmen Chaves (Athens: University of Georgia Press, 1994), 156–78; Patrick Lee Johnson, "Apalachee Identity on the Gulf Coast Frontier," *Native South* 6 (2013): 110–41.

13. Verner W. Crane, *The Southern Frontier, 1670–1732* (Durham: Duke University Press, 1929), 9–11; Amy Turner Bushnell, "Republic of Spaniards, Republic of Indians," in *New History of Florida*, ed. Michael Gannon (Gainesville: University Presses of Florida, 1996): 62–77.

14. Bishop Díaz Vara Calderón, *A 17th Century Letter of Gabriel Díaz Vara Calderón, Bishop of Cuba, Describing the Indians and Indian Missions of Florida* (Washington: Smithsonian institution, 1936); Bishop Diego Ebelino de Compostela, letter to the King, 28 September 1689, Havana, AGI, SD 151; John H. Hann, "Summary Guide to Spanish Florida Missions and Visitas." *The Americas* 66, no. 4 (1990): 417–513; Hann, *Apalachee,* 171.

15. "Junta de Guerra, July 13, 1704," in *Here They Once Stood*, 56–59; Hann, *Apalachee,* 203–5.

16. Calderón, *A 17th Century Letter*; Governor Laureano Torres y Ayala, 15 April 1696, AGI SD 228, in *Here they Once Stood,* 21–22.

17. Boyd, *Here they Once Stood,* 10.

18. Bonnie G. McEwan and Charles B. Poe, "Excavations at Fort San Luis," *Florida Anthropologist* 47, no. 2 (1994), 105.

19. Bonnie McEwan, "Hispanic Life on the Seventeenth-Century Florida Frontier," *Florida Anthropologist* 44, nos. 2–4 (1991): 255–67; Michelle M. Pigott. "The Materiality of the Apalachee Diaspora: An Indigenous History of Contact and Colonialism in the Gulf South," *Southeastern Archaeology* 41, no 1 (2022): 1–21.

20. Hann, "Summary Guide."

21. McEwan, "Hispanic Life"; Bonnie G. McEwan and John H. Hann, "Reconstructing a Spanish Mission: San Luis de Talimali," *OAH Magazine of History* 4, no. 4 (2000): 16–19; Bonnie McEwan, Michael W. Davidson, and Jeffrey M. Mitchem, "A Quartz Crystal Cross from Mission San Luis, Florida," *Journal of Archaeological Science* 24 (1997): 529–36.

22. John H. Hann, "Church Furnishings, Sacred Vessels and Vestments Held by the Missions of Florida: Translation of Two Inventories," *Florida Archaeology* 2 (1986): 146–64.

23. For the incredible variability of mission experience in Florida, see the better-excavated sites in Guale discussed in Rebecca Saunders, *Stability and Change in Guale Indian Pottery, A.D. 1300–1702* (Tuscaloosa: University of Alabama Press,

2000); Elliot Blair, "Making Mission Communities: Population Aggregation, Social Networks, and Communities of Practice at 17th Century Mission Santa Catalina De Guale" (Ph.D. dissertation, University of California, Berkeley, 2015); Carey J. Garland, Laurie J. Reitsema, Clark Spencer Larsen, and David Hurst Thomas, "Early Life Stress at Mission Santa Catalina De Guale: An Integrative Analysis of Enamel Defects and Dentin Incremental Isotope Variation in Malnutrition," *Bioarchaeology International* 2 (2018): 75–94.

24. McEwan, "San Luis De Talimali," 39.

25. McEwan, "San Luis De Talimali," 38.

26. For archaeological findings in St. Augustine that showcase women's properties and power, see Susan Richbourg Parker, "In My Mother's House: Dowry Property and Female Inheritance Patterns in Spanish Florida," in *Signposts: New Directions in Southern Legal History*, ed. Sally E. Hadden and Patricia Hagler Minter (Athens: University of Georgia Press, 2013), 26–46.

27. John F. Scarry and Bonnie G. McEwan. "Domestic Architecture in Apalachee Province: Apalachee and Spanish Residential Styles in the Late Prehistoric and Early Historic Period Southeast," *American Antiquity* 60, no. 3 (1995), 482.

28. McEwan, "Hispanic Life," 264; Alison Bruin, "A Comparative Study of Colonoware Ceramics from Two Spanish Mission Sites in the Apalachee Province, Leon County, Florida" (master's thesis, Florida State University, 2019); Jerry Lee, "Imported Ceramics and Colonowares as a Reflection of Hispanic Lifestyles at San Luis Talimali," in *Unearthing the Missions of Spanish Florida*, 167–214.

29. Albert C. Manucy, *The Houses of St. Augustine, 1565–1821* (Gainesville: University Press of Florida, 1992).

30. Amy Turner Bushnell, "Tomás Menéndez Márquez, Criollo, Cattleman, and Contador," in *Spanish Pathways in Florida, 1492–1992/Los Caminos Españoles En La Florida, 1492–1992*, ed. Ann L. Henderson and Gary R. Mormino (Sarasota: Pineapple Press, 1991), 118–39; Justin B. Blanton, "The Role of Cattle Ranching in the 1656 Timucuan Rebellion: A Struggle for Land, Labor, and Chiefly Power," *Florida Historical Quarterly* 92, no. 4 (2014): 667–84.

31. Jeffrey M. Mitchem, "Beads and Pendants from San Luis De Talimali: Inferences from Varying Contexts," in *The Spanish Missions of La Florida*, ed. Bonnie McEwan (Gainesville: University Press of Florida, 1993): 399–417; Elizabeth J. Reitz, "Evidence for Animal Use at the Missions of Spanish Florida," *Florida Anthropologist,* 44, nos. 2–4 (1991): 295–306. For a comparison with St. Augustine, see Judith A. Bense, "Spanish Florida's Eighteenth-Century Presidios and the Tale of their Ceramics," *Southeastern Archaeology* 40, no. 4 (2021): 231–47.

32. McEwan, "San Luis De Talimali," 55. For more on colonoware, see Vicki L. Rolland and Keith H. Ashley, "Beneath the Bell: A Study of Mission Period Colonoware from Three Spanish Missions in Northeastern Florida," *Florida Anthropologist* 53, no. 1 (2000): 36-61, and Charles R. Cobb and Chester B. DePratter, "Multisited Research on Colonowares and the Paradox of Globalization," *American Anthropologist* 114, no. 3 (2012): 446–61.

33. Vernon and Cordell, "A Distribution and Technological Study of Apalachee Colono-Ware from San Luis De Talimali," *Florida Anthropologist* 44, nos. 2–4 (1991): 316–27; Lee, "Imported Ceramics and Colonoware," 167–214.

34. See Deagan, "St. Augustine: First Urban Enclave in the United States," *North American Archaeologist,* 3, no. 3 (1982): 183–205; Deagan, "St. Augustine and the Mission Frontier," in *The Spanish Missions of La Florida,* 87–110; "From Santa Elena to St. Augustine: Indigenous Ceramic Variability (A.D. 1400–1700)," ed. Kathleen Deagan and David Hurst Thomas, *Anthropological Papers of the American Museum of Natural History* 90 (2009); Deagan, *America's Ancient City*; Deagan, *Artifacts of the Spanish Colonies of Florida and the Caribbean, 1500–1800* (Washington: Smithsonian Institution Press, 1987); and Deagan, "Mestizaje in Colonial St. Augustine," *Ethnohistory* 20, no. 1 (1973): 55–65.

35. As Enrique Rodríguez-Alegría and Setha M. Low have separately argued, there was not a clear Spanish rejection of Native material and utilitarian goods. See Rodríguez-Alegría, "Eating like an Indian: Negotiating Social Relations in the Spanish Colonies," *Current Anthropology* 46, no. 4 (2005): 551–73; and Low, "Indigenous Architecture and the Spanish American Plaza in Mesoamerica and the Caribbean," *American Anthropologist* 97, no. 4 (1995): 748–62.

36. Voss, "Gender, Race, and Labor in the Archaeology of the Spanish Colonial Americas," *Current Anthropology* 49, no. 5 (2008), 869; Nan A. Rothschild, *Colonial Encounters in a Native American Landscape: The Spanish and Dutch in North America* (Washington: Smithsonian Books, 2003), 31.

37. Scarry and McEwan, "Domestic Architecture in Apalachee Province," 491.

38. Hann, *Apalachee,* 176; "Juan Gómez de Engraba to Francisco Martínez, March 13, 1657," AGI SD 225.

39. Hayley Negrin, "Possessing Native Women and Children: Slavery, Gender, and English Colonialism in the Early American South, 1670–1772" (Ph.D. dissertation, New York University, 2018).

40. "Visitations," AGI Escribanía de Cámara (EC)-156 [60]; emphasis mine.

41. "Visitations," AGI EC-156 [60]; Jennifer Baszile, "Apalachee Testimony in Florida, a View of Slavery from the Spanish Archives," in *Indian Slavery,* 185–206; Hann, *Apalachee,* 165. For the effects of slavery on Native gender relations, see Michelene E. Pesantubbee, *Choctaw Women in a Chaotic World: The Clash of Cultures in the Colonial Southeast* (Albuquerque: University of New Mexico Press, 2005), 56–58.

42. "Visitation of Ivitachuco," 3 December 1694, Joaquín de Florencia, Visitation, 1694–1695, AGI EC 157, quoted from John H. Hann, "Visitations and Revolts in Florida, 1657–1695," *Florida Archaeology* 7 (1993), 170.

43. "Visitation of Santa Cruz de Capole," 5 December 1694, Joaquín de Florencia, Visitation, 1694–1695, AGI EC 157, quoted from Hann, "Visitations," 173. Emphasis mine.

44. "Visitation of San Martín Tomoli," 7 December 1694, Joaquín de Florencia, Visitation, 1694–1695, AGI EC 157, quoted from Hann, "Visitations," 175. Emphasis mine.

45. See my "Defying Indian Slavery: Apalachee Voices and Spanish Sources in the Eighteenth-Century Southeast," *William and Mary Quarterly* 75, no. 2 (2018): 295–322.

46. "Visitation to Our Lady of la Candelaria," 7 December 1694, AGI ES 157, in Hann, *"Visitations,"* 176. For good overviews of this violence, see Christina Snyder, *Slavery in Indian Country: The Changing Face of Captivity* (Cambridge: Harvard University Press, 2010), and Robbie Ethridge, *From Chicaza to Chickasaw: The European Invasion and the Transformation of the Mississippian World, 1540–1715* (Chapel Hill: University of North Carolina Press, 2010).

47. "Solana to Zúñiga y Cerda," 10 June 10 1704, AGI SD 858. For a summary of the violence in Apalachee, see "Extracts from ... an inquiry into the deaths of the Fathers in Apalachee ... June, 1705," in *Here They Once Stood*, 74–82, especially 81.

48. For the importance of Native women to Native foodways, see Jane Mt. Pleasant, "A New Paradigm for Pre-Columbian Agriculture in North America," *Early American Studies* 13, no. 2 (2015): 374–412, and Susan Sleeper-Smith, *Indigenous Prosperity and American Conquest: Indian Women of the Ohio River Valley, 1690–1792* (Williamsburg: Omohundro Institute of Early American History and Culture, 2018), 13–66.

49. See Hann, *Apalachee,* 271–75, and my "'All of Us Will Have to Pay for These Activities': Colonial and Native Narratives of the 1704 Attack on Ayubale," *Native South* 10 (2017): 1–18.

50. "Governor Zúñiga y Zerda to the Caciques of Yvitachuco," 24 April 1704, AGI SD 858, folio 275–76.

51. "Governor Zúñiga y Zerda to the Caciques of Yvitachuco," folio 275–76.

52. "Governor Zúñiga y Zerda to the Caciques of Yvitachuco," folio 275–76.

Metawney of Coweta, Muscogee Women, and Historical Erasure in the Eighteenth-Century Past and Our Present

BRYAN C. RINDFLEISCH

In April 1776, the Superintendent for Indian Affairs in the South—the Indian trader and merchant George Galphin—filed his last will and testament in the Ninety-Six district court in South Carolina. This document has since become a staple for scholars of the eighteenth-century South. More than a dozen pages long, the Galphin will reveals the intimate, familial dimensions of the deerskin trade and European-Indigenous interactions in the eighteenth-century South; the amassed wealth of a prosperous merchant, who was one of the largest slave-owners in the early South; kinship connections that included British, French, Irish, African, and Native family members on both sides of the Atlantic; and the vibrant community of hundreds of enslaved peoples, both African and Native. In short, Galphin's will is a stunning document that scholars have analyzed and scrutinized for more than a century.

The Galphin will is also remarkable for another reason: it names the Muscogee (Creek) woman with whom Galphin fathered three children and to whom he left most of his estate. As he stipulated in April 1776, "I will that the said Metawney do live at her said Children's Cowpen and be maintained and Cloathed by them, and I give to her … a Suit of Mourning." At the same time, he wished their children "be sent to Charlestown or Savannah to School." This was the only occasion in Galphin's life on which he ever named Metawney (at least in a way that made it into the documentary record), despite the fact she was the sole reason that Galphin had been able to ingratiate himself with Muscogee peoples for the previous three decades and so accumulate the wealth that he partitioned out in 1776.[1]

The importance of Galphin's naming of Metawney cannot be overstated. Time and again during the eighteenth century, Euro-American men like Galphin simply referred to Indigenous women as "Indian Wenches"—or, in Metawney's case, that "Creek Indian Woman" or "Galphin's Indian Wench"—and thereby silenced those voices in the historical archives, essentially writing out the important roles and labor that women like Metawney provided within both the Muscogee and the Euro-American worlds. As scholars of the Native South have been demonstrating since the late 1990s, Native American women have been relegated to what Theda Perdue terms the "historical shadows" by Euro-American men, which has distorted the ways in which historians have seen, interpreted, and understood these women's lives and the "historical events [that] affected them." As Perdue wrote in her seminal work on Cherokee women, the "historical sources obscure [these] women's experiences." And while scholars have recently challenged and nuanced our understandings of the Indigenous female presence in the eighteenth-century South (inspired in part by work on enslaved and freed Black women by Daina Ramey Berry, Kathleen Brown, Marisa Fuentes, and Jennifer L. Morgan, among others), historians are still limited in their ability to explore the gendered contours of the eighteenth-century Native South.[2]

Even though we know little to nothing about Metawney's life other than the fact that she was intimately involved with Galphin, gave birth to and raised their three children in the town of Coweta, and died in December 1777 (according to a codicil to the Galphin will), we can still draw upon the consensus of scholarship related to Native American history and eighteenth-century Indigenous societies, particularly work on the matrilineal structures of the Muscogee world, to contextualize what Metawney's experiences as a Muscogee women would have been like in the eighteenth-century South. While such a framework does very little to fill in the gaping holes regarding Metawney's specific past, we can use the fleeting appearances of other eighteenth-century Muscogee women in the archives to flesh out her life, despite the limitations of and glaring omissions in that same documentary record.

That said, it should be noted that while the majority of Muscogee women—and Indigenous women in general—were written out of the past, there were certain extraordinary individuals who at times defied this silencing, such as Mary Musgrove (Bosomworth), who proved a rather prolific figure throughout the American South in the eighteenth century. This certainly begs the question: what was it about Musgrove/Bosomworth that commanded so much more attention from Europeans than her Muscogee counterparts? On the one hand, Musgrove/Bosomworth was a woman of two worlds—half-Muscogee, half-English—and she proved to be one of the earliest and most successful political and economic intermediaries between the Muscogee and the British in the early eighteenth century, precisely because of her two-world heritage and the fact that she spent most of her childhood and adult life in the British colonies. Musgrove/Bosomworth became intimate with a number of individuals, including John Musgrove (an Indian trader), Jacob Matthews (a planter), and the Rev. Thomas Bosomworth, and she enjoyed the favor of prominent leaders in both Muscogee and settler society, including Brims and Malatchi of Coweta and James Oglethorpe. She was also an extensive land-owner—which later precipitated what is known as the "Bosomworth Controversy"—and an Indian trader in her own right. In short, Mary Musgrove (Bosomworth) was an extraordinary individual for her time, but one whose experiences did not represent those of the vast majority of Muscogee women—and Indigenous women more generally—in the eighteenth century.[3]

Finally, it is important to reflect on the reasons why Indigenous women like Metawney have been absent from scholars' studies of the past, reasons that are entirely symptomatic of the fact that Euro-American men deliberately wrote these women out of existence and that historians over the centuries, including myself, have perpetuated this violence of silence. In short, we—historians and other scholars—are every bit as responsible as eighteenth-century individuals like Galphin for silencing Indigenous women in the past and for the consequences that such silence has had for Native women in the present. It is hardly a coincidence that Native American women today experience higher rates of sexual violence, partner violence, and murder at the hands of non-Native men than any other group in the United States and Canada, a threat that goes largely unnoticed by people, unless they work in some capacity within Native/Indigenous studies.[4] This is why the Missing and Murdered Indigenous Women and Girls (MMIWG) movement exists, to intervene and stop the cycles of historical erasure and sexual violence that have been inflicted upon Indigenous female bodies and voices in both the past and present. As the Muscogee scholar Sarah Deer asserts, the historical erasure of Indigenous women and the sexual violence to which they are subject in the present are both part of a larger "historical and political" cycle that Indigenous women have experienced and endured throughout the centuries, and MMIWG is a means through which Indigenous women are taking back their bodies and stories in the face of such erasure and violence.[5]

In short, this essay is a brief exploration of the ways in which scholars of the eighteenth century can be more mindful and deliberate in their understandings of Native American history and particularly their depictions of Indigenous women in the past and present, which can inform both our research and our teaching. At the same time, those of us who are non-Native scholars must come to terms with the historical apathy, erasure, and violence that our discipline has perpetuated. Admittedly, this work is not easy or complete in any sense of the word; it is maddening, ambiguous, and at times sickening. Yet we can begin to piece together the story of an eighteenth-century Native woman like Metawney, and her critical importance to her family, community, and Muscogee society more broadly. Therefore, despite the history of violence that has silenced Metawney and so many other Indigenous women like her in the past, scholars of the eighteenth century must reassert and privilege the stories of such women and in the process come to terms with the colonialism that our archives, our profession, and our own research and teaching have perpetuated.

First of all, being a woman in a matrilineal society meant that Metawney was celebrated as a life-giver, based upon her ability to give birth and to sustain her people with food. This is why Muscogee *micos* [headmen] time and again described to Euro-Americans in the eighteenth century how they, both Native and non-Native peoples, "are one and the same people, [who] were nursed by the breast of the same Mother, [and] the same lands produced for [our] Subsistence." In other words, the Muscogee world revolved around its women, like Metawney, or, as the Tallassee King put it in November 1779, "this Ground is our Mother, it is from [her] [we] Grow from this Ground that we are all raised, [and] therefore we ought to be like one Woman's Son." Creation Stories also reflect such female-centricity and instilled such values among Muscogee peoples at the earliest ages. In several variations of the Corn Woman or Corn Mother story, eighteenth-century Muscogee recounted how she gave birth to their people in a distant past, while at the same time cultivating corn to feed and nourish their people for the future. In one particular variation, Corn Woman made corn of her own body, when "she rubbed herself as one rubs roasting ears and made bread of what came off," after which she informed the Muscogee that "I am your mother. You can eat bread made out of [my] white corn." And when Corn Woman disappeared the next day, her children—the Muscogee—ventured to the corncrib, which they found "full of corn." All of this is a testament to the fact that Muscogee women were the heart and soul of the Muscogee world.[6]

Of similar importance is the fact that women like Metawney were the primary sources of kinship within eighteenth-century Muscogee society. As one unusually astute Euro-American observer described in 1708, Muscogee peoples "reckon all their families from the mother's side and have not the least regard who is their father ... [and] it seems to be done with the greatest Judgment in the world thus reckoning kindred from the woman's side." Muscogee women thus connected their families and clans, which were the main sources of identity in Muscogee society. In Metawney's case, she belonged to her mother's family and clan and so too did her three children (George, Judith, and John), all of whom lived with Metawney's relatives throughout their lives, rather than with their father Galphin. This is why Galphin, despite stipulating in his will that Metawney's children "be sent to Charlestown or Savannah to School," had no power to actually compel his children to do so, and it explains why George, Judith, and John remained closely attached to their mother and her people in Coweta, rather than to Galphin in South Carolina. Similarly, Metawney's kinship ties protected her children and their relatives, as evidenced by Sohonoketchee of Coweta at a conference with U.S. agents in 1796, when he invoked his kinship ties to Metawney's son John as his "cousin," or clan relative. Sohonoketchee, by promising to "make it my duty ... to look after [John] in the future and see that he conduct himself properly," shielded John from U.S. officials who wanted to arrest him for horse-thieving.[7]

Muscogee women like Metawney were thus the anchors within their families. Within eighteenth-century Muscogee society, marriage consisted of a set of "relationships between kin groups as [much as] they were relationships between individuals," meaning marriage to a woman meant that her spouse was invited into a relationship with that woman's family and clan relatives, which included becoming beholden to her relatives' expectations. In Metawney's case, she enfolded Galphin into her family and clan, which is why he was, according to the Muscogee *mico* the Tallassee King, "looked upon as an Indian" thereafter by other Muscogee people. Muscogee women also enjoyed sexual autonomy prior to marriage and in the event a marriage ever soured, a woman could speedily end the relationship without consequence, so long as there had not been any adultery, which was punishable in Muscogee society with the "cropping" (or removal) of the offender's ears. Further, Muscogee women like Metawney were economically independent, meaning that they enjoyed custody over the property and lands of their spouse and household. This is why Muscogee men who married into a woman's family lived with her relatives within the matrilineage, or "lineage household," which was composed of several different *hutis* [homes] that all belonged to the woman's extended kin. Moreover, it was Muscogee women who provided the labor that sustained the matrilineage and the broader community, cultivating the food and resources they shared with their relatives and distributed to other townspeople, which ranged from corn—the main staple of Muscogee diets—to beans, sweet potatoes, other fruits and vegetables, and domesticated animals. And if a family ever harvested a surplus, the women of the matrilineage traded that extra food to weary travelers visiting Muscogee territories or at colonial centers like Augusta, New Orleans, Savannah, St. Augustine, and St. Marks. And more often than not, Muscogee women were able to charge "an extravagant price" for their corn and other food, which Euro-Americans, like the Spanish garrison at St. Marks, were forced to "buy … for the Troops."[8]

Women were also pivotal when it came to Muscogee cosmology and ceremony. For instance, the most important religious practice in the Muscogee world was the Busk, or Green Corn Ceremony, which occurred every year in August or September at the "ripening of the corn." The Busk embodied the efforts of Muscogee peoples to restore balance to their "social order"—in their relationships with one another, other Indigenous groups, and Euro-Americans—and was a time of renewal and reconciliation as "they forget and forgive all the causes of quarrels." Throughout this observance and celebration of the first fruits of the year (which could extend for a week or more), Muscogee women were the primary vehicles for restoring ceremonial order and cosmological balance to the Muscogee world. Throughout the Busk, women refused "every kind of Sustenance, except Water, for three Days," during which they "cleaned out their houses, renewing the old hearths, and cleansing all their culinary vessels" and disposed of any old corn. Even though most women were forbidden from joining the men in the rituals that took place in the town center, the most revered clan matrons—the mothers of all—"were allowed … to tread on the holy ground." Meanwhile, women such as Metawney would have "prepared the new corn for [the] feast" and brought it into the town center, which was then followed by the "Relighting of the [Sacred] Fire." After that, the "Master or Mistress of each respective Family … communicated [the Fire] by Torches" to their own homes, thereby signifying the beginning of a new year and forgiveness of all of the past year's transgressions. At the end of the Busk, Muscogee women feasted and danced with the men in the town center to celebrate the annual renewal.[9]

Yet one of the most important roles that women played in the Muscogee world was as political actors who influenced the negotiations between their people and Euro-Americans, but Euro-American men rarely, if ever, documented such actions. One historian puts it best: Euro-Americans invented a fiction that privileged the "visibility of male ambassadors, along with male dominance of formal rhetoric" among the Muscogee throughout the eighteenth century; this was a product of their own patriarchal sensibilities as well as their casual disregard for Muscogee women's political acumen. If we were to take Euro-Americans at their word, women were "never admitted" into the discussions between Euro-American and Muscogee men and were seldom "seen in the public square" where the two sides exchanged talk of peace and trade. Instead, it was only when Euro-American and Muscogee men concluded their discussions that the men "dine[d] with, gift[ed], and entertain[ed] the chiefs [with] their Women & their Children." Yet nothing could be further from the truth. As scholars like Robbie Ethridge have demonstrated, Muscogee women wielded tremendous political agency through "informal channels" to direct their peoples' negotiations with Euro-Americans, particularly by "influencing public opinion," which could then be used to contest or even remove a *mico* from his position of leadership, or by "influencing their male kin" behind closed doors by reminding them of their obligations to their families. It was also women like Metawney who performed the invisible labor of these formal negotiations in the first place; they always "received kindly and furnished" Euro-American visitors "plentifully" and, by being hospitable and gracious, exhibited their life-giving powers as women and their peoples' intent to set the stage for peaceful negotiation.[10]

There are also instances preserved in the archives in which Muscogee women were not only present for political negotiations, but also exerted their power in ways that defied Euro-American men's willful ignorance. Despite the efforts of Euro-American men to wipe Muscogee women—and Indigenous women more generally—from the narrative, women were *always* present at the formal and informal conferences between their people and Euro-Americans, even if Euro-American men did not care to document them. Since women were the primary sources of kinship and community in the Muscogee world, they attended these meetings as representatives of their families and clans and to remind the *micos* of their obligations to their respective families and clans. In addition, Muscogee women were present at these formal and informal discussions to claim their family's and clan's share of the gifts that Euro-American diplomats distributed at each congress. For example, when the *mico* Escotchaby of Coweta ventured to St. Augustine and met with Spanish officials in December 1777, he made sure to bring "with him his ... Mother," who accepted the Spanish governor's gifts on behalf of her son. Or when the *mico* Chigelli met with British authorities in 1736 and again in 1753, he was accompanied by "Three Women of Note, among which Number is [his] Daughter" and remarked that Muscogee men always "brought our wives and our Children ... to have trade" and presents from Euro-Americans. In fact, it was one of the main responsibilities of the *micos* to ensure that their female relatives—and so, by proxy, all of their relatives—were liberally supplied with goods and presents from these diplomatic exchanges. Indeed, it got to the point that *micos* often complained to Euro-American officials that they needed to receive large "Presents ... for their Wives and Children at home," lest they risk provoking ill will among their family members. And while British, French, Spanish, and U.S. agents all grumbled about the "common Ceremonys" of distributing gifts to each and every Muscogee delegation, they nonetheless paid the "usual Compliments" in the hope of maintaining a good rapport with Muscogee peoples, because they recognized that if they did not appease Muscogee women, they risked alienating Muscogee peoples altogether.[11]

Muscogee women also acted in discretely political ways that Euro-Americans could not wholly ignore or erase from the archives. Whether it was influencing male decisions behind closed doors as family and clan representatives or working behind-the-scenes to ensure a favorable outcome in their peoples' negotiations with Euro-Americans, Muscogee women played politics as much as their male counterparts. Take, for instance, the case of the Gun Merchant of Okchai, an Upper Town *mico* who grew frustrated with British authorities in May 1757 and flashed what the British termed a "chagrine of Temper." When the Gun Merchant appeared the next day, he apologized and explained his "Temper" was the result of "some domestic Disturbances between him and his Wife." While the British likely took the Gun Merchant at his word (i.e., it was just a "domestic disturbance"), what the Gun Merchant left unsaid was the fact that his wife had confronted him in private about his actions during the negotiations with the British. We can imagine that she likely reminded him of his obligations to her family and clan and thereby steered the Gun Merchant's decisions accordingly. Similarly, at the Picolata congress in 1765, Escotchaby—a Lower Town *mico*—apologized to the British, with whom he had "Promise[d]" to meet, that he could not be at Picolata "because his Wife was sick." But once again, if we read between the lines of what Escotchaby told the British, he likely remained at home not because his wife was "Sick," but because she and her family demanded that he do so. Why? Because if we further contextualize the Picolata congress, we learn that Escotchaby's wife's family had "more to do in Land Affairs, than any other Indian[s] of the Lower Creek," and Picolata was where the British hoped to extend their boundary lines into Muscogee territories. In short, Escotchaby's wife and her family made it clear to the other *micos* who went to Picolata that any negotiations to cede Muscogee land was off the table.[12]

Muscogee women occasionally wielded their political will publicly. In the case of the *mico* Judd's Friend, his "Wife" traveled alone by canoe to Fort Loudon in November 1757, where she notified the British officer

Raymond Demere that "her Husband had been sick and had killed Nothing yet ... and desired me to send him [bags] of Powder, and two of Bulletts which I could not refuse him." That is, it was Judd's Friend's spouse who demanded powder and bullets on behalf of her family and clan, but framed it in a way to appease Demere's patriarchal sensibilities. Needless to say, Demere complied with her request. Meanwhile, when British authorities attempted to enlist the Muscogee to join the Seven Years' War in 1757 and promised a "Reward for Scalps," several *micos,* including the Wolf of Mucclasse, intimated to the British that "it is by no Means proper that such a Thing should take Air at present as such a Thing might breed a good Deal of Disturbance, *and particularly with the Women*, who would alledge that I force them by such Encouragement to a War." This incident says it all, for the Wolf himself was considered one of the "greatest Warriour[s] in the Nation," and here he deferred to female authority. In this case, Muscogee *micos* like the Wolf not only relented to female pressure, particularly when it came to grave matters such as going to war against a Euro-American power, but articulated as much to Euro-Americans in public, who likely wondered what was really going on behind the scenes. In all of these ways and more, then, Muscogee women consistently demonstrated their political savvy and influence within the Muscogee world and in their peoples' negotiations with Euro-Americans throughout the eighteenth century, despite all efforts by Euro-American men to sanitize such female politics and remove Muscogee women from the narrative altogether.[13]

Maybe we should not be so astounded, then, by the lengths to which Euro-American men went to silence Muscogee women—and Indigenous women more generally—in the eighteenth century, nor by how the consequences of those efforts continue to reverberate throughout North America today. As Indigenous scholars like Devon Mihesuah (Choctaw) have articulated time and again, colonialism, in all of its manifestations, "continues to affect Indigenous females in countless ways," and that includes the historical erasure that has facilitated—to this day—"sexual violence and abuse at the hands of Euro-Americans." Today's MMIWG movement and the violence to which this movement is dedicated to eradicating is a violence that is undeniably linked to the eighteenth-century past, when Euro-Americans attempted to silence Native female presence, voices, and narratives. In short, MMIWG is not simply an Indigenous female movement in response to the epidemic of sexual violence in the United States and Canada committed (predominately) by non-Native men, but a movement that privileges, embodies, and asserts Indigenous female voices and stories to counter their historical erasure.[14] Historical erasure in the past and sexual violence against Indigenous women today are invariably connected, as troubling and sickening as it should be for us, and we should not see or treat them as separate phenomena. Again, as Sarah Deer discusses in her work, sexual violence in Native America is an issue rooted in the past that has affected Native female bodies, voices, and histories for centuries. And while we can only scratch the surface of such gendered erasure and violence in the eighteenth century, it is our responsibility as historians to intervene and stop this colonial cycle of erasure and violence.[15]

To conclude, I urge other historians of the eighteenth century—and the seventeenth, nineteenth, twentieth, and twenty-first centuries for that matter—to be mindful, urgent, and more inquisitive when it comes to the historical erasure of Indigenous women in the past and present, and not to evade the unsettling connections between past and present. I am not only talking about doing so in our research, but also in our teaching. As each and every one of us encounters hundreds—if not thousands—of students in our classrooms, how do we teach about Native American peoples and histories; what narratives do we privilege in that teaching—the settler narrative of erasure and violence, or an Indigenous narrative?; and how often do we present our Indigenous brothers and sisters as living and thriving in the present, as opposed to just living and dying in the past? Do we connect the past to the present in meaningful ways for our students that peel back the layers of colonialism that have silenced and continue to do violence to Muscogee and other Native women today? In short, are we as scholars and teachers participating in the colonial project, or are we going to do better? In the words of the Sovereign Bodies Institute and the Brave Heart Society, who work with the "Women Warriors" and "Survivors" of sexual violence today, it is only by "reclaiming [the voices] about who we are as Indigenous women, [that] we reclaim our bodies and our strength" and remind everyone "of the life sustaining power of [Indigenous] women," as "women warriors guide [others] to safety" and always have. Ironically enough, Muscogee women themselves have spoken such truths since the eighteenth century, when they articulated to any settler who was willing to listen, that "when white men have come into our nation, they have never studied the good of the women. ... All they have hitherto done is to make our situation more wretched."[16] It is time then for those of us who are non-Native scholars to end this insidious colonial cycle, both in our research and in our teaching.

Notes

1. Last Will and Testament of George Galphin, 6 April 1776, 000051 .L 51008, South Carolina Department of Archives and History. For further information about Metawney specifically, see my *George Galphin's Intimate Empire: The Creek Indians, Family, and Empire in Early America* (Tuscaloosa: University of Alabama Press, 2019).

2. David Taitt to John Stuart, 21 September 1772, in *Early American Indian Documents*, ed. Aldan T. Vaughan, et al., 20 vols. (Bethesda: University Publications of America, 1979–2004), 12:115 ("Indian Wench"); David Taitt to John Stuart, 21 September 1772, Board of Trade and Secretaries of State: Indian Affairs, 1763–1784, Folder 74, National Archives ("Woman," "Wench"); Perdue, *Cherokee Women: Gender and Culture Change, 1700–1835* (Lincoln: University of Nebraska Press, 1999), 5.

3. The most extensive biography of Mary Musgrove (Bosomworth) is Steven C. Hahn, *The Life and Times of Mary Musgrove* (Gainesville: University Press of Florida, 2012).

4. According to the U.S. Department of Justice, the National Congress of American Indians, and the National Institute of Justice, Native American women experience the highest rates of sexual assault, violence, and rape in North America, between two to three times greater than the national average. "Office on Violence Against Women (OVW)," Department of Justice Archives, https://www.justice. gov/archives/ovw/blog/protecting-native-american-and-alaska-native-women-violence-november-native-american; "Policy Insights Brief—Statistics on Violence Against Native Women," National Congress of American Indians, http://www. ncai.org/resources/ncai_publications/policy-insights-brief-statistics-on-violence-against-native-women; Andre B. Rosay, "Violence Against American Indian and Alaska Native Women and Men," National Institute of Justice, https://www.nij.gov/journals/277/Pages/violence-against-american-indians-alaska-natives.aspx.

5. Deer, *The Beginning and End of Rape: Confronting Sexual Violence in Native America* (Minneapolis: University of Minnesota Press, 2015).

6. Amelia Rector Bell, "Separate People: Speaking of Creek Men and Women," *American Anthropologist* 92, no. 2 (1990): 335 ("life givers"); To the Head Men and Warriors of the Creek Nation, 17 June 1777, in *Early American Indian Documents*, 18:232 ("same Mother"); George Galphin to the Tallassee King and Creek Beloved Men at Silver Bluff, 7 November 1779, in George Galphin Letters, 1778–1780, Edward E. Ayer Manuscript Collections, Vault Box Ayer MS 313, Newberry Library ("Ground"); Bill Grantham, *Creation Myths and Legends of the Creek Indians* (Gainesville: University Press of Florida, 2002), 240–41 ("I am your Mother," "full of corn"), 242–53 (Corn Woman/Mother); Jessica Yirush Stern, *The Lives in Objects: Native Americans, British Colonists, and Cultures of Labor and Exchange in the Southeast* (Chapel Hill: University of North Carolina Press, 2017), 25 (Corn Woman/Mother).

7. Thomas Nairne, *Nairne's Muskhogean Journals: The 1708 Expedition to the Mississippi River*, ed. Alexander Moore (Jackson: University Press of Mississippi, 1988), 60–61 ("reckon," "Judgment"); Proceedings of the Colerain Conference, 22 June 1796, United States Congress, in *American State Papers*, class 2: *Indian Affairs*, 2 vols. (Buffalo: W.S. Hein Publishers, 1998), 2:601 (Sohonoketchee, "cousin," "duty"); Charles Hudson, *The Southeastern Indians* (Knoxville: University of Tennessee Press, 1976), 184–88 (matrilineal kinship); Kathryn E. Holland Braund, "Guardians of Tradition and Handmaidens to Change: Women's Roles in Creek Economic and Social Life during the Eighteenth Century," *American Indian Quarterly* 14, no. 3 (1990): 240 (matrilineal kinship).

8. Hudson, *Southeastern Indians*, 190, 213 (matrilineage), and 312–13 (economic ownership); Braund, "Guardians of Tradition and Handmaidens of Change," 241 (matrilineage); Robbie Ethridge, *Creek Country: The Creek Indians and Their World* (Chapel Hill: University of North Carolina Press, 2003), 74–76 (*huti*); Benjamin Hawkins, "A Sketch of the Creek Country in the Years 1798 and 1799," in *The Collected Works of Benjamin Hawkins*, ed. Thomas Foster (Tuscaloosa: University of Alabama Press, 2003), 74s ("property"); Joshua A. Piker, *Okfuskee: A Creek Indian Town in Colonial America* (Cambridge: Harvard University Press, 2006), 143 (economic ownership); Indian Nancy to Raymond Demere, 12 December 1756, in *Documents Relating to Indian Affairs, 1754–1765*, ed. William L. McDowell, Jr. (Columbia: South Carolina Department of Archives and History, 1970), 269 ("buy Corn"); Hawkins to unknown recipient, 15 December 1797, in "Letters of Benjamin Hawkins, 1796–1806," ed. Thomas Foster, *Collections of the Georgia Historical Society* 9 (1916), 38 ("extravagant").

9. Thomas Brown to the Earl of Cornwallis, 16 July 1780, in *Charles Cornwallis Papers*, PRO 30/11/2, British National Archives ("ripening"); Hudson, *The Southeastern Indians*, 200 (Busk), 366–68 ("social order," separation of sexes, female labors); Louis Leclerc Milfort, *Memoirs, or a Quick Glance at My Various Travels*, trans. Ben C. McCary (Savannah: Beehive Press, 1959), 135 (old corn, "quarrels"); Hawkins, "A Sketch of the Creek Country in the Years 1798 and 1799," 76s ("feast," dances); *William Bartram: Travels & Other Writings*, ed. Thomas P. Slaughter (New York: Library of America, 1996), 510 ("solemnity"); Piker, *Okfuskee*, 162 (new fire) and 177–78 (Busk); David H. Corkran, *The Creek Frontier, 1540–1783* (Norman: University of Oklahoma Press, 1967), 36–39 (Busk, "sacred square"); John R. Swanton, "The Green Corn Dance," *Chronicles of Oklahoma* 10, no. 2 (1932): 179–80 (Busk).

10. Michelle LeMaster, *Brothers Born of One Mother: British-Native American Relations in the Colonial Southeast* (Charlottesville: University of Virginia Press, 2012), 31 ("visibility," "key role"), 33–38; *William Bartram: Travels*, 450 ("never admitted"), 455 ("seldom"); Joseph Wright to Henry Ellis, 4 July 1758, in William Henry Lyttleton Papers, 1756–1760, Box 8: July–October 1758, William L. Clements Library ("dine"); Ethridge, *Creek Country*, 105 ("informal channels," "public opinion," "male kin"); 3 December 1797, "Letters of Benjamin Hawkins, 1796–1806," 23 ("furnished").

11. Declaration of Juan Josef Eligio de la Puente, 26–28 December 1777, in *Synopsis of Official Spanish Correspondence Pertaining to Relations with the Uchiz Indians, 1771–1783*, Part II: 1776–1779, ed. James Hill www.unf.edu/floridahistoryonline/Projects/uchize/index.html ("Mother"); Proceedings of the Council Concerning Indian Affairs, 4 June 1753, in *Documents Relating to Indian Affairs, May 21, 1750–August 7, 1754*, ed. William L. McDowell, Jr. (Columbia: South Carolina Department of Archives and History, 1958), 410 ("Daughter"); Thomas Causton to the Trustees, 16 January 1735, in *Early American Indian Documents*, 11:41 ("trade"); legislative notice, 20 March 1756, in *Colonial Records of the State of Georgia*, ed. Allen D. Candler, 32 vols. (Atlanta: Franklin-Turner Company, 1906), 7:286 ("Compliments"); Talks with Malatchi, 18–19 August 1749, in *Early American Indian Documents*, 11:187 ("Ceremonys").

12. Kathryn Braund, *Deerskins & Duffels: The Creek Indian Trade with Anglo-America, 1685–1815* (Lincoln: University of Nebraska Press, 2008), 23–24 (influence, behind closed doors); Daniel Pepper to Governor William Henry Lyttelton, 7 May 1757, in *Documents Relating to Indian Affairs, 1754–1765*, 372 ("domestic Disturbances"); Proceedings of the Picolata Congress, 21 January 1766, in Thomas Gage Papers, 1754–1807, American Series, vol. 19, William L. Clements Library ("Promise," "Sick"); John Stuart to James Grant, 15 March 1769, in *The Indian Frontier in British East Florida*, ed. James Hill http://www.unf.edu/floridahistoryonline/Projects/Grant/index.html ("Land Affairs").

13. Paul Demere to Governor William Henry Lyttelton, 24 November 1757, in *Documents Relating to Indian Affairs, 1754–1765*, 417 ("Wife," "Nothing yet"); Daniel Pepper to Governor William Henry Lyttelton, 7 April 1757, in *Documents Relating to Indian Affairs, 1754–1765*, 364 (Wolf, "Scalps," "Encouragement," "Warriour").

14. This is not to dismiss the violence that Muscogee and other Indigenous women face today in their own communities, but the numbers (at least those that are reported and recorded) demonstrate that non-Native violence against Native women accounts for an overwhelming majority of the reported cases, between 65–75%. See "Office on Violence Against Women"; "Violence Against Women," National Congress of American Indians, http://www.ncai.org/policy-issues/tribal-governance/public-safety-and-justice/violence-against-women; "Policy Insights Brief; and Rosay, "Violence Against American Indian and Alaska Native Women and Men."

15. Devon A. Mihesuah, *Indigenous American Women: Decolonization, Empowerment, Activism* (Lincoln: University of Nebraska Press, 2003), 41.

16. Sovereign Bodies Institute & Brave Heart Society, *Zuya Winyan Wicayu'onihan—Honoring Warrior Women*, 25 November 2019, https://www.facebook.com/SunrisePrayerWarriorsMMIW/; Samuel Mitchell, "The Progress of the Human Mind from Rudeness to Refinement," *American Monthly Magazine and Critical Review* (September 1818).

Gunpowder and Creek Diplomacy in the Pre-Revolutionary Native South

JENNIFER MONROE McCUTCHEN

In her recent work on *The Lives in Objects*, Jessica Yirush Stern explores the social, cultural, and diplomatic nature of exchange in the Native South. While Stern's study details numerous gifts and commodities, her investigation of guns and gunpowder is particularly intriguing. Stern suggests that because guns required gunpowder, ammunition, and a British gunsmith to maintain and repair them, they could never be truly owned by the Native men who possessed them.[1] Gunpowder and ammunition were required to make firearms operational, which meant they were useless without steady and reliable access to those associated goods. The Creek *mico*, or headman, Bob Captain, said as much in 1766, when chastising the hostile actions of his young warriors. Questioning what Creek men would do with their guns if the British cut off the supply of gunpowder and ammunition to their communities, Bob Captain suggested that the Creeks "throw them at our enemies, and we shall find they will do no more execution than a stick or stone."[2]

Stern's argument is certainly thought-provoking and it raises questions about the ways in which Native peoples regarded European goods in the eighteenth-century Southeast. It illuminates how access to highly valued commodities shaped Native societies, inviting scholars to reframe commodity studies through an ethnohistorical lens. This reorientation is important, as it emphasizes the cultural, as opposed to the economic, impact of exchange and allows us to better understand how certain goods could influence Indigenous socio-political structures and community-based relationships. But an analysis of gunpowder, rather than guns, proves more useful for this type of exploration. While Stern is correct that the use of firearms depended on steady and reliable access to gunpowder and ammunition, her claims about ownership can be challenged by the fact that Creek men learned the art of gunsmithing, as well as how to cast bullets and make gunflints, following the introduction of guns into their communities in the late seventeenth century. Though the use of firearms required skill and frequent upkeep, all Native men learned basic maintenance and often used a single gun throughout their entire lives. These weapons were passed down to subsequent generations, making them a permanent, heirloom good among the Creeks and their Indigenous neighbors.

For the majority of the eighteenth century, Creek men desired gunpowder more than any other foreign manufacture, including guns. While weapons could be repaired and reused, gunpowder "was an expendable and perishable commodity, which only Europeans could supply."[3] Gunpowder manufacture was an extremely difficult and complex process, requiring technological expertise, considerable financial backing, and high concentrations of charcoal, saltpeter, and sulphur.[4] It was impossible to produce large quantities of gunpowder in Britain's North American colonies due to a lack of essential ingredients and the empire's mercantilist economic structure.[5] Dependence on gunpowder, therefore, became a part of everyday life for all inhabitants of the late eighteenth-century Southeast, not just Native peoples. Though colonial settlers also needed ammunition for hunting and defense, British officials were often forced to prioritize the procurement of gunpowder for Creeks, who would have interpreted any restrictions on their supply as a declaration of war. British leaders relied upon gunpowder to strengthen their diplomacy with Indigenous people, even though steady and reliable access to this commodity allowed Creeks to act violently toward their own settlers.

As contact with Europeans became more frequent and familiar, new economic pressures forced Creek men to reevaluate their societal roles and obligations. While hunting continued to maintain certain elements of pre-contact ritual, economic motivations increasingly gained importance, eventually coming to drive the practice. Guns and gunpowder transformed the Creeks and their Indigenous neighbors into commercial hunters, and "a steady hand and plenty of shot became essential" for men who hoped to meet the average deerskin yield of one hundred pounds per year.[6] By the late eighteenth century, Creek men produced half of the entire deerskin supply in the Southeast, leading hunters to correlate legitimacy, authority, and masculine power with their ability to provide foreign goods to their families. The increasing encroachment of white settlers onto Native lands following the Seven Years' War encouraged young Creek men to associate mature manhood more directly with boldness and physical aggression. Access to gunpowder proved necessary for warriors, who were increasingly using violence to preserve their collective independence and to exert masculine authority. A single commodity, such as gunpowder, could influence the ways in which men secured legitimacy and validation and so, in turn, gained authoritative power. Authority was subjective and fluid, varying depending on town interests, community needs, the actions of individuals, and the accessibility of important foreign goods. For the Creek Confederacy, a society comprised of culturally and linguistically diverse political entities among whom "membership was not fixed, institutions were not regularized, power was not centralized, and procedures were not codified," the maintenance of authority, "the raw calculus of power," was constantly in progress.[7]

Moving beyond the established historiography of "Indians and guns," this essay explores the sociocultural impact of gunpowder on Native communities during the period between the end of the Seven Years' War and the beginning of the American Revolution.[8] It focuses on Native peoples who were recognized by Europeans as members of the Creek Confederacy, the most formidable and well-armed Indigenous group in the region.[9] It posits that gunpowder, particularly the ability to access it, shaped the ways in which Creeks navigated the changes that the end of the Seven Years' War brought to their families and communities in order to protect their existing beliefs and practices surrounding authority and power.[10] In separating gunpowder from the existing firearms narrative and using it as an independent vehicle for ethnohistorical investigation, scholars can consider not just the causes of Indigenous cultural change, but also how Native peoples both collectively and individually interpreted and shaped the world around them as they adapted to the cultural, economic, and sociopolitical shifts of the Pre-Revolutionary period. Placing Creeks at the center of the narrative allows for the deployment of ethnohistorical methodologies that facilitate a deeper exploration of how specific European goods shaped Indigenous culture. This approach allows scholars to understand the ways in which European commodities could provide Native peoples with opportunities to maintain both individual and collective autonomy as they navigated the geopolitical shifts brought about by the end of the Seven Years' War.

Within this framework, the dialogues and negotiations between individual Creek leaders and British officials take on new significance. Their conversations are indicative of the changing sociopolitical and geopolitical landscape of the Native South during the 1760s and 1770s, as well as the ability of Indigenous peoples to adapt and adjust to these shifts. This is particularly evident in discussions between Emistisiguo, a prominent Upper Creek headman from the town of Little Tallassee, and British officials like John Stuart, the Superintendent of Indian Affairs. Emistisiguo "owed his rise to power chiefly to his firm alliance with the British" and enjoyed a close relationship with Stuart throughout the 1760s and 1770s.[11] Emistisiguo used this connection to bolster his individual, community-based power through traditional means, and to relay the importance of maintaining influence over his own people.[12] In a May 1764 talk, Emistisiguo reminded Superintendent Stuart that he had previously been "promised Ammunition, and other Articles for the old people to distribute to the young people by their Elders, and to acquaint them the reason of these presents, to Establish a good understanding between the English and us."[13] But their failure to receive these supplies of gunpowder led to an uptick in violence, with younger Creeks stealing horses and pilfering goods from the traders. Emistisiguo told Stuart that he could not exert his proper influence without access to the necessary goods, which fueled additional appeals for gunpowder and ammunition. These younger Creeks' actions continued, however, and in 1765, Superintendent Stuart asked Emistisiguo if he would pressure his fellow *micos* to put a stop to the young Creeks' aggressive behavior. Emistisiguo responded by deflecting Stuart's request until the Superintendent could deliver "the rum and powder he promised us at the late Congress at Augusta, which we have Often Wished for."[14] Emistisiguo reminded Stuart "it will be necessary to give them some presents, in hopes to remedy that evil. If that does not produce the desired Effect, I am afraid it is incurable."[15] Stuart agreed, sending Emistisiguo gunpowder, ammunition, and rum, among other goods. Stuart remained cautiously optimistic that through this approach, "the old Men will see the Madness of their young Men and correct them in Time."[16]

Emistisiguo and his fellow Creek headmen had no desire to forcefully discipline the younger generations, however. While *micos* might have denounced ongoing Creek-settler violence, they did so in order to insist that gunpowder and ammunition needed to enter Creek communities through them, rather than through the flood of inexperienced traders who were by then a constant presence in their towns and villages.[17] When questioned about the violent or aggressive actions of their warriors, *micos* often maintained that they were powerless to regulate the actions of their people; all they could do was to try to influence their behavior. In January 1766, Governor Grant of East Florida voiced his frustration with the Lower Creek leader Cowkeeper for failing to force his young people to behave favorably toward neighboring settler populations. Grant's irritation with Cowkeeper only grew as the latter repeatedly brushed off British anxieties. On more than one occasion, Cowkeeper responded to British concerns regarding Creek aggression by plainly stating that he knew "nothing of what his young men do."[18] Gun Merchant, an Upper Creek *mico*, said as much to Stuart in 1771, when he expressed hope that he would "be supplied with Plenty of goods especially Ammunition and guns, as their Mad Young men will thereby be Convinced of the White people's Intentions to Hold fast the Chain of Friendship and be more Inclined to listen to my Friendly Talks and Advice."[19] Together, these remarks reveal that Creek elites centered their discussions and cross-cultural negotiations with settler officials on gunpowder throughout the 1760s and 1770s, understanding that these goods could both bolster their traditional authority and successfully combat threats to their individual and collective power.

Diplomatic negotiations regarding gunpowder also highlight the prioritizing of local influence among Creek elites. Eighteenth-century Creek governance was community-based, and the protection of the *micos'* local authority largely eclipsed their desire to gain farther-reaching influence on European terms. The Creek world "was a world of towns," a fluid social and political space that valued *talwa*, or village, interests. Though Europeans referred to these peoples as "Creeks" or as members of a "Creek Confederacy" and recognized that certain family or clan linkages connected them together, the Creeks were not yet a coherent group. The individuals noted in British sources as Creeks would not have thought of themselves as such. Instead they would have identified themselves as members of specific communities, such as Coweta, Abeika, or Okfuskee. In this sense, European-created tribal labels "often obscure more than they reveal," especially with regard to Indigenous autonomy and power.[20] Because the Creek Confederacy was still forming as a unified political entity in the 1760s and 1770s, gunpowder reshaped the meaning of leadership while these developments were in flux.[21]

The persistence of diplomacy based on the (often diverging) interests of specific towns created space for Creeks to identify British weaknesses and use them to their advantage following the Seven Years' War. The protection of local priorities mimicked the Creeks' neutrality policy of earlier decades and provided openings through which the *micos* could directly replicate the European competition they had previously found so beneficial. Creek headmen adjusted their traditional playing-one-off-against-the-others strategy by forcing the British to balance the needs of separate Creek towns, factions, clans, and coalitions, thereby allowing individual *micos* to act in ways that would promote their personal influence and benefit their own townspeople. Emistisiguo, for example, often leaned into his advantageous relationship with Superintendent Stuart in order to achieve his goals. He welcomed British settlement at Pensacola and Mobile in 1764 by proclaiming that the French and Spanish "were the people who told Lies of the English to his Nation … and that as those Nations are now removed there would be no obstacles in the way to keep peace and quietness with the English and his Nation." He further expressed his "sincere desire … that a Strict Friendship should subsist between his Nation and the English," noting that this connection would bring gunpowder and ammunition closer to his people.[22] Emistisiguo's position was at odds with those of many Lower Creeks, especially those from the town of Coweta, who viewed Britain's movement into East and West Florida as a threat. Cowetas worked to shore up their security with additional diplomacy, maintaining connections with the Spanish by traveling to Cuba to procure gunpowder, ammunition, and other goods.[23] But divergent political and diplomatic interests ran deeper than the Upper and Lower divisions, with *micos* from neighboring towns often disagreeing with one another regarding the expansion of British influence in the region. The Wolf King, a headman from the Upper Creek town of Muccolossus, did not share Emistisiguo's enthusiasm regarding the British occupation of West Florida, blaming their settlement for a surge in violence among his people. As young men from Muccolossus and other Upper Creek towns traveled to Pensacola for supplies, they often encountered deceitful traders who used alcohol, intimidation, and force in their attempts to swindle Creek parties of their deerskins and other goods. But both sides instigated violence on the trade paths, which was exacerbated when gunpowder was in short supply. Following a series of recent Creek-initiated attacks, the Wolf King advised colonial and military officials to reject the demands of any non-elite Creek who arrived at Pensacola looking for goods. He argued instead that it would be more convenient for the headmen to receive gunpowder and ammunition directly in exchange for deerskins. This would "prevent the young people coming over here to trouble this place," but would also allow highly sought-after goods to enter Creek communities through the headmen, protecting their community-based authority and influence.[24]

It was not uncommon, however, for a *mico*'s affinity to shift or for a headman to feign interest in another European trade partner, particularly if gunpowder and ammunition were involved. In 1773, Emistisiguo informed Stuart that the Spanish, who had been meeting with groups of Cowetas in Havana, expressed interest in supplying his people in Little Tallassee with goods as well. "If they want to supply us," he told Stuart, "we want to have nothing to say to them, [but] If the Spaniards intend to send us anything I will accept nothing less than Six large Ships Loaded with Ammunition."[25] While Emistisiguo's expectation was unrealistic, his statement shows that even pro-British *micos* were not opposed to keeping their options open in the event that new allies might provide access to gunpowder and support their ambitions and goals. Proclamations such as this not only reminded the British of their weak position in the region, but also forced them to contemplate the sociopolitical implications of gunpowder and other goods entering Creek communities.

These strategies continued to serve Creeks well during the American Revolution, allowing them to play Rebel and Loyalist groups off of one another in a continuation of the competition between foreign powers from which they had benefited earlier in the eighteenth century. While some headmen chose to officially declare neutrality, the preservation of local sociopolitical practices allowed individual *micos*, towns, and villages to determine which side, if any, they would support. Stuart's strong relationship with Emistisiguo and his fellow *mico*, the Second Man, tilted Little Tallassee and a number of other Upper Creek towns in favor of the Loyalists.[26] Many Lower Creek communities, by contrast, actively worked to distance themselves from Stuart and British policies more generally. The Cowetas' continued contact with the Spanish, along with long-standing personal relationships with Rebel sympathizers Jonathan Bryan and George Galphin, pushed them and other Lower Creek towns toward either neutrality or the revolutionary cause.[27] These practices safeguarded community-based diplomacy and decision-making processes while guaranteeing that Creek headmen could determine the terms on which they would negotiate with those who were trying to secure their allegiance.

As the rebellion took shape, *micos* across the Creek Confederacy successfully manipulated both sides to secure a steady supply of trade goods that included gunpowder and ammunition. Discussions of gunpowder heavily influenced cross-cultural dealings during this period, as Rebels, Loyalists, and Natives each used the commodity to achieve their own goals. In September of 1775, Sempoyaffee of Coweta and a number of Lower Creek headmen, including Blue Salt of Cusseta, the Pumpkin King of Hitchiti, and a Chehaw headman named Long Warrior, sent a talk to Superintendent Stuart. "We hear there is some difference between the white people," Sempoyaffee began, "and we are all sorry to hear it." But the Rebels, he continued, "have sent us a handfull of powder and lead, and now we see your good talk and send us word to come down [to St. Augustine] and get more." Though the *micos* welcomed gifts of gunpowder and ammunition from both sides, they expressed their desire to remain "in friendship with all white men." "We all see now your talk is good," they informed Stuart, "and the talk from the beloved men from Georgia is the same. We like them both very well, and are not desired to Join any one party."[28] With this declaration of neutrality, Lower Creek leaders confirmed what Stuart and other colonial officials already knew: a decade of significant effort and expense had failed to establish British superiority in the region, rendering the Crown unable to assert control over the Creeks and their neighbors.

Emistisiguo had sent a similar talk to Stuart a few weeks earlier. Like his counterparts in the Lower towns, Emistisiguo's desire for peace amongst the colonial populations was directly connected to gunpowder supplies. The British, he said, had long agreed to support the Creeks with ammunition, and as "The great King Ordered the ships allways to come over with a Supply for us, we do not know the reason why they should now be hindered." While Emistisiguo was glad to hear that Stuart had secured some gunpowder and ammunition for his people, he expressed frustration that they would have to travel hundreds of miles from Little Tallassee to St. Augustine to retrieve it. Emistisiguo then informed Stuart that the long journey to St. Augustine for a "handful" of powder would not be feasible. "You must Consider," he concluded, "we are not a small people but many in Number and the Quantity of Ammunition will be too little."[29] Emistisiguo correctly understood that if the Revolution intensified, Indigenous access to gunpowder and ammunition would be severely compromised. While Emistisiguo's decision to snub Stuart's offer may appear impulsive and somewhat irresponsible, from the Creek perspective, this choice was strategically wise. By rejecting what he perceived to be a paltry gift of gunpowder, Emistisiguo reminded Stuart and other Loyalists that an alliance with his people was not a guarantee and that the Creeks were not as dependent on British gunpowder and ammunition as colonial officials tried to make them out to be. In making this point, Emistisiguo provided an Upper Creek counterbalance to the actions of the Cowetas and other Lower Creeks. Emistisiguo's approach supported larger Creek efforts to maintain a position of authority in cross-cultural diplomacy, often forcing Loyalists and Rebels to acquiesce to the demands of individual Native leaders.

The years following 1763 brought intense sociopolitical and cultural change to the Southeast, to which Indigenous peoples adapted in a variety of ways. While these adjustments altered Creek daily life, they also complicated ideas about legitimacy, authority, and power. Creek dialogues highlight how power and influence were shaped by access to European goods and reveal varying Native views on British expansion. The perspectives of these headmen encourage new questions about the negotiations and actions that went into accessing important commodities after the Seven Years' War, inviting ethnohistorians to analyze how certain goods, such as gunpowder, could shape Indigenous socio-political structures and community-based relationships.

Scholars have long ignored gunpowder and its significance within the larger historical frameworks of Native-European exchange. They have routinely conflated firearms and gunpowder within examinations of the impact of guns on Native life and, in so doing, have overlooked the specific role of gunpowder in Indigenous societies and cultures. Isolating gunpowder from the existing discussions of firearms is important because of its unique position as an exhaustible, but necessary commodity accessible only through trade and diplomacy with Europeans. By focusing on the actions of Creek *micos*, we can see how gunpowder played an important role in Indigenous adaptation and adjustment following the geopolitical shifts of 1763. Consequently, attention to gunpowder highlights the continued prioritization of local power within the Native South after 1763, despite the changes brought to Creek diplomacy by the ejection of the French and the Spanish from the region.

Placing Native peoples at the center of the narrative allows us to move away from historical interpretations that emphasize Indigenous dependence and cultural declension. Instead of undermining Creek agency, this approach challenges traditional perceptions of how cross-cultural diplomacy was conducted in the Pre-Revolutionary Native South, illuminating the ways in which European goods could provide the Creeks and their neighbors with opportunities to maintain both individual and collective autonomy. Given gunpowder's significance to the maintenance of Creek diplomacy, it is important that its role in preserving Indigenous power and independence be fully recognized.

Notes

1. Stern, *The Lives in Objects: Native Americans, British Colonists, and Cultures of Labor and Exchange in the Southeast* (Chapel Hill: University of North Carolina Press, 2017), 105.

2. "Tallapoosa Chiefs to Governor Johnstone, Reporting Execution of the Murderer of Goodwin and Davies," in *Georgia and Florida Treaties, 1763–1776*, Vol. 12 of *Early American Indian Documents*, ed. John T. Juricek (Bethesda: University Publications of America, 2002), 314.

3. Armstrong Starkey, *European and Native American Warfare, 1675–1815* (Norman: University of Oklahoma Press, 1998), 23.

4. For a detailed analysis of the creation of gunpowder, see David Cressy, *Saltpeter: The Mother of Gunpowder* (New York: Oxford University Press, 2012).

5. This system guaranteed that the English (and later the British) retained as much control over trade as possible, while simultaneously ensuring that the nation remained focused on exports, rather than imports. England/Britain sought to develop an empire of commerce, envisioning that wealth and raw materials would flow from the margins of the colonial world to the mother country for production. Manufactured goods would subsequently return to the colonies for sale or trade, thereby ensuring that all profits from the economic enterprise remained within the empire. Thus, in order to increase production and consumption, it was imperative that England/Britain settle as many colonies as possible; this would ensure the metropole both a steady supply of raw materials and a continuous increase in the number of guaranteed consumers for its manufactured goods. See Joyce Appleby, *Economic Thought and Ideology in Seventeenth-Century England* (Princeton: Princeton University Press, 1978).

6. Kathryn E. Holland Braund, *Deerskins & Duffels: The Creek Indian Trade with Anglo America, 1685–1815* (Lincoln: University of Nebraska Press, 1993), 66. Braund notes that "a very conservative estimate ... would place Creek production at an average of 100 pounds of deerskin per year per gunman for trade (about 50 deer per man, assuming each skin weighed 2 pounds). Doubtless those with more skill or luck would produce more, whereas others would do worse" (70–71).

7. Steven J. Peach, "Creek Indian Globetrotter: Tomochichi's Trans-Atlantic Quest for Traditional Power in the Colonial Southeast," *Ethnohistory* 60, no. 4 (2013): 9.

8. Numerous scholarly books have explored the relationship between Southeastern Native peoples and guns. Early work, like Richard White's *The Roots of Dependency: Subsistence, Environment, and Social Change among the Choctaws, Pawnees, and Navajos* (Lincoln: University of Nebraska Press, 1983), analyzed this topic as a matter of dependence, arguing that as the Choctaw became more integrated into the global market economy, their desire for European goods, especially guns, forced them to deplete their own natural resources. In *Deerskins & Duffels,* Braund explores how guns transformed and commercialized Creek hunting practices, but argues that, despite these changes, other aspects of Creek social and cultural life successfully endured. Braund's analysis illuminates how firearms did not automatically trigger declension, but rather provided Creeks with opportunities for cultural growth. In a sweeping overview of North American Indian history from first contact through the nineteenth century, David J. Silverman's *Thundersticks: Firearms and the Violent Transformation of Native America* (Cambridge: Harvard University Press, 2016) details how Indigenous peoples became fully aware of guns' potential to provide them with military and political power over other Native groups. He argues that following the introduction of guns to Native peoples, Indigenous arms races spread across the continent, escalating intertribal warfare and solidifying the significance of European technology in the Native American world.

9. Verner W. Crane, *The Southern Frontier, 1670–1732* (Tuscaloosa: University of Alabama Press, 1928), 184.

10. In the period before 1763, the Creek Confederacy's diplomatic policy of neutrality had allowed *micos* to play the British, French, and Spanish off of one

another in order to maintain access to multiple sources of foreign goods without committing to a strict alliance with any. But the end of the Seven Years' War ushered in a new era of diplomacy in the North American Southeast. The Treaty of Paris removed the French from the region and relegated the Spanish to New Orleans. Upper and Lower Creeks now found themselves forced to adapt to a new reality, limited to one European trade partner when they had previously benefited from relations with all three.

11. J. Russell Snapp, "Emistisiguo," in *Colonial Wars of North America, 1512–1763*, ed. Alan Gallay (New York: Routledge, 1996), 192.

12. Joshua A. Piker, "'White & Clean' & Contested: Creek Towns and Trading Paths in the Aftermath of the Seven Years' War," *Ethnohistory* 50, no. 2 (2003): 317.

13. "Upper Creek 'Great Talk' to Superintendent Stuart and Governor Wright," in *Georgia and Florida Treaties*, 213.

14. "Stuart and Wedderhorn to Indian Chiefs," in *Mississippi Provincial Archives, 1763–1766: English Dominion*, ed. Dunbar Rowland (Nashville: Brandon Printing Company, 1911), 201.

15. "Stuart and Wedderhorn," in *Mississippi Provincial Archives*, 201.

16. "Colonel Tayler's Talk to the Indians," in *Mississippi Provincial Archives*, 518.

17. Beginning in 1764, the British empire sought to implement changes that would regulate the Indian trade. Under their "Plan of 1764," any individual who wanted to trade with Native peoples could do so as long as they obtained a license from their colony. There was no official restriction on where they could trade, but the lack of restrictions and the widespread availability of permits rendered the trade less centralized. With nearly any colonist now free to trade away from the oversight of colonial officials, traditional methods of European-Indigenous exchange crumbled, negatively affecting relations between the British empire and the Creeks.

18. "Grant to Conway," R1; F289–290, James Grant Papers, David Library of the American Revolution.

19. "Upper Creek Headmen to Superintendent Stuart, Declaring Issue of Oconee Murders Settled and Complaining of Encroachments," in *Georgia and Florida Treaties*, 98.

20. Piker, "'White & Clean' & Contested," 332.

21. Because of the fluid nature of the Creek Confederacy, exact numbers of Creek towns and villages vary in the historiography. Joshua Piker estimates that fifty-six towns and villages made up the Creek Confederacy in 1763, whereas Robbie Ethridge puts the number closer to seventy-three (see Piker, *Okfuskee: A Creek Indian Town in Colonial America* [Cambridge: Harvard University Press, 2004], 6; Ethridge, *Creek Country: The Creek Indians and their World* [Chapel Hill: University of North Carolina Press, 2003], 31). Given the ephemeral nature of Creek life, both numbers could be correct. I have chosen to approximate the number of villages at fifty-nine, based on a report made by Francis Ogilvie, Interim Governor of West Florida from 1763 to 1764. Ogilvie noted fifty-nine Upper and Lower towns and 3,603 Creek "gun men" in the entire confederacy (Ogilvie, "A List of Towns and Number of Gun Men in the Creek Nation," in Thomas Gage Papers, 1754–1807, American Series, vol. 21, William L. Clements Library, University of Michigan).

22. "Emistisiguo and Other Headmen to Superintendent Stuart," in *Georgia and Florida Treaties*, 216.

23. See my "'More Advantageous to be with Spaniards': Gunpowder and Creek-Spanish Encounters in Cuba, 1763–1783," *Terrae Incognitae: The Journal of the Society for the History of Discoveries* 52, no. 3 (2020): 245–60.

24. "Captain Robert MacKinnen's Conference With, and 'Grant' From, The Wolf King and Other Tallapoosa Headmen," in *Georgia and Florida Treaties*, 219.

25. "Emistisiguo to Superintendent Stuart, Reporting Spanish Overtures via Lower Creeks," in *Georgia and Florida Treaties*, 121.

26. The Upper Creek towns were more conservative than their Lower counterparts, with most headmen favoring cautious, controlled interactions with the British. See David Corkran, *The Creek Frontier, 1540–1783* (Norman: University of Oklahoma Press, 1967), 269.

27. "Devolution and Revolution," in *Georgia and Florida Treaties*, 129.

28. "Lower Creek Reply to Superintendent Stuart, Declaring Neutrality," in *Georgia and Florida Treaties,* 177.

29. "Emistisiguo's Reply to Superintendent Stuart's Talk of August 15," in *Georgia and Florida Treaties,* 174–75.

Beauty, Voice, and Wit: Learning Courtship and Sex through Song in Early Eighteenth-Century England

ALISON DESIMONE

Nestled within John Walsh's *A Collection of the Choicest Songs & Dialogues* (1703) is a song by John Barrett describing the alluring Celinda. She performs for Cupid, who sits as judge to determine which of her charms is her most captivating feature:

> Celinda's Beauty Voice and witt for Cupids Empire vied,
> Who Thirsis chose, as Judge to sitt the Contest to Decide.
> And all the while stood Smiling by,
> To see that Doubtfull Chance
> Careless which got the Victory
> Since all his Pow'r advance.
> Thirsis Examining every Grace,
> No judgment could declare,
> So equally each Charm took Place,
> In finishing the fair.
> But whilst he Gazes, flames of Love surround the wondering Boy,
> His doubts as fatall to him prove, as Paris Judgment did to Troy.[1]

As pastoral characters, Celinda and Thirsis represent an archetypal heterosexual relationship for early eighteenth-century audiences. Cupid and Thirsis judge Celinda's charms: her beauty, her voice, and her wit compete for Thirsis's affections. Initially, it is Thirsis who holds the power; he has chosen the god Cupid to preside over the competition, as he stands silently by. Yet the balance of power shifts to Celinda by the end of the song; Thirsis succumbs to Celinda's charms, and the song ends with a terse warning: misjudging a woman may instigate a metaphorical Trojan War.

This song, and many others like it that were published in songbook miscellanies of the early eighteenth century, offered audiences something more than entertainment.[2] Songs that circulated in printed songbooks provided a means of learning about love in all of its forms. Love songs covered a wide range of subjects with advice that a man or woman could follow through the various stages of courtship. Those who purchased songbooks, and who sang and studied the lyrics of these works, could discover the best qualities in a husband or a wife. Songs revealed to young women how to use their charms to entice men; but others advised those same women to be chaste and obedient wives. As in Barrett's "Celinda's Beauty," warnings about lovesickness and heartache abounded for young men singing these pieces, cautioning them to spurn temptation. For both sexes, erotic and bawdy lyrics offered pornographic fantasies that could be indulged in the mind, as a means of increasing physical desire for the opposite sex. By purchasing and performing songs, Englishmen and Englishwomen learned ways of engaging with each other across a variety of romantic contexts.

The diversity of types of love songs published in the early eighteenth century reflected a contemporary transformation in how the English thought about and practiced courtship. The eighteenth century saw a reinforcement of supposedly "traditional gender roles" in marriage, with a focus on female subservience to male partners.[3] Conduct books, especially for women, reinforced these patriarchal attitudes by equating love with obedience and by describing the qualities a woman must possess in order to ensure a successful marriage.[4] Yet, the early eighteenth century also saw the continued circulation of explicit literary material devoted to sexual pleasure. Both men and women sought out advice on sexual activity from many different types of sources.[5] As Tim Hitchcock has argued, "discourses around sex in general became … more widely distributed, more explicit, and more modern" in this period, with growing emphasis on sexual activity beyond intercourse.[6] These disparate approaches to relationships between the sexes played out across the lyrics of love songs published in songbook miscellanies. As works for mostly private consumption in the home, love songs provided a secure outlet for exploration and engagement with topics that would have been inappropriate for mixed company. Through the printed song, young men and women could learn, safely, proper approaches to courtship and sexual relationships.

This essay explores the ways in which love songs provided an alternative means of learning about courtship and sex through musical performance. Recently, scholars of eighteenth- and nineteenth-century music have been reconstructing the ways in which both men and woman used domestic performance as a means of teaching themselves about political, social, and religious subjects.[7] Active performance of a song required more than just superficial engagement with lyrics or a melody. Often, a performer had to learn the notes, be able to sing the lyrics and play an accompaniment at the same time, and even determine where to place the lyrics within the melody for songs that had multiple stanzas (the lyrics were usually printed below the music itself).[8] As Julia Hamilton notes, this process "would have entailed spending time working through the lyrics," thereby ensuring a deeper understanding of the lessons imparted by the song texts.[9] Moreover, many songs in miscellanies had origins in the theater: publishers, such as John Walsh, reprinted theatrical songs from the engraving plates used in their initial publication, making the compilation of a songbook miscellany quick, easy, and in some cases cheaper than engraving new songs from scratch.[10] This meant even further engagement with the song's text, because the domestic performer may have been familiar with the piece from its original performance on stage.[11] In some cases, singing the lyrics may have brought to mind the plot of the play, or the character who performed the song; this aural recollection could have spurred further meditation on the lessons conveyed by the text.[12]

Songbook miscellanies were also expensive luxury items; if a family purchased one for their home, it most likely did not sit on the shelf gathering dust. David Hunter has shown that most songbooks retailed for 12*s* to 15*s* each.[13] If we follow Robert Hume's work on eighteenth-century income and purchasing power, such prices would make these books some of the more expensive on the market and thus available, at least through purchase, only to a small slice of Britain's population during the early eighteenth century.[14] Subscribers' lists for miscellanies from the 1720s make it clear that those most committed to purchasing them were typically titled aristocrats or members of the professional class (especially lawyers, scholars, and musicians).[15] Despite the expense, however, these songbooks were a long-term investment that provided a wide variety of music on many subjects. By owning one, a purchaser had access to a song for every occasion, including music lessons, private meditation, and social events in the home.

Most conduct books and at least some pornographic materials were cheaper than songbook miscellanies. Conduct books often reinforced "complementary" social roles, whereby men and women each cultivated a specific set of ideal behaviors as a means of attracting a husband or a wife.[16] Erotic or pornographic literature could similarly instruct, especially with regard to sexual activity (useful to both sexes before marriage). However, it also provided an outlet for inappropriate or illegal sexual fantasies, such as sexual assault or rape, and so ideally served to deter readers from actually committing those crimes.[17] Overall, these literary sources offered a more limited range of subject matter and a potentially less engaging, or more easily ignored, approach than the active performance of songs. Love songs covered the full gamut of what was to be found in conduct books and pornography, from courtship and marriage to explicit erotica. These songs reflected the tension between the possibility of sexual liberty and the behavioral rules and limitations placed on each sex—both sides of courtship that Englishmen and Englishwomen needed to learn and navigate successfully.

Teaching Courtship in Early Eighteenth-Century England

If a man or a woman wanted to learn about courtship—which is to say, any of the social, physical, or emotional aspects of engaging intimately with a prospective partner—they could turn to numerous literary sources published in the eighteenth century. Courtship was a necessary stage in a relationship, as it offered the only opportunity to determine the suitability of a partner before committing to them for life.[18] As Amanda Vickery notes, the elite were more likely to make arrangements they thought suitable for their sons and daughters, while members of the professional and propertied middling sort had more personal choice when deciding on partners.[19] Nevertheless, all were looking for "a good match [to satisfy] a range of criteria, including family advancement, the ideal of parity, character, and affection."[20] Early eighteenth-century authors such as Joseph Addison and Richard Steele openly advocated for a kind of courtship that built a foundation for friendship in marriage: "Those marriages generally abound most with love and constancy that are preceded by a long courtship. The passion should strike root and gather strength before marriage be grafted onto it."[21] To Addison, a "long courtship" of mutual affection and declaration would ultimately ensure a long-lasting marriage. In this way of thinking, courtship was an essential process to master; men and women had to learn the proper language and behavior to adopt in pursuit of a partner, which created a market for manuals that could advise on the process.

Conduct books flourished long before the eighteenth century, but achieved new prominence as attitudes towards marriage and sex shifted in the early 1700s.[22] These publications were often written by men to instruct an audience of women in an idealized version of womanhood. Ingrid Tague has argued that these books aimed to control the performance of femininity by encouraging women to cultivate specific qualities that would attract a good husband.[23] Conduct books described "a particularly unambiguous and ... increasingly dominant definition of femininity as docile [and] domestic."[24] Instead of promoting female emotional, financial, and sexual independence, conduct books transformed "subjection itself into a benefit"; the ideal woman avoided the "unnatural" state of public prominence.[25] While the audience for these books would have been young ladies on the cusp of marriageable age, it is likely that their mothers were the principal purchasers of these books for their daughters.[26] Conduct books would have been found in the libraries of middling and elite families; as Tague has argued, these sources are replete with admonishments to avoid both luxury activities, such as attending plays and operas, and behavior commonly gendered as feminine, such as engaging in gossip.[27] These books documented and offered advice on the ideal mode of conduct for women to follow, first in courtship and later in marriage, where properly behaving women could serve as models for their own daughters.[28]

While there are far too many conduct books to discuss here, the most popular examples offered similar descriptions of the ideal early eighteenth-century Englishwoman. Often, the subjects covered appear on the title pages of these sources, providing instruction even before the text itself had begun to be read. Take, for example, the title of the popular *The Whole Duty of a Woman: or, A Guide to the Female Sex, From the Age of Sixteen to Sixty, &c. Being Directions, How Woman of all Qualities and Conditions ought to Behave themselves in the various Circumstances of this Life, for their obtaining not only Present, but future Happiness.* The title is further enhanced by a thorough description of the contents of the book:

I. Directions how to obtain the Divine and Moral Vertues of *Piety, Meekness, Modesty, Chastity, Humility, Compassion, Temperance*, and *Affability*, with their Advantages; and how to avoid the opposite Vices.

II. The Duty of *Virgins*, directing them what they ought to do, and what to avoid, for gaining all the Accomplishments required in that State. With the whole art of Love.

III. The whole Duty of a Wife.

IV. The whole Duty of a Widow, &c.
Also choice Receipts in Physick and Chyrurgery. With the whole Art of Cookery, Preserving, Candying, Beautifying, &c.[29]

Here, the author lists the ideal qualities for which eighteenth-century women ought to strive. Other conduct books contain similar descriptions of proper female behavior. *The Young Ladies Conduct: or, Rules for Education* includes chapters on subjects such as "Of Temperance, Chastity, Industry, &c." and "Of Modesty and Chastity," thereby highlighting female comportment as something that required self-discipline, restraint, and humility.[30] Many conduct books approach the topic of female behavior from a distinctly Christian perspective. *The Virgin's Nosegay* directs women to cultivate virtues such as "fear of God, love of God, presence of God, piety, discretion, prayer, and austerity."[31] Throughout the eighteenth century, conduct books presented modesty—both before and after marriage—as the most desirable quality in a woman: "Modesty should not altogether be defaced, or laid aside in the Marriage State, but rather strengthen'd and improv'd, by a more solid Conduct and Management, to make it appear Awful and Becoming."[32] Books offering women advice on appropriate behavior and temperament abounded in the eighteenth century; even men could read these works to learn what virtuous qualities they should look for during the process of courtship.

Although conduct books promoted a certain type of genteel and sensible behavior, their prescriptions often diverged from actual social practice. Amanda Vickery argues that what was advocated for public behavior— the chaste obedience of a wife to her husband—became a more mutually balanced relationship in the privacy of the household, where women could assert themselves with more (although not total) equality.[33] Chris Roulston similarly acknowledges that "advice literature ... was not so much reflecting material reality as attempting to create an alternative, idealized domestic realm," which nevertheless still conveyed a set of "ideological parameters" to its readers, whether or not the advice was followed.[34] Read individually, conduct books offered the potential of an ideal world in which relationships between men and women were solidly defined. Read one after another, however, it becomes clear that creating this ideal space in practice was subject to debate, reflecting contemporary anxieties over how best to instruct readers who did not always follow the advice they were getting.[35]

Erotic or pornographic books, on the other hand, were a subversive type of reading, one suitable for private consumption and enjoyment, rather than public display of one's adherence to an ideal. Patricia Crawford contends that men and women probably sought out explicit literature for different purposes: women needed to learn about the aspects of sexual intercourse that would lead to successful reproduction, while books aimed at men gave titillating advice and stoked their sexual fantasies.[36] The market for these resources emerged simultaneously with an apparent increase in sexual activity beyond intercourse; Tim Hitchcock argues that the seventeenth and eighteenth centuries saw a proliferation in other kinds of sexual activity, including oral sex and foreplay.[37] Erotic literature, like conduct books, came in a variety of genres; by the mid-eighteenth century, men and women could purchase and read explicit poetry and novels and could engage with obscene visual images.[38] The most famous of these novels—and the first explicitly pornographic one in the English language—was John Cleland's *Memoirs of a Woman of Pleasure* (also known as *Fanny Hill*), published in 1748–49. Appearing as a counterpoint to pious moralism (including that of conduct books), *Memoirs of a Woman of Pleasure* offered its readers a fantasy of escape to a world in which sexual pleasure was not only desirable, but necessary and natural.[39] Yet most pornography focused less on explicit descriptions of sexual organs and acts and more on the workings of male desire.[40] Eighteenth-century obscene books and periodicals aimed both to stimulate their readers and to educate them in the mysteries of sexual behavior, respectable and otherwise.[41]

Although the literary marketplace offered a diverse array of advice on conduct and sexual behavior for both men and women, books and periodicals were not the only sources from which readers could get the information they sought on aspects of courtship and intimacy. Vocal music also offered the opportunity to consume advice in short, accessible, and memorable bits designed for private performance in one's own home, or sometimes communal spaces amidst company.[42] While purchasing single-sided sheet music was easier and cheaper than buying book after book, miscellanies of songs found an audience in the eighteenth century, and those who could afford them often purchased them. Because of the sheer number of songs they contained, songbook miscellanies offered good (and long-lasting) value, despite their initial price tag. As will be shown, songs had the flexibility to cover a wide range of topics pertaining to love, sex, and gendered behavior. Many songs included pornographic or erotic content, but others reflected on the difficulties of courtship, the emotional toll of heartbreak, and the pleasures and pains of marriage. In performance, men and women had the opportunity not only to sing lyrics, but also to reflect on them deeply and to choose which song(s) would be the most appropriate at any given stage in their personal lives.

Becoming and Courting a Partner through Song

Let us imagine how a young woman might have used a songbook miscellany in early eighteenth-century England. She is fifteen and from a well-to-do family; her father purchased John Walsh's *A Collection of the Choicest Songs & Dialogues* for 15*s* so that she could practice her keyboard skills and entertain the family or any suitors who might come calling. She thumbs through the collection, which includes over two hundred songs; it is organized alphabetically, rather than by theme or level of difficulty, so she must carefully read the lyrics and consider the melody of the song she chooses to sing. She settles on a love song by Richard Courteville, "A lass there lives upon the Green," on pages 18 and 19. There are three sections of text, and the song is in A major—a key that fits well with her light soprano voice. The melody is difficult; she will have to practice it many times to master the long runs of sixteenth notes that punctuate the vocal texture, but if she can successfully navigate through the serpentine melismas, she knows she will impress anyone who hears her.

Our hypothetical young lady is also drawn to the song because of the quality of its lyrics. The song approaches love from the male perspective; a swain sings of the beauty of an unnamed woman, focusing on her alluring qualities:

> A lass there lives upon the Green,
> Cou'd I her Picture draw;
> A brighter Nymph was never seen;
> That looks and reigns a little Queen
> That keeps ye Swains in awe.
>
> Her Eyes are Cupids Darts, & Wings,
> Her Eye brows are his Bow,
> Her silken Hair the Silver strings,
> That sure and swift destruction brings
> To all the vale below.
>
> If Pastorella's dawning light
> Can warm and wound us so,
> Her Noon will shine so Piercing bright,
> Each glancing Beam will kill out right,
> And every Swain subdue.[43]

From a scholarly perspective, musicologists may read Courteville's use of a highly decorated melody as a musical metaphor for the woman's beauty. But from our young lady's perspective, the lyrics have other enjoyable qualities. The woman described by the swain seems physically enticing and she easily holds the attention of others. For our young lady, these are qualities to cultivate as she begins to entertain male admirers of her own; she must also "keep ye Swains in awe" by singing and playing with ease, attending to her physical mien, and perfecting other aspects of her personality that will demonstrate her potential as a wife. This speculative sojourn into a young lady's experience singing from a songbook miscellany shows that the use of these songs required careful attention and consideration to both the lyrics and the melody; those who learned these pieces did so deliberately, likely gaining a deep understanding of the lessons imparted by their texts.

These songs allowed men and women to learn the vagaries and vocabularies of courtship. As Amanda Vickery explains, the process of courting or being courted came with a prescribed set of behavioral rules for romance. Men "had to plan a romantic campaign with military precision; its skirmishes and reverses [were] welcomed by the confident as a thrilling trial of their masculine audacity."[44] Women, on the other hand, welcomed courtship because it made them "the absolute centre of attention and often the protagonist[s] of a thrilling drama."[45] In order to embody the performance of courtship, both men and women had to learn about the roles that they would play. Love songs provided an interactive opportunity for men to understand the language of romantic love: how to flatter, woo, and ultimately claim the object of their affection. Women, on the other hand, could learn what qualities to cultivate in order to be most attractive to potential suitors. Though love songs are often written from a man's point of view, engaging with that perspective could help women master all of the personality traits and behaviors that would keep men engaged, interested, titillated, and determined.

In this way, love songs—like conduct books—presented a clear picture of the qualities desirable in both male and female partners. While the audience for conduct books was primarily young ladies on the cusp of entering society—and therefore opening themselves up to courtship from gentlemen, men would have learned from these books too, especially how to evaluate the women they pursued. "Modesty," "chastity," "temperance," "humility," and "affability" described the ideal bride. Similar accounts of female perfection can be found in many eighteenth-century love songs. Remember how John Barrett's "Celinda's Beauty," with which we opened, tells the story of Thyrsis evaluating Celinda's charms, only to find them all equally exquisite. These charms extended beyond her physical beauty to encompass all the other virtues that the ideal woman should cultivate. In Barrett's "Liberia," for example, the singer details how "Liberia's all yt I esteem & all I fear is her Disdain. / Her wit, her Humour, and her Face, please beyond all I felt before. / Oh! Why can't I admire her less, or Dear Liberia love me more."[46] Daniel Purcell's "Ofelia's Aire," which was originally sung as part of Colley Cibber's *Love Makes the Man*, insists that Ofelia's beauty is wholly intertwined with her other qualities:

> Ofelia's Aire, her Meen, her Face, & easy Shape conspire to Please,
> But when in moving scenes she shines,
> And to her beauty action joyns,
> From every Grace ye Arrows fly,
> And Crowds of gazing Lovers dye,
> Against variety of Charmes,
> Tis hard to find defensive Arms.
> Yet her bright eyes and tunfull voice,
> Give but imaginary Joyes,
> What reall ones she may bestow,
> The happy Swains can tell that Know.[47]

Ofelia here fulfills the typical requirements of female beauty, but she is more than the sum of her physical parts. Her "Aire" and her "Meen"—her character—add to her desirability; later, the singer cites her "Grace" and "variety of Charms" as well. In teaching conduct, a song such as Purcell's clearly advises that women should develop and perfect far more than just their physical characteristics; their mannerisms, behavior, and a "variety of Charms" will also help attract potential suitors.

One persistent theme in love songs is that a woman's eyes hold the key to her inner thoughts, feelings, and designs. Here too songs parallel conduct books. Weetenhall Wilkes's *A Letter of Genteel and Moral Advice* suggests that men used a woman's eyes as an invitation to courtship: "We look upon a Woman's Eyes to be the Interpreters of her heart; and we often gather more Encouragement from a pleasing Glance than from her softest Words."[48] John Weldon's song, written for Cibber's *She Wou'd and She Wou'd Not*, gives exactly the same advice: "But Celia when I saw those Eyes, / Twas soon determin'd there, / Stars might as well forsake the skyes, and Vanish into Air."[49] Jeremiah Clarke's "Ah! Fly" blames the unnamed woman's eyes for ensnaring the male singer: "Least while the Thefts your eyes commit, / And you make no return, / Not finding how to freedom yet, / Eternally they mourn."[50] Neither song highlights the word "eyes" melodically; but both include plenty of passages of embellished, melismatic singing as a means of musically illustrating the elusive beauty so attractive to the singer.

Songs, like conduct books, offered advice to both men and women that went beyond encouraging particular physical qualities and personality traits. While conduct books described how women should behave in order to attract an appropriate partner, they also admonished women not to entice men in whom they were not seriously interested. Wilkes notes that men will respond to every little flirtation: "Be careful how you give way to what many Ladies call *an innocent Liberty*; for here Civility may be taken for an invitation. The double Temptation of Vanity and Desire is so prevalent in our Sex, that we are apt to interpret every obliging Look, Gesture, Smile or Sentence of a Female we like to the hopeful Side."[51] Songs similarly warned men not to become ensnared by flirtatious women. These lyrics often depict the man as the unrequited partner, bitterly lamenting the one-sided relationship. Weldon's "At Noon in a sultry Summer's day," for example, tells the story of Strephon, who comes across a beautiful nymph sewing in the fields. She flirts with him, but then rejects him, asking him instead to do her chores.[52] Purcell's "Beneath a Gloomy Shade," originally written for Thomas Baker's *The Humour of the Age*, offers a warning from a man spurned in love: "Ah heedless Shepherds guard your hearts, / From womans fatall Eyes, / They wound us still with poisoned darts, / & he that's wounded dyes."[53] In the musical setting, the song opens with an embellished, speech-like section in which the singer offers context for the story of the rejected Lycidas. In the next section, Purcell uses a descending minor tetrachord on the words "The mournfull Flutes contend in vain, / To lull his Cares, to ease his pain," as a means of musically rendering the singer's distress.[54] Finally, the warning to all "Shepherds" (which, in pastoral, means all men) comes through in an upbeat, syllabic final section of music. Purcell sets the words "They wound us still with poisoned darts, / & he that's wounded dyes" higher in the singer's range, thereby making sure that the audience will hear the cautionary advice. More often than not, songs of unrequited love from the male perspective blame the woman for torturing men. Throughout these songs, the advice given to men remains constant: seek out those women whose virtues and intentions are pure and shun those who will tempt, but remain forever out of reach. Yet these songs have meaning for women as well: be careful that you do not give misleading attention to potential suitors, as that could result in disaster for both you and your family.[55]

Warnings aside, many songs offered women direct advice on how to invite courtship and what kinds of men they should seek out. Wilkes advises his female audience in *A Letter of Genteel and Moral Advice* not to respond to every compliment that they receive from the opposite sex, lest they be taken in by men of unscrupulous morals: "Be not over credulous in believing every obliging Thing your Admirer says; for that would expose you to his Artillery of Perswasions. When he praises your Beauty, Wit, Shapes or Temper, and tells you that in his Eyes you excel all others of your Sex, do not receive such Compliments as an homage due to your merit, without examining whether he be sincere or flatters."[56] Edward Keen's song, "Celias Bright Beautys," provides a similar lesson for women to learn as they negotiate flattery and attention from many different kinds of men:

> Celias bright Beautys all others transcend,
> Like Loves Sprightly Goddess she's flippant and gay,
> Her rival admirers in Crowds to attend,
> To her their devoirs and addresses to pay,
> Pert gaudy coxcombs the fair one adore,
> Grave dons of the law and queer Priggs of the gown,
> Close Misers who broode o're their treasure in store,
> And Heros for plundering of modern Renown.
> But men of plunder can n'ere get her under,
> And Misers all women despise,
> She baulks the pert fops in the midst of their hopes,
> And laughs at ye grave & precise.[57]

The melody of this song works differently than the embellished examples discussed above. Keen's song is set syllabically, save for one small scalar flourish toward the end. Set in G major, the song fits the female voice well, hitting a high A on the upper spectrum and dipping down to a D above middle C on the other; the song sits perfectly for a light soprano voice. The simple melodic setting, with small triadic leaps and scalar passages, indicates that the principal performer for this piece would have been a young lady accompanying herself at home. A song such as "Celias bright Beautys" would have been an entertaining way to poke fun at the relentless attentions of the opposite sex, while simultaneously learning what to avoid during courtship.

Earlier we considered love songs that narrate the experience of unrequited love from a male perspective. There are similar songs that do so from a woman's point of view. These works run the gamut, from complete heartbreak to somber reflections on the lack of female agency. John Eccles's song "Relieve, the fair Belinda said" was composed for Mary Pix's *The Beau Defeated*. Pix's comedy depicts love and marriage as a game between the sexes, in which the characters conspire with and trick one other in order to obtain favor from the objects of their affection.[58] Mrs. Fidget, played by Elizabeth Willis, probably sang this song in Act 5 as a "diversion" for some of the other characters.[59] Yet this diversion is also a moment of real contemplation regarding how women are controlled through all aspects of courtship and marriage:

> Relieve, the fair Belinda said,
> Relieve, ye gods, a lover's pain.
> Relieve a poor unhappy maid
> By faithless vows to love betrayed
> Yet not beloved again.
> Ah! If to love it be a pain
> What is't to be not loved again?

Till fifteen parents we obey,
Then lovers sigh and moan.
And leave us not till they convey
With am'rous sighs our hearts away,
So that they're ne'er our own.
How wretched are we women grown;
Our hearts and wills are ne'er our own,
No, our hearts and wills are ne'er our own.[60]

Within the context of the play, Mrs. Fidget reflects on aspects of the plot that have already transpired. A performance of this song at home, out of a songbook miscellany, might have reminded young ladies who were already familiar with the play of its plot and whatever moral lessons were to be drawn from it.[61] But young women may also have performed this song sincerely, believing in the text because they had lived the experience it narrates. In the early eighteenth century, young women of the elite ranks often had little choice over their partners.[62] Eventually, the Clandestine Marriages Act of 1753 enshrined this practice into law.[63] In "Relieve, the fair Belinda said," the singer laments how parents control their daughters when they're young, and, as soon as the young women have gained some measure of freedom, their hearts are immediately stolen by a lover: "Our hearts and wills are ne'er our own." This song offered, if not hope, then at least sympathy for a woman's plight and perhaps some comfort in the knowledge that hers was a common experience. While advice literature offered prescriptions for proper behavior when engaged in romantic pursuits, their hyperbolic language betrays how unachievable most of their admonitions were in real life. Songs, on the other hand, connected men and women to the realities of courtship through the performance of shared emotion that elaborated upon their personal experiences and showed them that others experienced the same thing.

Understanding Sex: Songs as Pornographic Fantasies

The first volume of John Cleland's *Memoirs of a Woman of Pleasure* opens with an epistolary appeal from Fanny Hill herself: "Truth! stark naked truth, is the word; and I will not so much as take the pains to bestow the strip of a gauze-wrapper on it, but paint situations such as they actually rose to me in nature, careless of violating those laws of decency, that were never made for such unreserved intimacies as ours; and you have too much sense, too much knowledge of the *originals* themselves, to snuff prudishly, and out of character, at the *pictures* of them. The greatest men, those of the first and most leading taste, will not scruple adorning their private closets with nudities, though, in compliance with vulgar prejudices they may not think them decent decorations of the stair-case or saloon."[64] Hill here justifies the intimate description of her sex life that follows by asserting the familiarity of such scenes. Despite the social expectation of outward decorum, Cleland makes clear that his readership would have far more extensive knowledge of sexual activities than they would necessarily admit. Cleland's ability to anticipate what readers wanted to consume in private is a manifestation of a larger phenomenon related to sexual activity in the eighteenth century. Tim Hitchcock notes that discussions about sex "focused on a more thoroughly interiorized self, creating people who were able to use their imaginations to liberate sexual desire from its immediate social context."[65] In other words, novels—and song lyrics—provided men and women with the opportunity to experience sex in their minds, rather than only in physical relationships. These experiences offered both titillation and excitement, but also provided the chance to learn about sexual activity in preparation for the realities of courtship, marriage, and intercourse.

Songbook miscellanies are rife with sexually charged songs. While some miscellanies would have been published for an exclusively male audience (such as books of catches and glees), miscellanies printed for mixed company also regularly included bawdy or outright explicit lyrics. Yet as with love songs, erotic songs came in a variety of styles, each suitable for a different occasion and each teaching a different approach to sexual activity. Many songs are not explicitly pornographic and instead provide stimulating narratives that remain, at least loosely, within socially appropriate territory. For example, John Eccles's song for *Women will have their Wills* describes Belinda as "all ingaging most oblidgeing / Whilst I'm pressing, clasping, kissing," all of which suggests a female partner more than willing to engage in erotic pleasure with the male singer.[66] In another example, Daniel Purcell's "On yonder Bed supinely Laid" presents the story of a young woman who is presumably having intercourse for the first time. She is scared, and cries, but the song also portrays her as a willing and consenting partner:

> On yonder Bed supinely laid,
> Behold the Loved Expecting Maid,
> In Tremor Blushes halfe in tears,
> Much She wishes, more she Fears.
> Take her to thy Faithfull arms,
> Hymen bestow thee all Her charms.[67]

The text does not explicitly describe the actual sex; instead, the singer (or listener) would have had to use their imagination to fill in the gaps, making the song an even more exciting experience. Purcell's music enhances the imagery in the text. The vocal line revels in the erotic fantasy; as a recitative in the English style, the singer would be able to take his or her time in working through the alluring description of the recumbent maiden. The long notes in the bass line also provide opportunities for extended dissonance (such as in measure 6, when the vocal line repeats an E-flat against a F in the bass). These moments of tension solicit resolution, an oft-used musical metaphor for sexual release. Purcell's setting enhances the erotic titillation of the text itself, allowing the singer and audience to experience the sexual anticipation of the two characters in the song.

Lyrics often taught aspects of consent to those singing and listening. Jeremiah Clarke's "'Tis sultry weather, pretty maid," performed by Richard Leveridge and Mary Lindsey in *The Island Princess*, was printed numerous times in the eighteenth century. Leveridge and Lindsey were a comic duo, and although, within the context of the semi-opera, the song functioned as humorous entertainment, once published, it became something an amateur performer could consider and study while learning the music.[68] Leveridge's character (the Town-Spark) implores Lindsey to join him under a tree, but she coyly refuses his advances:

> 'Tis sultry Weather, pretty Maid,
> Come, let's retire to yonder shade.
> > [*She stands bashfully hiding her Face.*]
> Pray, why so shy? Why thus do you stand?
> Sure 'tis no Crime to touch your Hand.
> Oh let me take a civil Kiss.
> > [*She curtsies when he kisses her.*][69]

The maid continues to refuse, until she finally proclaims: "When a Gentleman's Suiter, 'tis hard to say nay." By the end of the dialogue, the maid has successfully put off the Town-Spark. In the context of the play, it is simple entertainment; but performing this dialogue at home may have given women an example of how to refuse the continued advances of an unwanted admirer.

Some songs offer narratives of sexual activity between two clearly consenting adults. In John Eccles's "I Gently toucht her Hand," the male narrator guides the listener through his successful seduction of a willing woman.[70] The text uses phrases like "I gently toucht her hand" and "On her soft Breasts my hand I laid, / And a quick light Impression made," suggesting a slow and careful exploration of the woman's body, rather than something more crass and violent. Throughout Eccles's song, the woman is always consenting: "I prest her rebel Lips in vain, / They rose to be prest again," and the male narrator makes clear that he will not take his actions too far:

"Yet trust me, I no farther meant, / Then to be pleas'd and Innocent." Such a careful approach parallels the values encouraged in young men, including their approach to seduction.[71] Jeremiah Clarke wrote music for a pastoral text recounting, in even more detail, a consensual sexual encounter between a shepherd and a nymph. In "Young Corydon and Phyllis sate," the woman initiates the sexual activity and each stanza builds upon the previous one, becoming more and more erotically charged as the song continues:

> Young Corydon and Phyllis sate in a lovely Grove,
> Contriving crowns of Lillies; repeating Tales of Love.
> And something else but what I dare not name.
> But as they were a playing,
> She ogled so the Swain;
> It sav'd her plainly saying,
> Let's kiss to ease our pain:
>   And something else [&c.]
> A thousand times he kiss'd her,
> Laying her on the Green,
> But as he further pres'd her,
> A pretty Legg was seen:
>   And something else [&c.]
> So many Beauties viewing
> His ardour still increas'd
> And greater Joys pursuing,
> He wander'd o'er her Breast,
>   And something else [&c.]
> A last Effort she Trying,
> His Passion to withstand,
> Cry'd but 'twas faintly crying,
> Pray let me take your Hand:
>   And something else [&c.]
> Young Corydon grown bolder,
> The Minute wou'd improve,
> This is the Time he told her,
> To shew you how I love.
>   And something else [&c.]
> The Nymph seem'd almost dying,
> Dissolv'd in amorous Heat,
> She kiss'd and told him sighing,
> My Dear your Love is great:
>   And something else [&c.]
> But Phyllis did recover,
> Much sooner than the Swain,
> She blushing ask'd the Lover,

Shall we not kiss again:
>   And something else [&c.]
Thus Love his Revels keeping,
Till Nature at a stand,
From Talk, they fell to sleeping,
Holding each others Hand.
>   And something else [&c.]⁷²

Both Corydon and Phyllis engage in mutually pleasurable and consensual intercourse, but before they achieve orgasm, the two explore each other through foreplay (kissing and touching), an activity that was becoming increasingly prominent in sexual encounters in the early eighteenth century.⁷³ After both climax, the shepherd and nymph fall asleep in each other's arms, hands clasped. The casual refrain of "And something else ..." makes the music all the more singable and memorable. Whether men and women performed this song in mixed company, among members of their own gender, or alone in privacy, "Young Corydon and Phyllis sate" taught its singers and listeners how to have physically and emotionally fulfilling sexual intercourse (or at least that intercourse could be fulfilling in those ways).

Not all erotic songs involved consent. Many pornographic lyrics published in miscellanies and as single-sided sheet music depict rape fantasies, written to titillate a male audience and to warn a female one. A number of the latter are Scotch songs, mimicking Scottish brogue and including characters such as "Jenny" (a term for a Scottish sex worker) and "Jockey," a name for a wandering scoundrel. In "A Bonny Lad there was," Jockey persistently chases after "a lass," until he finally has his way with her:

A Bonny Lad there was, and Jockey was his Name,
He courted Long a Lass, but cou'd no wrong her fame.
He profer'd money, proferd Land,
He saw her night and Day,
But still she wou'd na understand, but answer'd Jockey nay.
But he a Cuning wary Loon
Found eance a pleasant hour,
Was me quo he,
I'se ho' my Boon, and tuke [bang/beat] her tell a Bowr.
He lig'd her on the Grass, where they had a Muckle Play,
And ever since the Bonny Lass has ne're Cry'd Jockey Nay.⁷⁴

Jockey attempts to seduce the lass through gifts, but to no avail. By the end of the song, her rejections lead him to simply take what he desires. The song is ambiguous in terms of how it depicts the lass's reaction; it does not explicitly state that she enjoys it, but the final words do emphasize her acceptance of the situation, if not necessarily her full consent, since she will "ne're Cry Jockey Nay." In a similar popular song, "The Maid of Lyn," a young man meets a girl on the road:

> On Brandon Heath, in sight of Muell Steeple
> In Norfolk, as I rode along,
> I met a Maiden, with Apples taden,
> & thus to her I urg'd my Song,
> Kiss me said I, she answer'd no,
> & still she cry'd I won't do so,
> But when I did my Love begin,
> Quoth she good sir, I live in Lyn. …
> Three times I try'd to satisfie this Maiden,
> And she perceiv'd her Lovers pain,
> Then I wou'd go, but she cry'd no,
> And bid me try it o're again,
> She cry'd my Dear, I cry'd forbear,
> Yet e'er we parted fain wou'd know,
> Where I might see this Maid agen,
> Quoth she good Sr I live in Lyn.[75]

At first, the maid protests and clearly says no; after three more stanzas, her protests have turned into swooning, as she not only gives into his desires, but begs him to stay and continue pleasuring her. The fantasy here is that these maids secretly desire the sexual attention forced upon them. Singing these narratives helps normalize such assault and enhance the allure (at least for other men) of male sexual dominance.

Some songs instead insinuate the destructive consequences of rape for women, rather than focusing solely on male fantasy. In Richard Leveridge's "Jenny long resisted":

> Jenny long resisted Wully's fierce desire,
> She the more persisted coyness rais'd his fire.
> When he'd reap'd the treasure and the virgins spoyls,
> He found such short pleasure answer'd not his toyls.
> Jenny lay neglected in her lover's arms,
> When she was rejected, she try'd all her Charms:
> Then she did discover, that no Trick, nor Art,
> Tho't might win a lover, could regain his Heart.[76]

While the song ignores the physical and emotional trauma that Jenny would have experienced from her rape, it hints at the social stigma attached to this kind of violence. In eighteenth-century England, a woman who had been raped would have had few options other than marrying her rapist in order to regain some of her social standing. As Laurie Edelstein has shown, most cases were not reported because of the social consequences of doing so.[77] Not only would women face a grueling trial, which would expose their private lives to public scrutiny, but if their assailants were convicted, the women, as "damaged goods," would have to face a life of dependence on (potentially judgmental or ashamed) family members, which might well be accompanied by a descent or further descent into poverty. In "Jenny long resisted," male pleasure and the male perspective dominate, with only veiled insinuations regarding the suffering and debilitating social trauma that women might experience from such an encounter.

Erotic and blatantly pornographic songs circulated with some frequency in published miscellanies and songbooks. Audiences of men and women could explore different kinds of sexual fantasies through the lyrics of those songs. Some of those fantasies were consensual, depicting the intimate exploration of a willing sexual partner; others involved taking women by force. That these songs were printed side by side with love songs, which offered advice on courtship and how to choose an appropriate partner, suggests that erotic songs also had an educational function. While engaging in sexual fantasy through pornographic lyrics, men and women also learned how to behave sexually and how to avoid situations that might tarnish their social standing and their ability to find an ideal husband or wife.

Songbook miscellanies offered consumers a cornucopia of different songs to suit any kind of occasion—from courtship, to processing feelings of unrequited love, to celebrating or complaining about marriage, to fantasizing about the opposite sex. Men and women alike could learn about love and sex through song. With a miscellany, singers and listeners would not have been expected to play through every song in the book; instead, they could pick and choose those lyrics that best suited their mood or situation for a given performance.[78]

Conduct books included consistent—if biased, conservative, and ultimately unattainable—advice for men and women on the art of courtship and proper behavior with the opposite sex. Erotic literature taught men and women about aspects of sex otherwise purposefully concealed from public view. Songs—published in miscellanies and anthologies—accomplished all of these things, repackaging social advice or sexual fantasy into discrete, accessible, and entertaining lyrics and melodies for a wide variety of emotions or occasions. As England's attitude towards courtship, marriage, and sex continued to change in the early eighteenth century, song culture offered a literary-musical genre to which men and women could turn in order to learn about and reflect upon these changes. Love songs were a bellwether that can help us better understand how men and women perceived and experienced lovemaking with both potential and actual partners in eighteenth-century England.

Notes

I would like to thank my anonymous reviewers for their detailed feedback.

1. John Barrett, "Celinda," in *A Collection of the Choicest Songs & Dialogues Composed By the most Eminent Masters of the Age* (London: I. Walsh, 1703), 29–31. The extant copies of this collection each slightly vary in their contents. All quotations in this essay will be from the British Library's copy (G.304).

2. A songbook miscellany is a collection of songs by many different composers, compiled by a publisher.

3. Ingrid Tague, "Love, Honor, and Obedience: Fashionable Women and the Discourse of Marriage in the Early Eighteenth Century," *Journal of British Studies* 40, no. 1 (2001): 79–80.

4. Tague, "Love, Honor, and Obedience," 85.

5. Patricia Crawford, "Sexual Knowledge in England, 1500–1750," in *Sexual Knowledge, Sexual Science: The History of Attitudes to Sexuality*, ed. Roy Porter and Mikuláš Teich (Cambridge: Cambridge University Press, 1994), 92–94.

6. Hitchcock, "The Reformulation of Sexual Knowledge in Eighteenth-Century England," *Signs* 37, no. 4 (2012): 824.

7. See, for example, Julia Hamilton, "'African' Songs and Women's Abolitionism in the Home, 1787–1807," *Studies in Eighteenth-Century Culture* 50 (2021): 153–68; and Elizabeth Morgan, "War on the Home Front: Battle Pieces for the Piano from the American Civil War," *Journal for the Society of American Music* 9, no. 4 (2015): 381–408. Both Hamilton and Morgan write somewhat speculatively about the later eighteenth century; there is even less evidence, in the early eighteenth century, of how songs would have been performed by their consumers. Yet the persistent publication of these types of songs and songbook miscellanies throughout the eighteenth century suggest that families of the middling sort and the gentry continued to purchase—and presumably use—them.

8. Hamilton reminds us of the many steps it takes to learn a song: "studying the meaning and sentiment of the song's text, singing the words of the first stanza to the tune, working to find suitable text-settings for later stanzas, and accompanying oneself while singing" ("'African' Songs and Women's Abolitionism," 154).

9. Hamilton, "'African' Songs and Women's Abolitionism," 154.

10. For more on the practical reasons why publishers reused plates and the legal implications of their doing so, see John Small, "The Development of Music Copyright," in *The Music Trade in Georgian England*, ed. Michael Kassler (Farnham: Ashgate, 2011), 256–93.

11. Songbook miscellanies sometimes printed the original singer's name at the top of the page. Sandra Mangsen discusses how this helped to memorialize performances from the theater; see her *Songs Without Words: Keyboard Arrangements of Vocal Music in England, 1560–1760* (Rochester: University of Rochester Press, 2016), 59–92.

12. In the absence of recording technology, these at-home performances of theatrical songs were one way in which audiences could remember specific performers and performances. See Mangsen, *Songs Without Songs*, 12–58.

13. Hunter, "The Publishing of Opera and Song Books in England, 1703–1726," *Notes: The Quarterly Journal of the Music Library Association* 47, no. 3 (1991): 648.

14. Hume, "The Value of Money in Eighteenth-Century England: Incomes, Prices, Buying Power—and Some Problems in Cultural Economics," *Huntington Library Quarterly* 77, no. 4 (2015): 383.

15. There are no subscribers' lists for the earliest songbook miscellanies. By the 1720s, however, John Walsh and other publishers were selling their books by subscription to the wealthiest segment of the population. See my *The Power of Pastiche: Musical Miscellany and Cultural Identity in Early Eighteenth-Century England* (Clemson: Clemson University Press, 2021), 106–7.

16. Tague, "Love, Honor, and Obedience," 85–86. Vivien Jones also discusses the various audiences for conduct books, arguing that they functioned not only as pedagogy, but also as literature and that therefore men were a likely part of their intended audience as well. See her "The Seductions of Conduct: Pleasure and Conduct Literature," in *Pleasure in the Eighteenth Century*, ed. Roy Porter and Mary Mulvey Roberts (New York: New York University Press, 1996), 108–32.

17. On the purpose and function of erotic and pornographic literature historically, see *The Invention of Pornography: Obscenity and the Origins of Modernity, 1500–1800*, ed. Lynn Hunt (New York: Zone Books, 1993).

18. Divorce was an expensive and legally complicated undertaking in the eighteenth century. Even annulments were rare, with the burden of proof often placed upon women. For examples, see Amanda Vickery, *The Gentleman's Daughter: Women's Lives in Georgian England* (New Haven: Yale University Press, 1998), 73–74. For a later example of a woman attempting to bring charges against her husband in an English court, see my "Musical Virtue, Professional Fortune, and Private Trauma in Eighteenth-Century Britain: A Feminist Biography of Elisabetta de Gambarini (1730–65)," *Journal of Musicological Research* 40, no. 1 (2021): 5–38.

19. Vickery, *Gentleman's Daughter,* 40–41.

20. Vickery, *Gentleman's Daughter,* 41.

21. [Addison], *The Spectator* 261 (29 December 1711).

22. See Roy Porter and Lesley Hall, *The Facts of Life: The Creation of Sexual Knowledge in Britain, 1650–1950* (New Haven: Yale University Press, 1995), 1–122. Kathleen Davis ascribes the origin of conduct books to Puritan writings of the seventeenth century that advocated for a marriage between "equal" partners. See her "Continuity and Change in Literary Advice on Marriage," in *Marriage and Society: Studies in the Social History of Marriage*, ed. R. B. Outhwaite (London: Europa, 1981), 58.

23. Tague, "Love, Honor, and Obedience," 79–80.

24. Jones, "Seductions of Conduct," 108.

25. Tague, "Love, Honor, and Obedience," 89, 86.

26. Tague, "Love, Honor, and Obedience," 82. These sources often described their reasons for publishing such advice in their prefaces. For example, in the preface to *The Virgin's Nosegay, or, The Duties of Christian Virgins* (London: M. Cooper, 1714), the author remarks that the "following Work was undertaken at the Request of

a few sober, discreet Ladies, who see, with pious Concern, the spreading Immorality and Infidelity of their country; and particularly the growing loose, forward and immodest Behaviour, and unthinking Conduct of the Youth of their own Sex" (i). There are also examples of parents writing and publishing conduct books for their own daughters; the most famous may be the Marquess of Halifax's *The Lady's New Year's Gift: or, Advice to a Daughter*, which went through multiple editions in the late seventeenth and eighteenth centuries.

27. Tague, "Love, Honor, and Obedience," 82–83.

28. On the ways in which conduct books created an idealized world for their readers, see Chris Roulston, "Space and the Representation of Marriage in Eighteenth-Century Advice Literature," *The Eighteenth Century* 49, no. 1 (2008): 27.

29. *The Whole Duty of a Woman: or, A Guide to the Female Sex,* 5th ed. (London: J. Gwillim, 1712).

30. [John Essex], *The Young Ladies Conduct: or, Rules for Education* (London: John Brotherton, 1722).

31. *Virgin's Nosegay*, table of contents.

32. *The Young Ladies Conduct*, 103.

33. Vickery, *Gentleman's Daughter,* 60.

34. Roulston, "Space and the Representation of Marriage," 27.

35. Marilyn Francus discusses how conduct books tend to vary in terms of the advice they gave, depending on the personal circumstances of the writer, the time period, and other contexts. See her "'Tis Better to Give: The Conduct Manual as Gift," in *The Culture of the Gift in Eighteenth-Century England*, ed. Linda Zionkowski and Cynthia Klekar (New York: Palgrave Macmillan, 2009), 79–106.

36. Crawford, "Sexual Knowledge," 82–84.

37. Hitchcock, "Reformulation of Sexual Knowledge," 826.

38. Visual pornography in the seventeenth and eighteenth centuries often conveyed political and religious messages. For examples, see Rachel Weil, "Sometimes a Scepter is Only a Scepter: Pornography and Politics in Restoration England," in *Invention of Pornography*, 125–56. Prose fiction and poetry also combined political satire with pornographic imagery. Quite frequently, erotica was used as a means of discrediting Catholicism. For an example of how the English used pornographic poetry to slander the soprano Catherine Tofts upon her move to Italy, see my "Equally Charming, Equally Too Great: Female Rivalry, Politics, and Opera in Early Eighteenth-Century London," *Early Modern Women* 12, no. 1 (2017): 73–103.

39. Randolph Trumbach, "Erotic Fantasy and Male Libertinism in Enlightenment England," in *Invention of Pornography*, 254.

40. Trumbach, "Erotic Fantasy and Male Libertinism," 259–60; Crawford, "Sexual Knowledge," 98.

41. Porter and Hall, *Facts of Life,* 20–22.

42. On the use of songbook miscellanies in the home, see my *The Power of Pastiche*, 99–166.

43. Courteville, "A Lass there lives upon the green," in *A Collection of the Choicest Songs & Dialogues*, 18–19.

44. Vickery, *Gentleman's Daughter,* 82.

45. Vickery, *Gentleman's Daughter,* 82.

46. Barrett, "Liberia," in *A Collection of the Choicest Songs & Dialogues*, 104.

47. Purcell, "A Song in the Comedy of Love Makes the Man," in *A Collection of the Choicest Songs & Dialogues*, 66–67.

48. Wilkes, *A Letter of Genteel and Moral Advice To a Young Lady* (London: E. Jones, 1740), 108.

49. Weldon, "Celia my heart," in *A Collection of the Choicest Songs & Dialogues*, 32–33.

50. Clarke, "Ah Fly," in *A Collection of the Choicest Songs & Dialogues*, 10.

51. Wilkes, *Letter of Genteel and Moral Advice*, 108.

52. Weldon, "At noon in a sultry Summer's day," in *A Collection of the Choicest Songs & Dialogues*, 6.

53. Purcell, "Beneath a Gloomy Shade," in *A Collection of the Choicest Songs & Dialogues*, 22–24.

54. For the descending minor tetrachord's long, symbolic history, see Ellen Rosand, "The Descending Tetrachord: An Emblem of Lament," *The Musical Quarterly* 65, no. 3 (1979): 346–59.

55. As Vickery notes, "many [women] walked a tightrope of romantic excitement: imprudent encouragement smacked of filial disobedience and could end in disinheritance and disaster, but a fastidious decorum might dishearten a suitor and lead to aching disappointment" (*Gentleman's Daughter,* 82).

56. Wilkes, *Letter of Genteel and Moral Advice*, 108.

57. Keen, "Celias Bright Beautys," in *A Collection of the Choicest Songs & Dialogues*, 35. This song includes two more stanzas, which describe additional kinds of men paying attention to Celia. The final stanza cleverly includes a political twist; Celia is being pursued by men trying to convince her to become a Jacobite, but she forsakes them and the "shrill capons Voice" (the castrati coming over from the Continent, who often stood in for Catholicism) in order to maintain her loyalty to the Hanoverians: "For these thought to have her, for whistling for / They courting with guts shew'd defect in their Brains, / And to the pretender to make her surrender, / By singing no favour she'l show, / For she'l not make Choice of shrill capons Voice, / For a politick Reason you know."

58. For an overview of Pix's play within the context of early eighteenth-century drama, see James E. Evans, "*The Way of the World* and *The Beau Defeated*: Strains of Comedy in 1700," *South Atlantic Review* 68, no. 1 (2003): 15–33.

59. *John Eccles: Incidental Music, Part I: Plays A–F*, ed. Amanda Eubanks Winkler (Middleton: A–R Editions, 2015), 58.

60. Eccles, "Relieve, the fair Belinda said," in *A Collection of the Choicest Songs & Dialogues*, 153.

61. Mangsen, *Songs Without Words,* 156–88.

62. Vickery, *Gentleman's Daughter,* 40–41.

63. Jones, "Seductions of Conduct," 113. On the Clandestine Marriages Act, see Rebecca Probert, "The Impact of the Marriage Act of 1753: Was it Really 'A Most Cruel Law for the Fair Sex?,'" *Eighteenth-Century Studies* 38, no. 2 (2005): 247–62.

64. [Cleland], *Memoirs of a Woman of Pleasure* (London: G. Fenton, 1749), 4–5.

65. Hitchcock, "Reformulation of Sexual Knowledge," 824.

66. Eccles, "Bellinda's pretty pleasing Form," in *A Collection of the Choicest Songs & Dialogues*, 25.

67. Purcell, "On yonder Bed supinely Laid," in *A Collection of the Choicest Songs & Dialogues*, 132–33. The second stanza continues: "Heaven to thee bequeath'd the Faire, / To raise thy Joy and lull thy care, / Heav'n made Greif if mutuall cease, / But Joy devided to increase, / To mourn with Her exceeds delight, / Darkness with Her, the Joy of Light."

68. On Leveridge and Lindsey's comic banter in Thomas Clayton's *Arsinoe*, see my *The Power of Pastiche*, 200–7.

69. Clarke, "'Tis sultry weather, pretty maid," in *A Collection of the Choicest Songs & Dialogues*, 191–92.

70. Eccles, "I Gently toucht her Hand," in *A Collection of the Choicest Songs & Dialogues*, 96–97.

71. Vickery, *Gentleman's Daughter*, 82.

72. Clarke, "Young Corydon and Phillis sate," in *A Collection of the Choicest Songs & Dialogues*, 224.

73. Hitchcock, "Reformulation of Sexual Knowledge," 826.

74. "A Bonny Lad there was," in *A Collection of the Choicest Songs & Dialogues*, 4.

75. "The Maid of Lyn," *A Collection of the Choicest Songs & Dialogues*, 55.

76. Leveridge, "Jenny Long resisted," in *A Collection of the Choicest Songs & Dialogues*, 94. I also discuss this song in *The Power of Pastiche*, 141.

77. Edelstein, "An Accusation to be Made? Rape and Malicious Prosecution in Eighteenth-Century England," *American Journal of Legal History* 42, no. 4 (1998): 353.

78. See my *The Power of Pastiche*, 101. On how people chose specific songs from songbooks, see also Mangsen, *Songs Without Words*.

Traveling Together as a Couple: Gender, Diplomacy, and Cultural Mediation in the Life of the Countess of Fernán Núñez, Spanish Ambassadress in Lisbon and Paris (1778–91)

CAROLINA BLUTRACH

"Several foreign diplomats went to the opera house and then to the home of Madame the ambassadress of Spain, where she held a circle."[1] This morsel of information about the Spanish *ambassadrisse*'s involvement in the cultural and social life of Paris was logged in the foreigner surveillance records kept by the city's police force on 1 January 1791. It is by no means an isolated reference to the lady in question. Although she was not herself the Spanish Crown's appointed representative in France, as the ambassador's wife, she was expected to assume certain duties and responsibilities. The police records, which kept track, among other things, of the movements of diplomats accredited by the French court, tell us much about the intense political, social, and cultural activity of these men and their wives. The Spanish ambassadress is mentioned several times, with reference to her participation in Parisian cultural events, both with and without her husband, and to her role as the hostess of social gatherings attended by a regular group of people (her *cercle* or *société*). Her name was María de la Esclavitud Sarmiento, and she was the wife of Carlos Gutiérrez de los Ríos, sixth Count of Fernán Núñez. Like many other noblemen's wives, she served as ambassadress consort, accompanying her husband as he took up his various diplomatic postings, which meant crossing geographical, linguistic, and cultural borders. When the Countess traveled with her husband to their first diplomatic posting in Lisbon in 1778, her level of education was not sufficiently sophisticated to enable her to move with ease in the transnational world that characterized courtly and aristocratic life in Enlightenment Europe. Through studies and experience, she gradually remedied this situation, to the extent that she was identified as an active and individualized agent with her own social circle in the exacting environment of the French court at the dawn of the Revolution. When she and her husband had to leave Paris, they left behind all their belongings, including two libraries of over 1,600 volumes, primarily in French, comprising the "books of his lordship" and those "of her ladyship." It was through the efforts of the widowed Countess some years later that these were finally transported across the Pyrenees and incorporated into the family library in Spain.

Travel, international courts, and embassies are all spaces traditionally linked to the study of cultural mediation, an issue that in recent years has begun to be considered from the perspective of the female experience. Cultural mediators, cultural brokers, "*passeurs culturels*," or "go-betweens" are all terms for agents who facilitated communication "between parties separated by physical, social, and political distances."[2] Because their role involved representation and negotiation, ambassadors sought to integrate themselves into the culture and society to which they had been sent, without losing touch with their homeland. Once posted, they had to operate at court and within the diplomatic community, but also in the urban spaces of aristocratic, *mondaine* sociability—all of which were, by their very nature, transnational stages. The cosmopolitan mindset of the aristocratic way of life was always conducive to the crossing of physical and virtual boundaries. Connections of kinship or friendship, linguistic skills, and participation in cultural communities of varying degrees of formality (such as academies, salons, or intellectual networks) resulted in the circulation of knowledge, ideas, and objects across borders.[3] Thanks to their social background and the nature of their diplomatic role, ambassadors—and ambassadresses—were among the leading agents of mediation. Tom Verschaffel and his collaborators have argued that "a cultural mediator can be considered as a person, as a function and as a discursive and practicing instance."[4] This essay will explore who this particular Spanish ambassadress was, what her social background and level of education were, in which formal and informal networks and spaces of sociability she moved—both alone and with her husband—during their travels and postings, and what concrete practices she employed in mediating between languages and cultures.

Methodologically, this case study has a number of distinctive features. Virtually nothing has been written about María until now, and the sources available are scarce and fragmentary. Born into a provincial aristocratic family in the far north-western Spanish region of Galicia, María left her home in 1777 when, at the age of 17, she married the sixth Count of Fernán Núñez. As his consort, she began a new, itinerant life, spending extended periods of time in Madrid, Lisbon, Paris, and Louvain. Hers became a life of travel and moving in courtly circles, of diplomatic obligations, book-collecting, and interests in lineage. María bore her husband nine children, six of whom survived into adulthood. Although María was the Count's constant companion for the rest of his life, there has been far less written about her than about her enlightened aristocrat of a husband, who was a well-known bibliophile, soldier, traveler, and the Spanish ambassador to Lisbon between 1777 and 1787 and to revolutionary Paris between 1787 and 1791. Not only did she accompany him on all his travels (the two diplomatic postings and the various journeys they undertook between leaving Paris in 1791 and returning to Spain in 1794), but, at his express wish, she remained head of the family after his death.[5] And yet she is either absent from or makes only a very marginal appearance in all of the works written about the Count. The Countess herself has been the subject of only a single article analyzing the correspondence she maintained after she was widowed with her stepson, Camilo Gutiérrez de los Ríos, in 1808, a particularly turbulent time in Spanish political life.[6] In addition to revealing that she was clearly well informed about the events of the day (through rumors, press reports, and news gleaned from influential friends and relatives), her letters also set out her opinions on these matters, demonstrating that she was "a woman of strong character, quite active in everything relating to the interests of her family, and fascinated by political affairs."[7]

The present essay will not only shed more light on the little-known figure of the sixth Countess of Fernán Núñez, particularly her years as ambassadress, but also aims to contribute to a better understanding of the role played by women as cultural mediators in the eighteenth century. This is a field opening up in various different areas of research, including the study of women travelers, the analysis of queens and their entourages as agents and catalysts of cultural transfer, and recent investigations into the role of the ambassadress. My account of the transnational life of María, Countess of

Fernán Núñez is intended to add to this discussion.[8] Her story also provides an opportunity for reflecting on the sources available for such an analysis. Women are less visible in official records, and although travel journals, letters, and other ego-documents written by women have been discovered and studied (and have facilitated access to the experiences of female subjects in the worlds of court culture, aristocratic sociability, and the "republic of letters"), materials of this type are not always available. This may be because they have not survived, or simply because such writing practices were more widespread among men, which is certainly true of travel journals. Where no letters or diaries exist, it is necessary to gather and interpret scattered, indirect, and fragmentary evidence and to read it critically with an eye toward the way in which the subject was seen by others—for the most part, men. This is the situation we face with the Countess of Fernán Núñez. Although plenty of documentation is available with which to analyze the Count's life, hers is much more elusive, especially as far as the years of their marriage are concerned. Any sources relating to her experience are both unquestionably fewer in number and more indirect in nature than those relating to the life and career of her husband, a reality that highlights the differences imposed by gender not only on the course of people's lives, but also on the records that remain of them. Despite the scarcity of documentary evidence, however, there are epistemological frameworks that enable us to reconstruct this woman's experience; contextualize her within the familial, cultural, and political history with which her life was interwoven; and analyze her role as a cultural mediator. Using the biographical information available and focusing on the function of the ambassadress and on the cosmopolitan aristocratic culture of the day, this essay aims to contribute to our knowledge about the gendered workings of diplomacy and cultural mediation, highlighting the transnational lives of ambassadors (both male and female) by looking at their sociable practices and their role as agents in knowledge circulation.

Consorts, Mobility, and Cultural Mediation

In recent years, gender studies has had a powerful impact on research into early modern travel literature, royal courts, diplomatic history, and cultural mediation. Analyses of women's experience of travel, which originally focused on the nineteenth century, have gradually broadened to include journeys made by nuns and noblewomen in earlier periods, with the stories of British female travelers garnering particular attention.[9] The fields of family history and court studies have been adding to our understanding for several decades now by incorporating the maternal line and female consorts into their narratives.[10] The journeys undertaken by princesses and their entourages have proved to be an especially fruitful area of research, one that has added significantly to our understanding of female travel and the political and cultural roles played by women. One of the issues that emerges when analyzing these women is their degree of mobility and its impact on political practices and cultural transfers. More often than not, it was women who left their families and (geographical and cultural) homelands behind in order to marry and be integrated into other dynasties. These princesses did not travel alone, but rather were accompanied by their courts. Female households—the entourages of female rulers—have also begun to be studied as transnational spaces of court politics and culture and as places and agents of cultural exchange.[11] As Giulia Calvi notes, "Transnational marriage alliances were indeed at the core of international relations, and a distinguishing feature in the study of early modern female elites is the systematic displacement which the marriage exchange produced."[12] These marriages thus became significant channels of cultural mediation, alongside other practices that have traditionally received more attention, such as travel and diplomacy, and analysis has shown that women of royal or noble families often played key roles as brokers in organizing such alliances.[13] The degree of power wielded by such women as politico-cultural mediators enabled them to serve as agents, instruments, and catalysts of influence and change.[14]

The agency of elite women in courtly culture and politics is today beyond dispute; this underlines the importance of taking informal spaces of political activity into account, spaces that were not exclusively feminine. As Jeroen Duindam contends, "the line between male and female does not match any division between formal and informal, with the single exception that women other than the queen regnant or regent were rarely expected to attend the council, a situation they shared with a large majority of males at court." Although women were excluded from formalized decision-making and thus almost invisible in official records, a ruler and his advisors could nonetheless elect to cast either men or women "in shady roles as intermediaries or agents in diplomacy and decision-making." Because women living at court were close to those in power and held positions of trust, they had opportunities to influence political decisions and to promote the interests of their families, friends, or clients. As Duindam concludes, "household and government, men and women in court office and politics, [and] politics and culture can be studied effectively only in their constant interaction."[15]

In the field of political history, the study of diplomacy has also been hugely enriched by the adoption of approaches based in cultural and gender studies. The New Diplomatic History has seen a profound revision in what kinds of sources, spaces, objects, subjects, and languages are considered when attempting to reconstruct the knowledge and practice of early modern diplomacy.[16] Attention to the everyday, go-betweens, gift-giving practices, and cross-cultural and cross-confessional exchanges are all now common elements in diplomatic studies.[17] While many works dealing with noblewomen, female rulers, female households, and dynastic marriages have shed light on the role of women in international politics, there continue to be a lack of studies specifically examining their place in the history of diplomacy. *Women, Diplomacy and International Politics since 1500* set out to redress this absence, and I hope to take its analysis still further. Spanning a broad chronological and geographical range, the cases considered in this collection highlight the agency of women, the importance of their family connections and friendships, and the use they made of correspondence and physical proximity (whether in the private apartments of palaces or the semi-public arena of salons)—resources and spaces that enabled them to operate as newsgatherers and political and cultural mediators, either alone or as part of a matrimonial team.[18]

The idea of a matrimonial team, or working couple, is particularly relevant when it comes to conceptualizing the role of the ambassadress consort. In recent years, the term *Arbeitspaar*—traditionally used to designate artisan, merchant, and peasant couples who formed a single unit of work and production in the pre-industrial economy—has been applied to royal or noble couples and, in diplomatic history specifically, to spouses incorporated into their husbands' profession, a phenomenon that has been studied with particular reference to the twentieth century.[19] Ambassadors' wives played a fundamental role in various aspects of early modern diplomacy, despite the precarious nature of their official status and the vagueness of the term *ambassadress*, which could refer to both the wife of an ambassador and a female diplomat. In fact, the word first began to be used in European courts in the sixteenth century as ambassadors' wives started taking on new ceremonial, social, and political responsibilities. According to Friedrich Karl von Moser's *L'ambassadrice et ses droits* (1752), the first woman to be recognized with that title was the Countess of Olivares, wife of the Spanish ambassador to Rome, in 1585.[20] That the term seems to have originated in Italy is not surprising, since the role of permanent ambassador itself also began there. The Italian roots of the word can be seen in Spanish dictionaries of the day. The *Tesoro de la Lengua Castellana* (1611) includes the word "embasjatrize" (halfway between Spanish "embajadora" and Italian "ambasciatrice"), which is defined as "an ambassador's wife." Significantly, it appears not as an entry in its own right, but rather as part of the entry for "embaxada" [embassy, in the sense of a diplomatic mission]. By contrast, in the *Diccionario de Autoridades* (1732) the word "embajadora" does appear, as a Spanish word and as its own entry. Here it has a dual definition:

a woman sent with credentials from one prince to another, or the wife of an ambassador.[21] It is therefore possible to trace the rise of the ambassadress as a force within diplomatic culture during the period following the creation of the role in the sixteenth century.[22] These women—either in company with their husbands or alone—crossed geographical, linguistic, and cultural borders, participated in ceremonial life at court and in elite society, played an active role in political communications and negotiations, and operated as cultural mediators in an extremely diverse range of ways and spaces. In what follows, I will analyze the ways in which the sixth Countess of Fernán Núñez assumed these functions, based on our knowledge of her presence in various spaces of sociability, her access to learning and knowledge, and her role in the recovery of two Enlightenment libraries built up over the course of her travels.

Lisbon: "This small embassy serving her as a school for those to come"

For María de la Esclavitud Sarmiento, marriage to the sixth Count of Fernán Núñez meant the start of a life of travel and her entry into the diplomatic world. This entailed not only the crossing of geographical and linguistic borders, but also, fundamentally, a socio-cultural transition. Her duties as the wife of a cultivated, high-ranking aristocrat demanded a level of education she did not initially possess. The environment of the Portuguese court, however, allowed her to acquire, through study and practical experience, the skills she needed in order to act as ambassadress consort. María (1760–1810) was the only daughter of Diego Sarmiento, fourth Marquis of Castel-Moncayo, and his wife Joaquina Cáceres. Before her marriage, she lived a provincial life, splitting her time between Galicia and the central-western region of Extremadura, where her family also owned land. In 1777, the year in which she married, she was 17 and had had a less sophisticated upbringing than her husband, who was then 35 and quite a man of the world. Carlos José Gutiérrez de los Ríos, sixth Count of Fernán Núñez, had been educated at the *Colegio de Nobles* in Madrid, then embarked on a career in the military, and completed his education by traveling around Europe in the style of the Grand Tour. Before their wedding, he went to Galicia to meet his future bride. After their first encounter, in Pontevedra, in which they exchanged "words without saying anything … sidelong glances, observations and all other things that are natural, allowed, and indeed necessary in such cases," both parties were left "content, in agreement, satisfied and on a footing of trust and friendly sincerity that promises constant happiness in the years to come, and which has banished—for the period before the wedding—the fear born of not knowing one another." During his visit, the couple breakfasted, lunched, and dined together and went to the opera, danced, and conversed with each other. The Count noted in his journal that he had taken leave of María with an embrace and that he felt that the 120-league journey, at a cost of 400 doubloons, had been well worth the effort.[23]

A few months later, he shared his impressions with an old friend, Prince Emanuel of Salm-Salm, with whom he had maintained a regular correspondence since 1768.[24] In a letter of 2 June 1777, he mentioned how good-natured his future wife and her family were, noting María's docile character; her noble, but gentle bearing; her talent for dancing (that marked her out from other ladies); and the sincere and amicable relationship he wanted to establish with her. He did, however, express regret about her lack of a refined education.[25] Not long after the wedding, Carlos was appointed Spanish ambassador to Portugal. On 23 September 1778, the couple left for Lisbon, the court at which they would live until 1787 and where four of their nine children would be born.[26] The first, Carlos, the future seventh Count and first Duke of Fernán Núñez, came into the world soon after their arrival in the Portuguese capital, the Countess having undertaken the journey during the seventh month of her pregnancy. Her new husband had suggested that she stay in Spain, given her condition, but she apparently insisted on accompanying him and was thus, in his words, "subject to the obligations of an ambassadress."[27]

The Count regarded Lisbon (where the demands of sociability at court and beyond were not excessive) as the ideal place for his wife to complete her education and prepare for life in the more high-profile embassies he had in his sights. In other words, as he explained to Prince Emanuel in a letter of 15 March 1779, in Lisbon she could "apply herself to French and the other points of education in which she is lacking and, this small embassy serving her as a school for those to come, we shall wait here for as long as it takes to progress to that of London or Paris ... I am very happy with her, since despite these minor deficiencies, born of her childhood, she has an excellent heart ... loves me dearly, and I flatter myself that with constancy, time, and patience the rest will come."[28]

In spite of the differences between them in terms of rank and education, as noted by the Count on various occasions, his marital relationship was cordial. It appears that the couple were gradually creating the intimate and happy friendship between husband and wife so fashionable in Enlightenment discourse. Having traveled from Lisbon to Madrid to deal with some political matters, the Count wrote to his friend on 15 March 1784 that "I am the happiest man in this world. I have been granted a wife virtuous in character and thinking, and entirely lacking in hypocrisy, fanaticism, and bigotry. She loves me, I love her, we are close friends, we walk together ... each consulting the other, each keeping the other's secrets."[29]

As far as their life at court is concerned, the Count told the Prince that he was spending quite a bit of time alone, both because of the "spirit of the country" and because of the ongoing consequences of the Lisbon earthquake of 1755. Diplomats, the Count explained, go to the royal palace only six or eight times a year and "although those of Spain, Naples, and Sardinia meet every Saturday, it is in private and scarcely anyone else is present." There were no public promenades or performances and no socializing in private homes. "Society is therefore reduced to the diplomatic corps," whose members came together in gatherings attended by a small number of Portuguese nobles. These circumstances obliged him to lead the life of a "semi-bourgeois ambassador," spending time with his wife in the intimacy of their home, where they took pleasure in their garden, books, and music and in looking after the house and attending to the upbringing of their children.[30] There were in fact separate spaces in their home specifically devoted to those activities. According to an inventory made in Lisbon in September 1783, they had a music room with "a large cupboard containing various instruments," in addition to the English pianoforte, organ, and harpsichord to be found in other rooms—as well as an ante-library and a library housing books, maps, prints, and drawings.[31]

Looking beyond the image created in his letters, however, it seems that the Count and Countess were in fact part of Lisbon social circles. During his ambassadorship, they formed a network of friendships with various other foreign diplomats and with Portuguese aristocrats, notably those associated both with other European courts and with the dissemination of Enlightenment ideas and practices. So far as we can deduce from the Count's correspondence and travel journal, Madame Lepselter (Isabelita Aranu) and her husband, Baron von Lebzeltern Collenbach, plenipotentiary minister of the Habsburg Empire at the court of Portugal, were their "good friends and constant companions." So too was Prince Rafadale, the Neapolitan ambassador to Lisbon. The Count also maintained close links with another friend of Prince Emanuel's: the Duke of Braganza (second Duke of Lafões), who had returned to his native Portugal in 1779 after years of traveling around Europe and forging links in Vienna and, after a stay in England, with members of the Royal Society in London. The Duke also spent time in Turkey and Egypt.[32] More names were gradually added to those mentioned by the Count in his correspondence of 1779. When he and his wife left Lisbon in 1787, he wrote in his travel journal of his sadness at leaving behind "many good friends," such as "the Duke of Alafoens [Lafões]; the Countess of Ficallo; the Count and Countess of Vimieiro; the Marquis and Marchioness of Tancos; *monsieur* and *madame* Lebzeltern, ambassador of the Emperor; Monsignor Belsiomi, nuncio of his Holiness; the Count of Front, the Sardinian ambassador; and others, who showed me with the most sincere affection the same friendship

I felt for them." As for royalty, he mentioned the Queen of Portugal; the Infanta Carlota, daughter of Charles IV of Spain, who married Prince João of Portugal; and her governess, the Countess of Lumiares, "our friend."[33]

This portrait of a Lisbon in which the aristocracy held few banquets, parties, or receptions and civilized society revolved instead around the city's merchants and ambassadors also emerges from the writings of other foreign visitors to Portugal, including adventurer, writer, and diplomat Giuseppe Gorani, who was in the service of the future Marquis of Pombal between 1765 and 1767, and French physician Joseph-Barthélemy-François Carrère.[34] Other sources, such as the letters of Arthur William Costigan (who visited Lisbon in the 1770s), and the diary of the wealthy traveler, collector, and writer William Beckford, or that of the French ambassador, the Marquis of Bombelles (both written in the 1780s), paint a picture of a more dynamic social scene.[35] In the journal covering his ambassadorship in Lisbon between 1786 and 1788, the Marquis described the receptions he and other ambassadors hosted, where the guests included figures such as the Count of Fernán Núñez, Baron von Lebzeltern, the Count of Front, Robert Walpole (the British envoy extraordinary and minister plenipotentiary), and Daniel Hogguer (the Dutch ambassador). It is worth noting the Marquis's description of the reception given by the Spanish ambassador and his wife at the Palácio das Necessidades, home to the Spanish embassy, on the occasion of the birthday of King Charles IV's son, Fernando, to which fifty-two guests came and at which, as well as good music, there was a very grand banquet. The Marquis adds to our knowledge of Lisbon sociability by mentioning, for example, a meeting between his children and those of the Tancos and Fernán Núñez families and the visits, promenades, and audiences of the ambassadresses consort. He recorded the visit paid by "the Spanish ambassadress" to his wife, and what he saw as the ambassador's excessive anger when the music at one party began before he and his wife had arrived and mentioned the disagreements between the Countess of Fernán Núñez and Mrs. Walpole, wife of the British envoy. He also wrote about receptions hosted by Portuguese nobles, such as the Duke of Lafões, the Count of Vimieiro, and the Marquesa of Penalva.

Significant figures who were part of the Count and Countess of Fernán Núñez's intimate circle, in addition to their fellow diplomats, included the Count and Countess of Vimieiro, Countess of Ficalho, and the Duke of Lafões, all leading lights in the social, political, and cultural life of Lisbon during the couple's time there: an age in which its elite came together at salons known as *assembleias*. The historiography on sociability in Enlightenment Portugal all points to the fact that, in addition to the sheer destruction it caused, the earthquake of 1755 also acted as a turning point. A new kind of social interaction emerged in the years that followed, one shaped by the growing number of foreign citizens who were settling in Lisbon, by an increasing awareness of the customs of other places (France, in particular), by the modernization policies implemented by the Marquis de Pombal and the latter's own experience of life elsewhere in Europe as ambassador to London and Vienna, and by the spread of a "new" Catholicism more open to the world, as expressed in the works of St. Francis de Sales. Lisbon's *assembleias* were invitation-only, mixed-gender gatherings that took place in private homes, generally on a weekly basis. They were organized and hosted by married women: a light meal was usually served, and there were readings, poetry improvisations, musical performances, singing, and dancing.[36] Queen María I's ascent to the throne in 1777 not only allowed many aristocratic families who had been exiled during the Pombal regime to return to the capital, but also placed questions regarding women's right to govern and the role they should occupy in society at the heart of intellectual and political debate. The Vimieiros were one of the families who came back to Lisbon in 1777, and the Countess, Teresa de Mello Breyner, was the hostess of one of the most prestigious *assembleias* of the time. One of her regular guests was the Duke of Lafões, who spent a lot of time with members of the diplomatic community and hosted his own gatherings attracting the cream of Lisbon society.[37] Another was the Abbé José Correia da Serra, the philosopher, diplomat, politician, statesman, and botanist who, together with Lafões, founded Lisbon's Academy of Sciences in 1780. The name of Teresa's husband, Sancho de Faro e Sousa, also appears on its list of founders, but hers does not, although she is known to have played a part in its establishment. There was a portrait of Lafões, meanwhile, in the Fernán Núñez residence in Lisbon, underscoring the close personal and intellectual connection the Count and Countess enjoyed with one of the leading figures of Enlightenment science in Portugal.[38]

Lisbon's *assembleias* enabled the formation of social networks of intellectuals (both male and female), whose ideas circulated either orally or in writing. They were also a forum for the dissemination of ideas from elsewhere, with letters from abroad being read aloud to all present. The Countess of Vimieiro's correspondents included Leonor de Almeida, Countess of Oyenhausen (and future fourth Marchioness of Alorna) and ambassadress consort in Vienna; Maria Wilhelmine, Countess Thun, also resident in Vienna; Marie-Caroline Murray, the Brussels-based author of a tribute to the Archduchess Maria Theresa that Vimieiro translated into Portuguese; and an Englishwoman named Johnston.[39] As for Lafões, he maintained a correspondence with the Emperor Joseph of Austria. Participating in these élite social gatherings gave attendees the relational, intellectual, and symbolic capital they needed in the struggle for power in court society.

We have no evidence to prove that the Count and Countess of Fernán Núñez were among Teresa de Mello Breyner's guests, but we do know they were closely connected to many of those in her circle. As well as hosting *assembleias*, the Count and Countess of Vimieiro were guests, in their turn, at receptions held by the Spanish and Imperial ambassadors.[40] Teresa de Mello Breyner mentioned the Spanish ambassador and his wife, and their banquets and parties, several times in her correspondence with Leonor de Almeida. In a letter of 16 December 1781, for example, she noted that the couple had held a dance for a select number of guests that had lasted until seven in the morning, although she herself had not been able to attend because she had been unwell. On 1 April 1783, she wrote to her friend that the ambassador had hosted a musical performance to which members of the nobility had been invited, but also many merchants' wives. On 26 April 1783, she again noted that the ambassador had been giving parties for various reasons and that so many people came to these events that they could not all be suitable guests—some were sincere, but others were foolish, quick-tempered, or indiscreet. Finally, on 11 April 1787, she relayed the news that the Count and Countess of Fernán Núñez had left Lisbon.

The connection between the Fernán Núñez and Vimieiro families extended to the Palace and the Portuguese royal family. On her mother's side, Teresa de Mello Breyner came from a line of women who had served the court. Her grandmother had traveled to Portugal from Austria as part of the retinue of the Archduchess Maria Anna, the bride-to-be of King João V, and Teresa's mother, Isabel Josefa de Breyner, was a lady-in-waiting, granted the title of Countess of Ficalho by Queen María I in 1780. At the time, plans were under way for a marriage between Princess Carlota Joaquina of Spain and Prince João of Portugal—a union in which the Count of Fernán Núñez played a key role. In 1785, Isabel was asked to become lady-in-waiting to Carlota, but she turned down the post for financial reasons. Brought up at court, her daughter Teresa received a good education in Latin and the sciences. She went on to forge contacts with the most important writers of the day, including António Dinis da Cruz e Silva, Father Manuel do Cenáculo (tutor of Prince João), and Correia da Serra, all of whom attended her *assembleia*, along with other members of the Academy of Belles-Lettres. Teresa de Mello Breyner wrote two texts vindicating the role of female rulers, both of which were published anonymously: the 1781 translation of Marie-Caroline Murray's work on Maria Theresa already mentioned, and a tragedy, *Osmia* (1788), which was awarded a prize by Lisbon's Royal Academy of Sciences, as well as being translated into Spanish and staged in 1798.[41]

While much of the Count of Fernán Núñez's time as ambassador was taken up with the negotiations and other political commitments associated with his role, the Count of Fernán Núñez did not neglect his domestic surroundings or his cultural and artistic interests. According to Antonio Vigara, while the Count was in Lisbon, he remained in regular contact with his nephew and friend, the twelfth Duke of the Infantado (Pedro de Alcántara de Toledo y Silva). Indeed, the Duke arranged for various books and works of art to be sent to the Count from Paris.[42] The Count was similarly assisted in purchasing furniture and porcelain from England by Thomas Robinson, second Baron Grantham, the British ambassador to Spain, and his brother Frederick.[43] And the Count himself acted as an intermediary in arranging for the transport of timber from Brazil to the Spanish court. A great bibliophile, he also continued to expand his library. When it came to buying books and cataloguing his latest acquisitions, the Count was helped by the distinguished Valencian cosmographer Juan Bautista Muñoz, founder of the General Archive of the Indies in Seville. In 1785, having been charged with writing an updated history of the New World, Muñoz was eager to consult archives in both Spain and Portugal. He and Manuel do Cenáculo (a member of Teresa de Mello Breyner's circle) had met in Valencia and continued to correspond with one another on a regular basis. Muñoz told Cenáculo that, on the advice of their mutual friend José Correia da Serra, he was going to visit various archives and libraries in Lisbon, including the holdings of the Count of Fernán Núñez, in search of materials about the Americas. And it was the Spanish ambassador who persuaded Queen Maria I to grant Muñoz permission to work at the Torre do Tombo, Portugal's national archive, where he was aided by Correia da Serra.[44]

As ambassadress consort, the Countess of Fernán Núñez both witnessed and participated in the various aspects of sociability just described and was part of the erudite culture of a court and society that, despite being situated on the periphery of Europe, nevertheless fostered close political, intellectual, and cultural ties with London, Vienna, Paris, and Madrid. María left no accounts of her journey to or time in Lisbon: no letters, journals, or any other kind of text. No catalog survives of the family library that Muñoz visited, and we have no direct evidence of her taste in books, only the assumptions we can make based on that of her husband and his mention of her need to improve her education. Interestingly, in the portraits painted of the Count and his wife during their Lisbon years by the Irish artist Thomas Hickey, both are dressed in the English style fashionable at the time, and the Countess has a book open on her lap.[45] In the refuge of their Lisbon home, she was able to devote herself to reading, music, and the art of intimate conversation. Together with the opportunities she had to interact with the city's aristocratic society (receptions, parties, dances, dinners, promenades, and audiences that required an awareness of protocol and diplomatic precedence), this reading and conversation enabled María de la Esclavitud Sarmiento to acquire tools and experience during her years in Lisbon that were unquestionably good training for her next destination.

Paris: Her own circle, her own books

The Fernán Núñez family had connections in Paris that worked in their favor. On his maternal side, Carlos was related to the Rohan Chabot family. His mother was Charlotte Félicité Rohan Chabot, daughter of Louis II Bretagne Alain de Rohan-Chabot, fourth Duke of Rohan and a Peer of France, and his wife, Françoise de Roquelaure. In fact, in her will of 1750, the widowed fifth Countess of Fernán Núñez had indicated that her children, Carlos and Escolástica, should be taken to Paris to be brought up as wards of her brother, Louis-Marie-Bretagne Dominique de Rohan-Chabot, who had by then inherited the title of Duke of Rohan. King Ferdinand VI was opposed to this idea, however, and took Carlos and his sister under his own protection instead. Thus, the sixth Count of Fernán Núñez first visited Paris in 1774, as part of the European travels he undertook before his marriage. According to his travel journal, he arrived in the city on 16 March, and stayed with his uncle and aunt until 6 April. The only purpose of his visit was that of "seeing and getting to know my relatives; I did not present myself at court and I spent all my time with the family and in society, without attempting to see all that this great crossroads of Europe has to offer."[46] He went back to the French capital on 21 January 1775 and this time was presented at Versailles, thanks to the mediation of the Spanish ambassador, the Count of Aranda.[47] His stay was shorter than he had planned because he was ordered by the court in Madrid to rejoin his regiment in Cartagena, from which a Spanish invasion of Algiers was about to be launched. The Count left Paris on 9 May, but this second visit did give him the opportunity to observe and write about the character of its inhabitants and some of the local customs: "Paris is the height of all that is both good and bad." He mentioned the wise, prudent, and mature conversations that could be had in the city, with many people of good sense and wide knowledge of the world, but he also warned of the many vices and intrigues to which one was exposed there. We know from his journal that there were many foreigners in Paris at the time and that it was essential to have an introduction in order to be admitted to the right homes. Parisians enjoyed gathering with their friends and moving freely about the city—under the watchful gaze of the local police. The Count also noted how careful you had to be in order to ensure that ladies did not give you a nickname that would bring you disgrace, and how, conversely, praise from one of them could make you the center of attention, sought after by all society.[48]

Twelve years later, on 7 October 1787, the Count returned to Paris as the Spanish ambassador, now accompanied by his wife and children, along with a retinue of no fewer than fifty people.[49] They stayed with his uncle, the Duke of Rohan, before setting up house in the luxurious Hôtel de Soyecourt.[50] Details of the arrival of the new ambassadorial couple and all of their movements thereafter were logged in the foreigner surveillance records that were kept by the Paris police and periodically reported to the Foreign Minister, the Count of Vergennes.[51] The police report on the arrival of the Count and Countess of Fernán Núñez includes a description of the new ambassador's rank and family background and details regarding his financial situation; it also mentions the cordial relationship he enjoyed with his wife, who is throughout referred to as "Mme l'ambassatrice d'Espagne." These records reveal the intense social activity into which they were swept up as members of the diplomatic community in Paris. In addition to describing their visits to Versailles, the reports catalogue the walks they took, the times they went out on horseback, their trips to the theater and the opera, and their attendance both at receptions held in the homes of foreign diplomats (the ambassadors of Venice, Sweden, Britain, Sardinia, and the Habsburg Empire, among others) and soirées and dinners hosted by the likes of Mme de la Reynière and the Countess of Boufflers, the patron of Jean-Jacques Rousseau. The Count and Countess of Fernán Núñez also frequently met up with the Duke and Duchess of the Infantado, both in Paris and at the ducal home in Issy, where the Fernán Núñez children spent long periods. While they were in Paris, María gave birth to three more children: twin sons, Luis and Antonio, on 24 August 1788, and a daughter, Bruna, on 31 October 1789. Many of the police reports explicitly note that the ambassador and his wife attended social activities together. Interestingly, from 1791 onwards there are also references to María hosting regular gatherings of her own "circle" at their home.[52] As well as these domestic *soirées*, the Countess would also go to the theater accompanied by those of her circle.[53]

The Count and Countess kept an open house and received visitors jointly, with Sundays set aside for fellow Spaniards who were part of the Society for the Preservation of the Language. Founded by Carlos on 1 January 1788, the latter was a forty-strong group whose number included his wife; other eminent members of the Spanish aristocracy living in and around Paris (the Duchess of the Infantado, the Count of Arboré, the Marquis of Ureña, the Marquis de la Rosa, the Duchess of Beaufort, and Antonia Galabert and Teresa Cabarrús—the wife and daughter, respectively, of the financier Francisco de Cabarrús); men of science and letters, such as Tomás de Veri and Agustín de Betancourt; and members of the military, including Juan Senén de Contreras and Jorge Juan Guillelmi. Its aim was to act as a space of sociability in which those present could help one another to improve their knowledge of the Spanish language and protect it from foreign influence. When in doubt, they deferred to the authority of the Dictionary of the Spanish Royal Academy, hence the motto of the Society: *Dudo, Consulto, Conservo* [I question, I consult, I preserve].

Paris made intense social demands on the ambassadorial couple, and the boundaries between professional and personal relationships and between political and recreational conversation were not always clear-cut. With its distinguished circles of sociability and wide-ranging leisure activities, the city offered many opportunities to pursue negotiations and consolidate connections. A year or two into her time there (after the birth of her remaining children), the Countess of Fernán Núñez, having built upon the formative experience of her time in Lisbon, possessed sufficient tools and skills to handle herself well, both at Versailles and in the wider social life of Paris.

The fast-moving political events in France, however, meant that the Spanish ambassador was removed from his post on short notice. On 17 September 1791, he and his family left Paris—María was again pregnant—and began a period of self-exile in various European cities before finally returning to Madrid in 1794. Their first destination was Louvain, where they arrived on 4 October, having made various stops along the way, including the Prince of Condé's castle, which, in his travel journal, the Count called "a home fit for a king," and the country house of René-Louis de Girardin in Ermenonville, where they found "one of the first and loveliest English gardens in France, famous because on its island is buried Juan Jacobo Rousea."[54]

Having departed in haste, with the Revolution raging around them, the family left behind most of their possessions, including their books, at the Hôtel de Soyecourt. Before leaving, the Count gave M. de Souvigny, his agent in France, detailed instructions about shipping the latter back to Spain. The Count left Souvigny expressly in charge of his library and asked him to draw up and send him a list of any books and pamphlets it contained relating to the Revolution.[55] However, this commission was not carried out immediately and the family's belongings ended up being confiscated by the Committee of Public Safety in August 1793.[56] The Count and Countess returned to Spain in late 1794, and soon afterwards, on 23 February 1795, Carlos died in Madrid, leaving a will that stated that his wife should have guardianship and care of their children and possessions.[57] It was the widowed María, therefore, who ultimately embarked on the process of negotiating for and recovering what remained, after public auction, of their assets in Paris, including their books and pamphlets.

The details of what was involved in reclaiming the family's economic, cultural, and symbolic capital can be found in the correspondence that the

Countess maintained, in French, in 1796 with her administrator in France, Roberto Vauquelin, whom the late Count had appointed from Louvain.[58] Among that correspondence is a list of the first shipment, which required 72 chests, 14 of which contained books and papers.[59] Vauquelin not only listed in which chests the books would be traveling, he also sent the Countess two separate and detailed lists of "the books of his lordship the Count of Fernán Núñez" and "the books of her ladyship the Countess of Fernán Núñez."[60] If we compare the two lists with an earlier surviving catalog of their library (from around 1778), everything seems to point to the fact that this was a collection built up during the couple's years in Portugal and France. We know they had a library in their Lisbon home and that the Count purchased books while resident there, but we do not know how many volumes he bought nor what they were. It is clear, however, that the books, like their owners, were well traveled: some moved from Madrid to Lisbon; others from Paris to Lisbon—these were volumes acquired with the help of the Duke of the Infantado and the botanist Antonio José Cavanilles, a friend of the Duke's and tutor to his children; quite a few went from Lisbon to Madrid; and others from Madrid to Paris, where the couple established their "Parisian library," to which they undoubtedly added during their years in the city.[61]

Beyond the issues relating to legal possession, or to the agency involved in the acts of buying, collecting, and reading, the distinction that Vauquelin drew between "the books of his lordship" and those "of her ladyship" would seem to suggest that husband and wife had separate collections that occupied different spaces within the family home, although each could and did access the other's books. The Count's Paris library was made up of 559 printed books and 20 manuscripts distributed across 1,349 volumes, while the Countess's consisted of 96 printed books across 323 volumes.[62] French is the predominant language in the Countess's library, which reveals a taste for and interest in French *belles lettres*, including books on manners, sentimental and educational novels, poetry, science, and satirical literature, including works of *libertinage érudit* and others banned in Spain by the Inquisition. It is a modern collection that, despite the presence of a few books on religious themes (ten at most, all of them in Spanish), is fundamentally secular in nature.[63] All 1,672 volumes of the couple's libraries were finally transported from Paris to Madrid in 1796, thanks to the Countess's efforts.

What we know of the Paris ambassadorship enables us, therefore, to paint a portrait of a woman who had her own library and was the hostess of her own circle. The letters she wrote to her administrator reveal a widow actively involved in reclaiming the belongings, including books, that she and her late husband had had to abandon when they left the embassy.

The Transnational and Transgenerational Mediation of a Female Aristocrat

By dint of their work, training, and mobility, travelers, ambassadors, scientists, writers, explorers, merchants, missionaries, soldiers, and bureaucrats all played key roles as brokers and go-betweens. In recent years, gender studies have helped bring a new balance to this narrative through an analysis of the transnational lives of the women who belonged to the same social and intellectual circles as these male go-betweens: princesses and their entourages, nuns, ambassadresses, and female writers, translators, and travelers.

There was a cosmopolitan dimension to the aristocratic way of life that encouraged a crossing of boundaries. Travel; diplomacy; a knowledge of other languages (French, at least, as the *lingua franca*); access to the latest literary, scientific, philosophical, and political thinking from other places; a set of shared aesthetic ideas; and a command of court manners and protocol—all of these were integral parts of an aristocratic culture built and maintained through transnational connections, networks, and family ties. María, Countess of Fernán Núñez moved among the political and cultural elite traveling with her husband across geographical, linguistic, and cultural borders. Her life and agency developed within a sociocultural world in which subjects negotiated their own identities in the space between the self and the other, learning to understand other cultures, ideas, and customs, to be receptive to new ideas and experiences, and to adapt easily to new circumstances (a skill particularly necessary for ambassadors), while not losing sight of their origins. The Countess gained first-hand knowledge of the manners and customs of the Portuguese and French nobility. She dealt with other ambassadors and ambassadresses and came into contact with aristocrats and leading intellectuals who were members of salons, transnational networks, and literary and scientific academies. She was invited to balls; attended the theater, opera, and receptions, both alone and with her husband; and hosted gatherings in their home. She also had at her disposal a secular modern library enabling her to keep abreast of the latest scientific, literary, philosophical, and moral writings, which she could then draw upon in conversation.

Unlike some other figures of the time, the Countess left no private documents that would allow us access to what she thought or how she dealt with her cultural encounters.[64] The study of diplomatic practices and travel in the early modern period draws primarily on contemporary journals and letters. María's husband kept a record of all his travels (not only those associated with his diplomatic postings, but also those relating to his earlier profession as a soldier and the Grand Tour-style journeys he undertook for educational purposes) in a handwritten journal dedicated to his children.[65] We have nothing, however, from the Countess concerning her own travels, her life in Lisbon or Paris, or the peripatetic years before the family's return to Spain. There are no letters like those written by Lady Mary Wortley Montagu during her years as the British ambassadress consort to the Ottoman Empire (1717–18), which circulated among select small groups of readers. Nor are there any diaries, such as those kept by Elizabeth Vassall Fox, Baroness Holland, regarding her European travels between 1791 and 1811. There are not even any of the shorter, more fragmentary texts that have survived from earlier periods, which were written by ambassadors' wives while en route to or from their husbands. For example, Lady Anne Fanshawe, wife of the English ambassador to Spain (1664–66), wrote about the travel associated with their diplomatic postings in the memoirs dedicated to her children that she compiled at the end of her life. In a different format, we also have the *Tagzettel* [daily notes] that Johanna Theresia Harrach sent to her husband, the Imperial ambassador to Spain, during her journey with her children from Madrid to Vienna in 1676, which are very different in tone from the travel journal kept by the ambassador.[66] Nor do we have any articles, such as those written and published in the Spanish press in 1797 for the use and benefit of her country by María Agustina Romana de Siles y Cuenca, who accompanied her husband as ambassadress consort to diplomatic postings in Stockholm, The Hague, and London.[67] The profile of the Countess of Fernán Núñez also differs from that of other polyglot, cultured aristocratic female travelers who, unlike the Countess, maintained epistolary exchanges and acted as writers, translators, and patrons of the arts. One such noble was the fourth Marchioness of Alorna, consort of the Portuguese ambassador to the Habsburg Empire; another was Irene de Navia y Bellet, Marchioness of Grimaldo (1726–86), an ambassador's daughter; and a third was the Marchioness of Osuna (1752–1834), patroness of artists, musicians, and writers, who presided over a famous salon in Madrid and traveled to Paris as ambassadress consort—the latter, as well as writing letters, also kept a travel journal which, sadly, has not survived.

Because of this lack of documentary evidence, the Countess of Fernán Núñez has rather sunk into historiographic neglect. Here, by using indirect and scattered references—from the official reports of the Paris police, mentions of her by third parties in a variety of writings (her husband's letters and journals; the diaries of the ambassadors she met, such as the Marquis of Bombelles; and the correspondence of people who moved in the same circles, such as the Countess of Vimieiro), and the letters she herself wrote to her administrator in Paris after the Count's death—it has been possible to reconstruct María's contribution to the Spanish ambassadorial couple's sociability during their postings and to characterize her involvement in the business of diplomacy. Whether with her husband or alone, the Countess paid visits to other ambassadors' wives and the ladies at court and participated in the social and cultural life of the cities and courts in which she lived. With the less demanding Lisbon acting as her "school," this woman from the provincial periphery mastered the tools and resources that enabled her to navigate court and aristocratic sociability with ease and to help her husband create the reputation and the network of contacts they both needed in order to successfully fulfill their political and cultural role. As time went on, she also handled life in Paris independently and with composure: she hosted her own circle and was clearly involved in the diplomatic dealings that went on in its informal, but no less political, spaces.

By birth, training, and experience, many aristocrats played leading roles in cultural transfer. The surviving sources relating to the Count make it easier to clearly identify his role as a cultural mediator during his ambassadorial postings: he facilitated the movement of books, ideas, artistic trends, works of art, other artifacts, and raw materials. There is no evidence regarding his wife's agency when it comes to buying books or acquiring works of art during these years. From that point of view, María becomes rather more visible after her husband's death, when she assumed the crucial role of cultural and transgenerational mediator by negotiating the return of the possessions the family had to leave behind in Paris. In arranging the transport of the 1,672 volumes that had graced their Parisian bookshelves, the Countess made a significant contribution to the establishment of the Fernán Núñez library. The role she played as mediator was both evident and critical, not so much in acquiring the books in the first place, but rather in rescuing and reuniting a collection of great value to her descendants. Unquestionably a substantial economic, cultural, and symbolic legacy, the Count's and Countess's Paris libraries had been amassed over the course of a shared life of travel and diplomacy and could now be passed on to the next generation, thanks to María's skill in mediation as she continued the teamwork that she had begun with her late husband.

Notes

This research has received funding from the European Research Council under the European Union's Horizon 2020 programme (CIRGEN, ERC Advanced Grant, Grant Agreement No. 787015).

1. "Plusieurs ministres estrangers ont été à l'opèra ensuit chez Madame l'ambassadrisse d'Espagne òu il y avait cercle." Archive du Ministère des Affaires Étrangères (subsequent citations will be made as AMAE), contrôle des étrangers, 1771–1940, 1 January 1789, Book 79, 12v.

2. Janie Cole, "Cultural Clientelism and Brokerage Networks in Early Modern Florence and Rome: New Correspondence between the Barberini and Michelangelo Buonarroti the Younger," *Renaissance Quarterly*, 60, no. 3 (2007), 748. For a revision of the go-between concept in the history of science, see Kapil Raj, "Go-Betweens, Travelers, and Cultural Translators," in *A Companion to the History of Science*, ed. Bernard Lightman (Oxford: Blackwell, 2016), 39–57.

3. Willem Frijhaoff, "Cosmopolitisme," in *Le monde des Lumières,* ed. Vincenzo Ferrone and Daniel Roche (Paris: Fayard, 1999), 31–40; Vanda Anastácio, "Women Writers in an International Context: Was the Marchioness of Alorna (1750–1839) Cosmopolitan?," in *Cosmopolitanism in the Portuguese-Speaking World*, ed. Francisco Bethencourt (Leiden: Brill, 2018), 132–43.

4. Verschaffel, et al., "Towards a Multipolar Model of Cultural Mediators within Multicultural Spaces: Cultural Mediators in Belgium, 1830–1945," *Revue belge de philologie et d'histoire*, 92, no. 4 (2014), 1257.

5. Will, memoirs, and military codicil of the sixth Count of Fernán Núñez, Archivo Histórico Nacional, Sección Nobleza (subsequent citations will be made as AHN-SN), Fernán Núñez, C. 491, D. 5 (clause 41).

6. Before his marriage to María, the Count fathered two illegitimate children with Italian opera singer Gertrudis Macucci: Ángel (born 1771) and Camilo (born 1772), both of whom he supported without publicly acknowledging them as his. It was his dying wish that his wife should continue to protect them. Ángel pursued a military career, while Camilo went into the diplomatic service. The Mutiny of Aranjuez (17–19 March 1808) brought about the downfall of prime minister Manuel Godoy and the abdication of King Carlos IV in favor of his son, Fernando VII. The *Dos de Mayo* Uprising (2 May 1808) was a popular revolt against the French military occupation of northern Spain and marked the start of the Spanish War of Independence (1808–14). Together, these events have been seen as the beginning of the Spanish Revolution.

7. Antonio Juan Calvo Maturana, "'Dios nos libre de más revoluciones': el Motín de Aranjuez y el Dos de Mayo vistos por la condesa viuda de Fernán Núñez," *Pasado y memoria: Revista de historia contemporánea* 10 (2011), 169.

8. *Translators, Interpreters, Mediators: Women Writers, 1700–1900*, ed. Gillian Dow (Bern: Peter Lang, 2007); *Early Modern Women and Transnational Communities of Letters*, ed. Julie D. Campbell and Ann R. Larsen (Farnham: Ashgate, 2009); *Readers, Writers, Salonnières: Female Networks in Europe, 1700–1900*,

ed. Hilary Brown and Gillian Dow (Bern: Peter Lang, 2011); "Enlightened Female Networks: Gendered Ways of Producing Knowledge (1760–1840)," ed. Anna Maerker, Elena Serrano and Simon Werrett, special issue of *Notes and Records of the Royal Society* 76, no. 4 (2022).

9. See "Voyageuses," ed. Rebecca Rogers and Françoise Thébaud, special issue of *Clio: Histoires, femmes, sociétés* 28 (2008); *British Women Travellers: Empire and Beyond, 1770–1870*, ed. Sutapa Dutta (New York: Routledge, 2019), among others.

10. See Fanny Cosandey, "De lance en quenouille: La place de la reine dans l'État moderne (XIVe–XVIIe siècles)," *Annales. Histoire, Sciences Sociales* 52, no. 4 (1997), 799–820; Cosandey, *La reine de France, symbole et pouvoir* (Paris: Gallimard, 2000); Cosandey, "Puissance maternelle et pouvoir politique: La régence des reines mères," *Clio: Histoire, femmes et sociétés* 21 (2005), https://journals. openedition.org/clio/1447; *Queenship in Britain, 1660–1837: Royal Patronage, Court Culture, and Dynastic Politics*, ed. Clarissa Campbell Orr (Manchester: Manchester University Press, 2002); *Queenship in Europe, 1660–1815: The Role of the Consort*, ed. Clarissa Campbell Orr (Cambridge: Cambridge University Press, 2004); *The Rule of Women in Early Modern Europe*, ed. Anne J. Cruz and Mihoko Suzuki (Urbana: University of Illinois Press, 2009); *Forgotten Queens in Medieval and Early Modern Europe: Political Agency, Myth-Making, and Patronage*, ed. Valerie Schutte and Estelle Paranque (London: Routledge, 2019). On Spanish queens specifically, see *La Reina Isabel y las reinas de España: realidad, modelos e imágenes historiográficas*, ed. María Victoria López- Cordón and Gloria Franco, vol. 1 (Madrid: Fundación Española de Historia Moderna, 2005), and *Queenship and Political Power in Medieval and Early Modern Spain*, ed. Theresa Earenfight (Aldershot: Ashgate 2005). The widespread interest in this field of study has resulted in the appearance of Palgrave Macmillan's "Queenship and Power" series, which has produced more than 60 titles since 2003.

11. *Le Donne Medici nel Sistema Europeo delle Corti, XVI–XVIII secolo*, ed. Giulia Calvi and Riccardo Spinelli, 2 vols. (Florence: Edizioni Polistampa, 2008), xviii. According to the editors, this two-volume work offers the first complete history of a dynasty from the perspective of its female members.

12. *Moving Elites: Women and Cultural Transfers in the European Court System*, ed. Giulia Calvi and Isabelle Chabot (Badia Fiesolana: European University Institute, 2010), 1. The transnational lives and cultural and political significance of female members of the Spanish royal family have also been the subject of study. See *Early Modern Habsburg Women: Transnational Contexts, Cultural Conflicts, Dynastic Continuities*, ed. Anne J. Cruz and María Gallistampino (Farnham: Ashgate, 2013).

13. See Bartolomé Yun Casalilla, "Aristocratic Women across Borders, Cultural Transfers, and Something More. Why Should We Care?," in *Early Modern Dynastic Marriages and Cultural Transfer*, ed. Joan-Lluís Palos and Magdalena S. Sánchez (London: Routledge, 2016), 237–57.

14. *Queens Consort, Cultural Transfer and European Politics*, ed. Helen Watanabe-O'Kellley and Adam Morton (London: Routledge, 2016), 3–4.

15. Duindam, "The Politics of Female Households: Afterthoughts," in *The Politics of Female Households: Ladies-in-Waiting across Early Modern Europe*, ed. Nadine Akkerman and Brigit Houben (Leiden: Brill, 2014), 367, 370.

16. John Watkins, "Towards a New Diplomatic History of Medieval and Early Modern Europe," *Journal of Medieval and Early Modern Studies* 38, no. 1 (2008), 1–14.

17. "Cross-Confessional Diplomacy and Diplomatic Intermediaries in the Early Modern Mediterranean," ed. Maartje van Gelder and Tijana Krstić, special issue of *Journal of Early Modern History* 19, no. 2–3 (2015); *Global Gifts: The Material Culture of Diplomacy in Early Modern Eurasia*, ed. Zoltán Biedermann, Anne Gerritsen, and Giorgio Riello (Cambridge: Cambridge University Press, 2018); "Diplomacia y Embajadas en la Edad Moderna: de lo Global a lo Cotidiano," ed. Laura Oliván Santaliestra, special issue of *Chronica Nova* 44 (2018).

18. *Women, Diplomacy and International Politics since 1500*, ed. Glenda Sluga and Carolyn James (New York: Routledge, 2016). See also *Gender and Diplomacy: Women and Men in European and Ottoman Embassies from the 15th to the 18th Century*, ed. Roberta Anderson, Laura Oliván Santaliestra, and Suna Suner (Vienna: Hollitzer Verlag, 2021).

19. *Gender and Political Culture in Early Modern Europe, 1400–1800*, ed. James Daybell and Svante Norrhem (Abingdon: Routledge, 2017), 3–24; Jennifer Mori, *The Culture of Diplomacy: Britain in Europe, c. 1750–1830* (Manchester: Manchester University Press, 2011); Laura Oliván Santaliestra, "Gender, Work and Diplomacy in Baroque Spain: The Ambassadorial Couples of the Holy Roman Empire as *Arbeitspaare*," *Gender & History* 29, no. 2 (2017), 423–45; Florian Kühnel, "'Minister-like cleverness, understanding, and influence of affairs': Ambassadresses in Everyday Business and Courtly Ceremonies at the Turn of the Eighteenth Century," in *Practices of Diplomacy in the Early Modern World, c. 1410–1800*, ed. Tracey A. Sowerby and Jan Hennings (London: Routledge, 2017), 130–42.

20. Moser, *L'ambassadrice et ses droits* (Berlin: Étienne de Bourdeaux, 1752), 8.

21. Laura Oliván Santaliestra, "Por una historia diplomática de las mujeres en la Edad Moderna," in *Autoridad, poder e influencia: Mujeres que hacen historia*, ed. Henar Gellego Franco and María del Carmen Herrero (Barcelona: Icaria, 2017), 70. On the equivalent word and its meanings in France, see Loïc Bienassis, "Ambassadrice," in *Dictionnaire des femmes des Lumières*, ed. Huguette Krief and Valérie André, 2 vols. (Paris: Honoré Champion, 2015), 1:51–57.

22. Gemma Allen, "The Rise of the Ambassadress: English Ambassadorial Wives and Early Modern Diplomatic Culture," *Historical Journal*, 62, no. 3 (2019), 617–38.

23. Journey to Galicia, AHN-SN, FN, C. 2033, D. 5 (fol. 23–24). The visit took place between late April and early May 1777.

24. Prince Emanuel was the son of Nikolaus Leopold of Salm-Salm, first Duke of Hoogstraten. His sister, Maria Ana, married the twelfth Duke of the Infantado, nephew of the sixth Count of Fernán Núñez. Prince Emanuel was an infantry colonel in the regiment of Brabant. For more on him, see Archivo Histórico Nacional, OM-

CABALLEROS_MONTESA, Exp.421. For more on the friendship between the two noblemen, see Alfredo Morel Fatio, *Etudes sur l'Espagne* (Paris: Honoré Champion, 1906), 26ff.

25. Alfredo Morel Fatio and Antonio Paz y Meliá, "Biografía del conde de Fernán Núñez," in *Vida de Carlos III*, 2 vols. (Madrid: Fundación Universitaria Española, 1988), 2:241.

26. The four children born in Lisbon were Carlos (1779), José (1780), Escolástica (1783), and Francisco (1786).

27. Morel Fatio and Paz y Meliá, "Biografía," 2:245 (Madrid, 23 September 1778).

28. Morel Fatio and Paz y Meliá, "Biografía," 2:246.

29. Morel Fatio and Paz y Meliá, "Biografía," 2:251.

30. Morel Fatio and Paz y Meliá, "Biografía," 2:247 (Lisbon, 15 March 1779).

31. AHN-SN, Fernán Núñez, C. 1676, D. 7.

32. Morel Fatio and Paz y Meliá, "Biografía," 2:245–49 (Lisbon, 15 March 1779). Nuno Gonçalo Monteiro and Fernando Dores Costa, *D. João Carlos de Bragança, 2º Duque de Lafões, Uma vida singular no século das Luzes* (Lisbon: Inapa, 2006). For more on Portuguese connections with the Royal Society of London, see Ana Cristina Araújo, *A Cultura das Luzes em Portugal* (Lisbon: Livros Horizonte, 2003).

33. Journey from Lisbon to Madrid, 9 April 1787, AHN-SN, FN, C. 2033, D. 10, fol. 12–13.

34. Maria Alexandre Lousada, "Sociabilidades mundanas em Lisboa. Partidas e Assembleias, c. 1760–1834," *Penelope* 19–20 (1998), 133.

35. Costigan, *Sketches of Society and Manners in Portugal: In a Series of Letters from Arthur William Costigan, Esq., late a captain of the Irish Brigade in the service of Spain, to his brother in London*, 2 vols. (London: T. Vernor, 1787); Beckford, *Italy: with sketches of Spain and Portugal* (London: R. Bentley, 1834); Marquis de Bombelles, *Journal d'un ambassadeur de France au Portugal, 1786–1788* (Paris: Presses Universitaires de France, 1979). On the conflicting accounts of sociability at the court of Lisbon, see Lousada, "Sociabilidades mundanas," and Maria Antonia Lopes, *Mulheres, espaço e sociabilidades: A transformação dos papéis femininos em Portugal à luz de fontes literárias (segunda metade do século XVIII)* (Lisbon: Livros Horizonte, 1989).

36. On *assembleias* see Lousada, "Sociabilidades mundanas"; Lopes, *Mulheres, espaço e sociabilidades*; Maria de Lurdes Lima dos Santos, *Intelectuais Portugueses na Primeira metade de Oitocentos* (Lisbon: Presença, 1988); Vanda Anastácio, "Cherchez la femme (À propos d'une forme de sociabilité littéraire à Lisbonne à la fin du XVIIIème siècle)," *Arquivos do Centro Cultural Portugues* 49 (2005), 93–101; and Anastácio, "Women and Literary Sociability in Eighteenth-Century Lisbon," in *Women Writing Back / Writing Women Back*, ed. Anke Gilleir, Alicia Montoya, and Suzan van Dijk (Leiden: Brill, 2010), 93–111.

37. Marquis de Bombelles, *Journal d'un ambassadeur,* 211–12.

38. AHN-SN, Fernán Núñez, C. 1676, D. 7; the portrait is one of the items listed in the inventory of their library.

39. Countess Thun's *Idéa de hum elogio histórico de Maria Theresa Archiduqueza de Austria ... escrita em francez por M. M***** was published in Lisbon by the Officina of Francisco Luiz Ameno in 1781. Marie-Caroline Murray's original had been published earlier that year in Brussels by J. Van den Berghen as *Essai d'un éloge historique de Marie-Thérèse, archiduchesse d'Autriche, impératrice-douairière ... par M. M*****. For more on the life of the Countess, see Raquel Bello and Elias Torres, "Teresa de Mello Breyner, Countess of Vimieiro (1739–1798?)," in *Women, Enlightenment, and Catholicism: A Transnational Biographical History*, ed. Ulrich L. Lehner (London: Routledge, 2018), 87–97. The Countess de Vimieiro's letters to Leonor de Almeida can be found in Raquel Bello Vázquez, *Uma certa ambiçaõ de gloria: Trajectória, redes e estratégias de Teresa de Mello Breyner nos campos intelectual e do poder em Portugal (1770–1798)* (Ph.D. dissertation, Universidad Santiago de Compostela, 2005), Appendix.

40. Raquel Bello Vázquez, "Sociabilidade e aristocracia em Portugal no último quartel do século XVIII," in *A questão social no novo milénio* (Coimbra: Faculdade de Economia da Universidade de Coimbra, Centro de Estudos Sociais, 2004), 1–12.

41. Mello Breyner, *Osmia: Tragedia portuguesa en cinco actos, premiada por la Academia Real de las Ciencias de Lisboa, y traducida al castellano por I. M. R. L.* (Madrid, 1798).

42. AHN-SN, Fernán Núñez, C. 787, D. 4. José Antonio Vigara Zafra, "La embajada del VI conde de Fernán Núñez en Lisboa (1778–1787): Un ejemplo de promoción social a través de la diplomacia," in *Embajadores culturales: Transferencias y lealtades de la diplomacia española en la Edad Moderna*, ed. Diana Carrió-Invernizzi (Madrid: UNED, 2016), 244.

43. Bedfordshire and Luton Archives and Record Service, Wrest Park (Lucas) Manuscripts, L 30/15/54–L 30/16/16.

44. Nicolás Bas, "Juan Bautista Muñoz (1745–1799): un ilustrado valenciano, autor de la "Historia del nuevo mundo" y fundador del Archivo General de Indias," *Estudis: Revista de historia moderna* 26 (2000), 245–62, especially 254; *El cosmógrafo e historiador Juan Bautista Muñoz (1745–1799)* (Valencia: Universitat de València, 2002), 128–29; Leon Bourdon, "Relations 'Littéraires' portugaises de Juan Bautista Muñoz (1784–1799)," *Arquivos* 8 (1975), 405–536.

45. The paintings date from some time between 1780, when Hickey arrived in Lisbon, and 1783, when they appear in the family's inventory of assets. Photographs of these paintings can be found at the Fototeca del Instituto del Patrimonio Cultural de España [Photo Library of the Spanish Cultural Heritage Institute], http://catalogos. mecd.es/IPCE/cgi-ipce/ipcefototeca?TITN=320142. Don Carlos Guitiérrez de los Ríos, Archivo Moreno, 06173_B, IPCE, Ministerio de Cultura y Deporte; and Doña María de la Escalvitud, condesa de Fernán Núñez, Archivo Moreno, 06174_B, IPCE, Ministerio de Cultura y Deporte.

46. AHN-SN, FN, C. 2033, D. 2/1, fol. 31–32.

47. AHN-SN, FN, C. 2033, D. 2/1, fol. 38.

48. AHN-SN, FN, C. 2033, D. 2/1, fol. 39–41.

49. After returning to Madrid and before traveling to Paris, the Countess of Fernán Núñez was admitted as a member of the Junta de Damas de Honor y Mérito,

the oldest secular philanthropic association in Spain. See *Society, Women, and Enlightened Charity in Spain: The Junta de Damas de Honor y Mérito, 1787–1823*, ed. Catherine M. Jaffe and Elisa Martín Valdepeñas Yagüe (Baton Rouge: Louisiana State University Press, 2022).

50. AHN-SN, FN, C. 2033, D.10, fol. 113.

51. AMAE, contrôle des étrangers, 1771–1940. See too Mónica Bolufer Peruga, "Vivir la civilidad: Diplomacia y cortesía en la experiencia de una pareja aristocrática," in *Arte y artificio de la vida en común. Los modelos de comportamiento y sus tensiones en el siglo de la Luces* (Madrid: Marcial Pons, 2019), 252–76.

52. "A circle was held at the home of Madame the ambassadress of Spain, at which most members of the diplomatic corps were present," 6 February 1791 ["Il y a eu cercle chez Mme l'ambassatrice d'Espagne, le pluspart des membres du corps diplomatiques s'y sont trouvés"]; "They spent the evening at the home of Madame the ambassadress of Spain," 20 and 27 March 1791 ["ont passé la soirée chez Mme l'ambassatrice d'Espagne"].

53. The Countess was out "with her company" on 11 March 1791 ["avec sa société"]. There are similar reports from 13 February, 20 February, 24 April, 15 May, 22 May, 19 June, 26 June, 7 July, 14 July, 17 July, 21 August, and 8 September 1789. On French sociability, see Antoine Lilti, *Le Monde des salons: Sociabilité et mondanité à Paris au XVIIIe siècle* (Paris: Fayard, 2005).

54. Paris-Louvain travel journal (1791), AHN-SN, FN, C. 2033, D. 13.

55. AHN-SN, FN, C. 1442, D. 1.

56. Archives du Département des Affaires Étrangères, Paris, Correspondance politique, Espagne, vols. 636 and 637.

57. The Count's death was announced in the *Gaceta de Madrid* on Tuesday, 24 March 1795, 328–29. AHN-SN, FN, C. 964, D. 12. AHN-SN, FN, C. 491, D. 5 (clause 41). On the guardianship, see also AHN-SN, FN, C. 177, D. 48 and C. 2150, D. 2. Of their nine children, only six were still alive in 1795: Carlos, José, Escolástica, Francisco, Luis, and Bruna.

58. The Countess negotiated not only with Vauquelin, but also with the representatives she sent to deal with him, agreeing which items (including furniture and carriages) were to be shipped to Spain and which were to be sold because of their condition. Her letters, written between May and July 1796, can be consulted at AHN-SN, FN, C. 1355, D. 13 and D. 19.

59. AHN-SN, Fernán Núñez, C. 1355, D. 19–33.

60. "Les livres du M. le Comte de Fernán Núñez" and "les livres de Madame la Comtesse De Fernán Núñez."

61. Nicolás Bas Martín, "A. J. Cavanilles en París (1777–1789): Un embajador cultural en la Europa del siglo XVIII," *Cuadernos de Geografía* 62 (1997), 223–24. Cavanilles was closely associated with various learned Spanish figures, including Juan Bautista Muñoz, who, as we have already seen, had his own connection with the Count. Cavanilles supplied books and journals to many noblemen and intellectuals, including the Count (231).

62. The list of the Countess's books can be consulted at AHN-SN, FN, C. 1355, D. 19–34, and that of the Count's at AHN–SN, FN, C. 1355, D. 19–35.

63. For an analysis of the Fernán Núñez library and the two lists of books, see my "Libros y vidas que viajan: género y mediación cultural en la biblioteca de los VI condes de Fernán Núñez," *Arenal: Revista de Historia de las Mujeres* 29, no. 2 (2022): 447–68.

64. On the role of writing, particularly letter-writing, in the construction of subjective experience, see Dena Goodman. *Becoming a Woman in the Age of Letters* (Ithaca: Cornell University Press, 2009).

65. See my "Autobiografía y memoria en el diario de viajes del VI conde de Fernán Núñez," *Espacio, Tiempo y Forma: Serie IV, Historia Moderna* 26 (2016), 65–84.

66. Laura Oliván, "Idas y vueltas de un matrimonio de embajadores: Memoria, identidad y género en los relatos de viaje de Fernando Bonaventura y Johanna Theresia Harrach (1673–1677)," *Espacio, Tiempo y Forma: Serie IV, Historia Moderna*, 26 (2016), 39–64.

67. Siles y Cuenta published in 1797 in the *Semanario de Agricultura y Artes destinado a los Párrocos* under the heading "Extracto de carta de una señora Española, cuyas observaciones en Suecia y en su viaje desde aquel país La Haya, nosh an parecido dignas de publicarse" [Excerpts of letters from a Spanish lady, whose observations in Sweden and on her journey from that country to The Hague we thought worthy of publication]." See Mónica Bolufer Peruga, "'Ver desde su retiro la extensión del mundo': La experiencia y el relato de viajes," in *El siglo XVIII en femenino*, ed. Manuel García Hurtado (Madrid: Síntesis, 2016), 224–25.

Matriarchal Economies: Women Inheriting from Women in Eighteenth-Century Wills, Courts, and Fiction

JOLENE ZIGAROVICH

While I acknowledge that a gendered economy was clearly harmful to women, this essay seeks to work with the fact that women in eighteenth-century Britain could regard property in a similar fashion as men and that in eighteenth-century wills and courts women found forms of economic agency. In *Law, Land and Family,* Eileen Spring has observed that heiresses are transmitters of inheritance, and scholars such as Allan Hepburn, Virginia H. Cope, and Susan Glover have shown how, despite the legal tradition of primogeniture, eighteenth-century English women did inherit money, land, and personal property.[1] We see this practice reflected in numerous novels (such as Samuel Richardson's *Clarissa*, Eliza Haywood's *The History of Miss Betsy Thoughtless*, Charlotte Lennox's *The Female Quixote*, and Frances Burney's *Evelina*), in which the deserving and moral heroines are rewarded for their virtue with an inheritance from a male relative. This essay will further interrogate the issues associated with primogeniture and illuminate the practice of female-to-female inheritance in wills, court decisions, and fiction. While female will-making persisted in the period, we will see that legal structures limited the prevalence of monied heiresses. Novels, in turn, seem to pick up the topic of female inheritance and the figure of the heiress, often depicting women who inherit, distribute, or are given money and property from other women, as witnessed in Lennox's *Henrietta*, Burney's *Cecilia*, and Charlotte Smith's *Emmeline*. Among the questions we will explore are: how rare was this cultural practice? And are these fictional cases imaginative fantasies of female economic independence and power?

This essay observes that matriarchal economies emerged in wills in which women wielded their power by directing their own inheritances to deserving daughters and female relatives. It then examines this practice in fiction, comparing the kinds of female friends and relations involved in the transmission of property. With both real and fictional examples, I compare the types of property willed, gifted, and inherited; examine the legal stipulations involved with female inheritance; and measure the success of property transmission between women. Despite the fact that in actual wills men directed much of their financial legacies to their male successors, both inheriting widows and daughters and never-married women found economic empowerment in the act of bequeathing to other women. Noting that the number of actual heiresses declined in the period, I examine how the heiress becomes a staple of fiction, central to debates about birthright and inheritance. While women of all classes made bequests to other women in actual wills, I argue that these female economies are primarily symbolized in female-authored fiction by the figure of the heiress and assert that in both actual and fictional cases women's financial legacies could successfully navigate (or at times, even circumvent) the patriarchal economic structures that often disenfranchised them.

Bequeathing and Inheriting Women

In both life and fiction, daughters inherited their portions when they married or reached the age of twenty-one. Susan Staves has demonstrated that these portions were increasingly left to daughters in the form of trusts—that is, they did not have direct access to the capital themselves.[2] In *Married Women's Separate Property*, Staves shows how changes in dower, jointure, pin money, and maintenance disempowered wives through an evasion of common-law provisions. Eileen Spring agrees and argues that common-law property rights for women eroded, noting that the heiress, widow, and younger children experience "a decline of women's rights over land."[3] This was frequently true in novels as well, in which we see a woman's portion paid when she is married and so in effect (because of coverture) given to her husband. However, fiction allowed women more possibilities for agency and economic identity than the law typically did. I wish to suggest that narrative became a more reliable space for women to actively participate in the economy and that their roles as heiresses who either inherit from or bequeath to other women reflects the productive workings of a matriarchal economy, a structure formed by women to navigate patriarchal interests and, where possible, financially empower other women.

As we will see in our discussion of actual wills, the majority of women making bequests to other women were from the middling and even working ranks of society. In literature, though, monied heiresses are ubiquitous. The propertied widow is an especially common figure, as in Haywood's *The History of Miss Betsy Thoughtless,* which features the wealthy widow Mrs. Blanchfield, who dies and bequeaths her fortune to Mr. Trueworth and her jewels to Harriot Lovit. This female-to-male gift (Trueworth "blushed at having so much more ascribed to him, than he would allow himself to think he deserved, and would gladly have been deprived of the best part of his fortune, rather than have received an addition to it by such fatal means") is balanced by the widow's female-to-female gift: "All my jewels I entreat you to accept,—they can add nothing to your beauty, but may serve to ornament your wedding garments."[4] Of course, Harriot isn't alone. The young, virtuous heiress—as found in Burney's *Cecilia,* Lennox's *The Female Quixote,* all six of Jane Austen's novels, and numerous other works—is the most common woman of means in the eighteenth-century novel. And as several studies have uncovered, plots involving female orphans and illegitimate daughters, as well as birthright and legitimized heiresses, are especially prevalent in the period.[5] The chief challenge for male heirs, such as *Evelina*'s Lord Orville and *Cecilia*'s Mortimer, is the affront to their honor involved in marrying beneath their rank or having to give up their family name, while the primary concern of heiresses is being courted for their wealth, rather than out of love. While Virginia Cope argues that often these moral and educated heiresses seek love matches and don't consider their property when choosing a husband (she terms them "heroines of disinterest"), I'm focusing on *interested* heiresses, as well as widows and minor female characters who play active economic roles in female-to-female inheritance plots.[6] While on the surface, propriety precedes property for these heroines, and so the eventual restoration of the family estate is a reward for their virtue and intelligence, I wish to claim that, especially in cases of female-to-female inheritance, the economically interested heroine benefits both morally and materially from her interest, and, as shown in actual cases of wills, she bestows economic power on other women.

Much like Samuel Richardson's *Clarissa; or, The History of a Young Lady* (1747-48), which dramatizes not only Clarissa's inheritance from her grandfather, but also Anna Howe's matriarchal inheritance, Charlotte Lennox's mid-century novels respond to concerns about female inheritance and matriarchal legacies. In *The Female Quixote; or, The Adventures of Arabella* (1752), the orphaned heiress Arabella lives on a country estate and has a large inheritance that attracts many suitors solely interested in her wealth. Her father's will declares that she must marry her cousin Glanville or else lose part of her estate, and so, as part of giving up her romance-reading and "delusions" at the end of the novel, she ultimately makes the "reasonable" decision to keep her inheritance and marry him. Yet it is Lennox's third novel, *Henrietta* (1758)—written after the 1753 Marriage Act that required public notice of a couple's intent to marry and no longer enforced private verbal promises to live together as man and wife—that fully explores the challenges of familial bequests.[7] Leaving the comfort of her family behind, Henrietta attempts to financially support herself as a lady's maid in London. This choice is prompted by a manipulative female legacy. Her aunt Lady Meadows wishes to bequeath a large inheritance to Henrietta, but she stipulates that she must convert to Catholicism. Her aunt directs: "If you retire to a convent, and put yourself into a way of being instructed in the true religion, I will pay your pension largely; and the day that sees you reunited to the faith, shall see you restored to my fondest affection, and made sole heiress to my whole estate."[8] Henrietta refuses to change her religion in order to retain her aunt's protection and inherit her fortune, and so rejects female-to-female inheritance that is tainted with moral compromise. Henrietta later marries a marquis and is rewarded for her Protestant ideals with a good fortune.[9] As with many novels during this period, the "heiress problem" plot unveils the anxieties raised by marriages of choice. The threat posed to landed families by the downward social mobility of the heiress is dramatized and then ultimately overcome.

Influenced by Lennox, Frances Burney's *Evelina; or, The History of a Young Lady's Entrance into the World* (1778) is a seminal example of the female birthright plot. After recognizing that Evelina looks exactly like her dead mother, her father, Lord Belmont, pronounces that she should "immediately take her place, according to [her] right, as Miss Belmont."[10] Evelina is quickly informed that he "will give you, immediately, £30,000; all settlements, and so forth, will be made for you in the name of Evelina Belmont."[11] Yet seemingly within hours of her legitimization, recognition of her birthright, and inheritance, Evelina bequeaths a large portion of her fortune to Polly Green, the daughter of a maid who replaced Evelina with her own infant daughter to be raised as Lord Belmont's. This "gift" was facilitated by a negotiation between her father and her fiancé, Lord Orville: "This noblest of men had insisted the so-long supposed Miss Belmont should be considered *indeed* as my sister, and as the co-heiress of my father! though not in *law*, in *justice*, he says, she ought ever be treated as the daughter of Sir John Belmont."[12] But it is Evelina who ultimately shares her portion with Polly Green. While Cope and others have argued that this gift demonstrates Evelina's indifference to wealth, I read Evelina as actively pursuing legitimation, and thereby property and wealth (albeit under the guise of indifference). She follows the advice of Mr. Villars, Mrs. Selwyn, and Lady Howard, allowing letters to be written to her father on her behalf and agreeing to confront him in person in the full expectation that she will be acknowledged as his legitimate daughter and therefore his heiress. Her passive-aggressive strategy is successful. In the end, Evelina regains her name, her relatives, and her rightful property, enabling her to bestow on another woman the gift of wealth and inheritance.

Burney concludes *Evelina,* however, not only with a female-to-female gift, but also with the legal reality that wives' inheritances were subsumed by their husbands upon marriage. In her subsequent novels, Burney continued to develop plots that dramatize the anxieties surrounding female possession. Burney rewrites *Evelina*'s heiress plot later in *Cecilia; or, Memoirs of an Heiress* (1782), but does so in reverse: *Cecilia* charts its heroine's dispossession in a "dismal commentary on women's potential for retaining individual property rights."[13] By robbing Cecilia of her inheritance, Burney effectively shifts the emphasis to the acquiring of autonomy through individual development and awareness, rather than proprietorship and economy. An heiress only because she is an orphan, Cecilia is trapped by the patriarchal economy: her uncle's will dictates that in order to receive £3000 per annum, she must continue the family name by bestowing the surname Beverley upon her future husband. This clause of the will ostensibly gives her the right to independent thought and action (upon marriage she will keep her surname and identity, have a certain amount of power in her marriage negotiations, and will be a female recipient of family wealth). But while she temporarily enters a matriarchal economy, helping other women in their business ventures so that they may gain a modest economic independence, she ultimately experiences disinheritance. Choosing love over fortune and interest, she marries and gives up her name and estate in what is seen as an "extraordinary sacrifice."[14] The narrator describes Cecilia's indifference to her inheritance: "At the proposal of parting with her uncle's fortune, which, desirable as it was, had as yet been only productive to her misery, her heart, disinterested, and wholly careless of money, was prompt to accede to the condition."[15] As Linda Zionkowski details, reviewers and admirers of the novel, such as Hester Chapone and Mary Delany, expressed frustration with Cecilia's choice to give up her fortune. In 1782, the writer in *The Critical Review* remarks, "Cecilia's conduct, in sacrificing so large a fortune to gratify the pride of the Delvile family, is an example which we would by no means wish to propose as an object of imitation for the fair sex."[16] We can certainly agree with contemporary and current readers of the novel that the heroine's indifference to fortune is a form of defeat and a diminishing of her agency. While Cecilia's economic sacrifice dominates the narrative, however, Burney simultaneously narrates an optimistic female bequest, illuminating financial forms of independence.

At the close of the novel, Burney reinstates Cecilia's economic power through a modest female inheritance: her husband Mortimer's maternal aunt, who admired the extraordinary sacrifice Cecilia made, "left to her, and to her sole disposal, the fortune, which almost from his infancy she had destined for her nephew."[17] This *deus ex machina* is extraordinary: Cecilia receives the fortune of this aunt—someone previously unknown to her—which enables the couple to live comfortably. Mortimer generously remarks that he was "delighted to restore to her through his own family any part of that power and independence of which her generous and pure regard for himself had deprived her."[18] While Zionkowski interprets Cecilia's charity as confined to the domestic and "limited gestures of good will that would not impinge upon the resources of the patriarchal household," I wish instead to emphasize the power of women investing in one another. With this unconditional female-to-female legacy, Cecilia benefits from a clearly discernible chain of female charity, perhaps fashioning a new model of economy that critiques patriarchal capitalism. She resumes her charitable works and marries Mortimer, whose future inheritance has suddenly been reduced.

Yet in the end, Cecilia remains disinherited from her paternal estate, which perhaps explains why the scene of Mortimer's aunt altering her will is only briefly addressed. In my reading, this suggestion that female virtue is somehow incompatible with property signals the historical waning of the heiress and her influence that has been recognized by Eileen Spring and others. It disallows the possibility of women gaining both economic and emotional independence, and it reflects a larger truth about the decline of the heiress and her bequeathing power over the course of the eighteenth century. But by placing an heiress at the center of these plots, authors like Burney, Lennox, and Charlotte Smith foreground the social tension created by the potential of successful female economies. Female-to-female bequests, in particular, complicate, disrupt, and problematize inheritance norms. And when these disruptions emerge in the novel, they both underscore these economic and social disruptions and offer new possibilities for how property might be transferred between women.

Cecilia depicts a successful system of female bequeathing and gifting. But how frequent was this in actual practice? Much of the information about women bequeathing to women comes from wills. In this period, a man had complete power to disinherit his children and wife. Because of the laws of coverture, married women were precluded from making a will except by special arrangement with their husbands. Therefore, the vast majority of women's wills were made by widows (about 80%), as we see in *Henrietta* and *Cecilia*, and single women (close to 20%).[19] In the seventeenth century, we can witness a slight, but measurable increase in female will-making. Richard T. Vann's work demonstrates that female bequests beyond their immediate families were on the rise. For example, out of 89 wills of women, 18% bequeathed to nieces, 40% to friends, and 7.9% to servants (all higher percentages than what was done by their male counterparts). In his study of the town of Banbury during this period, Vann observes that "almost a third of the wills proved locally were coming from women, as compared to about a quarter in the period from 1650-1724."[20] He suspects that this may "reflect increasing economic activity on the part of women, or at least of widows. The inventories show that many widows were active moneylenders, and some were at the center of quite large webs of credit."[21] In *Silent Partners: Women as Public Investors during Britain's Financial Revolution,* Amy Froide shows that women's capital was a critical component of Britain's financial and colonial dominance in the eighteenth century and that women not only invested for themselves, but also relied on other female relatives as their agents. In addition to investing cash, women also held land. M. K. Ashby observes, "England has always had large landowners who were women. In the village of Bledington, Gloucestershire in the early seventeenth century, daughters were handsomely treated, in both fathers' and mothers' wills; their legacies are usually equal to their brothers' except where one of the latter is going to carry on the farm with his mother."[22] Sheila M. Cooper, reporting on a broad cross-section of wills in late seventeenth-century King's Lynn in Norfolk, observes that daughters inherited as well as sons, but that daughters were more likely to inherit money and household goods than land, unless there were no sons.[23] The seventeenth century saw several advice books that reflected this practice, such as Elizabeth Richardson Cramond's *A Ladies Legacie to Her Daughters* (1645), which describes female bequests in the wills of women from all social classes.[24] Trusts and strict settlements were ways in which the customary restrictions on women's property could be lifted. As Davis recognizes, "Trusts could provide all single and married women with access to separate property, though in practice they applied only to those who belonged to the landed classes."[25] And trusts could be challenged in the Court of Chancery.

Yet Froide observes that assertive single women "could exploit a legal loophole to acquire property that would not have originally descended" to them.[26] One example she offers is that of Mary Lacy, who in 1736 went to court to enroll a deed in her own name and that of her sister in order to lay claim to Lomer manor and rectory, which Mary Bone had devised to Lacy's mother and thereafter William Moore. Lacy asserted that her mother was now dead and that Moore was a papist and so incapable of owning the property or receiving its income. She enrolled her claim to the land she thought rightfully belonged to her and her sister.[27] Similarly, the case of the widowed Elizabeth Williamson demonstrates how women capitalized on their power and often secured property rights to their daughters. Her case appears in manor court records as early as 1695, when she and her husband successfully sued a builder for poor work on a new house.[28] But it is her history of ownership and the bequests she made that is of interest for my discussion. Elizabeth was a joint tenant of her home with her first husband, inheriting it after his death. When she later married John Williamson, she remained the sole tenant, giving the tenancy to her daughter only after her second husband's death. Even then, she retained a life occupancy and rented out rooms to provide an income. The mortgage was cleared and the granddaughter to whom it eventually passed purchased the freehold. Two other properties that Elizabeth held as surviving joint tenant with her second husband passed at her death to her son. Her example demonstrates the manner in which savvy widows could not only redirect property among family members, but also ensure matrilineal lines of inheritance. Yet the practice of entail worked against such redirection in the service of maintaining patrilineal lines, especially in the eighteenth century. Entails had long been used to distribute land to younger children, but they were also used to keep land and property in the hands of male descendants, as we see in Jane Austen's *Sense and Sensibility* (which we will discuss later). Spring recognizes that "the increasing hostility to female heirs must have meant some use of such a weapon against them."[29] Since entails could specify the sex of the inheritor, females could summarily be cut out of inheriting land and property for a lifetime or even in perpetuity.

The Importance of Nieces

Yet while women from wealthy families may have been limited by entails, working- and middling-rank women routinely inherited and bequeathed portable property, real estate, and businesses. In the first half of the eighteenth century, we see single, female business owners take up will-making. Froide observes, "Of the 2 million wills which survive from the mid-sixteenth to the mid-eighteenth century, approximately one fifth (or 400,000) were made by women."[30] For Vann, the most striking aspect of the period between 1725 and 1800 is the increasing prominence of women as will-writers and inheritors.[31] Because various studies focus on different parishes or counties and differing time spans it is difficult to discern clear patterns, but in general the proportion of wills that were made by women grew only slightly over the early modern period. In her study of women's wills in Lancashire and Cheshire between 1660 and 1837, Amy Louise Erickson observes that women with estates under £40 decreased from 31 to 23%, and those with estates over £40 remained relatively consistent, between 18 and 22%.[32] Froide recognizes that "although never-married women and widows always left more legacies to kin, friends, and servants than did men, over the eighteenth century women began to leave two to three times more bequests to these individuals than did men."[33] In a study of wills in Southhampton, Froide observes that aunts helped their nieces by providing them with portions or property. For example, the widow Mary Carteret bequeathed two houses and the George Inn to her five nieces. Froide remarks, "Such property helped maintain at least one lifelong singlewoman, for Carteret's niece Frances Gollop was still single twenty-eight years after she had received her inheritance."[34] In her will from 1780, the never-married investor Mary Trevor left an annuity of £250 transferable at the Bank of England to her two sisters and then to her nieces.[35] In the absence of a husband or direct male heir, widows and non-married women controlled their own money and property, as Lennox's *Henrietta* and Burney's *Cecilia* depict.[36] While an absolute bequest to a wife was typically made with the understanding that the wife shared the same familial interest as her dying husband, widows could direct property and investments to other female relatives on their own accord and even redirect money destined for male blood relatives to non-blood-related women, such as a niece-in-law.

In fact, the twin situations we see in *Cecilia*—the uncle's will that bequeaths a large fortune to his niece, Cecilia, and the will of Mortimer's maternal aunt that bequeaths her fortune to Cecilia, a niece-in-law—were not that uncommon in actual practice. Nieces often receive special attention in wills from the period, as we saw in the case of Mary Carteret, yet they haven't received nearly as much scholarly attention as wives and daughters. In my work on Chancery cases of the period, I was struck by the number of nieces who used the court system to hold onto legacies (ranging from a £10 annual income to a £10,000 inheritance) not only from their uncles, but also from their aunts and other female relatives.[37] A few examples from the *English Reports* will underscore these practices and demonstrate the growing importance of aunt-niece legacies. In *Williams v. Jones*, we learn that Ann Jones left her nieces and nephews sizeable legacies, ranging from

£100 to £150, and her god-daughter £10. She also designated Mary Jones, her great-niece, as co-executrix of her estate. Upon Ann Jones's death in 1804, Mr. Williams, the co-executor, sued Mary Jones and several of the nephews and nieces who were Ann's next of kin to have the rights of the residual estate declared. The court first recognized that the will bequeathed to Mr. Williams "twenty pounds for his trouble" without any payment to Mary Jones for her role as co-executrix and then declared Mary Jones the recipient of the estate's residue.

In another case from the *English Reports*, nieces fought to keep annuities from both their aunt and uncle. In *Crompton v. Sale*, Thomas Boddington, in a will dated 20 August 1726, bequeathed money to numerous female relatives. He left his sister, Mary Potter, an annuity of £10 and his sister's daughter, Elizabeth Potter, an annuity of £5. To his niece, Martha Nicholls, Boddington left an annuity of £10 and to her daughter Elizabeth an annuity of £5. He gave another niece, Martha Dimmock, an annuity of £10 and her daughter, Elizabeth Dimmock, £5. All of the annuities were to be paid by his wife, Elizabeth Boddington, out of his personal estate tax-free, and Boddington made his wife his sole executrix and residuary legatee.[38] It's notable that Boddington recognizes numerous women and their daughters in his will. But what drew this case into court was its use of matriarchal legacies. In 1728, Elizabeth Boddington made her own will, giving Elizabeth Potter an additional £5 "to her and her heirs for ever, in case she should survive her mother Mary Potter, *and not otherwise.*" She gave Elizabeth Nicholls, the second daughter of her niece Martha Nicholls, an annuity of £5, her niece Martha Dimmock an annuity of £10, and to Martha's daughter, Elizabeth Dimmock, an annuity of £5. The question brought to the court was whether the annuities given by Elizabeth Boddington should be taken as a satisfaction of the similar annuities given to them by the will of Thomas Boddington ("they being bequeathed by her who having her husband's personal estate, was become a debtor in respect thereof, and consequently might intend the legacies in satisfaction of such debt") or whether the heirs should have the several annuities given to them by both wills? Citing numerous cases, the Lord Chancellor decided for the defendants: Martha and Elizabeth Dimmock, as well as Elizabeth Potter and Elizabeth Nicholls (if they should survive their respective mothers), should receive the annuities given to them by both wills.[39] He stated, "I see no reason why it may not be supposed the testatrix intended to be kind as well as just to her husband's relations, and to make an addition to what he had given them."[40] Therefore, the nieces prevailed in court, and were each granted both of the annuities bequeathed to them.

It comes as no surprise that women of the aristocracy were regularly involved in inheritance cases that eventually made it to Chancery. As I examined cases that involved female wills, it became clear that widowed heiresses demonstrated the importance of matriarchal legacies in their wills. *Lady Lincoln v. Pelham* is a notable Chancery case that reflects the economic power of the aristocratic heiress. Lady Catherine Pelham, in her will of 1 July 1775, bequeaths £4,000 each to her sons-in-law, the Duke of Newcastle and Lord Sondes, and £2,000 each to her two daughters, Lady Sondes and Mary Pelham (unmarried). She appoints another daughter, Frances Pelham (also unmarried), and Mary Pelham executrixes of her will and also bequeaths them "all the residue of her goods, chattels, and personal estate and effects ... equally to be divided between them."[41] In 1780, Lady Catherine made a codicil that revoked the legacy to the Duke of Newcastle. When she died in 1781, three petitions were presented to the court, including one from other sons of the Duke and the children of Lady Sondes suing for what they believed to be their rightful inheritance. The case would take over twenty years to settle. During this time, Mary Pelham died without issue and appointed her sister Frances to be her executrix. Unfortunately, Frances died in 1804 intestate, unmarried, and without issue. In his decision, the Lord Chancellor stated that the intention of the children's grandmother should be the primary consideration. He cited the will that designates that the "younger" children of her daughters inherit upon their mothers' deaths and finds that since there is only one surviving "youngest" child, he should receive three-quarters of the estate (£8,000) and the remaining portion should be distributed to those considered the "youngest" at the time of her death. Though a male grandson received the majority of the estate, Lady Catherine's steerage of her wealth and the legal trust set up to manage her bequests relied upon her daughters.

In *Henry Davis v. Henry Gibbs, Administrator of Elizabeth Gibbs* (1729), we see how Lady Boreman, in a will dated 1699, bequeathed "all her manors, messuages, lands, tenements, hereditaments, and real estate whatsoever in *Kent, Essex, Bucks, Bedfordshire*, or elsewhere within the kingdom of *England*, of which she was any way *seised or entitled* to, unto her nephew *Henry Davis* the appellant, and to her niece *Elizabeth* (the wife of the respondent *Gibbs*) for their lives equally, share and share alike; and after their decease, then the testatrix devised her said real estate to the heirs of her said nephew *Henry Davis* (the appellant) and of her said niece *Elizabeth Gibbs*, equally in equal parts, to hold them and their heirs, as tenants in common."[42] Her niece Elizabeth Gibbs died without issue and her husband was her administrator. Is Henry Davis entitled to his sister's inheritance? Or should it go to her husband? After years of delays and appeals ("the cause had been four times heard in Chancery"), the Lord Chancellor ultimately decided "that the same belonged to the respondent the husband, as administrator to his wife, and not her brother the appellant, as heir at law." While the niece's inheritance ended up in her husband's hands, and not another woman's, what is important here is the potential for transfers of property between women. In another niece case, *East et Maria Ux' v. Thornbury* (1731), Thomas Thornbury left his niece £300, payable a year after his death. Her brother, as executor, held onto the legacy for two years, eventually paying his sister, Mary Thornbury, £300 without interest. Mary sued for the interest and won, with her brother ordered to "pay the arrears of interest from the year after the testator's death, with costs of suit."[43] As this and so many other cases, both pre- and post-Hardwicke, demonstrate, women not only included daughters in their wills, but also nieces, who played critical roles in the transmission of legacies and often successfully defend their inheritances in court. This phenomenon is reflected in inheritance plots such as those of *Henrietta* and *Cecilia*, in which nieces and other extended female relatives who receive bequests demonstrate changes in kinship relations and economies. With their financial importance being challenged and their role in inheritance practices shifting, women sought additional paths for female legacies. Needing to expand the familial net for their bequests and investments, women increasingly saw nieces as critical to female-to-female inheritance systems.

Middling and Working Rank Bequests

One of the most fascinating discoveries of regional studies is the increase in the number of women's wills in industrial towns. As women gained new economic power, they became increasingly concerned with their legacies. Industrial development created opportunities for them to hold property and create wealth. Maxine Berg argues that in the new industrial towns, such as Birmingham and Sheffield, a higher portion of women owned real property and had substantial amounts of cash to bequeath to their children. In those metal-working centers, 22.8% of women in Birmingham and 18.1% in Sheffield, nearly all of them spinsters or widows, left wills over the course of the eighteenth century.[44] For example, in the 1789 "Will and Probate of Elizabeth Andrews of Sheffield, Widow," Andrews left a small legacy to the couple she lived with and listed six other women as legatees.[45] Christine Wiskin's study of urban businesswomen in the period shows that their wills specifically designated their daughters or nieces as much as their sons or nephews to "inherit the assets which would enable them to continue family enterprises."[46] Wiskin observes that "widows or daughters came into their own when they inherited the business. They were now in a position to choose whether to wind it up and live on the proceeds, or to continue it."[47]

Her study demonstrates that a "sizeable minority" of women who inherited businesses continued them. She describes widows who owned or managed properties and businesses as stand-ins for deceased husbands and who regarded spinster daughters as the "surrogate sons" of their parents. Wiskin asserts that "female life cycles explain why urban women had to provide for themselves; family circumstances were a form of empowerment, providing monetary and social capital for the widows and daughters of businessmen."[48] This economic power—typically regarded as male—would, in turn, provide opportunities for women to create matriarchal instead of patriarchal legacies. Indeed, women maneuvered their way through the inheritance system, many specifically bequeathing their inherited businesses to female relatives.

Though women bequeathed businesses, lent money, and otherwise participated in what was generally considered the male sphere of property exchange, the majority of women's wills bequeathed portable property, as entails and strict settlements limited the inheritance of land. Dorothy Howard's will from 1748 (not proved until 1760) reflects this practice. Though not wealthy, Howard was proud of her economic power and bestowed a legacy on her "poor servant who has given me undeniable proofs of her honesty uncommon fidelity and concern for me." She wrote: "I am persuaded my friend and relations will not blame me for bestowing upon my said servant all the residue of my estate I do therefore give devise and bequeath to the said Margaret White all the rest residue and remainder of my good cloaths money or securities."[49] From the mid-eighteenth century on, British women tended to bequeath more frequently to close female kin, friends, and servants than they had done previously (and more frequently than they did to men).[50] Even granddaughters saw increased visibility as inheritors. Mary Astell (not the celebrated writer) received a legacy from her grandmother, Mary Millington, which later became part of an inheritance dispute in *Bouchier v. Horngold* (1754). Ann Headlam's will of 1834 bequeathed a legacy to her niece, Mary Oates, who "was duly rewarded for many visits paid to her Aunt when she was sick." Mary received "linen, books, wine, wearing apparel and ornaments as well as a half share residual, which amounted to £145."[51] These detailed bequests show how women embraced one of the few forms of legal independence and power allowed them. Bequests given by women to daughters, granddaughters, nieces, and female servants and friends indicate not only the increasing importance of self-fashioning in the process of writing or dictating a will and choosing items (however small) to bequeath, they also reveal how the female testator can bestow economic power on other women. Working within a restrictive patrilineal system, both wealthy and ordinary women found ways to maintain and bequeath to other women both their personal and their real property. In so doing, female-to-female bequests provided future models for inheritance and the opportunity for inheriting women to continue this practice.

Of course, will-making is integral to this inscription of female economic power and legacy, which is why so many novels attend to the dangers of lost inheritances. A rewriting of *Evelina*, Georgiana, Duchess of Devonshire's scandalous *The Sylph* (1779) depicts a series of female heiresses who control formerly "male" estates; yet, like *Cecilia*, it narrates the loss of matrilineal lines of property. The history of the inheritance of a comparatively minor character, Maria Maynard, speaks to the narrative possibilities of female economies and the threat that they supposedly pose to patrilineage. Edward Grenville, the father of the novel's heroine Julia, writes to his daughter informing her of his previously untold past. Poor, yet of good blood, he fell in love with a young "heiress of upwards of thirty thousand pounds," and despite the protestations of her family, they married.[52] On the eve of her turning twenty-one, she suffered an attack of gout and died, leaving her will unsigned. The stipulations of her inheritance decreed that, should she die childless before she came of age, the large estate to which she was heiress would then "devolve upon a cousin": Maria Maynard. To intercept the estate and prevent its matrilinear transfer, Maria's father remarried, had a son with his second wife, and then falsely announced that Maria was dead, so that his son could inherit her fortune (Maria was so scarred from smallpox as to be unrecognizable).[53] Edward then sued on the theory that his former wife was entitled to her estate on the day of her marriage, despite being underage. Ultimately, Maria is disinherited and Edward recovers the estate, but in the meantime he eloped with Maria (who will become Julia's mother), which somehow softens the economic violence.

The Sylph thus dramatizes the male anxieties produced by female will-making and female-to-female bequests. Edward Grenville seeks legal counsel to uphold his claim on his former wife's estate, and Maria Maynard's father proceeds to remarry and father a child in the hope of intercepting his "dead" daughter's inheritance. Both cases involve litigation (though off-page). As women's roles as executrixes and administratixes increased, actual court cases from the period reflect a higher proportion of female litigants who were caught up in disputes over the estates of the deceased. A study of Chancery by Henry Horwitz found that women made up 14.4% of plaintiffs in 1627 and 21.2% by 1818-19.[54] In "Putting Women in Their Place: Female Litigants at Whitehaven, 1660-1760," Christine Churches examines regional court proceedings to show that "widows were often obliged to sue for maintenance."[55] Over half of the suits in Common Pleas and King's Bench records involved women "exercising administration of the effects of deceased husbands or brothers."[56] Churches remarks that "Widows' knowledge of property law and business strongly suggests their active participation in these areas of social life before their widowhood."⁵⁷ But while these regional studies demonstrate that women were active participants in litigation over their inheritances, studies such as those of Eileen Spring, Maxine Berg, and Eva König find that wealthy women increasingly favored private, rather than public legal proceedings over the course of the second half of the century, as we will see in *Emmeline*. I have highlighted some interesting cases that did go to court, but most suits, both in law and in equity, never progressed beyond the initial complaint and were generally settled through private agreement or arbitration.⁵⁸ Noting the increase in private legal structures, Berg argues that the decline of the widow-executrix, for example, reflects a shift in the management of household financial affairs to lawyers.⁵⁹ So while women certainly sought to litigate for their inheritances, they had to navigate the ever-growing realities of the legal doctrine of coverture, patriarchal court systems, and gendered notions of proper behavior.

Charlotte Smith, who notoriously fought in court for years for her own rightful inheritance and that of her children, places heiresses at the center of her plots in order to dramatize the financial strength of matriarchal economies.⁶⁰ A useful example is that of *Emmeline, The Orphan of the Castle* (1788), which opens with a complex legacy of female inheritance, symbolized by Mowbray Castle and its inhabitant Emmeline, the supposed "natural" (i.e., illegitimate) daughter of the deceased Mr. Mowbray. How Emmeline eventually secures her birthright and inherits the castle at the end of the novel is intricately detailed by Smith, as is the female role in the castle's ownership history. With the extinction of her family's male line, Lady Eleonore Delamere became "sole heiress, her husband took the name of Delamere; and obtaining one of the titles of the lady's father, was, at his death, created Viscount Montreville."⁶¹ In her will, Lady Delamere leaves her eldest son, Mr. Mowbray, "the large estate," and he then marries, having a son and two daughters. After Mr. Mowbray and his wife die, the castle passes to his younger brother, Lord Montreville, who finds it inhabited by the orphaned infant Emmeline. Since her parents eloped and were thought not to have been married when she was born, Emmeline is allowed to remain in the castle with its servants and is given the surname "Mowbray." Fifteen years later, Lord Montreville hands the castle (and its residents, including Emmeline) over to his son. While Lord Montreville and his son Delamere are confident that the castle's ownership is not at risk, Smith consistently gestures toward the Cinderella myth through Emmeline's sympathetic and disenfranchised position. As Eva König recognizes, Smith's protagonist must "both be impeccable in her behavior and yet become increasingly self-assertive as the narrative develops."⁶² At the close of the novel, Emmeline locates documents that not only prove her parents were indeed married (Mr. Mowbray married Miss Stavordale in France after Lady Delamere died), but also that Emmeline had been left the Mowbray estate by her father. After some legal intervention, Emmeline is declared owner of the estate. In fact, a set of lawyers helps Emmeline avoid a public lawsuit and instead reach a private agreement.[63]

Effectively, this legal intervention results in Emmeline disinheriting her uncle, Lord Montreville, and his son (her cousin), Delamere. Smith recognizes the financial triumph that this represents by stating that Emmeline "saw an infinite deal for which to be grateful, and failed not to offer her humble acknowledgements to that Providence, which, from dependance and indigence, had raised her to the highest affluence; given her, in the tenderest of husbands, the best and the most generous and most amiable of men; and had bestowed on her the means and the inclination to deserve, by virtue and beneficence, that heaven where only she can enjoy more perfect and lasting felicity."[64] Mowbray Castle has become a symbol of matrilineal bonds; from being a site of contestation, it eventually becomes the site of Emmeline's mastery and advantage. Loraine Fletcher writes that "Emmeline's intelligence and humanity make her, rather than the Montrevilles, the right person to inherit and renovate Mowbray Castle, and to use the power that goes with it."[65] I agree, but Fletcher doesn't address the female legacy that has enabled Emmeline's proper inheritance. Indeed, Emmeline becomes a heroine of economic *interest* and success; economic considerations are allowed to play a part in her marriage choice and her virtue is rewarded nonetheless. As in many of her novels, Smith envisions women's successful navigation and overthrowing of patriarchal property ownership. In *Emmeline*, Smith politicizes her heroine's position, thereby creating a powerful fantasy of disinheriting male property owners. Emmeline benefits from the fact that her cousin Delamere, the previous owner of the castle, died in a duel and from the legal documents that surface proving her parents' marriage and her right to inherit the castle and estate. Yet as we have seen in actual court cases, legal structures were in place that rewarded patrilineal inheritance, limited married women's property ownership (through coverture), and restricted female inheritance.

Smith's courtship novel *Celestina* (1791) similarly includes numerous occasions of female-to-female gifting and inheritance. Celestina de Mornay, poor and without family connections, financially assists the attractive servant girl Jessy, befriends the abandoned Sophy Elphinstone, and financially assists Sophy's sister, the destitute and dying prostitute Emily. Yet it is Lady Horatia Howard's financial generosity that fully dramatizes the power of matriarchal gifting. The affectionate and philanthropic Lady Horatia is so impressed with Celestina's education, sensibility, and virtue that she rewrites her will, intending to provide Celestina a sort of "pin money" for her future marriage:

> Her encreasing tenderness for Celestina, made her often reflect with uneasiness on her situation, and very earnestly wish to see her married ... she knew that after having taken her as her daughter, and accustomed her to share all the indulgencies which her own rank and income procured, it would be a very painful reverse of fortune were she to leave her in the narrow circumstances in which she found her. To save much out of her jointure had never been her wish, and was hardly now in her power. Her own fortune, in default of children, returned to her brother; and all she had to dispose of was about two thousand pounds. This she gave, by a will made in the fourth month of their being together, to Celestina; and with this, and what she before had, she thought that Celestina might, if married to Montague Thorold, enjoy through life that easy competence which was the utmost of her ambition.[66]

Lady Horatia navigates her own inheritance and finances, carefully ensuring that Celestina (who at this point in the novel has not yet been discovered to be a relative) is provided for, so that she may enjoy a form of financial independence in marriage. This virtuous gifting differs from the novel's patrilineal inheritance plot. Willoughby's uncle, Lord Castlenorth, settles a large sum of money on him when he becomes engaged to the Castlenorths' daughter, a reward for keeping both estates within the family. When Castlenorth dies without discovering that the engagement has been broken off, Willoughby keeps the money without any retribution or criticism. And when Willoughby eventually marries her, Celestina benefits from this inheritance as well.

While, as we saw, the success of Cecilia's and Celestina's inheritance and female gifting is tempered, *Emmeline* convincingly depicts female lines of succession and the inheritance of portable property that enables its heroine a certain amount of personal and economic agency. While Austen will pillory the Miss Bingleys and de Bourghs for their outspoken financial power, Smith rewards her virtuous, yet financially interested heroines with their birthrights, good husbands, and ultimately the keys to the castle.

The Decline of the Actual Heiress and the Rise of the Literary Heiress

By Jane Austen's day, English inheritance practices were largely patrilineal. The entail on Norland, which disinherits the Dashwood women in *Sense and Sensibility* (1811), and that on Longbourn in *Pride and Prejudice*

(1813), which results in the disinheritance of the five Bennet sisters, are two well-known fictional examples of the consolidation and retention of property. Non-portable property (houses, land) was primarily funneled to male children—or, in the case of Longbourn, to Mr. Collins, a male cousin—through entail. For many historians, this resulted in what has often been termed the "great decline of the female heiress." While historians such as Lawrence and Jeanne Fawtier Stone concluded that the percentage of English heiresses actually rose in this period (to a high of 17% of all heirs in 1760-79), more recent studies of wills and court cases tell the story of a deterioration in women's access to property.[67] In *Novel Relations*, Ruth Perry traces the legal disinheritance of daughters in the eighteenth century and fictional treatments of this phenomenon. Perry is reacting to studies, such as that of the Stones, which she believes are embedded in class bias and misleading, male-centered views of the eighteenth-century family. To counter such biases, she recovers traditional maternal constructions of the family, noting that "English society had always prized its daughters" and that through both the maternal and paternal lines "daughters inherited as well as sons, and widows had substantial property rights in their deceased husbands' estates. Daughters inherited property before collateral male relatives, and in landed families daughters were sometimes given land as their marriage portion."[68] Yet according to Perry, the seventeenth century witnessed a shift from this bilateral kin system to a lineage system defined primarily by male primogeniture and the marriage of first-born sons.[69] By mid-century, the erosion of provisions for daughters, wives, and widows in equity, manorial, and ecclesiastical courts as well as common law was evident.[70]

Provisions in common law began limiting women's inheritance of land, and a series of statutes in ecclesiastical law reduced what counted as a reasonable portion for a woman of her husband's or father's moveable goods from as much as two-thirds to one-third or less.[71] Spring argues that the proportion of families who, by chance, had no heirs at all and only female collateral relatives, combined with those who had only female heirs, adds up to between 25% and 40% of all inheritances.[72] Spring demonstrates how collateral male relatives (such as the brothers of a woman's father or even a nephew) were often placed in the line of succession if there were no male offspring in a family.[73] By the early eighteenth century, strict settlement became the primary means by which land passed between members of the gentry and aristocracy. Inherited property was transferred according to terms set out by property owners. According to Lloyd Bonfield, "Property holders were freer to fashion individualized strategies of inheritance than strict adherence to the customs of inheritance would have allowed."[74] Yet this partial freedom to individualize bequests had its drawbacks. Bonfield finds that "the considerable quantity of litigation over dispositions suggests that the designs of property holders were not always respected. Numerous suits were probably initiated and then settled, leaving the historian with some doubt as to the actual distribution of family property."[75]

Following strict settlement provisions, women's hereditary rights were ultimately made secondary since the agreements often followed primogeniture in entailing property through the successive eldest sons. Spring claims that aristocratic women's portions had been steadily shrinking over the course of the seventeenth century, and in the eighteenth century "inheritance would not be traced through [the heiress] except as a last resort … the interests of the patriline were uppermost."[76] She notes that by the end of the eighteenth century, "only 11 percent of peers' sons had married heiresses."[77] Similarly, in his seminal study of landownership, John Habakkuk finds that there was a decline in the number of heiresses from the mid-eighteenth century onwards "because of demographic changes," including attitudes that valued seeking dynastic advantage through marriage (i.e., the landed family had become commercial).[78] This shift diminished women as landowners, but emphasized their role as conduits in the patrilineal transmission of land. Perry recognizes the peril this posed, asserting that for numerous, interrelated reasons, "women of both the landowning and working classes lost economic power within the family and status in society in the course of the eighteenth century."[79] Women found themselves more powerful as wives than as daughters because as wives they could bring property into a family, whereas daughters only shared in the estate and so reduced what could be passed on to future generations.[80]

In addition to economic, demographic, and familial changes, there were numerous legal reasons for the decline of the heiress. Among its other purposes, Lord Hardwicke's Marriage Act was "aimed at preventing heirs or heiresses from being duped into marriage with persons (ostensibly fortune-hunters) who were socially and/or economically inferior."[81] While the Act benefited and protected women and helped to better regulate property, it may have also contributed to the commercialization of marriage by causing "property in land to become entangled to its detriment with self-interest."[82] By both limiting and protecting women's financial independence, these restrictions included the transference of power to parental and marital guardians. Essentially, under the guise of providing security, these Acts partly limited women's inheritance and financial independence.

With the rise of female economic power and the emergence of laws that attempted to stifle that power, it is no wonder that legal cases involving monied heiresses declined in the period; as we saw in Smith's *Emmeline*, women increasingly sought private, rather than public, legal means to negotiate their inheritances. An example of women's dispossession by the legal system may be found in *Dormer v. Parkhurst* (1740). John Dormer, a member of a collateral branch of the Dormer family, challenged the possession of land by three sisters identified in a will as heirs-general (a situation in which property passed to a new owner according to a fixed order of kinship). The courts dispossessed the three sisters after they had been in possession for twelve years.[83] Spring remarks, "We may be sure that had Fleetwood [Dormer]'s heirs not been female the case would never have arisen. John Dormer would not likely have challenged a male in the senior branch of the family who was in possession."[84] Noting that English landowners had moved from lineal to patrilineal principles, Spring recognizes that the heiress in gentry and aristocratic families experienced a great downward slide.[85] Contradicting studies such as that of the Stones, she claims that only 13% of inheritances between 1540 and 1780 went either to or through women.[86] Legal developments restricting heiresses' rights and favoring private legal arrangements over public court cases resulted in the transplantation of the heiress from the margins of legal discourse to the center of fictional plots. Virginia Cope, Cheryl Nixon, Eva König, and others recognize that, as a result of this shift, heiresses became abundant in fiction. They not only nostalgically reflect an earlier economic practice, they also speak to the growing anxieties about threats to patrilineal inheritance (such as illegitimate children). By centering plots on rightful heiresses and their birthrights, manipulative male relatives who sought to siphon off an heiress's property, and virtuous natural daughters who ultimately discover their true parentage and are rewarded with social and economic status, female authors reacted to patrilineage and biased legal structures by dramatizing successful matrilineal economies.

Austen's Female Economies

Numerous studies of Jane Austen have focused on the material disadvantages of women and the heroines in her novels.[87] We can agree that, although Austen certainly depicts notable heiress-heroines, such as Emma Woodhouse or Anne Elliott, and numerous minor heiresses (such as Miss Grey, Miss Bingley, or Mary Crawford), many of her heroines are socially and economically vulnerable (the Bennet sisters, the Dashwood sisters, Fanny Price) and threatened by relative poverty, despite the fact that they are often from genteel families. Yet embedded in these plots of economic danger that seems to offer no material benefit to women, there are some notable examples of successful matriarchal inheritance plots. For instance, the widowed Mrs. Ferrars, in *Sense and Sensibility*, is a wealthy, manipulative mother who commands her first son Edward with the threat of disinheritance.[88] In fact, she eventually disinherits him for refusing to marry an heiress—"the Hon. Miss Morton, only daughter of the late Lord Morton, with thirty thousand pounds"—and persevering in his engagement to Lucy Steele, who quickly transfers her affections to the now favored son, Robert. When Robert pursues the poor, sycophantic Lucy, Mrs. Ferrars is forced to accept the match and provide them with a thousand a year, which allows Edward to pursue his true love, Elinor Dashwood. Despite all this, we are supposed to somehow accept the novel's concluding statement regarding the alliance between Lucy, Robert, Mrs. Ferrars, and John and Fanny Dashwood: "nothing could exceed the harmony in which they all lived together."[89] In the end, not only is Lucy's economic self-interest rewarded, Austen also suggests that money-wielding widows cannot ultimately overpower young love. Mrs. Ferrars may not have the daughters-in-law she would like, but she can rest assured that her main responsibility has been achieved: the Ferrars' name and estate will continue in the patrilineal line.

With this reading of the powerful heiress-widow in mind, I wish to close by considering a similar economic situation, that of the de Bourgh women in *Pride and Prejudice,* who have received relatively little critical attention.[90] Extremely wealthy, Lady Catherine has been seen as a "larger comic target than the novel's more conventionally silly girls and women."[91] Elsie Michie recognizes that, for Austen, Lady Catherine and Miss Bingley "represent wealth's propensity to corrupt the moral sentiments."[92] While I agree that Austen caricatures these "vulgar," "indelicate" women, providing negative models for virtuous women to reject in terms of their attitudes toward property, I would also claim that we can look to the de Bourghs as powerful symbols of matriarchal economies. In fact, their financial situation perhaps simultaneously signals both a remembrance of lineal inheritance (now wasted and sickly because of the growing dominance of patrilineal practices) and a rejection of the entail practices that haunt the Bennets. The haughty and powerful widow, Lady Catherine de Bourgh, who presides over an elaborate estate, Rosings, wields her economic and social power throughout the novel, directing the Bennet family, approving of Mr. Collins's marriage, and in some ways controlling Fitzwilliam Darcy, her nephew. Should she survive her mother, the sickly Anne de Bourgh, the only child and invalid daughter of Lady Catherine, will inherit a massive fortune through the maternal line, including Rosings, an estate that is not entailed (Lady Catherine famously pronounces, "Otherwise I see no occasion for entailing estates from the female line. It was not thought necessary in Sir Lewis de Bourgh's family").[93] By anticipating that Anne will marry her maternal first cousin, Lady Catherine seeks to have her estate consolidated with the Darcy family's Pemberley. Such a match would result in significant material advantage, not only in terms of portable wealth, but also in land, an asset increasingly kept from women. Yet as with many cousin-couples in Austen, the match is never looked on as favorable and it never materializes.[94] Austen may focus on the resentments and damaging effects of inheritance, but with Mrs. Ferrars, Miss Bingley, and the de Bourghs, we are also reminded of the economic power that matriarchal inheritance can wield and endow.

Conclusion

Primogeniture made very wealthy heiresses a rarity, yet, as I have shown, matriarchal bequeathing—though often minimized in plots—abounded in eighteenth-century literature and society. Legal regulations may have attempted to control women's economic power and behavior, but will-making women often made female-to-female bequests, from small gestures transferring personal belongings to larger gifts of businesses, buildings, and land. While working- and middling-rank women's wills that included personal bequests to other women flourished in the period, the monied heiress saw a decline. In fiction, however, the figures of the business-minded, maternal heiress and the controlling, rich widow ultimately wielded the power of matrilineal inheritance. I see these female birthright and inheritance plots responding to the broader concerns about female economic power: the rightful heiress who financially supports or makes bequests to other women symbolizes the potential for women of all ranks to continue diverse forms of female bequests, despite the limitations placed upon them by gender norms and the law. These cultural anxieties about women, femininity, and the marketplace eventually produce a myriad of heiresses in the nineteenth-century novel, which further explores the moral conundrum of femininity and the amassing of wealth. Indeed, Jane Eyre is an exemplar of the heiress who gifts wealth and independence to her poor female relations. Yet it is in the emerging capitalism of the eighteenth century that we find these female economic forces first played out in fiction. And as women's reliance on the legal system to rightfully distribute bequeathed property waned, the novel took up these concerns about property and its proper regulation and transmission, allowing women to symbolically and literally hold the keys to the castle.

Notes

I wish to thank the two anonymous readers for their helpful suggestions, as well as Jakob Ladegaard for his detailed feedback on an early draft. I am grateful to Simon Stern and Lisa Cody for organizing the roundtable at the 2021 Virtual Meeting of the American Society for Eighteenth-Century Studies on "Law, Life, and Literature in the British Eighteenth Century," at which I presented the initial ideas for this essay.

1. Spring, *Law, Land and Family: Aristocratic Inheritance in England, 1300–1800* (Chapel Hill: University of North Carolina Press, 1993), 13.

2. Both married and unmarried women were active in the English economy as producers, consumers, lenders, investors, owners, and managers of property. See Staves, *Married Women's Separate Property in England, 1660–1833* (Cambridge: Harvard University Press, 1990), 27–55. Following Staves, Amy Louise Erickson, *Women and Property in Early Modern England* (New York: Routledge, 1993) and Amy M. Froide, *Never Married: Singlewomen in Early Modern England* (Oxford: Oxford University Press, 2005) and *Silent Partners: Women as Public Investors during Britain's Financial Revolution, 1690–1750* (Oxford: Oxford University Press, 2016) examine women's financial agency in the period.

3. Spring, *Law, Land and Family*, 93.

4. Haywood, *The History of Miss Betsy Thoughtless* (Oxford: Oxford University Press, 1997), 386.

5. See April London, *Women and Property in the Eighteenth-Century English Novel* (Cambridge: Cambridge University Press, 1999); Lisa Zunshine, *Bastards and Foundlings: Illegitimacy in Eighteenth-Century England* (Columbus: The Ohio State University Press, 2005); Virginia H. Cope, *Property, Education, and Identity in Late Eighteenth-Century Fiction: The Heroine of Disinterest* (New York: Palgrave Macmillan, 2009); Cheryl L. Nixon, *The Orphan in Eighteenth-Century Law and Literature: Estate, Blood, and Body* (New York: Routledge, 2011); and Eva König, *The Orphan in Eighteenth-Century Fiction: The Vicissitudes of the Eighteenth-Century Subject* (New York: Palgrave Macmillan, 2014).

6. "Disinterest" is a term with numerous meanings. The *OED* defines it as "that which is contrary to interest or advantage," as well as "impartiality" and "unconcern." The character type identified by Cope fits all of these definitions. In *Property, Education, and Identity*, she argues that the domestic novel reflects a "feminization of disinterest" (4) and that the heroine of disinterest is valued by her "attitude toward … property" and her recognition that property rights are "earned rather than bequeathed" (6). Cope's study does not take into account active, economically minded female characters or those whose disinterest is feigned.

7. An Act for the Better Preventing of Clandestine Marriages, popularly known as Lord Hardwicke's Marriage Act, required that weddings in England and Wales take place only in church and that couples had to be 21 years of age to marry without the consent of their parents. Scotland's refusal to accept the Act led to numerous couples in England fleeing to Gretna Green to marry.

8. Lennox, *Henrietta*, ed. Ruth Perry and Susan Carlile (Lexington: University Press of Kentucky, 2010), 132.

9. For an excellent assessment of Lennox's heroines and marriage plots, see Susan Carlile, *Charlotte Lennox: An Independent Mind* (Toronto: University of Toronto Press, 2018).

10. Burney, *Evelina, or, The History of a Young Lady's Entrance into the World*, ed. Edward A. Bloom (Oxford: Oxford University Press, 1982), 378.

11. Burney, *Evelina*, 378.

12. Burney, *Evelina*, 378. Burney does not disclose the exact amount of Evelina's inheritance. Lord Belmont's "gift" would be considered an *inter vivos* settlement, i.e., one that transmitted property or goods while the bequeather was still alive.

13. Cope, *Property, Education, and Identity*, 57.

14. Burney, *Cecilia, or Memoirs of an Heiress*, ed. Peter Sabor and Margaret Anne Doody (Oxford: Oxford University Press, 1999), 939.

15. Burney, *Cecilia*, 804.

16. *Critical Review* 54 (December 1782), 414. Margaret Anne Doody notes that "the approving review in this periodical may have been written by Charles Burney's old friend Thomas Twining" (*Frances Burney: The Life in the Works* [Cambridge: Cambridge University Press, 1989], 405 n66).

17. Burney, *Cecilia*, 939.

18. Burney, *Cecilia*, 939.

19. Froide, *Never Married*, 204. My essay examines personal bequests, but there are numerous women's wills from the period that bequeath funds to women's charitable associations, schools, and hospitals.

20. Vann, "Wills and the Family in an English Town: Banbury, 1550–1800," *Journal of Family History* 4, no. 4 (1979), 366.

21. Vann, "Wills and the Family," 366.

22. Ashby, *The Changing English Village: A History of Bledington, Gloucestershire in Its Setting, 1066–1914* (Kineton: Roundwood Press, 1975), 116.

23. Cooper, "Intergenerational Social Mobility in Late Seventeenth- and Early-Eighteenth-Century England," *Continuity and Change* 7, no. 3 (1992): 283–301.

24. Cramond, *A Ladies Legacie to Her Daughters* (London, 1645). For more on Cramond, see Lloyd Davis, "Women's Wills in Early Modern England," in *Women, Property, and the Letters of the Law in Early Modern England*, ed. Nancy E. Wright, Margaret Ferguson, and A. R. Buck (Toronto: University of Toronto Press, 2004), 219–36. Elizabeth Jocelin's *The Mothers Legacie* (London, 1624) is another example of an early modern advice book that engages with female economies, limitations, and will-making along with the spiritual and moral legacies that mothers undisputedly endow upon their children.

25. Davis, "Women's Wills," 222.

26. Froide, *Never Married*, 128.

27. Froide, *Never Married*, 128. The case referenced is Hampshire Record Office (HRO), Q 1/12, fols. 143–45.

28. Cheshire Record Office (CRO) D/Lons/W5/232 (Street Survey Book), entries for 20 Lowther Street, 4 Duke Street, and 7 Plumblands Lane, Whitehaven. For

more on the litigation history of the Williamsons, see Christine Churches, "Putting Women in Their Place: Female Litigants at Whitehaven, 1660–1760," in *Women, Property, and the Letters of the Law in Early Modern England*, 58–59.

29. Froide, *Never Married*, 28.

30. Froide, *Never Married*, 204.

31. Vann, "Wills and the Family," 366.

32. Erickson, *Women and Property*, 156. These figures are the complete value of the estate in question. They would have yielded, according to Erickson, about £13 per annum in income.

33. Froide, *Never Married*, 65.

34. Froide, *Never Married*, 65. She cites Southampton Record Office (SRO), SC 4/4/491/1–2. Froide's study does not emphasize the significance of nieces in female will-making and bequests.

35. The National Archives, Public Record Office (PROB) 11/1063, Mary Trevor, spinster, 1780, cited in Froide, *Silent Partners*, 124.

36. Lloyd Bonfield observes that "although the 'unity of person' concept obtained in England as a legal construct, diaries and letters demonstrate that married women often assisted their husbands in managing estates, even running businesses. Moreover, men often selected their spouses as executors of their wills, suggesting that they had reasonable faith in the managerial skills of their widows; such confidence could only have been gained through experience during marriage" ("Developments in European Family Law," in *The History of the European Family*, ed. David I. Kertzer and Marzio Barbagli, 3 vols. [New Haven: Yale University Press, 2001], 1:123).

37. For instance, John Gale's will from 1767 bequeaths the Manor of Isleworth and its estates, furniture, and other articles to Samuel Barnelsey and William Hargrave "in trust for the sole use and benefit of his niece Henrietta Maria, the wife of Henry Stables, for and during the term of her natural life" and "notwithstanding her coverture, all the rents, issues, and profits, arising from the aforesaid premises." Gale's will also states that this estate should be held in trust for Mary Gale Stables, his niece's daughter, "for her maintenances" when she comes of age. Gale thus bequeaths a substantial annual income first to Henrietta and then to Mary, and in so doing creates a significant matriarchal legacy. See *Reid v. Shergold* (1805), in Francis Vesey and John Eykyn Hovenden, *Reports of Cases Argued and Determined in the High Court of Chancery*, 20 vols. (Boston: C. C. Little and J. Brown, 1844), 10:370–81. In a fictional example, the Duchess of Devonshire's *The Sylph* concludes with the heroine receiving a large living inheritance from her deceased husband's uncle. While a widow, Julia receives two thousand a year, and if she chooses to marry, Mr. Stanley will settle upon her fifteen thousand pounds.

38. For details, see William Peere Williams and Samuel Compston Cox, *Reports of Cases Argued and Determined in the High Court of Chancery and of some Special Cases Adjudged in the Court of King's Bench*, 3 vols. (London: A. Strahan and W. Woodfall, 1787), 2:553–55.

39. The Lord Chancellor cited several preceding cases in his determination: *Seed v Bradford, Crompton v Dymock, Barret v Beckford, Duffield v Smith, Attorney General v Hird, Chidley v Lee, Duke of Somerset v Duchess of Somerset, Mackdowell*

v Halfpenny, Davison v Goddard, Hanbury v Hanbury, Meredith v Wynn, and *Wood v. Briant.*

40. Williams and Cox, *Reports of Cases,* 2:555.

41. Francis Vesey, *Reports of Cases Argued and Determined in the High Court of Chancery from the Year 1789 to 1817,* 19 vols. (London: S. Sweet and Stevens and Sons, 1827–33), 10:167.

42. *Henry Davis v. Henry Gibbs, Administrator Of Elizabeth Gibbs,* in Williams and Cox, 3:26–33.

43. *East et Maria Ux' v. Thornbury* (1731), in Williams and Cox, *Reports of Cases,* 3:126.

44. Berg, "Women's Property and the Industrial Revolution," *Journal of Interdisciplinary History* 24, no. 2 (1993), 233–50. See also Penelope Lane, "Women, Property and Inheritance: Wealth Creation and Income Generation in Small English Towns, 1750–1835," in *Urban Fortunes: Property and Inheritance in the Town, 1700–1900,* ed. Jon Stobart and Alastair Owens (Farnham: Ashgate, 2000), 172–94.

45. YWD 1695/3, https://discovery.nationalarchives.gov.uk/details/r/f0d5c2bf-5e67-4f40-a625-30eeeb7f3f6b.

46. Wiskin, "Urban Businesswomen in Eighteenth-Century England," in *Women and Urban Life in Eighteenth-Century England: 'On the Town,'* ed. Rosemary Sweet and Penny Lane (Ashgate, 2003), 98.

47. Wiskin, "Urban Businesswomen," 109.

48. Wiskin, "Urban Businesswomen," 98.

49. Quoted in Davis, "Women's Wills," 230.

50. See Froide, *Never Married,* 12.

51. Legacy receipt on the account of the personal estate of Ann Headlam, 13 April 1835, Oates Papers, quoted in R. J. Morris, *Men, Women and Property in England, 1780–1870: A Social and Economic History of Family Strategies amongst the Leeds Middle Class* (Cambridge: Cambridge University Press, 2005), 96.

52. Georgiana, Duchess of Devonshire, *The Sylph,* ed. Jonathan David Gross (Evanston: Northwestern University Press, 2007), 38.

53. Though I don't have the space to go into detail, Maria's inheritance plot reads like a Victorian sensation novel (especially Wilkie Collins's *The Woman in White*). Her father advertises her death and has the body of an unknown woman buried in a grave, directing that "a large quantity of quicklime" be "put into the coffin."

54. Horwitz, *Chancery Equity Records and Proceedings, 1600–1800: A Guide to Documents in the Public Record Office* (London: HMSO, 1995), 36–37.

55. Churches, "Putting Women in Their Place," 53.

56. Churches, "Putting Women in Their Place," 53.

57. Churches, "Putting Women in Their Place," 58.

58. One study of litigants in the early seventeenth century shows that women comprised 5% to 13% of all litigants. See Christopher Brooks, *Lawyers, Litigation and English Society since 1450* (London: Hambledon Press, 1998), 111.

59. Berg, "Women's Property," 239.

60. Smith was involved in a lengthy legal battle over her father-in-law's will. In fact, the inheritance was tied up in Chancery for almost forty years. Through

bypassing his profligate son and leaving a large portion of his estate instead to Smith's children, Smith's father-in-law created a legal quagmire that was supposedly the basis for the seemingly infinite legal proceedings in Charles Dickens's *Bleak House*. By the time Smith's legal case succeeded, most of her father-in-law's £36,000 estate had been spent. See Loraine Fletcher, *Charlotte Smith: A Critical Biography* (London: Macmillan, 1998).

61. Smith, *Emmeline, The Orphan of the Castle,* ed. Loraine Fletcher (Peterborough: Broadview Press, 2003), 45.

62. König, *The Orphan,* 153.

63. König points out that this private agreement resembles the Private Acts of Parliament, which upheld "a model of the law acting on behalf of the individual by creating a singular, non-transferable law that solves the unique problems of the unique individual." These individuated acts "approximate a legal individualism that parallels the individualism of the novel" (*The Orphan,* 75). For more on Private Acts, see Spring, *Law, Land and Family,* 55–62.

64. Smith, *Emmeline,* 476.

65. Fletcher, Introduction to Smith, *Emmeline,* 22.

66. Smith, *Celestina,* ed. Loraine Fletcher (Peterborough: Broadview Press, 1999), 385.

67. Stone and Stone, *An Open Elite? England 1540–1880* (London: Clarendon Press, 1984), 119.

68. Perry, *Novel Relations: The Transformation of Kinship in English Literature and Culture, 1748–1818* (Cambridge: Cambridge University Press, 2004), 40.

69. Perry, *Novel Relations,* 40.

70. Perry, *Novel Relations,* 46.

71. Perry, *Novel Relations,* 47. Perry's assessment of "the great disinheritance" relies on the previous work of historians such as Erickson, Staves, Spring, and John Habakkuk.

72. Spring, *Law, Land and Family,* 10–15.

73. Spring, *Law, Land and Family,* 14–15. Spring does not fully address the rising importance of "collateral female relatives," such as nieces.

74. Bonfield, "Developments in European Family Law," 1:120.

75. Bonfield also observes that "with the exception of rare cases in which a wife sued her husband for maintenance, there was little interspousal litigation in England. Most litigation involving married women's property rights was undertaken by wives in conjunction with their husbands, for example to claim a portion owed by brides' families; or by wives joined with male relatives against their husbands for intermeddling with their separate estate" ("Developments in European Family Law," 1:122–23).

76. Spring, *Law, Land and Family,* 18–19.

77. Spring, *Law, Land and Family,* 165.

78. Habakkuk, *Marriage, Debt, and the Estates System: English Landownership, 1650–1950* (Oxford: Clarendon Press, 1994), 200. Habakkuk places the seventeenth- and eighteenth-century heiress at the center of economic developments such as the rise and fall of the great estate. Habakkuk's view is that when an heiress married,

"the estate, as an entity, as the basis of a distinct landed family, disappeared as a result of her marriage" ("The Rise and Fall of English Landed Families, 1600–1800," *Transactions of the Royal Historical Society* 29 [1979], 189).

79. Perry, *Novel Relations*, 64.

80. For a comparison of property and inheritance among women in families, see Naomi Tadmor, "Dimensions of Inequality among Siblings in Eighteenth-Century English Novels: The Cases of *Clarissa* and *The History of Miss Betsy Thoughtless*," *Continuity and Change* 7, no. 3 (1992): 303–33; also see her *Family and Friends in Eighteenth-Century England: Household, Kinship and Patronage* (Cambridge: Cambridge University Press, 2001).

81. Eleanor F. Shevlin, "'Imaginary Productions' and 'Minute Contrivances': Law, Fiction, and Property in Eighteenth-Century England," *Studies in Eighteenth-Century Culture* 28 (1999), 144. See Rebecca Probert's *Marriage Law and Practice in the Long Eighteenth Century: A Reassessment* (Cambridge: Cambridge University Press, 2009) for an excellent assessment of how the Act benefited women. Probert notes that as the Act was debated in Parliament, "MPs harped on the risk of the heir marrying 'a common strumpet' or an heiress 'an infamous sharper'" (212 n37).

82. Shevlin, "'Imaginary Productions,'" 144. Perry also sees Lord Hardwicke's Act as contributing to "the great disinheritance" of women, since the privatization of marriage essentially transformed women into "property," thereby making over "property that they owned to their new masters" (*Novel Relations*, 195).

83. Spring, *Law, Land and Family*, 111.

84. Spring, *Law, Land and Family*, 112.

85. Spring, *Law, Land and Family*, 18–19.

86. Spring, *Law, Land and Family*, 15.

87. See Claudia Johnson, *Jane Austen: Women, Politics, and the Novel* (Chicago: University of Chicago Press, 1990); Perry, *Novel Relations*; Elsie B. Michie, *The Vulgar Question of Money: Heiresses, Materialism, and the Novel of Manners from Jane Austen to Henry James* (Baltimore: Johns Hopkins University Press, 2011); Lynda A. Hall, *Women and "Value" in Jane Austen's Novels: Settling, Speculating and Superfluity* (New York: Palgrave Macmillan, 2017); and *Law and Economics in Jane Austen*, ed. Lynne Marie Kohm and Kathleen E. Akers (Lanham: Lexington Books, 2019).

88. The novel's other widow, Mrs. Smith, likewise controls her nephew Willoughby's future fortune, casting him off (although she later restores her favor) when she learns that he has seduced and abandoned Colonel Brandon's ward, Eliza.

89. Austen, *Sense and Sensibility*, ed. John Mullan (Oxford: Oxford University Press, 2019), 367.

90. Some notable studies of inheritance in *Pride and Prejudice* include Jo Alyson Parker, "*Pride and Prejudice*: Jane Austen's Double Inheritance Plot," *REAL: Yearbook of Research in English and American Literature* 7 (1991): 159–90, and Marilyn Francus, "Jane Austen, Pound for Pound," *Persuasions: The Jane Austen Journal On-Line* 33, no. 1 (2012), https://jasna.org/persuasions/on-line/vol33no1/francus.html.

91. Richard A. Posner, "Jane Austen: Comedy and Social Structure," in *Subversion and Sympathy: Gender, Law, and the British Novel*, ed. Martha C. Nussbaum and Alison L. LaCroix (Oxford: Oxford University Press, 2013), 87.

92. Michie, *The Vulgar Question of Money*, 27.

93. Austen, *Pride and Prejudice*, ed. James Kinsley (Oxford: Oxford University Press, 2020), 126.

94. Mr. Darcy never considers the match with Anne, rejects the possibility of marrying the commercially wealthy Miss Bingley, and famously marries beneath his rank for love. Fanny Price's marriage to her first cousin, Edmund Crawford, at the end of *Mansfield Park* (1814) is one of the few "successful" (though somewhat discomforting) Austen cousin-marriages.

THE FEMALE *WUNDERKIND* IN THE EIGHTEENTH CENTURY

Introduction: The Female *Wunderkind* in the Eighteenth Century

JÜRGEN OVERHOFF

The eighteenth century, a progressive age that was obsessed with the prospects of learning and, accordingly, also filled with high hopes for newly devised educational methods, was very aptly styled by contemporaries as "our pedagogical century."[1] The questions of gender and the equality of women also gained new prominence in the discussion of enlightened educational principles, which is why, around 1800, prestigious schools for girls were established in many cities in both Europe and North America.[2] The foundational principles of an enlightened pedagogy were laid out at the threshold of the new epoch by John Locke in his 1693 *Some Thoughts Concerning Education*.[3] This influential treatise was primarily designed for the instruction of the sons of the gentry, but, as Locke pointed out, many of its educational precepts were obviously applicable to gentlemen's daughters as well.[4] Locke bragged that both boys and girls would learn "three times as much" when taught in the playful and stimulating fashion he proposed: all children could be very easily "cozen'd into ... Knowledge" without perceiving it "to be any thing but a Sport."[5] At times it seemed as if all talented children could perform wonders of learning, if only they were raised with the right kind of educational guidance.

The new educational methods propagated by Locke aroused great expectations. Child prodigies became the craze of the day. Throughout the eighteenth century, cases of wonderfully gifted children were reported and celebrated across Europe, prompting Jean-Jacques Rousseau to discuss the phenomenon of "ces petits prodiges" extensively in his famous educational treatise of 1762, *Émile*.[6] It was in this context that, in eighteenth-century Germany, the word *wunderkind* [wonder child] was first introduced and used to refer to child prodigies.[7] The term alluded, of course, to the pre-modern conception of a divinely blessed child working wonders in the Biblical sense, but it now meant something entirely new and different: a *wunderkind* was someone who exhibited a prodigious natural talent that had been decisively enhanced by a refined Enlightenment education. Even the most famous *wunderkind* of the age, Wolfgang Amadeus Mozart, performed musical miracles because his father, Leopold, had trained him during his early childhood according to the standards of Enlightenment pedagogy set by Locke and his German epigone, Johann Bernhard Basedow.[8]

Like a growing number of other eighteenth-century men who followed in the pedagogical footsteps of Locke, Basedow and Leopold Mozart were entirely convinced that not only could a highly talented boy turn out to be a prodigy, but a girl could be trained in the same way. And indeed Maria Anna Mozart was almost as accomplished a pianist as her younger brother, with whom she toured Europe while they were both still children. Emilie Basedow, the pedagogue's only daughter, was also presented by her father to large audiences as a "wonder" of learning, since she spoke several languages (including Latin) when she was only seven years old. In the wake of their astonishing successes, other female prodigies, both in Germany—like Dorothea Schlözer, the daughter of the Göttingen professor and historian August Ludwig Schlözer—and elsewhere in Europe, were promoted as wonders of their time.[9] Yet, far too often, female prodigies' own high hopes ended in disappointment when they had to marry and conform to the demands of traditional gender stereotypes. Was their fate a sign of the remarkable ambivalence of the age of Enlightenment, a century that promoted the need for female learning and emancipation, even as it perpetuated gender gaps that could not be fully overcome?

This cluster features three brief essays examining the lives of several examples of the female *wunderkind* in eighteenth-century Spain, Italy, and Austria. Collectively, they ask—with Rousseau, Immanuel Kant, and Michel Foucault—how and why the very idea of a female prodigy could also be regarded as a deviation from Nature. In so doing, we hope to open up a larger discussion, charting out new and interesting directions for research on gender, sexuality, feminism, and education in the long eighteenth century.

Notes

The contributions to this cluster originated in papers given at the 2021 Virtual Meeting of the American Society for Eighteenth-Century Studies. We thank all of the participants in our session for their interesting and thoughtful comments, which we have tried to incorporate in the published versions of these talks.

1. Johann Gottlieb Schummel, *Spitzbart, eine komi-tragische Geschichte für unser pädagogisches Jahrhundert* (Leipzig: Weygand, 1779).

2. See Christine Mayer, "Erziehung und Bildung für Mädchen," in *Handbuch der deutschen Bildungsgeschichte*, ed. Notker Hammerstein and Ulrich Herrmann, 2 vols. (Munich: C. H. Beck, 1996–2005), 2:134–68; Mary C. Kelley, *Learning to Stand and Speak: Women, Education, and Public Life in America's Republic* (Chapel Hill: University of North Carolina Press, 2006), 48–49.

3. Locke, *Some Thoughts concerning Education*, ed. John W. Yolton and Jean S. Yolton (Oxford: Clarendon Press, 1989).

4. See Roger Woolhouse, *Locke: A Biography* (Cambridge: Cambridge University Press, 2007), 204.

5. Locke, *Some Thoughts Concerning Education*, 135 and 209.

6. Rousseau, *Émile, ou de l'éducation*, ed. Michel Launey (Paris: Garnier-Flammarion, 1966), 130–35 (see also 130 and 188). Rousseau predominantly pointed to well-known examples of child prodigies in France and Austria.

7. Johann Christoph Adelung, *Grammatisch-kritisches Wörterbuch der hochdeutschen Mundart* (Wien: Bauer, 1811), 1622.

8. Silke Leopold, *Leopold Mozart, "Ein Mann von vielen Witz und Klugheit"*: *Eine Biografie* (Kassel: Bärenreiter, 2019), 127.

9. See my "Ein menschengemachtes Wunderkind: Emilie Basedow und die Ambivalenzen der philanthropischen Aufklärungspädagogik," in *Das Achtzehnte Jahrhundert: Zeitschrift der Deutschen Gesellschaft für die Erforschung des achtzehnten Jahrhunderts* 45, no. 1 (2021), 11–27.

Deviations from Nature's Rule: The Naturalization and Denormalization of the Female *Wunderkind* in the Eighteenth Century

TIM ZUMHOF AND NICOLE BALZER

Wunderkinder were often admired in the eighteenth century and the term itself tended to have positive connotations. However, the evaluation of child prodigies underwent a significant change over the course of the century, with the result that, toward the end of the century, an increasing number of voices discussed *wunderkinder* as examples of a disrupted natural order and of unnatural, pathological development. Following Michel Foucault, we wish to introduce a power-theoretical perspective on the female *wunderkind* in the eighteenth century. Our essay will be presented in two parts. First, we will briefly explain some central aspects of Foucault's power-theoretical approach and its relation to our topic. Second, we will address the question of what discourses are related to the discovery and, more specifically, the problematization and the devaluation of female child prodigies in the eighteenth century.

Foucault's notion of power cannot be captured fully in a short essay like ours. "Power" is a central concern in nearly all of Foucault's writings, and one that he was continually reconceptualizing. We will limit our explanations to those aspects of his thinking that are most important to the topic at hand, which Foucault primarily developed in *Madness and Civilization, Discipline and Punish,* and the first volume of *The History of Sexuality.*[1] What should be stressed first is that Foucault moves away from understanding power as a possession or capacity or "general system of domination exerted by one group over another."[2] Instead, Foucault thinks about power as relational: that is, as a relation between multiple forces and mechanisms: "It seems to me that power must be understood in the first instance as the multiplicity of force relations immanent in the sphere in which they operate and which constitute their own organization; as the process which, through ceaseless struggles and confrontations, transforms, strengthens, or reverses them; as the support which these force relations find in one another, thus forming a chain or a system, or on the contrary, the disjunctions and contradictions which isolate them from one another; and lastly, as the strategies in which they take effect."[3] Foucault also conceives of power as a productive assembly of mechanisms, discourses, and practices that have the capacity to constitute phenomena. He insists, "We must cease once and for all to describe the effects of power in negative terms: it 'excludes,' it 'represses,' it 'censors,' it 'abstracts,' it 'masks,' it 'conceals.' In fact, power produces; it produces reality; it produces domains of objects and rituals of truth. The individual and the knowledge that may be gained of him belong to this production."[4] As the latter part of this quotation implies, throughout his books Foucault challenges the idea that power and knowledge are separate from or opposed to one another. Rather, they "directly imply one another; … there is no power relation without the correlative constitution of a field of knowledge, nor any knowledge that does not presuppose and constitute at the same time power relations."[5]

Foucault analyzed a number of discourses as "power-knowledge relations" and, in the course of so doing, developed his much-cited thesis that "normalization becomes one of the great instruments of power at the end of the classical age."[6] Especially in *Madness and Civilization* and *Discipline and Punish*, Foucault demonstrates how discourses surrounding phenomena, such as madness, exert "power" through "normalization": they constitute and reconstitute phenomena by producing knowledge and hierarchizing qualities, skills, and aptitudes, and through this they also produce ideas of normality and draw the boundary between the normal and the abnormal. Moreover, Foucault argues that the *normal* is not only shaped and maintained through the definition of the *ab*normal, but also by being portrayed as *natural*, and that convincing people that certain phenomena are natural or *un*natural is one of the most effective ways in which to exercise power. According to

Foucault, however, there are no truly natural phenomena that lie behind those constituted discursively; phenomena that appear natural are in fact constructed through power-knowledge relations.

Thus, a Foucauldian perspective on the female *wunderkind* in the eighteenth century would consider that figure and her exceptional gifts as constituted or constructed, rather than natural. It would encourage us to suspect that the "discovery" of child prodigies in the period is not coincidence, but rather stems from specific discourses that should be understood as power-knowledge relations. Moreover, even if Foucault himself never showed much interest in gender and has often been criticized for neglecting it as a central category of analysis, his work can serve as an important tool for examining gender as part of the phenomenon of the child prodigy in eighteenth-century discourse. From a Foucauldian point of view, gender differentiations should be understood as social constructions with powerful effects that stem in part from their having been declared to be natural and biological.

Although Foucault frequently emphasized the interplay of practices and discourses, in what follows we will restrict our attention to discourses. Our overarching questions are: What discourses are related to the discovery of child prodigies in the eighteenth century? And what role does gender play, both in these discourses and in the construction of female *wunderkinder*? To answer these questions, it is important to emphasize once again that we have reason to suspect that the evaluation of child prodigies underwent a significant change in the late eighteenth century and that they came to be discussed as examples of a disrupted natural order and of unnatural, pathological development. For example, in 1786, Johann Georg Krünitz's *Oeconomisch-technologische Encyklopädie* stated that a child's early wisdom can be viewed as a disease.[7] Immanuel Kant described child prodigies—like Christian Heinrich Heineken, the so-called Lübecker *wunderkind*, and Jean-Philippe Baratier—in his *Anthropologie in pragmatischer Hinsicht* (1798) as "deviations from nature's rule, rarities for a natural history collection."[8] Kant's indication of the proper place for *wunderkinder* is telling: such natural history collections were often referred to as *Wunderkammern* [cabinets of wonders]. Both *wunderkinder* and the exhibits in *Wunderkammern* were presented to interested audiences.

However, child prodigies were discussed not only as a phenomenon contrary to the "normal" course of nature, but also as products of an unnatural upbringing. Mignon, for example, the androgynous *wunderkind* in Johann Wolfgang Goethe's *Wilhelm Meisters Lehrjahre* (1795–96) was the recipient of an education that makes her appear as an automaton without a soul and as a victim of childhood amnesia. In the novel, Goethe clearly comments on the period's conceptions of childhood and education. Within this discussion, Mignon embodies a lost, forgotten, and pathological childhood.[9] Joachim Heinrich Campe expressed a similar skepticism and warned of the dangers of an early education.[10] According to Campe, the child prodigy from Lübeck and others like him did not fulfill the public's expectations later on in life.[11] In fact, Heineken and Baratier, like Mignon, died at a very early age.

In light of this, we would like to propose that the differing evaluations of *wunderkinder* are related to two different and opposing understandings of childhood, child development, and the consequences of education for such development. On one hand, the widespread admiration of child prodigies in the eighteenth century represents an idea of childhood as an imperfect phase of life. To this way of thinking, child prodigies are the result of what the preformist model regarded as an accelerated development. In the seventeenth and eighteenth centuries, preformationism was a popular theory arguing that organisms grew from a miniature version of themselves. Preformationists like Charles Bonnet or Albrecht von Haller believed that the form of living things existed prior to their development.[12] Accordingly, child prodigies were seen as exceptional phenomena who progressed faster through the process of becoming who they were supposed to be. Education here only functions as nurture or care and ultimately has no effect upon a being's form or abilities.

The negative view of the *wunderkind* as a phenomenon contrary to the "normal" course of nature, on the other hand, relates to epigenetic notions of development, which challenged preformistic theories beginning in the middle of the eighteenth century. Epigeneticists such as Caspar Friedrich Wolff assumed that the development process occurs in several stages and that an organism's features are not preexisting, but rather come into existence and develop progressively over time. In his *Theorie von der Generation* (1764), Wolff describes the development of organisms as the gradual shaping of new forms out of formless matter.[13] However, epigenetic ideas not only prompted a reassessment of childhood as an indispensable stage in human development, they also inspired the anthropological and educational concept of *Bildung* as a process of unfolding an individual's indefinite potential through his or her interaction with the surrounding world.

In *Émile, ou De l'éducation* (1762), Jean-Jacques Rousseau writes of the "true course of nature" in human development and coined the term "perfectibility" as "the attribute which enabled human behaviour to develop in a progressive way within the lifetime of each individual and from one generation to the next."[14] For Rousseau, childhood was an integral part of the natural progression in human understanding. He came up with the idea of a *natural* education that followed the hidden course of nature and renounced any educational practices that would disrupt a child's natural development. Rousseau, and many of his disciples, regarded any kind of disciplining, conditioning, or training of children as unnatural. He believed that most child prodigies were only such in their parents' eyes. In his view, actual child prodigies were extremely rare.[15] Since their behavior and their abilities deviated from what was regarded as natural development, they were described as pathological phenomena.

Campe, a keen reader of Rousseau's works, was the first to use the word "frühreif" [precocious] to describe child prodigies. The term later found its way into nineteenth-century educational encyclopedias. For example, in 1860, Karl Adolf Schmid's *Encyklopädie des gesamten Erziehungs- und Unterrichtswesens* explains that "We are inclined to call a child precocious when he or she can read with understanding. The word evolved into the meaning of so-called child prodigies who achieve amazing things from an early age on, but afterwards either perished or lagged behind to never reach full maturity."[16] By the beginning of the twentieth century, psychologists saw in child prodigies like Heineken nothing more than the hideously distorted features of an elderly homunculus.[17]

We have been using Foucault's notion of power-knowledge relations to reflect upon the emergence of child prodigies in the eighteenth century. Following the idea that specific discourses served as crucial conditions for this emergence, we were trying to determine which discourses were related to the two markedly different assessments of child prodigies. However, we have not yet addressed the question of what role gender played in these discourses and in the evaluation of female child prodigies. It is important to note that the preformistic and epigenetic approaches each had a different conception of the body in terms of sexuality and gender.[18] Preformationists often reduced the female contribution to the act of conception to simply carrying and nourishing the embryo, which obviously further entrenched the longstanding bias toward women as the so-called weaker sex.[19] Although epigeneticists rejected this theory and presumed that men and women provided mostly equal contributions to the act of conception, they too had a dubious conception of gender, one that followed the tradition that Thomas Laqueur has described as the "one-sex model," in which female sexual organs were merely inverted versions of their male counterparts.[20] Once again, women come off as biologically inferior to men.

The fundamental shift in the late eighteenth century toward a difference model of sex (with all its attending consequences for gender roles) is one aspect of the larger sexualization of human "nature," which had repercussions for both the concept of *Bildung* and the education of women. Rousseau is again key. He promoted the idea that there was a natural difference between men and women and concluded that "once it is demonstrated that man and woman are not and ought not to be constituted in the same way in either their character or temperament, it follows that they ought not to have the same education."[21]

With this in mind, we propose that in the figure of the female *wunderkind* different social orders intersect. On one hand, there is a developmental order that differentiates between childhood and adulthood. On the other hand, there is a gendered order that differentiates between "women" and "men." Both gain their normative power through their reference to the (supposedly) natural order: the "natural" development of humans and the inherent nature of women, as compared to that of men. A striking example of these intersecting social orders can be seen in the case of Dorothea Schlözer (1770–1825), who was educated by her father in an attempt to prove that girls were as malleable as boys. Dissatisfied with Rousseau's notion of a natural difference between men and women, August Ludwig Schlözer conducted a pedagogical experiment with his daughter. He taught her to read and write at the age of three. Since August was a professor at the University of Göttingen, Dorothea was taught mathematics by her father's colleagues at the age of five. Later, she was allowed to listen to lectures at the university on philosophy and the natural sciences, but only from behind a curtain, hidden from the male students. At the age of seventeen, attired in bride-like white and with flowers in her hair (echoing the traditional connection between female scholarship and virginity), she was examined by the Göttingen faculty.[22] In a 1787 letter to Christian Gottfried Körner, Friedrich Schiller called Schlözer's experiment a farce. Although Dorothea successfully completed her examination and was the first woman in Germany to be awarded a degree in philosophy, she was not allowed to pursue a career as a scholar. Her academic and scientific endeavors abruptly ended when she reached a marriageable age, at which point she was supposed to shift to a gender-typical role as a wife and mother.

Against this background, we suspect that gendered ideas about human development inflect the discourse on female prodigies precisely because they are related to specific discourses on human development. However, to answer the question of what exact role gender played in the construction and discussion of female *wunderkinder* in the eighteenth century, further research is necessary. It should not only ask whether the discourse on female prodigies was founded in general on gendered hierarchies, but also in what specific ways a binary gender division was a precondition for the devaluation of female prodigies.

Notes

1. Foucault, *Madness and Civilization: A History of Insanity in the Age of Reason*, trans. Richard Howard (New York: Vintage Books, 1965); *Discipline and Punish: The Birth of the Prison*, trans. Alan Sheridan (New York: Vintage Books, 1979); and *The History of Sexuality*, vol. 1: *The Will to Knowledge*, trans. Robert Hurley (New York: Pantheon Books, 1978).

2. Foucault, *History of Sexuality*, 92.

3. Foucault, *History of Sexuality*, 92–93. See too Foucault, "The Subject and Power," in Hubert L. Dreyfus and Paul Rabinow, *Michel Foucault: Beyond Structuralism and Hermeneutics* (Chicago: University of Chicago Press, 1983), 208–26.

4. Foucault, *Discipline and Punish*, 194.

5. Foucault, *Discipline and Punish*, 27.

6. Foucault, *Discipline and Punish*, 27, 184.

7. Krünitz, *Oekonomisch-technologische Encyklopädie, oder allgemeines System der Staats-, Stadt-, Haus- und Land-Wirthschaft, und der Kunst-Geschichte*, 242 vols. (Berlin: Joachim Pauli, 1773–1858), 37:679.

8. Kant, *Anthropology from a Pragmatic Point of View*, ed. and trans. Robert B. Louden (Cambridge: Cambridge University Press, 2006), 122–23. The original phrase in German is "Abschweifungen der Natur."

9. See Ursula R. Mahlendorf, "The Mystery of Mignon: Object Relations, Abandonment, Child Abuse, and Narrative Structure," *Goethe Yearbook* 7 (1994), 23–39.

10. Campe, "Ueber die große Schädlichkeit einer allzufrühen Ausbildung der Kinder," in *Allgemeine Revision des gesammten Schul- und Erziehungswesens von einer Gesellschaft praktischer Erzieher*, 16 vols. (Wolfenbüttel: Schulbuchhandlung, 1785–88), 5:1–160.

11. See Campe, *Wörterbuch der deutschen Sprache*, 5 vols. (Braunschweig: Schulbuchhandlung, 1807–11), 5:786.

12. See Shirley A. Roe, *Matter, Life, and Generation: Eighteenth-Century Embryology and the Haller-Wolff Debate* (Cambridge: Cambridge University Press, 1981), 21–44.

13. See Heike Hartung, *Ageing, Gender, and Illness in Anglophone Literature: Narrating Age in the Bildungsroman* (New York: Routledge, 2016), 55.

14. Rousseau, *Emile, or On Education*, ed. and trans. Christopher Kelly and Allan Bloom (Hanover: University Press of New England, 2010), 37. See too Robert Wolker, "A Reply to Charvet: Rousseau and the Perfectibility of Man," *History of Political Thought* 1, no. 1 (1980): 81-90.

15. Rousseau, *Emile*, 240.

16. Schmid, *Encyklopädie des gesamten Erziehungs- und Unterrichtswesen*, 11 vols. (Gotha: Rudolf Besser, 1859–78), 2:563.

17. See August von Pestalozza, *Das Wunderkind: Ein Beitrag zur Psychologie der Hochbegabten* (Leipzig: Freytag, 1923), 15.

18. See Heinz-Jürgen Voß, "Determining Sex/Gender: Genes and DNA Precisely Do Not Predict the Development of a Genital Tract," in *Normed Children: Effects of Gender and Sex Related Normativity on Childhood and Adolescence*, ed. Erik Schneider & Christel Baltes-Löhr (Bielefeld: transcript Verlag, 2018), 141.

19. See Nancy Tuana, "The Weaker Seed: The Sexist Bias of Reproductive Theory," *Hypatia* 3, no. 1 (1988), 35–59.

20. Laqueur, *Making Sex: Body and Gender from the Greeks to Freud* (Cambridge: Harvard University Press, 1990), 8.

21. Rousseau, *Emile,* 538.

22. See Londa Schiebinger, *The Mind Has No Sex?: Women in the Origins of Modern Science* (Cambridge: Harvard University Press, 1991), 257–60.

Knowledge on Display: Aristocratic Sociability, Female Learning, and Enlightenment Pedagogies in Eighteenth-Century Spain and Italy

MÓNICA BOLUFER

In eighteenth-century Europe, while women were generally discouraged from participating in intellectual activities for moral, "natural," and even medical reasons, extraordinary exhibitions of female learning were, in some cases, given a place of honor in courtly, aristocratic, and academic rituals. These were particularly visible in Italy.[1] Several Italian women were admitted to literary, artistic, and scientific academies; a few were granted university degrees and even held teaching positions (particularly in Bologna). From Laura Bassi (1711–88) to Maria Clotilde Tambroni (1758–1817), these women became international cultural attractions for foreign intellectuals and travelers on their Grand Tour.[2] To a lesser, but still important extent, "exceptional" women (often young girls) from Spain and Portugal acquired local, sometimes national, occasionally international, and always ephemeral public celebrity, which has hardly been acknowledged by scholars. This essay will examine this phenomenon transnationally in order to explore several significant issues: how did gender, rank, and age intersect in such displays, what were the interests at stake, and how did they help build a European imaginary of women's learning that was fraught with ambiguities, but nonetheless may have fostered further aspirations on the part of women.

We will be focusing on the exhibition of humanistic learning (grammar, geography, cartography, history, modern and sometimes classical languages; more rarely, mathematics, natural philosophy, and natural history) in aristocratic and academic performances. These worked far differently than the appearance of musical *wunderkinder* in courts and concert houses for the entertainment of noble patrons or paying audiences, or the increasing display of female artistic "accomplishments" (drawing, painting, music, dancing) in genteel and middle-class domestic and polite circles.[3] In Italy, the families involved are nobles (in the case of Maria Delfini Dossi), but also aspiring merchants (Maria Gaetana Agnesi), low patricians (Mariangella Ardinghelli), lawyers (Laura Bassi), and even plebeians (Maria Clotilde Tambroni, Maria Dalle Donne). The Spanish cases cover a narrower social spectrum, ranging from courtly aristocrats to local nobles or patricians.[4] Described usually as "prodigies" of "extraordinary talent," these women were exhibited to prove their allegedly exceptional individual capacities, the intrinsic superiority of their noble blood, or their enlightened education. Those three elements, combining and complicating the distinctions and connections between nature and culture, were mixed in different proportions depending on the specific contexts (courtly, polite, or academic) in which these women were displayed, and also on when they were displayed, with education gaining more significance over the course of the eighteenth century.

Some girls performed alongside their brothers. Individual exhibitions of male "prodigies" were also held. The education of royal children was subject to public scrutiny: European intellectuals followed with great interest Étienne Bonnot de Condillac's reports of his (failed) efforts to educate Prince Ferdinand of Parma (1751–1802) as a child—and future monarch—of the Enlightenment.[5] Other educators used their own children as pedagogic experiments. In 1785 (and again in 1787), Juan Bautista Picornell had his three-year-old son tested by professors at the University of Salamanca, who compared him to the German *wunderkind* Christian Heinrich Heineken (1721–25) and expressed reservations about the effects of such precocious training, which echoed the growing enlightened suspicions toward "unnatural" education.[6] However, female demonstrations of learning were presented more emphatically as extraordinary and spectacular, even if some contemporary accounts went out of their way to declare that the girls were interrogated thoroughly and according to custom, as if to exclude any hint of paternalism or gallantry.

If a prodigy was someone who crossed "natural" boundaries, female prodigies were credited with not only surpassing the barrier of age, like their male counterparts, but also that of gender, thus connecting them to the robust tradition of "illustrious women" celebrated in early modern literature and art, particularly in aristocratic circles (in catalogues of women distinguished in letters, government, and arms; in works of the *querelle des femmes*; in tapestries, frescoes, and even tea sets). In the cultural universe of the Ancien Régime, the notion that blood was the vehicle for the transmission of superior moral and intellectual abilities justified the privileges of the nobility, setting it symbolically apart as a wonder in itself. Exceptionally talented noble girls were therefore presented as wonders among wonders, powerful images of the hierarchical and gendered system of knowledge and power. At the same time, public performances by highly educated girls and women conveyed the idea that culture could help nature to develop its full potential: with a proper education, the limitations of gender could be surpassed. Textual and iconographic emphasis on the exceptionality of these figures worked to contain their potentially disruptive implications by setting them up not as models to be imitated, but rather as prodigies to be admired. However, in the context of the ongoing debate regarding the extent to which men's and women's moral and intellectual abilities were natural (as opposed to the result of education), some women used these examples to justify their own intellectual ambitions by stressing the equal talents of their sex.

These celebrations were held and publicized in different countries in ways that show striking similarities and that were sometimes reinforced by symbolic or explicit propaganda. Cultural and political relations between the Spanish monarchy and the Italian peninsula were strong and self-conscious: three Spanish queen consorts in the eighteenth century were Italian-born, and there was a constant two-way flow of courtiers, artists, intellectuals, and clerics, with the artistic and literary academies of the two regions tightly interwoven. Personal and family connections reinforced those ties: at least one Spanish noble family that displayed their gifted daughter was of Italian origin, and members of the Bourbon and Farnese dynasties also participated in acts celebrating learned women. A portrait of Elisabeth Farnese, queen consort to King Philip V of Spain, presides over the engraving commemorating Maria Vittoria Delfina Dosi's defense of her legal thesis at the Collegio di Spagna in Bologna in 1722.[7] Her son Charles, the former Duke of Parma, was welcomed in 1735 as King of Naples and Sicily at the palace of the Prince of Tarsia by Eleanora Barbapiccola and Faustina Pignatelli, who were each internationally renowned patrons and disseminators of Cartesianism and Newtonianism, and by Mariangela Ardinghelli, a natural historian, translator, and facilitator of exchanges between French and Neapolitan circles of learning.[8] This experience must have weighed on his decision to award the daughter of one of his courtiers a university degree when he became King Charles III of Spain in 1759.

Charles hoped to prove that in his new kingdom women could "publicly demonstrate their progress," as they did in Italy.[9] Both Spain and Italy were considered by foreign travelers and intellectuals to be lagging behind France and Britain in their cultural achievements, and therefore the exhibition of learned women (the more extraordinary, the better) was for scholars, civic and academic authorities, and ruling dynasties a highly political gesture.

Displays of female "prodigies" sometimes took place through elaborate rituals presented to an elite audience distinguished by their social rank, learning, or public office. Sometimes they were also shown to cheering crowds and further publicized through programs for the event, newspaper articles, poems, engravings, medals, and word of mouth. They all embodied the strongly performative and spectacular qualities of Ancien Régime culture, but in ways that had differing gender connotations. In some cases, these spectacles were staged at court or in aristocratic and genteel residences, which were mixed-gender spaces in which the conspicuous consumption and exhibition of culture (a mixture of the learned and the polite) was an integral part of education, above all for gentlemen but also, to a lesser extent, for ladies. For example, Maria Gaetana Agnesi (1718–99) entertained distinguished guests in the family *palazzo* in Milan with her scholarly conversation, while her sister Maria Teresa played the harpsichord, thus aiding their socially ambitious father's ascent.[10] In 1763, the count and countess of Parcent exhibited the talents of their fourteen-year-old daughter, Cayetana de la Cerda (1748–1808), and their sixteen-year-old son, José, at a performance in Valencia that followed a highly theatrical script, organized into acts and scenes and punctuated with musical intervals. A contemporary poetical description highlights the siblings' equal learning: except for Latin (which was reserved for José), they were said to have both received the same lessons, and members of the audience were encouraged to ask questions of both of them. At the same time, the gender difference between the two was visually and textually marked: the brother and sister entered the stage from opposite ends (with the former gallantly giving preference to the latter) and were compared, respectively, to the shining Sun and the crescent Moon.[11] Emphasizing the girl's achievements added luster to their lineage precisely because it was considered an even more extraordinary proof of the family's distinction and the special care that her parents had taken in going beyond the customary education for noble girls. Twenty years later, King Charles IV of Spain and his queen, María Luisa (originally from Parma and educated, along with her brother, by Condillac), sought to impress the Portuguese court of Queen Maria I when their daughter, Carlota Joaquina (1775–1830), arrived in 1785 to marry Prince João They made Princess Carlota take a public examination that was praised by the press in both countries, thereby raising the Bourbons to the level of the (highly cultivated) Bragança and publicizing the political links between the two dynasties and the allegiance of Carlota to her new nation.[12]

A different approach was taken when female prodigies were being displayed at university or civic buildings. Like the polite performances we have just considered, these had some theatrical aspects (a conductor, music, a genteel audience). But they put more emphasis on the scholarly content of the demonstration and adopted solemn rituals that mimicked the *disputatio* of the (male-only) universities or the public examinations of pupils at the (equally male-only) schools that were promoted by the Jesuits and popularized during the eighteenth century. Laura Bassi's defense of her thesis, the subsequent conferral of a degree on her, and the public lectures she gave at the Archiginnasio and the anatomical theater in Bologna, all of which were internationally celebrated in the 1730s, may have influenced the examination of María Rosario Cepeda (1756–1816) in 1768 by ecclesiastics and teachers at the Royal Naval Academy in Cádiz, on a stage adorned with symbols of the sciences and the monarchy.[13] Contemporary engravings and textual descriptions certainly suggest that Italian precedents helped shape the presentation of María Isidra de Guzmán (1767–1803), who publicly defended her thesis and was awarded a degree at the University of Alcalá in 1785 at the express wish of Charles III—two years before Dorothea Schlözer received her degree in Göttingen. In two subsequent celebrations, she paraded through the city accompanied by university authorities and preceded by horsemen, drums, and bugles, in a carriage with glass windows so that the populace could see and cheer her.[14] This is the most lavish case of the spectacularizing of female learning, but it was operating within a cultural economy of spectacular science that, as many historians have shown, was an integral part of Ancien Régime society and that typically assigned women an iconic, often allegorical, but ultimately limited role.[15]

Several social and political forces intersected in the staging of these performances, in each instance with a different balance of complementary or competing interests. The girls' families were always heavily involved and sought to enhance their own social prestige and cultural capital by proving their commitment to refined, up-to-date educational practices. They were also, of course, showcasing their daughters' abilities as prospective wives, mothers, and hostesses. Both in Italy and Spain, fathers appear more conspicuously in the sources as the ones hiring tutors and seeking institutional support. However, the agency of mothers in promoting their daughters' education became more visible in cases in which they insisted on their status as the holders of noble titles in their own right or as widows. For example, in 1781, the Marquise of la Romana made her daughter,

Pascuala Caro (1768–1827), take a public exam that was primarily devoted to arithmetic and geometry. Pascuala had had the same education as her elder brothers, who were bound for military careers, where those skills were in high demand. However, the international prestige of female mathematicians like Bassi and Agnesi must have helped make the Marquise's unusual approach respectable.[16]

In a few cases, the girls' tutors were mentioned (generally if they were renowned pedagogues who counted on the prestige they would gain from their pupils' exams to advance their careers). More often, public credit was given to the girls' allegedly exceptional abilities or to the liberality of their aristocratic patrons. In the 1760s, girl prodigies (such as de la Cerda and Cepeda) were presented as embodying the intrinsic, "natural" superiority of their noble blood more than personal merit, individual effort, or pedagogic excellence. Exhibitions held in the 1780s and 1790s, on the other hand, put a heavier emphasis on education, as confidence in its powers grew. The most singular example of the latter was the public examination taken jointly in 1797 by the four elder children of the Duke and Duchess of Osuna: two girls (Joaquina, 1783–1817, and Josefa, 1784–1851) and two boys (Francisco and Pedro).[17] We know about this examination because of a description written by their tutor and probably supervised by the duchess herself, who was a formidable figure in Enlightened Spain and went to great lengths to secure the most modern education for her offspring. The Osuna examination is less a celebration of aristocratic exceptionalism than a declaration of Enlightened principles, one optimistic about how culture and nature could go hand in hand and a well-planned, genteel education could fully develop an individual's potential. Explicit statements regarding gender differences are conspicuously absent from this account, which can be read as an implicit proclamation of intellectual equality between women and men, in a time when emphasis on the complementarity of "two incommensurable sexes" was on the rise.[18]

What about the girls? Is it true that, in Marta Cavazza's words, "female figures played the role of pawns, though … not always passive pawns" in these displays that were often designed by their male family members or political authorities?[19] Cavazza and other scholars have proved otherwise. Maria Gaetana Agnesi and Laura Bassi offer two clear examples of women whose personal determination pushed them to choose a different path of life than what had been planned for them by their families and social circles. Agnesi rejected being exhibited as a prodigy of learning and instead devoted herself to celibate study and piety, while Bassi defied the iconic role allocated to her as the virgin *Minerva docta,* a living allegory of the learned city, in order to create for herself an unprecedented career as a married natural philosopher who taught in public.[20] In Spain, the girls were so young—most of them were just twelve to fourteen years old—that it is likely they were not personally directing their own lives and educations, although the absence of private writings makes that impossible to determine. María Isidra Guzmán, who was slightly older at eighteen, may have genuinely wished to obtain a doctorate (perhaps she was even inspired by the Italian precedents we have been examining), but how can a historian take her father's petition on her behalf at face value?[21]

As we have seen, the principal goal in the training of these young women was to display their knowledge in public at spectacular events that were emphatically staged as exceptional and thereby positioned their learning as part of the realm of accomplishments that would engage courtly or polite audiences, rather than as something be used for personal or practical ends. Once these female "wonders" stepped out of the limelight, their education did not generally allow them to become adult female intellectuals, who occupied an ambiguous and difficult position, even in Italy.[22] However, their experiences seemed to have helped them to assume more accessible roles, such as those of the devout writer or the Enlightened female patron, patriot, and social improver. Pascuala Caro pursued her intellectual dedication in a respectable way as a nun and religious poet famous locally for her knowledge of scripture. Others fulfilled their responsibilities to their noble families by marrying and raising children, sometimes far from the court (de la Cerda lived in the provinces; Cepeda in Mexico), thus disappearing from public view. Excluded from learned academies, with the exception of María Isidra de Guzmán (who was admitted to the Spanish Academy by royal request), several former prodigies participated in female patriotic societies (a distinctive feature of the Spanish Enlightenment), where they labored to promote social reforms and useful knowledge.[23] None of them left behind learned works. However, most continued to cultivate themselves in various ways, and some subscribed to enlightened journals or promoted the arts and letters as patrons.

At the same time, though, the public celebration and international circulation of these cases, particularly the Italian ones, disseminated powerful examples of the female intellect that may well have inspired other women to pursue their own intellectual dreams. If Diamante Medaglia Faini, a local legend in the small city of Salò, decided in 1774 to give up poetry for mathematics, inspired by the public presence of women in scientific institutions (as well as by the fictional female amateur scientists featured in literature "for ladies"), another poet, María Gertrudis Hore, envied how a fellow citizen of Cádiz, María Rosario Cepeda, was allowed to pursue "such noble studies," when she herself could not, "in spite of my longing."[24] Icons, even when not entirely real, can have unpredictable and inspiring effects.

Notes

This research has received funding from the European Research Council under the European Union's Horizon 2020 research and innovation program (Project CIRGEN, ERC Grant Agreement No 787015).

1. Jürgen Overhoff, "Ein menschengemachtes Wunderkind: Emilie Basedow und die Ambivalenzen der philanthropischen Aufklärungspädagogik," *Das Achtzehnte Jahrhundert* 45, no. 1 (2021), 11–27; Paddy Holt, "Performing in a different place: The use of a prodigy to the Dublin Philosophical Society," *British Journal for the History of Science* 53, no. 3 (2020): 371–88.

2. Marta Cavazza, "Between Modesty and Spectacle: Women and Science in Eighteenth-Century Italy," in *Italy's Eighteenth Century: Gender and Culture in the Age of the Grand Tour*, ed. Paula Findlen, Wendy Wassyng Roworth, and Catherine M. Sama (Stanford: Stanford University Press, 2009), 275–302; *Alma Mater Studiorum: La Presenza Femmenile dal XVIII al XX Secolo* (Bologna: Clueb, 1988).

3. Mélanie Traversier, *L'harmoie de verre et miss Davies: Essai sur la mécanique du succès au siècle des Lumières* (Paris: Seuil, 2021), 17–32. See too Waltraud Maierhofer's essay in this cluster and Ann Bermingham, "The Aesthetics of Ignorance: The Accomplished Woman in the Culture of Connoisseurship," *Oxford Art Journal* 16, no. 2 (1993): 3–20.

4. *Gaceta de Madrid*, 5 May 1800, 365.

5. Élisabeth Badinter, *L'infant de Parme* (Paris: Fayard, 2008), 33.

6. *Examen público, catechístico, histórico y geográfico, a que expone Don Juan Picornell y Gomila ... a su hijo Juan Antonio Picornell y Obispo* (Salamanca: Andrés García Rico, 1785). See too Tim Zumhof and Nicole Balzer's essay in this cluster.

7. Cavazza, "Between Modesty and Spectacle," 281–83.

8. *The Contest for Knowledge: Debates over Women's Learning in Eighteenth-Century Italy*, ed. Rebecca Messbarger and Paula Findlen (Chicago: University of Chicago Press, 2005); Paola Bertucci, "The In/Visible Woman: Mariangela Ardinghelli and the Circulation of Knowledge between Paris and Naples in the Eighteenth Century," *Isis* 104, no. 2 (2013): 226–49.

9. *Exercicio literario, que presenta al público la Señora Doña María Rosario Cepeda* (Cádiz: Manuel Espinosa de los Monteros, [1768], n.p. See also Juan Antonio González Cañaveras, *Relación de los exercicios literarios que la Sra. doña Maria del Rosario Cepeda y Mayo ... actuó los dias 19, 22 y 24 de septiembre del presente año* (Cádiz: Manuel Espinosa de los Monteros, 1768).

10. Massimo Mazzotti, *The World of Maria Gaetana Agnesi, Mathematician of God* (Baltimore: Johns Hopkins University Press, 2008).

11. *Relación que hace un amigo a otro de la célebre Literaria función que en el día 7 de Abril del presente año 1763 huvo en la Ciudad de Valencia, en la Casa de los Excmos. Señores Condes de Parcent, executada por sus Excmos. Hijos D. Joseph y Dᵃ Cayetana de la Cerda y Cernecio* (Valencia: Joseph Estevan Dolz, 1763).

12. *Gazeta de Lisboa* 40 (4 October 1784); *Gaceta de Madrid* 82 (14 October 1785), 669–70.

13. *Exercicio literario*.

14. See the contemporary sources in María Jesús Vázquez Madruga, *Doña María Isidra Quintina de Guzmán y de la Cerda, "Doctora de Alcalá": Biografía* (Alcalá de Henares: Ayuntamiento de Alcalá, 1999), 159–267.

15. Bertucci, "In/Visible Woman"; Cavazza, "Between Modesty and Spectacle"; *The Faces of Nature in Enlightenment Europe*, ed. Lorraine Daston and Gianna Pomata (Berlin: BWV-Berliner Wissenschafts-Verlag, 2003).

16. *Examen a que se presentará Doña Pascuala Caro y Sureda, hija de los señores marqueses de la Romana el día ... de abril de 1781* (Valencia: Benito Monfort, 1781).

17. Diego Clemencín, *Discurso leido en la abertura del examen público de las señoras doña Josefa y doña Joaquina Giron y Pimentel, y de los señores d. Francisco y d. Pedro, sus hermanos, hijos de los excelentísimos señores Duques de Osuna* (Madrid: Cano, [1797]).

18. See Thomas Laqueur, *Making Sex: Body and Gender From the Greeks to Freud* (Cambridge: Harvard University Press, 1992), 152.

19. Cavazza, "Between Modesty and Spectacle," 301.

20. Mazzotti, *World of Maria Gaetana Agnesi*, 144–51; Paula Findlen, "La Maestra di Bologna: Laura Bassi, una donna del Settecento in cattedra," in *Eredi di Laura Bassi: Docenti e ricercatrici in Italia tra età moderna e presente*, ed. Marta Cavazza, Paola Govoni, and Tiziana Pironi (Milano: FrancoAngeli, 2014), 63–94.

21. Petition dated 15 April 1785, in Vázquez Madruga, *Doña María Isidra*, 163–64.

22. Lorraine Daston, "The Naturalized Female Intellect," *Science in Context* 5, no. 1 (1992): 209–35.

23. Elena Serrano, *Ladies of Honor and Merit: Gender, Useful Knowledge, and Politics in Enlightened Spain* (Pittsburgh: University of Pittsburgh Press, 2022); *Society Ladies and Philanthropy during the Spanish Enlightenment: La Junta de Damas de Honor y Mérito, 1787–1823*, ed. Catherine M. Jaffe and Elisa Martín-Valdepeñas (Baton Rouge: Louisiana State University Press, 2022).

24. Paula Findlen, "Becoming a Scientist: Gender and Knowledge in Eighteenth-Century Italy," *Science in Context* 16, no. 1-2 (2003): 59–87; *Copia y recolección de los papeles, que en prosa, y verso han dirigido, algunos doctos ingenios de esta ciudad, en debido aplauso del desempeño que en sus actos literarios de los días 19, 22 y 24 de el mes proximo pasado, executó la señora Doña Maria del Rosario Cepeda* (Cádiz: Imprenta Real de Marina, [1768]).

Maria Theresia Paradis and Blindness as Opportunity

WALTRAUD MAIERHOFER

Maria Theresia Paradis (1759–1824) was an eighteenth-century child prodigy, pianist, and composer.[1] She was also one of the patients hypnotized by Franz Mesmer, first with spectacular success and then even more scandalous failure that Dr. Mesmer defended in his *Abhandlung über die Entdeckung des thierischen Magnetismus* [*Treatise on the Discovery of Animal Magnetism*].[2] Both have been the subject of several biographies, novels, and films; however, most of these works focus on the encounter between Paradis and Mesmer in 1777.[3] According to Mesmer, Maria Paradis, who had been blind since the age of three, regained her sight as a result of his treatment, but at the same time her musical abilities faltered and so her parents insisted on ending her therapy. Paradis relapsed and either remained blind or once again became so, although Mesmer started rumors that she was only pretending to be blind.[4] She became a celebrated pianist famous for her musical memory. Between 1783 and 1787, she went on an extended concert tour throughout Western Europe. Several contemporary articles, memoirs, and works of travel writing describe Paradis and her accomplishments.[5] Paradis did not publish her own account of her situation nor enter the debate over the education and human capacity of individuals with vision impairments—or of women more generally, for that matter.

Maria Paradis was celebrated as a *wunderkind* on the organ and piano, although she probably first performed in Vienna's musical circles no earlier than 1775, when she was sixteen. Prodigies were fashionable in the period and Paradis's parents may have wished for their own child celebrity. Her father, Joseph Anton [von] Paradis was the imperial secretary and a Court Councilor to Maria Theresia, Empress of the Holy Roman Empire. Paradis's mother, Rosalia Maria Paradis (née Levassori della Motta) was the descendant of several generations of court dancers and dance teachers. Maria remained their only child, a status she shared with other exceptional women of the eighteenth century, such as the painter Angelika Kauffmann.[6] In larger families, a disabled child would often be given to childless relatives, but, since she was an only child, Paradis was spared such a fate. Musical and performing professions had a long tradition in the Paradis family, and her father's connections made it possible for her to receive lessons from Vienna court musicians, including ones in composition and music theory from Antonio Salieri. Paradis was given the same type of education as a *wunderkind* as the Mozart siblings and other European prodigies: that is, her natural talent was enhanced with refined and goal-oriented instruction.

Vienna's musical circles celebrated the young pianist not just because she was female, but also because she was blind (or at least severely visually impaired). This brief essay argues that the more important *Wunder* exemplified by Paradis was not her early performance career, but rather the fact that her career stretched well into adulthood. Paradis has traditionally been seen as a pitiable victim of her impairment. I instead contend that she escaped the constraints of middle-class gender roles—what Leslie Fiedler termed the "tyranny of the normal"—because of it.[7] Her accomplishments as an organizer of so-called dilettante academies and a teacher in her own private music school deserve more recognition. It is important to examine how Paradis found appropriate venues for her musical interests after her initial appearances as a performing *wunderkind*, as well as how her musical work intersected with gender roles and her own disability. She organized semi-public concerts and continued to compose and perform. From about 1810 to the end of her life, she ran a private music school for girls. However, reports about her continued to pity her perceived deficiency and lack of children.

In what follows, I will briefly review the factors that made Paradis a prodigy and female, but not feminine. Enlightenment medicine developed what Michel Foucault calls, in *Power/Knowledge*, a "politics of health" and pursued a strategy of cure, rather than assistance, for mental and physical impairments.[8] Paradis's parents took the same approach when they sought Mesmer's help to have their daughter's eyesight restored. The widely publicized initial success (and later failure) of Mesmer's attempts at healing must be seen in the context of these politics. It is possible that Paradis made a decision, consciously or unconsciously, not to continue to pursue such a cure (Mesmer claimed that Paradis wished to be blind again).[9] Certainly in her later life, she emphasized assistance, rather than "cure," or what is today called "the social model of disability," as opposed to the medical model that emerged in the eighteenth century.[10] Paradis is said to have inspired the founding of special schools for the blind, both in Vienna and in Paris, and she helped develop reading and writing aids for the blind. A cure would have restored her femininity as a *wunderkind*. With her physical disability, however, she was able to avoid the role of a bourgeois woman and so was not limited to a life of marriage, reproduction, and housekeeping, as were Maria Anna Mozart and Dorothea Schlözer, whose creative and scientific work ended when they reached marriageable age.[11] Paradis was a living model for the success of education, and she contributed to bettering the living conditions of those with visual impairments.

Scholarship on disability in the eighteenth century has shown that the mark of a disability (then called a defect or deformity) overrode gender expectations. Despite the early Enlightenment's push for women's education, over the course of the eighteenth century gender roles in the middle class became more and more polarized, based on biological difference. Women's ability to bear children was declared to be their natural destiny and that, in turn, justified their being limited to a life as a dependent restricted to house and family. A physical or mental "defect" could override some of these expectations. A young woman with a physical or mental defect was not considered suitable for marriage even if her reproductive organs were fully functional. Being blind minimized Maria Paradis's "desirability as a woman" because it was "considered a defect or deformity of the body."[12] What scholars have found to be the case for many talented young female artists in the period applies even more to female musicians: their ambitions were curtailed, especially in the middle class, so that they would not hinder a marriage aimed at preserving the family wealth. Renate Berger summarizes the limitations for women artists and performers: in the middle class, having a *Versorger* [breadwinner] was more important than pursuing one's artistic ambitions. A bourgeois woman's only acceptable place was in the "house" with its many duties.[13] For Berger, marriage was "the coffin of female creativity in the eighteenth century."[14] The gender expectations of the period saw female sexuality as incompatible with creativity and so restricted creative expression to unmarried women.

As Tim Zumhof and Nicole Balzer argue elsewhere in this cluster, Foucault reminds us that we should understand prodigies within the context of power-knowledge relations. Paradis's "defect" was what allowed her to publicly perform on the piano and organ, both considered "male" and "aristocratic" instruments in the eighteenth century. By being (or rather by being known to be) blind, she was able to disregard the fact that she was being gazed upon, nor did she gaze back. She could remain unaffected by how the audience visually received her during her performances. Her music could replace the importance of seeing and being seen at a public event. She could be in front of an audience and the center of attention without being subject to the male gaze in the way that another woman in her position would be, and the same is true of her later work as the director of a private music school. She could perform without feeling shame for exposing her body to (male) desire. In his 1777 report on Mesmer's success in healing Maria, her father briefly hints that she suffered immensely before her blindness when she was exposed to curious onlookers and medical experts; he feared that her innate good temper had given way to "fits of melancholy" (a broad term for mental illness).[15] However, his report, like Mesmer's, narrativized and sentimentalized both her impairment and Mesmer's cure, linking them to "the bourgeois sensibility of individualism and the drama of an individual story."[16] Accordingly, they are not completely reliable sources for understanding disability's connection to gender in the late eighteenth century.

Audiences may have in part attended Paradis's concerts because of her anomalous nature as a blind performer. For several years toward the end of the eighteenth century, Paradis organized "dilettante academies," or weekly events held in the winter that introduced young musical talents to society; she also performed herself.[17] We know this from an annual publication on music in Vienna and Prague put out by Johann Ferdinand von Schönfeld, an art patron and retired publisher. Schönfeld praises Paradis's performances as masterful and her compositions as always original and striving for true expression of feeling.[18] These invitation-only events were highly regarded and a staple of musical life in Vienna. They often contained a mix of piano and vocal music, a style for which Franz Schubert became famous and that has been "underplayed" in research on music in Vienna before Schubert.[19]

It is likely that Paradis's parents continued to support her financially. She apparently gave lessons in piano and voice to girls in her home. Initially these were free, but an anonymous report in 1810 notes that she had begun to charge for the lessons, which went against expectations for women.[20] This was the beginning of her private music school. The report excused her engaging in commerce because of the death of her father, which presumably ended his financial support. It also reveals some remarkable gender expectations: although it praises her teaching methods as perfect, it nonetheless depicts her among her young (nine- to eleven-year-old) students as a mother with a loving demeanor that was reciprocated by the girls' utmost cordiality.[21]

Thus, her role as a compensated professional is overshadowed by the image of her occupying a motherly role. The report justified her school's concert by pointing out the lack of social activities during and after the war and the supposed feminine need for sociability as a replacement for family. Today, we acknowledge Paradis's independent, enterprising, and innovative spirit that encouraged girls to perform semi-publicly.

Another contemporary account offers useful insight into the effects of gender on the adult *wunderkind*. It suggests that Paradis's having adopted the feminine roles of educational motherhood and sociability did not change the ways in which her impairment excluded her from being perceived as female. Her younger friend, the popular conservative writer Caroline Pichler, mentioned in her memoirs that Viennese society loved and respected Paradis.[22] However, Pichler also described Paradis's visual impairment as her misfortune, although she praised Paradis's positive attitude toward her blindness as well as the fact that she had found happiness, joy, and comfort in music.[23] Her approbation implies that for a blind woman the usual sources of happiness—marriage and children—were not only unavailable, but unthinkable. Newer research suggests that the librettist Johann Riedinger, with whom she lived, was her partner in more than just musical undertakings, although contemporaries perceived their relationship to be no more than an asexual friendship.[24] Physical disability continued to be more important than gender, but it did not preclude all feminine roles for an adult woman.

Scholarship has only begun to examine cases of *wunderkinder,* such as Paradis, and how the Enlightenment view of blindness as a disease, the emerging medical model of disability, and changing middle-class gender roles affected her life and career. Considering the intersections of gender and "defect" in the eighteenth century allows us to conclude that it was her deficient eyesight that allowed Maria Paradis to continue her performing career beyond her teenage years. That is, she was able to do so not despite her blindness, but because of it. Her status as a blind person left Paradis unbound by many of the typical gender limitations, which allowed her to extend her status as a *wunderkind* into adulthood and become an organizer of academies and concerts and an independent teacher in her own private music school.

Notes

1. For a more substantial introduction, see Hidemi Matsushita, "Maria Theresia von Paradis (1759–1824)," in *New Historical Anthology of Music by Women*, ed. James R. Briscoe (Bloomington: Indiana University Press, 2004), 121–25, and Christian Fastl, "Paradis (Paradies), Maria Theresia (Marie Therese)," in *Oesterreichisches Musiklexikon*, https://www.musiklexikon.ac.at/ml/musik_P/Paradis_Maria.xml.

2. Mesmer, *Abhandlung über die Entdeckung des thierischen Magnetismus* (Karlsruhe: Michael Macklot, 1781).

3. The most recent biography is Marion Fürst, *Maria Theresia Paradis: Mozarts berühmte Zeitgenossin* (Vienna: Böhlau, 2005). For a fictional treatment, see Alissa Walser, *Am Anfang war die Nacht Musik: Roman* (Munich: Piper, 2010; translated as *Mesmerized*, trans. Jamie Bulloch [London: MacLehose Press, 2012]). For an overview of the ways in which Paradis and Mesmer's relationship has been understood, see Fürst, *Maria Theresia Paradis*, 200–25.

4. Enlightenment writing does not typically differentiate between degrees of impairment. Paradis's father recorded her as blind from the age of three, a diagnosis that Mesmer repeated at the beginning of his therapy, but she may not have been completely blind.

5. The appendix in Fürst, *Maria Theresia Paradis*, reprints these and other contemporary sources.

6. Space does not allow me to further explore the concept of the exceptional woman. For a useful account, see Mary Sheriff, *The Exceptional Woman: Elisabeth Vigee-Lebrun and the Cultural Politics of Art* (Chicago: University of Chicago Press, 1996).

7. Fiedler, *Tyranny of the Normal: Essays on Bioethics, Theology, and Myth* (Boston: David R. Godine, 1996).

8. Foucault, "The Politics of Health in the Eighteenth Century," in *Power/Knowledge: Selected Interviews and Other Writings, 1972–1977*, ed. Colin Gordon, trans. Colin Gordon, et al. (New York: Pantheon Books, 1980), 166–82.

9. See Mesmer, *Abhandlung*, 63–64.

10. See Colin Barnes and Geoffrey Mercer, *The Social Model of Disability: Europe and the Majority World* (Leeds: Disability Press, 2005).

11. See Tim Zumhof and Nicole Balzer's essay in this cluster.

12. Jess Domanico, "Reading 'The Blind Poetess of Lichfield': The Consolatory Odes of Priscilla Poynton," in *The Idea of Disability in the Eighteenth Century*, ed. Chris Mounsey (Lanham: Bucknell University Press, 2014), 208.

13. Berger, "'… denn meine Wünsche streifen an das Unmögliche': Künstlerinnen zwischen Aufklärung und Biedermeier," in *Zwischen Ideal und Wirklichkeit: Künstlerinnen der Goethe-Zeit zwischen 1750 und 1850*, ed. Bärbel Kovalesvski (Ostfildern-Ruit: Hatje, 1999), 16.

14. Berger, "'… denn meine Wünsche,'" 21 [my translation]. Berger's phrase, in German, is "die Ehe als Sarg weiblicher Kreativität."

15. Mesmer, *Abhandlung*, 63 [my translation]. Mesmer was reprinting a newspaper article that quoted Joseph Paradis. The latter's phrase, in German, is "melancholische Anfälle."

16. Lennard J. Davis, *Enforcing Normalcy: Disability, Deafness, and the Body* (London: Verso, 1995), 11.

17. [Johann Ferdinand von Schönfeld], "Dilettantenakademien," *Jahrbuch der Tonkunst von Wien und Prag* (Vienna: im von Schönfeldischen Verlag, 1796), 69–74. An English translation is available: Schönfeld, "A Yearbook of Music in Vienna and Prague, 1796," trans. Kathrine Talbot, in *Haydn and His World*, ed. Elaine R. Sisman (Princeton: Princeton University Press, 1997), 289–320.

18. Schönfeld, "A Yearbook of Music," 309.

19. David Wyn Jones, *Music in Vienna, 1700, 1800, 1900* (Woodbridge: Boydell Press, 2016), 1.

20. "Nachrichten (Auszug eines Schreibens aus Wien)," *Allgemeine Musikalische Zeitung* (Leipzig) 30, 25 April 1810, column 472, https://reader.digitale-sammlungen.de/de/fs1/object/display/bsb10527960_00270.html.

21. "Nachrichten," columns 473–74.

22. Pichler, *Denkwürdigkeiten aus meinem Leben*, 2 vols. (Vienna: Pichler, 1844), 1:45.

23. Pichler, *Denkwürdigkeiten*, 1:40, 1:217.

24. See, for example, Fürst, *Maria Theresia Paradis*, 170, 289.

BIOGRAPHY AND THE WOMAN WRITER REVISITED

Introduction: Biography and the Woman Writer Revisited

ELIZABETH NEIMAN AND YAEL SHAPIRA

The essays included in this cluster explore several themes that emerged in our two-part panel at the 2021 Virtual Annual Meeting of the American Society for Eighteenth-Century Studies: "Still Lives? Revisiting the Biographical in the Study of Eighteenth-Century Women's Writing." As part of introducing the cluster, we think it would be worthwhile to describe how and why we organized this panel and what questions we hoped to see investigated through it. We—Elizabeth and Yael—met some years back through our joint research interest in the Minerva Press, the infamously popular London publisher that brought out an unprecedented number of women novelists between 1785 and 1820. Our work on Minerva's long-ignored novels and novelists followed divergent routes: Elizabeth approached Minerva as a Romanticist, Yael as a scholar of the Gothic and the history of the novel. Yet we both found ourselves drawn to questions of biography and its utility, especially since Minerva's most popular and prolific writers were women about whom, in many cases, very little is known.

As we were both aware, however, reliance on biography comes with its own share of troubling questions. Biographical criticism became a crux of disagreement for feminist critics in the 1980s and 1990s, when poststructuralist claims about the death of the author prompted some feminist scholars "to agree … that the authorial presence is best set aside in order to liberate the text for multiple uses."[1] Others found the poststructuralist rejection of the author problematic, because it occluded the ways in which gender has historically shaped subjectivity as well as cultural notions of authorship and authority. Looking back at the dispute two decades later, Toril Moi noted that it was never resolved, which left theory and practice permanently out of sync, as "one half of the brain continues to read women writers while the other continues to think that the author is dead, and that the very word 'woman' is theoretically dodgy."[2]

Seeking a way to get beyond the theory/practice binary, critical uses of biography in feminist literary criticism have become increasingly self-aware: the dangers of essentialism and over-simplification have been countered by a recognition that the life stories of women writers—both those told about them and those they told themselves—call for a nuanced, historicized analysis in their own right. In this context, scholars have insightfully probed women's engagement with the author-construct: the operative conventions that, at any point in time, delimit, but also mobilize how authors define themselves, their lives, and their work. Take, for example, Jennie Batchelor's influential reassessment of women's self-effacing presentation of themselves and their careers, both in appeals to the Royal Literary Fund and in the prefaces to their published work. As Batchelor shows, the conventions of feminine humility mark, but also mask, women writers' negotiations with an increasingly masculinized discourse on authorship that influences how those writers have been memorialized, both in their day and our own.[3] Recent studies by Brenda Ayres and Susan Civele illustrate the continued resonance of this approach. According to Ayres, twentieth- and twenty-first-century biographers of nineteenth-century women writers frequently distort a writer's life in order to create the version of that writer that best accords with their own theses. But when read collectively and for gaps and points of conflict, biographies can offer a method for digging back into a writer's work and thus for writing more expansive literary histories.[4] Civele, in her turn, illustrates how Romantic-era women writers took up the emerging conventions of autobiographical writing, visibly shaping the genre and their own reception in ways that sometimes challenge twenty-first-century assessments of their work.[5]

Still, perhaps it is not surprising that as the literary field widens and more texts and writers—many of them previously unknown—are considered within its purview, unease over the place of biography in feminist scholarship persists. As Batchelor has asked, "how can we preserve the lives and reanimate interest in the texts of [women writers] who have been unjustly marginalized or misrepresented within literary history without making biography the 'master-text' to which their works are subordinated and thus replicating, albeit in a different guise, the antifeminist strategies of the past?"[6] Then again, do we ever read *un*biographically in our current critical practice? If, as Gillian Dow observes, "We cannot un-know what we know (or what we think we know) about the woman behind the writing," we can ask in turn, what then is the effect of continuing *not* to know about some writers what we do know about others?[7] And what of those many women writers about whom little to nothing *can* be known? Can or should we search their texts for reflections of their lives? Would we read their writing differently if we could fill in the biographical lacunae? What might these unreachable figures teach us about the limits, but also the possibilities, of biographical research in feminist literary studies?

The four essays in this cluster continue this conversation about biography and women's writing, exploring some of the directions that it is taking at the present moment. Rebecca Crisafulli returns to the feminist/poststructuralist debate described above, which she uses to chart a way forward through a flexible methodology that draws on both sides of the argument. Biographical information, Crisafulli suggests, is of value when it usefully expands how a given text can be read, but should be treated with caution when it reduces or misleads. Crisafulli illustrates this wary use of biography in discussing the *philosophe* Louise d'Épinay's epistolary novel, *L'Histoire de Madame de Montbrillant*, which has been generally dismissed as a thinly veiled autobiography, principally of value for what it reveals about d'Épinay's friendship with Jean-Jacques Rousseau. When the restrictive biographical reading is countered by attention to the novel's broader philosophical investments, Crisafulli contends, *L'Histoire de Madame de Montbrillant* can be newly understood as a *roman pédagogique,* which may even have influenced the writing of Rousseau's *Émile.*

Lise Gaston similarly considers both the possibilities and the limitations of biography by exploring the case of Charlotte Smith, who famously encouraged readers to treat her work as autobiographical. And yet Smith's biography in some places strains against her literary persona, as Gaston shows by analyzing Smith's matter-of-fact business negotiations concerning a family estate in Barbados, which depended on the labor of enslaved persons, toward whom her characteristic sensibility was notably absent. Pitting Smith's reliance on slavery as a metaphor for her own suffering against her brisk financial discussions of the enslaved persons she regarded as property, Gaston asks, "What do we do when the facts of a biography unsettle the aesthetic project?"

Andrew Winckles, in turn, raises a different and striking question with regard to the use of biography when he wonders, "If we still don't know enough about already well-known women, then why should we devote time and resources to exploring the lives of the obscure and forgotten? Why should we do the hard work of stitching together archival fragments and trying to recover the biographical details of women that few people have ever heard of?"

Though all of the contributors to the cluster consider the often intense labor of biography worth doing (including Winckles himself, in his discussion of religious writer and poet Sally Wesley), the very question highlights an important fact: dilemmas regarding biography now arise primarily for those who study forgotten or overlooked women, writers whose names are virtually unknown outside of very small circles of specialists. When it comes to canonical authors, the reliance on biography is an established fact of life, whether or not it is explicitly flagged as a methodological choice. Jane Austen's location among the "pseudo-gentry," Frances Burney's circle of literary acquaintances and patrons, and Mary Shelley's family history are mentioned in critical discussions of their work as a matter of course. Yet in the study of the obscure, as Winckles emphasizes, biography seems at once crucial and newly problematic.

Efforts to reconstruct the identities of forgotten women can be fruitful, as in Simon Macdonald's identification of the prolific popular novelist "Mrs. Meeke" as Frances Burney's stepsister, Elizabeth Allen, or in Lyndon Dominique's speculation that the author of the anonymously published *The Woman of Colour*—a circulating-library novel that has drawn considerable recent attention—may have been an actual woman of color named Ann Wright.[8] Yet, as Winckles suggests, to investigate forgotten women writers of this sort is to struggle constantly with sources that are fragmentary and incomplete, when available at all, while lacking the legitimizing assumption of a writer's perceived importance to literary history.

The challenge of working with only partial biographical evidence is made vivid in Kaitlin Tonti's essay on the letters that Esther Edwards Burr, Aaron Burr's mother, exchanged with her close friend Sarah Prince. As Tonti explains, "Early American women's biographies are always challenging to compile, as they are fragmented and thus representative of their hectic roles as wives and mothers." In the case of the Burr-Prince correspondence, the radically incomplete nature of the evidence is the result of a choice made by one of the women involved: Prince asked Burr to destroy her side of the correspondence. Tonti points to the gap created by Prince's missing letters as an opportunity to rethink how scholars might write biographically, challenging us to consider what can be learned from an epistolary exchange of which only one side survives.

Winckles offers a stimulating response to the challenge posed by fragmentary sources when he writes that "we need to create new methods for understanding these gaps—of living within and becoming comfortable with the in-between space of obscure women's texts, of getting to know texts like we know people and feeling similar assumptions about them in our respective guts." We are intrigued by his call for a renewed, but revised investment in the older humanist emphasis not only on the author's personhood, but also on the scholar's own intuition and unique voice.

Like the panels in which they originated, these four essays all ask how biography can serve as a tool that complicates, rather than simplifies: used thoughtfully, they show how biography can enable a fuller understanding of both particular texts and literary history more generally. In some cases, as Winckles and Tonti demonstrate, biographical research is a primary path to areas of writerly activity that would otherwise remain hidden. The archives and letters in which the lives of Sally Wesley and Esther Burr may be glimpsed are also points of access into forms of literary exchange and production that are otherwise missing from the historical record. In other situations, asking biographical questions can be a way of recognizing and challenging the stories that have already solidified around particular figures, literary genres, and historical conditions. In juxtaposing Smith's resolutely autobiographical "I" with the alternative view of her biography that emerges from her letters, Gaston reminds us of the fissures that can hide beneath well-known authorial personae. Crisafulli's discussion of d'Épinay, meanwhile, points to the ease with which stories of women writers can collapse into clichés and asks how too-easy assumptions about female subservience and apoliticism might inform (or, rather, misinform) interpretive practice.

In what follows, we recognize the potential of listening to incomplete, yet suggestive sources and of recognizing the limitations of one's own vision and voice within the emerging project of investigating eighteenth-century women's writing and lives. That project is ultimately collective: it relies on a collaborative approach that has, until recently, often seemed at odds with research expectations in the Humanities, where the fierce debate over the "death of the author" left Romantic ideas about the individualistic nature of critical work curiously intact. As part of an interdisciplinary recovery effort that is currently rewriting women's literary history, biography benefits profoundly from collaboration. Pooling labor and resources can be a way of confronting scarcity (fragmentary, limited, or scattered evidence), but also, conversely, the potentially overwhelming abundance of an expanding canon and growing set of bibliographic information. As Devoney Looser notes, the intersection of biography, "big data," and new technologies has enormous potential for the study of women's writing, and it calls for new ways of working together. The fruits of this approach are already evident in such resources as the *Orlando: Women's Writing in the British Isles* database or the annotated online edition-in-the-making of Elizabeth

Montagu's correspondence.[9] In Betty Schellenberg and Michelle Levy's view, moreover, collaboration is a source of vital sustenance, offering "the sociability and shared vision required to undertake and bring to completion the many tasks at hand."[10] The fact that our panels were convened on Zoom (as a result of the pandemic forcing our Annual Meeting to be held in a virtual format) made the gifts of collaboration immediate and tangible. As panelists presented their work, the chat quickly filled not only with expressions of interest and encouragement, but also with questions about the availability of editions and other materials relating to little-known women writers. Many of the queries were answered on the spot with references and links. The panels themselves—like this cluster, and our own co-authoring of this introduction—have thus made vivid how a revaluation of shared work and a renewed sense of a common mission might usher our investigations of the biographies of women writers into a new age.

Notes

1. Cheryl Walker, "Feminist Literary Criticism and the Author," *Critical Inquiry* 16, no. 3 (1990), 553.

2. Moi, "'I Am Not a Woman Writer': About Women, Literature, and Feminist Theory Today," *Feminist Theory* 9, no. 3 (2008), 264.

3. Batchelor, "The Claims of Literature: Women Applicants to the Royal Literary Fund, 1790–1810," *Women's Writing* 12, no. 3 (2005): 505-21.

4. Ayres, "Introduction, or *What You Will*," in *Biographical Misrepresentations of British Women Writers: A Hall of Mirrors and the Long Nineteenth Century*, ed. Brenda Ayres (London: Palgrave Macmillan, 2017): 1–16.

5. Civale, *Romantic Women's Life Writing: Reputation and Afterlife* (Manchester: Manchester University Press, 2019).

6. Batchelor, "Jane Austen and Charlotte Smith: Biography, Autobiography, and the Writing of Women's Literary History," in *Women's Life Writing, 1700–1850: Gender, Genre and Authorship*, ed. Daniel Cook and Amy Culley (Basingstoke: Palgrave Macmillan, 2012), 183.

7. Dow, "The 'Biographical Impulse' and Pan-European Women's Writing," in *Women's Writing, 1660–1830: Feminisms and Futures*, ed. Jennie Batchelor and Gillian Dow (London: Palgrave Macmillan, 2016), 194.

8. Macdonald, "Identifying Mrs. Meeke: Another Burney Family Novelist," *Review of English Studies* 64, no. 265 (2013): 367–85; Lyndon J. Dominique, "Introduction" to *The Woman of Colour*, ed. Lyndon J. Dominque (Peterborough: Broadview Press, 2007), 31.

9. Looser, "British Women Writers, Big Data and Big Biography, 1780–1830," *Women's Writing* 22, no. 2 (2015): 165–71; *Orlando: Women's Writing in the British Isles from the Beginnings to the Present,* https://orlando.cambridge.org; *Elizabeth Montagu Correspondence Online,* http://emco.swansea.ac.uk.

10. Schellenberg and Levy, "Hiding in Plain Sight," *Huntington Library Quarterly* 84, no. 1 (2021), 209.

Using the Miller-Kamuf Test to Evaluate the Role of Biography in Scholarship on Eighteenth-Century Women's Writing

REBECCA CRISAFULLI

A t least two women who talk to each other about something other than a man: these are the conditions a work of fiction must meet in order to pass the famous Bechdel Test. Pithy and easy-to-remember, the test has spawned countless analyses of books and films and has inspired the creation of other tests to evaluate the authenticity of a given representation, among them the Vito Russo Test for LGBTQ+ characters and the DuVernay Test for portrayals of People of Color. I propose a test that eighteenth-century scholars can use in their own work: the Miller-Kamuf Test. It evaluates the relative weight given to biography and textual analysis in the extant scholarship on a woman author with the goal of encouraging further research that would lead to a fuller, more accurate understanding of women authors' contributions to the Enlightenment.

The name Miller-Kamuf refers to a debate in the 1980s between two critics of French literature that stemmed from Roland Barthes's 1967 declaration of the death of the author and the emancipation of textual interpretation from the constraints imposed by an author's biography that that death made possible.[1] Nancy K. Miller observed that this shift happened just as texts by women were being deemed worthy of study and that it pushed them to the side once more. Peggy Kamuf argued that focusing on the identity, or signature, of women authors recreated a separate-but-unequal version of the western masculinist canon. It would thus be more productive to treat texts as texts without considering an author's biography. A particular point of contention was the *Lettres portugaises*. Long thought to have been written by a woman, twentieth-century critics revealed the author to be Gabriel de Guilleragues. To Kamuf, Guilleragues's gender did not matter; anyone could write from a woman's perspective. To Miller, it did matter because Guilleragues had written as a woman not to empathize with women, but rather to establish a contract of sympathy with a male audience, founded on the "neutralization of the Other": Woman.[2] Thus, in this text, Woman can "become a subject only upon the condition of her 'subordination.'"[3]

In the Miller-Kamuf Test, "Miller" refers to the relative weight that biography should be given vis-à-vis textual analysis (which is here given the shorthand of "Kamuf"). Consider how the test works in the following two cases:

Henriette *** wrote letters to Jean-Jacques Rousseau about his disparaging views on women's education.[4] She claimed to seek his blessing to study and to have intellectual discussions with educated men as a means of consoling herself because she could not achieve domestic bliss: as a noble over thirty with no dowry, she would not be able to marry. Nothing is known about her life; almost every study of her letters relies exclusively on textual analysis. Henriette*** scholarship thus scores high on the Kamuf side and zero on the Miller side.

Louise d'Épinay authored educational works, carried on a prodigious correspondence with leading Enlightenment thinkers, and contributed to the *Correspondance littéraire.* Her nearly 2,000-page epistolary novel, *L'Histoire de Madame de Montbrillant*, has always been classified as a thinly veiled memoir or autobiographical novel.[5] Nineteenth-century editors branded it a memoir in the interest of sales, because d'Épinay had personal relationships with Friedrich Melchior, Freiherr von Grimm; Denis Diderot; Voltaire; and Rousseau. Well into the twentieth century, many critics focused on d'Épinay's relationships with famous men and evaluated *Montbrillant* as a form of life writing.[6] D'Épinay scholarship scores low on the Kamuf side and high on the Miller side.

Measuring the balance between Miller and Kamuf is only a first step. In 2008, Toril Moi called for a renewed theoretical engagement with the issues at stake in the still-unresolved debate from the 1980s, pointing out that a woman writer still faces the same dilemma that Simone de Beauvoir warned us about: either "write as a woman or like a woman" or "write as a generic human being," which "opens up an alienating split between her gender and her humanity."[7] I do not have a solution, but I submit that even without one, we can use the terms of the debate to raise awareness as to how critics have sometimes harmfully deployed biography and textual analysis in studies of women's writing and to do better in our own scholarship by asking what might be gained by stepping away from biography? Or, conversely, what could a biographical approach contribute?

For the cases discussed here, doing better means undertaking projects to make the Miller and Kamuf scores more even. There may be cases in which an imbalance makes sense, but generally, the test would indicate where the scholarship needs more balance, because balancing textual analysis and biography can help us remember the difficulties that women faced in publishing or even writing in the first place, without imposing the very stereotypes that keep women's literature marginalized.

All too often, we bring assumptions to our study of eighteenth-century women's writing that are well-founded, but that can keep us from seeing everything that is going on in a text. One such assumption is that because many women were inadequately educated, they were capable of writing about their own experiences, but not of offering prescriptions for how best to change society. It can be tempting to assume that autobiographical writings are sincere, spontaneous, and personal, but they may be carefully constructed and written for a social purpose.

Henriette ***'s letters illustrate the danger of these assumptions because, in the absence of any biography, most critics have believed that she was who she claimed to be. However, Mary McAlpin has suggested that she "may well have been misrepresenting the circumstances of her life in her letters" and underscores that Henriette *** prepared her correspondence with Rousseau for publication. Such work contradicts her claim to have taken Rousseau's advice and withdrawn from the public eye, so it is probably not a good idea to take her at her word.[8] In this case, considering the low Miller score, we might focus our efforts on finding out, if we can, who she was, or else explore different biographical possibilities and their interpretive consequences. For example, if a man wrote them, or an established female author, or a group of people, the letters sound less earnest and more ironic, especially if Henriette ***'s letters were a *La Religieuse*-style hoax intended to get Rousseau to admit that his views on women were flawed.

In d'Épinay's case, biography has overshadowed textual analysis of *Montbrillant*. To raise its Kamuf score, I would set aside preconceptions about its genre and d'Épinay's biography. Reading this way, I would argue that *Montbrillant* is best understood as a *roman pédagogique* or educational novel inspired by d'Épinay's experiences, rather than as an autobiographical novel per se. The work presents readers with the exemplary life of Émilie, a poor noble, and chronicles her abusive marriage, her financial troubles, her quest to find a virtuous lover and friends, and the separation of her own assets from those of her husband. Especially important to the story are Émilie's struggles to obtain a proper moral and intellectual formation and, later, to devise and implement an idealized curriculum for her own children. *Montbrillant* grapples with some of the principal questions of education of the eighteenth century: Are parents or schools better suited to educate children? What is the best method? Can you raise children to be virtuous in a corrupt society? D'Épinay included caricatures of her contemporaries to critique their educational ideas.

Reading *Montbrillant* this way may seem like a subtle shift, because the work is still inspired by her experiences, but it changes how we understand d'Épinay's contributions to Enlightenment thought in at least three ways.

Scholars have noted that d'Épinay disagreed with Rousseau's views on women's education, but she is often considered to have learned from and reacted to his ideas.[9] *Montbrillant* was likely written over some years beginning in 1756, when d'Épinay provided Rousseau with housing on her property.[10] At this time, he was developing his ideas for *Émile* and the two talked daily. Reading *Montbrillant* as the novel of Émilie's education suggests that d'Épinay may have contributed much more to these discussions than we have traditionally realized. Indeed, there are views expressed in d'Épinay's *Lettres à mon fils* (1759) that anticipate those found in *Émile* (1762).[11]

This reading also reveals that d'Épinay was responding not just to Rousseau, but also to a wider pedagogical tradition, including the insights of women like Jeanne-Marie Leprince de Beaumont and Marie de Rabutin-Chantal, marquise de Sévigné. In the latter, for example, d'Épinay found a proponent of mothers educating their daughters at home, instead of warehousing them in convents until they were old enough to be married, and a model curriculum that would build girls' intelligence through reading, conversation, writing, and introspection. D'Épinay updated Sévigné's method with Enlightenment ideals.

Finally, this reading shows us d'Épinay's plans for transforming society. The women educated according to her model would bring a well-developed intellectual and moral foundation to their marriages. These qualities would stand in for a dowry and would make a woman the equal of her husband. By changing the emotional and financial bases of marriage, the curriculum was meant to transform a corrupt state nonviolently and thus serve as an alternative to revolution. D'Épinay makes recommendations regarding the public sphere and political economy, even calling for changing the taxation practices of the *ancien régime*. It would not have been possible to see these aspects of *Montbrillant* without turning away from her biography.

Though the Miller-Kamuf Test sidesteps the theoretical confrontation Moi calls for in favor of practical applications, as the case studies illustrate, resolution of the debate may lie in our collective scholarly responses to the test. The case of Henriette *** shows that considering potential biographies could open up new possibilities for textual analysis, while that of d'Épinay teaches us that textual analysis without biography can reveal previously hidden contributions, which, in turn, would change how we assess and use the author's biography. In these instances (and many others that await exploration), Miller and Kamuf are not at odds, but rather depend on one another to produce new knowledge.

Notes

1. For more on the issues at stake in the debate, see Kamuf, "Writing Like a Woman," in *Women and Language in Literature and Society*, ed. Sally McConnell-Ginet, Ruth Borker, and Nelly Furman (New York: Praeger, 1980), 285–86; Miller, "'I's' in Drag: The Sex of Recollection," *The Eighteenth Century* 22, no. 1 (1981): 47–57; Kamuf, "Replacing Feminist Criticism," *Diacritics* 12, no. 2 (1982): 42–47; Miller, "The Text's Heroine: A Feminist Critic and Her Fictions," *Diacritics* 12, no. 2 (1982): 48–53; and Kamuf and Miller, "Parisian Letters: Between Feminism and Deconstruction," in *Conflicts in Feminism*, ed. Marianne Hirsch and Evelyn Fox Keller (New York: Routledge, 1990), 121–33.

2. Miller, "'I's' in Drag," 50.

3. Miller, "Text's Heroine," 116.

4. *J-J. Rousseau Henriette *** Correspondance [1764–1770]*, ed. Yannick Séité (Paris: Éditions Manucius, 2014).

5. Louise d'Épinay, *Histoire de Madame de Montbrillant*, ed. Georges Roth (Paris: Gallimard, 1951).

6. For accounts of *Montbrillant*'s publication and reception history, see Odette David, *L'Autobiographie de convenance de Madame d'Épinay, écrivain-philosophe des Lumières: Subversion idéologique et formelle de l'écriture de soi* (Paris: L'Harmattan, 2007); Pierre Tyl, "*L'Histoire de Madame de Montbrillant* des *Mémoires de Madame d'Épinay* aux *Contre-Confessions*," in *L'Œuvre de Madame d'Épinay, écrivain-philosophe des Lumières. Actes du premier colloque international consacré à Madame d'Épinay, organisé par Jacques Domenech* (Paris: L'Harmattan, 2010), 69–78.

7. Moi, "I am not a Woman Writer," http://www.eurozine.com/i-am-not-a-woman-writer/.

8. McAlpin, *Gender, Authenticity, and the Missive Letter in Eighteenth-Century France: Marie-Anne de La Tour, Rousseau's Real-Life Julie* (Lewisburg: Bucknell University Press, 2006), 180, 182.

9. On d'Épinay learning from Rousseau, see Louise d'Épinay, *Les Conversations d'Émilie*, ed. Rosena Davison (Oxford: Voltaire Foundation, 1996), 10–15, and Mary Trouille, "La Femme Mal Mariée: Mme d'Épinay's Challenge to *Julie* and *Émile*," *Eighteenth-Century Life* 20, no. 1 (1996): 42–66. On the characterization of d'Épinay as a disciple of Rousseau, see Ruth Plaut Weinreb, *Eagle in a Gauze Cage: Louise d'Épinay, Femme de Lettres* (New York: AMS Press, 1993), 35–36.

10. Weinreb, *Eagle in a Gauze Cage*, 72–73.

11. Ruth Plaut Weinreb, "Émilie or *Émile*? Madame d'Épinay and the Education of Girls in Eighteenth-Century France," in *Eighteenth-Century Women and the Arts*, ed. Frederick M. Keener and Susan E. Lorsch (New York: Greenwood, 1988), 57–66.

Inviting Conflict:
Slavery and Charlotte Smith's
Biographical Aesthetic

LISE GASTON

Unlike many of her female contemporaries, who shunned public scrutiny of their private lives, Charlotte Smith invited biographical readings of her work. In prologues and prefaces, which engendered both sympathy and derision, Smith decries her position as a wronged wife and highlights her devotion as a working mother. Similarly suffering, saintly wives and abusive husbands populate her fiction, while the speakers of her popular *Elegiac Sonnets* bemoan their tragic lot. Critics still follow the author's invitation: Jacqueline Labbe shows how Smith "creates a parade of acculturated identities" in her poetry, while Melissa Sodeman asserts that "Smith's biography is critical to understanding her aesthetic."[1] However, what do we do when the facts of a biography unsettle the aesthetic project supposedly based upon it? This essay tackles this question by arguing that while Smith uses the figure of the slave in her writing as a rhetorical and aesthetic device to emphasize the often gendered injustice she faced, both her 1796 novel *Marchmont* and her letters reveal how the pathos produced by this figure collides with the monetary potential of the labor of enslaved persons.[2] We can therefore ask how far Smith's apparent invitation to read autobiographically really goes, and how, as critics, we should grapple with this approach when it produces conflicting accounts not only in her literary texts, but also within her biography itself.

Smith long framed herself as "the slave of the Booksellers," and used similar language to describe her marriage, writing to Mary Hays, "but I am—married—! … I am still in reality a slave & liable to have my bondage renewed."[3] In an earlier letter to Thomas Shirley, Smith confesses: "But really it is almost too much for me … to be compelled to live only to write & write only to live. While every body seems to think (I mean of the family) that I am bound to do it, forgetting that I was a mere child when they talk'd me into bonds, which I have found most insupportably heavy."[4] The marital contract here is something weighty, physical, and permanent. She is bound to writing in a different, yet equally permanent way: she is both (economically) chained to her desk and apparently fated to do it anyway, both by vocation and out of maternal duty. Like Smith's representation of her teenage self, "talk'd into bonds" and "sold" from her father's house at "not quite fifteen," her female characters are often merely the objects of male agreements made without their consent.[5]

Smith invokes slaves and slavery as rhetorical figures in her works to elicit pity, to blur the distinctions between duty and coercion, and to protest the indignity of bonds, including her own. We find anti-slavery sentiments in poems such as "The fire-fly of Jamaica, seen in a collection," which pities the "sighing slave" and "The recent captive, who in vain / Attempts to break his heavy chain."[6] This antislavery rhetoric follows her fictionalization of her own position as a long-suffering wife in numerous novels, not the least 1792's *Desmond*.[7] Determined to travel to revolutionary France at her vile husband's request, the titular hero's beloved Geraldine Verney writes: "If I get among the wildest collection of those people whose ferocity arises not from their present liberty, but their recent bondage, is it possible to suppose they will injure *me*, who am myself a miserable slave, returning with trembling and reluctant steps, to put on the most dreadful of fetters?"[8]

But we really see the problematic equation of an individual woman's life with being someone else's property in the rhetoric of enslavement and the presentation of slavery in *Marchmont*. After a series of misadventures, the titular hero and his wife arrive at the crisis of the novel. Marchmont is imprisoned at King's Bench for the enormous debts accrued by his deceased father. Althea, his dutiful wife, has joined him, in yet another echo of Smith's biography (she famously joined her husband in debtor's prison). Through a metaphoric structure of substitution, Marchmont's body stands in for his father's corpse, which stands in for his father's debts; Marchmont's wife's body then takes on her husband's constraints and suffering, until they are both released from bondage via the monetary value ascribed to other bound bodies: enslaved persons in the West Indies. The novel ends when Mr. Desborough—a rich, previously unknown uncle—pays Marchmont's debts and releases them. He also helps to secure a sudden inheritance for Althea. We learn that upon the death of Marchmont's aunt, her husband, Mr. Desborough, had departed for the West Indies to care for some property he inherited. However, "I could not endure to be master of slaves. The whole system of a plantation was repugnant to all my feelings, and all my principles. I sold my cane lands, and the unhappy people who worked them, to whom I would have given their liberty if I had been allowed to do it. It was a blessing I could bestow only on a few. I came home, rich for a man that wanted so little."[9] Marchmont, in prison, experiencing what Amanda Bailey calls "debt bondage as [a] corporal event," claims that his imprisonment is unjust.[10] Despite the fact that he has inherited his father's legitimate debts, Marchmont decries "the vile instrument of tyranny that has the injustice, the barbarity to confine me."[11] He repeatedly compares himself to an enslaved person with phrases like: "shall I bear it patiently, chained like a felon—like a galley-slave?"[12] Ironically, it is income from the unfree labor of enslaved persons (albeit on a plantation in the West Indies, not a galley in the Mediterranean) that ultimately enables his freedom, while the liberty of those who were actually, rather than simply metaphorically, enslaved is denied. Sodeman has suggested that the "slave for Smith is a purely formal figure, its referent not so much the displaced African of the slave trade as a figure from classical literature."[13] However, any classical figurations in *Marchmont* come up against literal, if unseen, enslaved persons in the contemporary West Indies, who are integral to an ending that illustrates Edward Said's claim that "the right to colonial possessions helps directly to establish social order and moral priorities at home."[14] Despite Mr. Desborough's (and Smith's) abolitionist sentiments, the continued unfreedom of enslaved persons is what makes possible the liberation of the "deserving" Englishman.

This irony reappears four years after the publication of *Marchmont*, when Smith negotiates the sale of Gays, a Barbados estate owned by a family trust, from which she planned to profit.[15] In her letters she demonstrates a concrete knowledge of the enslaved individuals included in the sale, and argues over their financial value with businesslike precision. Writing to William Prescod, she first laments the position of her family, before turning to the business at hand: "give me leave to state to you my hopes and expectations that you will consider the heavy Losses my Family have sustained. ... It is true the value of the Negroes is by death lessen'd; but only three of considerable value have died: a Man worth (as pr valuation of 1798) 70£ called Kit James, a young Woman called Catharina, stated to be worth £100, and a Woman called

Sarah or Sareey worth £80. The three other Girls or Women were of inferior value, and one Slave named Bennah, tho stated in the Managers Account to be a Man, was a very old Woman worth nothing; her death therefore & that of the old Men is rather a relief than a disadvantage to the Estate."[16] Her accounting continues, revealing that when Smith is operating as a business woman, rather than a sentimental author (though a glance at her letters to her publishers shows how she could conflate those roles), she values the enslaved laboring bodies—not in the abstract, but as specific, named individuals—in the same way that Marchmont does when he unquestioningly benefits from a similar financial transaction. Even the death of these persons (a seemingly perfect occasion for sentimental effusions) only results in further economic calculation. But the use of enslaved persons here and in *Marchmont* does more than just signal hypocrisy. The division between rhetorical sympathy and material gain follows her novels' pattern of repeated discrepancies between written or stated claims and felt bodily experience: Marchmont's metaphorical identification as a slave versus what actual enslaved persons in the world routinely underwent. This pattern of a division between what a character (or narrator) abstractly asserts and lived experience recalls the imaginary nature of value, which was a key element in the slave trade more generally. Smith's letter illustrates the truth of Ian Baucom's statement that "value exists not because a purchase has been made and goods exchanged but because two or more parties have agreed to believe in it."[17] Here, as in *Marchmont*, the agreed-upon value of bodies shifts, depending on the identity of who benefits.

Smith's unique invitation to read both her poetry and fiction biographically opens up a productive gap in her critical reception. This essay's turn toward the material, historical, and economic conditions of slavery, as a way of complicating the relation between the aesthetic and the biographical, is a brief attempt to respond to Tricia Lootens's call: "How can we experiment with readings intent on exploring the ways in which ... invocations of 'slavery' or 'slavishness,' even at their most abstract, may remain haunted by ultimately irreducible, ineffaceable, corporeal histories of transimperial human loss?"[18] We need not look far for the figures that haunt Smith's works—only perhaps not in the ways that the author intended.

Notes

1. Labbe, *Charlotte Smith: Romanticism, Poetry, and the Culture of Gender* (Manchester: Manchester University Press, 2003), 8; Sodeman, "Charlotte Smith's Literary Exile," *ELH* 76, no. 1 (2009), 134.

2. Smith is not alone in her use of this trope; for some of the other ways in which white British women writers employed antislavery writing in the service of their own political and domestic positions, see Moira Ferguson, *Subject to Others: British Women Writers and Colonial Slavery, 1670–1834* (New York: Routledge, 1992).

3. Smith, *The Collected Letters of Charlotte Smith*, ed. Judith Phillips Stanton (Bloomington: Indiana University Press, 2003), 79–80, 350.

4. Smith, *Collected Letters,* 23.

5. Smith, *Collected Letters,* 80. For more on the "performative gestures" of Smith's correspondence, see Jennie Batchelor, *Women's Work: Labour, Gender, Authorship, 1750–1830* (Manchester: Manchester University Press, 2010), 70.

6. Smith, "To the Fire-fly of Jamaica, Seen in a Collection," in *Conversations Introducing Poetry: Chiefly on Subjects of Natural History for the Use of Children and Young Persons* (Edinburgh: T. Nelson and Sons, 1863), 201 3.

7. For Smith's views on slavery as expressed in her fiction, see George Boulukos, "The Horror of Hybridity: Enlightenment, Anti-Slavery and Racial Disgust in Charlotte Smith's *Story of Henrietta* (1800)," in *Slavery and the Cultures of Abolition: Essays Marking the Bicentennial of the British Abolition Act of 1807*, ed. Brycchan Carey and Peter J. Kitson (Cambridge: D. S. Brewer, 2007), 87–109, and Eamon Wright, *British Women Writers and Race, 1788–1818: Narrations of Modernity* (Basingstoke: Palgrave Macmillan, 2005).

8. Charlotte Smith, *Desmond*, ed. Antje Blank and Janet Todd (Peterborough: Broadview Press, 2001), 303–4.

9. Smith, *Marchmont: A Novel,* ed. Mary Anne Schofield (New York: Scholars' Facsimiles & Reprints, 1989), 415.

10. Bailey, *Of Bondage: Debt, Property, and Personhood in Early Modern England* (Philadelphia: University of Pennsylvania Press, 2013), 10.

11. Smith, *Marchmont*, 311.

12. Smith, *Marchmont*, 311.

13. Sodeman, "Charlotte Smith's Literary Exile," 134.

14. Said, *Culture and Imperialism* (New York: Vintage Books, 1993), 62.

15. For more on the complex nature of the family's plantation holdings and her father-in-law's fraught will, see Loraine Fletcher, *Charlotte Smith: A Critical Biography* (New York: Macmillan Press, 1998), 291, and Elizabeth A. Dolan, "Financial Investments vs. Moral Principles: Charlotte Smith's Children's Books and Slavery," in *Time of Beauty, Time of Fear: The Romantic Legacy in the Literature of Childhood*, ed. James Holt McGavran (Iowa City: University of Iowa Press, 2012), 59, 65–66. Dolan blends the biographical with the literary, suggesting that Smith's "conception of herself as a slave and of her husband, the son of a West Indian planter, as her owner profoundly shapes her response to African slavery" (59).

16. Smith, *Collected Letters*, 353.

17. Baucom, *Specters of the Atlantic: Finance Capital, Slavery, and the Philosophy of History* (Durham: Duke University Press, 2005), 17.

18. Lootens, "Looking Beyond (and Before) *Ancient Ballads*: Toru Dutt's *Sheaf* and the Force of Abolition Time," *Victorian Studies* 61, no. 2 (2019), 274.

The Space in Between: Affect, the Archive, and Writing Women's Lives

ANDREW O. WINCKLES

A s scholars who work in literary biography, and especially as scholars who are interested in *women's* literary biography, many of us are used to working with fragments, ephemera, and the scraps that have somehow survived the centuries. For while we know a good deal more today about the lives and works of numerous eighteenth-century women writers than we used to, there is still a lot we do not know. Furthermore, while we still don't know important details regarding the lives and works of even very well-known women of the eighteenth century, we know even less about the women on the margins: women who may never have gained literary fame and fortune, who may even have preferred to circulate their works in manuscript among a select circle of friends. If we still don't know enough about already well-known women, then why should we devote time and resources to exploring the lives of the obscure and forgotten? Why should we do the hard work of stitching together archival fragments and trying to recover the biographical details of women that few people have ever heard of?

The answers to these questions are complicated. On the one hand, it seems clear that if we want a better picture of the past—if we want a better understanding of how women lived and worked in the eighteenth century, then it is not enough to focus only on the well-known or the clearly exceptional. On the other hand, the impulse towards recovery for recovery's sake brings with it its own set of methodological challenges and assumptions. For example, much recovery is rooted in archival work—in the attempt to find and piece together the fragments of the past into a coherent account. And yet, those of us who do archival work know that the archive often actively resists coherence; it is instead filled with gaps, with incomplete traces of lives that can never fully be tracked. As Anjali Arondekar points out in her analysis of South Asian LGBTQ archives, even though we recognize the "analytical limits of the archive," many of us "continue to privilege the reading practices of recovery over all others." Arondekar insists that we should instead devise "new reading practices that ... juxtapose productively the archive's fiction-effects (the archive as a system of representation) alongside its truth-effects (the archive as material with 'real' consequences), as both agonistic and co-constitutive."[1] In other words, in writing the lives of the women of the past we need to look past recovery and reconstruction as an end in itself and begin to think productively about how we interact with and represent the archives themselves, the information they contain, and (perhaps especially) the gaps in that information.

To illustrate what I mean, I want to use one very specific and brief biographical sketch that points toward some of the methodological difficulties of writing the biography of an obscure woman and then suggest how this particular case also potentially opens up new and important avenues for understanding the fragments that women have left behind. Specifically, I want to focus on the case of Sally Wesley and a network of religious and literary women that she developed during the late 1790s. This narrative is pieced together from Wesley's own correspondence, collected from multiple archives around the world, and, while I know (relatively speaking) more about the events of this period in her life than I do about other moments, there is a still a lot I don't know and likely will never know.

Sally Wesley was the daughter of Charles Wesley and the niece of John Wesley, the founder of Methodism. A gifted poet like her father, Wesley published little of her work, instead preferring to circulate most of it in manuscript to her friends and acquaintances. After Charles Wesley's death in 1788 and her uncle John's death in 1791, she became the primary caretaker for her mother, Sarah Gwynne Wesley, and the inheritor of a difficult financial situation. Sally's older brother, Samuel, had amassed large debts and, to make matters worse, the family was embroiled in a dispute with the Methodist Conference over the copyrights to Charles Wesley's work.

It was because of these financial problems that, in late 1796, Wesley took a job as governess to Thomas De Quincey's younger sister Mary at the family house in Green Hay, just outside of Manchester. It was at Green Hay that she became acquainted with the Rev. John Clowes. At some point, Clowes proposed marriage, writing to her that he felt "a particular Thankfullness to the Divine providence for having granted me the extraordinary privilege of being acquainted with, & especially of being so closely attached to a Mind like yours."[2] This intellectual and spiritual match did not appear to be enough for Wesley, however, and she rejected his proposal, writing that she believed that "the single State has appeared to be appointed for me since you were last in Town."[3]

Wesley's rejection of Clowes may also have had something to do with the manner in which her stay in Green Hay concluded. While there, Wesley planned a trip for herself and Mary De Quincey to visit her friend Martha Swinburne, wife of the noted travel writer Henry Swinburne, in Durham. A mutual acquaintance of Wesley and Swinburne—Rachel Fanny Antonina Lee—was also in Manchester and offered the use of her carriage for the trip. This led Sally to introduce Mrs. Lee to the De Quinceys, who invited her to Green Hay. Lee, however, was one of the most notorious women in England. The illegitimate daughter of Sir Francis Dashwood, Fanny Lee was a wealthy and freethinking woman who had obtained a divorce from her husband, possessed her own scholarly aspirations, and who spent much of her time and fortune attempting to prove that she was in fact the legitimate heir to her father's title. In 1804, Lee would become notorious after being kidnapped by (or eloping with) Loudon Gordon, assisted by his brother Lockhart, which led to a media circus of a trial that acquitted the Gordons on all charges and supposedly exposed Lee as an atheist (which she was not).

Predictably, the meeting between Mrs. Lee and the De Quinceys sometime toward the end of July 1797 did not go well. John Clowes was also invited to the dinner because Mrs. De Quincey had, in the words of Thomas De Quincey, "understood from Miss Wesley—that Mrs. Lee was a bold thinker; and that, for a woman, she had an astonishing command of theological learning."[4] The dinner conversation seems to have devolved into a debate over and defense of Christianity, with Lee forwarding her own unorthodox opinions and Clowes unable or unwilling to debate with her. Eventually, Thomas De Quincey writes, his mother's sensibilities were so shocked that "she suffered an alarming nervous attack."[5]

This disastrous meeting seems to have soured relations between Mrs. De Quincey and Wesley and, while Sally remained friendly with Lee, her time in Green Hay came to an end. Martha Swinburne wrote to her on 8 August, commenting that she seemed "so low," and going on to say that "Mrs. Q [De Quincey] has a narrow mind: first for suffering any displeasure received from an indifferent person to affect her health: and secondly for reproaching you with what you could not help."[6] Regardless, as a result of this ill-fated meeting, Wesley broke off her relationship with Clowes, chose not to continue as Mary's governess, and arranged to go stay with her friend Mercy Doddridge in Gloucestershire. Later Wesley at least drafted a letter to Mrs. De Quincey in which she admitted that "my dear mother's affairs are the present subject of my apprehensions and of my Vexations" and lamented the fact that De Quincey "should ever have suppos'd I came to Manchester for any purpose but instructing your Children ... there was no other motive."[7] By late August Wesley was at the Doddridges and by the beginning of October she was back in London, where she took a job working for Dr. George Gregory as a secretary and translator.

While I have been able to piece together quite a bit about this pivotal year in Wesley's life, there are still a lot of gaps. Why didn't she marry Clowes? What was the nature of their relationship? How did she really feel about becoming a governess? What was her friendship with Fanny Lee like? What role did religion play in these relationships? Some of these questions may be answerable with more research and visits to different archival collections, but some of them can never be answered: there are simply too many archival gaps. Despite what we don't know, it is also clear that there are a lot of important things we can learn about women's lives from this story: courtship, marriage, work, financial prospects, literary prospects, religious belief and religious difference, female sociability and correspondence, just to name a very few. We could pull at the Fanny Lee portion of the story and reveal a narrative about fame, trauma, female sexuality, and intellect in the eighteenth century. Or we could pull at the Sally Wesley/Mercy Doddridge relationship and learn more about women's roles in religious dissent in the eighteenth century. Or we could explore Wesley's literary career and output and how this brief stay in Green Hay affected her publication prospects. Or we could read the whole narrative as being about the financial state of women in the eighteenth century. This is the difficulty of writing this type of biography—not only are there gaps, but there are also multiple possible threads to pursue, each of which would lead us in a different direction.

Ultimately, though, writing this type of biography requires becoming comfortable with embracing and working within these gaps. Often women were separated by geography or their correspondence involved significant temporal lags. Other gaps arise from literal lacunae in their writings caused by illegibility, the deterioration of the paper, or the separation of materials within and across archives. As a result, we are often left with little to no context through which to make these womens' texts legible, and thus we need to create new methods for understanding these gaps—of living within and becoming comfortable with the in-between space of obscure women's texts, of getting to know texts like we know people and feeling similar assumptions about them in our respective guts. As scholars, we are understandably uncomfortable with this type of methodology. After all, we have been trained to base our work on verifiable facts and concrete historical records. What I am suggesting, however, is that there is an affect attached to working in the archive and with these types of materials. We learn to *feel* things in our readings of these manuscripts that have meaning and are worthy of further scholarly inquiry. In the case of Sally Wesley, for example, this year in her life is often treated much like Thomas De Quincey treats it in his memoirs—as an interesting footnote—and it would be easy to read her archive the same way, as a mere record of intriguing events. Yet, the manuscripts themselves are invested with so much more information if you know how and where to look. Both on the page and within the gaps, I can feel the heartbreak of this year (the end of her relationship with Clowes, the scandal of her friendship with Mrs. Lee, the constant worry evoked by her precarious financial situation), but doing so requires both prior knowledge of other aspects of Wesley's history and my own very subjective experiences with the traces of her in archives around the world. In other words, I had a subjective reaction to Wesley's manuscripts, and this emotional response, coupled with the more objective research I had already done, allowed me to piece together and make better sense of her actual experiences.

This type of affective archival practice has gained increasing currency, especially among scholars working in LGBTQ archives, postcolonial archives, and human rights archives. These archives are characterized by a tension between what is officially written down—legal documents, records, etc.—and what is not. There are gaps and silences inherent to these archives that often mean as much or more than what is actually written down. Maryanne Dever, for example, has argued that an archive of letters from Greta Garbo to her presumed lover, Mercedes de Acosta, is not evidence of "nothing" or that no romantic relationship existed between the two women (as was widely reported in the press), but instead is "evidence of another sort: evidence of the thing which does not exist."[8] She then proceeds to read the Garbo/de Acosta archive according to its structure and gaps—there are no overt professions of love or desire, yet de Acosta meticulously preserved every envelope or piece of stationary she ever received from Garbo, even an outline of Garbo's foot that the star mailed to her, so that de Acosta could order her the correct size of shoes. These gaps or lack of evidence become, in Dever's reading, evidence of the thing that is missing.

These types of archives are also often encoded with what Ann Cvetkovich characterizes as an "archive of feelings," which reads texts as "repositories of feelings and emotions, which are encoded not only in the content of the texts themselves but in the practices that surround their production and reception."[9]

Learning to read these archives, then, means attending to the affective fields that they produce: the affective power of the materials themselves; the ways in which they interact with various communities past, present, and future; and the way that we, as researchers, interact with the archival texts we're examining. In the case of my research on Sally Wesley, for example, I was always and inevitably reading her manuscripts through the lens of my own accrued experiences: my encounters with her other texts in other archives, my knowledge of how her manuscripts were produced and circulated among her friends, and even my own very personal engagement with Methodism. This approach allows us to begin to imagine a new means of biographical inquiry, one that aims not only to uncover traces of obscure women, but also the conditions of their obscurity: the social, cultural, historical, and archival practices that have rendered so many of their stories illegible to us. This method not only allows us to think more clearly about the past, but also to understand our own scholarly investments in the present, especially regarding how knowledge is produced, validated, and transmitted to future generations.

Notes

1. Arondekar, "Without a Trace: Sexuality and the Colonial Archive," *Journal of the History of Sexuality* 14, nos. 1 and 2 (2005), 12.

2. Clowes to Wesley, 5 June 1797, Wesley Family Series, Box WF4, Frank Baker Collection of Wesleyana and British Methodism, Duke University Libraries.

3. Wesley to Clowes, August 1797, Wesley Family Series, Box WF4, Frank Baker Collection of Wesleyana and British Methodism, Duke University Libraries.

4. De Quincey, *Autobiographic Sketches* (Boston: Tickner and Fields, 1859), 155.

5. De Quincey, *Autobiographic Sketches*, 158.

6. Swinburne to Wesley, 8 August 1797, Methodist Archives and Research Centre, John Rylands Library, DDWF 26/75.

7. Wesley to Mrs. Quincey, undated, Wesley Family Series, Box WF4, Frank Baker Collection of Wesleyana and British Methodism, Duke University Libraries.

8. Dever, "Greta Garbo's Foot, or Sex, Socks and Letters," *Australian Feminist Studies* 25, no. 64 (2010), 164.

9. Cvetkovich, *An Archive of Feelings* (Durham: Duke University Press, 2003), 7.

Reading Between the Silences in the Correspondence of Esther Edwards Burr and Sarah Prince

KAITLIN TONTI

In *Hamilton: An American Musical*, Aaron Burr sings about his parents in "Wait for It," proclaiming, "my mother was a genius, my father demanded respect."[1] Despite her status as a genius, however, there are no substantial biographies written about Esther Edwards Burr. There are at least six biographies written about her father, Jonathan Edwards, and seven on her son, Aaron Burr. The closest scholars have come to documenting Burr's life is in the introduction to Carol Karlsen and Laurie Crumpacker's edition of her letters, titled *The Journal of Esther Edwards Burr, 1754-1757.*[2] The collection includes Burr's letters to her closest friend, Sarah Prince. However, modern readers only have access to one side of the correspondence as Prince's letters have gone missing. Early American women's biographies are always challenging to compile, as they are fragmented and thus representative of their hectic roles as wives and mothers. In Burr's case, her letterbook offers the only means of constructing a biography for her, since she left few other writings when she died at the age of twenty-six.

Creating Burr's biography depends on an analysis of how Burr responded to Prince, but with none of Prince's thoughts available. In other words, their correspondence opens a space to consider how Prince's silences also help to construct Burr's character. Burr and Prince wrote to maintain a friendship through their mutual faith. However, without Prince's half of the correspondence, their relationship comes off as that of mentor and mentee, rather than a friendship based on equal footing. Prince's silences reveal Burr as a woman who appeared confident, but was often insecure in her role as a Godly mother and wife within a Puritanical hierarchy. In providing advice to Prince, the correspondence reveals how Burr romanticized her domestic role in order to seek out the validation she did not receive at home.

Before analyzing Burr and Prince's correspondence, it is necessary to examine the genre in which they were working Although diaries and letters are both umbrellaed under the term "life-writing," it is necessary to distinguish the two to understand why scholars should regard Burr's writing as part of a correspondence, rather than a diary. Karlsen and Crumpacker explain how, instead of sending individual letters, Burr and Prince sent several letters at a time in packets. They refer to Burr's letterbook as a diary and a journal, though "this was no ordinary diary; nor was it meant solely for her own eyes. She wrote the journal as a series of letters."[3] Philippe Lejeune suggests a simple definition of a diary: "you take some paper, or your computer, you write down the date, and then you write whatever you're doing, thinking and feeling."[4] With only Burr's side of the correspondence preserved, her writing certainly looks like a diary; however, modern readers must approach her writing in the knowledge that it was shaped by what Prince also wrote.

Although lost, Prince's half of the correspondence is highly significant for understanding Burr's personality. Liz Stanley notes that one distinctive feature of the letter is its dialogical nature, which informs the structure of the "unfolding communication between letter writers and readers."[5] At first glance, Burr and Prince's correspondence might not seem to be working this way, because its dialogical element is obscured by the fact that only Burr's letters have survived. However, that does not mean that there was no power dynamic established between the correspondents. Janet Altman suggests that the "I-you" function assumes there are two roles in correspondence: the sender and the receiver. The sender always writes as "I," and the "I" dictates how the receiver perceives the content of a letter. Altman argues that the "I-you relationship" that governs epistolary discourse also governs our perception of which figures are the principal agents in the unfolding dialogue. If the receiver fails to write back, thus becoming an "I" in turn, then he or she will not seem nearly as central as the sender.[6] In part because of the absence of Prince's responses, there is not a single agreed-upon way of describing Burr and Prince's writing. Roxanne Harde calls it a "journal."[7] Samantha

Tamulis calls it a "letter-journal."[8] I will refer to it as a correspondence, since Prince did write back, even if we no longer have access to her responses. Keeping the "I-you" roles of correspondence in mind will be especially helpful to considering the advice that Burr gave to Prince regarding how an average married woman experienced the day.

Prince was still single during their correspondence, and Burr often insisted that her life was inherently more complicated and more valuable as a mother and a pastor's wife. As Puritans, Burr and Prince knew that women were helpmeets to their husbands, with duties that included managing a home, parenting, and entertaining. In one letter, Burr describes having entertained Princeton College's trustees, writing "But I am realy tired of the World, and indeed such a day ... is enough to tire a person that loves it the most."[9] In many of her letters, Burr faces the challenge of balancing her worldly duties with Godly ones, yet she maintains to Prince that the role of being a helpmeet solidifies God's favor.

Burr's frustrations with entertaining and motherhood spill into her letters to Prince, but with the caveat that Burr knows that Prince, as a single woman, cannot fully share in her experience. In one letter, she worries about her daughter Sally's behavior, writing, "I had almost forgot to tell you that I have begun to govourn Sally. She has been Whip'd once on *Old Adams* account ... but none but a parent can conceive how hard it is to chastise your *own most tender self*" (*J* 95). In these instances, Burr assumes the "I" role in how she speaks to Prince from the perspective of a more experienced woman. Burr believes that Prince cannot identify with the hardships she faces in her domestic role and that Prince will only know God better when she herself becomes a wife and mother. As Tamulis suggests, motherhood shaped a woman's identity within the community.[10] Thus, Burr's reputation depended on the reputations of those with whom she socialized, making it necessary to encourage Prince to marry. In advising Prince, though, Burr also implies that she is looking for praise. Taking the time to detail her busyness becomes a means of validating the importance of her role. Despite Burr's insistence that she is of value domestically, her tutoring of Prince reveals that she felt unnoticed at home and so she used their correspondence to affirm her role as an adviser.

Burr expands on her knowledge of domesticity to educate Prince in marital customs. In a letter of 6 January 1755, she writes, "Miss Abigail is nere marrying, as is usual for all young people *but Miss Prince*" (*J* 78). Burr's emphasis on "Miss Prince" sounds less like advice and more like scolding. Matters of love seem to have brought out Burr's inner critic, who was annoyed by Prince's remaining single. In another instance, Burr chastises Prince for playing coy with a suitor, stating, "tis most likly that he thinks that you dislike him, or elce that you are a Mortal proud creture, which must sink you in his opinnion, … my dear no man likes a woman the better for being when she means the very thing she pretends to be shy off" (*J* 195). Burr reinforces the Puritan gender hierarchy, suggesting to Prince that there is a proper way to engage in a courtship. However, there are moments when Burr implies that she may not be the perfect Puritan helpmeet that she would like to imagine herself. On 21 June 1757, Burr writes, with respect to marriage, that "it requires some degree of prudence in a Woman that has been always used with the greatest Complesance and as if she was absolute Monarch, to be Gently blamed in some pretty artfull Way let kn[o]w that He is her Head and Governor" (*J* 265). Burr's suggestion that no man will appreciate Prince's coyness is at odds with her realization that women bound in marriage often feel as if men are depriving them of their premarital power. In another letter, Burr complains about how women are relegated to "set and see, and hear" the conversation, only making "observations" to themselves in social gatherings (*J* 54). Burr desires the same right as her husband to engage in conversation.

In Burr's moments of advising and directing Prince, she works out many of the feelings that she would not otherwise reveal or even admit to herself. In many of her letters, Burr pushes against the limitations of her religion. She often doubts that there is an all-loving God and then quickly retracts her doubts. To question her Puritan faith would imply that she also doubts the gendered hierarchy built upon the principles of the church. In the home, women like Burr recognized that their love for God came first, before their love for their husbands. In encouraging Prince's faith, however, Burr discloses to Prince her waning piety. On 25 October 1754, Burr marvels at "how much more Mercyfull has God been to me than others that are far better than I. Sometimes I am affraid I am to have my portion in this life, and what a miserable portion will that be" (*J* 57). Her religious uncertainty is also evident when she learns of her family's danger amidst the Seven Years' War. On 8 November 1754, she begs Prince to explain "why is it? Why does God suffer his own most dear children to be hunted about in this manner!" (*J* 61). Burr's doubts regarding God's protection extend to her concerns for her husband's health, as she writes, "I wish I could leve him in the hands of a kind and Gracious God who has preserved him, and me, so many journeys" (*J* 51). In wishing that she had faith that God would protect her husband, she reveals her desire to control the situation. She does not want to leave it in God's hands; however, in her position as the helpmeet, she also had no control over her husband's decisions.

Although Burr had little power in her everyday life, several letters suggest that Prince knew Burr was in a position of authority within their relationship.

On 1 November 1754, Burr writes, "You say I have excepted the office of *Monitor* but on no other conditions than that you be one to me. *Mind that.* I think it one of the great essentials of friendship [that] the parties tell one another their faults, … it is one of the best evidences of true friendship" (*J* 59). Although Burr maintains that their friendship is not unequal, Prince acknowledges Burr as an adviser or "monitor," which suggests that she sensed how Burr intended to write from the perspective of a wiser, married woman. However, Burr's felt superiority carries over into their disagreement as to what should happen with their letters. Burr wrote to advise and guide Prince, but her role in the larger community of Puritan sisterhood seems to have inspired a desire to have the letters printed.

Burr's wish to publish the letters resonated with her need to assert power. In her mentoring of Prince, Burr likely saw an excellent opportunity to guide more single women on their path to religious wifehood. Stanley writes about "epistolary community," or the notion that several people may read a single correspondence.[11] Burr wrote with the expectation that her letters would circulate between other close friends and eventually find a larger audience that would demand a printed version of the correspondence. These types of communities were not uncommon. Later, in Revolutionary Philadelphia, women's epistolary communities included the circulation of original poetry. For instance, Milcah Martha Moore's commonplace book preserved the verse of the women with whom she interacted in an epistolary community.[12] These communications ultimately created a meaningful and influential literary subculture that demonstrated women's awareness of politics; however, most of their writing went unpublished, and if it was printed, it was done under a pseudonym. In this light, a biography for Burr would focus not only on her devotion to mentoring, but also on her eagerness to participate in the larger culture of print, which would offer her greater authority than she would have in a strictly manuscript culture. Much of Burr's advice to Prince would apply to other evangelical women searching for husbands. If printed, Burr and Prince's correspondence might have read much like a conduct manual. Considering Burr's hope of printing, the issues of ownership and narrative control cast a shadow over the correspondence for modern readers. In Suzanne Bunkers's seminal "Whose Diary Is It Anyway?", she raises the question of who retains ownership of a diary once its creator has died.[13] Although what Burr writes is dictated in part by Prince's existence, the question of "whose letters are these anyway" applies to their correspondence. With Prince's half of the correspondence no longer extant, Burr maintains narrative control, which is evident in Karlsen and Crumpacker's titling of their edition, *The Journal of Esther Edwards Burr*, rather than *The Correspondence of Esther Edwards Burr and Sarah Prince*.

Burr asserted ownership and narrative control over the correspondence long before Prince's letters were lost. On 29 November 1754, Burr writes, "you are determined to prevent the publication of any of your Letters, but I imagine tis not soully in your power, which I desire to be thankful for" (*J* 67). The impetus to take ownership of the correspondence is grounded in Burr's initial role as an adviser or a monitor. Prince apparently did not see the point in printing their correspondence, whereas Burr felt the need to reassure Prince of the value of their letters by asserting that "Mr Burr" thought "*Miss Prince*[']*s*" writing was "Ten times as well worth Printing" as "Miss Joan's" (*J* 67). Burr goes on to advise her that "tis not worth your while to vex your self for nothing, for I believe we shall have some of em in the Press *first* or *last*" (*J* 68). Burr's sly comment, "but I imagine tis not soully in your power," suggests that she saw herself as having the ultimate say on what would become of the letters. Burr's decision regarding publication also weighs more powerful as she is Mr. Burr's wife. Whereas Prince has no husband to advise her, Burr takes it upon herself to assure her friend that an influential male figure has encouraged their letters' publication. Burr assumes that Prince is reluctant to publish because she is not confident in her writing, though Prince was more likely concerned with preserving her privacy as a still-single woman looking for a suitable husband.

Creating a biography for Esther Edwards Burr begins at the intersection of religion and friendship. Modern readers are only privy to Prince's silence, and in that silence we encounter Burr as a wife and mother who ultimately challenges the culture that would deem her a mere helpmeet. Prince's voice is not available to balance the correspondence, and thus an image of Burr as a mentor and adviser to Prince emerges. This is empowering for Burr because it gives her an authority she did not have at home with her husband. In advising Prince on marriage, motherhood, and faith, Burr appears confident. However, at the core of her thoughts lies an insecurity regarding her domestic role, which adds another complex layer to any portrait of her life. In a culture in which Burr's worldly goods belonged to her husband, Burr pushed against this insecurity by asserting ownership over her correspondence with Prince. Doing so confirms the validity of her voice, and so she subtly advocates for publication of the correspondence. Burr's biography, then, must go beyond the stereotypical image of an eighteenth-century woman whose meek nature was somehow characteristic of her essence. Instead, Burr presents a woman aware of her talent and confident in her ability to provide guidance to and find community among other women.

Notes

1. Lin-Manuel Miranda, *Hamilton: An American Musical* (Los Angeles: Warner/Chapell, 2016), 88.

2. Karlsen and Crumpacker, Introduction to *The Journal of Esther Edward Burr, 1754-1757*, ed. Carol F. Karlsen and Laurie Crumpacker (New Haven: Yale University Press, 1984), 3–42.

3. Karlsen and Crumpacker, Introduction, 3.

4. Lejeune, *On Diary*, ed. Jeremy D. Popkin and Julie Rak, trans. Katherine Durnin (University of Hawai'i Press for the Biographical Research Center, 2009).

5. Stanley, "The Epistolarium: On Theorizing Letters and Correspondences," *Auto/Biography* 12 (2004): 201–35.

6. Altman, *Epistolarity: Approaches to a Form* (Columbus: Ohio State University Press, 1982).

7. Harde, "'I don't like Strangers on the Sabbath': Theology and Subjectivity in the Journal of Esther Edwards Burr," *Legacy: A Journal of American Women Writers* 19, no.1 (2002), 18.

8. Tamulis, "The Birth Pangs of the American Mother: Puritanism, Republicanism, and the Letter-Journal of Esther Edwards Burr," in *Women's Narratives of the Early Americas and the Formation of Empire*, ed. Mary McAleer Balkun and Susan C. Imbarrato (Houndsmills: Palgrave Macmillan, 2016), 93–109.

9. Burr, *Journal*, 92. Subsequent citations will be made parenthetically as *J*.

10. See Tamulis, "The Birth Pangs of the American Mother."

11. Stanley, "The Epistolarium," 203.

12. Moore, *Milcah Martha Moore's Book: A Commonplace Book from Revolutionary America*, ed. Catherine La Courreye Blecki and Karin A. Wulf (University Park: Pennsylvania State University Press, 1997).

13. Bunkers, "Whose Diary Is It Anyway? Issues of Agency, Authority, Ownership." *Auto/Biography* 17, no.1 (2001): 11–27.

On the Playing Cards of the Dulac Brothers in the Year II

JEFFREY S. RAVEL

There are, of course, many possible approaches to the problem of the relationship between Revolution and private life. One could multiply endlessly both the 'angles of vision,' the private calendars, and the use of an ever-wider extent of personal case histories. It is unlikely, however, that one's conclusions would be any less tentative. In this frontier zone of history, much will remain unstated, a great deal has to be guessed at, often on very thin evidence, something may even have to be invented.
　　　　　Richard Cobb, *Reactions to the French Revolution*[1]

On 18 Frimaire Year II (8 December 1793 in the Gregorian calendar), the Committee of Public Safety in Paris issued an arrest warrant for Charles Dulac, a young officer serving as Secretary of the Representatives of the People for the Army of the Moselle. Four days later, armed with the order, a squadron of four men from a neighborhood surveillance committee arrived at Dulac's Parisian residence on the Right Bank, near the *Bibliothèque nationale*. They arrested Dulac and led him off to the Luxembourg Prison to await an appearance before the Revolutionary Tribunal. They also seized over two hundred papers in his possession and, curiously, 120 used playing cards with handwritten notes on their backs.[2] The papers confiscated that day were mostly written in the two years prior to his arrest. They hint at a collective biography of Charles and his older brother, Gregory, in 1792–93, including details of their entanglements with revolutionary politics and warfare, their personal finances, and, in the case of Charles, his romance with a young noblewoman in their native Auvergne. In contrast, the annotations on the backs of the 120 playing cards do not testify directly to the brothers' revolutionary experience. The vast majority of them are brief quotations excerpted from the Bible, several pagan authors from antiquity, the sixteenth-century skeptic Michel de Montaigne, and a variety of eighteenth-century sources, including Jean-Jacques Rousseau, Gabriel Bonnet de Mably, and the *Encyclopédie* of Denis Diderot and Jean Le Rond d'Alembert. In some instances the cards contain political slogans appropriate to the revolutionary moment. A Nine of Clubs, for example, proclaims: "Despotism begins where liberty ends" [see Figures 1 and 2].[3] Reading through the backs of the cards, which appear to have been annotated by Gregory, one does not encounter a coherent set of philosophical principles or a consistent moral creed by which to lead one's life, but rather a set of aphorisms that might be shuffled and reshuffled according to circumstances.[4]

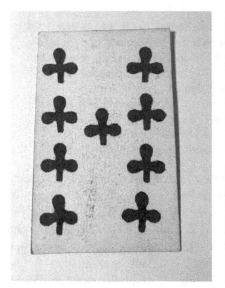

Figure 1. Dulac playing cards, Nine of Clubs, recto, late eighteenth century. Stencil on paper, 8.5 cm x 5.4 cm. Archives nationales de France, AF II 34, dossier 284, #119.

Figure 2. Dulac playing cards, Nine of Clubs, verso, late eighteenth century. 8.5 cm x 5.4 cm. Archives nationales de France, AF II 34, dossier 284, #119.

Playing cards, it turns out, served many purposes in eighteenth-century France beyond gaming and gambling. Some people used them for practical purposes, such as recording debts, advertising professional services, cataloguing books, labeling legal files, and teaching French grammar. Others used these small pieces of paper, blank on one side, to capture fleeting thoughts and transcribe meaningful sayings. One might dismiss the scribblings on the backs of these playing cards as random *bons mots* that made a momentary impact on Gregory, enough so that he took the time to jot them down in rushed, crabbed handwriting. But one might also argue that they represent a self-curated snapshot of a cultural heritage that resonated with these two young men, a type of evidence that is more revealing of their intellectual and emotional predispositions than if the guards had found the collected works of Rousseau or Voltaire or the complete *Encyclopédie* in their Parisian apartment. Their used playing cards constitute a portable, unbound commonplace book from the end of the Enlightenment with which one might better understand the revolutionary motivations of the brothers. The writings on these 120 playing cards help to illuminate the unexpected experiences of Gregory and Charles Dulac during the French Revolution. In their ability to evoke the mundane as well as the profound, used playing cards like the ones found in the possession of the Dulac brothers offer insight into the material and intellectual worlds of individuals who lived through the revolutionary upheavals at the end of the eighteenth century.

Pursuing Military Careers During a Political Revolution

By itself, the story of the two brothers' efforts to build military careers in the midst of political chaos is remarkable. It featured a renunciation of the social privileges and economic advantages their family had under the Old Regime, active participation in the political controversies of the period, and career-building efforts that relied on patronage from major revolutionary political and military figures. These included the Marquis de Lafayette; Charles-François Dumouriez, the hero of the Battle of Valmy in September 1792; Francisco de Miranda, a Venezuelan military leader and revolutionary; and Georges Auguste Couthon, a legislator from the Auvergne who served on the Committee of Public Safety during the Terror. More than once, the brothers faced career setbacks with potentially devastating consequences; the imprisonment of Charles in December 1793 was the final chapter in the tale of their efforts to recast themselves as military officers in revolutionary France.

Gregory and Charles were the third- and fourth-born sons of a noble family with deep roots in the Auvergne, a province in the south of France whose largest city is Clermont-Ferrand. Their parents, Claude Dulac de Puydenat and Anne-Charlotte du Floquet, had four sons between 1760 and 1770. In 1767, Claude Dulac purchased the Château de Cluzel, an ancient, substantial country estate in the Auvergne, which he added to the family's hereditary lands near the town of Brioude, seventy kilometers southeast of Clermont-Ferrand and outside the smaller town of Courpierre, northeast of Clermont.[5] The two oldest brothers, André-Grégoire Nicolas René and Georges-Cathérine, were born in 1760 and 1763; their father destined them both for careers in the military.[6] The two younger sons, Gregory and Charles, were born in 1768 and 1770. Gregory, a student in the King's Artillery Corps in 1785, joined the Royal Artillery Regiment stationed in Strasburg that same year as a second lieutenant and followed Georges-Cathérine into the Knights of Malta. Charles, the youngest son, was born in 1770. By the start of the Revolution, he had also joined the Knights of Malta.[7] The papers of the two younger brothers confiscated by the revolutionary authorities in December 1793 contain speculations regarding battlefield strategy, detailed plans for provisioning military units, and handwritten solutions to math problems, all of which indicate a fascination with the strategic and logistical problems encountered in combat.[8]

The onset of the Revolution splintered the family along political lines. By 1791 at the latest, the family patriarch and his two eldest sons had fled the country, unwilling to support a regime that nullified their aristocratic privileges and seized the feudal property that the family had accumulated over generations. André-Grégoire, the eldest son, signed the counter-revolutionary Act of Coalition of the Nobility of the Auvergne in Fribourg on 10 April 1791, thereby proclaiming his open hostility towards the Revolution. The flight of the father and the elder brothers to the Holy Roman Empire triggered the confiscation of the family's holdings by French authorities. In the second half of 1793, the names of Claude and his two oldest sons appeared on a list of émigrés drawn up by the republican officials in Clermont-Ferrand.[9]

Gregory and Charles, however, stayed behind. The first documented trace of their break with family expectations dates to mid-May 1790, when Gregory challenged the authority of his commanding officer in the Strasburg royal regiment, in which he had served since 1785.[10] The colonel in charge of the regiment, Armand-Marc-Jacques Chastanet, Marquis de Puységur, better known for his mesmerist writings, was almost twice as old as Gregory in 1790.[11] The difference in age and experience did not prevent the young Dulac, however, from sending a petition to the Minister of War in Paris, in which he asserted that Puységur, seventeen years his elder, was not qualified to command the unit. It was a shocking charge from a junior officer, made even more radical by his decision to address his complaint directly to the Minister and to publish an account of the response of Puységur and the other officers in the regiment. Dulac's attack on his commanding officer led to a divisive scene within the regiment, with some officers and enlisted men joining the challenge mounted by Gregory to the established regimental order. Within two days of the initial encounter between Puységur and Gregory, the latter was placed under arrest. By the end of May the affair had found its way to the National Assembly in Paris, where Alexandre de Lameth, a representative from the department of the Jura, spoke up in favor of Puységur, recommending that the Assembly reconfirm him as the unit's commanding officer."[12] Convinced by Lameth's argument, the Assembly wrote to the regiment to confirm the representatives' satisfaction with Puységur's command. Having lost the battle before the legislative tribunal, Gregory resigned his post in the Strasburg royal regiment that July and returned to the Auvergne.

In his printed pamphlet, Gregory affirmed his rejection of the commanding officer's legitimacy but stopped short of rejecting monarchical authority, claiming: "I am always subordinated, always ready to serve the king, ready to obey. But elsewhere, my comrades, elsewhere—*we are all equals.*"[13] By the following summer, after leaving the King's service and returning to the Auvergne, he was prepared to denounce Louis XVI as well. Upon his return to Clermont, he frequented increasingly radicalized political circles. During the night of 20–21 June 1791, Louis XVI and his family tried to flee the country to join counter-revolutionary émigrés living across the eastern frontier. The royal family was caught before reaching the border and returned to Paris. Although apologists for the king claimed that he had been kidnapped, many in Paris and the provinces interpreted the flight to Varennes as evidence that a constitutional monarchy headed by Louis XVI was untenable. In Clermont, Gregory gave a fiery speech on 25 June to the city's *société populaire*, less than a week after the King had attempted to flee the nation. In his oration, subsequently published by an Auvergnat printer as *Reflections on the Conduct of Louis XVI Bourbon*, he spared no rhetorical flourishes in attacking the king: "Answer me, Louis XVI! You can no longer exist, stripped of the honor of being able to tyrannize twenty-five million people? Being loved by them, doing good for them, succoring the poor, that is not good enough for you? ... Thirty-five million pounds cannot sustain the splendor of your throne! Vile man!"[14] For Gregory, the emerging realities of French citizenship were incompatible with the notion of divine right monarchy. "If my fatherland continues to recognize Louis XVI Bourbon as its constitutional leader," he declared, "I will no longer consider myself French."[15]

Gregory's revolutionary sympathies in 1790 and 1791, however, did not bring his military career to an end. Shortly after his return to the Auvergne in the summer of 1790, he enlisted as a regular in the National Guard division in his family's home district of Courpierre, and the following summer, soon after publishing his attack on Louis XVI, he enrolled in a newly formed volunteer battalion in the Puy-de-Dôme, the revolutionary department in which Clermont-Ferrand was situated. By September 1791, he had been named an officer in the battalion, and in the winter and spring of 1792, as this battalion was attached to the Armies of the Center and the North, Gregory became an aide-de-camp in the revolutionary armed forces. In short, in the two years after leaving the King's army, he realigned himself politically and managed to obtain the rank of an officer within the command structure of the emerging revolutionary armies. His younger brother Charles followed suit, first obtaining a post as sergeant in the Puy-de-Dôme volunteer battalion in September 1791, then following his older brother into the newly constituted revolutionary forces, where he also served as an aide-de-camp in the Army of the North by the spring of 1792.[16]

While the *ci-devant* aristocratic brothers had found posts in the revolutionary officer corps by the summer of 1792, they now faced the challenge of navigating the various political factions in Paris. By the summer of 1792, the distrust between the legislators in Paris and the officers on the battle front was already evident. The politicians knew they would need the generals to preserve the Revolution from its internal and external enemies, but they also feared that these men might turn on them, using their armed followers to seize power for themselves, or to restore the Bourbon dynasty. Lower-level officers like the Dulac brothers had to heed the political currents back in Paris, even as they sought to serve the nation on the battlefield. In the summer of 1792, Gregory, who had so vehemently denounced the king the previous summer, was under the command of Gilbert de Motier, Marquis de Lafayette, the hero of the American Revolutionary War. Lafayette, also a native of the Auvergne, had reached into the region's volunteer battalions to staff his officer corps and fill out his regiments. On 10 August 1792, for example, he confirmed Gregory's appointment as Sub-Lieutenant in an infantry regiment.[17] But that same day an armed crowd invaded the Tuileries Palace in Paris, threatening Louis XVI and effectively ending the constitutional monarchy. Lafayette, already compromised by his association with the royal court since 1789, was labeled a traitor and fled to the Austrian Netherlands. On 24 August 1792, Gregory was suspended from duty, because of his affiliation with Lafayette, and he was arrested the next day.[18]

Imprisoned in the military garrison in Valenciennes on the northern border of France, Gregory once again found himself the subject of an inquiry in Paris, where legislators weighed a report on his conduct from the commissioners of the National Assembly assigned to the Army of the

North.[19] The Lafayette connection also affected Charles, who had been anticipating a promotion. He too was suspended from service, pending the outcome of his brother's case. Faced with the sudden demise of their military careers, the brothers began a campaign to have the Assembly dismiss the allegations of "Fayettism" lodged against Gregory.[20] In an interview with the commissioners in the Valenciennes prison, and then in an appearance that he and Charles made before the National Assembly in Paris in early September, Gregory reminded the commissioners of his public denunciation of Louis XVI after the flight to Varennes the previous summer. In order to demonstrate their patriotism, he and Charles offered to contribute one-fifth of their combined wealth to the National Treasury, proposed to continue their military service as volunteers, and renewed their revolutionary oaths. While these actions certainly carried weight, the decisive factor may have been an endorsement from Charles-François Dumouriez, a general in the Army of the North whose star was on the rise in the wake of Lafayette's defection. Testifying on Gregory's behalf before the Assembly's commissioners, Dumouriez confirmed Gregory's patriotism and underlined his utility in the coming military struggles: "I am persuaded, sir, that your repentance is sincere and that you have too much intelligence to fail to appreciate the crimes of Lafayette that misled you and that unjustly defamed me. I forgive your errors in my regard and I sincerely embrace you. If the honorable commissioners are indeed willing to consent to it, you will serve under me and I will obtain for you a post in the regiment."[21] Dumouriez's testimonial, along with the brothers' pledges of loyalty to the Revolution, was enough to prompt the Assembly to lift Gregory's suspension. On 20 September, the final report on Gregory's case noted that Lafayette had "misled his opinion without corrupting his heart." A decree from the National Assembly that same day permitted Gregory to rejoin the military; shortly thereafter, Charles received a promotion comparable to the one that had been canceled upon his brother's arrest.[22]

In the short term, the brothers were well served by the patronage of Dumouriez. Two days after Gregory's release from prison, French forces under the command of the general won a critical victory at Valmy that staved off invasion by the Austrian and Prussian armies. His troops then went on the offensive in the North, pushing the enemy forces well back into the Austrian Netherlands by the end of the year. In the beginning of October, Charles was named a deputy adjutant general in the Army of the North, a special assignment for officers at the level of lieutenant-colonel or colonel. By the middle of the month, Gregory, his reputation now restored, had received a similar commission.[23] For the remainder of 1792 the brothers carried out various military assignments designed to consolidate the victories of the

French forces on the northern front and prepare for further advances into the Low Countries. Soon after the first of the year, however, the French position on the northern front began to deteriorate, due to an overly aggressive initiative led by Dumouriez and another leading general, Francisco de Miranda, a Venezuelan officer and republican sympathizer who would later become known as one of the liberators of Latin America. By the beginning of March, the French troops were in disarray, the generals had begun to accuse each other of treason, and the politicians back in Paris were making inquiries into the setbacks on the northern front.

Once again, the Dulac brothers found themselves caught up in a military controversy aggravated by revolutionary politics. Although it had been Dumouriez who had vouched for Gregory when the latter was accused of Fayettism in the summer of 1792, by March 1793 the brothers had taken the side of the Venezuelan general Miranda. On 8 March 1793, the latter extended orders first issued in January that allowed both Gregory and Charles to take a leave of absence "in order to restore their health."[24] In fact, it appears that Miranda encouraged the brothers to investigate the actions of Dumouriez in order to exonerate the Venezuelan from responsibility for the military failures in the North.[25] In early April, Charles rushed back from the front to denounce Dumouriez to the Convention as a traitor to the Republic for his actions in the theater of war.[26] The following month Charles denounced another officer serving on the Northern front named John Skey Eustace, a citizen of the United States, for aiding the Austrians and the Prussians. He also testified that month in favor of Miranda in the trial that led to Miranda's exoneration.[27] Charles, learning from his brother's imprisonment the previous summer, understood that military service was inseparable from the politics of the capital.

After the fall of Dumouriez, the revolutionary career paths of Charles and Gregory, so tightly intertwined since the fall of 1791, began to diverge. Gregory stayed in Paris, monitoring developments in the Convention and the political clubs and maintaining connections with influential political and military figures. He mused about withdrawing from the military to become a man of letters, complained about his health, and urged Charles to join him in a return to their native Auvergne, where they could re-enlist in the volunteer battalion as patriotic foot soldiers, sheltered from suspicions of political disloyalty. He appeared to be tiring of the strains of revolutionary politics and warfare.[28] Charles, meanwhile, carried out various military missions in the provinces, eventually being appointed to the post of Secretary of the Representatives of the People for the Army of the Moselle. Only a month before his arrest, Charles was actively involved in the consolidation of selected battalions in this army due to "the general disorder" of the troops.

The Committee of Public Safety ordered him to suspend at least eleven officers for offenses ranging from drunkenness to unauthorized home visits for childbirth.[29]

At the end of July 1793 Gregory was back in the Auvergne, attending to the finances of the brothers and reconnecting with local revolutionaries who remembered his denunciation of Louis XVI in Clermont-Ferrand two years earlier. The most powerful political figure in the Auvergne that summer was Georges Auguste Couthon, an obscure lawyer before 1789, who was elected to the National Assembly in 1791 and joined forces with the Montagnard faction led by Maximilien Robespierre and Saint Just in 1793. He was appointed to the Committee of Public Safety, the *de facto* ruling body of France during the Terror, in July. At the end of August, he returned to his native Auvergne to organize reinforcements for a siege of the city of Lyons to the east, which was in full-blown rebellion against the government in Paris. Couthon was well acquainted with the Dulac brothers; he had a hand in exonerating Gregory from charges of Fayettism in 1792, and later that year the brothers solicited his support for a petition they submitted to the Assembly regarding their father's estates.[30] In need of help to mobilize the citizens of the Auvergne for the siege of Lyons, Couthon did not hesitate to ask Gregory to return these favors. Gregory complied, summoning soldiers, gathering provisions, and participating in the siege itself. The engagement reinvigorated Gregory's revolutionary passions; in a letter to Charles from Lyons at the end of September, he exulted in the victory of the forces he had helped to rally: "Let us rejoice, my friend—liberty has triumphed, equality will soon reign! ... The month of September of this year will be just as disastrous for the despots and for the aristocracy as September last year [when the monarchy ended], with the difference that this time I hope it will be the last time!"[31]

Neither brother, however, could have anticipated that the presence of Gregory in Lyons would once again derail their careers. Back in Paris after the siege, a dispute broke out between Couthon and Edmond Louis Alexis Dubois-Crancé, a member of the National Convention and military veteran who had overseen the siege in its earlier stages. After the surrender, Couthon accused Dubois-Crancé of failing to act fast enough to secure the defeat of the city, a charge that led to the latter's arrest. In response Dubois-Crancé submitted a lengthy defense to the Convention, in which he referred to Gregory Dulac as "a well-known Fayettist," who had perhaps been bribed. In turn, Couthon admitted that Gregory had "distanced himself from the spirit of the Jacobins," and had frequently sided with the wrong factions.[32] Under the pressure of factional conflict in Paris, Couthon could only muster an equivocal endorsement of Gregory, one that did not overlook his aristocratic origins or his ties to the disgraced Marquis de Lafayette. The brothers' carefully scripted efforts to recast themselves as good revolutionaries were coming undone.

Back in the Auvergne in November, Gregory learned of the attack on his revolutionary *bona fides* by Dubois-Crancé and did his best to control the damage, making the rounds of the local political clubs to confirm his dedication to the Revolution.[33] In a letter to Charles, he recounted his service to the local *sociétés populaires*, his denunciations of local aristocrats who were subsequently arrested, and the satisfaction he derived from the friendship of a few local *sans-culottes*. Nonetheless, he wrote, "never has slander so bitterly pursued me."[34] In Paris, Dubois-Crancé kept up his attacks on Couthon's patronage of Gregory during the siege of Lyons. On 8 December at the Jacobin Club, when Couthon renewed his criticism of Dubois-Crancé's military leadership, the latter responded that he was chagrined to see "a man such as Dulac at the head of a column where his influence might become dangerous."[35] Couthon noted that Gregory had alternated between being an aristocrat and a patriot, but that he had successfully recruited a citizen army in the Puy-de-Dôme that summer to march on Lyons. Nevertheless, Couthon confirmed, he had eventually stripped Gregory of his military role. This attack in the Jacobin Club was apparently the final straw for Couthon, who may have feared charges of moderation based on his patronage of Gregory. That same evening the Committee of Public Safety issued an arrest warrant for Charles, who was then in Paris. While the Committee did not leave behind a record of its deliberations, it is reasonable to imagine that Couthon insisted on imprisoning Charles in order to distance himself further from Gregory, whose tainted past was too tempting for Couthon's enemies to ignore. Four days later, Charles found himself in the Luxemburg prison in Paris awaiting a hearing before the Revolutionary Tribunal, and a potential death sentence.[36] In the Auvergne, Gregory's revolutionary credentials were in shreds.

As the lethal politics of the Terror accelerated, there proved to be no place for the scions of an aristocratic family in the officer corps of the new army, no matter how strenuously they proclaimed their devotion to revolutionary principles. The story of the two brothers, though, is more complex than this account of their military fortunes from 1790 to 1793 would suggest. Why did they choose to break with their father and older brothers? How complete was that break, and what were the intellectual and emotional currents driving their actions? And what was the fate of Charles, now subject to revolutionary justice? To answer these questions, we turn next to the 120 playing cards confiscated when Charles was arrested in December 1793, and to a general survey of the uses of playing cards before the Revolution.

Playing Cards in Eighteenth-Century France

The most obvious use for playing cards in eighteenth-century France was that of gaming and gambling.[37] Decks of playing cards were manufactured throughout the kingdom and were widely available at all levels of society. By the second half of the reign of Louis XIV, a chamber devoted to high-stakes gambling was one of several prominent rooms set aside for courtly pleasures at Versailles, as recorded in the engravings of the royal apartments by Antoine Trouvain in the 1690s [see Figure 3]. His image of the *Seconde Chambre* shows the Dauphin surrounded by other courtly gamblers; the postures of the players, and the intensity with which several of them hold our gaze, evokes the rigid court etiquette that prevailed at Versailles in the second half of the Sun King's reign.

Playing cards circulated well beyond aristocratic circles; a century after Trouvain recorded the courtiers at play, for example, a market for used cards had developed in Paris that brought reconstituted decks of cards to the neighborhood bars and wine shops of the capital, a development echoed in other towns throughout the kingdom.[38] Condemnation of gambling spread just as widely throughout the century. An earlier eighteenth-century engraving by Nicolas Guérard makes these criticisms clear [see Figure 4].

Figure 3. Antoine Trouvain, *Seconde Chambre des Apartements*, c. 1695. Copper engraving, 39.2 cm x 49.9 cm. Wikimedia Commons.

Figure 4. Nicolas Guérard, *Riche au matin et gueux au soir*, c. 1703. Copper engraving, 27.7 cm x 19 cm. Cabinet des estampes de la Bibliothèque nationale de France.

Guérard depicts a young nobleman, who, due to his gambling addiction, was "wealthy in the morning, but beggared by nightfall." The shower of playing cards fluttering from his right hand to the ground accentuates the wig flying off his head. In case the message was not clear enough for the viewer, the engraver has inscribed several epithets that reinforce the dangers of card-playing. The lines on the overturned table at the lower left of the image assert that "a little gambling is never troubling, since one is always cheerful, win or lose; but a big bet leaves one open to losses and often reduces the gambler's entourage."[39] The engraver further suggests that such uncontrolled gambling risks the loss of one's life, as well as one's wealth; the caption above the two dueling figures on the right notes that "gambling often makes enemies out of friends."[40] Claims about the immorality of gambling were widespread and an important part of how French men and women thought (or at least were told to think) about playing cards.

Gaming, gambling, and moral depravity were not, however, the only meanings conjured up by playing cards before the Revolution. Decks of cards, produced on large sheets of composite paper with specialized stenciling processes, were also part of the world of print and visual media in prerevolutionary and revolutionary France.[41] A *trompe l'oeil* broadsheet from 1714, attributed to a little-known French engraver named Dumesnil, suggests some of the associations that people in eighteenth-century France might have made between playing cards and other printed, commercial objects [see Figure 5]. In this engraving, we see a jumble of images affixed to a letter rack. Most of them depict important political and military events of 1713, the final year of the disastrous War of the Spanish Succession, while others contain notes that relate to other happenings, or refer to the sale of almanacs. One sheet at the bottom of the page is a musical score entitled "New Dance by Surenne." Peeking out from the unsorted pile of images and texts are portions of five playing cards, which immediately attract attention because of the blocks of red, yellow, blue, and black that vividly stand out against the otherwise monotone composition. The fully visible King of Hearts in the center of the composition, intended to represent Charlemagne, may have gestured toward the ever-present imperial ambitions of the aging Sun King, whose propaganda needs were served by the images and texts behind him. The Jacks of Spades and Clubs at the top of the image serve as a surrogate for viewers, gazing down expectantly at the collage of the past year. I would suggest that the engraver placed the cards in the composition to emphasize the random order of the year's events, shuffled as though they were a deck of cards. Viewers of this engraving might have juxtaposed the self-absorbed, private play of gamblers, suggested by the colorful playing cards, with the significant diplomatic and military events represented in the

Figure 5. Dumesnil, *Évènements de l'année 1713*, 1714. Copper engraving, 55 cm x 41 cm. Cabinet des estampes de la Bibliothèque nationale de France.

engravings that threaten to spill out of the image. Randomness marks both games of chance and the news of the day; the promise of the broadside is that the well-designed almanac to follow will bring order to the chaotic events of the previous year, just as the rules of play provide structure for card games.[42]

A printed game board, first created in the late seventeenth century and reissued several times after 1700, offers another way to think about the uses of playing cards [see Figure 6]. Throughout the seventeenth and eighteenth centuries, designers and educators created high-end decks of cards intended to instruct users on topics such as world geography, French heraldry, and, in this case, military theory and practice. This game of fortifications takes the form of a broadside. It is laid out as a spiral path, beginning with the Ace of Diamonds at the lower left-hand corner and ending with the King of Hearts in the center of the print, just before the game's endpoint, a fully fortified citadel. Players roll a die to advance along the game board; each space contains information about military design and strategy for the player to study. But each space is also a unique playing card that features a miniature version of the card in the upper right-hand corner; space 47, for example, the Eight of Hearts, also provides an image and description of an arsenal [see Figure 7]. Owners of this broadsheet might have kept it intact to play the board game, or they might have cut it into fifty-two cards to be studied separately and used for other gaming or training purposes. The broadside contains features more commonly associated with a codex, such as the alphabetical index of military terms found in the left-hand margin. The gaming function of playing cards could also be appropriated for educational purposes, and designers and manufacturers wagered that the medium of the playing cards might prove as conducive to instruction as a bound book. The broadside fixes the cards in sequence, similar to the way in which a codex orders its pages. But it also offers the option of cutting and shuffling them, emphasizing the many purposes to which playing cards might be put.

The non-gaming meanings of playing cards are further in evidence in the genre paintings of Jean-Siméon Chardin that portray adolescent boys building architectural structures with playing cards left behind by adults. Chardin executed four paintings on this theme in the 1730s, including a canvas from 1736–37 entitled *The House of Cards* [see Figure 8]. Michael Fried has argued that Chardin's human figures, including this one, represent a level of absorption intense enough to ignore the presence of the viewer.[43] Others have seen the playing cards and the coin on the table as a moralizing caution to the youth against the temptations he will face once he reaches adulthood. But one might also consider the materiality of Chardin's playing cards. This boy seems to have stumbled upon the cards, left on a gaming table after adult card players have exited the scene. The boy is indifferent

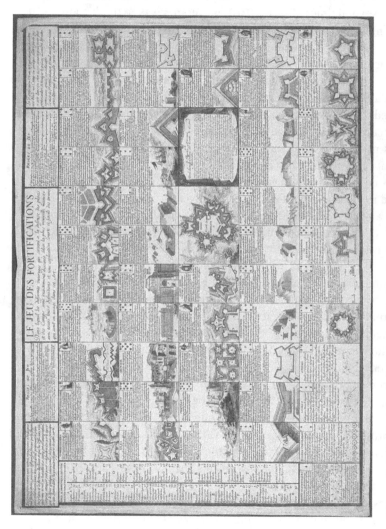

Figure 6. Gilles Jodelet de la Boissiere, *Le Jeu des fortifications*, late seventeenth century. Reprint by Jean Mariette, Paris, after 1691. Copper engraving, hand-colored, 55 cm x 74 cm. The Trustees of the British Museum.

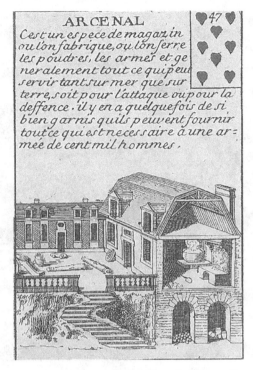

ARCENAL

Cest un espece de magazin
ou l'on fabrique, ou l'on serre
les poudres, les armes et ge
neralement tout ce qui peut
servir tant sur mer que sur
terre, soit pour l'attaque ou pour la
deffence. il y en a quelquefois de si
bien garnis qu'ils peuvent fournir
tout ce qui est necessaire à une ar=
mée de cent mil hommes.

Figure 7. *"Arcenal / eight of Hearts,"* detail from Gilles Jodelet de la Boissiere, *Le Jeu des fortifications,* late seventeenth century. Reprint by Jean Mariette, Paris, after 1691. Copper engraving, hand-colored, 8.5 cm x 5.4 cm. The Trustees of the British Museum.

to the abstract games that the grown-ups had been playing. He repurposes these pieces of paper, two of which he has folded along a vertical axis, to build a rudimentary house and the beginnings of a wall-like structure, both of which are in danger of collapse. Unlike the cards on the *trompe l'oeil* image or those depicted in the fortifications game, most of the cards that Chardin represents feature their blank backs. The white planes that make up the bulk of the card house stand out; if not for the gaming table and the two upright bent cards that feature Spades and Clubs, or the top of a red pip card sticking out from behind the card structure, it might not even be possible to recognize the bits of paper as playing cards.

The Chardin images suggest a reality of everyday life in Old Regime France that has since been obscured: the scarcity of paper, and the fact that decks became worn and could no longer be used for gambling, meant that playing cards had a second life after the gaming table. Their blank backs

Figure 8. Jean-Siméon Chardin, *The House of Cards*, 1736–37. Oil on canvas, 60.3 cm x 71.8 cm. National Gallery, London.

could be used for purposes that had nothing to do with games of chance. We know from tax collection procedures and other archival sources that elite households and gambling parlors bought new decks by the dozens every season to replace those that were no longer serviceable. The discards, rather than being tossed out, were sometimes given to servants or sold to those who could not afford new decks. In some instances, cards were sold by the pound or given to individuals who wanted to use the blank backs for a wide variety of purposes.[44] In various archives in France, the United Kingdom, and North America one can find used cards from the eighteenth century that served as receipts, IOUs, business cards, lists of household expenditures, and even a recipe for a laxative. Any time individuals needed to make lists, keep track of financial obligations, or advertise their services, these small rectangular pieces of paper were convenient and plentiful.[45]

Furthermore, playing cards could record information, or be used for instructional purposes, as we have already seen with the fortifications game. Worn or discarded playing cards turn up as card catalogues in private libraries. A catalogue of over 200,000 eighteenth-century playing cards is still held at the Mazarine Library in Paris, and Edward Gibbon left behind over 1,600 playing cards, now housed at the British Library, that itemized his personal book holdings.[46] Used playing cards might also serve as flash cards for learning languages, or as models for handwriting lessons. Cards were also repurposed as labels to identify bound legal documents. This use, as a filing system for court cases, appears to have been the second-most prevalent in the eighteenth century, after library card catalogues. The information theorist Markus Krajewski has argued that these efforts to catalogue and file are the precursors to online databases, giving eighteenth-century people access to what we might today call enhanced data storage and retrieval systems.[47]

It was not only amateur notetakers and professional cataloguers whose speculations appear on the backs of blank cards. Late in his life, Jean-Jacques Rousseau kept a handful of used playing cards in his pocket, allegedly so that he could jot down ideas that occurred to him during his solitary walks. The University Library in Neufchâtel holds twenty-seven of these cards today, including a Queen of Clubs with Jean-Jacques's musings about the existence of a deity scribbled on the back.[48] These twenty-seven cards with Rousseau's annotations are dwarfed, however, by an archive of over 35,000 playing cards left behind by the eighteenth-century Genevan physicist Georges-Louis Le Sage. Their content has been studied exhaustively by the historian of science Jean-François Bert, who has concluded that Le Sage became increasingly obsessed with recording, organizing, and sorting the tiniest details of his inquiries into the natural world, to the extent that he was not able to proceed from the details to generalizations that would allow him to publish his work.[49] Le Sage's recorded correspondence with d'Alembert and other Enlightenment scientists has been studied, but the dense, byzantine nature of his playing-card files has left him on the outskirts of histories of eighteenth-century science, where, according to Bert, he probably belongs. On a Ten of Clubs in Le Sage's files, for example, we find a "provisional agenda" for classifying observations about the motion of fluids that involves using ink and pencil to take note on different aspects of his observations.[50] Le Sage's obsessions with note-taking and procedure extended to his own mental processes as well, which he recorded in exhaustive detail on the backs of the used playing cards he most likely bought in bulk in Geneva. One packet, labeled "Plans (for myself only) of my literary and psychological notes on myself. Undated," is revealing. A Three of Spades contains a series of complaints on both sides of the card about "the weakness of my attention span" and a set of strategies to record his observations on the playing cards so that he could keep track of them; sort them into a logical, hierarchical order; and, perhaps someday, organize them into a narrative explanation of his own psychology.[51] In this example of the use of playing cards, we find poor Le Sage lost in a confusing mental maze worthy of a story by Jorge Luis Borges, unable to find an exit, or to remember where he entered. It is left to Bert to contextualize both the medium of his note-taking and the pathology of his intellectual activity.

With the Rousseau and Le Sage annotations in mind, let us now turn to the 120 playing cards confiscated from the Paris residence of the Dulac brothers in late 1793. The manufacturer of these cards was Jean Ducamus, whose name we can see on several of the face cards preserved in the archives, including on the left margin of a King of Spades [see Figure 9]. Ducamus was a card-maker in Clermont-Ferrand in the late eighteenth century from whom someone in the Dulac family most likely purchased the cards, either directly or through an authorized commercial vendor. Although the archival dossier contains 120 cards, it is missing an Ace of Clubs, a Queen of Clubs, a Six of Diamonds, and a Three of Spades. In contrast, there are six examples of the Eight of Clubs and five each of the Ten of Diamonds and the Seven of Spades. This random distribution, when coupled with the local origins of the cards, suggests that one of the brothers had grabbed a fistful of them from the family's stash of worn-out cards. Alternatively, it is possible that some of the cards may have been lost by the brothers or removed from the stack. Whether these events happened before or after 1789 is unclear. The design of the face cards, such as the King of Spades in Figure 9, conforms to the pattern that was mandated by the crown in the Auvergne before 1789. Cards produced after the Revolution initially did away with signs of royalty such as crowns and scepters and in 1793 replaced kings, queens, and jacks with post-monarchical motifs.[52]

While we can date the manufacture of the Dulac brothers' cards to the prerevolutionary period, it is harder to determine whether the annotations on the back of the cards were made during the Revolution. The vast majority of the quotations are from sources published before 1789, but it is certainly possible that Gregory scribbled at least some of them on the backs of the cards after the Revolution broke out. Not all 120 cards feature pithy sayings on their backs; a dozen have bibliographic citations of works by Montaigne, Pierre Gassendi, and Jean de La Fontaine, while eight more sport definitions of words such as *ichtyophage* (one who eats fish), *impéritie* (incompetence; this is repeated a second time on another card), and *pédérastie* (pederasty; "shameful and vile passion between men").[53] In all, 95 cards offered quotations on the back, twelve had bibliographical citations, eight copied dictionary definitions, and five recorded miscellaneous thoughts.

Among the 95 cards that feature quotations on the back, the most popular sources are eighteenth-century authors, the pagan authors of antiquity, and

Figure 9. Dulac playing cards, King of Spades, recto, late eighteenth century. Stencil on paper, 8.5 cm x 5.4 cm. Archives nationales de France, AF II 34, dossier 284, #107.

sayings from the Book of Proverbs and the Book of Wisdom in the Bible. I have been unable to determine sources for twenty-three of the quotations. Among those cards with quotations whose origins I have identified, the Book of Proverbs is the most frequently cited source, appearing on sixteen cards. The Roman stoic philosopher Lucius Annaeus Seneca is next with eleven citations. Somewhat surprisingly, Mably, the eighteenth-century political theorist of republicanism, appears six times on the back of the Dulac cards, while quotations from Rousseau are copied only four times. This analysis suggests a mental horizon for the brothers that extended beyond the secular, republican sentiments of the post-1789 period and even beyond the canonical works of the Enlightenment, to works of ancient stoicism, sixteenth-century skepticism, and Christian morality.

We might think of these 95 cards as an informal, unbound version of a commonplace book. Commonplacing dates at least as far back as the Renaissance, when humanists, such as Desiderius Erasmus, compiled examples of effective rhetoric excerpted from the writers of classical antiquity. At the end of the seventeenth century, John Locke published a work, initially in French in 1686 and then translated into English and published posthumously in 1706, that offered a new, more structured method for recording and organizing snippets culled from one's reading.[54] The Lockean method found a devoted following on both sides of the Channel throughout the eighteenth century. Indeed, the anonymous 1765 *Encyclopédie* article on "*recueil*" [collection] offered a summary of Locke's commonplacing technique.[55] The Dulac cards do not constitute a strictly Lockean commonplace exercise. They are not bound up as a book, and they do not appear to have an organizing structure, as Locke had insisted they should. Robert Darnton has suggested that the continuing popularity of commonplacing throughout the Enlightenment indicates a "segmented" method of reading in which readers jumped from book to book, rather than reading one volume after another sequentially.[56] An easily retrievable collection of quotations might suit the practical needs of eighteenth-century individuals better than a handsomely bound set of collected works in folio. The evidence from these 120 playing cards suggests that this may have been Gregory's preferred method of reading, and perhaps that of his brother as well. We should take the playing cards seized from the Dulacs in December 1793 as a distilled, portable library into which one or both of the brothers could dip as needed, shuffling the cards in order to find advice or consolation.

When and how did Gregory, and perhaps Charles, consult these 120 playing cards? Unfortunately, nothing in the papers seized along with the playing cards provides any direct evidence regarding their use. Did the cards travel to the battlefield with the brothers? Did they consult them by candlelight as they struggled with the political and personal choices they faced in the midst of a Revolution that tore apart not only the nation, but also their own family? We do not know. A clue from the report on the arrest of Charles in December 1793, however, offers some insight into the motivation for this commonplacing practice. The official report of the arrest noted that among the papers seized was a small envelope labeled as follows: "A packet discovered and sealed, having an inscription bearing these words—notes containing good sense [*notes du bon sens*]." The packet referenced here most likely contained the playing cards.[57] The phrase "*bon sens*" had multiple meanings in eighteenth-century France, as Sophia Rosenfeld has explained.[58] Some understood it to mean the practice of thinking "philosophically," following rationalist, Cartesian principles. In the seventeenth century, this form of thought had been deployed to dismiss skeptical, potentially atheistic thought. By the eighteenth century, however, propagators of *bon sens* argued that it could serve as the basis for a secular moral order that would replace the teachings of Catholicism. Those engaged in this type of reasoning according to "good sense" sought to establish certain basic truths that they claimed were self-evident to anyone educated. The sources of this reasoning were the literary, religious, and philosophical cultures of literate France towards the end of the Enlightenment. In other words, this was an approach to truth that was rooted in books and other forms of instruction available primarily to the kingdom's elites, rather than in the lessons of everyday life available to all. One eighteenth-century publication written by Jean-Baptiste de Boyer, marquis d'Argens, an author excerpted several times on the back of the Dulac playing cards, even referred to this approach as a "Philosophy of Good Sense."[59] These efforts prompted a backlash at the time from the anti-philosophical party that claimed its version of *bon sens* reinforced Christian authority against the unfounded speculations of the *philosophes*. The Dulac playing cards, which drew on both secular and religious authorities, would seem to reflect this conflicted understanding of *bon sens* that emerged in the last decades of the Old Regime.

What "good sense" did this unbound collection of commonplaces contain? Consider some of the aphorisms recorded on the cards that treat the moral meanings of wealth. A Three of Spades, for example, contained the following line from Mably: "Oh, how wealth is humiliating for the poor, who lack everything! And what moral flaw almost always allows those who should be revolted by such wealth to be dazzled by it?"[60] One can imagine these words, published in a 1789 work entitled *On the Rights and Duties of the Citizen*, inspiring youthful aristocrats who were dismayed by the economic injustices of the Old Regime. But such enlightened pleas for economic equality were also mixed in with sentiments drawn from scripture and the ancient Stoics. A Six of Hearts recorded Proverbs 11:24: "One gives freely and becomes even richer, while another fails to do good because of avarice, and impoverishes himself."[61] While the Mably quotation empathizes with the poor and attacks those who are blinded by lucre, the biblical proverb lays out the benefits for those who share their wealth and the consequences for those who do not. Meanwhile, on a Nine of Hearts Gregory recorded the following sentiment from Seneca: "There is no need for a law to punish an ingrate; the horror that accompanies ingratitude is his torment. One must give, solely for the pleasure of having given."[62] In this stoic view of life, charity is its own reward; the one truly benefited is the donor, not the recipient.

This sampling of *pensées* copied on the backs of the Dulac playing cards suggests that Gregory pondered a variety of sources, both contemporary and traditional, to arrive at his own understanding of *bon sens*. These dictums of good sense were not only applicable to the politics and economics of the revolutionary moment; they also offered guidance on personal matters and the ethical choices that the brothers had to negotiate after 1789. For at the same time as the brothers sought a place in the military order of the new regime, they faced daunting struggles in their private lives without the guidance and support of their *émigré* parents and extended family. How did they replace the Old Regime support structures that they had rejected? How did the revolutionary principles they had embraced shape their search for life-partners? If anything, the answers to these questions proved to be even more challenging than the trials the brothers encountered in the armies of the Revolution.

"Dulac-Style Love"

As historians have noted in recent decades, the rebellion against absolutist monarchy and socio-economic inequality was also understood by the revolutionary generation to be a crisis in paternal authority and the ways in which it structured relations within the family.[63] The history of the Dulac family after 1789 illustrates this theme. While there are no traces of the *émigré* Dulacs in the papers seized in the Parisian apartment of the younger brothers in December 1793, there is a draft of a letter from Gregory to his two older brothers that sheds light on the family's dynamics after the outbreak of the Revolution.[64] This draft, most likely written in the spring or summer of 1793, begins by denying an assertion that Gregory and Charles remained attached to their cause only because they saw no way to exit safely from the revolutionary path they had chosen. Gregory responds, not without affection for his brothers, that it is natural for the latter to believe reports that the two younger sons wish to return to the bosom of their family. The remainder of his letter, however, clearly lays out the sentiments that bound Gregory and Charles to the revolutionary cause. Gregory admits that he has been guilty of egotistical pride and a partisan spirit that at times made him lose sight of the revolutionary principles that inspire him. He acknowledges that he has suffered because of his estrangement from the family in exile. Nevertheless, he insists, he cannot make common cause with his brothers, even if he is tempted to do so by the memory of their mother. The "cause of humanity," above all else, motivates him to continue the revolutionary struggle. The elder brothers, unable to live without their noble privileges, have sought refuge outside of France, rather than working to better their homeland from within. He concludes by invoking their common religious upbringing: "If the gospel, if religion has retained its hold on you, then do not allow the prayers of your [younger] brothers to be in vain. We well understand that the constitution does not suit you, but we never could have conceived that you would dare to attack it with weapons in hand. I can write no more. May God comfort you."[65] The letter reveals depths to Gregory's revolutionary sentiments that were absent in his printed attacks on the noble privilege of Puységur in 1790 or the Bourbon monarchy in 1791. By 1793, he has distilled his political ideology into an ardent support for the abstract cause of humanity and separated it from the faults of the partisan-minded advocates with whom he had formerly been allied. He speaks to his brothers in the language of family and religion in which they had been raised, despite the backlash against paternalist ideology and the dechristianization efforts of the most radical revolutionaries. And while Gregory cannot deny the ties of blood that he shares with his brothers, he decries the attempts that they and other *émigrés* have made to mislead the French people and to threaten the nation with military invasion and destruction. In short, it is a letter that reveals how deeply rooted Gregory and Charles were in their family's heritage, and how much it has cost them to renounce it.

One consequence of that renunciation was financial instability. In late 1790, for example, Gregory received a letter from an anxious creditor in Malta, where the brothers had apparently spent time with other members of the Order before 1789.[66] In 1792 and 1793, once the revolutionary government had seized the estates left behind by their *émigré* father and brothers, Gregory and Charles pursued a variety of strategies to reclaim some of their lost revenue. Their efforts led to some success: in August 1792, the authorities in the department of the Haute-Loire granted the brothers an annual pension of six hundred pounds from the largest estate their father held in the region. But in mid-summer 1793, Gregory and Charles were still receiving dunning letters from Malta, and Gregory, who by then was back in the Auvergne, was filing claims for unpaid wages from his time in the revolutionary army.[67] The rhetorical strategies the brothers employed when seeking financial relief framed their difficulties in terms of the betrayal of their family and their devotion to the Revolution. The minutes of the National Assembly in Paris for 16 August 1791, for example, record that the following letter from Gregory and Charles was read to the legislators: "we believe we must inform you that although we were previously knights in the Order of Malta, we were and we are French citizens, soldiers of liberty. We prefer this title. It is the only one worthy of a free man, even above that of 'prince' that one finds in enslaved countries. If we have long held the title of 'knight' with all of its prejudicial assumptions, it was only because we believed that the Order would forgive our debts."[68] The brothers concluded their letter to the representatives of the people by pledging funds formerly destined for Malta to the upkeep of the National Guard, an offer that reportedly drew applause from the Assembly. The formula of "soldiers of liberty" found its way into other pleas for relief that the brothers wrote. In an undated letter, they were at pains to distinguish themselves from their father and elder siblings in the eyes of revolutionary administrators: "The aristocratic virus does not always infect all the members of the same family—a father might hate the Revolution while his sons become soldiers of liberty."[69] The brothers, now risking their lives for the Revolution, renounced their father's authority and their privileged status; in turn, they asked not to be judged for his crimes, and not to be entirely deprived of their ancestral wealth, given their devotion to the revolutionary cause.

Although the brothers denounced the paternal authority of the Bourbon king and of their father in many public and private speeches and letters, they did not imagine a world without father figures. Some passages in their correspondence show them recasting their relationship as one of father and son, in the absence of their biological father. In these epistolary exchanges, Gregory sought to fill the role of paternal advisor vacated by their *émigré* father, even though he was only two years older. He often refers to his younger sibling as *mon cher fils* [my dear son], and Charles frequently calls him *mon bon père* [my good father], or even *mon père moral* [my moral father], an epithet that again evokes religious sentiments. In sixteen letters written in 1792 and 1793, Gregory offers Charles advice on many matters. In late May 1793, in the wake of the Dumouriez/Miranda affair, for example, he chides his younger brother's denunciations, which he considered impetuous: "I have recognized great qualities in you, but they have not hidden your flaws ... you give me sufficient proof that your selfishness exists not only when you yield to your anger, but that it even extinguishes your good sense."[70] Two months later, he advises Charles to decline his role as the people's representative to the armies in the north as too dangerous politically. He counsels Charles instead to follow in his own footsteps and return to the volunteer army in the Auvergne as a foot soldier, "where you will be sheltered from suspicion and from slanderers, and you will have no other passion than the love of the fatherland that will propel you towards a republican career."[71] In short, in the second half of 1793, Gregory pleaded with Charles to abandon the perils of military service at the national level, return to their home, and rejoin the local militia. Gregory repeatedly advises Charles on how to make his way in the world; similar sentiments are also present on the backs of their used playing cards. Gregory's exhortation to care for his reputation and friendships finds an echo in a quotation from the Book of Wisdom on a King of Clubs: "A good reputation is preferable to great wealth, and friendship to gold and silver."[72] Seneca, for his part, had advice on the regulation of emotions that Gregory noted on a Ten of Clubs: "He who masters his passions finds the calm that all the world seeks."[73] While the brothers framed the renunciation of their father in the anti-paternalist politics of the moment, Gregory also reached back to biblical morality and the stoicism of the ancients in an effort to guide his brother through the treacherous maelstrom of the Revolution.

Charles apparently sought this advice from Gregory, the only figure whose counsel he could seek after the other members of their family had fled. While the younger sibling exuded revolutionary enthusiasm and confidence on the front lines and in Paris, his private correspondence with his brother offers examples of despair. In an undated epistle, Charles wrote of his inner agony: "I sense only too bitterly the flaws, the crimes of which I am guilty; I see clearly how they debase me in this moment."[74] In another letter to Gregory, written in May 1792, Charles welcomes "the true, the soul-shredding remorse that provides a proper baptism" and makes a distinction between his head and his heart: "My head, my puny head, misled me. The heart, the heart alone is enough all by itself. ... The ability to distinguish between good and evil belongs perhaps to judgement, and in that sense to the mind, and to the head. But to the heart, to the heart alone sentiment is given and attributed. From this sublime gift springs everything that teaches us to hate evil and to love that which is good."[75] His conclusion is that one should not rely on intellect. Instead, Charles coaches himself, he needs to privilege the passions, and trust his heart. This approach may well have come from the sources, both biblical and secular, that one finds on the backs of the playing cards. An Ace of Diamonds in the brothers' possession quotes the Book of Wisdom on the virtues of the heart: "Love justice, you who are the terrestrial judges; take from God sentiments worthy of Him, and seek them with a simple heart."[76] A Five of Diamonds, meanwhile, cites Rousseau's *Emile*, which preaches that "a simple being who can live without passions, without attachments is hardly a man; such a creature is either a brute or a god."[77] Charles's moral universe extends beyond a sense of the civic duty one owes to one's fellow Republican citizens. His meditations are not limited to the secular political philosophy of 1789, nor to the dechristianization movement of 1793. Elsewhere he writes that he seeks a "moral baptism." Charles confesses to his brother that he wants a spiritual purity derived from Christian teachings and describes a form of penance based on cleansing his heart, rather than rigorously applying the rule of reason.

Gregory was particularly forthcoming with advice about Charles's romantic life. He reminded Charles that he had more experience with women, and he tried to allay his brother's self-doubts by focusing on a romantic relationship that Charles was pursuing with Annette Alinde, a twenty-year-old noble neighbor who lived near the Dulac family estate outside Brioude: "Oh my son!" he wrote in October 1793, "your friend will assure your happiness, live, live for her."[78] Seven letters from Annette to Charles have survived in the archives; unfortunately, none of Charles's letters to her remain. Even so, Annette's writings and Charles's laments to Gregory make it clear that the two were infatuated with one another. To take one example, revolutionary correspondence in 1793 often featured the phrase, "Year IV of the Republic, One and Indivisible" at the top of the first page. In the heading of her letter to Charles of 14 August 1793, Annette playfully parrots this revolutionary device, reminding Charles that it is "Year IV of our Love."[79] Still, their relationship was not an easy one. Annette's noble family was not pleased by her attachment to one of the revolutionary Dulac brothers; like Charles, two of her brothers had already gone into exile by 1792. When her mother accidentally read one of Charles's epistles to her daughter, Annette had to resort to a secretive transmission network to continue their correspondence. Later, in summer 1793, with the rise of Jacobinism in the Auvergne, Annette warned Charles that her family might soon be imprisoned for its residual royalist sympathies, in which case their correspondence would be cut off.

For his part, Charles was torn between his revolutionary enthusiasms and his desire for Annette, the daughter of a noble family. In the summer of 1793, he drafted a three-and-a-half page missive to the local authorities in the Puy-de-Dôme which he titled "Every Man Owes His Fellow Citizens an Account of his Conduct."[80] Much of the draft was taken up with a defense of the actions he and Gregory had taken over the last three years of their military service. Towards the end of this polemic, however, he asserts that he would be willing to die at the hands of his enemies, if not for the love of the woman he would leave behind: "She would live in the midst of the Republic, while I, who preferred duty to the most vivid and pure love, my death would leave me the regret of having served neither the cause of freedom nor that of my love, she who was everything to me. ... The Republic and my lover, or death!" Tellingly, though, in the final version of his narrative, he left out this paean to Annette and focused solely on his public actions and those of Gregory.[81] In a letter to Annette from around this time, Gregory insisted on the depth of the love that Charles felt for her, but also tried to excuse his brother's devotion to the Revolution by arguing that his most important debt was to the people, not his romantic partner: "Charles would not be worthy of you or of himself if he had remained calmly at home. He would not have obtained happiness, it would not exist in the midst of his remorse."[82] He then counseled her to read Plutarch, Montaigne, and Rousseau, especially the latter's *La Nouvelle Héloïse* and *Discourse on Inequality*, to understand why men like Charles had to sacrifice everything for their love of the fatherland. Perhaps he had in mind a saying from Rousseau's *Émile* regarding remorse that he had copied on the back of one of his playing cards: "Sadness and misfortune respect sleep, leaving the soul some respite. Only remorse never leaves one alone."[83]

Annette, it would seem, came to the conclusion that Charles had chosen his revolutionary passions over their relationship and was unhappy with his decision. However, it was evident that she was also in love with him. She signed one letter in December 1792 with "I love you more than I can say, and I am yours for life."[84] Nevertheless, she made it clear that as a member of the nobility and as a woman she did not share all of Charles's views. In October 1792, she told him: "I am not political. I follow the voice of my heart, and I fear that no matter what you might say to control my conduct ... it would be impossible for me to love someone who oppresses the weak and the innocent."[85] In her last letter to Charles in September 1793 she upbraided him, writing: "I have made it a habit to expect nothing more of fortune than the cruelest blows; I am philosophical enough to understand that a man animated by the desire for glory can easily neglect a woman and only think of her in his moments of leisure. This is what is called republican-style love, and therefore also known as Dulac-style love."[86] She then turned to his most recent letter, in which Charles had apparently shared an epigram worthy of being inscribed on the back of a playing card: "A woman's heart is more loving but less firm than a man's; absence weighs heavily upon her."[87] She categorically rejected this assertion, telling him that if he believed this, he did not know her well. It was not his absence that left her distraught, but the fear that his feelings for her did not reciprocate those she had for him. Throughout these two tumultuous years she was tormented by the thought that what she characterized as his "republican-style love" would be inadequate.

In the romantic realm as well as the revolutionary one, therefore, the brothers' dedication to the new regime placed them in conflict with their past lives and other current pursuits. On one of Gregory's playing cards, by chance an Ace of Hearts, he had captured the following quotation from Mably's 1763 *Entretiens de Phocion*: "Impose silence on your passions in order to consult your reason, and it will teach you all the manly duties."[88] Charles struggled with this advice, and Annette would certainly never have accepted it. At the end of 1793, with Charles facing a death sentence because he had tried to fulfill "all the manly duties," Mably's dictum seemed horribly misguided.

Dénouement: A Pseudonym, a Suicide, a Marriage

Although the tempestuous courtship recorded in the letters of Annette reads like a potentially tragic love story set against the backdrop of a cataclysmic revolution, the plot did not resolve itself as one might expect. For one thing, "Annette" had been writing to Charles under a pseudonym. There is no archival trace of an Alinde family in the Auvergne in the late eighteenth century, or indeed in earlier periods. In Brioude, however, after the passage of the Law of Suspects by the National Convention on 19 September 1793, the local revolutionary officials chose to detain anyone publicly known to be royalists, as well as anyone related by birth or marriage to an *émigré*. During late October and early November the authorities rounded up eighty-seven suspects who allegedly met these criteria, including twelve women between the ages of 18 and 32. Two of them were 20 years old, the age that "Annette" claimed to be at the time of her letters to Charles. Other archival traces lead to the conclusion that Annette Alinde was, in reality, Anne-Claude de Labro, the fifth of seven daughters of Guillaume de Labro, a nobleman who had been mayor of Brioude before the Revolution.[89] Two of her brothers, François Marie and François Maurice, had fled soon after the start of the Revolution to join the *émigré* armies, as "Annette" had mentioned in her letters to Charles. She had also predicted her family's detention in her last letter to Charles, written only two days before the passage of the Law of Suspects. The municipal records relate that Anne-Claude was released on 5 November 1794, approximately a year after the authorities had arrested her.[90]

At the time of his imprisonment in Paris, therefore, Charles's beloved "Annette" was also under house arrest in the Auvergne. We do not know if Anne-Claude learned of her lover's incarceration under orders from the Committee of Public Safety, nor do we know if the news of her provincial detention had reached Charles by the time of his arrest. Archival records in Paris, however, record the outcome of his time in jail: he spent three and half months in Luxemburg prison without ever appearing before the Revolutionary Tribunal. On 6 Germinal Year II (26 March 1794), some of the papers that had been seized in the raid at the end of 1793 were returned to him, after which he appears to have left Paris.[91] Following his escape from the shadow of the guillotine, he finally took Gregory's advice and returned to the Auvergne to enmesh himself in local affairs. There he found his *père moral* also fixated on a love interest. In July 1793, Gregory had mentioned a new love in his missives to Charles, coyly reporting that he had "made himself into a young lover whose pure morals and excellent heart are worthy of a young woman who was in turn worthy of him, and who would make him even more worthy of serving the fatherland for whom he had sacrificed everything."[92] Gregory did not mention her name, but we know that by spring of the following year he was seeing a noblewomen in Clermont-Ferrand named Marie Silvie Saulnier. The latter had married a Clermont lawyer and notary named Jean-Baptiste Espinasse in August 1786, when she was eighteen years old. Espinasse filed for divorce, on grounds of "*incompatabilité d'humeur*," a new category in the civil law created by the Revolution on 1 April 1794. At that point, Saulnier was twenty-six years old, the same age as Gregory and two years older than Charles.[93] Around this time, the latter returned to the Auvergne, where he would have been able to confirm that Anne-Claude was under house arrest in Brioude with the rest of her noble family. Given his recent release from prison in Paris and the suspicions of treason that had never ceased to haunt the brothers, it would have been dangerous for Charles to continue his courtship of Anne-Claude. Perhaps by then the ardor of one or both of the young lovers had cooled.

Soon after Charles's return to the Auvergne, he too began to take an interest in Marie Silvie Saulnier. We have only one source for what transpired in late spring and summer between the two brothers and Marie Silvie: an August 1794 deposition given by a Clermont doctor named Michel Menestier.[94] According to Menestier, Gregory had become obsessed with the idea of marrying Marie Silvie; whether he began to press his case before or after her husband divorced her is unclear, as are the intentions of Charles at that moment. The recent *divorcée*, however, firmly rejected Gregory's suit. Plunged into despair, he tried to kill himself by consuming a vial of opium that Marie Silvie kept on hand to calm the convulsions that Gregory's attentions were causing her; Menestier remarked that "the nerves of this young *citoyenne* [had become] very irritable."[95] The doctor reported that he arrived on the scene in time to purge the drug from Gregory's system, thereby saving his life. "A while later," Gregory returned to Clermont from the Dulac family estate near Courpierre, only to learn that Charles, his brother and "son," was having much greater success in courting his desired bride. Gregory, furious, abruptly left Clermont, but returned to the city a week later, where he once again attempted suicide. Again, the good doctor saved his life. The third time, however, Gregory was not so fortunate. On 14 August, he traveled from Thiers to Clermont. Before he left, he wrote a brief note to a friend named Gilibert in which he enclosed a key to an armoire in a room he rented in Thiers. He instructed Gilibert to retrieve "the letters and papers which I entrust to your friendship."[96] The next morning, 28 Thermidor Year II (15 August 1794), Gregory succeeded in killing himself via poison at the Clermont residence of Marie Silvie. And a little over a month later, Charles married Marie Silvie in Clermont-Ferrand in front of a town official and five witnesses.[97]

While official sources in the archives confirm that these events transpired, I have not found documents that would allow one to make sense of this unanticipated turn of events. As Richard Cobb argued more than a generation ago, much remains unknowable about the relation between the experience of revolution and the private lives of French men and women like the Dulac brothers, Marie Silvie Saulnier, and Anne-Claude de Labro in the 1790s. One might speculate that Gregory was emulating notable Roman republicans who had committed suicide for political reasons, such as Seneca, whom he had quoted eleven times on the backs of his playing cards, or Marcus Porcius Cato (Cato the Younger), whose death many revolutionaries considered exemplary. Or he may have had eighteenth-century fictional characters in mind, such as the protagonist of Johann Wolfgang von Goethe's *Sorrows of Young Werther*, who also ended his life after being spurned in a love triangle. But without direct testimony from Gregory, it is difficult to know how his political and personal circumstances led to his decision. Even if one were to discover more archival traces, they still might not provide a satisfying explanation for this unexpected dénouement. The interior journey that led Gregory from the roles of a revolutionary firebrand and surrogate father to that of a suicidal suitor of a recent *divorcée* may simply not be recoverable almost 230 years later. It may not have been understandable at the time.[98] Nor is it easy to imagine the range of emotions that Charles must have felt as he buried his brother and then married the woman whose heart he had captured at the expense of his brother's life.[99] Had the brothers' republican and fraternal solidarity foundered on their romantic rivalry? How should we imagine the feelings experienced in the Year II by Marie Silvie, who had just escaped one marriage only to find herself caught between two brothers vying for her affections? And what happened to the love of Charles for "Annette," locked away in detention in Brioude where she was unavailable to receive or return his affections?[100] Sometimes the archives remain silent, in spite of our best efforts.

They do, however, occasionally offer unexpected views found in unanticipated places, such as the backs of used playing cards. At some point before the events that led him to take his own life, Gregory had been struck by complementary quotations from Marcus Tullius Cicero and Montaigne that suggested that the philosopher's all-consuming, life-long task was to prepare for death. He recorded the sayings together on the back of an Eight of Clubs [see Figures 10 and 11]. The Ciceronian quotation, derived from Plato, might be rendered as "The whole life of the philosopher is a meditation upon death." The well-known adage from Montaigne is similar: "To ponder philosophy is to learn how to die."[101] The experiences of the brothers during the Revolution played out in a confusing sequence of factionalism, personal peril, and emotional trauma in ways that defy coherent political or moral interpretation. Perhaps one or both of them intuitively understood how difficult it would be to make sense of their revolutionary experiences, which is why they held on to the playing cards that have sat silently in the archives for over two centuries. The writing on the backs of the cards allowed them, and permit us, to connect with those who have philosophized before us, even when we cannot divine their deepest, most troubling thoughts. They offer ways, perhaps illusive, to make sense of the fate that awaits us all.

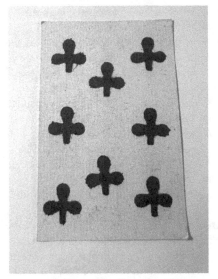

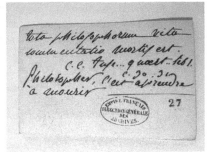

Figure 11. Dulac playing cards, Eight of Clubs, verso, late eighteenth century. 8.5 cm x 5.4 cm. Archives nationales de France, AF II 34, dossier 284, #27.

Figure 10. Dulac playing cards, Eight of Clubs, recto, late eighteenth century. Stencil on paper, 8.5 cm x 5.4 cm. Archives nationales de France, AF II 34, dossier 284, #27.

Notes

Thomas Concy and Simon Macdonald have provided invaluable research assistance for this article, allowing me to overcome the geographical limitations imposed by the COVID pandemic. I have benefited from comments on earlier versions of this essay by members of the MIT History Faculty Seminar, the Boston French History Group, and respondents to the Presidential Address I presented at the 2021 Virtual Annual Meeting of the American Society for Eighteenth-Century Studies, as well as insights from Cristelle Baskins, Thierry Depaulis, Simon Macdonald, Kenda Mutongi, and Charles Walton.

1. Cobb, *Reactions to the French Revolution* (London: Oxford University Press, 1972), 128.

2. For an account of the arrest and the seizure of Dulac's papers, see Archives nationales (subsequent citations will be made as *AN*) AF II 34, dossier 281, #9–10. This essay is based in large part on those papers, which can be found at *AN* AF II 34, dossiers 279–84.

3. "Le despotisme commence où finit la liberté" (*AN* AF II 34, dossier 284, #119). All translations from French are mine.

4. I base the assertion that Gregory annotated the backs of the playing cards on a comparison with the examples of his handwriting in the dossiers in the *AN*.

5. On the family's origins, dating back to the thirteenth century, see Gustave Chaix d'Est-Ange, *Dictionnaire des familles françaises anciennes ou notables à la fin du XIXe siècle*, 20 vols. (Evreux: Charles Hérissey, 1903–29), 15:12. For details of the family's land holdings before the Revolution, see Francisque Mège, *Le Puy-de-Dôme en 1793 et le proconsulat de Couthon* (Paris, 1877), 190. On the Château de Cluzel, a thirteenth-century fortress that had been considerably expanded and remodeled in the seventeenth century, see Antoine de Bouillé, *Manoirs abandonnés* (Paris, 1950, unpaginated digital version); George Paul, "Le Cluzel près St. Eble," *Almanach de Brioude et de son arrondissment* 39 (1959), 71–84; and "Château de Cluzel," https://www.pop.culture.gouv.fr/notice/merimee/PA00092705.

6. On the birthdate of and a post in the royal stables at Versailles for André-Grégoire Nicolas René, see Chaix d'Est-Ange, *Dictionnaire des familles,* 12; on the birthdate of Georges-Cathérine, see Archives départementales du Puy-de-Dôme (subsequent citations will be made as *ADPD*) 63 1 Q762; on admission to the Order of the Knights of Malta for the three youngest Dulac sons, see Nicolas Viton de Saint Allais, *Catalogue général et alphabétique des familles nobles de France admises dans l'Ordre de Malte, depuis l'institution de cet Ordre jusqu'a présent, suivi de la nomenclature générale des Chevaliers de Malte* (Paris, 1815), 151.

7. There is some confusion about Gregory's birthdate. Mège, *Le Puy-de-Dôme en 1793*, 190, gives a birthdate of 1762 for Gregory, but in a publication three years later the same author indicates that he was born in 1768 (see *Les Bataillons de volontaires, 1791–1793* [Paris, 1880], 186). Most other sources, however, including Chaix d'Est-Ange, *Dictionnaire des familles*, 12, and *AN* AF II 34, dossier 282, #25, indicate the later birthdate. Gregory's entry into the royal military academy is mentioned in Chaix d'Est-Ange, *Dictionnaire des familles*, 12; his move to the Strasburg artillery regiment is recorded at *AN* AF II 34, dossier 281, #17. Gregory's birthname was Nicolas-Charles Dulac, while Charles was christened Charles-Grégoire Dulac. The documents seized by the Parisian guard in December 1793 make it clear, however, that Nicolas-Charles was known in the Auvergne by the name of "Grégoire," while his younger brother was commonly referred to as "Charles." I will use the anglicized version of Grégoire's name in this essay. Charles's birthdate in October 1770 is confirmed in Chaix d'Est-Ange, *Dictionnaire des familles*, 12; and *AN* AF II 34, dossier 281, #26.

8. *AN* AF II 34, dossiers 279 and 280 include reflections by the brothers on battlefield strategy, plans for military provisioning, and, in two cases, solutions to math problems. On efforts more generally to apply enlightened thought to the Old Regime and revolutionary French military, see Ken Alder, *Engineering the Revolution: Arms and Enlightenment in France, 1763–1815* (Chicago: University of Chicago Press, 1997) and Christy Pichichero, *The Military Enlightenment: War and Culture in the French Empire from Louis XIV to Napoleon* (Ithaca: Cornell University Press, 2017).

9. On André-Grégoire's activities as an *émigré* in 1791, see Antoine de Bouillé, *Manoirs abandonnés*, unpaginated digital version. A "liste des émigrés du district

de Thiers" of 2 July 1793 includes Claude Dulac and his two sons among those who had fled the region since the start of the Revolution (*ADPD* 1 Q 2631).

10. On Gregory's service record, see *AN* AF II 34, dossier 282, #25. On the incident in the Strasbourg Regiment in May 1790, see *Pétition de Grégoire Dulac, officier au régiment de Strasbourg, artillerie, à M. de La Tour-Du-Pin, ministre de la Guerre* (n.p., n.d) preserved as Bibliothèque nationale de France [subsequent citations will be made as *BnF*], 8-LN27-6605; and *Archives parlementaires de 1787 à 1860. Première série (1787 à 1799)*, ed. Jérôme Mavidal and Émile Laurent, 102 vols. (Paris, 1879–2012), 16:19–21 [subsequent citations will be made as *AP*].

11. The Marquis de Puységur was thirty-nine years old in 1790 when this incident took place; Gregory Dulac was twenty-two. On Puységur's mesmerism, see Adam Crabtree, "1784: The Marquis de Puységur and the Psychological Turn in the West," *Journal of the History of the Behavioral Sciences* 55, no. 3 (2019): 199–215.

12. *AP*, 16:21.

13. "Je suis toujours subornné, toujours prêt à obéir. Mais ailleurs, ailleurs, mes camarades—*tous égaux*" (Grégoire Dulac, *Pétition*, 8).

14. "Réponds-moi, Louis XVI: tu ne peux donc vivre déchu de l'honneur de pouvoir tyranniser vingt-cinq millions d'hommes? Celui d'être aimé d'eux, celui de faire le bien, de secourir le pauvre. Celui-là n'est pas digne de toi? … Trente-cinq millions ne peuvent soutenir le splendeur de ton trône! Infâme!" (*Réflexions sur la conduite de Louis XVI Bourbon, depuis le 20 juin 1791* [n.p., n.d.], 2; preserved in the Bibliothèque du patrimoine in Clermont-Ferrand as A 10652).

15. "S'il était possible que ma Patrie reconnût encore constitutionellement Louis XVI Bourbon, pour son chef … je ne me regarde plus comme Français" (Dulac, *Réflexions*, 3). On revolutionary political culture in the department of the Puy-de-Dôme more generally, see Philippe Bourdin, *Des Lieux, des mots, les Révolutionnaires. Le Puy-de-Dôme entre 1789 et 1799* (Clermont-Ferrand: L'Institut d'études du Massif Central, 1995). He discusses Gregory's 1791 diatribe against Louis XVI on 369–71.

16. On Gregory's transition into the armies of the Revolution, see *AN* AF II 34, dossier 282, #25. On Charles's enlistment in the National Guard battalion in the Puy-de-Dôme in September 1791, see *AN* AF II 34, dossier 281, #32; on his military progression through the summer of 1792, see *AN* AF II 34, dossier 281, #31.

17. *AN* AF II 34, dossier 281, #23.

18. *Chronique de Paris*, 28 August 1792, 964, notes the arrest of Gregory on 25 August 1792.

19. *AP*, 49:120, 49:132–33.

20. *AN* AF II 34, dossier 282, #1–2 contain transcriptions of and extracts from letters written by Gregory while imprisoned to representatives in the Assembly and other influential people on his behalf.

21. "Persuadé, Monsieur, que votre repentir est sincère et que vous avez trop d'esprit pour ne pas apprécier les crimes de Lafayette qui vous avait égaré et qui m'a injustement calomnié, j'oublie vos torts envers moi et je vous embrasse sincèrement. Si messieurs les commissaires veulent bien y consenter, vous servirez auprès de moi où je vous ferai obtenir de l'emploi dans un regiment" (*AP*, 49:473).

22. "Lafayette avait égaré son opinion sans corrompre son coeur" (*AP,* 50:174). *AN* AF II 34, dossier 282, #9–10 contains two versions of the Assembly's decree ordering the release of Gregory from the Valenciennes military prison. *AN* AF II 34, dossier 281, #31 records the delayed military appointment of Charles because of his brother's detention.

23. On Charles's appointment in October 1792, see *AN* AF II 34, dossier 281, #29; on Gregory's appointment, see *AN* AF II 34, dossier 283, #28.

24. The January and March 1793 orders can be found at *AN* AF II 34, dossier 281, #18–19, and *AN* AF II 34, dossier 282, #22–23.

25. Dumouriez is often demonized for his conduct in the spring of 1793, but see the revisionist account of his goals, and French foreign policy more generally in this moment, in Patricia Chastain Howe, *French Foreign Policy and the French Revolution: Charles-François Dumouriez, Pierre LeBrun, and the Belgian Plan, 1789–1793* (New York: Palgrave MacMillan, 2008).

26. See the account of Charles's testimony in *AP,* 51:293. *AN* AF II 34, dossier 281 #28 is Charles's handwritten version of this denunciation. See also *AN* AF II 34, dossier 282, #20, which is Gregory's account of the actions he and Charles took in March and April 1793 that culminated in testimony against Dumouriez and in favor of Miranda.

27. *AN* AF II 34, dossier 281 #27. On Eustace, see Yvon Bizardel, *Les Américains à Paris sous Louis XVI et pendant la Révolution. Notices biographiques* (Paris: Libraire historique Clavreuil, 1978), 56–57. On the trial of Miranda, see John Moreau, "The Trial of Francisco de Miranda," *The Americas* 22, no. 3 (1966): 277–91.

28. *AN* AF II 34, dossier 283, #21–22, 25–26.

29. *AN* AF II 34, dossier 281, #2, 7–8.

30. Robert Palmer, *Twelve Who Ruled: The Year of the Terror in the French Revolution,* 3rd ed. (Princeton: Princeton University Press, 1971), 130–59, remains a good summary of Couthon's actions in the Auvergne and in Lyons in the summer and fall of 1793. His account is based primarily on Mège, *Le Puy-de-Dôme en 1793.* On Couthon's patronage of the brothers in 1792, see *AP,* 49:132; *AP,* 53:4; and *AN* AF II 34, dossier 283, #28.

31. "Réjouissons-nous mon ami, la liberté triomphera! L'égalité planera bientôt! ... Le mois de septembre de cette année sera aussi funeste aux despots et à l'aristocracie que celui de l'année dernière à cette différence je l'espère que ce sera pour la dernière fois" (*AN* AF II 34, dossier 283, #33).

32. *AP,* 77:274.

33. See *AN* AF II 34, dossier 283, #37 for Gregory's reaction to the news that he had been denounced in Paris by Dubois-Crancé and his concern for the repercussions this attack might have on Charles, still active on the Eastern front.

34. "Jamais la calomnie ne m'a aussi âprement poursuivi" (*AN* AF II 34, dossier 283, #30).

35. "Dubois-Crancé répond qu'il avait dû voir avec chagrin, un homme comme Dulac, à la tête d'une colonne où son influence pouvait devenir dangéreuse" (*Gazette nationale, ou Le Moniteur universel,* 12 December 1793).

36. From April to November 1793, the first eight months during which the Revolutionary Tribunal in Paris operated, 508 cases resulted in 159 capital sentences, or a 31% execution rate. Beginning in December 1793, the month in which Charles was arrested, and continuing for the next eight months until the fall of Robespierre and his followers in July 1794, the Revolutionary Tribunal heard 3,524 cases, almost seven times as many as in the first eight months of its operation. These cases resulted in 2,466 executions, an execution rate of 70%, or more than twice the deadly pace of the first eight months. See http://www.justice.gouv.fr/histoire-et-patrimoine-10050/la-justice-dans-lhistoire-10288/le-tribunal-revolutionnaire-22842.html.

37. On these topics, see John Dunkley, *Gambling: A Social and Moral Problem in France, 1685–1792* (Oxford: Voltaire Foundation, 1985); Thomas M. Kavanaugh, *Enlightenment and the Shadows of Chance: The Novel and the Culture of Gambling in Eighteenth-Century France* (Baltimore: Johns Hopkins University Press, 1993); Francis Freundlich, *Le Monde du jeu à Paris, 1715–1800* (Paris: Albin Michel, 1995); Elisabeth Belmas, *Jouer autrefois: Essai sur le jeu dans la France moderne, XVIᵉ–XVIIIᵉ siècle* (Seyssel: Champ Vallon, 2006); and *Jeux de princes, jeux de vilains*, ed. Ève Netchine (Paris: Bibliothèque nationale de France and Seuil, 2009).

38. See my "Accommodation: The Policing of Used Playing Cards in Late Eighteenth-Century Paris," in *Paris, Policing, and Urban Sociability in Eighteenth-Century Paris*, ed. Pascal Bastien, forthcoming in *Oxford University Studies in the Enlightenment*. Freundlich, *Le Monde du jeu*, 73–136, and Belmas, *Jouer autrefois*, 108–86, discuss the social spread of card-playing in Old Regime France.

39. "Un petit jeu ne déconcerte, on est toujours gai, perte ou gain; mais un gros jeu rend sensible à la perte et réduit le joueur souvent à petit train."

40. "Le jeu fait souvent des deux amis deux ennemis."

41. Work on print history and visual culture in eighteenth-century France in the last generation is voluminous. One study I have found particularly useful in the context of playing cards is Richard Taws, *The Politics of the Provisional: Art and Ephemera in Revolutionary France* (University Park: Pennsylvania State University Press, 2013).

42. See the notes on this engraving in *A Kingdom of Images: French Prints in the Age of Louis XIV, 1660–1715*, ed. Peter Fuhring, et al. (Los Angeles: Getty Research Institute and Bibliothèque nationale de France, 2015), 290–91. For a stimulating discussion of similar Anglo-Dutch images of the period, see Dror Wahrman, *Mr. Collier's Letter Racks: A Tale of Art and Illusion at the Threshold of the Modern Information Age* (Oxford: Oxford University Press, 2012).

43. Fried, *Absorption and Theatricality: Painting and Beholder in the Age of Diderot* (Chicago: University of Chicago Press, 1988), 46–53. On Chardin's "house of cards" paintings more generally, see Kate E. Tunstall, "Chardin's Games," *Studies on Voltaire and the Eighteenth Century* 8 (2000), 131–41, and Katie Scott, "Chardin and the Art of Building Castles," in *Taking Time: Chardin's Boy Building a House of Cards and Other Paintings*, ed. Juliet Carey (London: Paul Holberton Publishing, 2012), 36–52.

44. See my "Accommodation."

45. Important collections of eighteenth-century playing cards with verso annotations can be found in repositories in France, the United Kingdom, and North America. The most extensive collection of historical French playing cards is held by the *Cabinet des estampes* in the *BnF*. In the Archives départementales du Rhône (Lyons) one finds a foot-long box (call number 1 J 389) containing eighteenth-century playing cards with many different verso annotations, including business receipts, shopping lists, the laxative recipe, and a surprisingly accurate comparison of Chinese and European demographics in the period. The Prize Papers in the British National Archives contain a cache of cards used as IOUs that were captured from French trading ships. In North America, the Rare Book and Manuscript Library of Columbia University holds the Albert Field Collection of Playing Cards, while the Beinecke Library at Yale University houses the Cary Collection of Playing Cards, both of which contain prerevolutionary French playing cards with various verso annotations.

46. On the cards at the Mazarine Library, see the note by Thierry Depaulis, "Les 200.000 cartes de la Bibliothèque Mazarine," *L'As de Trèfle*, 49 (1992): 4. On Gibbon's cards, see Depaulis and Ulrich Schädler, "Gibbon's Swiss Playing Cards," *The Playing Card*, 45, no. 4 (2017): 209–18.

47. Krajewski, *Paper Machines: About Cards and Catalogues, 1548–1929,* trans. Peter Krapp (Cambridge: MIT Press, 2011), 27–47. See also Judith Hopkins, "The 1791 French Cataloguing Code and the Origins of the Card Catalogue," *Libraries and Culture* 27, no. 4 (1992): 378–404.

48. Recto and verso images of the cards are reproduced, with notes, in Rousseau, *Oeuvres completes*, ed. Raymond Trousson and Frédéric S. Eigeldinger, 24 vols. (Geneva: Slatkine, 2012), 3:601–57; the Queen of Clubs is on 636–37. See also Robert Ricatte, "Un nouvel examen des cartes à jouer," *Annales de la société Jean-Jacques Rousseau* 35 (1959): 239–62.

49. Bert, *Comment pense un savant? Un physicien des Lumières et ses cartes à jouer* (Paris: Anamosa, 2018).

50. Bert, *Comment pense un savant?*, 116–17.

51. Bert, *Comment pense un savant?*, 70–71.

52. My *"Plus de rois, de dames, de valets"*: Playing Cards During the French Revolution," *Oxford University Studies in the Enlightenment*, forthcoming, studies the changing iconography of French playing cards in the revolutionary decade of the 1790s. See also Thierry Depaulis, *Les Cartes de la Révolution: Cartes à jouer et propagande* (Issy-les-Moulineaux: Musée français de la carte à jouer, 1989).

53. This is the definition Gregory provides on the card. The 1762 and 1798 editions of the *Dictionnaire de l'Académie française* both define pederasty as *"Passion, amour honteux entre des hommes"* [passion, shameful love between men]. See these definitions in the ARTFL *Dictionnaires d'autrefois* project, https://artfl-project.uchicago.edu/content/dictionnaires-dautrefois.

54. For an introduction to the history of commonplacing, see Helmut Zedelmaier, "Excerpting / Commonplacing," in *Information: A Historical Companion*, ed. Ann Blair, et al. (Princeton: Princeton University Press, 2021), 441–48. On Lockean commonplacing techniques, see Richard Yeo, "John Locke's New Method of

Commonplacing: Managing Memory and Information," *Eighteenth-Century Thought* 2 (2004): 1–38. On commonplacing in eighteenth-century France specifically, see Élisabeth Décultot, "L'art de l'extrait: définition, évolution, enjeux," in *Lire, copier, écrire*, ed. Élisabeth Décultot (Paris: Editions CNRS, 2003), 7–28.

55. "Recueil," in *Encyclopédie, ou dictionnaire raisonné des sciences, des arts et des métiers, etc.*, ed. Denis Diderot and Jean le Rond d'Alembert, 19 vols. (Paris, 1765), 13:868–70.

56. Darnton, "Extraordinary Commonplaces," *New York Review of Books*, 21 December 2000, 82–87.

57. "Paquet trouvé cacheté ayant une inscription portant ces mots—notes du bon sens" (*AN* AF II 34, dossier 281, #10). The report on the arrest and seizure does not specifically mention the playing cards. An attentive reading of the report suggests that this phrase is the most likely reference to the playing cards seized that day; the other documents swept up were carefully categorized and labeled, but none of them might be accurately characterized as "notes containing good sense."

58. Rosenfeld, *Common Sense: A Political History* (Cambridge: Harvard University Press, 2011), especially Chapter 3, "The Radical Uses of *Bon Sens*." Rosenfeld also argues that during the French Revolutoin, "*bon sens*" came to be associated with a counterrevolutionary, Christian, and populist critique of revolutionary ideology, but it is unlikely that this is the meaning the Dulac brothers intended when one of them labeled their playing cards as a source of "good sense."

59. Rosenfeld, *Common Sense*, 111–15.

60. "Que ce luxe est humiliant pour les pauvres qui manquent de tout! Et par quelle maladie de l'esprit, les hommes qu'il devrait révolter en sont-ils presque toujours éblouis?" Mably, *Des droits et devoirs du citoyen* (Paris, 1789), 36. Playing card annotation at *AN* AF II 34, dossier 284, #31.

61. "L'un donne libéralement et en devient plus riche; l'autre omet par avarice de faire le bien, et il s'appauvrait" (*AN* AF II 34, dossier 284, #73).

62. "Il ne peut y avoir de loi pour punir l'ingrat, l'horreur qui accompagne l'ingratitude fait son supplice. Il faut donner, pour le plaisir seulement d'avoir donné" (*AN* AF II 34, dossier 284, #67).

63. Among works on this topic, see Lynn Hunt, *The Family Romance of the French Revolution* (Berkeley: University of California Press, 1992); Suzanne Desan, *The Family on Trial in the French Revolution* (Berkeley: University of California Press, 2004); and Jennifer Ngaire Heuer, *The Family and the Nation: Gender and Citizenship in Revolutionary France, 1789–1830* (Ithaca: Cornell University Press, 2005).

64. *AN* AF II 34, dossier 283, #70. The draft is undated, but a reference to military deployment in Alsace and threats of *émigré* invasion of France suggests that it was written after the fall of Dumouriez in spring 1793.

65. "Si l'évangile, si la religion ont conservé sur vous quelqu'empire, que les supplications de vos frères ne soient pas vaines. Nous concevons bien que la constitution ne vous convient pas; mais nous ne concevons jamais que vous osiez l'attaquer les armes à la main. Je n'en puis plus. Dieu veuille vous secourir"; *AN* AF II 34, dossier 283, #70.

66. *AN* AF II 34, dossier 283, #59. Their debts included back payments for life insurance, interest on a loan, and the cost to repair a broken window in a house they owned on the island. This discussion of the finances of the Dulac brothers in the early 1790s is necessarily incomplete due to gaps in the archival record, but enough evidence exists to suggest that the brothers had financial problems.

67. *AN* AF II 34, dossier 283, #73 records the 600 *livre "pension alimentaire"* accorded to the brothers by the Haute-Loire government. See *AN* AF II 34, dossier 283, # 9 and #63 on midsummer 1793 claims from Malta; and *AN* AF II 34, dossier 283, #24 on Gregory's claims for back pay from the revolutionary armies.

68. "Nous croyons devoir vous prévenir que ci-devant chevaliers de Malte, nous étions et nous sommes citoyens français, soldats de la liberté, nous préférons ce titre; seul digne de l'homme libre, à ceux de princes dans des contrées asservies. Si nous avons porté plus longtemps cette décoration des préjugés, c'est dans la croyance que l'ordre serait tenu de nous rembourser nos frais de réception" (*AP*, 29:471).

69. "Le virus aristocratique ne possède pas toujours tous les membres d'une même famille—tel père haît la revolution dont les enfants sont soldats de la liberté." *AN* AF II 34, dossier 283, # 15. See also *AN* AF II 34, dossier 283, #14.

70. "Je vous ai reconnu de grandes qualités; ells ne me dissimulait pas vos défauts ... vous me donnez une suffisante preuve que chez vous l'égoïsme n'existe pas seulement dans les emportements de la colère, mais qu'il y éteint la sensibilité." *AN* AF II 34, dossier 283, #22.

71. "À l'abri des soupçons et des calomniateurs, que nulle autre passion que l'amour de la patrie ne nous a pulsé dans la carrière républicaine" (*AN* AF II 34, dossier 283, #25).

72. "La bonne réputation est préférable aux grandes richesses; et l'amitié à l'or et à l'argent" (*AN* AF II 34, dossier 284, #75).

73. "Celui qui se rend maître de ses passions a trouvé le repos que tout le monde cherche" (*AN* AF II 34, dossier 284, #37).

74. "Je sens trop amèrement les fautes, les crimes dont il m'a rendu coupable, pour ne pas reconnaître s'il m'avilait en ce moment" (*AN* AF II 34, dossier 283, #5).

75. "Ma tête, ma chétive tête, m'avais égaré. Le coeur, le coeur est tout par lui seul ... le discernement du bien et du mal appartient peut-être au jugement, et en cela à l'esprit, à la tête. Mais au coeur, au coeur seul est attribué lui seul et donné du sentiment. De ce sublime don vient tous qui nous porte à haïr le mal, et à aimer le bien" (*AN* AF II 34, dossier 283, #46).

76. "Aimez la justice, vous qui êtes le juge de la terre; ayez de dieu des sentiments dignes de lui, et cherchez-le avec un coeur simple" (*AN* AF II 34, dossier 284, #78).

77. "Quel être simple peut vivre sans passions, sans attachements ce n'est point un homme; c'est une brute ou c'est un dieu" (*AN* AF II 34, dossier 284, #117).

78. "Ô mon fils ... ta femme fera ton bonheur, vif, vif pour elle" (*AN* AF II 34, dossier 283, #29).

79. "L'an quatre de notre amour" (*AN* AF II 34, dossier 283, #48).

80. "Tout homme doit à ses concitoyens le récit de sa conduit" (*AN* AF II 334, dossier 280, #27).

81. "Elle vivrait au sein de la République, et moi, qui ai préféré le devoir à l'amour le plus vif comme le plus pure, ma mort me laissa le regret de ne servirait ni la liberté, ni ma femme, celle qui était tout pour moi … La République et ma femme, ou la mort!" (*AN* AF II 34, dossier 280, #27). The final version of this document, only one page in length and without reference to Annette, is at *AN* AF II 34, dossier 280, #31.

82. "Charles ne serait digne ni de vous, ni de lui, s'il fût resté tranquille dans ses foyers. Le bonheur, il ne l'eut même pas obtenu, il n'existe plus là où commence le remords" (*AN* AF II 34, dossier 283, #18).

83. "La tristesse et l'infortune respectent le sommeil et laissent du relâche à l'âme; il n'y a que les remords qui n'en laissent point" (*AN* AF II 34, dossier 284, #110).

84. "Je vous aime plus que je ne pourrais le dire et suis pour la vie votre amie" (*AN* AF II 34, dossier 283, #40).

85. "Je ne suis pas politique, je suis la voix de mon coeur et je ne crains pas quoique vous m'en diriez de me garer en me conduisant … il me serait impossible d'aimer celui qui opprime le faible et l'innocent" (*AN* AF II 34, dossier 283, #38).

86. "Je me suis fait une habitude à n'attendre de la fortune que les coups les plus affreuses, assez philosophe pour croire qu'un homme animé du désir de la gloire peut aisément négliger une femme et ne penser à elle que dans ses moments de loisir, voilà ce qui s'appelle aimer à la républicaine et par conséquent à la Dulac" (*AN* AF II 34, dossier 283, #44).

87. "Le coeur de la femme est plus aimant mais moins ferme que le nôtre; l'absence peut beaucoup sur elle" (*AN* AF II 34, dossier 283, #44).

88. "Imposez silence à vos passions pour interroger votre raison et elle vous apprendra tous les devoirs de l'homme" (*AN* AF II 34, dossier 284, #95).

89. The meaning of her pseudonym, if there was one, is unclear. Perhaps Anne-Claude meant it to be read as "*Annette à l'Inde,*" or "Annette in the Indies," indicating that she was in a place far away from Charles.

90. On the Labro family and their detention in 1793–94, see Paul Fontanon, "Destinée et descendance des jeunes filles nobles recluses à Brioude durant la Terreur," *Almanach de Brioude et de son arrondissment* 81 (2001): 63–101. On Anne-Claude's release in November 1794, see Fontanon, "Les victims brivardoises de la Révolution," *Almanach de Brioude et de son arondissement* 77 (1997): 63. For more on the Labro clan, see also Béatrix de La Rochette de Rochegonde, "La Terreur à Brioude (1793–1794)," *Almanach de Brioude et de son arondissement* 56 (1976): 19–56. I am grateful to Thomas Concy, who searched in vain for traces of an Alinde clan in the Auvergnat archives, then discovered these articles and suggested the compelling "Labro" thesis.

91. There is some confusion about the precise timing of Charles's release from prison and return home. *AN* AF II 34, dossier 282, #29 indicates that twenty-two of his documents were returned to him on 6 Germinal Year 2. Archives de la Préfecture de Police de Paris Ab 308 is a register indicating that Charles was released from prison on 14 Brumaire An 3 (4 November 1794), but as we will see below he was back in the Auvergne no later than mid-September 1794.

92. "Je me suis fais un jeune ami dont de moeurs pures, d'un excellent coeur, digne amant d'une femme digne de lui, plus digne encore de servir une patrie à qui il a tout sacrifié" (*AN* AF II 334, dossier 283, #24). Gregory also mentions his mysterious, unnamed lover in a letter that he wrote to Charles the same day (*AN* AF II 334, dossier 283, #25).

93. For the 1786 marriage act between Espinasse and Saulnier, see *ADPD* 6 E 2161; for the divorce act, see *ADPD* 6 E 113 110. Saulnier did not appear for the divorce hearing on 1 April 1794, in spite of receiving a summons.

94. The original of the Menestier deposition at the *ADPD* has been lost. The account that follows is based on a partial transcription of the document reproduced in Mège, *Le Puy-de-Dôme en 1793*, 191–92.

95. "Il … eut recours à un flacon contenant de l'opium dont on avait usé pour calmer les convulsions fréquentes que la véhémence de ses propos causaient à cette jeune citoyenne dont le nerf est très irritable" (Mège, *Le Puy-de-Dôme en 1793*, 192).

96. The full text of Gregory's message to Gilibert is as follows: "Je t'envoie mon cher Gilibert la clef de l'armoire de chez Dufand [the owner of the auberge] où je te prie d'aller de nuit cherchez les lettres et papiers que je confie à ton amitié. Je t'embrasse en ami. N.C.G. Dulac." The note to Gilibert, as well as the report by the Thiers officials based on their search of the room two days later, are at *ADPD* 63 L6341. Unfortunately, the contents of the armoire were not catalogued and do not appear to have survived.

97. Gregory's death certificate, at *ADPD* 6 E 113 189, confirms the time and place of his death, as well as the method by which he committed suicide. See *ADPD* 6 E 113 110 for the marriage act between Charles and Marie Silvie signed on 20 September 1794.

98. On suicide in eighteenth-century France, see Richard Cobb, *Death in Paris: The Records of the Basse-Geôle de la Seine, 1785–1801* (Oxford: Oxford University Press, 1978); Jeffrey Merrick, "Patterns and Prosecution of Suicide in Eighteenth-Century Paris," *Historical Reflections / Réflexions historiques* 16, no. 1 (1989): 1–53; Patrice Higonnet, "Du Suicide sentimentale au suicide politique," in *La Révolution et la mort*, ed. Elizabeth Liris and Jean Maurice Bizière (Taur: Presses universitaires du Mirail, 1991), 137–49; and Dominique Godineau, *S'abréger les jours. Le Suicide en France au XVIIIe siècle* (Paris: Armand Colin, 2012). While these studies tally cases of suicide by method, age, gender, and class, and offer rich general theses about the phenomenon of suicide in the eighteenth century, too little is known about Gregory's decision to end his life to relate their arguments to his specific case.

99. I have been unable to learn much about Charles's life after his marriage to Marie Silvie, although he appears to have resumed his revolutionary military career. The latest records that I have found are a pamphlet that he published in 1799 attacking a military contractor whom he thought was overcharging the army for cured animal hides (see *Aperçu de la conduite et de la science d'Armand Seguin* [Paris, Year VII], available at *BnF* L27N-18778); and a mention of his service as an artillery captain and commander in the Napoleonic armies in Italy in 1801 and 1802 (Antoine de Bouillé, *Manoires abandonnés*, unpaginated digital version).

100. Anne Claude de Labro married Pierre Jean Luc César, Marquis de Pons de Frugères, on 12 October 1803; her husband was an *émigré* who did not return to France until 1799 (Fontanon, "Destinée et descendance des jeunes filles nobles," 86). See Archives Municipales de Brioude, 1D5 for their marriage certificate. Anne-Claude died in 1845, at the age of 72.

101. Cicero: "Tota philosophorum vita commentatio mortis est"; Montaigne: "Philosopher, c'est apprendre à mourir." I thank my MIT colleague Professor William Broadhead for the translation from Latin.

The Jumbal: Cookies, Society, and International Trade

CHRISTOPHER E. HENDRICKS

M ary Randolph (1762–1828), a member of one of colonial Virginia's most prominent families, published what is arguably the first truly American cookbook in 1824: *The Virginia House-Wife*.[1] Her book emerged out of a well-established eighteenth-century tradition of women collecting recipes and snippets of household advice for their own use and then copying them down to pass along to their daughters. Randolph's first edition of *The Virginia Housewife* (the hyphen disappeared in the fourth edition of 1840) includes more than 430 recipes.[2] In the midst of this remarkable assemblage is a relatively straightforward recipe titled "TO MAKE JUMBALS":

> To one pound of butter and one of flour, add one pound of sugar,
> four eggs beaten light, and whatever spice you like; knead all
> well together, and bake it nicely.[3]

The precise origins of the jumbal, the prototype of the modern cookie, are unclear and speculative. But it developed in Europe during the Middle Ages and had become a baking staple in England by the early seventeenth century. As an example of material culture, the jumbal is rife with historical significance, demonstrating female agency and expression, the introduction and spread in Europe and America of non-native agricultural products, such as sugar and spices from South and East Asia, the development of new trade routes, and the evolution of culinary traditions. Given this, it is possible to use Mary Randolph's simple recipe as an entrée into the history and society of the long eighteenth century.

From her formative years growing up in elite Virginia society, to her surprising and unexpected career as an innkeeper, as well as her fame as a celebrated cook and author of a cookbook, Mary Randolph provides a particularly interesting focal point for this study. The recipes she chose to include in *The Virginia Housewife* grew out of eighteenth-century English traditions as they were transmitted to the North American British colonies and shared between generations of women. Furthermore, she used them to cook both privately and professionally. The focus of this study is not to analyze jumbal recipes in their evolutionary journey or to carefully compare contemporaneous jumbal recipes in all their permutations. Rather, with the confluence of its author's heritage, education, professional career, and ambition, Mary Randolph's simple recipe becomes a perfect springboard for examining larger themes.

In collecting her recipes, Randolph was following in a long tradition among the female members of Virginia's elite families. For generations, women had collected recipes for dishes they learned, created, or simply enjoyed from cookbooks. Frequently, they either bound the pages together or copied them into blank books, often intending to pass them along to their daughters when they got married. Martha Washington inherited such a manuscript from her first mother-in-law, Frances Parke Custis. The pages included late seventeenth-century recipes that Custis probably had copied from her own recipe collection. Washington added to those over the next fifty years, at the end of which she presented a bound copy of the collection to her granddaughter, Nelly Parke Custis Lewis.[4] At least two similar manuscripts passed through the Randolph family, the first dating to the beginning of the eighteenth century and the second assembled by Jane Bolling Randolph in 1743.[5] But in publishing her collection, Mary Randolph broke tradition and stepped into new realms.

Mary, or Molly as her family called her, was the oldest of thirteen children. She and her brothers and sisters were tutored privately, and the girls received training in domestic skills and household management. Molly was well prepared to run a large plantation by 1780, when at the age of eighteen, she married her cousin, David Meade Randolph.[6] While David worked to build a political career, Molly ran their domestic life, overseeing their Presqu'île plantation home at the confluence of the James and Appomattox rivers, supervising forty enslaved servants and managing the household accounts.[7] By necessity she had to be knowledgeable in a broad range of skills, including the mastery and intimate knowledge of food production, preservation, preparation, and presentation. At Presqu'île this included supervising, instructing, and inspecting the work of the enslaved cooks who prepared the meals on a daily basis. Molly explained, "If the mistress of the family will every morning examine minutely, the different departments of her household, she must detect errors in their infant state, when they can be corrected with ease."[8]

Financial difficulties forced the Randolphs to sell their landholdings, including Moldavia, the grand home they had built in Richmond in 1798. His political career in shambles, David pursued interests in coal mining and traveled to Britain in 1808. He stayed for seven years. Meanwhile, Molly made the bold choice of stepping forward to support her family in their dire circumstances and opened a boarding house in rented quarters located on Cary Street in Richmond. For a woman of her social standing, this was a risky move, but her friends supported her, and because of the demand for good accommodations when the General Assembly was in session, she could be extremely selective regarding her guests.[9]

The business was a success and Molly operated her boarding house in at least two locations from 1807 to 1819, even after her husband returned home from Britain. However, the couple eventually decided the time had come to retire, and they moved to the Washington home of one of their sons, William Beverly Randolph. David puttered about working on various projects and spent time across the Potomac at Arlington, the home of their cousins George Washington Parke Custis and his wife Mary Ann Randolph Fitzhugh Custis. Meanwhile, Molly had a project of her own. Having achieved fame as an excellent cook during her time as both a society hostess and an innkeeper, Molly decided to publish a cookbook filled not only with the recipes she had collected over the years, but also with helpful hints regarding the best way to keep a home.[10] If the book was successful, it could help shore up the family finances. But Molly may also have had an ulterior motive. As the Randolphs had no daughters survive to adulthood, this may have been her way of maintaining the tradition, well established in eighteenth-century Virginia, of passing on her culinary knowledge and management skills to the next generation.

Randolph assembled her cookbook, including the jumbal and other cookie recipes, based on years of personal experience. Indeed, she explained in the preface to *The Virginia Housewife*, "The greater part of the following receipts have been written from memory, where they were impressed by long continued practice."[11] Above all, she hoped her recipes and words of advice would have broad appeal. She wrote, "Should they prove serviceable to the young inexperienced housekeeper, it will add greatly to that gratification which an extensive circulation of the work will like to confer."[12] The book was a tremendous success and appealed to the experienced and inexperienced alike. When Martha Jefferson Randolph, who had married Molly's youngest brother Thomas, was assembling a manuscript recipe collection to pass on to her own daughter, she included at least fifty recipes from *The Virginia Housewife*.[13]

When she wrote her book, Mary Randolph was following in a long tradition of female authors dating to the late sixteenth century. In France, male chefs dominated the cookbook trade and wrote for other men, but it was different in England. There, while some of the earliest women writers of cookbooks used male pseudonyms, by the mid-eighteenth century, they began publishing under their own names, albeit discreetly, sometimes only using their initials or inserting their trade cards into the volumes. Later in the century, female cookbook authors in Britain took full credit for their work and sometimes used their reputations for marketing purposes. These later writers tended to be servants, while female authors in the first half of the century had mostly come from the upper classes. The market for these female-authored cookbooks spread among women of all ranks, expanding as literacy increased. In fact, women published around 425 different cookbooks in Britain during the eighteenth century, selling an estimated 531,250 copies.[14]

Only two cookbooks were produced in North America before Randolph's. The first one was an edition of Mrs. E. Smith's *The Compleat Housewife; or, Accomplished Gentlewoman's Companion*, first published in London in 1727. In 1742, William Parks, the editor of *The Virginia Gazette*, printed a version in Williamsburg based on the fifth edition of 1732 and included Smith's recipe for jumbals, which adds a little milk and uses crushed caraway seeds instead of the traditional cinnamon.[15] The book was extremely popular and Park's successor at the press, William Hunter, produced a reprint ten years later. It was the only American-produced cookbook for fifty years.[16] Then, in 1796 Amelia Simmons produced *American Cookery* in Hartford, Connecticut. Simmons is often credited with being the first American cookbook author. The trouble with that assertion is the fact that she copied the majority of the recipes from an English cookbook, Susannah Carter's *The Frugal Housewife* of 1772. Still, the volume sold well, and while she did not include a cookie recipe specifically designated a *jumbal*, Simmons did add what she called a "*butter drop*" cake—essentially, a jumbal recipe using mace and rosewater—that did not appear in Carter's book.[17] There were at least a dozen reprints and pirated editions of Simmons's book prior to 1830, but it was twenty-eight years before another significant cookbook and the first truly American cookbook came out: Mary Randolph's *The Virginia Housewife*.[18]

Randolph had difficulty locating a publisher for *The Virginia Housewife* at first, but it became a bestseller once it appeared. Interestingly, Randolph's name did not appear on the title page of the work, but rather at the end of the preface, where she reverted to the earlier tradition of signing herself with the ambiguously gendered "M. Randolph."[19] The book sold so well that Randolph produced a second edition with "amendments and additions" just a year later and was working on a third edition when she died in 1828.[20] But Randolph's death was not the end of *The Virginia Housewife*. Her son saw the third edition through the press, with Randolph's name finally appearing on the title page as Mrs. Mary Randolph.[21] Then a Baltimore publisher printed editions of the book in 1831 and 1838, and the book moved further north when a Philadelphia publisher came out with a version in 1850. Before the Civil War broke out, at least nineteen editions had appeared.[22] A recipe for jumbals appears in them all.

The English word *jumbal* (which appears in many different variations: jombil, jamble, jumboll, jumbold, jumball, jemelloe, gemmel, jumble) entered into parlance around the turn of the seventeenth century. The *Oxford English Dictionary* dates its first use to Gervase Markham's cookbook, *The English Hus-Wife* of 1615, although an earlier use appears in Thomas Dawson's *The Second Part of the Good Hus-Wives Jewell* in 1597, which includes a recipe called, "To make Jombils a hundred."[23] But the baked good to which the name refers may be even older. According to legend, in 1485, after the last battle of the War of the Roses, soldiers rifling through the detritus of King Richard III's army found his cook's recipe for jumbals. But there does not seem to be any source for this tale before the mid-nineteenth century, so it was probably concocted as a clever marketing ploy by a Market Bosworth bakery outfit.[24] Nevertheless, the longevity of the jumbal is astounding. A recipe even shows up in Irma von Starkloff Rombauer's *The Joy of Cooking,* which first came out in 1931.[25] Interestingly, *jumble* as the term for a mixture of things postdates the cookie and may have originated from the act of blending the ingredients together.[26]

The ancestry of the jumbal may lie in the Middle East, where the proximity to sugar production made the local diet comparatively high in sugar content for the time, although it pales when compared to modern American cookie recipes. Unlike European baked goods, this Middle Eastern precursor was heavily spiced with things like anise seed, caraway seed, coriander, cardamom, saffron, or cinnamon, all of which would have been exceedingly rare and prohibitively expensive for most Europeans during the Middle Ages. In one sense, the jumbal was a traveling cake, meaning that it was meant to keep for extended periods of time, up to a year according to some early accounts. The original crossed into Europe via Spain, thanks to the Moors, and then spread throughout the continent, evolving into the biscuit or cookie. The cookies made their way into Italy where bakers frequently included nuts, usually almonds. These early jumbals were also boiled prior to baking, rather like bagels.[27] The jumbal probably arrived in Britain via France. Its name originates from the Latin word for twin, *gemellus*, via the Old French word, *gemel*.[28] This is a reference to the hoops in which the cookie was originally shaped, which were similar to the then-fashionable gimmal rings.[29]

The jumbal would have been a rather expensive baked good to make, as is evident from examining the list of ingredients that Randolph used in her recipe: flour, sugar, spice, eggs, and butter. However, through probate inventories, widows' allowances, cookbooks, account books, and archaeology, it is easy to determine that these ingredients were readily available in eighteenth- and early nineteenth-century North America.[30] Additionally, American newspapers regularly advertised these precise items. For example, in 1772, John Powell, advertising in the *Virginia Gazette*, announced that he had cinnamon and other spices—the most expensive ingredient on Randolph's list—declaring they were "IMPORTED ... *and to be sold very cheap by the Subscriber who has just opened a Druggist and Apothecary's shop in the Upper End of* Richmond."[31]

The English word "flour" originates from the Old French word, "flur," meaning flower/blossom or fine grain. Interestingly, it was common to spell flour f-l-o-w-e-r until at least the late 1730s, by which time people began to separate the spelling of the two words for clarity.[32] In medieval England, wheat grain had to be boulted or sifted as part of milling to remove the bran, although millers never got their flour to be more than about 80 percent pure. Still, the British referred to this as fine flour and used it when baking premium goods. It would have been significantly more expensive than everyday flour, not only because of the extra labor involved, but also because of the greater quantities of wheat necessary to produce the same volume of finished product.[33] In Virginia, colonists began to experiment with planting wheat in the seventeenth century and by 1750, they were exporting the crop to Europe and the West Indies. Crop failures in Britain and the Seven Years' War led Parliament to drop import restrictions and begin buying Virginian wheat in such quantities that it caused wheat prices to rise back in Virginia.[34] But while fine flour would have been relatively expensive in eighteenth- and early nineteenth-century Virginia, it paled in comparison to the next two ingredients, both of which had to be imported.

Sugar used to be so rare in Europe that, until the tenth century, Europeans reserved it for medicinal uses. During the Middle Ages, Arabs, who had been growing and processing sugar for some time, began to adopt milling and refining techniques developed in India and expanded production throughout the Middle East, parts of North Africa, Sicily, and Southern Spain.[35] In medieval England, sugar was comparable in cost to tropical spices. But the price of sugar began to drop after the Portuguese introduced sugar cane to Brazil and established sugar plantations. By 1540, they were operating almost three thousand cane-grinding mills.[36] Once the sugarcane was milled, the resulting liquid simmered for hours, while workers skimmed off impurities. When thickened, the resulting molasses was poured into molds where it crystallized. These molds were cone shaped so that the crystallized sugar could be removed more easily. The highest-grade sugar came in loaves five inches tall. Loaves that came out of larger molds did not crystallize as well. But mid-range sugar could come in loaves as tall as three feet. Sugar was so valuable it was stored in locked caskets. When people required sugar, they cut pieces off the sugarloaf using sharpened tongs called sugar nips.[37] The sugar could be served in lumps or ground to various degrees of fineness in a mortar and pestle.

Sugar production spread quickly into the Caribbean, where the Spanish, French, Dutch, and English all pursued its development, and during the colonial period, the British even brought limited production to mainland North America as far north as Maryland.[38] Accompanying the spread of sugar and other cash crops came the explosion of the African slave trade after European diseases decimated Native populations and the number of indentured servants could not meet labor demands. By the time Brazil ended slavery in 1888, some 12.5 million people had been ripped from their homes and brought to the New World.[39]

The expansion of sugar into the Caribbean had a profound effect on the development of the Atlantic economy in the eighteenth century. Plantation owners clearcutting the islands in order to put every acre of viable farmland into production with cash crops like sugarcane, cocoa, and coffee relied on the importation of goods from the mainland colonies to feed and house the enslaved population. American colonists shipped rice produced in South Carolina and Georgia, wheat from Pennsylvania, New York, and New Jersey, and fish and timber from New England to the islands. New Englanders, desperate for items to exchange for finished products and other imported goods such as tea, transformed the molasses and sugar they bought in the Caribbean into rum to trade with Britain.[40]

The use of sugar expanded dramatically in Britain during the eighteenth century, with consumption per capita growing 400 percent from 1709 to 1809. By the middle of the eighteenth century, sugar passed grain as the most valuable trade good, making up 20% of all European imports. This was a boon to both Britain and France, whose colonial possessions produced 80 percent of the sugar that Europe imported at the end of the century. For the second half of the eighteenth century, sugar was Britain's most valuable import. The growing availability of sugar (and the resulting decrease in its price) meant that sugar use spread to all classes, and intake exploded, causing, among other things, a dramatic increase in the number of cavities, along with a decline in nutrition as poorer families in Britain substituted sweetened tea for healthier foods.[41] In eighteenth-century Virginia, sugar was considered one of the "status-laden foods" and remained relatively expensive until the U.S. Civil War, although its use was widespread.[42]

As noted earlier, bakers used a variety of spices to flavor their jumbals, including cinnamon. Much as they did with sugar, Europeans originally reserved cinnamon for medicinal uses, but quickly began using it as a meat preservative and to flavor food. Arab traders brought the spice, a tree bark native to Southeast and South Asia, overland into Europe. To maintain a monopoly, they closely guarded the secrets of the cinnamon trade. Portuguese and Spanish explorers were desperate to discover the origin of the valuable product. In fact, Columbus took samples of what he mistakenly thought was cinnamon back to Madrid after one of his voyages. Finally, around 1518, Portuguese traders discovered cinnamon in Sri Lanka, conquered the island, and enslaved the inhabitants, forcing them to produce the spice until the Dutch defeated them in 1638. The Dutch controlled the European cinnamon trade for the next century and a half until 1784, when the British defeated them in turn during the Fourth Anglo-Dutch War and seized control of the island. But by the turn of the nineteenth century, cinnamon production had spread to other parts of the world and the spice was no longer the expensive, rare commodity it had once been.[43]

The value of eggs is a little harder to pin down. When the jumbal arrived in Europe, chicken ownership among peasant households was fairly common. One fourteenth-century record shows peasants owning an average of three to five hens, each of which would have produced between seventy and one hundred eggs a year.[44] As time passed, eggs became increasingly important in the ordinary person's diet and by the eighteenth century, eggs were a common staple in both British and American households among members of all classes. In eighteenth-century Virginia, the "proliferation of country stores" grew to such an extent that products such as eggs and butter became "widely available" to "rural consumers of lesser status."[45]

Butter was by far the most common ingredient found in Randolph's recipe, spreading to all classes during the Middle Ages, particularly in England. It was particularly popular among the peasantry as a cheap source of nutrition, but the elite relished how cooking dried meats in butter could restore their flavor, particularly during the winter months.[46] By the eighteenth century, butter was a huge industry. In fact, butter was such an important part of the Irish economy that exporters established a Butter Exchange in Cork in 1770. Barrels of ancient Irish butter, which were often buried in peat bogs for aging, frequently show up in archaeological digs.[47]

As mentioned previously, the jumbal may have originated as a traveling cake. Because it had no leavening agents, it could be packed and stored for extended periods of time. But it also got very hard, thus necessitating its original shape as a ring or series of connected rings, which could be broken into edible-sized portions relatively easily. By the late sixteenth century, jumbals were being formed into sometimes quite elaborate pretzel-like shapes. Indeed, they were frequently referred to as "knots."[48] Such sculpted baked goods were both commonplace and celebrated in Elizabethan England, and there was room for bakers to be quite creative in terms of shape. The so-called Bosworth Jumbles were purportedly made in S shapes.[49]

Various scholars working in women's and gender studies, such as Susan Frye, are currently exploring women's expression through sewing and handwriting in Renaissance England. Frye argues that a woman's repertoire of thread knots and needlework stitches, as well as her skill in forming letters, served as an indication of her class and taste.[50] Wendy Wall connects these same handwriting and sewing skills to the culinary arts. She posits that although women in elite households oversaw cooks who did most of the actual food production, they frequently took charge of preparing desserts themselves, drawing on their skills to create individualized marzipan and baked goods.[51] Of course, such self-expression made eighteenth-century women increasingly complicit in the "commerce and colonialism that kept people of African descent enslaved as laborers in sugar cane fields in the Americas," whether they knew it or not.[52] It is ironic that while Britain ended the transatlantic slave trade in 1807, through its colonial possessions and the purchase of cotton and other staples from the American South, it helped to perpetuate the institution of slavery.

An interesting thing happened to the jumbal in North America. By the middle of the eighteenth century, while jumbal recipes on both sides of the Atlantic remained remarkably similar, the jumbal lost its shape. While British bakers were still busy knotting their jumbals, in the British American colonies, many recipes directed bakers simply to dollop the batter into rough lumps, similar to dropped biscuits. In a handwritten recipe for jumbals included in her collection, Martha Washington instructed bakers to roll out and cut the dough into shapes, or as she put it, "roule them into rouls & make them in what forms you please."[53] In her recipe, Mary Randolph trimmed down the instructions even further, just telling her readers to "knead all well together, and bake it nicely."[54] This could be due to a change in expectations in terms of how soon the jumbals would be consumed (immediately, rather than in the distant future). But it could also be that Americans were already increasing the amount of sugar they used in their recipes and beginning to add leavening agents, which would take the jumbal on to its next evolutionary stage, transforming it into the sugar cookie.

What all is imbedded in the jumbal, this staple of the eighteenth century and essentially the proto-cookie? It tells a story of the development of crop production and foodways. Its ingredients reveal a complex history of cultural exchange, labor systems, human bondage, colonialism, and the development of an elaborate system of trade involving five continents. Its baking provides insight into questions of social class, gender roles, and female agency. As recipes for jumbals were passed hand to hand and generation to generation, they followed social traditions and aided in the creation of an important genre: the cookbook. And with the development of the British tea ceremony in the eighteenth century, the jumbal made the perfect accompaniment: a tea cake ready at a moment's notice when guests arrived. This seemingly simple recipe for a cookie grants an unusual entrée into many aspects of life in the long eighteenth century and provides an answer to an important question: Is it truly possible to understand the eighteenth century without knowing what it tasted like?

A modern adaptation of Mary Randolph's "TO MAKE JUMBALS"

Cinnamon Jumbals

Makes 2 to 3 dozen

Jumbals are cookies or teacakes, traditionally formed in a love knot, but they can be rolled and cut in any shape.

3½ cups flour

1 cup of sugar

1 teaspoon cinnamon

2 large eggs

¾ cup melted butter

Preheat an oven to 350 degrees.

In a large bowl, sift together the flour, sugar, and cinnamon.

In a separate bowl, beat the eggs and stir in the butter. Knead this egg mixture into the flour mixture to form a dough.

On a floured surface, roll the dough out very thin. Cut in desired shapes and bake 10–12 minutes, until brown.[55]

Notes

1. Randolph, *The Virginia House-Wife: Method is the Soul of Management* (Washington: Davis and Force, 1824).

2. Karen Hess, "Historical Notes and Commentaries on Mary Randolph's *The Virginia House-wife*," in *The Virginia House-wife by Mary Randolph: A Facsimile of the First Edition, 1824, Along with Additional Material from the Editions of 1825 and 1828, thus Presenting a Complete Text* (Columbia: University of South Carolina Press, 1984), 227; Randolph, *Virginia House-Wife*, iii–viii.

3. Randolph, *Virginia House-Wife*, 157.

4. *Martha Washington's Booke of Cookery and Booke of Sweatmeats*, ed. Karen Hess (New York: Columbia University Press, 1995), 3, 7.

5. Katharine E. Harbury, *Colonial Virginia's Cooking Dynasty* (Columbia: University of South Carolina Press, 2004), xiii–xvi.

6. Harry Haff, *The Founders of American Cuisine* (Jefferson: McFarland, 2011), 38.

7. Haff, *The Founders of American Cuisine*, 38; Janice Bluestein Longone, "Introduction to the Dover Edition," in Mary Randolph, *The Virginia Housewife or, Methodical Cook: A Facsimile of an Authentic Early American Cookbook* (New York: Dover Publications, 1993), 7; Hess, "Historical Notes," xi, xl.

8. Randolph, *The Virginia Housewife*, iii–iv.

9. Ann T. Keene, "Randolph, Mary," *American National Biography*, ed. John A Garraty and Mark C. Carnes, 24 vols. (New York: Oxford University Press, 1999), 18:132; Jonathan Daniels, *The Randolphs of Virginia* (Garden City: Doubleday & Company, 1972), 197, 202; Samuel Mordecai, *Richmond in By-Gone Days* (Richmond: George M. West, 1856), 97.

10. Sue J. Hendricks and Christopher E. Hendricks, *Old Southern Cookery: Mary Randolph's Recipes from America's First Regional Cookbook Adapted for Today's Kitchen* (Guildford: Globe Pequot Press, 2020), 37–39.

11. Randolph, *Virginia Housewife*, iv.

12. Randolph, *Virginia Housewife*, iv.

13. Hess, "Historical Notes," viii–ix.

14. Gilly Lehmann, *The British Housewife: Cookery Books, Cooking and Society in Eighteenth-Century Britain* (Blackawton: Prospect Books, 2003), 61–66.

15. Smith, *The Compleat Housewife: or, Accomplish'd Gentlewoman's Companion* (Williamsburg: William Parks, 1742), 73.

16. Janice B. Longone and Daniel T. Longone, *American Cookbooks and Wine Books, 1797–1950* (Ann Arbor: Clements Library, 1984), 1; Eric Quayle, *Old Cook Books: An Illustrated History* (New York: Brandywine Press, 1978), 131–32.

17. Simmons, *American Cookery, or the Art of Dressing Viands, Fish, Poultry and Vegetables, and the Best Modes of Making Pastes, Puffs, Pies, Tarts, Puddings, Custards, and Preserves, and All Kinds of Cakes, from the Imperial Plumb to Plain Cake. Adapted to this Country. And All Grades of Life* (Hartford: Hudson & Godwin, 1796), 36; Susannah Carter, *The Frugal Housewife or Complete Woman Cook* (London: F. Newbery, 1772), vi–vii.

18. Hess, "Historical Notes," xix–xx; Longone and Longone, *American Cookbooks*, 1–2; Quayle, *Old Cook Books*, 138.

19. Randolph, *Virginia House-Wife*, i, xi.

20. Randolph, *The Virginia House-Wife*, 2nd ed. (Washington: Way & Gideon, 1825), i.

21. Randolph, *The Virginia House-Wife*, 3rd ed. (Washington: P. Thompson, 1828), i; Margaret Husted, "Mary Randolph's *The Virginia Housewife*: America's First Regional Cookbook," *Virginia Cavalcade* 30, no. 2 (1980): 82.

22. John L. Hess and Karen Hess, *The Taste of America* (Columbia: University of South Carolina Press, 1989), 89; Haff, *Founders*, 37–38, 40–41.

23. "Jumbal/jumble, n.," *OED Online*; and Thomas Dawson, *The Second Part of the Good Hus-Wives Jewell* (London: Edward White, 1597), 19–20; and "Jumble (cookie)," *Alchetron*, https://alchetron.com/Jumble-(cookie). Sources sometimes mistakenly credit the recipe to the first part of Dawson's work, which appeared in 1585. See, for example, Regula Ysewijn, "Jumbles on the Battlefield," *Miss Foodwise—Celebrating British Food and Culture*, https://www.missfoodwise.com/2017/04/jumbles-boiled-biscuits.html/; and Juan Alejandro Forrest de Sloper, "Bosworth Field," *Book of Days Tales*, https://www.bookofdaystales.com/tag/bosworth-jumbles/.

24. "Bosworth Jumbals," *The Foods of England Project*, http://www.foodsofengland.co.uk/bosworthjumbels.htm.

25. Ania Kleczek, "Spiced Jumbals (Early American)," *Holly Trail*, https://hollytrail.com/2017/09/03/spiced-jumbals-early-american/.

26. "Jumble, n.1," *OED Online*; "Jumble (cookie)," *Alchetron*.

27. Bertrand Rosenberger, "Arab Cuisine and Its Contribution to European Culture," in *Food: A Culinary History from Antiquity to Present*, ed. Jean-Louis Flandrin and Massimo Montanari, trans. Albert Sonnenfeld (New York: Columbia University Press, 1999), 219–20; "Sugar Cookies: Jumbles & American Sugar Cakes," *The Food Timeline*, https://www.foodtimeline.org/foodcookies.html#sugarcookies; "Jumbles—The First Cookies?" *Plate & Pencil*, https://www.plateandpencil.com/blog/recipes/jumbles-the-first-cookies.

28. "Gemel," *OED Online*.

29. "The Gimmal Ring," *Arthur's Home Magazine* 20 (1862): 283–84.

30. Lorena S. Walsh, "Consumer Behavior, Diet, and the Standard of Living in Late Colonial and Early Antebellum America, 1770–1840," paper presented to the Institute of Early American History and Culture, Williamsburg, Virginia, 25 September 1990, 1.

31. *Virginia Gazette* (Purdie and Dixon edition), 10 September 1772, 2. Powell advertised a similar list of merchandise the next year. See *Virginia Gazette* (Purdie and Dixon edition), 17 June 1773, 3, and *Virginia Gazette* (Rind edition), 17 June 1773, 2.

32. "Flour," *OED Online*.

33. "Medieval Flour and Pastry," *Oakden*, https://oakden.co.uk/medieval-flour-and-pastry-article/. For a general history of flour production, see Fran Gage, "Wheat into Flour: A Story of Milling," *Gastronomica* 6, no. 1 (2006): 84–92.

34. Gaspare John Saladino, "The Maryland and Virginia Wheat Trade from its Beginnings to the American Revolution," (Master's thesis, University of Wisconsin, 1960), 1, 3, 13, 124–25; Walsh, "Consumer Behavior," 12.

35. Sidney W. Mintz, *Sweetness and Power: The Place of Sugar in Modern History* (New York: Penguin Books, 1986), 30; J. H. Galloway, "The Mediterranean Sugar Industry," *Geographical Review* 67, no. 2 (1977): 179–81.

36. Antonio Benitez-Rojo, *The Repeating Island* (Durham: Duke University Press, 1996), 93.

37. Mintz, *Sweetness and Power*, 49; Meghan Budinger, "All About Sugar Cones," *Lives & Legacies: Stories from Kenmore and George Washington's Ferry Farm*, https://livesandlegaciesblog.org/2018/12/13/all-about-sugar-cones/; Richard S. Dunn, *Sugar and Slaves: The Rise of the Planter Class in the English West Indies, 1624–1713* (Chapel Hill: University of North Carolina Press for the Institute of Early American History and Culture, 1975), 188–96; Michael J. Stoner, "Codrington Plantation: A History of a Barbadian Ceramic Industry" (Master's thesis, Armstrong Atlantic State University, 2000), 23–30.

38. Mintz, *Sweetness and Power*, 32–35.

39. "Trans-Atlantic Slave Trade—Estimates," *Slave Voyages*, https://www.slavevoyages.org/assessment/estimates.

40. For a detailed exploration of colonial goods and trading patterns, see John J. McCusker and Russell R. Menard, *The Economy of British America, 1607–1789* (Chapel Hill: University of North Carolina Press for the Institute of Early American History and Culture, 1985).

41. Mintz, *Sweetness and Power*, 67; McCusker and Menard, *Economy*, 144–45, 158–59; Clive Ponting, *World History: A New Perspective* (London: Chatto and Windus, 2000), 510; Joseph Imorde, "Royal Cavities: The Bitter Implications of Sugar Consumption in Early Modern Europe," Getty Center, https://blogs.getty.edu/iris/royal-cavities-the-bitter-implications-of-sugar-consumption-in-early-modern-europe/.

42. Walsh, "Consumer Behavior," 5, 30–31.

43. "Cinnamon: A History as Rich as its Flavor," *SPICEography*, https://www.spiceography.com/cinnamon/; Sheldon Greenburg, "Spices and the Shaping of Our World," in *Food in Motion: The Migration of Foodstuffs and Cookery Techniques*, ed. Alan Davidson, 2 vols. (Stanningley: Prospect Books, 1983), 2:45.

44. Philip Slavin, "Chicken Husbandry in Late-Medieval Eastern England, c. 1250–1400," *Anthropozoologica* 44, no. 2 (2009): 43, 52.

45. Walsh, "Consumer Behavior," 11.

46. Harold McGee, *On Food and Cooking: The Science and Lore of the Kitchen* (New York: Scribner, 2004), 33, 589.

47. David Kearns, "Irish Bog Butter Proven to be '3500 Years' Past its Best Before Date," *University College Dublin*, https://www.ucd.ie/newsandopinion/news/2019/march/14/irishbogbutterproventobe3500yearspastitsbestbeforedate/.

48. Dawson, *Second Part*, 19–20; Marissa Nicosia, "Knots, Cookies, and Women's Skill," *Folger Shakespeare Library*, https://shakespeareandbeyond.folger.edu/2019/12/03/knots-cookies-recipe/.

49. Sloper, "Bosworth Field."

50. Frye, *Pens and Needles: Women's Textualities in Early Modern England* (Philadelphia: University of Pennsylvania Press, 2010); Nicosia, "Knots, Cookies, and Women's Skill."

51. Wall, *Recipes for Thought: Knowledge and Taste in the Early Modern English Kitchen* (Philadelphia: University of Pennsylvania Press, 2005); Nicosia, "Knots, Cookies, and Women's Skill."

52. Nicosia, "Knots, Cookies, and Women's Skill."

53. *Martha Washington's Booke of Cookery*, 348.

54. Randolph, *Virginia House-Wife*, 157.

55. This recipe is taken from Hendricks and Hendricks, *Old Southern Cookery*, 197.

Raw Movement: Material Circulation in the Colonial Eighteenth Century

SARAH R. COHEN, CYNTHIA KOK, BRITTANY LUBERDA, AND SOPHIE TUNNEY

The eighteenth-century world economy played out on an oceanic stage. Maritime trade networks circulated a vast range of extractive goods including mahogany, silver, cotton, ginseng, sugar, and other earth-drawn substances. Swifter ships, strategic ports, the increasing use of enslaved labor, and an insatiable desire for the rare and curious on the part of a swelling consumer market supported the systematic distribution of raw materials in bulk.[1] While the concept of global transportation in the eighteenth century applies broadly to trade, immigration, and exploration, the focus of this study is the transformation of raw materials into commercial products under European colonialization.[2] Here, "raw" materials signifies "immature; unripe" goods exchanged in bulk.[3] Either crude or partially processed, such substances underwent months-long voyages before arriving at a port of trade. In eighteenth-century parlance, as recorded by Samuel Johnson, bulk describes both a quantity—as in "magnitude; size"—and "the main part of a ship's cargo; as, to *break bulk*."[4] Once bulk raw materials arrived at a port, they were subject to various forms of further refinement as manufacturers prepared them for the agricultural, commercial, and luxury sectors. Using the maritime global supply chain of the eighteenth century as an organizing principle, this article examines how four raw materials—silver, seeds, shells, and sugar—interplay with the political, scientific, artistic, and social concerns operative in a number of European countries.

Although European control of the extraction and commodification of each of the materials addressed here has deep historical roots, the eighteenth century offers a particularly useful site for critical inquiry. By this point, the commodity chain of global circulation had reached unprecedented heights of profiteering and sophistication, yet at the same time was revealing severe points of fracture and inadequacy. From the point of view of our respective raw materials, we each critically examine a case study of such paradoxes for the insights it yields into the quandaries and potential gains at stake in the European market for globally sourced and manipulated raw substances. Some materials successfully moved across the globe, often supported by Indigenous knowledge of geography or cultivation, while others were blocked by the Europeans' inadequate understanding of their material composition or the most suitable mode of transportation. In still other cases, the Atlantic Revolutions deeply disrupted the movement of raw materials that fed and financed European powers, returning the exchange of materials to the Indigenous communities that had produced them for centuries. Various forms of environmental depletion and devastation further interfered with productivity in the latter part of the century and led to ecological and social crises that continue to escalate.

Equally consequential are the still unresolved, global injustices resulting from slavery. All the raw materials considered here relied on coerced, enslaved labor at some stage of the supply chain. In Viceregal Peru, silver mining was carried out in part by unpaid Indian workers; in Mauritius and Cayenne, enslaved Africans and disenfranchised Native peoples harvested spice plants; in India and Indonesia, Indigenous laborers were forced to dive for pearl shells; and the sugar plantations of the West Indies were staffed by enslaved African people kidnapped and then shipped across the Atlantic through the same interconnected networks as the raw materials. Examining diverse materials at different states of the global trade network thus reveals many points of instability in the control of resources, technical knowledge, long-term sustainability, and, ultimately, the desires and responses of consumers. Each stage of the transportation of raw material highlights how matter and knowledge did not, in fact, flow seamlessly as objects circulated around the globe.

Building upon the rich and growing bodies of scholarship that address the eighteenth-century circulation of global commodities, this study uses a collaborative approach to address four raw elements, each examined by one of us at a particular point in its global journey.[5] We are dividing the circulation cycle into four stages: Extraction, Transportation, Manipulation, and Reception. In "Extraction," Brittany Luberda surveys the history of drafted labor and environmental exploitation in the silver mines of Potosí, in what is now Bolivia. This mine was a leading source of the world's specie, powering a bullion economy from its sixteenth-century beginnings to the end of the mine's real productivity. By the eighteenth century, Viceregal control of production had become obstructed by the skills and ingenuity of Native Andean miners, who conducted their own extraction and refining before silver was delivered to maritime ports. In the second section, Sophie Tunney examines the logistics of transporting live plants on a six-month journey across temperature zones. Beset by salty waters and unwelcome pests, this journey showcases France's repeated attempts to introduce spice plants into its Caribbean and South American colonies. Studying the movement of these plants provides vital insight into France's expanding (and faltering) colonial ambitions, both before and during the French Revolution. In "Manipulation," Cynthia Kok considers the trial-and-error process through which the "raw" becomes "polished." Kok traces how Netherlandish artisans transformed mother-of-pearl from a by-product of pearl harvesting into a desirable luxury object in its own right. Experimenting directly with mother-of-pearl's material capabilities, makers adapted established craft skills, such as metalworking techniques, and tested new methods, like chemically delaminating an oyster's layers in order to sculpt the shell fragments into resilient snuffboxes for luxury use. In "Reception," Sarah Cohen examines the refining of sugar into a white, powdered form suitable for *sucriers* [sugar shakers] that were used in French dining and display. Centering her analysis on two silver objects that take the form of enslaved people hauling harvested sugar cane, Cohen charts how the coerced labor of cultivation was unexpectedly visualized as a luxury product. Crafted in silver ultimately sourced from colonial exploitation in the Americas, the French *sucriers* demonstrate European efforts to extract, refine, and deliver the raw matter they cultivated through colonial exploitation, while at the same time exposing how human beings and their labor were instrumentalized for the ultimate purpose of European consumption.

In linking four separate histories of raw goods extracted, transported, and subsequently refined for European use in the eighteenth century, our essay seeks to explore the numerous ways in which human intervention complicated the consumer desires that prompted the global journeys of various resources. Colonial control, coerced labor, regulation of foreign territories, and a plethora of inadvertent mishaps, discoveries, and exposures point toward a far less coherent picture of raw goods and their subsequent refinement than a traditional Eurocentric survey might imply. In adopting a form of scholarly writing that directly reflects our composite subject, we offer a model for analyzing the transmission of eighteenth-century material culture that was itself multi-layered, interactive, and fraught with colonialist ambition.

Extraction: Mining Independence in Potosí

The *Cerro Rico*, or "Rich Hill," rises 15,750 feet high on a desolate plateau, casting a shadow over the city of Potosí. Until 1545, when Diego Gualpa, a Native Andean, told Spanish colonists about veins of silver below the mountain's surface, the land lay undisturbed.[6] Gualpa's knowledge marked the beginning of colonial-funded mass mining in this remote area of the Viceroyalty of Peru, which grew to be one of the largest metropolises in the world by the seventeenth century. Inspired by the hope of personal gain or forced to work for global profit, Native and foreign merchants, miners, enslaved workers, royal emissaries, and religious figures from as far away as Baghdad descended upon the bustling international center of silver. For about 250 years, the local inhabitants and seasonal laborers dug into the mountain for ore, refining enough to provide 20% of the entire amount of silver in circulation between 1545 and 1810.[7] By 1573, the city's coat of arms touted: "I am rich Potosí, Treasure of the world, I am the king of all mountains and envy of all kings."[8] Dominican friar Domingo de Santo Tomás, however, offered a dissenting voice among the celebrations of unimaginable wealth. He authored a harrowing account in 1550, describing the moral and mortal consequences of mining: "there was discovered a mouth of hell, into which have entered … a great quantity of people, which by the greed of the Spaniards they sacrifice to their god, and these are some silver mines they call Potosí."[9] For several centuries, the impressive peak or "mouth of hell" was carved by a labor system comprised of Native Andean draftees, enslaved Africans and Asians, and free miners and mine owners, both male and female. Santo Tomás's early denunciation of extraction's atrocities proved prescient, as the massive amount of Potosí silver that was transformed into objects and specie across the globe was tainted with the cruelties of enslavement and exploitation, until the means of extraction were largely reclaimed by Native Andean entrepreneurs in the eighteenth century.

Between 1545 and 1650, Potosí's silver extraction transitioned from what began as a largely Native enterprise into a draft system of enforced labor orchestrated by the Spanish Viceroyalty. Mining technologies in the Andean Mountains were well-developed by the time of the colonists' arrival as part of the highly advanced metallurgical practices of pre-Hispanic Native societies. Under the Inka Empire, mining was often done by *yanacona*, members of a servant class who undertook paid work as part of a reciprocal relationship with a governing member of society. At Potosí, the first two decades of production primarily came from mines that were owned or overseen by Native people and excavated by *yanacona* or *mingas*, paid day laborers.[10] Under this Indigenous leadership, ore was refined on the mountainside using perforated ceramic vessels called *guayra*, which harnessed wind power.[11] *Yanacona* extracted enormous amounts of silver, which attracted the attention of empires as far away as China and the Middle East. By the 1570s, however, the easily accessible veins were depleted and the *guayra* refinement process became less lucrative.

To continue profitability, Francisco de Toledo, fifth Viceroy of Peru, enacted a law in 1573 capitalizing on another longstanding pre-Hispanic social-labor structure called *mita* in Quechua. Traditionally a system of communal corvée labor, *mita* was reconfigured into the legally enforced servitude of Indigenous people.[12] Because *mita* obligations were tied to the local community, Toledo divided and relocated 1,077,695 Native Andeans into regional groups based on 614 (often bastardized) *ayllus*, or kin groups.[13] These regional groups owed tribute to the Viceregal government and were required to send draft laborers, or *mitayo*, to mine Potosí. The number of workers demanded varied in relation to their proximity to the mountain; a group from the Canchis Province, which is about 600 miles from the mountain, for example, sent one seventh of their male labor force between the ages of 18 and 50 each year.[14]

The working conditions were extraordinarily dangerous. The typical itinerary for a *mitayo* included a two-month journey to Potosí for four months of labor. Upon arrival, a miner was assigned to a mine owner, usually Spanish, or a Native overseer. The miner accessed his workplace via a common tunnel and a series of ladders, sometimes descending 750 feet below the surface.[15] Mine owner Luis Capoche described the physical toll of removing ore in 1585: "The Indians take out the ore, amounting to some *arrobas* [approximately 50 lbs] in blankets belonging to them, tied around the chest and the ore [borne] across their shoulders, they climb up three by three, and the one in front carries a candle in one hand by which they see where they are climbing and descending, as the mines are dark and without any visibility."[16] The work was completed in weekly shifts, with periods of rest between descents and rotations between mining and refining.[17] A second-hand illustration of mining in Potosí that was published in Frankfurt in 1601 emphasizes the workers' plight, showing the backbreaking weight, minimal light, thin bodies, and laborious heaving of heavy rock up step-by-step [see Figure 1]. Around the mountain, bags of ore were carried on the backs of llamas to mills. In addition to extracting ore, a *mitayo* might

Figure 1. Theodor de Bry, *Mining in Potosí,* engraving, published in *Historia Americae sive Novi Orbis,* Part IX, 1601. Creative Commons.

be assigned to one of the mills, where the ore was crushed and underwent a mercury amalgamation process. Distilling silver with mercury required the labor of either *mingas* or *mitayos* who used their feet to mix mercury, copper sulfate, iron, salt, and pulverized ore in a large box.[18] Exposure to these toxic materials (and similar ones encountered within the mine and during the crushing of ore) slowly poisoned Native workers on top of the malnourishment and exhaustion they were already experiencing. News of the unforgiving exploitation of Indigenous communities by Spanish colonizers in the "mouth of hell" followed the silver as it circulated, serving as propaganda against the Habsburg Empire and castigating its rulers for their crimes against humanity.

Drafted *mita* labor was not unpaid, but the compensation was meager and so required workers to bring food for the season or to sell untaxed, unrecorded silver extracted by additional labor on the weekends.[19] The bustling market of Potosí was almost as famous as the mine itself. There, secondary trade was crucial to the preservation of some measure of Indigenous culture and autonomy under colonial rule. Situated in the Plaza del Metal (also known as the *Gato de las Indias,* or market of Indian women), the market was comprised of a vibrant square and the adjoining streets, which were packed with storefronts and peddlers engaged in the exchange of silver or ore for food, supplies, llamas, oil, honey, coca, and *chica* [corn beer]. There was also a flourishing market for silver itself, and individual miners were able to use whatever they earned on top of their *mita* obligation to augment their standard of living, buy out their servitude, or support their families. Potosí's population was always predominantly Indigenous, and the year-round market offered a place for community and economic opportunity through subeconomies of credit and transfer. As Jane Mangan has argued, Potosí's massive urban market flourished outside of the Spanish colonial economy, and its reliance on kin and cultural networks helped propel Indigenous and a few African vendors (many of them women), to success in small-scale trade that was collectively influential.[20] Wealth-building through the market over the course of the seventeenth century led to increased freedom for draftees and a subsequent labor shortage for colonial overseers.

Although various reforms to the *mita* labor system were proposed by multiple Viceroys, it continued to be the primary, albeit failing, source of colonial silver extraction into the eighteenth century.[21] In addition to the labor shortage, economic upheavals and floods disrupted productivity and interrupted the global supply of silver. For example, in the 1640s, a Potosí corruption scandal rocked the international market when a special Royal inquisition into mine administration revealed that the Potosí mint was engineering the export of vast quantities of pesos, the weight and purity of which had been falsified. The cross-continental scheme, which stretched from the local assay officers to the port officials, resulted in a ban of Potosí coins in Antwerp and Genoa; coins were similarly rejected at ports in India and Southeast Asia.[22] Silver was recalled across the Spanish Empire, and the credit market in Potosí itself crumbled. The global outrage toward Potosí's fraudulence destabilized colonial-led mining operations. However, despite these perceptions and a depleted supply of ore, fantasies of an impending revival attracted Spanish and foreign investment in the excavation of silver well into the eighteenth century. The speculation surrounding the South Sea Company is just one of the better-known examples of these hopes.

Of the forces that revived Potosí mining in the early eighteenth century, however, the expansion of independent mining by Native-born laborers was paramount.[23] *Mitayos* were able to buy out their obligations. While at first this provided a welcome influx of cash to mine owners, it also decreased the number of drafted laborers entering the mines each year. At the start of the eighteenth century, *mita* labor had decreased to fewer than 4,000 workers, from a height of 14,000 workers in the late sixteenth century.[24] From the *mitayos*, a new class of entrepreneurial miners emerged called *kajchas*.[25] *Kajchas* were Native Andeans who had profited by working additional hours in the mines and no longer owed tribute. The *kajchas* established their own mills or worked with Native owners of makeshift, horse-powered mills, called *trapiches*, where they refined ore.[26] The success of this independent movement is illustrated in the growing ranks of registered *kajcha*, who numbered over 2,000 in an important revolt by Native workers in 1751–52, and in their receiving official recognition.[27] In 1754, the bank began to record two columns of transactions, the guild members of Spanish or Creole descent and the *kajchas, trapiche* owners, and other free laborers. The resources of Potosí continued to tempt the Spanish crown, and successive Bourbon kings cultivated the local economy by lowering taxes and attempting to reform the banking and refining systems. In truth, though, obtaining the best ore and thus the biggest profits depended primarily on Andean will and expertise (it is estimated that while *kajcha* miners only extracted 5% of the ore, those particularly rich deposits yielded some 40% of the silver).[28]

Because of this increasing Native wealth and freedom, by the eighteenth century, Potosí was a highly blended society. For many, loyalties to *allyus* no longer governed their actions, and different networks fostered trade relations, marriages, and community. The city was now a place where families of all classes had lived for generations. While Potosí was still a Spanish colony, the many cultures drawn in by mining (voluntarily or otherwise) helped the city develop a geographic identity marked by its hybridity with Andean practices. A silver tray attributed to a Potosí silversmith working in the second quarter of the eighteenth century (a rare survival of a silver object actually made in the region) shows that hybridity permeating art [see Figure 2]. The tray's corners are ornamented with Native or *mestizo*—biracial—musicians. The bands feature Baroque European flowers and foliage, but also faces of a sort found in colonial Andean design.[29] The stippled stigmata in the center represent the local Jesuit order, but the blood dripping from the wounds resembles Andean textiles. Indeed, this very combination of liturgical and secular themes itself indicates a location cognizant of its many sources.

Potosí never again reached sixteenth-century levels of output, but its miners generated a steady supply of silver for more than two hundred years until the mine was exhausted in the early decades of the nineteenth century. Ingots or coins were transported by mule or llama over mountains to ports, where they were distributed to wholesale markets in Goa, Manila, Seville, Lyons, and Antwerp, after which they were melted and fashioned into specie or luxury objects. Potosí remained a source of capital for the global Spanish Empire until Simón Bolívar reached the city in 1825 and the *mita* was abolished as part of Bolivia's gaining independence. At the Cerro Rico, speaking for the whole of South America, Bolívar pronounced: "Standing here on this silver mountain of Potosí, whose rich veins were Spain's treasury for three hundred years, I must declare my belief that this material wealth

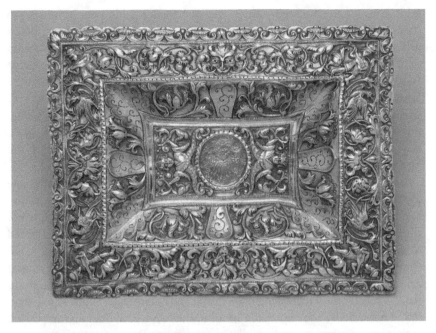

Figure 2. Tray, attributed to an anonymous silversmith working in Potosí, Bolivia, c. 1725–50, silver, 39.4 × 30.5 cm. The Baltimore Museum of Art, 2020.9.

is as nothing compared with the glory of bearing the ensign of freedom."[30]

From the mountain to the sea, transportation from port to port was key to eighteenth-century global exchange. In the next section, Sophie Tunney examines the complexities of moving plants across the sea. As hundreds of trees and seeds set sail for the Indian Ocean, colonial knowledge was tested against weather, pests, and rot. Our exploration of the supply chain continues as she traces the disparities between French imperial aspirations and botanical reality.

Transportation: The Global Journey of Potted Plants and Seeds between l'Ile de France and Cayenne

News spread in Paris in 1783 that botanists from the Jardin des Pamplemousses [Garden of Grapefruits], on l'Ile de France (present-day Mauritius) had successfully acclimatized and reproduced nutmeg and clove. Since 1715, France had attempted to secure a variety of spices from the regions surrounding the Indian Ocean and to transport them back to the metropole.[31] According to Sarah Easterby-Smith, France finally acquired a few live specimens of nutmeg, clove, and cinnamon in the 1770s. The location of these plants was kept under "lock and key."[32] Now that the garden on l'Ile de France had reproduced the spice plants, more could be sent to Paris. But the head-gardener on l'Ile de France, Jean-Nicolas Céré, had a different plan.[33] He hoped to diversify the island's agricultural production by introducing French fruits and vegetables for everyday use. In exchange for these spice plants, Céré requested that the Jardin du Roi [Garden of the King] send a large shipment of plants and seeds to l'Ile de France. The size of Céré's request was unprecedented.[34] Transporting hundreds of potted plants and seeds across the globe required extensive logistical planning. After five years of negotiations, Céré's proposal gained the support of the Navy, the monarchy, and the Jardin du Roi.

Many historians in the field of colonial botany have argued that the eighteenth century saw an important expansion in botanical exploration and extraction. The editors of *The Botany of Empire in the Long Eighteenth Century* contend that the "roots of a global botany of empire have been traced to the 1670s with the emergence of sugar plantations run on slave labor in the Caribbean and South America," which coincided with "'state-run colonial science' in France at the Académie Royale des Sciences and the Jardin du Roi." Accordingly, "increasing plant traffic and commercial exploitation were made possible by the expansion of administrative networks and improved technologies of transportation."[35] The editors use Bruno Latour's theory of accumulation in order to understand this vast movement of plants from the periphery to the center. But when we trace the history of botanical specimens as they moved from one colony to another, the evidence highlights severe ruptures in their transportation, accumulation, and the transfer of knowledge concerning them. By following the movement of plants between Paris, l'Ile de France, and Cayenne (on the northeastern coast of South America), we can see that botanists and state officials had lofty ambitions for their expeditions. However, the material history of these plants suggests staggering amounts of loss. The eighteenth century can thus be better understood as seeing both an expansion in botanical aspirations *and* a history of repeated failures and disruptions.

In February 1788, César Henri Guillaume de La Luzerne, the minister of the Navy, instructed M. Pouget, Intendant des classes de la Marine [the civil servant who oversaw naval conscription], to "confer with M. Thouin on the plan to send plants from the Jardin du Roi to l'Ile de France, and to bring them back, as well as other objects of the same kind."[36] André Thouin, head gardener of the Jardin du Roi, then became one of the central organizers of the expedition. With growing institutional support, de la Luzerne, Pouget, and Thouin wrote back and forth through February, March, and April of 1788 to figure out how to get all the necessary provisions and materials ready to ship plants and seeds from Paris to l'Ile de France.

When Céré originally wrote to the Navy, he requested a large shipment of fruit trees and other agricultural plants and seeds that could be of use to the island's population and economy. After discussing the request at length with both Pouget and de la Luzerne, Thouin drafted a proposal that encompassed 217 different species of plants, including almond trees, cherry trees, garlic bulbs, and artichokes.[37] Thouin clearly supported Céré's desire to expand the island's food supplies by importing a variety of different edible plants.

While the organizers publicly discussed the shipment of potted plants and seeds to l'Ile de France, a second portion of the expedition was secretly being planned. In exchange for these plants, Céré agreed to ship to Cayenne a variety of spice plants, including nutmeg, pepper, cinnamon, and clove.[38] On the eve of the French Revolution, France was attempting to create a new industry in their Caribbean and Atlantic colonies. If successful, it would disrupt the Dutch monopoly over spice production by first bringing these spices to Cayenne and then distributing them to French plantations across the Caribbean.

Thouin needed the specimens he was shipping to survive the six-month journey to l'Ile de France. As a result, he proposed a new method for packing trees and smaller plants. He argued that live plants needed space to grow during the voyage and light and air to prevent rot. Accordingly, he assembled a list of what should guarantee the successful transport of these specimens, writing "they will occupy boxes of 4 feet long by 2½ feet wide and about 4 feet high. The perennials will be easily contained in two grilled crates 3 feet long by 2 feet wide and 18 inches high."[39] Thouin and the other organizers hoped that with this design, the trees and seeds would survive the trip. But bringing the plants to the Indian Ocean was only half of the battle. Once they made it to the colony, the trees and seeds needed to acclimatize to their new environment, which depended on Céré and his team of gardeners.

Once the crate's design was approved, the organizers turned their attention toward hiring a gardener to accompany the plants at sea. Thouin knew that if these plants were to make it to l'Ile de France, they would require constant care from the moment they left Paris until they arrived at the Jardin des Pamplemousses. Thouin immediately thought of Joseph Martin, who was an apprentice-gardener at the Jardin du Roi. If something went wrong, and the plants were under duress, Martin might be able to save the plants from just rotting away.

On 28 March 1788, the plants were ready to leave. Thouin gave Martin detailed instructions for the thirty crates of plants, alongside the 107 "barrels" filled with bushes, smaller plants, and seeds.[40] Thouin provided guidance regarding how to care for the plants, but also gave Martin detailed instructions on his larger mission of securing spice plants for Cayenne.[41] As Martin was going all the way to l'Ile de France, he could acquire plants from the entire region and bring them back to France. This endeavor would take over a year to accomplish, and they hoped it would mark France's entrance into the spice trade.

As soon as Martin arrived on the island on 26 July 1788, he and the crew transported the plants to the royal garden and, with the help of Céré, began the acclimatization process. On 7 August 1788, Martin wrote to Thouin: "The plants have arrived in a good state. There is only the 5th box where lots have perished. … The majority of the potato roots ate up all the earth, so much so that there was no subsistence left for the other plants, which have died."[42] By 7 August 1788, Martin reported back that "451 chestnut trees sprouted, several grew 12 to 15 inches long and about 400 almond trees" have been planted.[43] With the new crate design, Thouin's detailed instructions, and Martin's care, the journey from Paris to l'Ile de France was an immense success.

As soon as Martin and the plants arrived in July 1788, Céré prepared a collection of spice plants for Cayenne, Martinique, and Saint-Domingue. Half of the spice plants were to be sent in 1788 and the other half would accompany Martin when he sailed from l'Ile de France to Cayenne. Since the Jardin du Roi had lived up to its end of the deal, Céré gave the green light for this transfer of plants. On 7 August, the first installment of spice trees was loaded onto a ship heading for the Caribbean.[44] However, a botanist was not accompanying this shipment, making it less likely that the plants would survive the journey. And, in a letter written on 19 May 1789, Martin alerted Thouin that this shipment of clove and nutmeg had indeed arrived in very poor condition: "Three expeditions in a row, we have sent them useless things."[45] Even with improved crate designs and careful packaging, the spice plants rotted away before they could arrive in Cayenne. The careful planning of the Jardin du Roi proved useless without a gardener on each leg of the expedition.

For the rest of 1788, Martin began the preparations for his own trip to Cayenne. He loaded the ship with more spice plants, including nutmeg, clove, and pepper, that had recently arrived from India. After the plants were all on board, they set sail for Cayenne on 6 March 1789. Immediately after departure, the plants were attacked by an army of rats. Martin was forced to make quick decisions on how best to relocate the crates. He writes, "I had to bring the pepper crates down to the other bridge because of these sad and destructive animals. They cut three pepper plants and continue to destroy the crates."[46]

When the ship finally landed in Cayenne on 15 May 1789, the majority of the plants had been destroyed. The plantation owners greeted them and asked that they unload and distribute the spice trees. Martin lamented that "these colonists desire most particularly nutmeg and pepper that we brought them in small numbers."[47] Martin did not specify how small those numbers were, after the immense loss of plants that had occurred during the voyage to Cayenne. The distribution of spice plants in Cayenne proved immensely disappointing, with most plantation owners left unsuccessfully clamoring for more.

After dropping off the plants and seeds destined for Cayenne, Martin and the crew then set sail for Martinique, Saint-Domingue, and finally Le Havre. The voyage from the Caribbean to France again involved severe loss. Martin wrote, "The plants are in a sorry state. They were damaged by the rats, which remain on board, they devastate us all. You will see much evidence of this when they arrive in Paris."[48] By the time the ship landed in Le Havre, the collection of "foreign" plants for the Jardin du Roi had been almost entirely destroyed. Martin arrived in Paris on 23 August 1789 with the remnants of the plants that he had collected over the previous year.[49] The results spoke for themselves: Martin only brought back eighty-eight species of plants, many in the form of seeds, which was vastly disappointing both for the Jardin du Roi and for the government's imperial ambitions. What ultimately made it to Paris was a mere fraction of the 217 species (and thousands of specimens) had been sent out to l'Ile de France.

In 1790, Martin was sent back to Cayenne to help plantation owners produce spice plants. This expedition ultimately resulted in the creation of clove and pepper nurseries in French Guiana. This process took several years, but when the transplantation and reproduction finally worked, it yielded thousands of clove and pepper trees.[50] Between 1791 and 1793, Martin distributed over 7,144 clove trees in Cayenne, as well as 525 pepper plants. But the success of this new endeavor was not the result of his labor alone. During the French Revolution, the Jardin du Roi de Cayenne was closed. The New Colonial Assembly seized monarchical land and Martin became the director of the Gabrielle Plantation.[51] The plantation grew over 5,000 clove trees using enslaved labor. France's newly renamed Jardin des Plantes [Garden of Plants] was directly involved in the running of a plantation that connected botany to the most brutal institution of the French Empire. By 1802, Martin planned to send over three thousand potted plants to the Jardin des Plantes. After years in Cayenne, his mission had succeeded. When Martin and his collection of plants set sail for France in May 1803, his ship was captured by the British. Martin was imprisoned and his collection of plants was sold. While he ultimately did make it to France, he arrived empty-handed, for the second time.

Transporting botanical specimens during the eighteenth century was a risky enterprise. Thouin's correspondence, now housed at the Muséum national d'histoire naturelle, is filled with a myriad of similar accounts. Botanists angrily wrote to Thouin about captains of ships refusing to take crates of botanical specimens. Gardeners ran across cities in France searching for missing plants only to discover them rotting away in the customs bureau. When foreign plants and seeds arrived, gardeners often did not have the knowledge to properly care for the specimens. By tracing the movement of plants on individual expeditions, we can see, almost in real time, the messy process of colonization and colonial extraction. These letters are filled with accounts of unreliable shipping techniques, highlighting the contrasts between the aspirations of empire and the messy reality on the ground.

While transporting live specimens between continents remained a conundrum, other, more stable materials regularly arrived in Europe and became integrated into local crafts. Focusing on mother-of-pearl in the Low Countries, Cynthia Kok examines how access to new resources prompted a culture of experimentation. Removed from its native context, mother-of-pearl became a malleable material on which European craftspeople could test different techniques and project their ideas. Her work highlights the ingenuity and flexibility of makers, as they transformed the raw into the refined.

Manipulation: Mother-of-Pearl Boxes in Netherlandish Craft

The rise of the Dutch East India Company [Verenigde Oost-Indische Compagnie or VOC] brought once-rare resources, like mother-of-pearl, to Europe in bulk. While mother-of-pearl was already a valued material in northern Europe, it was much less accessible prior to 1600 and primarily appeared in religious carvings. VOC control of pearl fisheries gave makers across Europe a chance to experiment directly with unprocessed nacre and learn—via hands-on manipulation—how to use its unusual properties. Although craftspeople in the Netherlands already had some experience working with mother-of-pearl, by the eighteenth century, the material had become integrated into the domestic landscape of the Netherlands in the form of objects like buttons, fans, and snuffboxes as makers came to more fully understand nacre's capabilities.

Mother-of-pearl constitutes the body of many types of shells, including both nautiluses and pearl oysters. Unlike nautilus shells, which could not be farmed, mother-of-pearl in the form of *Pinctada margaritifera* or *Pinctada maxima*—two types of oysters found throughout the Indo-Pacific—was easily accessible as a by-product of the pearl trade [see Figure 3]. Coastal communities on the Indian subcontinent and in what is now Indonesia had

Figure 3. *Pinctada margaritifera* shell, inside and out. Didier Descouens. Creative Commons.

farmed pearl oysters long before European merchants established imperial outposts in those areas. Writing in the late sixteenth century, Jan Huygen van Linschoten observed that pearls were brought up "by divers twenty or thirty fathoms [roughly 35 to 55 meters] deep under the water [where they] grow in the oysters on the bottom of the sea" surrounding Sri Lanka.[52] Pearl divers would stay in the water for up to half an hour at a time, bringing up four or five hundred shells per day.[53]

The process of pearl extraction was dangerous and violent, both for the (frequently enslaved or otherwise coerced) pearl divers and for the environment. Dutch traders relied heavily on local knowledge and labor to gather the pearls, yet only allowed the divers limited agency. VOC officials like the Dutch commander at Jaffnapatnam considered forcing "four good pearl divers with their tools and implements" to travel from India and Ceylon to the Banda Islands (upwards of 3,500 miles east) in search of an exploitable pearl bank.[54] Additionally, pearls were an intermittent resource that took time to develop; trading companies' prioritization of resource extraction and profit exposed pearl oyster banks to the possibility of overfishing—and risked disturbing a vulnerable ecosystem.[55] Between 1722 and 1790, the years covered by the 55 surviving volumes of the Bookkeeper-General of the VOC's colonial administrative center in Batavia (present-day Jakarta), the VOC transported just over 373,000 pounds of mother-of-pearl from Batavia to the Netherlands.[56] Extant ship manifests, inventories, and advertisements mention "barrels of mother-of-pearl [*tonnen parelmoer*]" alongside "crates of tea [*kisten thee*]" arriving in Amsterdam.[57] In 1749, for example, the *Amsterdamse Courant* specified that the ship *Tolsduyn* had 3,000 pounds of mother-of-pearl in its cargo.[58] Once trading ships arrived in Amsterdam, makers could purchase mother-of-pearl wholesale at sites like the East India House and the Amsterdam Exchange.[59]

The extensive labor behind pearl and mother-of-pearl production was obscured to European consumers as pearl oyster shells underwent further processing in the workshop of European makers. The shells are covered in a dull yellow or brownish outer "skin" (*periostracum*), which craftspeople had to chemically strip and polish away to access the inner pearly layer. The 1743 *Dictionary; or, General Treatise of Various Medicines* describes how oysters formed pearls and mother-of-pearl with an incremental building up of nacre: the material is "produced by natural additions ... of very thick and shiny layers ... in the manner of onion skins, which afterwards have hardened."[60] At the microscopic level, these layers are actually aragonite platelets laid down in parallel waves and held together with an organic binder. This structure of semi-translucent platelets not only accounts for the iridescence of mother-of-pearl, but also the material's flexibility, strength, and impermeability.

Early modern engagement with mother-of-pearl illustrates how direct handling of material shaped how people learned about unfamiliar resources. Recent art historical scholarship has turned toward a deeper investigation of artistic understanding of materials and their significance.[61] In *The Body of the Artisan*, Pamela Smith coined the phrase "artisanal epistemology" to discuss the embodied—and so unwritten—knowledge that craftspeople possessed about their materials.[62] Mother-of-pearl craftspeople needed to work with the shell in order to gain a deep familiarity with its unusual properties; they developed their embodied knowledge through direct experimentation. By working closely with the raw material, these makers began to understand nacre's capabilities and limits, as well as how it could be usefully manipulated.

While makers often preserved the spiral formation of nautilus shells, they were more willing to cut and reassemble the more plentiful oyster shells.[63] In his 1734 *Locupletissimi Rerum Naturalium Thesauri Accurata Descriptio* (a thesaurus of animal specimens based on his own collection), Albertus Seba describes mother-of-pearl as a natural resource that local makers transformed into art. In addition to oyster shell specimens, the *Thesaurus* includes engravings of twenty-two carved shell roundels. The text accompanying this plate acknowledges that the mother-of-pearl is sourced from the Indies, but also emphasizes the work of the craftsperson in converting the raw material into a usable object. By delaminating and polishing the shell, the maker reveals the "sheen of silver" and transforms the shell from a "dirty brown" container for pearls into an object "remarkable for the beauty of the engravings with which they have been adorned"—that is, *made* remarkable by the craftsperson.[64]

Not only is mother-of-pearl visually striking, its unusual flexibility and chemical stability made it suitable for personal handheld objects.[65] In the process of delaminating and polishing, makers also learned that the shell was malleable enough to cut and carve without shattering. By the eighteenth century, artisans like Norbert Heylbroeck specialized in engraving flat panels of mother-of-pearl that were often later assembled into small boxes [see Figure 4]. Heylbroeck inscribed the panels of the box with complex figural scenes depicting an allegory of art and mythological figures, including Galatea, Venus, and Neptune.[66] He then blackened the engravings with ink

Figure 4. Norbert Heylbroeck, snuffbox, c. 1750–60, mother-of-pearl, gold. Museum of Fine Arts, Boston. Photo: © 2023 Museum of Fine Arts, Boston.

or charcoal to make the lines more visible and signed the base of the box "N. Heÿlbrouck Fecit. Graveur de sa Majesté, de la Monnoÿe A Bruges." A variety of similar boxes survive, with some lids retaining a shell shape and others cut into round or octagonal plaques. Some featured elaborate bas-relief carving and blackened engravings—often depicting a biblical or mythological scene, but many were unsigned and undecorated, suggesting that makers offered these boxes at a range of price points.

Despite the growing popularity of mother-of-pearl, no professional organization developed to regulate mother-of-pearl workers. Many carvers trained as gold- or silversmiths. Metal itself was a popular material for small boxes; brass and copper boxes presented an affordable alternative to silver, for those who wanted one.[67] Metalsmiths would engrave box lids with shallowly carved decorations, similar to printing plates. Jan Bernhard Barckhuysen, whose plaques are represented in Seba's *Thesaurus*, officially worked as an engraver at the Gelderse Mint in Harderwijk.[68] Heylbroeck, similarly, was nominated to be mintmaster in Bruges in 1749 (although he was transferred to the Mint in Brussels a decade later after being accused of counterfeiting).[69] Makers like Barackhuysen and Heylbroeck adapted their metalsmithing skills, using burins, hammers, and chisels to carve and engrave on shell.[70]

In addition to connections to metalsmithing, mother-of-pearl plaques must also be situated in the context of a broader interest in experimenting with the capabilities of materials. Unlike metal, mother-of-pearl is chemically stable: the material has no taste or smell that could contaminate the contents of a box, which was particularly important in the case of snuff. Snuff was often scented with oils and it was essential to limit its exposure to air in order to maintain the powder's potency and fragrance.[71] Not only was the polished iridescent mother-of-pearl visually striking, its inert materials protected the box's contents from the environment without reacting with them.

Other materials with comparable plastic qualities include whale baleen, horn, and tortoiseshell. As early as the seventeenth century, the States General in the Netherlands granted makers exclusive patents to experiment with such materials to create airtight, waterproof containers.[72] Like mother-of-pearl, baleen, horn, and tortoiseshell were all durable, waterproof, and chemically inert. Additionally, they were moldable when heated. Horn, for example, was boiled or placed in hot embers until the layers could be prised apart. The layers would then be immediately pressed between hot metal plates in order to make flattened sheets before they were cut it into objects like lanterns, combs, and cutlery.[73] Baleen, similarly, was shaped into boxes, frames, medallions, and other small decorative objects.[74] While mother-of-pearl usually still required a metal frame, horn and baleen could be glued together to create a container without any risk of tarnishing. Such surviving examples feel remarkably like modern oil-based plastics: durable and stable enough to protect their ephemeral contents and to withstand regular contact.

Although not heat moldable, mother-of-pearl was likewise valued for its flexible durability. In the eighteenth century, these intimate, handheld mother-of-pearl boxes were part of daily rituals, integrating the foreign material into everyday life. Such boxes were not only markers of fashionability, but also sites of encounter between people and their increasingly globalized material worlds, in which both makers and consumers thought carefully about the qualities they could expect (or demand) of natural resources.

Underlying European access to raw mother-of-pearl, however, were exploitative labor practices and immense environmental damage that continue to plague modern economic structures and global supply chains.[75] Although hidden behind a polished façade in the case of mother-of-pearl snuffboxes, the same elements of European trading companies' abusive approach to acquiring global resources are visualized—and even glorified— in other arenas, such as the sugar casters made in the form of African laborers that are discussed in the following section. Examining these casters, Sarah Cohen sheds light on the complex relationship between raw materials, ornamentation, and power that underlay the European extraction of natural resources.

Reception: Sugar, Silver, and Enslaved Labor Staged for the French Elite

Employed sparingly in Europe until the early modern era, refined sugar gained increasing prominence on elite dining tables in the sixteenth and especially the seventeenth centuries, reaching an apogee around the turn of the eighteenth century, when its properties as a sweetener came to highlight a meal's final course or a separate collation of fruits and confections.[76] Inseparable from the rise of sugar within the economies of international trade in Europe was the Atlantic slave trade: in France, whose primary source of sugar was its colony of Saint-Domingue (present-day Haiti), the trade in enslaved persons swelled directly in tandem with the commerce in sugar through the 1730s and beyond.[77] The business of buying and selling human beings for enforced labor was, indeed, so intertwined with the business of buying and selling sugar for European consumption that the steep rise in sweetened desserts in French cuisine between the mid-seventeenth century and the late eighteenth century could simply not have occurred without the concomitant escalation in enslaving Africans.[78] But because all of the steps involved in harvesting and producing sugar, apart from some of the most elaborate refining processes, were carried out in the distant island colonies,

Figure 5. Claude II Ballin (attrib.), pair of sugar casters, c. 1730–40, silver. Louvre, Paris. Photo: © RMN - Grand Palais / Art Resource, NY.

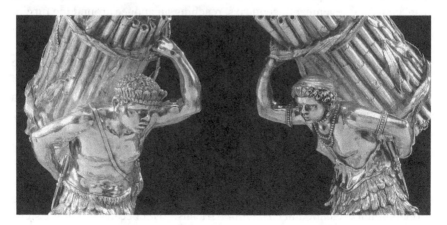

Figure 6. Detail of Figure 5.

such interdependency, to say nothing of the coerced labor it entailed, was largely invisible on the French table.[79]

A startling exception to this invisibility may be found in a pair of silver sugar casters that depict a man and woman laboring beneath bundles of sugar cane, as if physically "delivering" their sweet crystals to the elite dining table [see Figures 5 and 6]. Almost certainly commissioned by Louis-Henri, duc de Bourbon, they would have appeared amongst the duke's many other worldly goods on display at the château of Chantilly in the 1730s.[80] The figures would have been identifiable as an African man and woman through their carefully modeled physiognomies, which reflect incipient French understandings of racial types. Their bodies are cast in solid silver, glistening as they strain beneath their bundles of realistically portrayed cane. These hollow bundles are, in fact, the sugar canisters themselves, pierced at the top to allow the powdered sweetener to be dispensed. Weighing over four times the royally decreed limit for silver sugar casters (or *sucriers*), the casters also depart notably from other examples of this kind of luxury tableware, whose baluster design typically references their placement and use on the table, rather than the source of the product they contain [see Figure 7].[81] Indeed, while many *sucriers* in the early eighteenth century joined other condiment containers as part of table centerpieces (or *surtouts*) these two large figures were clearly designed to occupy their own place on a dessert or collation table.[82]

Although, unusually, the casters carry no maker's mark (or *poinçon*), Gérard Mabille has attributed them to the royal metalsmith Claude II Ballin, a renowned designer of silver figural *surtouts* and tableware, and has assigned them a tentative date of 1730-40, a time when Ballin was active in this genre and the duc de Bourbon himself was greatly expanding his collecting and commissioning enterprises.[83] With their bundles of cane dispensing actual sugar, their sculpted physiques seemingly well adapted to labor, and their gleaming silver surfaces, the duc de Bourbon's sugar casters emblematize the interconnected global trade in cultivated commodities and human beings that was galvanizing the French economy in the 1730s. The *sucriers*' high level of visual refinement, which complemented the ultra-purified sugar they proffered, translates blunt economic realities into modern French "taste," pleasing eye and palate alike.[84] Indeed, visual design was coming to be as important as flavor when the *officier* (the elite household's dessert steward) composed the sensory spectacle that constituted this aspect of dining.[85] Shine was especially important: since the later seventeenth century, silver had been typically used in elite settings not only for the luxury baskets and trays on which fruit was decoratively stacked, but also for the *sucriers* that furnished the sugar, the granular, reflective properties of which were themselves appreciated as part of the show, especially when illuminated by

Figure 7. Nicolas Besniers, pair of sugar casters, 1728–29, silver. Metropolitan Museum of Art, New York. Photo: © Metropolitan Museum of Art / Art Resource, NY.

candelabras positioned on the dessert tables for nighttime meals.[86] Indeed, elaborately modeled and molded sugar sculptures, a fixture of elite European table displays in the early modern era, shared much in common with the cast silver centerpieces and other gleaming tableware that were becoming newly fashionable in the first third of the eighteenth century.[87]

The laborer-casters quite literally embodied this multi-faceted, glittering symbiosis between sugar and silver, while also revealing contemporary European assessments of the Black African body as an aesthetic object whose shine signaled its status as a prized commodity. In his "New Division of the World According to the Types or Races of Men," which appeared in the *Journal des Sçavans* in 1684, François Bernier characterized the African race as exhibiting, in addition to dark skin, wooly hair, thick lips, and short, flat noses, a shiny and polished glow of the skin, enhanced by teeth "whiter than ivory" and oral cavities "red as coral."[88] Such references to costly and ornamental artifacts are displayed in Jean-Marc Nattier's portrait of the duc de Bourbon's sister, Mademoiselle de Clermont, in the Orientalizing role of a "Sultana" [see Figure 8].[89] Bracketing the diverse group of darker-skinned

Figure 8. Jean-Marc Nattier, *Mademoiselle de Clermont, Princess of the Blood, as a Sultana, Served by some Slaves*, 1733, oil on canvas. Wallace Collection, London. Photo: By kind permission of the Trustees of the Wallace Collection, London / Art Resource, NY.

"slaves" who serve their white mistress are two figures whom Bernier would have identified as African: their dark, shiny skin shows off to advantage the glow of the pearls they wear and hold, while Nattier makes sure to show us the ivory white teeth of the attendant on the right.[90] In the *sucriers*, it is silver that simulates the gleam of polished skin and refined sugar that epitomizes its commodified value.[91]

At the château of Chantilly, to which the duc de Bourbon had retreated following his dismissal as Prime Minister to Louis XV in 1726, the caster-laborers would have uniquely enhanced the duke's display of his own scientific and worldly knowledge through his extensive collections of globally sourced natural wonders and imported luxury goods, above all Japanese porcelain.[92] The laborers' costumes, drawn largely from print culture, signaled their dual geography in the European imagination: both figures wear the feather skirts familiar from personifications of "America," including a feather crown and bow and arrows on the part of the male figure, while the female figure wears beads and elegantly worked arm bracelets which probably were supposed to conjure up the idea of gold, a commodity long associated with Africa.[93] Combined with their physiognomies that would have appeared distinctively "African" to the duke and his guests, their realistically portrayed hauling of sugarcane, and, above all, the actual sugar they dispensed, the caster-laborers would have assumed a modern aura enhanced by the doubly commodified gleam of their surfaces.[94]

Produced at just the moment when France was beginning to rapidly expand its symbiotic trade in enslaved persons and sugar, the *sucriers* embody a concomitant artistic transition from courtly spectacle to elite domestic encounter. As Meredith Martin and Gillian Weiss have discussed, spectacles staged in the court of Louis XIV featured both actual enslaved men (most often the so-called *esclaves turcs*, or captive Ottoman Turks) and hired staff performing as "slaves" in order to physically enact royal authority on both land and sea.[95] In 1683, the duc de Bourbon's great-grandfather, Louis, prince de Condé, had produced in his apartments at Versailles a lavish masquerade in honor of the king that included a collation of elaborate fruits served by twelve *officiers* dressed "en Maures" [as Moors].[96] Two actual *esclaves turcs* meanwhile sat across the room in decorative chains, thus blurring the distinction between real and simulated bondage to the great amusement of the court.

By contrast, spectacles of consumption staged by eighteenth-century nobles, including the duc de Bourbon at Chantilly, highlighted pastoral characters and picturesque imagery through a lighter form of pageantry whose emphasis upon surface effects is at once complimented and ruptured by the silver *sucriers*. To welcome the duc de Bourbon's new wife, Caroline de Hesse-Reinfels, to the château of Chantilly in 1728, the duke's Master of Ceremonies arranged a long succession of performing villagers, gardeners, guardians of the Menagerie, and other pastoral folk to present the young bride with fruits, live animals, and prepared meats staged as a movable "*fête galante.*"[97] When, a few years later, the *sucriers* became part of the permanent display of luxury exotica at Chantilly, the enslaved workers they depict, theatrically clothed as "Indiens," in effect joined this procession, dispensing the super-refined sweet product of the shimmering cane they bear on their backs. But by revealing the coerced labor of humans forced into service as just another form of commodity, these *sucriers* exposed what had previously been masked in French display culture. It is perhaps no wonder that the *sucriers'* immediate European successors, porcelain sugar bowls ornamented by relaxed Black servers gesturing or lounging playfully, retained the association between the Black body and sugar, while at the same time suppressing any implications of work, let alone physical distress [see Figure 9].[98]

Figure 9. Franz Anton Bustelli, pair of sugar boxes, Nymphenburg Porcelain Manufactory, c. 1760, hard-paste porcelain. Metropolitan Museum of Art, New York. Photo: © Metropolitan Museum of Art / Art Resource, NY.

The silver *sucriers*, strangely poised as they are between high-end luxury product and the brutal reality of sugar production by enslaved Africans, may well be explained by the interests of the duc de Bourbon himself, who, in addition to his fascination with collecting and imitating the products of foreign lands, also held successive posts as vice-protector and vice governor of the French *Compagnie des Indes*, in which he also had significant financial holdings for a while.[99] But when viewed through the larger perspective of global trade, these unusual objects also reveal a paradox at the heart of the luxury market: the conflicted position of sugar in elite French dining—at once redolent of foreign trade and bent on refining away its own "raw" origins and the coerced labor its production entailed. Although almost certainly intended to be displayed with pride by their worldly owner, the *sucriers*, like the other commodities examined here, reveal the instability of human interventions in the process of extracting, transporting, transforming, and ultimately consuming global products for a European market.

Concluding Remarks

The diverse material histories of silver, seeds, shells, and sugar presented here are just a few examples of the ways in which eighteenth-century Europeans sought to transform raw mineral and organic matter from elsewhere in the world into products consumable at home. The problems and paradoxes each venture entailed—political, environmental, technical, ideological—offer multiple points of departure for further inquiry into the complexities of the exploitation, transportation, manipulation, and interpretation of "raw" materials in the process of their transformation and delivery. Seen holistically, the life-threatening toil of the Potosí miner that lies within specie and silver luxury objects ultimately resulted in artifacts like the duc de Bourbon's sugar casters. These, in turn, overtly refer to the coerced labor of enslaved Africans in the sugar-producing colony of Saint-Domingue. The environmental devastation caused by over-mining at Potosí also finds a distant echo in the unexpected challenges Martin encountered in attempting to transplant unfamiliar plants from one part of the world to another for the facilitation of French colonial enterprise. Ever eager to exploit the possibilities of natural resources, enterprising Northern European merchants and artisans manipulated "plastic" mother-of-pearl into luxury consumer goods. As historians of art, material culture, science, and the environment continue to investigate the intertwined problems raised by the sourcing, transportation, and use of raw materials in the eighteenth century, we hope that the case studies presented here will encourage still other connections and cross-evaluations.

There is, moreover, ample evidence to suggest that the problems and paradoxes raised in our case studies continue to plague the globalized world of today, most notably in the continued exploitation of workers and the environment in various extractive industries. Over ninety percent of goods worldwide are currently transported by sea using bulk containers.[100] Recent problems with such containers, mostly notably the March 2021 blockage of the Suez Canal, in addition to numerous COVID-19 pandemic-related shortages in everything from computer chips for car manufacturers to personal protective equipment for frontline medical workers have highlighted our dependence on global supply chains and the consequences of its disruption.[101] Although miners had already extracted the vast majority of the silver beneath Potosí by 1700, the mining of other natural resources (copper, zinc, lead, asbestos, and lithium) continues to drive the Bolivian economy. This comes at the cost of the health and education of the population, resulting in high premature male death rates. In 2014, the Bolivian government passed a law requiring a minimum age of 12 to work in the mines in order to combat child labor.[102] Saint-Domingue, for its part, had, by the end of the eighteenth century, almost completely depleted its forests due to the voracious burning of wood and the redirecting of water to the cultivation and refinement of sugar; today, Haiti is just 1% forested. There is, moreover, fierce and unsustainable competition for resources in Haiti that ultimately stems from the outsized forced immigration that took place during the early modern era.[103] As James Walvin and other historians of the global impacts of sugar production have underscored, when sugar industries shifted their operations to other parts of the tropical world (Cuba, Louisiana, Hawai'i, Fiji), a similar pattern of human and environmental degradation ensued: indentured laborers from Asia eventually replaced enslaved Africans in undertaking the harsh work of cultivating the cane. Meanwhile, the devastations wrought upon the human body due to overconsumption of sugar fall disproportionately upon the global poor, and among this group it is still people of the African diaspora, in particular women and children in the United States, who are suffering the most.[104]

Understanding the consequences of manipulating the "raw" is becoming ever more timely as we face a cataclysmic environmental future and many people around the globe continue to suffer from injustices visited by competition for high-demand resources. Examining the many ways in which European consumption of raw goods functioned in an eighteenth-century context should factor into our current search for solutions at once environmental, social, and creative. Seeking sustainability in our own era demands not only a rethinking of consumptive practices (and the social justice such practices demand), but also, perhaps surprisingly, looking back to the eighteenth century itself for inspiration. Mother-of-pearl is a prime example: as recently as 2019, biologists at the University of Rochester discovered how to layer crystalized calcium carbonate from the bacteria *Sporosarcina pasteurii* with a sticky polymer to make biocompatible artificial nacre in an inexpensive and environmentally conscious way.[105] Especially as we learn more about the damaging effects of producing and consuming petroleum-based plastics, reexamining historically used resources can suggest alternative ways of developing durable everyday materials. While historians often see such eighteenth-century technological innovations as James Watt's coal-powered steam engine as the generative force behind many of the most urgent problems that now confront the globe, our research sees the eighteenth-century supply chain as both a fundamental part of these problems and, perhaps, a seed of the solution as well.[106]

Notes

This collaboratively written essay originated in a panel on the "Raw: Materials, Merchants, and Movement in the Eighteenth Century" at the 2021 Virtual Annual Meeting of the American Society of Eighteenth-Century Studies. Brittany Luberda's research was conducted as part of the Baltimore Museum of Art's acquisition of a silver tray attributed to an unknown Potosí maker. She would like to thank Deborah Spivak for her expertise in Andean history and culture. Sophie Tunney's research would not have been possible without the support and guidance of David Troyansky and the advice of Barbara Naddeo and Helena Rosenblatt. Cynthia Kok's contribution has greatly benefited from the advice of Dr. Edward S. Cooke, Jr. Sarah Cohen would like to thank Mimi Hellman, Philippe Malgouyres, Kristel Smentek, and especially Michèle Bimbenet-Privat for their help with research and bibliography.

1. We acknowledge that in addition to raw materials, ideas, languages, mannerisms, and value systems moved about the world and that reckoning with that movement will be key to constructing a network theory of global trade. For more on such a theory, see Prasannan Parthasarathi and Giorgio Riello, "The Indian Ocean in the Long Eighteenth Century," *Eighteenth-Century Studies*, 48, no. 1 (2014), 8–10.

2. For consumer desires, credit and speculation, and the mentalities of merchants, see Daniel A. Rabuzzi, "Eighteenth-Century Commercial Mentalities as Reflected and Projected in Business Handbooks," *Eighteenth-Century Studies* 29, no. 2 (1995): 169–89, and Natasha Glaisyer, "'A Due Circulation in the Veins of the Publick': Imagining Credit in Late Seventeenth- and Early Eighteenth-Century England," *The Eighteenth Century: Theory and Interpretation* 46, no. 3 (2005): 277–97.

3. "Raw," *Johnson's Dictionary Online*; https://johnsonsdictionaryonline.com/1755/raw_adj.

4. "Bulk," *Johnson's Dictionary Online*; https://johnsonsdictionaryonline. com/1755/bulk_ns_(1).

5. For more on the circulation of global commodities in the eighteenth century, see *The Mobility of People and Things in the Early Modern Mediterranean: The Art of Travel*, ed. Elisabeth Fraser (New York: Routledge, 2020); *Eighteenth-Century Art Worlds: Global and Local Geographies of Art*, ed. Michael Yonan and Stacey Sloboda (New York: Bloomsbury, 2019); Yao-Fen You, Mimi Hellman, and Hope Saska, *Coffee, Tea, and Chocolate: Consuming the World* (New Haven: Yale University Press, 2016); *Early Modern Things: Objects and Their Histories, 1500–1800*, ed. Paula Findlen (New York: Routledge, 2012); Philippe Malgouyres and Jean-Luc Martinez, *Venus d'Ailleurs: Matériaux et objets voyageurs* (Paris: Seuil for the Musée du Louvre, 2021); *The Global Lives of Things: The Material Culture of Connections in the Early Modern World*, ed. Anne Gerritsen and Giorgio Riello (New York: Routledge, 2016); and *Art, Commerce and Colonialism, 1600–1800*, ed. Emma Barker (Manchester: Manchester University Press, 2017).

6. Silver was heavily mined and refined across pre-Hispanic South America. Spanish colonial sources report that the Inka ruler Huayna Capac, in the late fifteenth century, attempted to mine Potosí, but was warned to cease by a god-like voice.

7. Kris Lane, *Potosí: The Silver City That Changed the World* (Oakland: University of California Press, 2021), 8.

8. Claudia A. Cornejo Happel, "Decadent Wealth, Degenerate Morality, Dominance, and Devotion: The Discordant Iconicity of the Rich Mountain of Potosi" (Ph.D. dissertation, The Ohio State University, 2014), 134–35; my [Luberda's] translation of "Soi el rico Potosí, Del Mundo soi el Tesoro, Soi el Rey de los Montes Y embidia soi de los Reies" (Bartolomé Arzáns de Orsúa y Vela, *Historia de la Villa Imperial de Potosí*, ed. Lewis Hanke and Gunnar Mendoza, 3 vols. [Providence: Brown University Press, 1965], 1:title page).

9. Quoted and translated in Lane, *Potosí*, 32.

10. Happel, "Decadent Wealth," 41, and Lane, *Potosí*, 51. Enslaved African workers are recorded as early as 1559, but as servants, vendors, or craftspeople, not miners.

11. Jane E. Mangan, *Trading Roles: Gender, Ethnicity, and the Urban Economy in Colonial Potosí* (Durham: Duke University Press, 2005), 31.

12. See Jeffrey A. Cole, *The Potosí Mita, 1573–1700: Compulsory Indian Labor in the Andes* (Stanford: Stanford University Press, 1985).

13. Donald L. Wiedner, "Forced Labor in Colonial Peru," *The Americas* 16, no. 4 (1960): 358.

14. Cole, *The Potosí Mita*, 7.

15. Wiedner, "Forced Labor," 371.

16. Capoche, *Relación general de la Villa Imperial de Potosí*, quoted and translated in Lane, *Potosí*, 53.

17. See Rossana Barragán, "Extractive Economy and Institutions?: Technology, Labour, and Land in Potosí, the Sixteenth to the Eighteenth Century," in *Colonialism, Institutional Change and Shifts in Global Labour Relations*, ed. Hofmeester Karin and De Zwart Pim (Amsterdam: Amsterdam University Press, 2018), 220 for a chart illustrating the shift schedule.

18. Barragán, "Extractive Economy," 217.

19. Lane, *Potosí*, 72.

20. Mangen, *Trading Roles*, 19

21. Jeffrey A. Cole, "An Abolitionism Born of Frustration: The Conde de Lemos and the Potosí Mita, 1667–73," *Hispanic American Historical Review* 63, no. 2 (1983), 307–33.

22. Lane, *Potosí*, 134.

23. For an eighteenth-century account of Potosí, see Orsúa y Vela, *Historia de la Villa Imperial de Potosí.*

24. Barragán, "Extractive Economy," 223.

25. Lane, *Potosí*, 151.

26. Lane, *Potosí*, 151.

27. Barragán, "Extractive Economy," 225.

28. Lane, *Potosí*, 151. Lane cites Enrique Tandeter, *Coercion and Market: Silver Mining in Colonial Potosí, 1692–1826* (Albuquerque: University of New Mexico Press, 1993), 124, which records that *kajcheo* mining made up one-third of all Potosí production.

29. See Cristina Esteras Martín, "Acculturation and Innovation in Peruvian Viceregal Silverwork," in *The Colonial Andes: Tapestries and Silverwork, 1530– 1830*, ed. Elena Phipps, Johanna Hecht, and Cristina Esteras Martín (New York: Metropolitan Museum of Art, 2004), 58–71.

30. Capoche, *Relación general de la Ville,* ed. Lewis Hanke (Madrid: Atlas, 1959), 5.

31. On Mauritius in the eighteenth century, see Megan Vaughan, *Creating the Creole Island: Slavery in Eighteenth-Century Mauritius* (Durham: Duke University Press, 2005). The Jardin du Roi in Paris was one of the "centers of calculation" that participated in expanding the extraction of resources across the globe (see Bruno Latour, *Science in Action: How to Follow Scientists and Engineers in Society* [Cambridge: Harvard University Press, 1987]). For more on the Jardin du Roi, see Emma Spary, *Utopia's Garden: French Natural History from Old Regime to Revolution* (Chicago: University of Chicago Press, 2000); *Colonial Botany: Science, Commerce, and Politics in the Early Modern World*, ed. Londa Schiebinger and Claudia Swan (Philadelphia: University of Pennsylvania Press, 2005); Sarah Easterby-Smith, *Cultivating Commerce: Cultures of Botany in England and France, 1760–1815* (Cambridge: Cambridge University Press, 2018); *Visions of Empire: Voyages, Botany, and Representations of Nature*, ed. David Philip Miller and Peter Hanns Reill (Cambridge: Cambridge University Press, 1996); and *The Botany of Empire in the Long Eighteenth Century*, ed. Yota Batsaki, Sarah Burke Cahalan and Anatole Tchikine (Washington: Dumbarton Oaks Research Library and Collection, 2016).

32. Easterby-Smith, "On Diplomacy and Botanical Gifts: France, Mysore, and Mauritius in 1788," in *Botany of Empire,* 199.

33. J. P. F. Deleuze, "Notice sur M. De Céré," *Annales Museum d'Histoire Naturelle Paris* 16 (1810), 332. In 1775, Céré was appointed director of the monarchy's official garden on the island. On botany in Mauritius, see Madeleine Ly-

Tio-Fane, *Pierre Sonnerat, 1748–1814: An Account of his Life and Work* (Mauritius: Imprimerie & Papeterie Commerciale, 1976), and Ly-Tio-Fane, *Mauritius and the Spice Trade: The Odyssey of Pierre Poivre* (Mauritius: La Haye, 1958).

34. Sarah Easterby-Smith has traced a second expedition from Paris to L'ile de France that was supposed to go all the way to Mysore on the Indian subcontinent. The Jardin du Roi and César Henri Guillaume de la Luzerne, the minister of the Navy, agreed to send specimens of nutmeg and clove as presents to Tipu Sultan, but when the botanists arrived on l'Ile de France, Céré refused to give them any ("On Diplomacy and Botanical Gifts," in *Botany of Empire*, 202).

35. Batsaki, Cahalan, and Tchikine, Introduction, in *Botany of Empire*, 4, 6.

36. Muséum national d'Histoire naturelle [subsequent citations will be made as *MNHN*], MS 47 (note, 18 February 1788, Paris).

37. *MNHN*, MS 47 (Thouin, "Etat des Végétaux utiles qui se trouvent en France et qui manquent à nos colonies des Isles de France et de Bourbon en 1788," Paris).

38. This was not the first attempt to acclimatize spice plants to Cayenne. Between 1781 and 1789, France sent several shipments of plants and seeds from l'Ile de France. In "Tableau des Plantes apportés depuis l'Epoque de 1773 en Désignant ceux qui ont peris and la traversée & ceux qui existent au Jardin Botanique" (Archives Nationales d'Outre Mer [subsequent citations will be made as *ANOM*], COL, C14 62, fol. 315, 14 August 1789, Cayenne), we can catch a glimpse of the previous failed attempts. In the 1784 shipment, 24 cinnamon trees were sent; 14 died during the crossing and the last 10 died after arrival in Cayenne. During that same year, 24 pepper plants were shipped; 19 died during the crossing, 2 more after arrival, which left only 3 alive at the Jardin Botanique in Cayenne.

39. *MNHN*, MS 47 (Thouin, "Etat des Végétaux").

40. *MNHN*, MS 47 (Thouin, "Instructions pour server aux 30 caisses et 105 Bariques d'arbres, plantes et graines remises au Sieur Martin pour le Jardin Royal des Plantes de Paris," 1788, Paris).

41. *MNHN*, MS 47 (Thouin, draft of "Instructions pour server aux 30 caisses et 105 Bariques d'arbres, plantes et graines remises au Sieur Martin pour le Jardin Royal des Plantes de Paris," 1788, Paris).

42. *MNHN*, MS 47 (letter from Martin to Thouin, 7 August 1788, Ile de France).

43. *MNHN*, MS 47 (letter from Martin to Thouin, 7 August 1788, Ile de France).

44. *MNHN*, MS 47 (letter from Martin to Thouin, 7 August 1788, Ile de France).

45. *MNHN*, MS 47 (letter from Martin to Thouin, 19 May 1789, Cayenne).

46. *MNHN*, MS 47 (letter from Martin to Thouin, 4 March 1789, Ile de France).

47. *MNHN*, MS 47 (letter from Martin to Thouin, 19 May 1789, Cayenne).

48. *MNHN*, MS 47 (letter from Martin to Thouin, 31 July 1789, Le Havre).

49. *MNHN*, MS 47 (letter from Martin to Thouin, 23 August 1789, Paris).

50. *MNHN*, MS 48, ("Tableau des plantes à épices et autres, délivrées des jardins et pépinières coloniales de Cayenne, aux habitans de cette colonie et autres endroits, depuis le 26 Avril 1791 jusqu'au 25 Juin 1793," Cayenne).

51. *ANOM*, Col C14 69, fol. 154 (letter from Martin to de La Luzerne, 18 February 1792, Cayenne).

52. "De peerlen comen van Ormus ende Ceylon ende andere wegen; worden gevischt van duyckers 20 ofte 30 vademen die ponder water, ende groeyen in de oesters op de gront van de zee." Jan Huygen van Linschoten, "copie van eenen brief, die een soon scrijft," 1585, Rijksarchief, Aanwinsten 1882, 212 B, 136-8, quoted in Jan W. Ijzerman, *Dirck Gerritsz Pomp, alias Dirck Gerritsz China, de eerste Nederlander die China en Japan bezocht (1544–1604)* (The Hague: Nijhoff, 1915), 12.

53. Nicolas Lémery, François van Bleyswyck, Cornelius van Putten, Isaäc de Witt, and Jan Daniel Berman, *Woordenboek of algemeene verhandeling der enkele droogeryen ...: in 't Fransch beschreven* (Rotterdam: Jan Daniel Berman, 1743), 437.

54. *Instructions from the Governor-General and Council of India to the Governor of Ceylon, 1656–1665*, trans. Sophia Anthonisz (Colombo: Government Press, 1908), 121–22; Samuel Miles Ostroff, "The Beds of Empire: Power and Profit at the Pearl Fisheries of South India and Sri Lanka, c. 1770–1840" (Ph.D. dissertation, University of Pennsylvania, 2016), 78.

55. Ostroff, "The Beds of Empire," 27.

56. Most shipments averaged between 500 to 1,000 pounds, with occasional shipments of more than 10,000 pounds of shells; see the data in Judith Schooneveld-Oosterling, Gerrit Knaap, Nicolien Karskens, et al., "Boekhouder Generaal Batavia. Het Goederenvervoer van de VOC in de achtiende eeuw," Huygens ING, https://bgb. huygens.knaw.nl/; VOC traders had access to pearl fisheries along the Coromandel Coast and in Sri Lanka and Indonesia and had access to additional sources in the South China Sea and the Gulf of Mannar, between India and Sri Lanka. See Ostroff, "The Beds of Empire," 5–6. A 1682 Dutch report recorded thirty-one pearl oyster banks off the coast of India; a later survey identified forty-seven. Verenigde Oost-Indische Compagnie, VOC: 1.04.02 7911, Nationaal Archief; Verenigde Oost-Indische Compagnie, VOC: 1.04.02 1570.

57. Jan Verleij. Minuutacten, 1750, Filegroup 4618244, Amsterdam City Archives, Amsterdam, Netherlands.

58. *Amsterdamsche Courant*, 10 May 1749.

59. Claudia Swan, *Rarities of These Lands: Art, Trade, and Diplomacy in the Dutch Republic* (Princeton: Princeton University Press, 2021), 76.

60. "Zy zyn 'er door natuurlijke aanvoegingen of t'zamenvoegingen van zeer dunne en blinkende lagen of plaatjes op de wijs van uijenschellen voortgebracht, die daar na hard geworden en versteent zijn; hare stoffe is deselve als die van 't Paerlemoer," in Lémery, et al., *Woordenboek*, 437.

61. Arjun Appadurai, "The Thing Itself," *Public Culture* 18, no. 1 (2006): 15; Ann-Sophie Lehmann, "How materials make meaning," *Nederlands Kunsthistorisch Jaarboek* 62, Materiaal en Betekenis, 1400–1800 (2012): 6–27; *Ways of Making and Knowing: The Material Culture of Empirical Knowledge*, ed. Pamela H. Smith, Amy R. W. Meyers, and Harold J. Cook (New York: Bard Graduate Center, 2017).

62. Smith, *The Body of the Artisan: Art and Experience in the Scientific Revolution* (Chicago: University of Chicago Press, 2004).

63. Georgius Everhardus Rumphius mentions that the shape of nautiluses was reminiscent of boats, referring to the keel and stern of the shell (*The Ambonese*

Curiosity Cabinet, trans. and ed. E. M. Beekman [New Haven: Yale University Press, 1999], 88).

64. "Presque toutes celles que l'on travaille ainsi sont de ces bivalves dans lesquelles on trouve les Perles. ... Ces Coquilles nous viennent des Indes, & on les appelle mères Perles, à cause du précieux ornement qu'elles renferment. Leur surface extérieure, lorsqu'elles sont encore chargées de la crouté qui les envéloppe, est d'un brun sale, & n'offre rien d'agréable à l'oeil: mais leur intérieur a l'éclat de l'argent; & elles ont la même couleur en dehors lorsqu'on a enlevé cette croute épaisse dont je viens de parler, & qu'on les a polies; ce qui est le cas de celles qu'on voit dans cette Planche, & qui de plus sont remarquables par la beauté des gravures dont on les a ornées," in Albertus Seba, *Locupletissimi rerum naturalium thesauri accurata descriptio, et iconibus artificiosissimis expressio, per universam physices historiam: opus, cui, in hoc rerum genere, nullum par exstitit,* ed. H. D. Gabius, P. Massuet, L. Jancourt, and P. van Musschenbroek, 4 vols. (Amsterdam: J. Wetstenium, Gul. Smith, and Janssonio-Waesbergios, 1734–65), 3:176–77.

65. Catherine Jestin, *Powder Celestial: Snuff Boxes, 1700–1880* (New Haven: Yale Center for British Art, 1990), 4.

66. Anne-Marie Claessens-Peré and Leo DeRen, *Dozen om te niezen: Belgische en Franse snuifdozen en tabaksraspen uit de 18de eeuw* (Antwerp: Executive Board of the Province of Antwerp Council, 1996), 17.

67. Daniëlle Kisluk-Grosheide, "Dutch Tobacco Boxes in the Metropolitan Museum of Art: A Catalogue," *Metropolitan Museum Journal* 23 (1988): 202.

68. W. H. van Seters, "Parelmoerkunstenaars in de 18de Eeuw: Het Werk van J. B. Barckhuysen, J. C. Konsé en C. La Motte," *Nederlands Kunsthistorisch Jaarboek* 17 (1966): 249.

69. Heylbroeck had already been accused of counterfeiting in Ghent in 1726. Although he was condemned to death for this crime in 1731, his sentence was commuted to imprisonment after his wife pled for clemency. See Paul van de Weijer, "Norbert Heylbrouck sr. herontdekt: 'Zinneprikkelende' snuifdoos (1732–1749) van een meestergraveur," *Ghendtse Tydinghen* 45, no. 1 (2016): 20.

70. Kisluk-Grosheide, "Dutch Tobacco Boxes," 203.

71. Jestin, *Powder Celestial,* 4.

72. See Adèle Schaverien, "Horn, Medals and Straw: A Little Known Link," *The Medal* 32, (Spring 2007): 32; Wassenaer, fol. 86v–88r, in P. J. J. van Thiel, "Hollandse lijsten van balein," *Miscellanea I.Q. van Regteren Altena*, ed. J. Zadoks-Josephus (Amsterdam: Scheltema and Holkema, 1969), 106.

73. Schaverien, "Horn, Medals and Straw," 31–38.

74. Marloes Rijkelijkhuizen, "Whales, Walruses, and Elephants: Artisans in Ivory, Baleen, and Other Skeletal Materials in Seventeenth- and Eighteenth-Century Amsterdam," *International Journal of Historical Archaeology* 13, http://link. springer.com/article/10.1007/s10761-009-0091-0/fulltext.html.

75. Molly Warsh details the European reliance on Indigenous labor, as well as the environmental impacts of pearl fishing in the sixteenth- and seventeenth-century Spanish pearl trade. See her *American Baroque: Pearls and the Nature of Empire, 1492–1700* (Chapel Hill: University of North Carolina Press, 2018).

76. On the development of sugar as part of the European meal see Jean-Louis Flandrin, *Arranging the Meal: A History of Table Service in France*, trans. Julie E. Johnson with Sylvie and Antonio Order (Berkeley: University of California Press, 2007), 80–83; Sidney Mintz, *Sweetness and Power* (New York: Penguin, 1985), 131.

77. Robert Louis Stein, *The French Sugar Business in the Eighteenth Century* (Baton Rouge: Louisiana State University Press, 1988), 17–39; Mickaël Augeron, "La Traite des Noirs et le Sud-Ouest français: Des origins à l'abolition," in *Bordeaux, La Rochelle, Rochefort, Bayonne: Mémoire noire; Histoire de l'esclavage*, ed. Caroline Le Mao (Bordeaux: Mollat, 2020), 17–54.

78. See Flandrin, *Arranging the Meal*, 87, fig. 12; Marie-France Noël-Waldteufel, "Manger à la Cour: Alimentation et gastronomie aux XVIIe et XVIIIe siècles," in *Versailles et les Tables royales en Europe XVIIème–XIXème siècles*, ed. Jean-Pierre Babelon (Paris: Réunion des musées nationaux, 1993), 74–76.

79. See Stein, *French Sugar Business*, chapters 2 and 7; Jean-Baptiste Labat, *Nouveau Voyage aux isles de l'Amérique*, 2 vols. (La Haye: P. Husson, T. Johnson, et al., 1724), 1:224–323.

80. See Gerard Mabille, "Deux Sucriers à poudre," in Musée du Louvre, *Nouvelle acquisitions du département des Objets d'art 1990–1994* (Paris: Réunion des musées nationaux, 1995), 163–65. My research on the intertwined commerce of luxury goods and globally sourced materials has benefited from a growing body of scholarship in this area. See Madeleine Dobie, *Trading Places: Colonization and Slavery in Eighteenth-Century French Culture* (Ithaca: Cornell University Press, 2010); *The Mobility of People and Things*; *The Global Lives of Things*; and *Eighteenth-Century Art Worlds*.

81. See Louis XV, *Déclaration ... concernant la vaisaille d'argent* (Paris: L'Imprimerie royale, 1721), 5. The sumptuary control reflected in this document was probably instituted after the fall of John Law in 1720; see Hélène Cavalié, "Paris, capitale d'or et d'argent à l'époque des Lumières, Un siècle de production d'orfevrerie," in *Le Commerce du luxe : Production, exposition et circulation des objets précieux du Moyen Âge à nos jours*, ed. Natacha Coquery and Alain Bonnet (Paris: Mare et Martin, 2015), 126. See also Alain Gruber, *Silverware*, trans. David Smith (New York: Rizzoli, 1982), 167–73; and Mabille, "1690–1800: La Table à la française," in Pierre Ennès, Gérard Mabille, and Philippe Thiébaut, *Histoire de la table: les arts de la table des origins à nos jours* (Paris: Flammarion, 1994), 177–78. A number of later eighteenth-century tablewares featured costumed figures "serving" a condiment, but none made the explicit reference to enslaved African sugar harvesters found in Ballin's silver *sucriers*.

82. Gérard Mabille, "Les Surtouts de table dans l'art français du XVIIIe siècle," *Estampille* 126 (1980): 62–73.

83. Mabille, "Deux Sucriers à poudre," 163–65. For examples of Ballin's various commissions for silver surtouts, see Mabille, "Les Surtouts de table," 67–68, and Mabille, "1690–1800," 141, no. 195. On the duc de Bourbon and his artistic practices at Chantilly, see Mathieu Deldicque, "Louis Henri of Bourbon-Condé and the Chantilly Porcelain Manufactory," in *Meissen and Chantilly Porcelain: La Fabrique de L'Extravagance*, ed. Mathieu Deldicque, trans. Sharon Kerman (Saint-Rémy-

en-l'Eau: Editions Monelle Hayot, 2020), 42–77; Gustave Macon, *Chantilly et le Musée Condé*, 2nd ed. (Paris: Henri Laurens, 1925), 131–58; Jean-Pierre Babelon, *The Château of Chantilly*, trans. Judith Hayward (Nouvelle Éditions Scala for the Domaine de Chantilly, 2014), 109–33; Manuela Finaz de Villaine, Nicole Garnier-Pelle, and Eléonore Follain, *Singes et Dragons: La Chine et le Japon à Chantilly au XVIIIe siècle* (Institut de France and Domaine de Chantilly, 2012); Nicole Garnier-Pelle, Anne Forray-Carlier, and Marie-Christine Anselm, *The Monkeys of Christophe Huet: Singeries in French Decorative Arts*, trans. Sharon Grevet (Los Angeles: J. Paul Getty Museum, 2011).

84. The powdered sugar used for dispensing over fruit at the collation represented the most advanced stage of purification, when the sweetener achieved its finest texture and whitest coloration. See Labat, *Nouveau Voyage aux isles de l'Amérique*, 1:283–316; Stein, *The French Sugar Business*, Chapter 7.

85. Noël-Waldteufel, "Manger à la Cour," 76; Barbara Ketcham Wheaton, *Savoring the Past: The French Kitchen and Table from 1300 to 1789* (New York: Touchstone, 1996), 106–8, 184.

86. See *Mercure galant*, October 1677, quoted and translated by Wheaton, *Savoring the Past*, 143; Joseph Gilliers, *Le Cannameliste français, ou Nouvelle instruction pour ceux qui désire d'apprendre l'office* (Nancy: Cusson, 1751), 73.

87. See Ivan Day, *Royal Sugar Sculpture: 600 Years of Splendour* (County Durham: The Bowes Museum, 2002), 31.

88. "Leurs dents plus blanches que l'yvroie le plus fin, leur langue et tout le dedans de la bouche avec leurs levres aussi rouges que du Corail." Of the Africans' black skin, Bernier writes, ""Leur peau … est comme huileuse, lice [i.e., lisse], et poli, si l'on excepte les endroits qui sont rôtis du Soleil" (François Bernier [attrib.], "Nouvelle Division de la terre," *Journal des Sçavans* 14 April 1684, 135).

89. On the colonialist and racist implications of this portrait, see Jennifer L. Palmer, "The Princess Served by Slaves: Making Race Visible through Portraiture in Eighteenth-Century France," *Gender & History* 26, no. 2 (2014): 242–62; Anne Lafont, *L'Art et la race: Africain (tout) contre l'oeil des Lumières* (Dijon: Les Presses du Réel, 2019), 515–16, 260–65.

90. When the painting was exhibited in the Salon of 1742, it appeared under the title, *Portrait de feuë Mademoiselle de Clermont, Princesse du Sang ... représentée en Sultane, sortant du bain, servie par des Esclaves*; Palmer, "The Princess Served by Slaves," 258 n1. See also Lafont, *L'Art et la race*, 16, 260–63.

91. The *sucriers'* ornamental transformation of the enslaved body, highlighting dazzling, shiny surfaces that obviate the fact of physical abuse, finds resonance in many other eighteenth-century arts in which African laborers are depicted. In the case of sugar casters, the heightened luxury of the enslaved laborers' polished silver "skin" recalls the way in which Black Africans' bodies were shined for sale in the early modern slave trade in order to conceal signs of prior torture. See Krista Thompson, "The Sound of Light: Reflections on Art History in the Visual Culture of Hip-Hop," *The Art Bulletin* 91 (2009): 488.

92. Macon, *Chantilly et le Musée Condé*, 147–60; Manuela Finaz de Villaine, "Le Goût de l'Extrême Orient à Chantilly," in *Singes et Dragons*, 3–10; Babelon, *Château of Chantilly*, 109–22. The duc de Bourbon also emulated the production

of foreign luxuries, establishing his own manufactories for soft-paste porcelain, "Indian" painted cottons, and imitation Chinese lacquers; Deldicque, "Louis Henri of Bourbon-Condé and the Chantilly Porcelain Manufactory"; Macon, *Chantilly et le Musée Condé*, 147–49.

93. As David Dabydeen and Catherine Molyneux have illuminated, generic or even faceless "Black" characters dressed in feathered crowns and skirts were also beginning to appear in early eighteenth-century British trade cards, shop signs, and other commercial imagery marketing American tobacco. David Dabydeen, *Hogarth's Blacks: Images of Blacks in Eighteenth Century English Art* (Athens: University of Georgia Press, 1987), 85–86, 124–25; Catherine Molineux, *Faces of Perfect Ebony: Encountering Atlantic Slavery in Imperial Britain* (Cambridge: Harvard University Press, 2012), 1–17, 146–77. See also the African dressed as an Indigenous "American" who supports the portrait of the Abbé Jean-Baptiste Labat in the frontispiece to the 1742 edition of his eight-volume *Nouveau Voyage aux isles de l'Amérique*. For examples of earlier European prints featuring African women wearing beads and arm bands, see Rebecca Parker Brienen, "Albert Eckhout's Painting of the 'wilde natien' of Brazil and Africa," *Nederlands Kunsthistorisch Jaarboek/Netherlands Yearbook for History of Art* 53 (2002): 120–27. On the associations of gold, see Herbert S. Klein, "Economic Aspects of the Eighteenth-Century Atlantic Slave Trade," in *The Rise of Merchant Empires: Long-Distance Trade in the Early Modern World, 1350–1750*, ed. James D. Tracy (Cambridge: Cambridge University Press, 1990), 289; Jacques Savary, *Le Parfait négociant, ou Instruction générale pour ce qui regarde le commerce de toute sorte de marchandises, tant de France que des pays estrangers*, 2 vols. (Paris: L. Billaine, 1675), 2:141.

94. On Bernier's primary audience, see Pierre H. Boulle, *Race et esclavage dans la France de l'Ancien Régime* (Paris: Perrin, 2007), 58.

95. Martin and Weiss, "Enslaved Muslims at the Sun King's Court," in *The Versailles Effect: Objects, Lives, and Afterlives of the Domaine*, ed. Mark Ledbury and Robert Wellington (New York: Bloomsbury, 2020), 153–76; Meredith Martin and Gillian Weiss, *The Sun King at Sea: Maritime Art and Galley Slavery in Louis XIV's France* (Los Angeles: J. Paul Getty Trust, 2022).

96. *Mercure galant*, March 1683, 326.

97. *Mercure de France*, August 1728, 1905.

98. See Adrienne Childs, "Sugar Boxes and Blackamoors: Ornamental Blackness in Early Meissen Porcelain," in *The Cultural Aesthetics of Eighteenth-Century Porcelain*, ed. Alden Cavanaugh and Michael E. Yonan (Farnham: Ashgate, 2010), 159–77. In subsequent decades, at least two new pairs of cane-bearing laborers ostensibly serving as *sucriers* joined the world of innovative tableware in France: cast from the same set of molds, one in silver and the other in bronze, both pairs feature youths dressed in "Asian" robes cold-painted in bright colors and patterns (Wadsworth Atheneum, Hartford, and J. Paul Getty Museum, Los Angeles). Casually transferring the implications of enslavement from the African to the Asian body, while tapping into the vogue for "Chinese" subjects and styles in the decorative arts, these *sucriers* raise complicated questions of their own regarding global relations and exchange. I am currently preparing another study focused upon these objects.

99. Philippe Malgouyres, "Deux Sucriers en forme d'esclaves," in Philippe Malgouyres and Jean-Luc Martinez, *Venus d'Ailleurs: Matériaux et objets voyaguers* (Paris: Musées du Louvre and Seuil, 2021), 147; Albert Girard, La réorganisation de la Compagnie des Indes 1719–1723 (suite et fin)," *Revue d'histoire moderne et contemporaine* 11, no. 3 (1908): 177–97.

100. Anna Nagurney, "Our Economy Relies on Shipping Containers. This is What Happens when They're 'Stuck in the Mud,'" *World Economic Forum*, 1 October 2021, https://www.weforum.org/agenda/2021/10/global-shortagof-shipping-containers/.

101. Peter S. Goodman and Niraj Chokshi, "Why the World Has Run Short of Everything," *New York Times*, 22 October 2021.

102. Kenneth Dickerman and Simone Francescangeli, "What life is like for the teenage miners of Potosi, Bolivia," *Washington Post*, 14 September 2018, https://www.washingtonpost.com/news/in-sight/wp/2018/09/14/what-life-is-like-for-the-teenage-miners-of-potosi-bolivia/.

103. Urmi Engineer, "Sugar Revisited: Sweetness and the Environment in the Early Modern World," in *The Global Lives of Things*, 198–220; Philip D. Curtin, *The Rise and Fall of the Plantation Complex: Essays in Atlantic History*, 2nd ed. (Cambridge: Cambridge University Press, 1998), 174.

104. Walvin, *Sugar: The World Corrupted, From Slavery to Obesity* (New York: Pegasus Books, 2018), 51–61, 119–27, 140–73, 189–215; Curtin, *Rise and Fall of the Plantation Complex*, 173–203.

105. Lindsay Valich, "Researchers create artificial mother-of-pearl using bacteria," *phys.org*, 23 April 2019, https://phys.org/news/2019-04-artificial-mother-of-pearl-bacteria.html.

106. P. J. Crutzen and E. G. Stoermer, "The Anthropocene," *IGBP Newsletter* 41 (2000): 12. See also J. R. McNeill, "Introductory Remarks: The Anthropocene and the Eighteenth Century," *Eighteenth-Century Studies* 49 (2016): 120–22.

Pope and the Reformation of the Oral:
The Iliad in the History of Mediation

ANDREW BLACK

As Alexander Pope approached his monumental translation of *The Iliad*, he saw in Homer what he describes as a "wild paradise," a "copious nursery," rather than an "ordered garden" in which beauty might be distinctly displayed. "If some things are too luxuriant it is owing to the richness of the soil," he explains, "it is only because they are overrun and oppressed by those of a stronger nature." Yet Homer's virtues "border on some imperfection" without overrunning those borders completely.[1] Pope's task then is to contain those energies, to temper them where necessary, while still retaining the spirit that makes Homer endure. The Homeric world presents Pope with startlingly vital scenes of energy and passion in the form of an agonistic, warrior ethos that was incompatible with the manners of the 1710s; these were the tensions that Pope had to manage in order to reframe Homer for a modern world. As Howard Weinbrot has written, Pope privileges "the superior human values of his own age" in the face of "ancient literary and moral depravity."[2] This reportedly caused Richard Bentley, the preeminent classicist of the day, to scoff that Pope wrote "a pretty poem ... but you must not call it Homer."[3]

Pope's translation has been read in many ways: as a late, but definitive volley in the *querelle* between Ancients and Moderns; as an attempt to modernize a poem that didn't need to be modernized; as "the noblest version of poetry which the world has ever seen."[4] It is clear that Pope was more invested in producing a unique poetic achievement than in producing a faithful translation. He hoped to rival not only previous versions of *The Iliad*, but also the greatest literary productions in English. In this essay, I evaluate Pope's *Iliad* translation as a significant moment in the history of mediation. An aggressive print marketplace, one in which Pope's *Iliad* would meet with major and definitive success, prompted thinkers of the period to put pressure on the ethics, efficacy, and integrity not only of print, but also of oral communication. This led to what Paula McDowell has described as a "heightened degree of self-conscious reflection on orality and its actual and potential intersections with an unrestrained press."[5] As a "wild paradise," *The Iliad* is a poem replete with speakers and speeches, many of them delivered in a violent or coercive way, embedded with deceitful motives and disruptive purposes.

Pope's work is not only a translation, however, but also works as an extensive critical exploration of *The Iliad* through lengthy notes and scholarly essays that defend Pope's decisions and often challenge the earlier translations to which his might be compared. The scholarly apparatus that he appends to the translation testifies both to a need for a consensus about Homer's moral value and a concern for the potential misinterpretation that might ensue from his popular translation.[6] In these sections, we find a thorough examination of persuasive moments in Homer's text. In effect, Pope is theorizing the way that oral persuasion should and should not occur and how it might be muted. At stake for Pope in *The Iliad* is a recurrent post-Lockean anxiety regarding the way in which mediation, both oral and written, is not only used to corrupt, but also is itself innately corrupted. Maynard Mack argues that Pope's *Iliad* translation is neither "narrowly Augustan nor uniquely Homeric." Pope similarly oscillates between valorizing and rejecting the oral dynamics that Homer presents.[7] In *The Iliad*, Pope exhibits a vexed nostalgia for the primacy of the spoken word in the classical world. Pope's process of translation attempts to isolate and contain the potentially dangerous persuasive and cultural energies that the oral provokes. It also uses print technology strategically to manage and reorient those tensions for the eighteenth-century reader. Separating orality from its tendency to provoke slippery abstraction and mystical interpretation and restricting the mechanistic agency of the printing press to those who would most wisely utilize it, Pope's *Iliad* works as part of a broader impulse to evaluate print and theorize its ethics by engaging with the fraught values of oral discourse.

Throughout this essay, I do not use the words "orality" and "rhetoric" (or its close synonym "oratory") interchangeably. Rather, I use orality to describe what Jonathan Swift's Hack would call "a Force, or energy" that could be manipulated and employed in nefarious ways by those most gifted in its delivery.[8] Rhetoric, then, is the disciplinary boundary imposed on oral practices, either correcting or refining them through an educational system often organized around the classical heuristics of Aristotle and Marcus Tullius Cicero. Rhetoric can heighten the power of language, as in Aristotle, yet it can also be used to limit and regulate language. In what was essentially an institutionalization of oral practice, Aristotle's rhetorical program paved the way for the study and practice of rhetoric as something reputable and rational. This led Walter Ong to claim that the "deeply agonistic roots" of rhetoric were compromised as part of the "inevitable migrat[ion] from the oral to the chirographic world."[9] To study rhetoric was to learn how to produce *eloquence,* which, as Adam Potkay explains, was a term eighteenth-century thinkers linked to "an imagined *scene* of ancient oratory in which the speaker moves the just passions of a civic assembly and implants a sense of community with his words."[10] It is that movement of the audience with a "force or energy," either unpracticed or not, that Homer represents, and it is that movement to which Pope turns with an attentive, yet anxious eye.

The elusive nature of the oral, in particular, was what provoked so much anxiety and desire for reform in the early eighteenth century. Devious orators could be potentially tamed by the polite models and critique that print provided, but that also created space for fugitive voices offering "new conceptions of the oral."[11] And yet it is obvious that those voices and the people who spoke them could appear liberating and empowering in their evanescence and freedom from constraint. Ever sensitive to human finitude and the power of poetry, Pope's impulses toward polite transformation are haunted by the affecting and atavistic power of the oral.

"This Gibberish": The Problem with Oral Discourse

In all the versions of *The Dunciad,* Pope sets his satirical sights on John "Orator" Henley, whose "Oratory" flourished in the 1720s as a site in which Henley both modeled and taught the art of persuasive speaking. Amongst a gallery of exultant dunces, Henley receives particular notice for his contributions to the vociferous and indecipherable noise that characterizes Dulness's kingdom: "Tuning his voice, and balancing his hands. / How fluent nonsense trickles from his tongue!" (3:198–203).[12] Yet Pope still acknowledges Henley's ability to "break the benches," while the more reputable clergy, like Edmund Gibson, "preach in vain." Even if he lacks the authority of the latter, Henley's voice is louder, sweeter, and makes even nonsense sound fluent. It may be oratory at its worst, but it is bafflingly successful.[13] Henley's spoken words also provoke an immediate response, which Pope feared his own writing often could not. No great speaker himself, Pope told Joseph Spence that he "never could speak in public," recalling an occasion when, "though I had but ten words to say, and that on a plain point … I made two or three blunders in it."[14] And, of course, Pope's inability to speak to women is well-chronicled: there is a telling note of resignation when he dispatches his 1717 *The Works of Mr. Alexander Pope* to Lady Mary Wortley Montagu, writing that he is sending her "all that I am worth, that is my Works."[15]

In his mockery of Henley and throughout *The Dunciad*, Pope expresses a contempt for contemporary oral practices with the same ferocious invective as he uses for the dangerous and insipid printed texts that he claims were corrupting the public. For instance, in Dulness's throne room, we are presented with the sad image of "fair Rhetoric languish'd on the ground. … And shameless Billingsgate her robes adorn" (4:23–25). Rhetoric's consignment to the feet of Dulness suggests two equally grim possibilities: either Rhetoric is what Dulness has corrupted in order to trumpet her own power or it is a once-virtuous discipline for which Dulness and her followers have no need. For Dulness to thrive, her charms must be enhanced by an army of her followers who will—to modify a phrase from *An Essay on Criticism*—"hide with ornaments [her] want of art" (line 296). Her existence and persistence are the result of her subjects' continual praise. Dulness relies on a cadre of those most skilled in the contemporary practices of mediation: booksellers, theater owners, patrons, painters, pamphleteers, publishers, editors, literary critics, preachers, and orators. She is first introduced in "clouded majesty" (1:45), a phrase that emphasizes how her vacuity is obscured and rhetorically reinvented as "majesty." As in the representation of Henley, bad rhetoric is presumed to be undeniably effective on those drawn more to show than substance. In this mock-celebration tinged with anxiety, Pope also demonstrates the degree to which ornamentation and excess have made it nearly impossible to distinguish reality from the glistening rhetorical façade that enhances or conceals it.

In *The Dunciad*, Pope's satirical invective cannot mask an apocalyptic fear of the new age of print and the potential demise of the fading aristocratic attitude toward authorship that regarded commercial success as shallow and opportunistic.[16] As the representation of Henley reveals, Pope's view of the oral is equally grim. Occupied with the ethics, efficacy, and integrity of both media, Pope turned his poetic attention toward the critical interests of a growing group of what we might today call media critics. As Marshall McLuhan noted, Pope is a "serious analyst of the intellectual malaise of Europe," whose writings anticipate McLuhan's own work on the printing press as a deeply problematic avatar of Enlightenment rationalism that fostered a radical and private individualism, even as it helped its intellectual advancements to proliferate.[17] James McLaverty has written about "the Pope who loved print and the Pope who hated it."[18] As an analyst of media, Pope frequently attacked the tools that made him a poetic superstar, often for highly personal reasons stemming from feuds, and even more often to defame those who found commercial success by manipulating print as a tool of mass communication. And as this essay contends, Pope's engagement with media extended to the oral as well.

This aversion to the oral and to the use of rhetoric can be linked to John Locke's highly influential presumptions about semantic instability. In *An Essay Concerning Human Understanding* (1689), the gulf between word and thing cannot be resolved merely through the kind of disciplinary stabilization that rhetoric might offer. Indeed, rhetoric only makes things worse. As John Guillory explains, Locke's "radical antipathy" toward language results in a belief that its inaccuracy "prevent[s] us from achieving a world in which knowledge and peace prevail."[19] Locke contends that even the most "distinct set of terms" used by "sect[s] in philosophy" are "gibberish," which "serves so well to palliate men's ignorance, and cover their errors."[20] As a vain attempt at systemization, rhetoric only further corrupts, working to "insinuate wrong ideas, move the passions, and thereby mislead the judgment." For Locke, rhetoric and its tools "are perfect cheats."[21] In *Some Thoughts Concerning Education* (1693), Locke proposes that students should focus on writing more than speaking because oral discourse is contaminated by "transient faults, dying for the most part with the sound that gives them life, and so not subject to a strict review," which means that they "more easily escape observation and censure."[22] Locke's empirical thinking pervades and sometimes even confounds Pope's poetry, as Pope continually locates a gulf between what can be known or expressed and the real and ideal. For Pope, rhetoricians (like those employed by Dulness) can only capitalize on, rather than correct, the inherent instability of language.[23]

As McDowell has shown, in a necessary qualification of McLuhan, oral tradition and print culture are cultural constructs; far from being ontologically prior to culture, they are analytically created and that creation comes about through reflections on mediation, rather than being outgrowths or consequences of the media in question. Since "printing and letters were being reduced to mere market-oriented trades without adequate moral, legal, and economic safeguards," writers such as Pope and Swift depicted the apocalyptic effects of the unfettered proliferation of Grub Street texts.[24] Yet in the mouths of the elocutionists whom Pope abhorred, the oral was itself a "market-oriented trade," as well as a path to social distinction and the cult of celebrity. As McDowell explains, the primary offenders were marginal or "fugitive" figures operating outside the borders of politeness: women, dissenting preachers, balladeers, street performers, and celebrity elocutionists like Henley.[25] Through satirical reprimands, Pope and Swift fantasize about a regulation and reevaluation of the oral, along with putting it under the control of a polite and enlightened domain and exposing those who would manipulate the slippery, yet hypnotic and persuasive modes of orality. The very act of representing a problematic orality reflects the desire to tame and domesticate the subversive voice.[26]

Could mediation be salvaged and redeemed from its abusers? For some, the solution could potentially be found in the polite rediscovery of a classical past to which the dangers of the oral could be safely consigned. The unrestrained press exacerbated, accelerated, and inflected discussions about the oral, prompting attempts to distinguish the facets of a "primary," or perhaps primal, orality from the mélange of media with which contemporary thinkers were confronted.[27] It is no coincidence that this effort happened concomitantly with an intense reflection on the relationship between classical and modern literary forms. Adam Potkay describes the means by which the "tension between the ideals of ancient eloquence and modern manners" prompted creative and anachronistic revisions. Eighteenth-century writers called for the revival of the eloquence of Cicero and Demosthenes, yet betray a lurking anxiety about its effects. What resulted in terms of persuasive activity in the "Age of Hume" was a polite style that, as Potkay notes, sought "to placate or stabilize rather than, as with eloquence, to make things happen."[28] This conciliatory impulse is inherent within the shift from the humanist reverence for classical eloquence to an emerging politeness, as well as in the work of polite rhetoric itself, which seeks civil consensus, rather than passionate arousal. In strikingly similar ways, Potkay and McDowell chronicle the responses to classical texts that provoke not merely veneration or imitation, but significant discussion regarding their relationship to modernity. At stake is not merely the question of whether the oral should be revived and made part of contemporary life, but how and by whom. The classical corpus could be sifted through and strategically redeployed to create contemporary avatars of politeness, but first they had to be purified of potentially extravagant or dangerous excesses.[29]

Because *The Iliad* is replete with speakers and speeches, these problems are inherent in the Homeric presentation of oral communication and persuasion. In *The Iliad* alone, 7,018 of its 15,690 lines are direct speech, much of it delivered in a violent or coercive way, embedded with deceitful motives and disruptive intentions.[30] As Nancy Worman explains, "Whether warriors vaunt on the field of battle or dispute in assembly, their threats, taunts, and slanderous labels broadcast superiority and coerce actions."[31]

Ulysses is a prime example and so an "obvious prototype for the classical orator" because of his "verbal dexterity, strategic mentality, and talent for coercion and control."[32] In *The Iliad,* speeches can be more powerful than spears, particularly when delivered by a god or goddess who uses hypnotic and "winged words."[33]

Homer's imaginative construction of the way in which mediation occurs clashes with Pope's vision of the way in which it should occur. In Homer, persuasion appears not at the behest of any moral philosophy, but as a coercive and often amoral means of gaining what one wants when one wants it. Homer avoids the abstract and presents persuasive moments as purely narrative acts, thereby submerging any theorization of rhetoric in story and presenting it through intense and immediate action. For Homer, rhetorical activity is characterized by its violence. The totalizing power that oral persuasion can have in Homer's texts prompts Pope to revise and comment, often at length. For Pope and his contemporaries, the effect of rhetoric can destroy the polite fabric of the sociable domains that his work both parodied and attempted to instruct. His *Iliad* project serves as one intervention.

"Easy Art": Rhetorical Performance in *The Iliad*

In Book 3 of *The Iliad*, there is a scene of oral performances that prompted Pope to revise. The captive beauty Helen, wife of the Spartan King Menelaus, stands at the walls of Troy with King Priam of Troy and a company of nobles. Helen offers her captors inside information: identifying the Greek commanders and describing their virtues and deeds. When she comes to Odysseus, the Trojan elder Antenor recalls a moment before the war when Odysseus and Menelaus came to try to persuade the Trojan council to return her and so avoid war. In Antenor's account, Menelaus delivered a brief, lucid, but ultimately unimpressive speech. However, when Odysseus rose, Antenor was struck by his oddly powerful eloquence. What follows is the most vivid image of the orator in either of Homer's poems. As a point of reference to clarify the alterations that Pope and his contemporaries would make, here is what might be considered the most literal translation of the passage:

> he would just stand and stare down, eyes fixed on the ground beneath him
> nor would he gesture with the staff backward and forward, but hold it
> clutched hard in front of him, like any man who knows nothing.
> Yes, you would call him a sullen man, and a fool likewise.
> But when he let the great voice go from his chest, and the words came
> drifting down like the winter snows, then no mortal
> man beside could stand up against Odysseus. Then we
> wondered less beholding Odysseus' outward appearance.[34]

Odysseus's speech is paradoxically both gentle and overpowering. He captivates his audience and causes them to overlook his odd manner and "outward appearance." Antenor remembers Odysseus's rhetorical force, even if he does not remember his exact words. Odysseus's actual presence is replaced by the more suggestive mental one that he creates for his listeners through his performance. Despite his unpromising appearance (he is older and smaller than Menelaus), his speech gives him real power. Odysseus uses words that flow like "the winter snows" and separate him from all other mortals.

In seventeenth-century translations, which Pope regarded as inadequate, this scene is reduced to its most basic description.[35] Antenor offers little in the way of moral commentary, and so neither do the translators. In his 1660 translation, John Ogilby emphasizes only the metaphorical "snow" and the soft fluency with which Odysseus/Ulysses spoke:

> A torrent swift as feather'd snow
> Not any with Ulysses durst contend
> Though we his gesture could not much commend.[36]

In this abbreviated version, Ogilby still conveys the fundamental aspects of Antenor's description: Ulysses's gesture is strange, but his words are strong. However, Ogilby ends by inverting the sequence of Antenor's narration, closing with the strangeness of the gesture, rather than its transformation through Ulysses's oral skill. George Chapman offers a similar approach. Though noted for his protracted and hyperpoetic stylings, Chapman nonetheless summarizes this scene in a single heptameter couplet:

> And words that flew about our eares like drifts of winter's snow,
> None thenceforth might contend with him, though nought admird
> for show.[37]

These versions are faithful in their attention to how Ulysses's rhetorical superiority is contrasted with his strange appearance and preserve the comparison of words to falling snow, yet they remove what the translators viewed as extraneous details.

When Pope turns to this scene, he gives a noticeably longer description than his predecessors:

> But, when he speaks, what Elocution flows!
> Soft as the Fleeces of descending Snows,
> The copious Accents fall, with easy Art;
> Melting they fall, and sink into the Heart!
> Wondering we hear, and fix'd in deep Surprize,
> Our Ears refute the Censure of our Eyes. (3.283–88)

Pope's revision immediately comes across as a glowing encomium to the orator and his skills. However, his description of the effects of speech inscribes the scene with new implications. These added details are significant to his vivid portrait of the classical orator, bringing in a modern sensibility and casting the scene as a cautionary example, rather than a rhetorical triumph. The connotations of "Elocution," a word no prior translator uses, are highly anachronistic. In Cicero and Quintilian, elocution equated to style, rather than delivery (*pronunciato*), which is the context in which Pope utilizes the term. Pope's use of "Elocution" mirrors its use in the emerging Elocutionary movement (with which Henley was associated). Pope presents this scene as every bit as contrived as Henley's oratory, though Ulysses's rhetorical ability is far superior to Henley's. In the next couplet, Pope continues to describe Ulysses's skill by using terminology that characterizes him as a modern, rather than ancient, orator: his "Accents" fall with "easy Art," a term that does not have any clear corollary in Homer's Greek. After introducing Ulysses's "art," Pope immediately describes its effect through a series of illusory images that conclude with sound refuting sight. The words melt and sink, and appearance overcomes reality through the vehicle of persuasive speech. The language that Pope here uses emphasizes the threat that he later denounces in *An Essay on Man,* where such artifice is a "trick to show the stretch of human brain" and so we must "Expunge the whole, or lop th' excrescent parts" (lines 47, 49).

Pope's description of Ulysses anticipates his later description of Henley through its characterization of rhetorical practice as dedicated to show, rather than substance. Pope preserves Antenor's commendation, but makes these striking additions that qualify and refocus the passage in order to emphasize the orator's potential to disrupt. The final couplet shows the chaos that results from such rhetoric: nothing is as it seems, and meaning and coherence have been so unsettled that the orator can create and control an artificial reality to his own benefit. In Pope's hands, Ulysses is an example of what Richard Lanham has called the "rhetorical man," who "is trained not to discover reality but to manipulate it."[38] When Antenor describes the result of persuasion as "Our Ears refute the Censure of our Eyes," he calls attention to the hypnotic transformation that has been brought about through artifice. The performance dominates the senses and bypasses the reason. By augmenting the simile of "fleeces of descending snow," Pope's translation reveals the totalizing power of rhetoric when exploited by a gifted speaker like Ulysses.

This extended, even anachronistic, description of Ulysses is made all the more dramatic by Pope's prior revision of Antenor's account of Menelaus's rhetorical abilities. When Menelaus speaks, Pope has Antenor describe the virtues of his plainness:

> When Atreus' Son harangu'd the list'ning Train,
> Just was his Sense, and his Expression plain,
> His Words succinct, yet full, without a Fault;
> He spoke no more than just the Thing he ought. (3.275–78)

Unlike Ulysses, Menelaus speaks with clarity and precision; his words are short, yet "full." In the second couplet, Pope emphasizes the propriety of the speech: it is "without a Fault." Antenor's description reveals that, despite Menelaus's apparent brevity or simplicity, his speech is composed with more attention to substance than to style. Antenor's description of Ulysses focuses on the performance itself, the way the words melt like snow and overwhelm the listeners. By contrast, Menelaus's concision reflects his "just" sense and underscores his virtue.

In his commentary on this passage, Pope directly challenges George Chapman's earlier translation and explains why he is presenting Menelaus's plainness as a virtue. Chapman's Antenor describes Menelaus as "passing loud, small, fast, yet did not reach / To much."[39] In a note, Chapman writes that this brevity "maketh even with his simple character at all parts—his utterance being noisefull, small or squeaking, an excellent pipe for a foole."[40] Pope frames his own commentary as a direct response to Chapman's analysis of Menelaus as a "foole":

> Chapman in his Notes on this Place and on the second Book, has described *Menelaus* as a Character of Ridicule and Simplicity. He takes advantage from the word ... here made use of, to interpret that of the *Shrillness* of his Voice, which was apply'd to the *Acuteness* of his Sense; He observes that this sort of Voice is a Mark of a Fool ... In short, that he was a weak Prince, play'd upon by others, short in Speech, and of a bad Pronunciation, valiant only by fits, and sometimes stumbling upon good Matter in his Speeches, as may happen to the most slender Capacity. This is one of the Mysteries which that Translator boasts to have found in *Homer*. But as it is no way consistent with the art of the Poet, to draw the Person in whose behalf he engages the World, in such a manner as no Regard should be conceiv'd for him; we must endeavour to rescue him from this Misrepresentation.[41]

After summarizing the supposed deficiencies of Menelaus, Pope counters Chapman with classical sources that will "rescue [Menelaus] from this Misrepresentation." Pope then moves to a more general discussion of Menelaus's virtues before concluding, "Thus his Character is compos'd of Qualities which give him no uneasy Superiority over others while he wants their Assistance, and mingled with such as make him amiable enough to obtain it."[42] While in other cases Pope revises or qualifies Homer, the commentary on Menelaus's style allows him a move toward fidelity. With the contention that such brevity is eloquent, Pope's long defense reframes what Chapman views as an affective failure into an appropriate rhetorical protocol.

Menelaus is characterized by his "eloquence," even if the speech he gives does not match a conventional definition of the term. Pope continues by invoking Cicero and Quintilian, who regard Menelaus's terseness as a good thing. Both describe his style as appropriate for the occasion and as an example of a pithy kind of eloquence. We might assume that Pope is merely doing the same in reclaiming Menelaus's propriety from misguided previous translators, like Chapman. Yet Pope's defense of Menelaus throughout Book 3 is so meticulous that it extends well beyond a simple act of philological commentary. In an earlier note that appears at the beginning of Antenor's narration, Pope claims that the "close Laconick Conciseness of the one, is finely oppos'd to the copious, vehement, and penetrating Oratory of the other."[43] That opposition works to celebrate Menelaus at the expense of Ulysses. Pope refuses to see Menelaus through the deficiencies that previous translators have assigned to him. If Chapman connects the "*Shrillness* of his Voice" with "the *Acuteness* of his sense," Pope's notes aim to "rescue him from this Misrepresentation." In so doing, Pope emphasizes that Menelaus's plainness should not be read as uncouth, but as an intentional rhetorical choice that reflects well on his integrity and prudence.

While Menelaus offers one positive model of rhetorical style removed from ornamentation and premeditation, Pope valorizes a different kind of rhetoric and its effects through the character of Nestor. In Homer's text, Nestor is depicted as a wizened, eloquent mentor, whose ends are often best furthered by serving in an advisory capacity. Like Menelaus, Nestor has integrity, but he uses it in more violent scenes that require his calming presence. Further, Nestor's persuasive activity allows Pope to theorize what he regarded as appropriate rhetoric in the figure of an orator whose impulse is to quell, rather than to incite, who provokes rational thought by dissecting and placating passionate impulses. Throughout the poem, Nestor exemplifies the pacifying function that Potkay locates at the heart of polite rhetorical protocols. While these actions are in the original Homeric text, Pope's translation displays a special ardor for Nestor's oratory. When Nestor intervenes in the feud between Achilles and Agamemnon, Pope commends him in a lengthy note: "The Quarrel having risen to its highest Extravagance, Nestor the wisest and most aged Greek is raised to quiet the Princes, whose Speech is therefore fram'd entirely with an opposite Air to all which has been hitherto said, sedate and inoffensive. He begins with a soft affectionate Complaint which he opposes to their Threats and haughty Language; he reconciles their Attention in an awful manner, by putting them in mind that they hear one whom their Fathers and the greatest Heroes had heard with deference."[44] Crucially, Pope adds that Homer invokes Nestor in "all the great Emergencies of the Poem." Nestor is able to bring about change in a way that Ulysses and Menelaus cannot. Pope locates the power of Nestor's eloquence in his ability to reconcile, rather than arouse passions. He combats "threats and haughty language" with affection and sensibility. In addressing the violence between Achilles and Agamemnon, he reminds them of their mutual respect and appeals to transcendent virtues. As the final line of the passage above reveals, he is a manager of disputes. Nestor's valor is situated in his ability to intervene with "softness" amongst violent words.

Much like Pope's own goals as a translator, Nestor's aim is to contain and calm the energies that threaten to prevail. Through his irenic presence, he give voice to the prudence that Pope hopes his translation will increase and clarify. Pope attempts to defuse violent argumentation and the animosity that could ensue by valorizing Nestor's more modest and productive goals. Again, Pope's extensive commentary reveals his attention to these orators and the potential effects of their rhetoric. Concerned with Ulysses's ability to replace one reality with another through his "melting" words, Pope makes a case for the unadorned and straightforward speech of Menelaus. Nestor's intervention is necessary to combat the inherent violence of Agamemnon's language. In *The Iliad,* moments of persuasion are always vexed. If they offer the possibility of positive change, they do not fulfill their potential. If they are the product of artful composition, their impulses are to be distrusted. For Pope, rhetoric is bound up in a dense matrix of intention and effect. Even as Ulysses's performance is magnificent, Pope elaborates on its disruptive potential through his phrasing and critical commentary.

The competing figures of Ulysses and Nestor represent, respectively, the problem of oral persuasion and the ways in which that problem could be solved through rational and restrained speaking practices. However, Pope's Achilles offers a striking example of how to listen and respond to a rhetorical performance. In Book 9, after Ulysses delivers a glowing encomium to Achilles with the hope of persuading him to return to war, Achilles is defiant:

> Ulysses, hear
> A faithful speech, that knows nor art nor fear;
> What in my secret soul is understood,
> My tongue shall utter, and my deeds make good. (9.406–9)

Achilles pits "faithful" speech against Ulysses's "art." In a note on this speech, Pope writes that "nothing is more remarkable than the conduct of *Homer* in this Speech of Achilles."[45] While elsewhere Pope condemns

Achilles for his irrational rage, at this point he justifies Achilles's "more sedate Representation of his past Services" because "Ulysses had dealt artfully with him, which in two Periods rise into an open Detestation of all artifice." Pope's sympathy throughout this commentary wavers and turns at moments to critique, but toward the end he nonetheless declares that "Exaggeration is a Figure extremely natural in Passion."[46] Achilles concludes by insisting that he is "unconquer'd still." The elderly Phoenix responds in a way that Pope frames as a language of true emotion, as opposed to the "art" of Ulysses:

> Then *Phoenix* rose;
> (Down his white Beard a Stream of Sorrows flows)
> And while the Fate of suff'ring *Greece* he mourn'd,
> With Accent weak these tender words return'd. (9:558–61)

The humility of Phoenix arises from his seeming inability, or at least unwillingness, to perform rhetorically. The "Accent weak" with which Pope introduces Phoenix's speech could not be more different than the "copious accents" that Ulysses had used in Book 3. As Morgan Strawn has recognized, Pope's translation here echoes the language of an emerging sentimentalism and would be read that way by many eighteenth-century readers, as Pope "intensifies" an "emotional turnabout."[47] As Phoenix's speech ends, Pope analyzes Achilles's answer in a note, claiming that his character is "everywhere of a Piece," as Homer "draws the Heat of his Passion cooling by slow Degrees, which is very natural."[48] Pope also implies that Achilles's aggravated response to Ulysses is an appropriate reaction to the "vehemence" that the latter commonly exhibits.

In their anachronism, the frequent references to Ulysses's "art" convert his supposed improvisation into examples of rhetoric as it was understood in Pope's time. Odysseus is an orator in the same way that Henley was and so typifies a daunting and dangerous individuality that reveals itself through oral practices. Much like Achilles, the listener must constantly be on guard against orators, interpreting rhetorical fluency with a wary eye toward the "angel tongue" that hides the inconsistencies on which it thrives.

"A more tolerable copy": Pope's Poetic Engineering

In the preface to the *Iliad,* Pope contends that "Homer makes us hearers, and Virgil leaves us readers."[49] However, a common criticism of Pope was that he does not let us *hear* Homer. John Dennis admits that he had not read the translation, but contends nonetheless that it is "as Ridiculous to pretend to make these Shine out in English *Rhimes* as it would be to emulate upon a Bag-pipe, the Solemn and Majestick Thorough Basse of an Organ."[50] Similarly, in an 1861 lecture, Matthew Arnold criticizes Pope's translation for "an artificial evolution of thought and a literary cast of style" that had "passed through a literary and rhetorical crucible, and come out highly intellectualized."[51] For these readers, Pope's versification lacked what John Keats found in Chapman: a "pure serene" that "speak[s] out loud and bold."[52] In a statement of praise that still implicates Pope, Gerard Manley Hopkins writes, "When one reads Pope's Homer with a critical eye, one sees, artificial as it is, in every couplet that he is a great man."[53] In 1791, William Cowper would even produce his own translation of Homer into blank verse in what many critics have seen as an attempt to provide a corrective improvement to Pope, whose translation had become dominant.[54] Yet Pope insistently defends what Hopkins thought "artificial" as a necessary part of bringing Homer's poem into line with contemporary standards of moral propriety and poetics. Pope's ultimate point is that Homer will not only survive this assimilation, but that his text will be stronger for having its indecencies removed.

For Pope's critics, *The Iliad* had a fraught existence in the commodity culture of the English literary marketplace, which undercut its participation in more abstract and seemingly high-minded debates about classicism and its translator's desire to produce a definitive work. In his reframing of the oral character of the poem, Pope establishes *The Iliad* as one of the most ambitious written performances of the eighteenth century. He embraces what Walter Ong calls the "closure" that printed texts allow, a consumer-oriented "tidiness and inevitability" that "makes for a different relationship between the reader and the authorial voice in the text." Further, print "embed[s] the word in space more definitively."[55] In his early career, Pope had little say over how his texts would appear when published, while in his later career he had an almost unprecedented amount of creative control. *The Iliad* can be seen as a transition point between those two phases, as it began almost simultaneously with Pope's 1717 *Works*.

Pope deploys what McDowell calls the "classical oral" in order to comment on the problems and possibilities of print, and so meditate on mediation itself. This required an authoritative rendering of Homer's text that only print could provide. Pope's text works through what Elizabeth Eisenstein has described as the apparatus that allow printed texts to secure their own stability.[56] Though Pope was not the first translator of *The Iliad* to provide notes and scholarly essays, his text was the most ambitious yet. The lengthy preface and "Essay on Homer" help constitute Pope's authority and that of his translation; so too do the extensive notes and critical commentary. Further, Pope's transformation of Homer's verse into heroic couplets makes it conform to contemporary poetic practice that further facilitates the recasting of Homer's language as polite. Bentley's reductive classification of Pope's translation as a "pretty poem" ignores all this elaborate textual work and fails to recognize how Pope uses print to control, reform, manipulate, and rehabilitate the oral.

By the middle of the 1710s, as Pope shepherded his *Iliad* translation through the press, revised and added to *The Rape of the Lock*, and prepared his 1717 *Works* for publication, he worked to "protect his poem[s] and enhance [their] powers of expression."[57] In the case of *The Rape of the Lock*, Pope removed his poem from the elusive and unmanageable context of the miscellany in which it had previously been published in order to "occupy all these potentially hostile zones himself."[58] And while Pope's relationship with Bernard Lintot would later fall apart over the financial terms Lintot was willing to offer for the 1725 translation of *The Odyssey*, at this point they still had a thriving, mutually beneficial arrangement. For example, Lintot's willingness to include illustrations in the 1714 version of *The Rape of the Lock* enhanced its popularity and playfulness, which in turn served as visual testimony to Pope's creativity.

Pope's *Iliad* was a publishing phenomenon: it brought him significant income and was typographically innovative.[59] Working with Lintot, Pope would produce some of the most handsome and sought-after books of the early eighteenth century. The six volumes were issued on a subscription model between 1715 and 1720. Each had to be purchased separately. Pope hoped to make six hundred guineas per volume. Pope also exercised almost unprecedented control over the typography, headpieces, and illustrations of the edition. The process was so involved and ambitious that Pope worked with several assistants—primarily William Broome, Elijah Fenton, and Thomas Parnell—to assist with the translation and summarize prior commentary. Maynard Mack notes that Pope aimed for an "infinitude of detail" and was "unsparing in his efforts to be accurate in his maps, ... his references to Homer's geography, ... [and] his descriptions of ancient ceremonies—responsibilities that he felt earlier translators had too much ignored."[60] However, Pope did little to acknowledge his most significant sources, presumably in an attempt to avoid provoking the ire of critics who would see such assistance as only further underscoring Pope's lack of credentials as a classicist. In concealing his indebtedness, particularly to Anne Dacier's pioneering translation of Homer into French prose, and mostly not acknowledging his assistants, Pope worked to definitively establish *The Iliad* as an Alexander Pope production.

Before arriving at Homer's invocation of the muse, subscribers who received Volume 1 of *The Iliad* in 1715 would pass through two title pages, an authorization to print, an eight-page list of subscribers, Pope's forty-one page preface, and sixty-two pages of an "Essay on Homer" (co-written with, and mostly by, Parnell). Pope's notes for the first book alone take up thirty-eight pages, while the translation they accompany is only forty pages. These elaborate paratexts "manage readers" by situating the text's authority in the overall project of the translation more than in the translated text itself.[61]

In his design of the book, Pope was most likely influenced by John Ogilby. The title page of Ogilby's 1660 translation notes that it is "Adorn'd with Sculpture and Illustrated with Annotations." What follows is a dedication to the recently restored Charles II, a fifteen-page "Life of Homer," five pages describing the various editions of Homer's works in Greek, four pages of laudatory epigrams about Homer, ten pages on the "Country & Time of Homer," and a poem in both Greek and English titled "Upon Homer's Statue Cast in Brasse." The translation itself then begins on page 52. Its pages are cluttered with marginalia that are primarily explanatory and contextual [see Figure 1]. In effect, they serve as a sort of dictionary of mythological references, rather than the critical and philological notes that Pope provides. For example, a note glosses the brief mention of "Caeneus" by explaining who he was and offering a quotation from Rhodius Apollonius (both in Greek and translated into English) regarding his "disastrous end" [see note y on the left side of Figure 1]. Pope rarely offers such explanations, assuming that his reader either already knows or does not care. Pope instead uses his notes to justify aspects of his translation and to offer commentary on the nature of poetry itself. Pope begins his first note for Book 1 by remarking, "It is something strange that of all the Commentators upon *Homer,* there is hardly one whose principal Design is to illustrate the Poetical Beauties of the author."[62] Pope often continues this critique by pointing out how previous translators and commentators have erred: e.g., in Book 3 where he comments that "It is remarkable that Mr. *Hobbes* has omitted [a] beautiful Simile."[63] Even when Pope is respectful toward his predecessors, his apparatus frequently works to publicize how his translation is correcting and improving on previous efforts as part of his catering to a sophisticated contemporary audience. His readers, Pope suggests, do not desire philological or antiquarian details, but rather extensive commentary to contextualize and distinguish the translation they are reading.

While Pope dismissed Ogilby's edition as "too mean for Criticism," it nonetheless served as a negative model. The "mean" qualities that Pope scorned in Ogilby help showcase the verbal elegance of the new translation. One of Pope's key ambitions in the project was to keep alive the "spirit and fire of Homer" (which Ogilby's version apparently lacked), even as the poem was made fit for polite readers through the refinement of its production and its use of heroic couplets. Ogilby also used couplets, with occasional

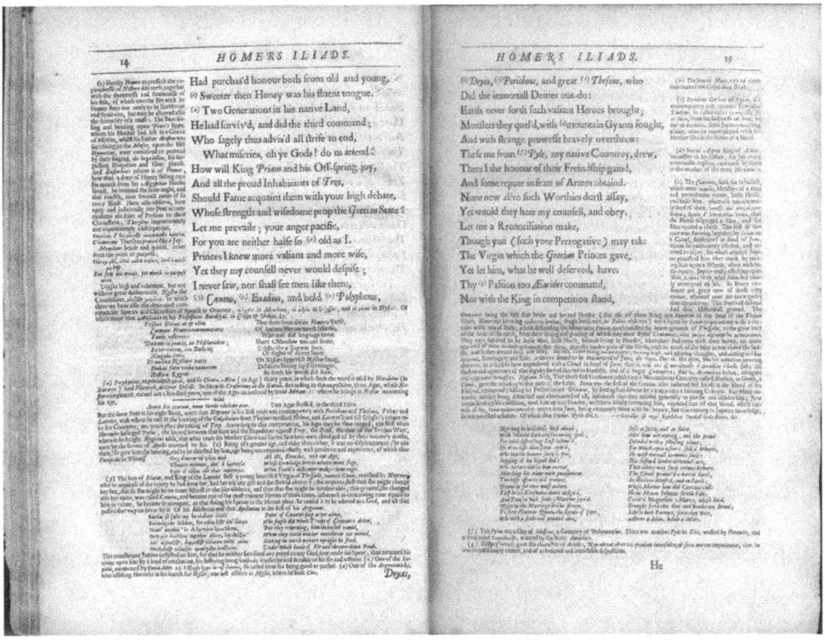

Figure 1. An opening from *Homer His Iliads Translated, Adorn'd with Sculpture, and Illustrated with Annotation by John Ogilby*. Courtesy of the Rare Books and Manuscripts Library, Thompson Library Special Collections, The Ohio State University Libraries.

enjambment, but in 1660 the form had not yet acquired the complexity and sophistication that it would acquire by the end of the seventeenth century (e.g., in Dryden's later work). Pope further accuses Ogilby of "extracting new meanings out of his Author," which implies that Pope will be respecting Homer's intentions (although Pope was, ironically, later accused of the very same thing).[64] Indeed, Pope prefaces his critique of earlier translations by announcing his ambition to "giv[e] a more tolerable Copy ... than any entire Translation in Verse has yet done."[65] In describing the text as "copy," Pope underscores the printed character of his work, and the adjective "tolerable" both degrades the earlier versions as "intolerable" and suggests that the ways in which his translation will be presented will not get in the way of his readers' engagement. Additionally, when Pope began his work, he saw himself as in competition with a highly anticipated translation by Thomas Tickell that had been encouraged (and perhaps assisted) by Joseph Addison.[66] Tickell's reputation as a more serious and learned classicist prompted many to expect and argue that his translation would be superior. Tickell, however, would eventually complete only one book.

When Pope is not commenting on poetics or methods of translation, his notes often resemble moral philosophy. He evaluates characters and practices in *The Iliad* on the basis of whether they could conform in appropriate ways to the modern world or if they should remain part of a superseded antiquity. In the preface, Pope notes that "Defects will be found upon Examination to proceed wholly from the Nature of the Times [Homer] liv'd in. Such are his *grosser Representations* of the *Gods*" and his "vicious and *imperfect* System" of theology, though "there are several Rays of Truth streaming through all this Darkness."[67] Many of Pope's notes can be read as attempts to remove what is obstructing those "Rays." One of the more vivid examples occurs in his lengthy "Essay on Homer's Battels" at the beginning of Volume 2. This piece explains and compares ancient and modern ideas of anatomy and military science, wondering, for instance, about the likely anachronism of the use of chariots. However, Pope repeatedly returns to the ethical character of Homer's depiction of war and the responses it raises in the reader. "What farther relieves and softens these Descriptions of Battles," he writes, is their ability to "raise a different movement in the Mind ... I mean Compassion and Pity."[68] Pope also notes that Homer is expert at portraying "every Turn of Mind or Emotion a Hero can possibly feel."[69] Pope's Homer sees battle as an opportunity to explore deeper moral concerns, and Pope's notes reflect a desire for the text to produce what he regards as correct interpretations, on both philological and philosophical levels. They also betray an anxiety that this most anticipated of publications not offend the politeness of the new literary marketplace.

Pope's imposition of heroic couplets further reflects the attempt to order this "wild paradise." The formal symmetry of the couplets, as well as what John Sitter calls their "epigrammatic effect," unifies and moralizes Homer's language in a way that prior translators had not attempted.[70] Pat Rogers has described how Pope employs the heroic couplet "as a placing and a discriminating device."[71] Rather than the complicated and potentially distressed syntax of Miltonic blank verse, the heroic couplet offers an "unassuming, inconspicuous amenity" that Pope perfects into "a marvelously supple piece of phonetic engineering."[72] Much like the dynamics of print itself, the couplet produces a level of closure that allows Pope to channel and "engineer" the heathen passions of Homer within its formal confines. This level of poetic contrivance, Pope writes, is a moderating force; it is "the graceful and *dignify'd* Simplicity" that he pursues in contrast to prior translators who have "swell'd into Fustian in a proud Confidence of the *Sublime*."[73] Attempts to maintain sublimity all too often slip into a "rusticity" that is inappropriate for a polite reader. The heroic couplet thus serves as a literary technology that Pope can use to trim the "wild garden" into something that will conform to the print market in which it will endure.[74] The arrangement of the couplet instills not only technical, but moral order. In artificializing, it smooths and dignifies, albeit at the expense of potential sublimity, and thus replicates what Mack calls "a generalized Western metaphysic for human action."[75] Its intended result is a text that thrives on the printed page. For Bentley, these transformations reduced the poem to the merely "pretty."

When Volume 6 arrived to subscribers in 1720, it contained only three books (the previous volumes had at least four). Following the final page of Book 24, Pope included twenty-nine pages of notes, a thirteen-page "Index of Persons and Things," a thirteen-page "Poetical Index," a five-page "Index of Arts and Sciences," and three pages of errata. Collectively, these create a "reader-friendly" apparatus that directs readers not only to specific moments, but also to key themes and concepts depicted in the poems. While indexes were not uncommon in eighteenth-century books, the depth to which Volume 6 goes supports David McKitterick's statement about the way in which the spatial dimensions of printed texts could be used to shape a reader's interpretation through a typographic design that "offer[s] a greater measure of coherence among different geographical, intellectual, or social loci."[76] The indexes also highlight the moral and philological stability that opposes the problematic aspects of Homer's "wild paradise." As a mark that the book is ending, it invites readers to recall the central themes and moments by returning to the text to re-read. Since Pope's translation was divided into six volumes that came out over the course of five years, the indexes work as a directive to readers who have already read the translation in its entirety and wish to return to particular parts.

More than any other component of the text, the indexes reflect Pope's desire to present an orderly *Iliad* with moral implications that are not only obvious and unambiguous, but also easily accessible. Pope's index serves more like a modern-day "topic map," which relies on digital technology to index and collate information through "several overlapping hierarchies which are rich with semantic cross-links."[77] Indexes provide readers with the "greater measure of coherence" that Pope desired. While the "poetical index" mainly directs readers to passages in which they can find "Descriptions of Persons" or "Descriptions of Things," some of its headings collect "Descriptions of the Internal Passions, or of their visible effects," and still others emphasize the moral and even political impulses behind Pope's choices. For the reader, these cross-references create a selective reading of *The Iliad* akin to the devotional use of a Biblical concordance: they guide readers to passages on which they might ruminate. For instance, underneath the heading of "Policy" is a section on *"Kings,"* which directs readers to fifteen different passages, ranging from how they "Derive their Honor from God" to the "Character of a great Prince in War and Peace" [see Figure 2]. The topics are not listed in the sequence in which they appear in the text, but rather seem to be arranged in order of importance. In the poetical index, a lengthy heading directs readers to "Descriptions of the Internal Passions, or of their Visible Effects" [see Figure 3]. While the list is concise in locating scenes of "Anxiety," "Grief," and "Hate," the index again controls interpretation by isolating and limiting the scenes that are appropriate for a reader to explore. Unlike the sections on sovereignty and kingship, the section on "Internal Passions" describes both negative and positive examples and also returns readers to Pope's extensive commentary that, in Slights's terms, works to "translate" the primary text into deeper strata of meaning. In its impulse to neatly discriminate between topics, the index reflects the emerging desire that Alvin Kernan locates in Samuel Johnson's "eagerness to strip whatever meaning [books] may have ... as quickly and efficiently as possible."[78]

In 1720, as Pope was moving on to the less-involved project of *The Odyssey,* he authorized the production of a new edition in duodecimo that converted the endnotes of the folio edition into footnotes [see Figures 4 and 5]. In the duodecimo edition, Homer's translated language floats above the more densely printed notes, which include all of Pope's "Observations," even though they are not tied to any specific line, but rather unfold Pope's "chief design" for including notes in the first place. The result is that the first fourteen lines of the poem require a full six pages. While the folio edition preserves Homer's text as its own entity, free from editorial intrusion, the commentary in the duodecimo presses up against the Homeric text to the point that it resembles *The Dunciad Variorum*'s parody of such apparatus. Future editions of *The Iliad* only expanded this use of ever more blatant visual cues. In many cases, it would be nearly impossible to separate Pope the Homeric commentator from Pope the poet-translator, as the expansive notes would make the reading experience seem less of a polite, gentlemanly activity and more like a scholarly endeavor bound to the new possibilities of print.

The disingenuous letter to Arabella Fermor that Pope included in the 1714 edition of *The Rape of the Lock* describes as frivolous an anxiety that Pope elsewhere found very real: "as it was communicated with the Air of a Secret, it soon found its Way into the World."[79] In this formulation, the oral whisper—spoken, uncontrollable, and easily misunderstood—is a coy stand-in for the poem itself. For the rest of his career, it would be his poetry's "Way into the World" that Pope would attempt to manage and control through a medium that seemed both his greatest friend and worst enemy.

POETICAL INDEX.

MECHANICKS.

Archery, Making a Bow, and all its Parts described, 4 136. &c.
Chariot-making. A Chariot described in all its Parts, 5. 889, &c. 24. 335.
Poplar proper for Wheels, 4. 554.
Sycamore fit for Wheels, 21. 44.
Clockwork, 18. 635.
Enamelling, 18. 635.
Ship-building, 5. 80.——15. 475.
Pine, a proper Wood for the Mast of a Ship, 16. 592.
Smithery, Iron-work, &c. The Forge described, 18. 435, 540. Bellows, 435, 482, 540. Hammer, Tongs, Anvil, 547.
Mixing of Metals, *ibid.*
Spinning, 23. 890.
Weaving, 3. 580. 6. 580
Embroidery, 6. 361.——
Armoury, and Instruments of War.]
A compleat Suit, that of *Paris*, 3. 410, &c. of *Agamemnon*, 11. 22,——&c.
Scale-Armour, 15. 629——
Helmets, with four Plumes, 5. 919——
——without any Crests, 10. 303——
——lin'd with Wool, and ornamented with Boars Teeth, of a particular make, 10. 311.——
——lin'd with Furr, 10. 397——
Bows, how made, 4. 137——
Battel-Ax, describ'd, 13. 766.
Belts, crossing each other, to hang the Sword and the Shield, 14. 468.
Corselets, ornamented with Sculpture, 11. 33.
——how lin'd, 4. 165——
Mace, or Club, 7. 170——15. 816.
Shields, so large as to cover from the Neck to the Ankles, 6. 145—— How made and cover'd, 7. 267. describ'd in every particular, 11. 43, &c.
Slings, 13. 890.
Spears, with Brass Points, 8. 617.
Ash fit to make them, 16. 143···19. 422.
How the Wood was join'd to the Point, 18. 618.
Swords, how ornamented, with Ivory, Gems, 19. 400.

ORATORY.

See the Article Speeches *in the Poetical Index.*

POLICY.

Kings.] Derive their Honour from God, 2. 233.——1. 315. Their Names to be honour'd, 2. 313. One sole Monarch, 2. 243. Hereditary Right of Kings represented by the Sceptre of *Agamemnon* given by *Jove*, 2. 129. Kings not to be disobey'd on the one hand, nor to stretch too far their Prerogative on the other, 1. 365. &c. Kings not absolute in Council, 9. 133. Kings made so, only for their excelling others in Virtue and Valour, 12. 377. Vigilance continually necessary in Princes, 2. 27·· 10. 102. Against Monarchs delighting in War, 9. 82, &c.—— 24. 55. The true Valour, that which preserves, not destroys Mankind, 6. 196. Kings may do wrong, and are oblig'd to Reparation, 9. 144. Character of a great Prince in War and Peace, 3. 236.
Councils.] The Danger of a Subject's too bold Advice, 1. 103. The Advantage of wise Counsels seconded by a wise Prince, 9. 101. The Use of Advice, 9. 137. The singular Blessing to a Nation and Prince, in a good and wise Counsellor, 13. 918. The Deliberations of the Council to be free, the Prince only to give a Sanction to the best, 9. 133.
Laws] deriv'd from God, and Legislators his Delegates, 1. 315. Committed to the Care of Kings, as Guardians of the Laws of God, 9. 129.
Tribute paid to Princes from Towns, 9. 206.
Taxes upon Subjects to assist foreign Allies, 17. 266.
Ambassadors, a sacred Character, 1. 435—— 9. 261.
Volunteers, listed into Service, 11. 904.

See the Article Art Military.

PHYSICK.

The Praise of a Physician, 11. 637.
Chiron learn'd it from *Æsculapius*, 4. 251.
Machaon and *Podalirius* Professors of it, 2. 890.
Botany.] Profess'd by skilful Women, *Agamede* famous for it, 11. 877.
Anatomy.] Of the Head, 16. 415, &c.
The *Eye*, 14. 577.
Under the *Ear*, a Wound there mortal, 13. 841.
The Juncture of the *Head*, and its *Nerves*, 14. 544.
The Juncture of the *Neck* and *Chest*, the *Collar-Bone* and its Insertion, the disjointing of which renders the Arm useless, 8. 393. &c.
The *Spinal Marrow* express'd by the Vein that runs along the Chine, a wound there mortal, 13. 692——20. 559——
The *Elbow*, its Tendons and Ligaments, 20. 554.
Blood, a great Effusion of it, by cutting off the Arm, the cause of immediate Death, 5. 105——
The *Heart* and its Fibres, 16. 590.
The force of the Muscle of the Heart, 13. 554.

S f f   A Wound

Figure 2. The entry on "POLICY" in the "POETICAL INDEX" of *The Iliad of Homer, Translated by Mr. Pope*. Courtesy of the Rare Books and Manuscripts Library, Thompson Library Special Collections, The Ohio State University Libraries.

POETICAL INDEX.

Descriptions of TIMES *and* SEASONS.

Day-break, 10. 295——
Morning, 2. 60—— 7. 515—— 8. 183——
9.833——11.1——11.115——19.1——
Sun-rising, 11. 871——
Noon, 16. 938——
Sun-setting, 1. 716——7. 556——8. 605
Evening, 16. 942——
Night, 2. *init.* 10th *Book throughout.* A ſtarry Night, 8. 687.
Spring, 14. 3 5——
Summer, 18. 637.
Autumn, 18. 651. 5. 1060——22. 40.
Winter, 12. 175. 331.

MILITARY *Descriptions.*

An Army deſcending on the Shore, 2. 117.
An Army marching, 2. 181. 940. The Day of Battle, 2. 458. A vaſt Army on the Plain, 535, &c. to 563. An Army going forth to Battel, 2. 976—— 13. 59——16. 255——19. 377.
A Chariot of War, 5. 890, &c.
Confuſion and noiſe of Battel, 16. 921——
A ſingle Combate, with all the Ceremonial, 3. 123, &c.
The Combate between *Paris* and *Menelaus*, 3. 423.
——of *Hector* and *Ajax*, 7. 250, to 335.
——of *Hector* and *Achilles*, 22.
Squadrons embattled, 4. 322—— 5. 637——8. 260——
Firſt Onſet of Battel, 4. 498, to 515.
A Circle incloſing the Foe, 5. 7/2.
Stand of an Army, 7. 75. Joining in Battel, 8. 75, &c. 13. 422——A Rout, 11. 193——14. 166——16. 440, &c. 21. 720——A Fortification attack'd, 12. 170, 201. 304. A Breach made, 12. 485. An obſtinate cloſe Fight, 12. 510——15. 860. An Army in cloſe Order, 13. 177, to 185——17. 406. An Attack on the Sea ſide, 14. 452——Levelling and paſſing a Trench, 15. 408. Attack of the Fleet, 15. 677, &c. 786. 855, &c. A Hero arming at all Points, *Agamemnon*, 11. 21. *Patroclus*, 16. 162. *Achilles*, 19. 390. Siege of a Town, 18. 591, &c. Surprize of a Convoy, *ibid.* Skirmiſh, *ibid.* Battle of the Gods, 20. 63, to 90. Two Heroes meeting in Battel, 20. 192. The Rage, Deſtruction and Carnage of Battel, 20. 574, &c.

Descriptions of the INTERNAL PASSIONS, *or of their viſible* EFFECTS.

Anxiety, in *Agamemnon*, 10, 13, &c. 100, &c.
Activity, in *Achilles*, 19. 416.
Admiration, 21, 62——24. 800——
Affright, 16, 968——
Amazement, 24. 590.
Ambition, 13. 458.
Anger, 1. 252.
Awe, 1. 430.
Buffoonry in *Therſites*, 2. 255, &c.
Contentment, 9, 520.
Conjugal Love, in *Hector* and *Androm.* 6. 510, &c.
Courage, 13. 109. 366——17. 250.
Cowardiſe, 13. 359—— 16. 488——
Curioſity, in old Men, 3. 194, &c.
Deſpair, 22. 377.
Diffidence, 3. 280.
Diſtreſs, 8. 290—— 9. 12, &c. 10. 96.
Doubt, 14. 21, &c. 21. 651, &c. 22. 138——
Fear, 10. 443——24. 441——
Fear in *Priam*, 21. 615. For his Son, 22. 43. 51, &c. Fear of a Child, 6. 596.
Fidelity, in *Lycophron*, Servant of *Ajax*, 15. 502——*Caleſius*, Servant of *Axylus*, 6. 20.
Grief in a fine Woman, 1. 150——3. 185——1. 450——
Grief of a Siſter for her dead Brothers, 3. 300, &c.
Grief in two Parents in tenderneſs for their Child, 6. 504.
Grief occaſion'd by love of our Country, in *Patroclus*, 16. *init.*
Grief for a Friend in *Achilles* for *Patroclus*, 18. 25—— 100, &c. 19. 335——22. 482——24. 5——
Furious Grief, 18. 367.
Frantic Grief, 24. 291.
Grief of a Father for his Son, in *Priam*, 22. 522, &c. 24. 200. 275. 291.
Grief of a Wife for her Husband, 22. 562. to the end, the Epiſode of *Andromache*, and again, 24. 906.
Grief out of gratitude, in *Briſeis*, 19. 319. in *Helen*, 24.
Haſte, expreſſ in *Hector*, 15. 395. 402, &c.
Hate, in *Achilles* to *Hector*, 22. 335. 433, &c.
Hardneſs of Heart, 9. 750——
Inſolence, in *Tlepolemus*, 5. 783. in *Epeus*, 23. 767.
Joy, its viſible Effects, 23. 678.
Love, in *Helen* and *Paris*, 3. 551, &c. in *Jupiter* and *Juno*, 14. 332, &c. 357——
Conjugal Love, in *Hector* and *Androm.* 6, &c.
Love of a Mother to her Son, in *Thetis* to *Achilles*, 18. 70——24. 117.
Q q q   Brotherly

Figure 3. The entry on "*Descriptions of the* INTERNAL PASSIONS, *or of their visible* EFFECTS" in the "POETICAL INDEX" of *The Iliad of Homer, Translated by Mr. Pope*. Courtesy of the Rare Books and Manuscripts Library, Thompson Library Special Collections, The Ohio State University Libraries.

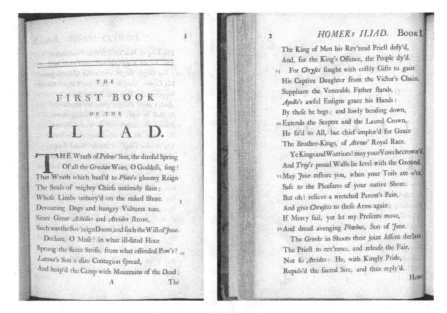

Figure 4. The recto and verso of the first leaf of the poem in the folio edition of *The Iliad of Homer, Translated by Mr. Pope*. Courtesy of the Rare Books and Manuscripts Library, Thompson Library Special Collections, The Ohio State University Libraries.

James McLaverty contends that the 1717 *Works* above all announce that "This is Pope's book and *Pope*": they attempt "to shape every Pope or *Pope* the public might encounter … *The Works* is less an attempt to resist and regulate the new currents than to do something exciting and risky with them himself. The volume gave Pope the opportunity to fashion a large book that was to represent the author himself."[80] It is no coincidence that Pope continued to work on his translation of the *Iliad* as the *Works* came together. Pope seized the opportunity to make his Homer a part of his oeuvre and to extend his own fame through its framing and presentation. And it is equally no coincidence that after the success of both the *Iliad* and the *Works*, he designed the 1720 duodecimo edition of *The Iliad* to capitalize on the ways in which he was now intertwined with Homer.

Penelope Wilson notes that "'Homer' before the eighteenth-century colonization of the classics was a more composite and more uncertain entity."[81] The continued life of Pope's *Iliad* attests not only to Pope's enduring popularity across the eighteenth century, but also to the degree to which his interpretation became the dominant way of both reading Homer and reading *about* Homer. Matthew Arnold's lecture in 1861 only confirms

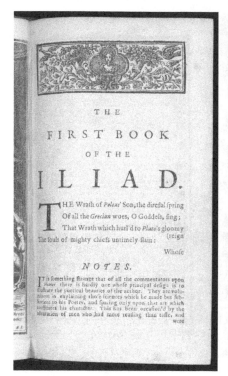
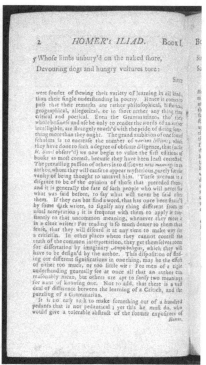

Figure 5. The recto and verso of the first leaf of the poem in the duodecimo edition of *The Iliad of Homer, Translated by Mr. Pope.* Courtesy of the Bodleian Libraries, University of Oxford, shelfmark 2391 f. 65 vol. 1.

the lasting influence of Pope's translation by challenging its aesthetic. It is likely that the success of Pope's translation prompted other philological projects to explore the historical personhood and poetics of Homer in such works as Thomas Blackwell's *Enquiry into the Life and Writings of Homer* (1735), Robert Wood's *An Essay on the Original Genius of Homer* (1769), and F. A. Wolf's field-defining *Prolegomena ad Homerum* (1795). Whether that "colonization" was brought about through the work of classicists or by modernizing poets such as Pope, the eighteenth-century veneration of Homer went hand-in-hand with his assimilation into eighteenth-century political, social, and religious paradigms. Pope's own classicizing gesture was shaped by these debates as he confronted a primal, even dangerous orality that could either stimulate or corrupt the polite regimentation of print.

For Pope, the uncontrollable oral mirrors his own anxieties about the reception of his work and the distressing possibility that his career as an author would be dependent not on the texts that he produced, but rather on the rumors about the man who produced them. The oral was a medium that Pope could not personally master, which deepened and complicated his disdain for and ridicule of the Henleys, Whartons, and Ulysseses who could perform in a way that was impossible for him. Pope's diagnosis, in his later poems, of how people could be contaminated by a violent "ruling passion" would only deepen this critique. In print, Pope could find a new existence, an empowered subjectivity detached from his own bodily condition and supplanted by the physical space of the book. Carolyn Williams has perceptively argued that Pope "perceived his own lifelong struggles for dignity, high social status, and political independence as a battle between manly virtue and effeminate corruption," and his engagement with classical antiquity was inflected by his deepest desires and fraught with various absences and excesses.[82] Orality, and its institutionalization and performance through rhetoric, provoked precisely these feelings in Pope: a sense that something was simultaneously absent in himself and excessive in others. *The Iliad* project gave him the power to order both kinds of affect through the centripetal force of print.

Notes

1. Pope, *The Iliad of Homer*, ed. Maynard Mack, in the Twickenham Edition of the Works of Alexander Pope, gen. ed. John Butt, 10 vols. (New Haven: Yale University Press, 1943-70), 7:2. All citations of Pope refer to this edition. However, I will be citing the verse parenthetically by book, canto, and line numbers (as appropriate) in order to facilitate reference to other editions. Pope's prose and the scholarly apparatus of the Twickenham Edition will be cited by page number in the notes.

2. Weinbrot, *Britannia's Issue: The Rise of British Literature from Dryden to Ossian* (Cambridge: Cambridge University Press, 2007), 303.

3. Quoted in Samuel Johnson, "Pope," in *The Lives of the Poets*, ed. John H. Middendorf (New Haven: Yale University Press, 2010): 1180.

4. Johnson, "Pope," 1076.

5. McDowell, *The Invention of the Oral: Print Commerce and Fugitive Voices in Eighteenth-Century Britain* (Chicago: University of Chicago Press, 2017), 15.

6. See Kirsti Simonsuuri, *Homer's Original Genius: Eighteenth-Century Notions of the Greek Epic, 1688–1798* (Cambridge: Cambridge University Press, 1979), 49: "The *Iliad's* straightforward morality of war and necessity appeared too simple and crude to the people of the early eighteenth century who had been used to peace and valued subtlety and sophistication in their human interaction."

7. Mack, Introduction to *The Iliad of Homer*, 7:clxxxvii.

8. Swift, *A Tale of a Tub and Other Works*, ed. Marcus Walsh (Cambridge: Cambridge University Press, 2010), 180.

9. Ong, *Orality and Literacy: The Technologizing of the Word* (London: Routledge, 2012), 111, 116.

10. Potkay, *The Fate of Eloquence in the Age of Hume* (Ithaca: Cornell University Press, 1994), 2.

11. McDowell, *Invention of the Oral*, 5.

12. All quotations from *The Dunciad* come from the 1742 version that the Twickenham Edition has designated as "B."

13. See Potkay, *The Fate of Eloquence,* particularly chapter 5. For Potkay, Henley is "more or less abstracted into an emblem of debased eloquence," just "another player in possession of oratory's lost prerogative" (108, 109).

14. Spence, *Observations, Anecdotes, and Characters of Books and Men*, ed. James M. Osborn, 2 vols. (Oxford: Clarendon Press, 1966), 1:102–3.

15. Montagu, *Correspondence*, ed. Robert Halsband, 3 vols. (Oxford: Clarendon Press, 1965), 1:428.

16. See Alvin Kernan, *Samuel Johnson and the Impact of Print* (Princeton: Princeton University Press, 1989). In *The Dunciad,* according to Kernan, "print ... replaces the literary arrangements of the old regime with those more in the spirit of its own mechanical, democratic, and capitalistic tendencies, creating a new world of writing, Grub Street" (9).

17. McLuhan, *The Gutenberg Galaxy: The Making of Typographic Man* (Toronto: University of Toronto Press, 1962), 258. In order to mimic McLuhan's tendency toward mystified abstraction, I have intentionally reified the printing press as an agent in this sentence.

18. McLaverty, *Pope, Print, and Meaning* (Oxford: Oxford University Press, 2001), 1.

19. Guillory, "Genesis of the Media Concept," *Critical Inquiry* 36, no. 2 (2010): 334.

20. Locke, *An Essay Concerning Human Understanding*, ed. Alexander Campbell Fraser (New York: Dover, 1959), 133.

21. Locke, *Essay Concerning Human Understanding*, 146.

22. Locke, *The Educational Writings of John Locke*, ed. James L. Axtell (Cambridge: Cambridge University Press, 1968), 299.

23. See Courtney Weiss Smith, "Political Individuals and Providential Nature in Locke and Pope," *Studies in English Literature, 1500–1900* 52, no. 3 (2012): 609–29. Pope's engagement with Locke is philosophical and ignores Locke's Whiggish political views. As Smith observes, both Locke and Pope are "skeptical about the infallibility of any human construct at the same time as they claim some kind of suprahuman sanction for these constructs" (614).

24. Paula McDowell, "Mediating Media Past and Present: Toward a Genealogy of 'Print Culture' and 'Oral Tradition,'" in *This is Enlightenment*, ed. Clifford Siskin and William Warner (Chicago: University of Chicago Press, 2010), 235.

25. I take the striking phrase "borders of politeness" from Paul Goring's chapter regarding "Bodies on the Borders of Politeness" in *The Rhetoric of Sensibility*

in Eighteenth-Century Culture (Cambridge: Cambridge University Press, 2005). This project is informed by Goring's discussion of the ways in which the poles of enthusiasm and politeness came to align.

26. See Robert Markley, *Fallen Languages: Crises of Representation in Newtonian England, 1660–1740* (Ithaca: Cornell University Press, 1993). Markley notes that seventeenth-century language projects "testify to the ideological urgency ... to control the dialogical and subversive tendencies of language" (72). Representations of disruptive orators, however satirical, mark this anxiety.

27. See Ong, *Orality and Literacy*. Primary orality is "the orality of cultures untouched by literacy" (5), as opposed to a "secondary" orality that persists in advanced, technologized cultures. Ong contends that a "new orality" emerges out of cultures that rely on writing and script (10–11).

28. Potkay, *Fate of Eloquence*, 5.

29. See, for instance, Mr. Spectator's claim that he prefers to be a "spectator of Mankind, than ... one of the Species" (*The Spectator*, ed. Donald F. Bond, 5 vols. [Oxford: Clarendon Press, 1965], 1:4). Both Addison and Steele invoke classical models to justify this non-interventionist approach. In *Spectator* 10, Mr. Spectator famously invokes Socrates to justify his goal of bringing philosophy "to dwell in Clubs and Assemblies, at Tea-Tables, and in Coffee-Houses" (1:44). In the comparison, Mr. Spectator at once elevates his own mission and playfully mocks the grand ambition of Socrates. Though Socrates may offer an ideal of serious intellectual pursuit, his radical energy has no place in polite society, while the modest goals of Mr. Spectator are an appropriate form of social improvement.

30. Jasper Griffin, "The Speeches," in *The Cambridge Companion to Homer*, ed. Robert Fowler (Cambridge: Cambridge University Press, 2004), 156 n1.

31. Worman, "Fighting Words: Status, Stature, and Verbal Contest in Archaic Poetry," in *The Cambridge Companion to Ancient Rhetoric*, ed. Erik Gunderson (Cambridge: Cambridge University Press, 2007), 29.

32. Worman, "Fighting Words," 30.

33. While "winged words" [*epea pteroenta*] is an epithet frequent in many Homeric translations, Pope never uses it. Instead, the epithets, which work as signals of orality, are integrated through various strategies into Pope's texts. On this epithet and its interpretation, see Françoise Létoublon, "*Epea Pteroenta* ('Winged Words')" *Oral Tradition* 14, no. 2 (1999): 321–35.

34. Homer, *The Iliad of Homer*, trans. Richmond Lattimore (Chicago: University of Chicago Press, 2011), 123. For all of the passages we'll be considering, I have consulted the Greek text and its facing-page translation in the Loeb edition (Homer, *Iliad*, trans. A. T. Murray [Cambridge: Harvard University Press, 1999]) and Lattimore's translation, which attempts to render the Homeric text word-for-word and line-by-line. Unless otherwise noted, my quotations are from Lattimore's translation. For a defense of his fidelity, see Simeon Underwood, *English Translators of Homer from George Chapman to Christopher Logue* (Plymouth: Northcote House in association with the British Council, 1998).

35. In the preface to his own translation, Pope discusses (and ultimately dismisses) earlier translations by George Chapman, Thomas Hobbes, and John Ogilby. Pope praises John Dryden's partial translation ("He has left us only the first Book and

a small Part of the sixth" [22]) and notes that he would not be attempting his own version had Dryden completed his.

36. Ogilby, *Homer His Iliads Translated, Adorn'd with Sculpture, and Illustrated with Annotation by John Ogilby* (London, 1660), 80. Henceforth, I will refer to Odysseus by its Roman equivalent ("Ulysses"), as was standard in seventeenth- and eighteenth-century translations. For the issues at stake in the choice of names, see Phillip Young, *The Printed Homer* (Jefferson: McFarland, 2008), 86–87.

37. Chapman, *The Iliad*, in *Chapman's Homer*, ed. Allardyce Nicoll, 2 vols. (New York: Pantheon Books, 1956), 1:80.

38. Lanham, *The Motives of Eloquence: Literary Rhetoric in the Renaissance* (Eugene: Wipf & Stock Publishers, 2004), 4.

39. Chapman, *Iliad*, 1:80.

40. Chapman, *Iliad*, 1:89.

41. Pope, *The Iliad of Homer*, 7:206 n278.

42. Pope, *The Iliad of Homer*, 7:206 n278.

43. Pope, *The Iliad of Homer*, 7:205 n271.

44. Pope, *The Iliad of Homer*, 7:104 n339.

45. Pope, *The Iliad of Homer*, 7: 452 n406.

46. Pope, *The Iliad of Homer*, 7: 457 n500. Steven Shankman argues that Pope's engagement with the contemporary discourse of the passions "enabled him to represent, with less distortion and with greater ethical immunity than had Chapman, the rise and abatement of Achilles' wrath" (*Pope's Iliad: Homer in the Age of Passion* [Princeton: Princeton University Press, 1983], 29).

47. Strawn, "Homer, Sentimentalism, and Pope's Translation of *The Iliad*," *Studies in English Literature, 1500–1900* 52, no. 3 (2012): 595.

48. Pope, *The Iliad of Homer*, 7:469.

49. Pope, *The Iliad of Homer*, 7:8.

50. Dennis, *A True Character of Mr. Pope and His Writings* (London, 1716), 17.

51. Arnold, *On Translating Homer: Three Lectures Given at Oxford* (London, 1861), 18.

52. Keats, *The Poems of John Keats*, ed. Jack Stillinger (Cambridge: Belknap Press of Harvard University Press, 1978), 64.

53. Hopkins, *Gerard Manley Hopkins: Selected Letters*, ed. Catherine Phillips (Oxford: Clarendon Press, 1990), 28.

54. See Robin Sowerby, *The Augustan Art of Poetry: Augustan Translations of the Classics* (Oxford: Oxford University Press, 2006).

55. Ong, *Orality and Literacy*, 122.

56. See Eisenstein, *The Printing Revolution in Early Modern Europe* (Cambridge: Cambridge University Press, 1993), 64.

57. McLaverty, *Pope, Print, and Meaning*, 14–15.

58. McLaverty, *Pope, Print, and Meaning*, 14.

59. Maynard Mack notes that "Subscription editions had appeared before … but never one like this" (*Alexander Pope: A Life* [New York: W. W. Norton, 1988], 267).

60. Mack, Introduction to *The Iliad of Homer*, 7:xli.

61. William W. E. Slights, *Managing Readers: Printed Marginalia in English Renaissance Books* (Ann Arbor: University of Michigan Press, 2001), 64.

62. Pope, *The Iliad of Homer*, 7:82 n1.

63. Pope, *The Iliad of Homer*, 7:201 n201.

64. Pope, *The Iliad of Homer*, 7:12–13.

65. Pope, *The Iliad of Homer*, 7:21.

66. See Joseph M. Levine, *The Battle of the Books: History and Literature in the Augustan Age* (Ithaca: Cornell University Press, 1991). Levine writes that Tickell's translation was a "response [to], rather than the cause of" Pope's project, but that the "rivalry undoubtedly added to the peculiar public interest that surrounded Homer at this time" (194).

67. Pope, *The Iliad of Homer*, 7:67, 7:68.

68. Pope, *The Iliad of Homer*, 7:255.

69. Pope, *The Iliad of Homer*, 7:255.

70. Sitter, *The Cambridge Introduction to Eighteenth-Century Poetry* (Cambridge: Cambridge University Press, 2011), 34.

71. Pat Rogers, *An Introduction to Pope* (New York: Routledge, 2014), 13.

72. Rogers, *An Introduction to Pope*, 15.

73. Pope, *The Iliad of Homer*, 7:18.

74. See Shankman, *Pope's Iliad,* 131–65.

75. Mack, Introduction to *The Iliad of Homer*, 7:clxxxvi.

76. McKitterick, *Print, Manuscript and the Search for Order, 1450–1830* (Cambridge: Cambridge University Press, 2005), 227.

77. Lars Marius Garshol, "What Are Topic Maps," *Xml.com*, September 11, 2002, http://www.xml.com/pub/a/2002/09/11/topicmaps.html?page=1. See also Jeffrey M. Binder and Collin Jennings, "'A Scientifical View of the Whole': Adam Smith, Indexing, and Technologies of Abstraction," *ELH* 83, no.1 (2016): 157–80. Following Binder and Jennings's account of the apparatus and reception history of Smith's *The Wealth of Nations,* I see a connection between Smith and Pope in their similarly idealized conception of the index as a tool that furthers the "rhetorical enterprise" of "systematic exposition in which abstract concepts are built up through the use of multiple concrete examples" (160).

78. Kernan, *Samuel Johnson and the Impact of Print*, 217.

79. Pope, *The Rape of the Lock and Other Poems*, ed. Geoffrey Tillotson, in the Twickenham Edition, 2:142.

80. McLaverty, *Pope, Print, and Meaning*, 53, 56.

81. Penelope Wilson, "Homer and English Epic," in *The Cambridge Companion to Homer*, ed. Robert Fowler (Cambridge: Cambridge University Press, 2004), 275.

82. Williams, *Pope, Homer, and Manliness: Some Aspects of Eighteenth-Century Classical Learning* (London: Routledge, 1993), 5.

THE DESERTED VILLAGE AT 250

Introduction: *The Deserted Village* at 250

MICHAEL GRIFFIN AND DAVID O'SHAUGHNESSY

Published on 26 May 1770, Oliver Goldsmith's long poem *The Deserted Village* has been a staple in many survey courses of British and Irish literature. It has, however, been a difficult poem to categorize, and readers' and critics' responses have been diverse: to some, it is too conservative in its worldview to animate readers; to others, it has a radical quality that is somewhat undercut by its own aesthetic and formal traditionalism. To still other readers, it is a fascinating work because of the difficulties that it poses and the craftsmanship employed in the service of those difficulties. More than any of Goldsmith's other poetic works (including *The Traveller, or a Prospect of Society*, which Samuel Johnson preferred and thought the best poem in English since the work of Alexander Pope), *The Deserted Village* has, for 250 years, widened and deepened in terms of its critical heritage, moving between an appreciation of its Augustan poise, its Romantic subjectivism, its Tory hierarchicalism, and its radical critique of an emergent imperialist capitalism. The essays in this cluster stem from a panel at the 2021 Virtual Annual Meeting of the American Society for Eighteenth-Century Studies convened (a year later than intended because of the COVID-19 pandemic) to consider the poem afresh on its 250th anniversary. Together, they allow us to view the poem in the round, raising and exploring further questions: are the key qualities of the poem pictorial? political? imperial? anti-imperial? proto-ecological? allusive? auditory?

The Deserted Village is a beautiful piece of work, with many allusions carefully embroidered into it, but its beauties and allusions may distract ultimately from the objects of its ostensible critique. Even the elements of protest running through the poem have had their motives questioned. Raymond Williams saw *The Deserted Village* as a "self-regarding poetic exercise": a lament for the loss of the social conditions that could foster poetry.[1] Commercial society had abstracted poetry from social relationships, and regret at the loss of rural virtues might be understood as no more than regret for the depreciation of Goldsmith's literary vocation. That vocation involves a form of labor, however, and Joshua Wright's essay defends that labor as being of a kind with that of the laboring swain in the poem. Wright suggests an emphasis on the "lost acoustic world" evoked by the poem's language, and indeed by the emphases of its imagery. The hollow-sounding bittern, making its sounds at a remove from human civilization, is a powerful emblem of the desolation with which the poem is so concerned. The lapwing serves a similar role. This essay alerts us to the centrality of "sweet" sounds throughout the poem—the village murmur rising, the mingling notes, the lowing herd, the geese gabbling, the baying watchdog, the loud laugh that spoke the vacant mind—and to Goldsmith's craft in rendering them. To Marxisant readers, Wright's core argument—that the critique of the poem's elision of labor ignores the poetic labor involved in the poem's construction—may be contentious, but the alignment of literary and agricultural labor is one that goes back to Theocritus and Virgil. It has long been a key element in the pastoral.

From pastoral sounds to allusive verbal images. Denys Van Renen's close reading of the poem's spatial arrangements treats its seeming resignation to an early capitalist sublime, or its acceptance of the replacement of an English sublime with an American, as ultimately a form of resignation within which Goldsmith's intertextualities may recognize the prospect of a wider ecological catastrophe set in motion by human activity and movement. The image of the pastoral clerical intelligence rising to a soulful peace above the weather, for instance, could stand, in a sense, for thinking beyond the immediate displacements of people to the consequences of those displacements understood in ecological time, though it could equally be read as an occasion for no more than an ostentatious intertextuality on Goldsmith's part. The literary provenance of this epic simile has attracted substantial commentary from Goldsmith's editors. In the Anglophone tradition there are, alongside Pope, the possible influences of John Dryden and Edward Young. Van Renen's noting of an echo of Joseph Addison, however, is new and highly suggestive, and his discussion of that allusion here adds greatly to our understanding of both the colonial and the ecological dimensions of the poem. Further, he argues that literary allusion disguises an ambivalence regarding mass displacement and its effects, an ambivalence that goes to the question of the poem's possible fatalism, its acceptance that some of the changes it decries cannot be reversed. It is noteworthy that Van Renen's and Wright's readings of the same passages vary so considerably: the contrast neatly demonstrates the poem's remarkable and enduringly generative qualities.

It is appropriate that Timothy Erwin's concluding piece makes reference to John Montague, whose thoughts on Goldsmith have been so influential. In a 1973 interview with fellow Irish poet Eavan Boland for the *Irish Times*, Montague relayed his sense of his own poem *The Rough Field* as "a poem about a threatened way of life." Boland thought it "not surprising that so contemporary a poet should turn back to one so superficially outdated as Goldsmith." Montague insisted that Goldsmith was "the first to state this great theme ... it's a lament for a way of life, but a celebration of it at the same time."[2] Montague's account of the poem has shaped subsequent, more worldly assessments, in which the pastoral is understood as a genre with global and post-colonial reach. In a 2014 reading, for instance, Shirley Lau Wong defended pastoral poetry from charges that it aestheticizes the harsher realities of agricultural labor, arguing instead that in Montague's *Rough Field,* Goldsmith's pastoral is updated to articulate an ambivalence towards more recent forms of modernization.[3] This ambivalence is poignantly articulated in *The Rough Field*'s concluding elegiac sequence, which alludes pointedly to Goldsmith in its envisioning of an older—and harsher—rural order giving way to a more efficient mode of production, with "Fewer hands, bigger markets, larger farms. / Yet something mourns." Montague saw *The Deserted Village* as "a sort of rural Wasteland," with a resonance not unlike that of T. S. Eliot's modernist classic. Goldsmith did not seek to associate Auburn with Ireland specifically, preferring instead to view it as a "universal village," through which he could consider the apparently inverse relationship between the health of rural society and the extent of imperial expansion. Montague's analysis broadens the appeal and relevance of the poem, seeing its preoccupations as not simply or merely local, but rather as expressing an international concern that is both historically specific *and* transhistorical.

Erwin's contribution helps us to think about the poem in new interdisciplinary ways that draw upon studies of visual culture outside the realm of what might be called high art history. His essay participates in an intensifying consideration of book illustration. At the outset, he issues a timely reminder that no poem in English apart from John Milton's *Paradise Lost* and James Thomson's *The Seasons* has been illustrated more often than *The Deserted Village*. The nineteenth-century tradition of illustrating

Goldsmith is fascinating, and Erwin insightfully suggests a continuity between the habit of illustrating the poem and the ways in which it was read. Indeed, there are insights here into how Goldsmith's oeuvre as a whole has been received. For example, Erwin's study invites us to consider the poem alongside *The Vicar of Wakefield* and the traditions of illustration that attend upon that strange novel.

Erwin begins his story with William Blake's innovative method for combining text and image in a more profound manner than Gérard Genette's term "paratext" will allow; Erwin proposes the more satisfying concept of "imagetext." This salutary starting point helps the rich culture of illustration that Erwin is exploring to escape the limiting logic of supplementarity. Much like Montague's description of the poem as *ut pictura poesis*, Erwin's essay allows us to visualize aspects of the poem's politics, while enhancing and embodying still more its deictic language: what was yonder, what was at that very spot, etc. Erwin traces the lineage of the poem's illustration from its first publication to James Gillray and John Keyse Sherwin through to Francis Wheatley's gorgeous pictures, showing how those images illuminate contemporary and early nineteenth-century understandings of the poem and adding to our own understanding of the ways in which readers have interacted with the text.

In another piece for the *Irish Times,* Boland argues that the tragedy of *The Deserted Village* was that it predated the revolutionary age in which it would have been able to break free of earlier eighteenth-century restraints: "'The Deserted Village' contains all the outrage, all the imaginative force of the Romantic crying out against the destruction of a pastoral myth and a personal world. Unlike any Romantic, however, [Goldsmith] must in this poem and 'The Traveller' continually salute a concept of order which his romantic instinct must have sensed did not exist, but which his Augustan skills had trained him to inherit."[4] In this passage Boland again catches the oddity of *The Deserted Village*, its simultaneous belatedness and innovation, its craft and its political endurance. Our cluster addresses these points of discussion from a variety of aesthetic and political perspectives and poses anew key questions: what do the poem's language, allusions, and sonic and visual elements ultimately tell us about its resonance, both at its moment of initial publication and now (a quarter-millennium later)? Is it a radical or a conservative poem? Is it an effective poem, or is it too fatalistic? Is it an English or an Irish poem? Is it an Augustan or a Romantic poem? Is the act of making such distinctions zero-sum? The critical fate of *The Deserted Village* is still unfolding.

Notes

1. Williams, "Nature's Threads," *Eighteenth-Century Studies* 2, no. 1 (1968), 53.

2. Boland, "The Tribal Poet: John Montague," *Irish Times*, 20 March 1973, 10.

3. Wong, "Country Bumpkin and Cosmopolitan: Some Versions of Postcolonial Pastoral," *Global South* 7, no. 2 (2014), 153–72.

4. Boland, "Oliver Goldsmith: 1730–1774," *Irish Times*, 9 April 1974, 10.

"Sweet was the sound": The Acoustic World of Oliver Goldsmith's *The Deserted Village*

JOSHUA WRIGHT

In the opening lines of *The Deserted Village*, Oliver Goldsmith gives an extended description of the village of Auburn's bucolic charms, before revealing that "all these charms are fled" in the poem's present.[1] *The Deserted Village* structures itself around such temporal oscillations, moving frequently between the past, present, and future. Notably, one sense dominates the poem's first return to the pastoralized past after the revelation of the village's present, degraded state: sound. The speaker reminisces: "Sweet was the sound when oft at evening's close, / Up yonder hill the village murmur rose," before cataloging the village's lost soundscape (*DV* 113–14). Later in the poem, the speaker poignantly recollects the way the village's blacksmith would "Relax his ponderous strength, and lean to hear" the conversation at the village's alehouse (*DV* 246). The blacksmith's attentiveness to listening models, I believe, a productive approach to Goldsmith's poem—a work suffused with sounds and deeply invested in their relationship with time, space, and the labor of poetry and memory.

Attuning ourselves to the poem's use of sound opens up space for a fresh perspective on many of the longstanding debates that have dominated the poem's critical history. The poem provides a surfeit of aural details that lovingly reconstruct, or create, the soundscape of Auburn, and in the process draw our attention to the ways in which the rhythms of life are constituted by sound. Goldsmith evokes the pain caused by the rupture or cessation of those rhythms, those ways of living, and those sounds. And yet, sound contains promise in the poem as well; if the bucolic past is marked by its murmurings, then sound (and the poetic voice committing it to the page) may also have the power to prevail over time's entropic forces.

I situate this essay within the context of a strain of literary-historical scholarship that seeks to recover various lost acoustic worlds. In offering a summary of such influential works as Alain Corbin's *Village Bells*, John Picker's *Victorian Soundscapes*, and Mark Smith's *Listening in Nineteenth-Century America*, Judith Pascoe writes that "All ... these writers ... suggest that modes of listening are intertwined with self-identity; that in re-creating a past soundscape, we might re-create a way of being in the world."[2] The speaker of *The Deserted Village* may be attempting just such a recreation. In *The Invention of the Oral*, Paula MacDowell asserts that "eighteenth-century texts are a valuable register of our predecessors' experiences of different aural environments. As these texts powerfully show, the consumption of sound is at once physiological and psychological. Social and personal factors influence not only what we hear but what it means."[3] The importance of the soundscape of Auburn cannot then be overstated; indeed, the details of the acoustic environment speak to many of the critical debates that have emerged surrounding the poem.

Although the poem famously opens with a bygone bucolic vision, Goldsmith's first prominent use of sound introduces the village's deteriorated present state. Goldsmith writes, "Along thy glades, a solitary guest, / The hollow sounding bittern guards its nest; / Amidst thy desert walks the lapwing flies / And tires their ecchoes with unvaried cries" (*DV* 43–46). The sounds the poem's speaker hears in this passage are negatively coded. Melissa Bailes notes that, "With adjectives emphasizing the 'solitary' and 'hollow' scene, every line evacuates the landscape of human presence, and even the birds, though active, embody this changed nature."[4] Bailes astutely notes the evacuation of space in the passage; however, it should be noted that it is not the scene that is described as hollow, but the sound of the bittern's cry itself. Noting this particularity emphasizes the power of sound in the poem—the emptiness of the bittern's cry deepens, or in the context of the poem creates, the emptiness of the scene. Whereas the village's past soundscape is one dominated by the noisy rhythms of life, the present is dominated by empty silences punctured by distinctive and meaningful noises.

The lapwing's cries, too, are suggestive. Bailes argues that "through conventional associations between birdsong and verse, [the lapwing's 'unvaried cries'] suggest a prevailing poetic monotony that foreshadows the destitution of Britain's poetry as well as of its working class."[5] Despite the poem's concern for the losses incurred amidst change, the lapwings' "unvarying" cries emphasize the village's present desolation. Although the poem dwells in the realm of memory, the involuntary echo represents a form of monotony and poverty—an echo is devoid of effort. The poet's imaginative efforts are depicted as being part of a more active process: Goldsmith writes, "Remembrance wakes with all her busy train, / Swells at my chest, and turns the past to pain" (*DV* 81–82). Here, memory is active and affective—the lines emphasize the embodied nature of memory, which cause the speaker physical pain. Later, when remembering the village's lost alehouse, the speaker makes a telling word choice: "Imagination fondly stoops to trace / The parlor splendors of that festive place" (*DV* 225). Imagination replaces memory in these lines, accentuating the degree to which the two are often interrelated. The word "stoops" further reinforces the idea that imagining and remembering are active and physical processes; they demand exertion and effort. Critiques of the poem's sentimentalizing often focus on the lack of labor depicted in it.[6] Yet, I propose that the imaginative acts of remembrance that suffuse the poem constitute a kind of labor. This idea, the conflation of rural and poetic labor, can be traced back all the way to Virgil's *Georgics*. As Kurt Heinzelman puts it: "Plows turn the land (*vertere terrarii*), but verses also inscribe, etymologically grounded as they are in the turns (*versus*) that plows make at the end of furrows."[7] Although often identified as a pastoral due to the obliqueness of its depictions of rural labor, *The Deserted Village* exemplifies this Georgic equivocation between rural and poetic labor through the poet's memorial efforts. While the lapwing's "unvaried cries" suggest a monotonous poetic present, the poetic labor of conjuring past sounds might offer a corrective—something that I will return to later.

But first, it is important to consider the soundscape of Auburn's heyday. The poem's speaker invokes sound to immerse himself and the reader in the village's past after the poem's first move to the hollow-sounding present. "Up yonder hill the village murmur rose," Goldsmith writes, before beginning a long succession of lines describing the auditory life of the village that has since been silenced (*DV* 114). Goldsmith describes the sounds of singing, laughter, gabbling geese, and children playing: "These all in sweet confusion sought the shade, / And filled each pause the nightingale had made" (*DV* 123–24). Once again, sounds exhibit a spatial dimension in this passage: whereas the bittern's hollow-sounding cry serves to further evacuate the deserted village of life, here, the susurrations of the rural scene tellingly "fill" the natural pauses. The nightingale's song alone would not be enough to enliven Auburn, but when balanced with the sounds of the village's denizens an evocative soundscape is created, one that can help the poem's speaker fully immerse himself and the poem's readers in the past.

The soundscape that Goldsmith evocatively constructs gives readers a sense of the rhythms of the inhabitants' rural lives through the rhythms of the poem's sounds. The sense of Auburn as a place resides in this rhythmic soundscape, as does the poet's sense of belonging to the village and its past. As Tim Edensor notes, "a combination of sonic rhythms gives a distinctive texture to place, contributing to the affective intensities and sensory orientations of belonging."[8] The poem's speaker notes, as he passes through, that the "mingling notes" of the village's auditory environment "came softened from below." The word "mingling" warrants particular attention here, suggesting as it does a coming together, a harmonious sense of belonging (*DV* 116). The sounds interact agreeably with one another: "the swain" is described as "responsive as the milk-maid sung," a responsiveness that indicates not only a harmony in song, but also in life (*DV* 117). The sounds of the village and nature complement one another—laughter, song, and the lowing of cows all constitute important elements of Auburn's lively auditory world.

This harmonious rhythm departed with Auburn's inhabitants, as Goldsmith laments: "But now the sounds of population fail, / No cheerful murmurs fluctuate in the gale" (*DV* 125–26). The village's auditory life comes and goes in the poem with a murmur—a telling word choice, suggestive of softness and indistinctness. The speaker's imaginative effort brings out the specific sounds that constitute Auburn's murmuring rhythms, giving a sense of them both independently and as a collective hum. The silencing of Auburn's sounds marks the end of its ways of living. As Edensor notes, "In addition to revealing the distinctive temporal phases and spaces of place, sonic rhythms also evoke the historical transformations of place."[9] The domesticated geese have been replaced by the wild bittern's cry. A life full of rhythmic sound has been supplanted by a spoiled present in which noises only rupture the silence and further evacuate the space of the deserted village. This destruction of rhythm has political dimensions. Declan Kiberd writes that, "Like many Gaelic poets of his day, Goldsmith was appalled by the rupture of traditional values and natural rhythms by a predatory class which knew the price of everything."[10] These values are audible in the poem.

The political potential of sound reveals itself again in Goldsmith's subsequent denunciation of accumulated luxury: "Proud swells the tide with loads of freighted ore, / And shouting Folly hails them from the shore" (*DV* 269–70). While previously in the poem, attention was paid to the harmonious intermingling of sound, Folly's shout emphasizes the disruptive force of luxury and accumulated wealth. This shout of pride and "Folly" reinforces sound's spatial dimensions in the poem: "The man of wealth and pride, / Takes up a space that many poor supplied; / Space for his lake, his park's extended bounds, / Space for his horses, equipage, and hounds; / The robe that wraps his limbs in silken sloth, / Has robbed the neighbouring fields of half their growth" (*DV* 275–80). Whereas once the rural poor filled the village with sound, now the solitary figure of the landlord extends beyond his bounds and takes up more space than he needs. Yet despite his sprawling occupation, the fields have been silenced and are now half empty: the space taken up by the landlord has been hollowed out, not unlike the bittern's call. Goldsmith's soundscapes suggest that by listening closely to aural rhythms and ruptures we can become more attuned to changing ways of life.

The murmurs of Auburn are echoed in the poem as it moves towards futurity. While critics have rightly noted the poem's primarily binary structure, turning on the movements between Auburn's past and its present, there is also a movement outward, both spatially and temporally, at the poem's conclusion and it too is marked by the presence of sound. Goldsmith writes of the villagers' departure for British North America: "To distant climes, a dreary scene, / Where half the convex world intrudes between, / Through torrid tracks with fainting steps they go, / Where wild Altama murmurs to their woe" (*DV* 341–45). The Altamaha River in Georgia echoes the previous murmur of Auburn. The word "murmur" here may have a double meaning expressing not only the discontent of the woeful emigrants, but also providing the slow, continuous, filling sound that previously characterized the idyll of village life. Despite its introduction of the poem's frightening and bleak depiction of the American landscape, the repetition of "murmurs" hints at the possibility for a positive conclusion. The absence of birdsong might also surprisingly point toward hope: Goldsmith writes of "matted woods where birds *forget* to sing, / But drowsy bats in silent clusters cling," a phrasing that emphasizes the connection between sound, memory, and finally poetry (*DV* 349–50, emphasis mine). If the birds have forgotten to sing, then the poet's art, the imaginative labor of remembering, might teach them how to open their beaks once again to fill the forests of the American Southeast with sound and life. The silence of the bats and birds underscores the degree to which sound can indicate the rupture of traditional rhythms and even induce changes in a place. Goldsmith's America is silent and brutish, but contains murmurs of potential.

Indeed, the poem concludes with such a vision of the future. Bailes writes that "the 'new-found worlds' to which Auburn's villagers immigrate harbor opportunities for immediate, prosperous growth and civilization through cultivation," a prosperous growth foretold and enabled by the emergence of the poetic voice and the return of sound.[11] Goldsmith mourns the departure of the poetic voice from English shores: "thou loveliest maid, / Still first to fly where sensual joys invade" (*DV* 407–8). Yet, he also wishes poetry well in its travels outward to America and onward toward the future. Indeed, Goldsmith concludes on this hopeful note, imagining a new beginning, in which the poetic voice revives after having fled the Old World and so commences the work of redressing the harm suffered by the villagers. The poetic voice may contain within itself the power to correct in the New World the mistakes of the Old. The poem's complicated spatial and temporal movements end here, with the suggestion that the future might rectify the faults of the past and one place might remedy the mistakes of another, with all of these changes evidenced in the sonic record of verse.

Goldsmith's poem constructs a soundscape and asks its readers to listen to the past, suggesting that through imagination, memory, and poetry a voice might be raised that can draw attention to, and perhaps even reverse, some of the damaging developments in society—the excesses of wealth and luxury—that have depopulated and silenced the village life of Auburn. Only the poetic voice preserves this world through the dual labors of imagination and memory, the effort of conjuring for others a sense of a place through the sounds, rhythms, and ruptures of the life once lived there. Goldsmith saturates his poem with sound and asks his readers to lean in and hear, so that his poetic voice may prevail over time to speak out from the past and help correct these wrongs in the future.

Notes

1. Oliver Goldsmith, "The Deserted Village," in *The Collected Works of Oliver Goldsmith*, ed. Arthur Friedman, 5 vols. (Oxford: Clarendon Press, 1966), 4:287–304, line 34. Subsequent citations will be made parenthetically as *DV*, followed by the line number(s) in question.

2. Pascoe, *The Sarah Siddons Audio Files: Romanticism and the Lost Voice* (Ann Arbor: University of Michigan Press, 2013), 14.

3. McDowell, *The Invention of the Oral: Print Commerce and Fugitive Voices in Eighteenth-Century Britain* (Chicago: University of Chicago Press, 2017), 19.

4. Bailes, "Literary Plagiarism and Scientific Originality in the 'Trans-Atlantic Wilderness' of Goldsmith, Aikin, and Barbauld," *Eighteenth-Century Studies* 49, no. 2 (2016), 268.

5. Bailes, "Literary Plagarism," 268.

6. Even a defender of the poem like John Barrell concedes that "It is perfectly true that, for example, Goldsmith hardly seems to mention the labor his villagers perform except to show them not actually performing it" (*The Dark Side of the Landscape: The Rural Poor in English Landscape Painting, 1730–1840* [Cambridge: Cambridge University Press, 1980], 78).

7. Heinzelman, "Roman Georgic in the Georgian Age: A Theory of Romantic Genre," *Texas Studies in Literature and Language* 33, no. 2 (1991): 192.

8. Edensor, "The Sonic Rhythms of Place," in *The Routledge Companion to Sound Studies*, ed. Michael Bull (Abingdon: Routledge, 2018), 165.

9. Edensor, "Sonic Rhythms," 162.

10. Kiberd, *Irish Classics* (London: Granta Books, 2000), 121.

11. Bailes, "Literary Plagarism," 268.

"Eternal Sunshine": Intertextuality as Environmental History in Oliver Goldsmith's *The Deserted Village*

DENYS VAN RENEN

This essay explores the intertextual connections between Alexander Pope's *Eloisa to Abelard* (1717), Joseph Addison's *Cato, a Tragedy* (1713), and Oliver Goldsmith's *The Deserted Village* (1770). I aim to demonstrate how intertextuality functions as both an escape from and a recognition of environmental depletion. Goldsmith's poem, with its allusions to these two works from earlier in the eighteenth century, highlights the speaker's anxiety about the "desolation" of a rural village, but it also discloses larger issues with eighteenth-century attitudes toward the environment that exacerbate, or capitulate to, destructive economic practices.[1] Midway through the poem, Goldsmith refers to how, like a "tall cliff" on which "Eternal sunshine settles" as momentary storms assail lower elevations, the village parson can escape the earthly cares of his parishioners through his relationship with God (*DV* 189, 192).

In a poem about widespread environmental degradation caused by human activity, Goldsmith's allusion to Pope's famous image of the "eternal sunshine of the spotless mind" reminds readers of an era in which storms were a constant menace to agricultural society, but were nonetheless natural occurrences and part of seasonal changes. One could perceive them as "rolling" or take an almost scientific interest in cloud formation as a natural—and not human—phenomenon. In fact, the simile reinforces that relationship: human actions (in this case, villagers pleading their economic distress) are like, but do not produce, clouds gathering about a mountain. Alfred Lutz has examined poets' and critics' reception of Goldsmith's poem by pointing out how they ignored "Goldsmith's careful juxtaposition of the village of the past and the deserted village, an opposition on which the political energy of the poem depends."[2] Goldsmith's "radical" poem critiques an economic system that renders parishioners unable to use or rely upon the land.[3] Goldsmith's allusions, however, may inscribe a counterhistory as they refute the "barren splendour" of the land that the poem directly indicts (*DV* 286). Allusions call readers' attention to the environmental conditions of earlier eras, but they also speak to a literary fertility in which later works emerge figuratively from the seeds of earlier ones, providing the illusion that literary continuity can substitute for sustained ecological health.

While I would like to conduct a more thorough excavation of the many readings of *The Deserted Village*, this brief essay will center on the relationship between intertextuality and the early recognition of the socio-economic consequences of the Anthropocene. First, I will discuss Pope's poem in more detail and describe what I would like to call Goldsmith's "peasant" aesthetics. Tobias Menely asserts that some poems from the long eighteenth century are, "in their allusive density, ... like the earth's strata, diachronic objects that record change and continuity across relatively long (in human time scales) durations of geohistory."[4] In Goldsmith's verse, however, readers can also witness how allusions serve as forms of consolation, compensation, and deferral. In *The Deserted Village*'s echo of *Eloisa to Abelard*, the allusion underlines an option no longer available to the speaker, for whom environmental extremes are caused by human activity and efforts to escape or ignore "rolling clouds" or bad weather only worsens them. In addition, the poem suggests that intertextual connections can resemble capitalist systems, as allusive networks appear potentially limitless. Then I will discuss a possible counterexample: Goldsmith's reference to Addison's *Cato*, a work that looms over the eighteenth century. In this case, Cato increasingly imagines the weather as a human construct: "The gods, in bounty, work up storms about us / That give mankind occasion to exert / Their hidden strength."[5] Accordingly, he spurns Juba's offer to enlist "our remotest kings," whose military might stems from the enormous power of the Nile (*C* 2.263). Juba, in short, is interested in "new alliances" between the human and the nonhuman worlds, rather than the "heroic" parameters of the human (*C* 2.259). The play serves as the eighteenth-century template for Europeans' disavowal of Indigenous knowledge about Earth systems. Goldsmith's poem evokes Addison's play to reconsider the ecological toll of commercial and imperial enterprises. That is, while the allusion to Pope signals that different environmental conditions existed in 1717 than in 1770, Goldsmith's nod to *Cato* concedes that there is insight in Numidian (and so non-European) attitudes toward natural processes. In so doing, the poem offers new modes to reorient its readers with respect to the relationship between land-use practices, representational systems, and climatological processes.

Pope and Goldsmithian "Peasant" Aesthetics

In *The Deserted Village*, people can establish a self-contained atmosphere apart from the surrounding "storms." The poem articulates a fantasy that, despite climatic extremes, one can always forge some sort of (aesthetic or physical) sanctuary. In a long section that includes the allusion to Pope, for example, Goldsmith likens the village preacher to a mountain about which "the rolling clouds are spread." Although he attends to the various cares his flock brings to him, these worldly concerns exist as passing storms. The soothing cycle of storms forming and dissipating manifests "over there," "a reified thing in the distance," as his "serious thoughts rest in Heaven" (*DV* 188): "As some tall cliff that lifts its awful form / Swells from the vale, and midway leaves the storm, / Tho' round its breast the rolling clouds are spread, / Eternal sunshine settles on its head" (*DV* 189–92).[6] The climatological analogy reinforces how, like seasonal storms, the villagers' cares serve as a constant background from which the parson can escape and then return to as his vocation requires. As Timothy Morton points out, the weather can serve as "a larger temporary backdrop" (at least until climate change "enters the scene").[7] The poem is about how unchanging human experiences—village life or "familiar" Earth systems—suddenly vanish or radically shift. Goldsmith's lines also allude to Pope's *Eloisa to Abelard,* in which Eloisa extols the "blameless vestal's lot" as she basks in the "Eternal sunshine of the spotless mind!"[8] While Pope speaks in strictly moral terms, Goldsmith's epic simile—in which he combines ethical, religious, and environmental considerations—suggests that not only earthly cares, but also Earth systems encumber the reader and poem (if not the parson). That is, "Eternal sunshine"—or any climatological phenomenon—is difficult to access without also thinking about all the human consequences that the poem explores.

The Deserted Village is well-known for its anxious account of villagers alienated from their traditional lands. However, it also articulates how allusions "resettle" readers in familiar discursive networks, rather than restore them to their home. Land-use practices, in short, cause environmental damage—as the poem discloses—and, therefore, displacement, but the poem already, in effect, anticipates (and participates) in this alienation. Svetlana Boym explains how "*Topos* refers both to a place in discourse and a place in the world." Memory then involves "connecting places in the familiar environment (physical *topoi*) to stories and parts of discourse (rhetorical *topoi*).[9] "Sweet Auburn" is effaced not only through aesthetic reengineering, but also through the substitution of new frameworks for conceptualizing space and time. In his "peasant" aesthetics, however, Goldsmith attempts to contain capitalist excesses through, for example, simulating the fragmentation of local communities and thereby insisting that representational practices can conceptualize and critique vast economic and imperial systems that already seem inevitable. He identifies how uncaring landlords and the villagers' consequent immigration to British North America weaken personal and national histories; only a "widowed, solitary thing," for example, remains as the "sad historian" of the village (*DV* 129, 136). For history and poetry are best evoked through the preservation of a place in living memory, but now the "very spot / Where many a time he [the preacher] triumphed, is forgot" (*DV* 216–18).

The poem foregrounds, then, the hidden socio-cultural, economic, and environmental effects of global commerce. The fantastic wealth created in the later eighteenth century staggers the mind: "Hoards, even beyond the miser's wish abound, / And rich men flock from all the world around" (*DV* 271–72). But in terse half lines, Goldsmith asks his readers to qualify their approval of these enormous mounds of gold and resources: "Yet count our gains" (*DV* 273). Insofar as the production of practical foodstuffs and goods goes, England remains stagnant: "This wealth is but a name / That leaves our useful products still the same" (*DV* 273–74). The notion of "wealth" masks the real losses in manpower and national unity; these "Hoards, even beyond the miser's wish" serve as sublime objects that delight the senses, but degrade the mind. After emphasizing the importance of "useful products," the poet reiterates how England exports "each needful product" and imports "all the luxuries the world supplies" (*DV* 283–84). Goldsmith here warns against the likelihood that glittering objects will distort our perceptions, much as Raphael in *Paradise Lost* cautioned Adam to "consider first, that Great / Or Bright inferrs not Excellence."[10]

In particular, the meter of the passage about wealth makes the nouns seem to dominate over the other parts of speech, and the repetition of the abstract concept of "space" reinforces the vast disproportions the speaker witnesses: "The man of wealth and pride, / Takes up a space that many poor supplied; / Space for his lake, his park's extended bounds, / Space for his horses, equipage, and hounds" (*DV* 275–78). This transition from the concrete place of the village to the abstract notion of space points to the real losses experienced by persons, animals, and plants. Goldsmith splits his lines in two ("Space for his lake, his park's extended bounds"), and then three ("Space for his horses, equipage, and hounds"). Through these caesuras, Goldsmith simulates the abstract divisions of land that have displaced the persons and objects formerly on the estate, nudging his readers to reject the capitalist sublime and to recognize how many lives it has upended, especially in "Sweet Auburn."

However, the somewhat strained simile comparing "some fair female" to the ruined land that immediately follows relinquishes much of the ground the poem had just gained (*DV* 287). With its claims that poetry can "redress the rigours of th' inclement clime" and insulate readers from the environmental "devastation" spread by luxury, *The Deserted Village*'s attempt to recreate environmental conditions that no longer exist would seem, at best, an exercise in futility (*DV* 422, 395). Eventually, the poem resigns itself to sensational and exaggerated descriptions of ecocatastrophes, "savage" conditions in North America that Goldsmith likens to what the speaker witnesses in England: vast scenes of devastation in lands that have squandered their once vigorous civilization. The second half of the poem is an aesthetic morass in which the speaker realizes that the atmosphere no longer exists as an unchanging backdrop to ordinary life and so replaces it with poetic commonplaces and inflexible tropes. Indeed, the couplet before the stanza on "some fair female" announces this environmental collapse: "While thus the land adorned for pleasure all / In barren splendor feebly waits the fall" (*DV* 285–86). As Goldsmith observes, the English fetishize the ornaments that disguise its "barren" land. The country teeters dangerously close to a wasteland because the English, awed by extravagance, now seek similarly heightened aesthetic experiences: "Thus fares the land, by luxury betrayed / In nature's simplest charms at first arrayed; / But verging to decline, its splendours rise, / Its vistas strike, its palaces surprize" (*DV* 295–98).

The capitalist sublime appears differently "arrayed," to use Goldsmith's metaphor, as the poet assigns the same "strik[ing]" aesthetics to the physical environment of North America. The stanza about colonial Georgia, in particular, overflows with depictions of its environmental and climatological extremes—"torrid tracts," "various terrors of that horrid shore," "blazing suns"—that pronounce it an inhospitable and formless wasteland (*DV* 343, 346, 347). Indeed, Goldsmith attempts to underline the vast differences between England and British North America by describing the hemispheric division between Europe and the Americas as a boundary across which the former villagers must pass, only to end up in "a dreary scene, / Where half the convex world intrudes between" (*DV* 341–42). The "dreary scene" reiterates how the villagers' new dwelling place is unamenable to poetry. Goldsmith drives home the discontinuity between the two worlds with his emphasis that, as Michael Griffin describes, the "vital strength" of colonials erodes when they settle on "that horrid shore" (*DV* 346).[11]

Cato and the Restoration of an Intertextual (Eco)system

Like Addison's *Cato*, *The Deserted Village* tries unsuccessfully to contain the devastations of the world offshore in the colonies. While the poem avers that the sounds emitting from American land and water systems seem incomprehensible, it nonetheless characterizes them as discordant, abandoning in the process the "peasant" aesthetics through which the poet had been teaching the reader to cherish the "simplest charms" (*DV* 286). The poem remains susceptible to the very same sensations that Goldsmith criticized in England because of his repurposing of the aesthetics of ecological disaster that he had earlier associated with its landed estates. Goldsmith describes a fundamental incompatibility between the settlers and their new surroundings. Turned away by the landed elite in England, villagers emigrate to Georgia, but the "wild Altama [the Altamaha River] murmurs to their woe" (*DV* 343). Rather than being fellow poets who sing about the landscape, the local animals remain silent ("Those matted woods where birds forget to sing, / But silent bats in drowsy clusters cling"), serving as surrogates for a poet who, because he is busy naturalizing the man-made environmental disasters of England, disavows the very etiology he has established (*DV* 349–50). The well-known line "The country blooms—a garden, and a grave" underscores how the wealthy have created conditions in England that have led to both economic and environmental refugees (*DV* 301). Rampant commercialism that prioritizes showy excess at the expense of a rural society that used to only take from the land what it actually needed has brought about a "desolation" in England that is supposedly inherent to America (*DV* 38). Goldsmith thus exacerbates the colonial destruction of "foreign" lands as he pronounces the landscape and inhabitants of America to be totally alien and thus separates England from the very devastation it has caused.

While Melissa Bailes cites Goldsmith's *An History of the Earth, and Animated Nature* as context for examining how *The Deserted Village* "represents America as a place of death and degeneration … reversible according to Enlightenment notions of improvement," I focus on *Cato* as a precedent for the poem's environmental attitudes.[12] Goldsmith notably concludes his depictions of extreme weather and the "silent" land with a depiction of the utter formlessness of America: "While oft in whirls the mad tornado flies, / Mingling the ravaged landscape with the skies" (*DV* 357–58). Before analyzing this couplet, I want to cite some parallel lines from *Cato* about North Africa: "The helpless traveler, with wild surprise, / Sees the dry desert all around him rise, / And smother'd in the dusty whirlwind, dies" (*C* 2.525–27). Note the similar word choices, imagery, and even rhymes between Goldsmith's lines about America and Addison's regarding Juba's homeland. *Cato* demonstrates how imperial imaginations are short-sighted: erasing or simply refusing to understood other peoples, regions, and weather systems in the service of implementing European worldviews eventually impoverishes the metropole as well as its colonies. Addison's play also suggests that Indigenous people in North Africa comprehend and are shaped by the link between lands and climate across vast distances. By alluding to *Cato*, Goldsmith enfolds his poem within wider discursive and environmental networks.

Indeed, Syphax, the Numidian general who speaks these lines about the "helpless traveler," exposes how Cato not only disavows the notion of climatological determinism, but also underestimates the Numidian troops precisely because they gain their power from "impetuous hurricanes" and "circling eddies" (*C* 2.522, 2.523). Cato, as the "helpless traveler," will always be an interloper because he transmutes weather systems into constructs that only "speak" in a specific discursive and political register. Being "smother'd" in clouds of dust encompasses a range of fears beyond ecological catastrophes and economic crises. Cultural and social aphasia result when one does not understand and therefore cannot draw upon the local environment. Like many Anglophone authors of the eighteenth century, Goldsmith articulates how England's "genius" is nourished by "lawns ... that scorn Arcadian pride, / And brighter streams than fam'd Hydaspis glide."[13] When the climate is rendered "foreign" by human activity or the climate of other regions is perceived as indecipherable, authors, through these already established allusive networks, can also foreground impediments to piecing together literary and environmental histories. Goldsmith alludes to Addison's play in which Indigenous characters recognize the relationships between people and climate, but the main character, Cato, disavows them. Does Goldsmith compound that disavowal as he reuses poetic templates to generalize weather events across colonial or (to the British) peripheral spheres? Or does the poem's allusion to *Cato* plunge its readers into the "eye of the storm"—an allusive knot and psychological and discursive aporia—in order to prompt his readers to rechart literary (and environmental) history?

Even if *The Deserted Village* draws on allusions to other poems, including pastoral traditions, to enclose and protect the villagers of Auburn (and, by extension, its own readers), those allusions can also disclose wider worlds and ecologies. In England, laborers formerly enjoyed "the cooling brook, the grassy vested green, / The breezy covert of the warbling grove, / That only sheltered thefts of harmless love" (*DV* 360–62). Goldsmith isolates his villagers in an imaginary and counterproductive "covert." Indeed, it would be difficult to come up with a more literarily and physically secluded spot than he here creates in just three lines. "Harmless love" would seem to foreground the sterility of this seclusion (the "love" does no harm, but also creates no children). On one hand, Goldsmith's intertextuality helps demonstrate how poets can take refuge in an allusive system or literary tradition in which equilibrium is always maintained and, in so doing, deny the dynamic relationship between people, culture, and land and so refuse to reinvent their own aesthetics in order to draw upon other cultures or account for environmental crises. Goldsmith's allusion to *Cato*, on the other hand, asks readers to resolve these impasses before subsequent texts can do the hard work of attuning their readers to radically changing environmental conditions.

Notes

1. Goldsmith, *The Deserted Village,* in *The Collected Works of Oliver Goldsmith,* ed. Arthur Friedman, 5 vols. (Oxford: Clarendon Press, 1966), 4:287–304, line 38. Subsequent citations will be made parenthetically as *DV*, followed by the line number(s).

2. Lutz, "The Politics of Reception: The Case of Goldsmith's 'The Deserted Village,'" *Studies in Philology* 95, no. 2 (1998): 174, 196, 185.

3. Lutz, "'The Deserted Village' and the Politics of Genre," *Modern Language Quarterly* 55, no. 2 (1994): 149–68.

4. Menely, *Climate and the Making of Worlds: Toward a Geohistorical Poetics* (Chicago: University of Chicago Press, 2021), 15.

5. Addison, *Cato,* in *The Broadview Anthology of Restoration and Early Eighteenth-Century Drama,* ed. J. Douglas Canfield and Maja-Lisa von Sneidern (Peterborough: Broadview Press, 2011), 2.1.283–85. Subsequent references will be made parenthetically as *C,* followed by the act and line number(s).

6. The first two phrases quoted are from Timothy Morton, *The Ecological Thought* (Cambridge: Harvard University Press, 2012), 3.

7. Morton, *Hyperobjects: Philosophy and Ecology after the End of the World* (Minneapolis: University of Minnesota Press, 2013), 102.

8. Pope, "Eloisa to Abelard," in *Alexander Pope: The Major Works*, ed. Pat Rogers (Oxford: Oxford University Press, 2008), pp. 137–47, lines 207 and 209.

9. Boym, *The Future of Nostalgia* (New York: Basic Books, 2001), 77.

10. John Milton, *Paradise Lost*, ed. John Leonard (London: Penguin, 2003), 8.90–91.

11. Griffin, *Enlightenment in Ruins: The Geographies of Oliver Goldsmith* (Lewisburg: Bucknell University Press, 2013), 41.

12. Bailes, "Literary Plagiarism and Scientific Originality in the 'Trans-Atlantic Wilderness' of Goldsmith, Aikin, and Barbauld," *Eighteenth-Century Studies* 49, no. 2 (2016), 272.

13. Goldsmith, *The Traveller; or, a Prospect of Society*, in *Collected Works*, 2:243–69, lines 319–20.

Book Illustration and
The Deserted Village

TIMOTHY ERWIN

B ook illustration is having a moment. The history of the book now routinely takes up graphic art alongside printing techniques, and entire monographs are devoted to the pictorial rendering of major texts. Few book illustrations fall within the traditional category of fine art. Most remain beyond the purview of the discipline of Art History and belong instead to the study of visual culture. Like the paratext as theorized by Gérard Genette, book illustrations condition how we read. From as early as the third edition of 1770, Oliver Goldsmith's *The Deserted Village* featured a title-page illustration, and by the mid-nineteenth century, dozens of images of its rustic characters appeared regularly alongside the verse. During the last two decades of the eighteenth century, three graphic artists reimagined Goldsmith's narrative as a tragedy, and their transformations help demonstrate the need for a term that highlights how images can complement, rather than merely supplement, a text. I suggest that we adopt what Sally Bushell has called the "imagetext."[1] An avatar of this kind of fluid interplay between image and text would be William Blake, who pointed out the possibilities with a crucial discovery in the mid-1780s. Advances in relief etching allowed him to incise words and pictures onto the waxed surface of a single plate. This novel fusion of letterpress printing and copperplate engraving made possible the prophetic poetics of *Songs of Innocence and Experience* and eventually set the stage for contemporary text artists with their practice of incorporating words, phrases, and narratives into a range of visual media.[2]

Apart from *Paradise Lost* and *The Seasons*, no poem in English has been illustrated more often than *The Deserted Village*, and none of its characters was more often pictured than the one Goldsmith calls "the sad historian of the pensive plain."[3] She first appears in the 1770 title-page vignette [see Figure 1], an image that serves simultaneously as both paratext and imagetext. A widow foraging for her supper, she plays the dual role of survivor and eyewitness. Isaac Taylor captures her in conversation with a traveler wondering what has become of sights like the "decent church that topp'd the neighbouring hill" (*DV* 12). Behind him wind the bare banks of a dwindling brook that the speaker remembers as "never-failing" (*DV* 11). Gesture is the speech of images, and the widow includes the ruined chapel in an eloquent sweep of general decline. Where Samuel Johnson invokes the laughing Democritus in *The Vanity of Human Wishes,* Goldsmith recalls the universal flux of melancholy Heraclitus. In the distance an emigrant ship sets sail for the "various terrors" that await its passengers, the victims of a disastrous bargain (*DV* 346).[4]

The Deserted Village has always invited a visual reading. Goldsmith describes the poem as the fond tracing of village life, nor is he above a pun in recalling how the village alehouse served "nut-brown draughts" (*DV* 221), the phrase evoking sepia sketches. When readers are pointed to "yonder copse where once the garden smiled" and later told to look just "there" or are asked to behold "the very spot" of the schoolmaster's triumph, the deictic language affirms a geography of the gaze (*DV* 137, 139, 217). The dispositional rhetoric asks us to map the vanished pleasures of the village, and the fact of their disappearance makes the call to witness all the more urgent.[5] Goldsmith dedicated the poem to Sir Joshua Reynolds, telling him in a prefatory letter that he remained a professed ancient when it came to the so-called progress of modernity. Reynolds responded with a painting entitled *Resignation* [see Figure 2]. Johnson defines the term "resignation" as "submission without murmur to the will of God,"[6] and the tableau is a *beatus ille* scene of "blest retirement" (*DV* 97). Swathed in darkness and flanked by columns symbolizing steadfastness, an allegorical figure awaits the end of life with Christian stoicism. While admirable, his attitude falls short of the "eminent instance of heroick action or heroick suffering" that Reynolds describes as the subject matter of history painting.[7] Similarly, of the two alternating timeframes in *The Deserted Village*, the first encompasses a state of contentment that reaches back to the Middle Ages and extends up to the speaker's departure as a youth. The second comprises the speaker's

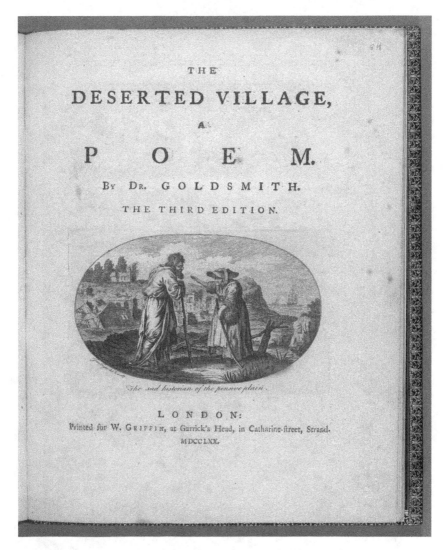

Figure 1. Isaac Taylor, title page, *The Deserted Village*, 3rd ed., copperplate engraving, London, 1770. Courtesy of the Huntington Library, Art Galleries, and Botanical Gardens.

subsequent decades of exile, during which the village of Auburn experienced its unforeseen decline. Neither includes a particularly heroic or suspenseful action. The misfortunes of the villagers began well before the return of the speaker, and his arrival fails to change their fate.

Figure 2. Thomas Watson after Sir Joshua Reynolds, *Resignation*, mezzotint, London, 1772. Yale Center for British Art, Paul Mellon Collection.

John Montague has suggested that *The Deserted Village* reflects "a personal development of the classical Augustan doctrine of 'ut pictura poesis,'" the notion that a poem should resemble a painting.[8] From at least the later seventeenth century, painting and poetry were considered sister arts. Although they use different means, one involving spatial arrangement and the other temporal succession, they reach similar representational ends. Each approaches the mimetic aims of the other: poetry through vivid verbal description, and painting by flanking the primary narrative moment depicted with hints of earlier and later events. In the process, they double their representational power. Around the time of Blake's discovery, three other graphic artists superimposed aspects of sentimental tragedy on the then-and-now structure of *The Deserted Village*. On hiatus from caricature, James Gillray created a visual narrative that was quickly adopted by John Keyse Sherwin, engraver to King George III. Each created a pair of prints showing the village as it once was and again as it now appears in its present state of decline. Surprisingly, they both identify an individual from the opening of the poem, the bashful virgin, with a figure from the close, the dutiful daughter. Both also show the daughter leaving behind a lover in order to emigrate with her family. As a third artist, Francis Wheatley, makes clear, the assimilation of the virgin to the daughter lends the poem the weight of history painting. Freestanding illustrations like these are imagetexts in a double sense. They adopt a mixed-media format found in art prints from the sixteenth century forward—Gillray and Sherwin quote liberally from the poem in the two columns of print ranged beneath each image—and they stand apart from the poem to interpret as well as to frame it.

"The Village Train" by Gillray portrays lost innocence by setting its soft rounded forms securely within an oval frame [see Figure 3]. In the background, the townsfolk engage in blind man's buff and wrestling, the "succeeding sports" of the opening verse paragraph (*DV* 20). At the center, a young couple dances to a country tune. Seated just below them we see another couple. With her hands crossed in her lap, the young woman casts an amorous glance toward the young man to her left. She represents the bashful virgin with "sidelong looks of love," and the figure on her right is the matron who "would those looks reprove" (*DV* 29–30). In the companion print [Figure 4], the rounded forms give way to angularity, and the bashful virgin reappears as a dutiful daughter who must forsake "a lover's for a father's arms" (*DV* 378). We can recognize her as the same person because the young man bidding her good-bye is the same fellow we saw courting her in the first print, accompanied by the same canine symbol of fidelity. Gillray weaves through his paired images a storyline consolidating figures who lived decades apart and who are separated by some three hundred and fifty lines of verse.

Figure 3. James Gillray, *The Village Train*, stipple engraving and etching, London, 1784. Courtesy of The Lewis Walpole Library, Yale University.

Figure 4. James Gillray, *The Deserted Village*, stipple engraving and etching, London, 1784. Courtesy of The Lewis Walpole Library, Yale University.

Sherwin tells much the same story. "The Happy Village" [see Figure 5] retains the young maiden with her hands folded. As before, she is seated to the right of the dancers and flanked by her chaperone and her suitor. A piper leans against a tree to play his tune and the pines atop the distant hills seem to notate the melody. In a composition evocative of Raphael's dancing cupids, a group of young people circle the tree in celebration of spring. A merry pair in the foreground glance back in invitation and a space momentarily opens for the seated couple. The suitor urges his shy beloved to join the dancing, but her chaperone prevents her. A walking stick behind the matron suggests a hidden diagonal intersecting the garland held aloft at left, and the ribald implication is that, unable to dance herself, the chaperone means to thwart more than a simple turn around a tree. The tone is very different in the second print, "The Deserted Village" [see Figure 6], as a family of six gather in a downward-sloping arrangement. Again, the parting lovers at center are the same couple seen in conversation decades before. As he hands her the reins of an ass, she shifts the infant sibling in her arms. Together their movements draw the gaze to her empty womb, implying their forfeiture of what the poem later calls "connubial tenderness" (*DV* 404). The shade tree about to be felled and the roof being cleared of thatch symbolize the "business of destruction" that, according to the poem, is already half-done (*DV* 396). Gillray and Sherwin display the human cost of disrupting natural cycles with an interpolated tale of longing and dismay. The equation of the bashful virgin with the dutiful daughter collapses the dual timeframe of the poem into a dramatic, desperate present. The visual rhetoric affirms *The Deserted Village*'s striking pathos by lending it a fraught personal dimension, and what Goldsmith call his "persuasive strain" becomes even more compelling (*DV* 423).

It was left to Francis Wheatley to depict the family's (and the village's) reversal of fortune in a single engraving [see Figure 7]. The family appears poised on the cusp of disaster. The mother comforts the children, the father prays on behalf of them all, and at center the daughter reluctantly leaves her beloved behind. The play of hands from left to right signals their reaction—"clasp[ing] close," bidding farewell, and trusting to heaven—and articulates the fate of the yeomanry (*DV* 382). The same gestures divide the upper half of the image from the lower. The left half with its flowering hollyhock and vine belongs to a fertile past, the right half to a barren future, and the shared effect is a cruciform arrangement. Like Hercules between virtue and vice, the daughter appears torn between contrary choices, and the family temporizes for her sake. Wheatley exhibited a painting of *The Deserted Village* at the Royal Academy in 1800 and the same year published two illustrations in the elegant F. J. Du Roveray edition of the poem. The first retains the family grouping from five years earlier [see Figure 8]. At right are the mother and children, the boy holding the reins of a donkey-cart. The

Figure 5. J. K. Sherwin, *The Happy Village*, stipple engraving and etching, London, 1787. Reproduced by permission of the British Museum. © Trustees of the British Museum.

father leads the way on the left with hands interlaced in prayer. The action, now slightly further advanced, again centers on the choice of the daughter, who steps forward to accuse viewers of being complicit in the displacement of the villagers. As an ensemble, these images from Gillray, Sherwin, and Wheatley answer the invitation to picture the poem by sketching out a narrative complete with a singular heroine, an early complication, dramatic conflict, and a tragic conclusion. As Montague suggests, they draw upon theories of *ut pictura poesis* in order to create a pictorial synthesis of space and time before bringing the refined sensibility of later empiricism to bear on the result. In Joseph Addison's day, the empirical aesthetic had kept its distance from the formal discourse of the arts, so this is new. Then again, the visual reception of the literary work often reveals the unexpected, and these same images lay bare a metaphor of the female body beneath the despoiled and neglected land.

In later decades, pictures of the village preacher, the old soldier, and the schoolmaster in the poem serve as genial examplars of generosity,

Figure 6. J. K. Sherwin, *The Deserted Village*, stipple engraving and etching, London, 1786. Courtesy of The Lewis Walpole Library, Yale University.

independence, and learning. The early visual record draws attention, by contrast, to a woman's sensibility, at first via the helplessness of the widowed survivor, and then in the suffering of the dutiful daughter. Along with keen sentiment, the widow represents the firsthand observations of Lockean epistemology. As images of ruined structures cede place to a story of family ruin, the plight of the daughter takes central stage, placing observation now in the service of feeling. For the Victorians, the widow became an icon of compassion, rather than a witness, and the dutiful daughter retreated into her alter-ego, the bashful virgin, seldom subject to the matron's gaze and then only as an anecdotal detail.[9] Meanwhile, another female figure, the ruined maid, became an emblem of visual-verbal collaboration.

Wheatley's second illustration for Du Roveray depicts a seduced and abandoned young woman dressed in white leaning against the pillar of a portico [see Figure 9].[10] She regrets ever trading her spinning wheel for the glitter of the city, the poem tells us, and she looks the very epitome of sorrow. Her expression recalls the coded discourse of the passions from the French *Académie royale*. Following Charles Le Brun's description of

Figure 7. Francesco Bartolozzi after Francis Wheatley, *The Deserted Village,* hand-colored engraving, 1795. Yale Center for British Art, Paul Mellon Collection.

how "Sadness" should be depicted, her brows are "more elevated toward the middle of the Forehead," her mouth is "somewhat open and the corners down," and her head is "negligently hanging upon one Shoulder."[11] As in *The Deserted Village* itself, the abandoned figure here allegorizes the landscape as victim.[12] The sentiment of sadness is general for all three of the women pictured here (the virgin, the daughter, and the ruined maid), whether it stems from the frustration of long-sanctioned courtship ritual or the threat of sexual violence. They each point out how suffering gets gendered in the text. During the peroration, the muse of poetry is called upon to lead the way to virtue, and though the "melancholy band" she guides was often pictured, she herself was not (*DV* 401).[13] It may be that the muse was already visually familiar and so was figured instead as a voice, a call for poets of the New World to resist the havoc wrought by luxury. In that sense, she is part of the poetic soundscape described earlier in this cluster by Joshua Wright. A poem can certainly be visionary without illustrations and may sometimes even render

Figure 8. Anker Smith after Francis Wheatley, etching and engraving on p. 52 of *The Poems of Oliver Goldsmith* (London: F. J. Du Roveray, 1800). Courtesy of the Huntington Library, Art Galleries, and Botanical Gardens.

Figure 9. Anker Smith after Francis Wheatley, etching and engraving on p. 54 of *The Poems of Oliver Goldsmith* (London: F. J. Du Roveray, 1800). Courtesy of the Huntington Library, Art Galleries, and Botanical Gardens.

them redundant. In this essay, we have examined but a few snapshots from a large scrapbook. The reception of *The Deserted Village* involved the creation of dozens of images, some of them humble lithographs meant for popular publications and others expensive engravings commissioned for limited editions. The promise of illustrations like these is that by uncovering latent structures, advancing implied values, and tracing lively new horizons, they can reveal much more than we would otherwise know about the complex interrelations of the text and its many imaginings.

Notes

1. On the relation of the terms, see Bushell, "Paratext or Imagetext? Interpreting the Fictional Map," *Word and Image* 32, no. 2 (2016): 181–94.

2. For a survey, see Simon Morley, *Writing on the Wall: Word and Image in Modern Art* (Berkeley: University of California Press, 2003). Morley takes up text artists working in movements from Dada to postmodernism.

3. The edition cited here is Oliver Goldsmith, *The Deserted Village*, in *The Collected Works of Oliver Goldsmith*, ed. Arthur Friedman, 5 vols. (Oxford: Clarendon Press, 1966), 4:273–304; line 136. Subsequent citations will be made parenthetically as *DV*, followed by the line number(s).

4. The emigrant ship also appears as a motif in the frontispiece engraving by James Mitan after Richard Westall for the title page of *The Deserted Village* (London: John Sharpe, 1816) and in an engraving by T. A. Creswick for *The Deserted Village of Oliver Goldsmith* (London: Etching Club, 1841), plate 37.

5. In a classic reading, Raymond Williams calls *The Deserted Village* a "baffling poem" for foregrounding the narrator and linking protest to nostalgia (*The Country and the City* [London: Chatto & Windus, 1973], 74). Illustration naturally limits the role of the narrator, and though the nineteenth century often viewed the poem as a brief for nostalgia, early illustrators focus on people no longer able to fulfill their social roles.

6. Johnson, *A Dictionary of the English Language*, 2 vols. (London: J. and P. Knapton et al., 1755), vol. 2, *s.v.* resignation.

7. Reynolds, *Discourses on Art*, ed. Robert R. Wark (New Haven: Yale University Press, 1975), 57.

8. Montague, "Exile and Prophecy: A Study of Goldsmith's Poetry," in *Goldsmith: The Gentle Master,* ed. Sean Lucy (Cork: Cork University Press, 1984), 56.

9. For a later depiction of the widow, see Hammatt Billings, *The Deserted Village* (Boston: J. E. Tilton, 1866), 19. For a later rendering of the bashful virgin, see Edward Austin Abbey, *The Deserted Village* (New York: Harper and Brothers, 1902), 9.

10. The abandoned maiden appears again in *Dalziel's Illustrated Goldsmith* (London: Ward and Lock, 1865), 201, and twice in *The Deserted Village* illustrated by Billings, 37 and 38.

11. Charles Le Brun, *A Method to Learn to Design the Passions*, trans. John Williams (London: J. Huggonson, 1734), 40.

12. Wheatley adapts the composition of an earlier print by Sherwin, "The Forsaken Maid" (1791). Its stark chiaroscuro only highlights her expressiveness.

13. For the emigrant train, see the engraved frontispiece after Richard Westall for *The Deserted Village* (London: John Sharp, 1816); the edition illustrated by Billings, 44; and the edition illustrated by Abbey, 99.

From Manual to Digital:
Women's Hands and the Work of
Eighteenth-Century Studies

MATTIE BURKERT

In 1994, Martha Woodmansee called the academic arts and humanities the "last bastion" of the Romantic conception of the author—that solitary and original genius with a proprietary relationship to his or her unique ideas. Writing at the dawn of the Internet era, Woodmansee speculated that the digital revolution might force the humanities to reconsider this stance on intellectual property: "As the collaborative nature of contemporary research and problem-solving fosters multiple authorship in more and more spheres, electronic technology is hastening the demise of the illusion that writing is solitary and originary."[1] Nearly three decades later, digital resources, workflows, and methods have indeed pushed humanities fields toward increasingly capacious understandings of scholarly collaboration, attribution, and credit.[2] Yet the myth of the heroic individual researcher persists, most notably in the continued emphasis on solo-authored articles and books as the gold standard for academic hiring, promotion, and tenure. Critics have argued for years that this lingering Romantic view of authorship immobilizes our fields in the face of ongoing publishing, employment, and social crises that relate both directly and indirectly to the rise of digital technologies.[3]

Less well recognized are the ways in which this concept of authorship helps to render humanities scholars inexcusably complicit in global networks of labor exploitation.

In this essay, I call on eighteenth-century scholars to own our fields' inheritance of and ongoing reliance on digital tools, datasets, and research materials produced by casualized, precarious laborers in technology industry sweatshops. I further insist on our responsibility to challenge deep-seated understandings of intellectual property on which the global information economy depends and to which our period of study gave rise. It was the long eighteenth century, after all, that defined communicative expression as intellectual property, knowledge as a source of extractable economic value, and its production as a form of alienable labor. These constructions relied and continue to rely on the figure of the hand, a synecdoche that has helped to police the shifting boundaries between agential and alienated knowledge work. The hand in "handwriting" signifies authorial presence and individuality; in "handiwork," it indicates labor grounded in the body rather than the mind, in tradition rather than originality. The hand also has etymological links to the terms "manual" and "digital," the former now associated with the work of the body, the latter with the seemingly intangible products of binary computation—produced, of course, largely through the operations of fingers (digits) assembling hardware and devices, entering data, or writing software on a keyboard.[4] As a figure for the women who largely perform this work, the hand looms large in the history of efforts to feminize and devalue some kinds of knowledge work and elevate others.

The following discussion begins with an account of the digital infrastructure of eighteenth-century studies today and of recent research that uncovers the hidden histories of Google Books, the HathiTrust Digital Library, Early English Books Online, Eighteenth-Century Collections Online, and the Text Creation Partnership. Building on this work, I offer a new case study of an offshore outsourcing project commissioned by and for eighteenth-century studies: the digital transcription, in 1970, of the eleven volumes of *The London Stage, 1660–1800*. This work, performed by women keypunchers at China Data Systems Corporation, forms the largely invisible foundation of the NEH-funded digital humanities project that I lead: the *London Stage Database*.

What would it look like to recognize workers like the women of China Data Systems among the many hands at work in our scholarship? What forms of solidarity would such a recognition demand? To answer these questions, I turn to an eighteenth-century woman whose plays have come down to us as the workmanlike products of a workaday writer: Susanna Centlivre. In a receipt documenting her sale of three copyrights to Edmund Curll, I find a story of creative and economic agency and alienation—one richly suggestive of how we might articulate the relationality of scholarly labor in our own time. As I will argue, doing so requires us to go beyond even the reimagining of humanities norms around authorship, collaboration, and publication that has been championed in the digital and public humanities for years. It demands that we divest from notions of labor and property embedded in copyright law, scholarly communication, and technocapitalism; historicize the split between creativity and its material expression; unpack the rhetorical figures that uphold that split today; and, ultimately, radically reconsider our field's foundational assumptions about the nature and value of scholarship. Such a reckoning requires nothing less than a full-scale reevaluation of our labor as such and in relation to the labor of others.

Most eighteenth-century scholars now operate within a copyright regime that defines a "work" as a form of property, the value of which inheres in the novelty or singularity of the individual expression of an idea. This legal framework is putatively designed to protect the economic rights of the author, but the direct economic value of humanities scholarship is marginal, at least as expressed in book sales figures or royalties. Instead, intangible value is conferred on our ideas within an economy of prestige and then transmuted by our institutions. The reputational gains associated with an acceptance at a top-tier journal, the imprimatur of an academic press, or the citations that follow publication are made manifest in a salaried position, a fellowship, a merit raise, or a promotion.

Recognizing these professional advancements as the primary benefits of authorship in the academic humanities, writers typically transfer most of the pecuniary interest in a work's success to their publishers, though they often reserve certain moral rights in the work as part of the publication agreement. These moral rights—to be credited for the work and to see its integrity protected—are codified by law in many countries. In the United States, by contrast, they are protected weakly and only where they converge with an economic view of copyright as a fundamentally proprietary relationship to a commodity. The site of this convergence is reputation: if a writer's ideas are plagiarized or misrepresented, the logic goes, their personal brand is damaged, and they suffer from lost opportunities to profit from their intellectual property in the future.[5]

Of course, scholarly works never reflect solely on the author, nor are they ever truly solitary achievements, a fact that has become all the more visible with the rise of digital humanities (DH) methods and electronic publication venues. Digital scholarship is not necessarily more collaborative, but its orthogonality to existing institutional structures forces scholars to confront material and social realities streamlined into invisibility within the established workflows of traditional humanities research. For example, scholars have long relied on the expertise of catalogers to navigate archives and then claimed undue credit for "discoveries" made there—hence, the old joke among librarians about a researcher consulting a finding aid and then calling the subsequent encounter it facilitates "serendipity." Those same scholars may now find themselves in active collaboration with their counterparts in libraries and archives as they navigate the complex legal and technical landscape around high-resolution imaging, metadata curation, and file hosting for a digital exhibit. The day-to-day working conditions in fields like book history and DH have positioned these fields as leaders in the push for humanities academics to better recognize and compensate collaborators across roles and ranks, including students, staff, technologists, librarians, archivists, editors, and community partners. At their best, such efforts help to debunk the myth of Romantic authorship and to embrace instead a "vision of the relational author as a participant in a process of cultural dialogue and exchange" like that for which Carys Craig has been calling.[6]

Roopika Risam, however, warns that self-congratulatory celebrations of DH's collaborative ethos can serve as a smokescreen for the field's continued dependence on uncredited technology workers: "While there has been some interrogation of the ethics of collaboration between roles among those within the Global North—to varying effect—there has been far less critical interrogation of the role of exploited and casualized labor from the Global South in supporting digital knowledge production in the Global North."[7] Jacqueline Wernimont and Elizabeth Losh enumerate a few of the kinds of outsourced labor on which DH depends: "digitizers scanning pages from books and journals, call center operators fielding customer service questions, assembly line workers manufacturing components, and extraction technicians mining raw materials."[8] Risam, for her part, is particularly concerned with the growing and uncritical use of anonymous workers for labor like data entry and transcription, compensated at pennies per task through services like Amazon's Mechanical Turk. Digital projects turn to such services because the limited options for commissioning time-intensive, monotonous work on a large scale and at low cost push the existing humanities infrastructure beyond its limits.[9] While the turn to "Turkers" may be specific to researchers working at computationally enabled scale, however, the hypocrisy around labor and credit is not unique to DH. Rather, as Risam makes clear, it signals the field's entrenchment within a broader academic culture that centers faculty expertise and subsumes all other kinds of work in the service of a few privileged researchers' agendas.

Eighteenth-century studies is no exception. For scholars working on our period of study, an enormous amount of research begins in databases, like the HathiTrust Digital Library and Eighteenth-Century Collections Online, that are built on invisible, largely offshore labor. The workers behind these resources typically assign the intellectual property in their work to their employer, retaining no moral or pecuniary right to the texts, data, and software they produce. Courts have ruled that such "work-for-hire" agreements are necessary supports to the information economy. Yet these arrangements do far more than just protect the commercial interest of companies in the intellectual property generated by their employees; they also allow those companies to disguise the work of uncredited humans as impossibly seamless user experiences, ostensibly automated content moderation, and too-perfect algorithms.

A particularly striking example of this phenomenon is the Google Books project, which is a central part of the architecture of the HathiTrust Digital Library. Out of the millions of page images, a small, but captivating fraction include accidental glimpses of fingers or hands—traces of the workers on Google's ScanOps team. As peeks into the Internet's hidden processes, these images have fascinated artists like Krissy Wilson, whose *Art of Google Books* blog frames "the adversaria of Google Books"—marginal notes, bookmarks, and other user traces, including those left by the scanning staff—as aesthetically pleasing tidbits of media history.[10] More than merely whimsical testaments to the collaborations and frictions between humans and machines, though, these inadvertent manicules are compelling precisely because they subvert Google's concerted efforts to conceal the workers behind these images—as evidenced in the company's termination of contractor Andrew Norman Wilson for capturing footage of the ScanOps team, most of them Black and Latino, using a separate entrance to access the Google campus.[11] In the "disembodied, anonymous, brown and black hands" of Google Books, many of them feminine in appearance, Andrea Zeffiro sees "the persistence of bodily acts in data infrastructures" that seek to occlude them.[12] Joseph Yannielli reads in these images "'the invisible hand' of the market … laid bare" and compares them to other hands, also feminine, that were captured accidentally as part of microfilming books in the middle of the twentieth century: "Like the women who programmed the first computers, their work was both invisible and glaring."[13] Indeed, the Google Books project makes it impossible to ignore the inconvenient truth that a vast majority of the essential work of the information economy is performed by women—often women of color, caregivers, and elders—whose labor is systematically devalued and hidden.[14]

In designing the cover image for a 2020 special issue of *PMLA* on "Varieties of Digital Humanities," Allison Booth and Miriam Posner were inspired by the large and growing body of art and criticism in which the hands of Google Books figure tangled relations of technology, scholarship, global capitalism, race, and gender. Booth and Posner's team created an image that evokes these accidental testaments to the laboring body. It offers an ironic echo of Google's stated aim to "put the world's printed heritage at our fingertips," one that the scholars intend as "a critique of the legacy of colonialism in the global production of textual data."[15] Booth and Posner leverage the hand—a figure that mediates between human and non-human actors in the collective imaginary surrounding digitization—to call for more widespread acknowledgment of technology workers as part of scholarly networks of production.

As a visual argument, the *PMLA* cover is part of a long tradition of feminist scholarship that attempts to reclaim invisible labor, recognizing, as Lauren Klein puts it in the same special issue, that "it is both a cause and an effect of this invisibility that these forms of labor are undervalued and undercredited (or uncredited altogether) in the end result. The project of infusing value and credit into invisible labor—of making this labor visible to the eyes and to the economy—is a feminist one because, among other reasons, the primary example of invisible labor is unpaid domestic work, which has historically been performed by women."[16] Yet counter-histories of "women's work" often fall into the trap of recovering devalued labor within the same masculinist frameworks through which it was initially marginalized. Recent celebrations of women's roles in early computing, for example, have focused largely on the engineers and scientists who broke barriers in professions dominated by men.[17] Mar Hicks cautions that these triumphalist narratives obscure the reality that the vast majority of mid-century women "computers" performed various technical jobs that were considered more akin to low-level administrative work than to professional careers.[18] Kate Ozment identifies a similar pattern in revisionist histories that reclaim female archivists, librarians, indexers, and catalogers as bibliographers, a title that was traditionally applied only to members of an almost exclusively male professoriate. These studies risk overwriting the fact that this classification system devalued women's work by design, rather than by accident.[19] Hicks and Ozment challenge us to understand the vitality of women's knowledge work, not by reframing it in historically gendered or classed terms, but rather by resisting a hierarchical division of agential work from alienated labor.

This division is implicitly reinforced by feminist and decolonial critiques of Google Books that turn on the figure of the hand—a loaded image that elicits distinctions between the work of the body and that of the mind, between manual and digital labor. To demonstrate how the hand does this ideological work, I turn now to two specific digital resources with particular importance for our period of study: Eighteenth-Century Collections Online

(ECCO), a database of facsimiles of primary texts in English or produced within the Anglophone world published by Gale; and the subset of materials from ECCO that have been transcribed and published to the open web through the Text Creation Partnership (TCP), known collectively as ECCO-TCP.

For two decades, ECCO and ECCO-TCP have made it significantly easier to access page images and transcriptions of many eighteenth-century books, enabling both day-to-day research and teaching and exciting large-scale analyses.[20] The centrality of these resources to scholarly workflows is reflected in the recent decision by the American Society for Eighteenth-Century Studies to purchase an institutional subscription on behalf of its members. Yet a growing number of scholars have sounded the alarm about the failure or refusal of publishers like Gale to document their collection priorities and processes.[21] Their lack of transparency poses serious epistemological, methodological, and ethical problems for humanities researchers who wish to account for the contours and biases of their datasets or to understand the material and human costs of access to these digitized documents. In his archaeology of the *Victorian Newspapers Database*, Paul Fyfe argues persuasively that "the efficacy of our scholarship depends upon a largely missing source history of these digital collections," a history that "weaves through variously sold and reconfigured companies, links big data to microfilming and micropublishing projects from the 1920s onwards, and blends labor practices from library acquisitions to the technical work outsourced to the global economy."[22] Understanding how, by whom, and for whom these resources came to be is every bit as essential as documenting the provenance of an archival collection with which one might work.

Stephen H. Gregg has recently undertaken a line of investigative work not unlike Fyfe's into the history of ECCO and ECCO-TCP, uncovering details about the reliance of those projects on offshore outsourcing.[23] For its plain-text transcriptions, the Text Creation Partnership contracts with Apex CoVantage and Straive (formerly SPi Global), based, respectively, in India and Singapore.[24] These companies appear to specialize in the production of large-scale digitization projects for academic and cultural heritage institutions. Apex, for example, comes up in Fyfe's history of how the British Library's nineteenth-century newspapers made their way online. Given their pervasive, yet hidden presence in humanities academe, Bonnie Mak has recently called these companies "the offshore sweatshops of the digital humanities."[25] It might be more apt to call them "the offshore sweatshops of the humanities," full stop.

While the TCP's relationships with its vendors are not exactly a secret, it is nearly impossible to uncover details about the people behind these operations or their working conditions. The British Library and the TCP are equally evasive about this stage in the process, while the companies themselves offer little information about their operations on the ground.[26] A tour of Apex's Hyderabad office posted on YouTube in 2020 offers hints as to the kind of workplace in which ECCO-TCP transcriptions may have been produced. The video is designed to tout the state-of-the-art facility, but it also reveals a strongly gendered workforce: a majority of software engineers, supervisors, and managers appear to be men, while the cubicle farm referred to as the "production floor" is populated predominantly (although not exclusively) by women.[27]

While the actual workers behind the transcriptions are hidden from view, a rhetorical construction of those workers is paramount to the TCP's self-representation as an ethical and innovative public-private partnership. The TCP was founded in 1999 as a collaboration between ProQuest, the Council on Library and Information Resources (CLIR), and libraries at the University of Michigan and Oxford to meet the need for machine-readable texts in early modern studies. While Optical Character Recognition (OCR) programs can facilitate automatic recognition of printed characters in page images, these algorithms are trained on modern fonts and are ill-suited to deal with older typefaces. OCR technology powers Gale's full-text search for ECCO, but the extent to which the search yields useful results is a function of scale; manual correction is necessary to render individual texts or small subsets of the total collection suitable for reading or analysis. As opposed to projects that aim to improve existing OCR technologies or to pilot new techniques for computer vision, the TCP espouses a production model that is emphatically dependent on human workers.

To produce high-quality plain text of books printed in eighteenth-century typefaces, the TCP engages two different workers to each type the text by hand. A program then collates the resulting transcriptions, encoding any conflicts as a chit ($\cdot$), which can prompt researchers to check the facsimiles in ECCO for themselves or, if working at scale, can trigger various actions to probabilistically infer the missing or garbled text.[28] The TCP website promotes this method as producing uniquely accurate and useful datasets for researchers, and they have long touted their process with particular recourse to the figure of the hand. For example, a 2012 status report by a University of Michigan Research Librarian, Rebecca Welzenbach, bears the inspirational title "Transcribed by Hand, Owned by Libraries, Made for Everyone"—a slogan that appeared on the TCP's landing page as recently as September 2019.[29] The passive voice does important work here, as the hand becomes the actor behind the transcription, erasing the specificity of the worker to whom it belongs. The hand evokes the human touch behind seemingly automated technological processes, while simultaneously reducing the workers' contributions to merely mechanical labor, evacuated of intellect or agency. This figure thus helps to relegate transcription to the realm of manual labor and to displace these workers' contributions to scholarship onto the implicitly more creative and intellectual contributions of the TCP team members based in North America, as well as the cultural heritage institutions that ultimately own the product of all this labor. The story of the TCP illustrates how the field of eighteenth-century studies is entangled with the technology industry's gendered and racialized labor practices, which depend on an ongoing exploitation and erasure of digital-age "women's work"—an erasure achieved, in part, through the overdetermined figure of the hand, which we can see at play both in the TCP's rhetorical self-representation and in the accidental glimpses we encounter in Google Books.

The TCP's history resonates with the origins of a digital project that I lead: the London Stage Database (https://londonstagedatabase.uoregon.edu). Launched in 2019, this open-access resource recovers and revitalizes the London Stage Information Bank, a previously lost project from the days when the digital humanities were known as humanities computing. With funding from the National Endowment for the Humanities, the American Council of Learned Societies, and the National Science Foundation (among others) and with a mandate from the editorial board of the five-part (in eleven volumes), 8,000-page set of reference books, *The London Stage, 1660–1800*, the Information Bank team set out to digitize and make searchable a massive calendar of all the known theatrical performances in London from the Restoration through the end of the eighteenth century.[30] After considering several options, they ultimately arrived at the same solution as EEBO-TCP would employ decades later: hand-typed transcriptions produced by offshore workers—in this case, women keypunchers based in Hong Kong.

In his memoir, *Travels in Computerland*, project director Ben Ross Schneider, Jr. styles himself a kind of Gulliver, a literature professor washed up on the unfamiliar shores of mainframe computing. To explain how he came to contract with an offshore keypunching firm, Schneider first recalls the domestic options he considered, offering in the process a revealing glimpse of attitudes towards women's work in the 1970s. One possibility he explored was to retain the services of a typing pool he calls the "MT/ST [Magnetic Tape / Selectric Typewriter] girls," who worked for the local Institute for Paper Chemistry.[31] He also considered the university-adjacent "cottage-industry of faculty wives, typists in academic offices, and local housewives who type dissertations at home" (*TC* 96). Particularly promising were the services of a faculty secretary who "could type your letters, handle your wife's phone calls, and direct a book salesman while she discussed last night's TV with her assistant" (*TC* 112) and a stay-at-home mother who "paid such perfect attention to both the children and me at once, that neither had cause to feel deprived by her ministrations to the other" (*TC* 110). In the guise of praising these women's capabilities, he suggests that document preparation is the kind of mindless work that can be juggled with other, equally feminized tasks, such as caring for children and fielding phone calls. At one point, Schneider himself attempted and failed to perform a batch of typing, discovering, to his surprise, that it was more cognitively and physically demanding than it looked (*TC* 68). This incident is treated, however, as a merely entertaining anecdote that does little to soften the pervasive misogyny.

This devaluation of women's work collides with racial fantasy when Schneider learns of New York-based China Data Systems (CDS) and its overseas keypunching operation, Hong Kong Data Processing. In an advertisement placed in the trade magazine *Business Automation*, Schneider recalls, "I found a picture of a beautiful pair of Oriental eyes gazing over the top of an IBM card" (*TC* 98). This encounter had so strong an impact on Schneider's decision-making process that he reproduces, in his memoir, much of the text from the full-page ad, which bears the headline "Meet the grand old man of off-shore keypunching" [see Figure 1]. The "grand old man" turns out to be both the woman behind the punch card and her employer: "Cindy Luk is one of our best keypunch operators. She was with us when we pioneered in off-shore keypunching, and she's still with us. That was only a year or so ago. But so much has happened in the off-shore keypunching field since we began that Cindy is a real old-timer. So are we. And so are the rest of the highly-educated, English-speaking operators in our Hong Kong keypunch center." The advertisement positions CDS as simultaneously a "pioneer" in a new field and the "grand old man" of that field, invoking a colonialist and masculinist imaginary in which it is possible to be both a trailblazing young buck and an esteemed patriarch. The company can occupy this seemingly paradoxical state thanks to the work of women like Cindy Luk, who is "a real old-timer" after a year on the job.

The ad copy emphasizes that Luk and her colleagues are "highly-educated" and "English-speaking"—a point so critical that it is reiterated almost immediately: "our keypunch operators come from one of the most efficient and best-educated work forces in Asia. They average more than 12 years of education in English-speaking schools." The ad appeals three times to the typists' education and twice to their English skills, insisting that they are the products of a good colonial education system and so can be entrusted with the same work as their white women counterparts in the U.S. These women of color have a key advantage, however, which is that they can be paid less: "We've cut our turnaround time and our costs. We'll

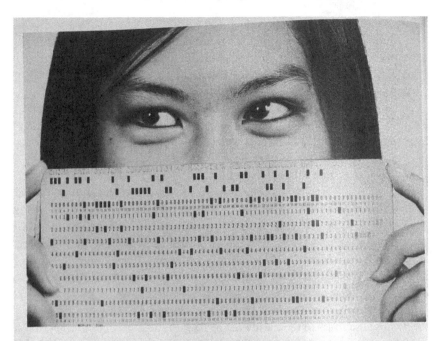

Meet the grand old man of off-shore keypunching.

Cindy Luk is one of our best keypunch operators. She was with us when we pioneered in off-shore keypunching, and she's still with us.

That was only a year or so ago. But so much has happened in the off-shore keypunching field since we began that Cindy is a real old-timer.

So are we.

And so are the rest of the highly educated, English-speaking operators in our Hong Kong keypunch center.

That's why we've been able to handle jobs for major U.S. clients of all sizes, from world-wide banks to retail chain stores, tire companies to international charities, both directly and through service bureaus.

Because our keypunch operators come from one of the most efficient and best-educated work forces in Asia. They average

more than 12 years of education in English-speaking schools. And they're all selected and trained through IBM tests and programs.

In the past year, our keystroke capacity has grown to the size of the largest American installations.

We've cut our turnaround time and our costs. We'll keypunch cards for half the U.S. price or less, with a 10-day turnaround time.

But our biggest asset is still Cindy and the rest of our smart, careful girls. Because they let us guarantee 99.8% accuracy . . . a guarantee that most off-shore companies can't make. And that quality is the same whether the size of the job is 5,000 cards or a million.

Our nation-wide sales organization picks up and delivers at your offices. That makes dealing with us just like dealing with somebody next door . . . no confusion or extra work for you.

Circle 227 on reader information card

Call or write us for more information or quotes. And watch for some of the new services we're going to be offering in the next few months. They'll be at a technological level that may startle you.

After all . . . when you're the grand old man in your field, you can't just stand still.

Right, Cindy?

china data systems corporation

485 Fifth Ave.
Room 1042
New York, N. Y. 10017
(212) 986-9680

Palo Alto, Calif. (415) 328-714C
Seattle, Wash. (206) 632-3222

China Data Systems Corporation is actively seeking representation in every major U.S. city, interested individuals or service bureaus may contact any of the above offices.

32

BUSINESS AUTOMATION

Figure 1. "Meet the grand old man of off-shore keypunching" [advertisement for China Data Systems Corporation]. Reproduced from *Business Automation* 17 (1970), 32.

keypunch cards for half the U.S. price or less, with a 10-day turnaround time." In fact, the price difference appears to have been even starker in the case of the London Stage Information Bank: Schneider notes in his memoir that CDS charged him roughly one-fifth of the cost quoted by the U.S.-based CompuScan.

Given the speed, accuracy, and efficiency with which they produce these results, the ad declares that "our biggest asset is still Cindy and the rest of our smart, careful girls." Here, the women are objectified as "assets" and as "girls," a contrast in both gender and age to the "grand old man" that CDS has become on the basis of their work. The visual rhetoric of a veiled young woman of color, paired with the implicitly male gaze and voice of the advertisement, encourages masculinist and Orientalist fantasies of power (echoed in Schneider's description elsewhere of his project as "my little empire" [*TC* 147]), even as it lays bare the economic logic at the heart of offshore keypunching. The enabling condition of the women's alienated labor is the existence of an intellectual property regime that understands information, ideas, and their expression as economic resources. The existence of a specialized creative class, capable in theory (if not always in practice) of owning the fruits of their knowledge work, is a necessary corollary to the expectation that a massive casualized labor force will produce texts, data, and code without retaining any such rights. Hence, Cindy Luk has been "with us" (the management) since CDS's inception, and she and her colleagues are referred to possessively as "our keypunchers" and "our biggest asset," even as their speedy typing becomes "our keystroke capacity."

The feminization, racialization, and accompanying devaluation of skilled technical work at CDS echoes Lisa Nakamura's history of the recruitment of Navajo women to assemble electronics for Silicon Valley in the 1980s. The myth that Indigenous women had a unique aptitude for circuitry work based on their experience of weaving blankets was applied to East Asian women as U.S.-based corporations moved their supply chains abroad; both groups, as Nakamura points out, were praised for their "nimble fingers."[32] The image of dexterous digits evokes pliability and diminutive physicality, thereby eroticizing handicraft. Although neither Schneider's memoir nor the China Data Systems advertisement refers explicitly to Cindy Luk's or her coworkers' fingers, their hands are ever-present in the repeated term "keypunching," a manual operation that transforms information for computational access—digitization in more than one sense of the word.

The figure of the hand activates racialized tropes about Asian women's sexuality that help to naturalize typing as women's work, and the description of the typists as "smart, careful girls" further suggests their innate aptitude for the "care" necessary to do this work. Indeed, "careful" seems to have been a byword for the employment of women computers in early DH projects. The uncredited punch-card operators who encoded the works of St. Thomas Aquinas for Father Roberto Buso's *Index Thomisticus* in the 1950s were recruited for strikingly similar reasons. Project archivist Marco Carlo Passarotti recalls: "I was told by Father Busa that he chose young women for punching cards on purpose, because they were more careful than men."[33] Here, "care" denotes the precision needed to perform detailed work, but it also suggests idealized feminine qualities associated with the invisible labor of tending to and maintaining vulnerable bodies, environments, and systems that require constant attention. The emphasis on women technologists' aptitude for "care" mediates between traditionally feminized roles—such as mother, homemaker, or weaver—and these women's suitability for employment as manufacturers or operators in an industrialized technology sector.

The figure of the hand helps to ground knowledge work in the raced and gendered body, allowing it to be recast as manual labor and therefore as alienated wage work, outside the realm of intellectual property that might need to be appropriately compensated and credited. These mental moves turn on assumptions that took shape in, but were not yet settled during the long eighteenth century—which makes them easier to see and their alternatives easier to imagine when we turn to the archives of our period. Let's consider a piece of ephemera from the first decade in which authors in England had a statutory right to their own work, and to one of the first workaday women writers in London: dramatist, poet, and Whig panegyrist Susanna Centlivre.

One of the only surviving copies of Centlivre's handwriting is preserved in the papers of antiquarian William Upcott, who collected (among other things) four scrapbooks of autographs from "Distinguished Women" like Margaret Cavendish, Sarah Fielding, Ann Radcliffe, Hannah More, Anna Letitia Barbauld, Frances Burney, Hester Chapone, Maria Edgeworth, and Madame de Staël.[34] While many of these autographs are part of letters, Centlivre's hand appears on a receipt that documents the sale of her copyright in three plays to Edmund Curll and subsequently tracks the distribution of shares in those works among other booksellers [see Figure 2].[35]

Under the 1710 copyright statute, authors like Centlivre were considered to be the original owners of their work, the sale of which was understood to be a one-time transaction that transferred all legal and financial right to publish and profit from the printed text for fourteen years.[36] The receipt documents three such sales, recording three payments of 20 guineas each to Centlivre for the "Copy"—i.e., the copyright—to her plays *The Wonder* (1714), *The Cruel Gift* (1717), and *The Artifice* (1722):

Figure 2. Receipt documenting Susanna Centlivre's sale of three copyrights to Edmund Curll, 1715. British Library Add MS 78686 fol. 68. © British Library Board. Photography by British Library Imaging Services.

> May 18th: 1715. Then Recd of Mr: Curll Twenty
> Guineas in full for the Copy of my Play
> call'd, <u>The Wonder: a Woman keeps a Secret</u>. Recd
> the Same Sum for <u>The Cruel Gift</u>, Susanna CentLivre
> & the same for <u>The Artifice</u>. —
> (In both wch Plays Mr: Bettesworth
> has a half share EC) in ye Last Mears & Payne a 3d.

Given the publication dates of the three plays and the date of the receipt itself, Curll appears to have assumed ownership of these copyrights over the course of several years, maintaining an ongoing relationship with Centlivre at the height and tail end of her career.

Curll also appears to have sold shares in these three copyrights to Arthur Bettesworth, William Mears, and Thomas Payne.[37] While the author's labor had a fixed monetary value established when the copyright was sold, the publisher's investment in a work was speculative, premised on the hope of future profits that might or might not be realized. Sharing the ownership of copyrights with other booksellers helped distribute the risks as well as the potential rewards.[38] In the years that followed, editions and collections of Centlivre's works appeared from each of these booksellers, sometimes in collaboration. For example, the first edition of *The Cruel Gift* was published and sold concurrently by Curll and Bettesworth, as was a 1734 reprint.[39] The first edition of *The Artifice* came out from Payne, but Mears, as his equal sharer in the rights, reissued it in 1735 as a standalone edition and repackaged it as part of a collection of *Four Celebrated Comedies Written by … Mrs. Centlivre.*[40]

As mentioned above, the timing of these three plays' publication would suggest that this receipt was either backdated or updated on at least two occasions.[41] Variations in handwriting and ink color, as well as the increasing crowding on the paper, support the latter interpretation. As I read the receipt, the original draft followed the 1714 publication of *The Wonder* and would have read:

> May 18th: 1715. Then Recd of M[r]: Curll Twenty
> Guineas in full for the Copy of my Play
> call'd, <u>The Wonder: a Woman keeps a Secret</u>.
> Susanna CentLivre

In 1717 or so, around the time *The Cruel Gift* was published, the receipt appears to have been updated in two places (italicized for emphasis):

> May 18th: 1715. Then Recd of M[r]: Curll Twenty
> Guineas in full for the Copy of my Play
> call'd, <u>The Wonder: a Woman keeps a Secret</u>. *Recd*
> *the Same Sum for <u>The Cruel Gift</u>,* Susanna CentLivre
> *(In both w[ch] Plays M[r]: Bettesworth*
> *has a half share EC)*

A final set of emendations appears to have been made around 1722, when "& the same for <u>The Artifice</u>" and "in y[e] Last Mears & Payne a 3[d]" were squeezed in to reflect the sale of the final play's copyright. Read this way, the receipt tells the story of how Curll originally invested on his own in Centlivre's work and then gradually recruited partners to share in the risks and rewards of two of her later plays. Curll evidently seized an opportunity when he "poached" Centlivre from rival publisher Bernard Lintot, buying the rights to *The Wonder* at double Lintot's rate.[42] Curll then brought his frequent collaborator Arthur Bettesworth on board as an equal sharer in time for a second print run, and the two went in together on her next offering, *The Cruel Gift*.[43] A few years later, Curll again purchased the copyright of one of Centlivre's plays, this time sharing the rights to *The Artifice* three ways with Mears and Payne, instead of splitting the venture with Bettesworth.[44]

Like these editions, the receipt itself is the work of many hands. The signature appears to be genuine; it matches that on a 1710 letter signed by Centlivre and held at the Billy Rose Theatre Division of the New York Public Library [see Figure 3].[45] It is likely that the initials "EC" are Curll's. The rest of the writing appears to be in two or three hands and in slightly different inks. None of it resembles surviving examples of Curll's handwriting, although it could have been produced under his auspices by an apprentice or clerk.[46] If so, the receipt may have been maintained in-house

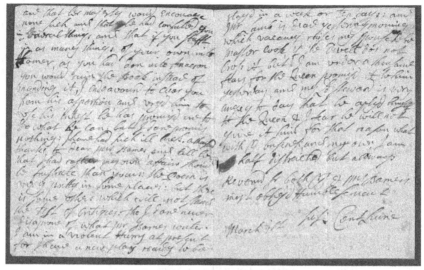

Figure 3. Letter from Susanna Centlivre to Joshua Barnes, 1 March 1710. Billy Rose Theatre Division, the New York Public Library. T-Mss 2001-065, Box 1, Folder 21.

as an ongoing financial record of transactions related to Centlivre. This would help explain how the receipt ended up in the possession of Upcott, who collected records from several publishers. If the receipt was updated and maintained within Curll's operation, however, he does not seem to have acquired Centlivre's initials to document her confirmation of the two later payments. Another, more intriguing possibility is that this was Centlivre's own copy of the transaction record. The notations concerning *The Artifice* are written in a darker ink and a more open hand than the rest of the receipt, with lettering that exhibits certain key similarities to Centlivre's letter.[47] If this speculation is correct, Centlivre may have kept this copy of the receipt after receiving her payment from Curll in 1715, had his clerk update it and him initial it in 1717, and then made her own notation about the copyright sale for *The Artifice*.

Why might she have done so? *The Wonder* was first published in May 1714, a full year before the date on this receipt; if Curll was not forthcoming with his promised payment, that may help explain Centlivre's desire to maintain a detailed record of her dealings with him moving forward.[48] Yet she not only recorded the sums of money that changed hands, after which point she had no further rights to the plays; she also noted the names of Curll's partners on those projects, information that might have been useful as she considered where to shop her next play. Indeed, although Centlivre and Curll maintained an ongoing working relationship, the arrangement was not exclusive; she published frequently with other booksellers throughout this same period.[49] Michele Levy suggests that women writers who worked with multiple publishers did so because the gendered power dynamics of these professional exchanges made it difficult to maintain a productive and mutually beneficial relationship with any single bookseller.[50] Centlivre's receipt, however, may complicate this characterization of women writers as aspiring, if failed, monogamists. It shows how the appearance of an author working with multiple publishers may result from collaborations between booksellers themselves and how a playwright's apparent reputational disarray may in fact reflect an abundance and variety of interest in her success. It suggests that the writer in question might try to track that interest and monitor changes in her personal brand—a kind of intangible property that remained her own, no matter who owned the rights to publish her plays.[51] Centlivre's receipt dramatizes the split between the emergent ideal of proprietary authorship and the economic reality of writing as a form of alienated labor. It documents the transformation of Centlivre's plays into fungible and transferable assets, even as her signature assertively announces her connection to the work. It hints at the ways in which the concept of reputation reduces moral rights to a pecuniary concern, enlisting the author's collaboration in the commodification and alienation of her labor. And it hints at the collective material reality that lies beneath all that authorial bluster: like the decontextualized fingers in Google Books, unidentifiable hands crowd the margins of the receipt, enacting the transactions and materializing their effects in the world.

The figure of the hand returns us, finally, to the circumstances of the receipt's preservation—in a scrapbook of signatures gathered by the antiquarian widely credited with originating the practice of collecting autographs—and to the ways in which that practice has been used to devalue women's knowledge work. The fetishization of a writer's autograph epitomizes the Romantic idealization of the author as a singular, irreducible individual, even as it grounds the legibility of that individuality in a mark made by the body. Centlivre has been framed by modern critics as a figure of resistance to Romantic authorship. Jacky Bratton, for instance, has argued that nineteenth-century critics erased Centlivre from the literary canon because they did not value her "intertheatrical" sensibility—an approach to dramatic writing that recognized actors, audiences, and the material conditions of performance as crucial collaborators in constructing the meaning of a play. Her work, notable for its innovative use of the resources of the stage and cast, was denigrated as "commercial, entertainment, professional, feminine, and in all possible ways both inferior and dangerous to true art."[52] Held up to an ideal of aesthetic achievement as masculine and autonomous, Centlivre was dismissed as a mere workmanlike producer of crowd-pleasing scripts. Even as recently as 1983, a revival of *A Bickerstaff's Burying* met with hostility from critics who called Centlivre "a journey-woman of the theatre" and an "industrial playsmith."[53] Centlivre's image today remains that of a skilled craftsperson—deft at manipulating her materials, to be sure, but lacking the spark of individual genius that differentiates the artist from the artisan.

These links between Centlivre's gendered embodiment and her status as a laborer were forged in her own lifetime. For example, she received this backhanded praise from Richard Steele on the occasion of the premiere of *The Wonder*: "it is no small Satisfaction to me, that I know we are to be entertained to Night with a Comedy from the same Hand that writ *the Gamester* and *the Busie Body*. The deserved Success these Plays met with, is a certain Demonstration that Wit alone is more than sufficient to supply all the Rules of Art. The Incidents in both those Pieces are so dexterously managed, and the Plots so ingeniously perplexed, as shew them at once to be the Invention of a Wit and a Woman."[54] The "same Hand" that Steele mentions serves here as a synecdoche for the playwright herself and suggests the reputational value that has accrued to her work as a result of her previous successes: though she did not consistently publish under her own name, she usually at least published as "the author of" hit works like *The Gamester* (London, 1705). In Steele's usage, the "Hand" also helps to figure Centlivre as a manual laborer, an association reinforced by the description of her plotting as "dexterous." The qualities of the work that show it to be the work of many hands (such as the complexity of the stage business in *The Wonder*) become signs of Centlivre's ingenuity, rather than her expertise, when they are framed within an understanding of good authors as singular creators.

Centlivre paid forward Steele's condescending endorsement of her embodied creativity, describing her actor-collaborators in similar terms and in ways that privileged her status and agency as the playwright. The preface to *The Wonder*, for example, famously attests to the interdependence of playwrights and actors:

> I Don't pretend to write a Preface, either to point out the Beauties, or to excuse the Errors, a judicious Reader may possibly discover in the following Scenes, but to give those excellent Comedians their Due, to whom, in some Measure the best Dramatick Writers are oblig'd. The Poet and the Player are like Soul and Body, indispensibly necessary to one another; the correct Author makes the Player shine, whilst the judicious Player makes the Poet's Fame immortal. I freely acknowledge my self oblig'd to the Actors in general, and to Mr. Wilks, and Mrs. Oldfield in

particular; and I owe them this Justice to say, That their inimitable Action cou'd only support a Play at such a Season, and among so many Benefits. Let this encourage our English Bards to Write, furnish but the artful Player with Materials, and his Skill will lay the Foundation for your Fame.[55]

Centlivre describes the writer as "oblig'd" to the actor, not once, but twice; her debt to Robert Wilks and Anne Oldfield is insistently economic, described as the comedians' "due" and as the "Justice" they are "owed." Yet the acknowledgement performs a kind of *noblesse oblige*. "Poet and Player" may be as interdependent as "Soul and Body," but the word order suggests that it is the Poet who is the Soul to the Player's Body. Reinforcing the association of acting with the labor of the body, Centlivre describes the Players as "artful" and as possessing the "Skill" to work with the "Materials" with which they are furnished. In context, it is clear that the sense of the word "art" invoked here is that of craftsmanship—the practical application of technical skill.

To consider the actors' well-trained and laboring bodies as essential collaborators in the creative process could be radical, were Centlivre to frame her own efforts in the same way. But she does not. The actors "lay the Foundation" for the writer's "Fame," a phrase that echoes her earlier statement that "the judicious Player makes the Poet's Fame immortal." Centlivre smugly congratulates herself for being willing to "freely acknowledge" the actors' contributions and to admit that they are "in some Measure" essential to her success, but she does not entertain the possibility that they might be truly co-equal co-creators. They are, instead, in a "support" role. Humanities academics today likewise gesture towards more inclusive forms of acknowledgment, but in ways that remain fundamentally wedded to existing models of intellectual property and hierarchies of labor. At a moment when many of our ways of knowing are dismissed, ridiculed, and attacked in the public sphere, scholars are understandably hesitant to relinquish frameworks of knowledge production in which our expertise is central and understood to be valuable, both socially and economically. Yet, as I have argued, the Romantic model of authorship to which our fields cling both enables and obfuscates our dependence on uncredited, undercompensated, offshore workers to produce the databases we all use.

The figure of the hand helped define the woman writer as a mere craftsperson and the woman computer as a manual laborer. As a synecdoche for the body, the hand situates gendered knowledge workers on the boundary between agential and alienated labor and highlights how they are essential to the production of information that they do not own. The enduring scholarly fascination with the fingers that appear in Google Books attests to the ongoing overdetermination of this hand, and to the ways our understandings of labor, property, and the body remain bounded by terms established in the eighteenth century. It is our particular responsibility as scholars of the period to unpack the rhetorical figures that uphold unjust labor structures; to conceive of ourselves as knowledge workers, rather than proprietors; and to join in solidarity with the many other hands at work in eighteenth-century studies.

Notes

This essay is dedicated to the memory of Scott Enderle, whose visible and invisible labors made the intersection of book history and digital humanities a richer, more playful, and more humane place to work. I would like to acknowledge the contributions of the following individuals and institutions: the British Library, the V&A Archives, the Folger Shakespeare Library, the Lawrence University Archives, the Houghton Library, and the Billy Rose Theatre Division of the New York Public Library; the Center for Women and Gender at Utah State University; Leah Benedict, Karen Britland, Franny Gaede, Stephen H. Gregg, Chelsea Phillips, Doug Reside, Carrie Shanafelt, John Unsworth, Jane Wessel, Claude Willan, and one of the anonymous reviewers of this essay for the journal. None of this research would be possible without the women of China Data Systems Corporation, nor without the dedication of Todd Hugie, Lauren Liebe, and Derek Miller to recovering their work.

1. Woodmansee, "On the Author Effect: Recovering Collectivity," in *The Construction of Authorship: Textual Appropriation in Law and Literature*, ed. Martha Woodmansee and Peter Jaszi (Durham: Duke University Press, 1994), 25.

2. *Digital Technology and the Practices of Humanities Research*, ed. Jennifer Edmond (Cambridge: Open Book Publishers, 2020): http://books.openedition.org/obp/11899.

3. See, for example, Kathleen Fitzpatrick, *Planned Obsolescence: Publishing, Technology, and the Future of the Academy* (New York: NYU Press, 2011).

4. Richard Holden traces the evolution of the term "digit" and how it came to refer to the discrete numeric values in binary code ("digital," *OED Blog*, 16 August 2012: https://public.oed.com/blog/word-stories-digital). See also Matthew G. Kirschenbaum, *Mechanisms: New Media and the Forensic Imagination* (Cambridge: MIT Press, 2008), 12.

5. Roberta Kwall, *The Soul of Creativity: Forging a Moral Rights Law for the United States* (Stanford: Stanford University Press, 2010), 30–31.

6. Craig, *Copyright, Communication, and Culture: Towards a Relational Theory of Copyright Law* (Cheltenham: Edward Elgar, 2011), 3.

7. Risam, "The Stakes of Digital Labor in the Twenty-First-Century Academy: The Revolution Will Not Be Turkified," in *Humans at Work in the Digital Age: Forms of Digital Textual Labor*, ed. Shawna Ross and Andrew Pilsch (London: Routledge, 2020), 245.

8. Jacqueline Wernimont and Elizabeth Losh, "Introduction," in *Bodies of Information: Intersectional Digital Humanities*, ed. Elizabeth Losh and Jacqueline Wernimont (Minneapolis: University of Minnesota Press, 2018), xxii; https:// dhdebates.gc.cuny.edu/read/untitled-4e08b137-aec5-49a4-83c0-38258425f145/ section/466311ae-d3dc-4d50-b616-8b5d1555d231#intro.

9. See Emily C. Friedman, "Ownership, Copyright, and the Ethics of the Unpublished," in *Access and Control in Digital Humanities*, ed. Shane Hawkins (London: Routledge, 2021), 226; and Tim Causer, Kris Grint, Anna-Maria Sichani, and Melissa Terras, "'Making such Bargain': *Transcribe Bentham* and the Quality and Cost–Effectiveness of Crowdsourced Transcription," *Digital Scholarship in the Humanities* 33, no. 3 (2018): 469.

10. Wilson, *The Art of Google Books*: https://theartofgooglebooks.tumblr.com.

11. Andrew Norman Wilson, *Workers Leaving the Googleplex* (2011), http:// www.andrewnormanwilson.com/WorkersGoogleplex.html. Wilson has continued to explore similar themes through the critically acclaimed art exhibit *ScanOps* (2012–the present).

12. Andrea Zeffiro, "Digitizing Labor in the Google Books Project: Gloved Fingertips and Severed Hands," in *Humans at Work in the Digital Age*, 133–54, 137, 140.

13. Joseph Yannielli, "The Secret History of the Severed Hands," HASTAC, 22 November 2014, https://digitalhistories.yctl.org/2014/11/21/a-feminist-history-of-computing/.

14. On the makeup of this labor force, see Shawn Wen, "The Ladies Vanish," *The New Inquiry* (11 November 2014), https://thenewinquiry.com/the-ladies-vanish. See also Lisa Nakamura, "Indigenous Circuits: Navajo Women and the Racialization of Early Electronic Manufacture," *American Quarterly* 66, no. 4 (2014): 919–41; Catherine D'Ignazio and Lauren Klein, *Data Feminism* (Cambridge: MIT Press, 2020), Chapter 7, https://data-feminism.mitpress.mit.edu/ pub/0vgzaln4#n2vrr0fw1rc; and Mary Gray and Siddarth Suri, *Ghost Work: How to Stop Silicon Valley from Building a New Global Underclass* (New York: Houghton Mifflin Harcourt, 2019).

15. Booth and Posner, "Introduction: The Materials at Hand," *PMLA* 135, no. 1 (2020): 14, 15.

16. Klein, "Dimensions of Scale: Invisible Labor, Editorial Work, and the Future of Quantitative Literary Studies," *PMLA* 135, no. 1 (2020): 24.

17. See, for example, James Essinger, *Ada's Algorithm: How Lord Byron's Daughter Ada Lovelace Launched the Digital Age* (Brooklyn: Melville House, 2014); Janet Abbate, *Recoding Gender: Women's Changing Participation in Computing* (Cambridge: MIT Press, 2012); Liza Munda, *Code Girls: The Untold Story of the American Women Code Breakers of World War II* (New York: Hatchette, 2019); and Margot Lee Shetterly, *Hidden Figures: The American Dream and the Untold Story*

of the Black Women Mathematicians Who Helped Win the Space Race (New York: William Morrow, 2016).

18. Hicks, *Programmed Inequality: How Britain Discarded Its Women Technologists and Lost Its Edge in Computing* (Cambridge: MIT Press, 2018), 5–9, 17. See also Jennifer S. Light, "When Computers Were Women," *Technology and Culture* 40, no. 3 (1999): 455–83.

19. Ozment, "Rationale for Feminist Bibliography," *Textual Cultures* 13, no. 1 (2020): 167.

20. Michael Gavin, "How to Think about EEBO," *Textual Cultures* 11, nos. 1 and 2 (2017): 70–105; see also Peter C. Herman, "EEBO and Me: An Autobiographical Response to Michael Gavin, 'How to Think About EEBO,'" *Textual Cultures* 13, no. 1 (2020): 207–16; and Gavin, "EEBO and Us," *Textual Culture* 14, no. 1 (2021): 270–78.

21. Ian Gadd, "The Use and Misuse of Early English Books Online," *Literature Compass* 6, no. 3 (2009): 680–92; Bonnie Mak, "Archaeology of a Digitization," *Journal of the Association for Information Science and Technology* 65, no. 8 (2014): 1515–26; and Cassidy Holahan, "Rummaging in the Dark: ECCO as Opaque Digital Archive," *Eighteenth-Century Studies* 54, no. 4 (2021): 803–26.

22. Fyfe, "An Archaeology of Victorian Newspapers," *Victorian Periodicals Review* 49, no. 4 (2016): 548, 549–50.

23. Gregg, *Old Books and Digital Publishing: Eighteenth-Century Collections Online* (Cambridge: Cambridge University Press, 2020), and "Eccentric Connections: Towards a Decolonial (Digital) Book History," *Eighteenth-Century Fiction* 34, no. 4 (2022): 471–82.

24. SPi Global was based in the Philippines. These companies also maintain offices in the U.K. and the U.S. and additional centers in countries including China, Nicaragua, and Vietnam. See "About," Apex CoVantage, https://apexcovantage.com/about/; "Contact Us," Straive https://www.straive.com/contact-us; and "Contact Us," SPi Global, as preserved in the Internet Archive: https://web.archive.org/web/20210119205839/https://www.spi-global.com/contact-us.

25. Mak, "Confessions of a Twenty-First-Century Memsahib: The Offshore Sweatshops of the Digital Humanities," paper presented at the MLA Convention, Austin, Texas, January 2016. An abstract of the paper is preserved on the personal website of Andrew Pilsch: https://oncomouse.github.io/mla16.html.

26. Margaret Maurer has found the TCP website rife with grammatical sleight-of-hand seemingly crafted to give the misleading impression that transcription occurs in house; "EEBO-TCP's Keyers and the Scholarly Labor of Digitization," Shakespeare Association of America (pre-circulated paper, 2021), 7.

27. Apex CoVantage, "Meet the Team at Apex CoVantage," https://www.youtube.com/watch?v=5EKLInwwUrY.

28. "The Results of Keying Instead of OCR," Text Creation Partnership, https://textcreationpartnership.org/using-tcp-content/results-of-keying/.

29. Homepage, Text Creation Partnership, 15 September 2019, as preserved in the Internet Archive: https://web.archive.org/web/20190915042804/http://www.textcreationpartnership.org:80.

30. *The London Stage, 1660–1800: A Calendar of Plays, Entertainments and Afterpieces, Together with Casts, Box-Receipts and Contemporary Comment. Compiled from the Playbills, Newspapers and Theatrical Diaries of the Period*, ed. William Van Lennep, et al., 11 vols. (Carbondale: Southern Illinois University Press, 1961–68).

31. Schneider, *Travels in Computerland; or, Incompatibilities and Interfaces: A Full and True Account of the Implementation of the London Stage Information Bank* (Reading: Addison-Wesley, 1974), 53; see also 67 and 133. Subsequent citations will be made parenthetically as *TC*.

32. Nakamura, "Indigenous Circuits," 933–34.

33. Passarotti, quoted in Melissa Terras and Julianne Nyhan, "Father Busa's Female Punch Card Operatives," *Debates in the Digital Humanities 2016*, ed. Matthew K. Gold and Lauren F. Klein (Minneapolis: University of Minnesota Press, 2016), https://dhdebates.gc.cuny.edu/read/untitled/section/1e57217b-f262-4f25-806b-4fcf1548beb5. Nyhan's book, *Hidden And Devalued Feminized Labour in The Digital Humanities: On The Index Thomisticus Project, 1954–67* (London: Routledge, 2023) promises to reveal further findings from this research.

34. On the provenance of these items, see Michelle Levy, "Do Women Have a Book History?" *Studies in Romanticism* 53, no. 3 (2014): 304–5; and Theodore Hofmann, Joan Winterkorn, Frances Harris, and Hilton Kelliher, "John Evelyn's Archive at the British Library," *The Book Collector* 44, no. 2 (1995): 200–6. See also the collection description at http://searcharchives.bl.uk/IAMS_VU2:IAMS033-002037628, and Janet Ing Freeman, "Upcott, William (1779–1845), antiquary and autograph collector," *Oxford Dictionary of National Biography* (Oxford University Press, 2004).

35. Evelyn Papers, Vol. DXIX, British Library Add MS 78686, fol. 118, recto.

36. Playwrights like Centlivre were not granted legal property in performances of their work until 1833, although they customarily received the profits from an author's benefit performance every third night of its initial run, and in some cases at subsequent benefit performances as well. See Jane Wessel, *Owning Performance | Performing Ownership: Literary Property and the Eighteenth-Century British Stage* (Ann Arbor: University of Michigan Press, 2022), and Derek Miller, *Copyright and the Value of Performance, 1770–1911* (Cambridge: Cambridge University Press, 2018).

37. I have identified the booksellers based on the title pages of the plays in question, in consultation with the *Oxford Dictionary of National Biography*, the Stationers' Company records published by *The Records of London's Livery Companies Online* (https://www.londonroll.org), and the Stationers' Company Register, Microfilm 985/6, British Library.

38. Terry Belanger, "Publishers and Writers in Eighteenth-Century England," in *Books and Their Readers in Eighteenth-Century England*, ed. Isabel Rivers (Leicester: Leicester University Press, 1982), 5–25; Adrian Johns, *Piracy: The Intellectual Property Wars from Gutenberg to Gates* (Chicago: University of Chicago Press, 2009), 41; Paulina Kewes, *Authorship and Appropriation: Writing for the Stage in England, 1660–1710* (Oxford: Clarendon Press, 1998). Splitting ownership

of a copyright at the point of its entry into the Stationers' Register was common enough that the latter included a column for "Shares."

39. See the English Short Title Catalogue (ESTC) entries: http://estc.bl.uk/T34448 and http://estc.bl.uk/T25994.

40. See ESTC entries: http://estc.bl.uk/T26858, http://estc.bl.uk/T26867, and http://estc.bl.uk/N31922.

41. Joseph Haslewood, writing under the pseudonym "Eu. Hood" for *The Gentleman's Magazine*, included this receipt in a list of interesting items from Upcott's collection and asserted that "The last two plays were added to the receipt at a later period," citing the initial performance dates of *The Cruel Gift* and *The Artifice* as evidence that the receipt could not have been written all at once in 1715; see "Literary Contracts … From MSS. In the possession of Mr. Upcott, of the London Institution," *Gentleman's Magazine* 94, no. 1 (1824): 319. Haslewood evidently clipped this description of the receipt and pasted it into the entry on Centlivre in his annotated copy of the first volume of Giles Jacob's *The Poetical Register* (British Library General Collection C.45.d.17), 33. For the ascription of the work of "Eu. Hood" to Haslewood, see Emily Lorraine de Montluzin, *Attributions of Authorship in The Gentleman's Magazine, 1731–1868: An Electronic Union List* (Charlottesville: Bibliographical Society of the University of Virginia, 2003), https://bsuva.org/bsuva/gm3/GM1824.html; see also Alan Bell, "Haslewood, Joseph (1769–1833), bibliographer and antiquary," *Oxford Dictionary of National Biography* (Oxford University Press, 2004).

42. Paul Baines and Pat Rogers, *Edmund Curll, Bookseller* (Oxford: Oxford University Press, 2007), 50. On Lintot's relatively meager copyright payments to Centlivre, see my *Speculative Enterprise: Public Theaters and Financial Markets in London, 1688-1763* (Charlottesville: University of Virginia Press, 2021), 119 and 221n105.

43. The first edition of *The Wonder* exists in two versions: one that lists only Curll as publisher, and another that lists both Curll and Bettesworth (http://estc.bl.uk/N36132 and http://estc.bl.uk/T26870). John O'Brien speculates that "the different imprints reflect the two men's different financial stakes in the first edition, with Curll taking the lead role from the start"; see "A Note on the Text" in *The Wonder: A Woman Keeps a Secret*, ed. John O'Brien (Petersborough: Broadview Press, 2004), 33. The 1719 second edition (http://estc.bl.uk/T26869) lists both men on the title page, as does the 1717 first edition of *The Cruel Gift* (http://estc.bl.uk/T34448). *The Cruel Gift* was also advertised as being available for purchase in the shop of Rebecca Burleigh, a frequent collaborator of Curll's; see *The Daily Courant* 4743 (2 January 1717), verso.

44. The title page of *The Artifice* (http://estc.bl.uk/T26858) is dated 1723 and lists only Payne as its publisher. However, newspapers advertised its availability at London bookshops beginning in October 1722 and indicated that it was printed for and sold by Mears, Payne, Curll, and several others booksellers; see, for example, *The Post Boy* 5183 (11 October 1722), verso. The second edition was printed in 1735 for Mears "and the proprietors" (http://estc.bl.uk/T26867 and http://estc.bl.uk/N5590). The same year, *The Artifice* was also included in Mears's *Four Celebrated Comedies Written by the Late Ingenious Mrs. Centlivre*.

45. To my knowledge, only two handwritten copies of any of Centlivre's literary works survive from her lifetime, and both appear to be professional transcripts, rather than autograph manuscripts. The first is a formal presentation copy of an unpublished work, "A Poem on the Recovery of the Lady Henrietta Holles from the Small Pox," held, though not yet fully catalogued, at the British Library (Harley MS 7649, ff 7r–10r). A c. 1709 manuscript of *The Busie Body* is located in the Houghton Library at Harvard University (MS Thr 39). The catalogue notes that the hand is "unidentified," but it again appears scribal.

46. Curll was not a member of the Stationers' Company and any apprentices he may have had were not legally bound and so left no paper trail with the Company; see Baines and Rogers, *Edmund Curll*, 325 n10. Samples of Curll's hand are reproduced in Claude Willan, "'Mr Pope's Penmanship': Edmund Curll, Alexander Pope, and Rawlinson Letters 90," *The Library* 12, no. 3 (2011): 259–80.

47. Centlivre's letter exhibits several different ways of forming repeated letters and combinations of letters, making comparison somewhat difficult; however, both samples exhibit a rapid, informal hand, more angular than rounded in appearance, with comparatively open lettering.

48. For a notice of the initial publication, see *The Post Boy* 2962 (4 May 1714), verso.

49. During the years encompassed by the receipt, Centlivre's farce, *The Gotham Election* (London, 1715), was published by S. Keimer (http://estc.bl.uk/T26854) and republished by J. Roberts as *The Humours of Elections* (http://estc.bl.uk/T26876), and her hit, *A Bold Stroke for a Wife* (London, 1718), was printed for Mears along with J. Browne and F. Clay (http://estc.bl.uk/T22948).

50. Levy, "Do Women Have a Book History?" 303, 308.

51. As Jane Wessel points out, "Research into eighteenth-century celebrity culture is seldom connected to questions of intellectual property law," even though "performance and celebrity were increasingly valued as forms of intellectual property" ("Mimicry, Property, and the Reproduction of Celebrity in Eighteenth-Century England," *The Eighteenth Century* 60, no. 1 [Spring 2019]: 66). On Centlivre as a celebrity, see my *Speculative Enterprise*, 80–81 and 212–13 nn3–9.

52. Bratton, "Reading the Intertheatrical, or, The Mysterious Disappearance of Susanna Centlivre," in *Women, Theatre and Performance: New Histories, New Historiographies*, ed. Maggie B. Gale and Viv Gardner (Manchester: Manchester University Press, 2000), 20.

53. Peter Hepple, "Ragbag of a Production," *Stage and Television Today*, 8 December 1983; John Barber, "Epicene Island," *Daily Telegraph*, 30 November 1983. These reviews have been preserved in the production files for *Wedlock/Deadlock*, dir. Fidelis Morgan, King's Head Theatre Club, London, now housed in the V&A Theatre Collection.

54. Marmaduke Myrtle [i.e., Steele], *The Lover* 27 (27 April 1714), verso. This issue exists in two versions, only one of which includes commentary on *The Wonder*.

55. [Susanna Centlivre], *The Wonder: A Woman Keeps a Secret. A Comedy. As It Is Acted at the Theatre Royal in Drury-Lane. By Her Majesty's Servants. Written by the Author of The Gamester* (London: E. Curll and A. Bettesworth, 1714). The full text is

available through ECCO-TCP at http://name.umdl.umich.edu/004798029.0001.000. The transcription derives from Gale Document Number CW0110075278, which is a facsimile of the British Library's copy (http://estc.bl.uk/T26870). Centlivre's name does not appear on the title page, but she signed the dedication and was, by 1714, well known as the author of *The Gamester*.

Contributors to Volume 52

Kathleen Tamayo Alves is Associate Professor and Deputy Chair of English at Queensborough Community College of the City University of New York. Her research centers on eighteenth-century literature, culture, and medicine, and she has recently published in *Aphra Behn Online, Eighteenth-Century Fiction, The Journal of the Assembly for Expanded Perspectives on Learning,* and *The Rambling.* Her book-in-progress, *Body Language: Medicine and the Eighteenth-Century Comic Novel,* explores how medicine shaped and was shaped by comic language through fictional dramatizations of female-specific bodily phenomena, such as menstruation, hysteria, and pregnancy.

Nicole Balzer is an academic senior counselor at the Institut für Erziehungswissenschaft and in the department of General Educational Science at the Westfälische Wilhelms-Universität Münster. She co-edited, with Jens Beljan and Johannes Drerup, *Charles Taylor: Erziehungs- und bildungsphilosophische Perspektiven* (mentis Verlag, 2020).

Andrew Black is Associate Professor of English and Philosophy at Murray State University. His scholarship focuses on the intersection between literature and rhetorical theory in the long eighteenth century. His work has appeared in *Eighteenth-Century Life, Restoration, Style,* and *The Seventeenth Century.* His current book project, tentatively titled *Shaping Sighs,* examines representations of orators and orality in eighteenth-century literature and rhetoric.

Carolina Blutrach works as a Postdoctoral Researcher on the project, CIRGEN: Circulating Gender in the Global Enlightenment: Ideas, Networks, Agencies (ERC2017 Advanced Grant 787015) at the Universitat de València. She received her Ph.D. in History and Civilization from the European University Institute in Florence. She has also held a Postdoctoral Fellowship for Researchers and Cultural Creators from the BBVA Foundation. She is the author of *El III conde de Fernán Núñez, 1644–1721: Vida y memoria de un cortesano práctico* (Marcial Pons-CSIC, 2014), editor of a special issue of *Revista Espacio, Tiempo y Forma: Serie IV, Historia Moderna* on *El viaje y su memoria en la construcción de identidades, siglos XVI–XIX* (2016), and co-editor, with

Giulia Calvi, of a special issue of the *European Review of History* on *Sibling Relations and Family History: Conflicts, Co-operation, and Gender Roles in the Sixteenth to the Nineteenth Centuries* (2010).

Mónica Bolufer is Professor of Modern History at the Universitat de València and Principal Investigator of the project, CIRGEN: Circulating Gender in the Global Enlightenment. Ideas, Networks, Agencies (ERC2017-Advanced Grant 787015). Her research interests include women's writing; discourses on gender, politeness, sensibility, and the self; and travel narratives, in comparative and transnational perspective. She has recently co-edited, with Elizabeth F. Lewis and Catherine M. Jaffe, *The Routledge Companion to the Hispanic Enlightenment* (Routledge, 2019).

Mattie Burkert is Assistant Professor of Digital Humanities in the Department of English at the University of Oregon. She is the author of *Speculative Enterprise: Public Theaters and Financial Markets, 1688–1763* (University of Virginia Press, 2021) and director of the NEH–funded London Stage Database project (https://londonstagedatabase.uoregon.edu). Her recent essays have appeared in *Theatre Survey*, *Restoration*, *Digital Humanities Quarterly*, and *Intermediate Horizons: Book History and Digital Humanities* (University of Wisconsin Press, 2022).

Allison Cardon earned her Ph.D. in English literature from the University at Buffalo, State University of New York, in 2021. She is now Visiting Assistant Professor at the College of Wooster. She has published an article on Samuel Richardson's *Pamela* and injury in *Novel* and is working on a book manuscript, *Writing Wrongs: Injury, Rights, and Injustice in Eighteenth-Century British Literature*. Her contribution to this volume of *Studies in Eighteenth-Century Culture* won the 2021 Race and Empire Caucus Graduate Student Essay Prize from the American Society for Eighteenth-Century Studies.

Emily C. Casey is Hall Assistant Professor of American Art and Culture in the Kress Foundation Department of Art History at the University of Kansas. Her current book project critically examines British and American visual and material culture to reveal how the world's oceans became a space through which networks of empire and capital were imagined and constructed. She has received grants and fellowships to support her research from the Metropolitan Museum of Art, the Smithsonian American Art Museum, the Omohundro Institute of Early American History and Culture, the Peabody Essex Museum, the Library Company of Philadelphia, and the National Maritime Museum in London. She currently serves on the board of the Association of Historians of American Art.

Tita Chico is Professor of English at the University of Maryland and Director of its Center for Literary and Comparative Studies. Her most recent book, *The Experimental Imagination: Literary Knowledge and Science in the British Enlightenment* (Stanford University Press, 2018), tells the story of how literariness came to be distinguished from its epistemological sibling, science, as a source of truth about the natural and social worlds. Her current book project, *Wonder: Literature and Science in the Long Eighteenth Century* (under contract with Cambridge University Press), looks at wonder as a defining epistemology for what we now understand as literature and science in the period. She has received numerous grants and fellowships, including a Visiting Fellowship at New College, University of Oxford; a Senior Research Fellowship, Queen Mary Centre for Eighteenth-Century Studies; and fellowships from the Institute of English Studies at the School for Advanced Study; the Harry Ransom Center; the Folger Institute; the National Humanities Center; the Newberry Library; Chawton House Library and Research Centre; and the Ford Foundation. Since 2001, she has served as Editor of *The Eighteenth Century: Theory and Interpretation*. She has also served as a member of the Executive Board of the American Society for Eighteenth-Century Studies.

Sarah R. Cohen is Professor of Art History and Chair of the Department of Art and Art History at the University at Albany, State University of New York. Her books include *Art, Dance, and the Body in French Culture of the Ancien Régime* (Cambridge University Press, 2000); *Enlightened Animals in Eighteenth-Century Art: Sensation, Matter, and Knowledge* (Bloomsbury, 2021); and *Picturing Animals in Early Modern Europe: Art and Soul* (Harvey Miller/Brepols Publishers, 2022).

Rebecca Crisafulli is Assistant Professor of French at Saint Anselm College. She earned her Ph.D. from the University of Chicago and is currently working on a book project regarding Louise d'Épinay.

Pichaya (Mint) Damrongpiwat is Lecturer in English and Comparative Literature at Columbia University. She recently received her Ph.D. in English from Cornell University. An article derived from her dissertation, "Fictions of Materiality in *Clarissa*," appeared in *The Eighteenth Century: Theory and Interpretation*. In 2021-2022, she was a Diamonstein-Spielvogel Fellow at the New York Public Library, where she conducted research for her new project, "'Every morsel of blank': Paper Recycling as Literary Practice in Women's Archives."

Alison DeSimone is Associate Professor of Musicology at the University of Missouri-Kansas City. She is the author of *The Power of Pastiche: Musical Miscellany and Cultural Identity in Early Eighteenth-Century England* (Clemson University Press, 2021), and the co-editor of *Music and the Benefit Performance in Eighteenth-Century Britain* (Cambridge University Press, 2020). She has published articles in the *Journal of Musicological Research*, *A-R Online Anthology*, *Händel-Jahrbuch*, and *Early Modern Women*. In 2018, she won the Ruth Solie Prize for an Outstanding Article on British Music from the North American British Music Studies Association.

Alejandra Dubcovsky is Associate Professor of History at the University of California, Riverside. Her first book, *Informed Power: Communication in the Early American South* (Harvard University Press, 2016), won the Michael V. R. Thomason Book Award from the Gulf South Historical Association. Her new work, *Talking Back: Native Women and the Making of the Early South* (Yale University Press, 2023), examines the roles and power of Native women in the early South.

Erica Johnson Edwards is Associate Professor of History at Francis Marion University. She is author of *Philanthropy and Race in the Haitian Revolution* (Palgrave, 2018) and co-editor of *The French Revolution and Religion in Global Perspective* (Palgrave, 2017).

She has published articles in *Studies in Religion and the Enlightenment, The History Teacher, Southern Quarterly,* the *Journal of Transnational Studies,* and the *Journal of the Western Society for French History.* She is one of the editors of *Age of Revolutions,* an open-access, peer-reviewed academic journal.

Timothy Erwin is Professor of English at the University of Nevada, Las Vegas. He is the author of *Textual Vision: Augustan Design and the Invention of Eighteenth-Century Visual Culture* (Bucknell University Press, 2015), a rhetorical study of competing analogies between text and image in Alexander Pope, Samuel Johnson, Henry Fielding, Samuel Richardson, William Hogarth, and Jane Austen. He is a former editor of *Studies in Eighteenth-Century Culture.* Recent articles include "Alexander Pope and a Carracci Venus at the Court of James II and Mary of Modena" in *Huntington Library Quarterly,* and "Discours sur l'Œil: *Roméo et Juliette* et *Marriage A-la-Mode* de William Hogarth," in the <u>*Actes des Congrès de la Société Française Shakespeare*</u>.

Robbie Ethridge is Professor Emeritus of Anthropology at the University of Mississippi. In addition to editing four anthologies and writing numerous articles and book chapters on the history and ethnography of the Native peoples of the American South, she is the author of *Creek Country: The Creek Indians and Their World, 1796–1816* (University of North Carolina Press, 2003) and the Mooney Award-winning book, *From Chicaza to Chickasaw: The European Invasion and the Transformation of the Mississippian World, 1540–1715* (University of North Carolina Press, 2010). Most recently, she has co-authored, with Robert J. Miller, *A Promise Kept: The Muscogee (Creek) Nation and McGirt v. Oklahoma* (University of Oklahoma Press, 2023). She is best known for her work on the sixteenth- and seventeenth-century colonial disruptions in the American South and the resultant shatter zone that transformed the lives of its Native inhabitants. Her current research continues this examination as she reconstructs the 700-year history of the pre-colonial Mississippian world, including the rise of chiefdoms, the transformation of that world as a result of European contact, and the restructuring of Native societies that occurred as they became an instrumental part of the colonial South.

Lise Gaston is a Social Sciences and Humanities Research Council of Canada Postdoctoral Fellow at Concordia University. Her work on late eighteenth- and early nineteenth-century women writers has appeared in *European Romantic Review, Nineteenth-Century Studies,* and *Nineteenth-Century Contexts.* She is the author of *Cityscapes in Mating Season* (Signature Editions, 2017).

Michael Griffin is Associate Professor of English at the University of Limerick. He is the author of *Enlightenment in Ruins: The Geographies of Oliver Goldsmith* (Bucknell University Press, 2013). He is the editor of *The Selected Writings of Thomas Dermody* (Field Day Press, 2012) and *The Collected Poems of Laurence Whyte* (Bucknell University Press, 2016) and co-editor, with David O'Shaughnessy, of *The Letters of Oliver Goldsmith* (Cambridge University Press, 2018). He is currently editing a volume of Goldsmith's poetry for a new Cambridge University Press edition of Goldsmith's works, co-edited with David O'Shaughnessy.

Christopher E. Hendricks is Professor of History at the Armstrong Campus of Georgia Southern University, where he has been teaching since 1993. He is the author of numerous publications, including *The Backcountry Towns of Colonial Virginia* (University of Tennessee Press, 2006).

Elizabeth Hutchinson, Associate Professor of Art History at Barnard College of Columbia University, is the author of *The Indian Craze: Primitivism, Modernism, and Transculturation in American Art, 1890–1915* (Duke University Press, 2009) and several essays on portraits of Native American diplomats made in the Early Republic. Her recent work has focused on two themes: decolonizing and Indigenizing museums and exhibitions and postcolonial/posthumanist approaches to the visual cultures of the American West.

Cynthia Kok is a Ph.D. candidate in the History of Art at Yale University. She is currently working on a dissertation that focuses on sensorial engagement in making and craft experiments with mother-of-pearl in the early modern Dutch world. Her other research interests include history and specimen collecting, crafting under European colonial governance, and mimetic material practices. She is the 2021–23 Kress History of Art Institutional Fellow at the Leiden University Centre for the Arts in Society.

Anne Lafont is an art historian and *directrice d'études* at L'École des Hautes Études en Sciences Sociales in Paris. Her research focuses on race and visual culture in the early modern era, the encounter between African objects and Western aesthetics in the eighteenth and nineteenth centuries, and the art of the Black Atlantic at large. Her most recent book is *L'art et la race: L'Africain (tout) contre l'oeil des Lumières* (Les presses du réel, 2019). Her contribution to this volume of *Studies in Eighteenth-Century Culture* originated as the James L. Clifford Lecture at the 2021 Virtual Annual Meeting of the American Society for Eighteenth-Century Studies.

Brittany Luberda is the Anne Stone Associate Curator of Decorative Arts at the Baltimore Museum of Art, where she oversees European and American silver, ceramics, furniture, and glass from 2200 BCE to the present. She has recently presented on the global circulation of materials and colonization at the Materializing Race Unconference, the International Society for Eighteenth-Century Studies, and Washington University of Saint Louis's Eighteenth-Century Salon. Her writing can be found in *Journal18*, *Furniture History Society Newsletter*, *Faenza*, and *Northwestern Art Review*.

Waltraud Maierhofer is Professor of German and Global Health Studies at the University of Iowa. She has published widely on German literature and culture since the eighteenth century, with a major focus on Goethe, narrative prose, and the intersections between gender, the visual arts, book illustration, and history. Her introduction to the life and work of the painter Angelika Kauffmann (Rowohlt, 1997) and her edition of Kauffmann's correspondence—*Angelica Kauffmann: "Mir träumte vor ein paar Nächten ich hätte Briefe von Ihnen Empfangen"* (Libelle, 2001)—are of importance to the study of *wunderkinder*. Her edited collection, *Women against Napoleon* (Campus Verlag, 2007), and her editions of Johann Heinrich Ramberg's adaptation of the Reynard the Fox fable (VDG, 2016) and of the *Life of Strunk the Upstart* (Schnell und Steiner, 2019) examine other aspects of social mobility and celebrity in the early nineteenth century. Her research has earned several awards from the Alexander von Humboldt Foundation.

Patrícia Martins Marcos is UC Chancellor's Rising to the Challenge Postdoctoral Fellow at UCLA's Department of History and the Bunche Center for African American Studies. She is a scholar of Portuguese colonialism and postcolonialism working at the intersections of the histories of race, science, medicine, and visual culture in the Afro-Luso-Brazilian Atlantic. She is the Associate Editor of the *History of Anthropology Review*. Her work has been supported by the Consortium for the History of Science, Technology, and Medicine; the Huntington Library; the American Philosophical Society; the John Carter Brown Library; and the Center for Black, Brown, and Queer Studies. She is the author of "Blackness out of Place: Black Countervisuality in Portugal and its Former Empire," which appeared in the *Radical History Review* in 2022.

Jennifer Monroe McCutchen is Assistant Professor of History at the University of St. Thomas in St. Paul, Minnesota. She specializes in early American history and ethnohistory, with a focus on gender, power, exchange, and diplomacy. She is the author of "'More Advantageous to Be With Spaniards': Gunpowder and Creek-Spanish Encounters in Cuba, 1763–1783," which appeared in *Terrae Incognitae: The Journal of the Society for the History of Discoveries* in 2020.

Elizabeth Neiman is Associate Professor of English and Women's, Gender, and Sexuality Studies at the University of Maine. While she considers herself a Romanticist, she entered the field sideways through her work on the popular and much-maligned novels of the Minerva Press. Her first book, *Minerva's Gothics: The Politics and Poetics of Romantic Exchange, 1785–1820* (University of Wales Press, 2019), makes the case for an exchange (albeit unequal) between Minerva novels and now-canonical political and literary texts. She remains interested in how marginalized women authors engage with Romantic texts and contexts and with the implications of those engagements, both in their day and our own. She is working on a new book project that explores how Romantic-era women writers (both canonical and lesser-known) adapt representations of sympathy and sublimity in ways that expose the gendered and racialized limits of empathy.

David O'Shaughnessy is Professor of Eighteenth-Century Studies at the University of Galway. He is the author of *William Godwin and the Theatre* (Pickering & Chatto, 2010). Most recently, he is the co-editor, with Ian Newman, of *Charles Macklin and the Theatres of London* (Liverpool University Press, 2021); the editor of *Ireland, Enlightenment, and the English Stage, 1740–1820* (Cambridge University Press, 2019); and the co-editor, with Michael Griffin, of *The Letters of Oliver Goldsmith* (Cambridge University Press, 2018). He is currently editing a volume of Goldsmith's theatrical writings for a new Cambridge University Press edition of Goldsmith's works, co-edited with Michael Griffin.

Jürgen Overhoff is Professor of the History of Education at the Westfälische Wilhelms-Universität Münster. From 2018 to 2022, he was President of the Deutsche Gesellschaft für die Erforschung des 18. Jahrhunderts [the German Society for Eighteenth-Century Studies]. His recent monographs are *Friedrich der Große und George Washington: Zwei Wege der Aufklärung* (Klett-Cotta Verlag, 2011) and *Johann Bernhard Basedow: Aufklärer, Pädagoge, Menschenfreund, Eine Biografie* (Wallstein, 2020). He has edited *William Penn: Früchte der Einsamkeit*, trans. Joachim Kalka (Cotta, 2018), and co-edited, with Anne Overbeck, *New Perspectives on German-American Educational History: Topics, Trends, Fields of Research* (Verlag Julius Klinkhardt, 2017).

Jeffrey S. Ravel is Professor of History at the Massachusetts Institute of Technology. He is the author of *The Contested Parterre: Public Theater and French Political Culture, 1680–1791* (Cornell University Press, 1999) and *The Would-Be Commoner: A Tale of Deception, Murder, and Justice in Seventeenth-Century France* (Houghton Mifflin, 2008). With Sylvaine Guyot, he co-edited <u>Databases, Revenues, and Repertory: The French Stage Online, 1680–1793</u> || <u>Données, recettes et répertoire. La scène en ligne, 1680–1793</u> (MIT Press, 2020), an online, open-access, bilingual collection of essays based on the Comédie-Française Registers Project (https://cfregisters.org/). He is currently writing a book about the history of playing cards in France. In 2019–20, he served as President of the American Society for Eighteenth-Century Studies (ASECS). His contribution to this volume of *Studies in Eighteenth-Century Culture* originated as the Presidential Address at the 2021 Virtual Annual Meeting of ASECS.

Robbie Richardson is a member of the Pabineau Mi'gmaw First Nation (Oinpegitjoig L'Noeigati) and Assistant Professor of English at Princeton University. He is the author of *The Savage and Modern Self: North American Indians in Eighteenth-Century Literature and Culture* (University of Toronto Press, 2018) and is working on a monograph on the collection of Indigenous objects in Europe up to 1800.

Bryan Rindfleisch is Associate Professor of History at Marquette University. He is the author of *George Galphin's Intimate Empire: The Creek Indians, Family, and Colonialism in Early America* (University of Alabama Press, 2019) and *Brothers of Coweta: Kinship, Empire, and Revolution in the Eighteenth-Century Muscogee World* (University of South Carolina Press, 2021).

Yael Shapira is Senior Lecturer in the Department of English and American Literature at Bar-Ilan University. She is the author of *Inventing the Gothic Corpse: The Thrill of Human Remains in the Eighteenth-Century Novel* (Palgrave Macmillan, 2018). Her current research, which focuses on the non-canonical Gothic fiction of the Romantic period, has appeared in *Romantic Textualities* and *Eighteenth-Century Life*. She has also contributed chapters on forgotten women writers to *The Cambridge History of the Gothic* (Cambridge University Press, 2020) and *Women's Authorship and the Early Gothic: Innovations and Legacies* (University of Wales Press, 2020).

Kaitlin Tonti holds a Ph.D. from Indiana University of Pennsylvania in early American literature. Her scholarship focuses on early American women's life-writing, including diaries, commonplace books, and letters. She is the author of "Milcah Martha Moore's Commonplace Book and the Early American Editorial Function," in *Women's Studies* and was featured on the Conversations at the George Washington Library podcast, where she discussed her recent scholarship on the political poetry of Hannah Lawrence Schieffelin. She is currently a lecturer in the English department at Albright College.

Sophie Tunney recently received her Ph.D. in History from the Graduate Center of the City University of New York. Her dissertation traced the French botanical network of the seventeenth and eighteenth centuries, focusing on the day-to-day lives of different botanists (and their plants) across France, its colonies, and the wider world. In 2022, she joined the History department at the Horace Mann School.

Denys Van Renen is Professor of English at the University of Nebraska, Kearney and the author of *The Other Exchange: Women, Servants, and the Urban Underclass in Early Modern English Literature* (University of Nebraska Press, 2017) and *Nature and the New Science in England, 1665–1726* (Liverpool University Press, 2018). He is also the co-editor of *Beyond 1776: Globalizing the Cultures of the American Revolution* (University of Virginia Press, 2018). His latest article on mid-eighteenth-century drama appeared in *Comparative Drama*.

Andrew O. Winckles is an independent scholar living in Adrian, Michigan, with his wife, three children, and six cats. He is the author of *Eighteenth-Century Women's Writing and the Methodist Media Revolution: "Consider the Lord as Ever Present Reader"* (Liverpool University Press, 2019) and the co-editor, with Angela Rehbein, of *Women's Literary Networks and Romanticism: "A Tribe of Authoresses"* (Liverpool University Press, 2017).

Joshua Wright received his Ph.D. from the University of Notre Dame in 2022. He is currently a postdoctoral fellow at the University of Notre Dame. The primary focus of his research is British Romantic poetry. He was named a co-winner of the 2021 Graduate Student Conference Paper Prize from the American Society for Eighteenth-Century Studies for an earlier version of his contribution to this volume.

Chi-ming Yang is Professor of English at the University of Pennsylvania. Her recent articles include "Crusoe's Goat Umbrella" (in *1650–1850: Ideas, Aesthetics, and Inquiries in the Early Modern Era*) and "The Song of the Rice Bird, A Plantation Ekphrasis" (in *Eighteenth-Century Fiction*). Her most recent book, *H is for Horse: Otherworlds of the Young Octavia E. Butler,* is forthcoming from Oxford University Press.

Jolene Zigarovich is Associate Professor of English in the Department of Languages and Literatures at the University of Northern Iowa. She is author of *Writing Death and Absence in the Victorian Novel: Engraved Narratives* (Palgrave Macmillan, 2012) and editor of *Sex and Death in Eighteenth-Century Literature* (Routledge, 2013) as well as *TransGothic in Literature and Culture* (Routledge, 2018). Her *Death and the Body in the Eighteenth-Century Novel* had the support of the National Endowment for the Humanities and is forthcoming from the University of Pennsylvania Press. She has recently been a visiting research fellow at the Institute for Advanced Studies in the Humanities, University of Edinburgh, and a fellow at the Netherlands Institute for Advanced Study, Amsterdam. These fellowships were in support of *Necropolitics: Legislating the Dead Body and the Victorian Novel* which considers the posthumous life of characters uncannily bound by regulation. This essay stems from her other work in progress, a book tentatively titled *Legal Bodies: Women, Economies, and the Law in Eighteenth-Century Fiction.*

Tim Zumhof is Associate Professor of Education at the Universität Trier. He co-edited, with Nicholas K. Johnson, *Show, Don't Tell: Education and Historical Representation on Stage and Screen in Germany and the USA* (Verlag Julius Klinkhardt, 2020).

ASECS Executive Board, 2022–23

President
Wendy Wassyng Roworth
University of Rhode Island

First Vice President
Lisa A. Freeman
University of Illinois, Chicago

Second Vice President
Paola Bertucci
Yale University

Past President
Rebecca Messbarger
Washington University in St. Louis

Treasurer
Joseph Bartolomeo
University of Massachusetts, Amherst

Executive Director
Benita Blessing

Members-at-Large
Lisa Cody, Claremont McKenna College
Emily Friedman, Auburn University
Catherine Jaffe, Texas State University
Ourida Mostefai, Brown University
Romita Ray, Syracuse University
Meghan Roberts, Bowdoin College

For information about the
American Society for Eighteenth-Century Studies, please contact:

ASECS
2397 Northwest Kings Boulevard
PMB 114
Corvallis, Oregon 97330
Telephone: (845) 202-0672
Email: asecsoffice@gmail.com
Website: https://www.asecs.org

American Society for Eighteenth-Century Studies

Sponsor and Lifetime Sponsor Members, 2022–23

Richard Shane Agin
Stanford Anderson
Samuel Baker
Eve T. Bannet
Joseph F. Bartolomeo
Robert Bernasconi
Thomas F. Bonnell
Mark Boonshoft
Martha F. Bowden
Theodore E. D. Braun
Jane K. Brown
Laura Brown
Marshall Brown
Vincent Carretta
Michael J. Conlon
Robert DeMaria, Jr.
William F. Edminston
Daniel Timothy Erwin
Jan Fergus
Lisa A. Freeman
Gordon Fulton

Charles E. Gobin
Susan E. Gustafson
Donald M. Hassler
Catherine Ingrassia
Margaret C. Jacob
Alessa Johns
George Justice
Deborah Kennedy
Heather King
Jocelyne Kolb
Sue Lanser
Elizabeth Liebman
Devoney K. Looser
Jack Lynch
Elizabeth Mansfield
Jean I. Marsden
Paula McDowell
Maureen E. Mulvihill
Melvyn New
Douglas Lane Patey
Jane Perry-Camp

Adam Potkay
Joseph R. Roach
Laura J. Rosenthal
Wendy W. Roworth
Treadwell Ruml, II
Peter Sabor
J. T. Scanlan
Betty A. Schellenberg
Harold Schiffman
William C. Schrader
Volker Schroder
John Sitter
G. A. Starr
Ann T. Straulman
Astrida Orle Tantillo
Randolph Trumbach
Raymond D. Tumbleson
Kathleen Wilson
William J. Zachs
Linda Zionkowski

Institutional Members, 2022–23

American Antiquarian Society
Colonial Williamsburg Foundation, *John D. Rockefeller, Jr. Library*
Newberry Library
Omohundro Institute of Early American History and Culture, *Kellock Library*
Stanford University, *Green Library*
UCLA, *William Andrews Clark Memorial Library*
University of Kentucky, *Young Library*
Yale University, *Lewis Walpole Library*
Yale University, *Center for British Art*

527